METHODISM
IN THE
NORTHWEST

By
ERLE HOWELL

Forty-eight years a member of Pacific Northwest Annual Conference

Edited by
CHAPIN D. FOSTER, President,

*Historical Society, Pacific Northwest Annual Conference.
Former newspaper publisher and Executive Director, Washington State
Historical Society.*

THE PARTHENON PRESS, PRINTERS
Nashville, Tennessee
1966

DEDICATION

To Those Pioneer Northwest Ministers and Laymen Who Went in Jeopardy of their Lives, this History is Dedicated with Gratitude and Affection.

COMMEMORATING THE BICENTENNIAL OF AMERICAN METHODISM

1766-1966

"Forever Beginning"

Bishop and Mrs. Everett W. Palmer

INTRODUCTION

No man, least of all a Christian, can be trusted with the future who is uninstructed by the past.

The story of early Methodism in this far corner of America has an epic grandeur that matches our mountains. It tells of enterprise and achievement, courage and persistence which only faith makes possible and only love sustains.

Who can read this account of our forbears and not be inspired to nobler thoughts and braver actions?

Like a tree, nothing of consequence long endures without roots deeply planted in the soil from which it springs. So, the life of Methodism in the Pacific Northwest is dependent upon our remembering from whence we come and how!

The role of memory may be likened to the robot pilot which directs the course of airplanes and ships at sea. Once the craft is set on a proper course, the automatic pilot takes over, enabling the ship to move steadily toward its goal despite contrary pressures of wind or current. So, the recollection of a noble past serves to keep us faithful to our high calling in Christ Jesus.

We who harvest the fruits of godly men and women who here toiled for Christ and Church find reason to say with the writer of Hebrews, "Therefore, seeing we are surrounded by so great a cloud of witnesses, let us lay aside every weight and the sins which cling so closely and let us run with perseverance the race that is set before us, looking to Jesus the pioneer and perfecter of our faith."

And surely we join to express our thanks to Mr. Chapin D. Foster, President of the Pacific Northwest Conference Historical Society, and to the distinguished author of this book, the Reverend Mr. Erle Howell, who have labored long with both great love and diligence to bring forth this history. For what these two stalwart men have done to equip us for the years ahead, Methodism in the Northwest will always be in debt.

EVERETT W. PALMER
Bishop, Seattle Area
The Methodist Church

PREFACE

The preparation of this manuscript has been a delightful adventure in research, and fellowship with many persons, without whom this work could not have been completed.

Special acknowledgment of indebtedness is due librarians at University of Washington, Seattle Public Library, Seattle Pacific College, University of Puget Sound, Oregon Historical Society, and Willamette University. Especial thanks go to Mrs. Daniel Bigelow, of Olympia, for drawing the map of early Methodism in the Northwest for the back jacket of this volume.

Gratitude is due Rev. Everett W. Palmer, Bishop of the Seattle Area, and his cabinet, for encouragement, advice, and faith. Rev. Paul J. Beeman, conference director of public relations, placed the writer under obligation by his counsel. The editors of The Methodist Publishing House, Nashville, Tennessee, have been frank and gracious in their constructive suggestions. Click Relander, city editor of The Yakima Republic, was most helpful in providing information regarding The Yakima Indians, and in criticising the manuscript for Chapter Five.

The work of laymen and pastors of the Pacific Northwest Annual Conference, in collecting data concerning the histories of local churches, has been invaluable.

A debt of untold gratitude is due the writer's wife, Bettie Bell, and his daughter Virginia Day, for the many months spent in research and typing notes and manuscript.

A debt of gratitude to the members of the Historical Society of the Pacific Northwest Annual Conference is heartily acknowledged.

Worthy of inexpressible gratitude is Chapin Foster, president of the Historical Society. It is due to him, more than to any other man, that this record of Methodism in the Northwest became a reality.

The writer long has been aware of the indispensable place of the layman in the success of every project of the church. But through this experience with Mr. Foster, this writer has come to a new appreciation of the meaning of teamwork with a strong layman. May the church always have such a man for every critical task.

To Chapin's wife, Mary, also is due much credit for the encouragement she gave and the cheerful manner in which she denied herself many an activity to permit her husband to give time to the promotion of this book.

ERLE HOWELL

Seattle, Washington
January 15, 1966

ERLE HOWELL
Author—Historian

CONTENTS

9

APPENDICES

List of Illustrations

THE CONFERENCE HISTORICAL SOCIETY

"No future is safe where the past is forgotten" may sound like a hollow phrase to some, but to those deeply interested in the future of our country it holds a challenge that cannot be slighted.

Methodists have had a part in the past of the Northwest and will play an important role in shaping the future of our Northwest—to the extent that they know the history of this important area and accept the responsibilities of constructive citizenship.

Those who study Northwest history come across, at every turn, such words as "plains, dust, ruts, chuckholes, sickness, death, hardships, mountains, snow, rain, forests, trails," but too often Methodists of today do not realize that Methodists of yesterday came in contact with all of these realities.

METHODISM IN THE NORTHWEST endeavors to present a graphic picture of the role Methodists played in the development of this area—religious and political development.

The Pacific Northwest Conference Historical Society has endeavored to render an important service in sponsoring the publication of this volume, and is deeply indebted to the author, Rev. Erle Howell, and to all others who have had a part in its production. In format this book has endeavored to blaze some new trails, and from it we are confident will come better Methodists and better citizens. The Northwest of the future can use both if it is to meet the challenge it faces in the development of a great nation facing a world in need of constructive leadership.

CHAPIN D. FOSTER, President

> *Not to know what has been*
> *transacted in former times*
> *is to continue always a child.*
> *If no use is made of the*
> *labors of past ages, the*
> *world must remain always in*
> *the infancy of knowledge.*
>
> *Cicero*

13

15

Chapter I

*In 1834, the Rockies and disputed owner-
ship of Northwest were virtually insurmountable barriers to the area. Activities
of Jason Lee during following ten years
proved him to be—*

A Man To Match The Mountains

Men of Courage Undertake a Daring Mission

The history of Northwest Methodism began when Rev. Jason Lee arrived in Oregon in 1834. Although most of his labors were outside the present State of Washington and Northern Idaho, knowledge of his activities is essential to the understanding of the history of Methodism within the bounds of the present Pacific Northwest Annual Conference.

The mission upon which Jason Lee and his companions set out, from Independence, Missouri, April 28,[1] was as daring as that undertaken by the First Century Christians. First, there were the "Stony Mountains," as some called the Rockies at that time. Leading American statesmen often referred to the range as the insurmountable natural boundary between the United States and the wilderness beyond. Among other barriers was the fact that the area to which the missionaries had started was a sort of no-man's-land, in dispute between the United States and Great Britain, in governing which neither at that time was particularly concerned.

Other mountain-like obstructions were soon to be encountered by the heroic missionary band. Rev. Wilbur Fisk, as much as any other Methodist leader of his day, was aware of these seemingly impassable walls, but, seeing in Lee a man to match the mountains, he recommended him to the mission board, and was not disappointed.

The Oregon Mission had its inception in 1831 when four Indians from west of the Rockies arrived at St. Louis inquiring about the white man's religion.

Much confusion has arisen about the identity of these Indians. The best authorities, however, agree that at least one was a Nez Perce, whose tribe resided on the western slopes of the Rocky Mountains, roaming over territory now lying in Eastern Washington and Northern Idaho.

The Indians appeared at the office of General William Clark, superintendent of Indian affairs for tribes in the Missouri River country, laying before him the object of their quest.

The General reported the incident to the Catholics in St. Louis, and sent word of it to the Methodist Episcopal Conference meeting in the town that week.

Indirect credit for getting the incident before the Church goes to William Walker,[2] a Wyandotte Indian interpreter, living on the Sandusky Indian Reservation in Northern Ohio. He visited St. Louis and, hearing of the event, wrote a letter to his friend, D. P. Disosway, a New York merchant, in which he asserted that he had met three of the Indians in General Clark's office.

A fourth Indian had died a few days previously and another passed away the same month. Two started to return to the West, but since one of these died near the mouth of the Yellowstone River, only one, the Nez Perce, reached his people beyond the mountains.

Disosway was a founder of the Missionary Society of the Methodist Episcopal Church. Being impressed, he forwarded the letter to the editor of the Christian Advocate and Journal in New York. It appeared March 1, 1833, and was copied by Zion's Herald, another Methodist publication, and organs of other denominations in America and Europe.

LEE ACCEPTS THE CALL

Methodist reaction to the dramatic incident was spearheaded by Dr. Wilbur Fisk, President of Wesleyan University, Middletown, Connecticut, one of the strongest leaders in the denomination.

FIRST, VANCOUVER—1848

Rev. William Roberts reported class at Vancouver, 1848. In 1852, Rev. C. O. Hosford first resident pastor. Following year, Rev. Gustavus Hines served. During second pastorate, Rev. C. O. Hosford, 1857-59, church building erected. Dedicated, Rev. John F. De-Vore, 1859-61. Attendance grew, Sunday school prospered.

First parsonage, begun, 1870, completed following year. Rev. W. I. Cosper. Ladies Mite Society became Ladies Aid, 1871.

Second church building erected 1883, Rev. F. M. Roberts, pastor. Church incorporated, July 17, 1883. Trustees: Harvey H. Gridley, S. R. Whipple, John Jaggy, Samuel P. Marsh, Amos Evans, Silas D. Maxon, W. Byron Daniels.

Prominent early pastors included Rev. T. E. Elliott, Rev. George C. Wilding, Rev. John Parsons, Rev. A. J. Joslyn.

In 1933, church celebrated fifty years in building. In 1944, building fund started, Rev. Dan Taylor, pastor. First unit started 1948, Rev. Olin M. Graham. Building dedicated, 1956, Rev. John C. Soltman, pastor. In 1959, main building started, costing $295,000. Consecrated, November 6, 1960, Rev. Dan Taylor, delivering address.

In 1964, Rev. Frank E. Brown, pastor, fourth year. Rev. F. L. Waller, eighth year. Members 1640. Church school, 1086. Woman's Society members, 310. Paid $287. Building value, $553,000. Parsonage, $28,000.

THESE BLAZED THE TRAIL FOR NORTHWEST MISSIONS

Rev. Jason Lee

Hi-Youts-To-Han
(Rabbit-Skin-Leggings)
Indian who returned

Anna Marie Pittman
Mrs. Jason Lee

Circuit Rider

His letter, advocating immediate action, was published in the Christian Advocate and Journal, March 22, 1833. He recommended Jason Lee, a student at Wilbraham Academy while Fisk was its principal in 1829. Lee was selected as "Missionary to the Flat Heads" in late spring of that year.

Lee's ancestral roots reached back two hundred years in Massachusetts. Yet he was born near Stanstead, Lower Canada, June 28, 1803, and grew up in that locality. At the time of his birth his parents supposed they were residing in territory belonging to the United States. At the age of 23 he was converted in a Wesleyan Methodist revival. In 1829 he entered Wilbraham Academy to prepare for the ministry. There he met Wilbur Fisk, who, seeing in Lee qualities of strong leadership, became his champion.

An insight into Lee's personality is suggested by a statement made by a classmate of this time, Osman C. Baker.[3] "Jason Lee was a large, athletic young man, six feet, three inches in height, with a fully developed frame and a constitution like iron.

"His piety was deep and uniform, and his life, in a very uncommon degree, pure and exemplary. In those days of extensive and powerful revivals, I used to observe with what confidence and satisfaction seekers of religion would place themselves under his instruction. They regarded him as a righteous man whose prayers availed much; and when there were indications that the Holy Spirit was moving in the heart of the sinner within the circle of his acquaintance, his warm Christian heart would incite him to constant labor until deliverance would be proclaimed to the captive."

Lee accepted the appointment and began to prepare for the adventure. He was accompanied by his nephew, Rev. Daniel Lee, of the New Hampshire Conference; Cyrus Shepard, a teacher, of Lynn, Massachusetts; P. L. Edwards and Courtney M. Walker, laymen, of

OLYMPIA, FIRST CHURCH—1852

First Methodist service at Olympia by Rev. William Roberts and Rev. James Harvey Wilbur, in 1852. Next year, Rev. Benjamin Close, appointed to Puget Sound Mission District, took up residence at Olympia, preaching there occasionally. Organization date of church uncertain, but Rev. William Roberts, presiding elder, 1854-55 left Olympia to be supplied, evidently by himself. In 1855, he reported 16 members.

Lots and cabin purchased, 1855. Rev. John F. DeVore, pastor that year, led in building first church, one room with lean-to for Sunday school. New building, at Fifth and Adams Streets, was erected in 1884. Old building moved and used as "Wesley Hall Annex." Former property sold.

A new building erected, 1900, was raised, 1914, and basement installed. New parsonage erected that year. Pipe organ installed, 1924. Church building damaged by earthquake, 1949, was condemned. New church became necessity. Ground broken, 1952, and 100th anniversary first preaching observed. Rev. William E. Callahan pastor. Congregation occupied the new building, 1954. Rev. Robert A. Uphoff, pastor, 1957-60. New structure already too small for growing congregation.

In 1964, Rev. Walter A. McArthur, pastor, fifth year. Members, 1360. Church school enrollment, 1368. Woman's Society, members, 283. Gave $2,478.

20

Independence, Missouri. The latter were for the secular department.

Lee had become acquainted with Nathaniel J. Wyeth, a fur trader of the Rockies. Learning that the trader planned to leave Missouri for the Westward Journey in April, he agreed to ship his supplies by the latter's brig, the May Dacre, around Cape Horn to the Columbia, and to accept Wyeth's invitation to travel overland with him.

The party, consisting of 70 men and 250 horses, mules and cattle, arrived at Fort Hall, on the Snake River near the present city of Pocatello, Idaho, July 14. There, Wyeth paused to construct a trading post, and the missionaries welcomed the opportunity to rest.

DELIVERED FIRST PROTESTANT SERMON WEST OF ROCKIES

The first Protestant sermon heard west of the Rocky Mountains was delivered by Jason Lee, at Fort Hall, July 27. The text was "Whether therefore ye eat or drink, or whatsoever ye do, do all to the glory of God."

After Lee delivered this sermon, a number of Indians went racing with some of Wyeth's men and a half-breed named Kinseau was killed. Next day Lee read the burial service and laid the man to rest.

Thus, with the proclamation of the Christian message on the Pacific side of the Rockies and the declaration of God's mercy over the dead, Jason Lee already had conquered the first mountain athwart his pathway.

The missionaries arrived at Fort Walla Walla, September 1, and were kindly received by P. C. Pambrun, Hudson's Bay official at the fort. Four days later, on a barge provided by their host, the company started down the Columbia River, arriving at Vancouver September 15.

Dr. John McLoughlin, Chief Factor for the Hudson's Bay Company on the Pacific Coast, met the weary travelers, extending to them his hospitality.

The Chief Factor has been described

COUPEVILLE—1853

First Methodist sermon on Whidbey Island was delivered by Rev. Benjamin Close, presiding elder of Puget Sound Mission District April 25, 1853, in the home of Grove Terry. Church organized, July 1853 first in Washington. The Rev. W. B. Morse, pastor.

W. D. Nichols, teacher and local preacher, built first Methodist church on Whidbey Island in 1859. Building valued at $650, was on land obtained from Grove Terry.

In 1872, church was moved to site donated by Thomas Coupe. New building was erected under Rev. W. H. McMillan in Coupeville at a cost of $2,500. Rev. T. J. Massey presiding elder. This building destroyed by fire in 1893 a week after insurance lapsed. New building was completed in 1894. A parsonage was erected in 1889 under the pastorate of Rev. C. C. Culmer. In 1908, under Rev. Robert C. Hartley, boys club was erected. Under Rev. Raymond Partee the building altered again. In 1949, Rev. Henry Cross, pastor, improvements costing $15,000 made. Parsonage erected in 1953 under Rev. Ritchie D. Ocheltree, Sr. In 1956, under Rev. Wayne D. Wright building further remodeled. In 1964, Rev. Truman H. Cotton was pastor. There were 298 church members, 212 in Sunday school, and 51 in Woman's Society of Christian Service.

as a large man, above average in height, with white hair, grayed from early manhood. He possessed a friendly heart and exhibited a fatherly concern for the missionaries. During the two weeks the travelers remained at the fort he and Lee developed a friendship that lasted throughout their lives.

WILLAMETTE VALLEY IS SELECTED

Although the Indians of the Willamette had nothing to do with the request of the Inland Tribes for the white man's religion, Lee decided to settle there. Considerations leading to this decision were several: A better opportunity to gather these Indians around him for instruction; the conviction that the Willamette Valley would be the center of that civilization which he already foresaw; French Canadians, former employees of the Hudson's Bay Company, who had settled on nearby French Prairie, had children needing education; and Dr. McLoughlin advised the location.

Dr. McLoughlin's advice, however, was not without prejudice. He and his company wished to keep the Americans south of the Columbia. Even at that early day, they sensed the implication for future national dominance in the coming of the Americans to the Northwest.

The May Dacre, with mission supplies aboard, had cast anchor at the mouth of the Willamette the day following Lee's arrival at Fort Vancouver. Therefore, having determined to locate the mission on the Willamette, the group left Vancouver, with the blessing of McLoughlin, September 29. They began construction of the mission house in early October, moving into the incomplete building, November 3. The building was 18 by 32 feet in dimensions.

The object of Lee's mission in Oregon was the conversion of the Indians. Yet, his sense of Christian citizenship, and vision of an oncoming empire, led him

SALMON CREEK—1853

First Methodist preaching at Salmon Creek, 1853. Sunday school and worship conducted in log house belonging to Joseph Hill. Rev. Samuel Matthews, first preacher. Rev. James Gerrish first pastor, 1853-55. Small church, erected, 1855. In 1860, another school used for church. In 1894 new school used for Methodist services.

Church built, 1900, land donated 1885 by Ansel S. Marble. Church incorporated April 12, 1897. Trustees: Rev. William J. Rule, John A. Goddard, Mrs. Jennie Warrell, Franklin Warrell, Peter Rasmussen. In 1910, Rev. Philip H. Raymond first occupied new parsonage.

Ladies Aid Hall, added, 1912, kitchen, 1919. Salmon Creek mostly on Vancouver Circuit, in 1910-50 had resident minister, who served other churches. Church, moved 100 feet, 1941, make room for Federal highway. Trustees: W. L. Galbraith, George W. Goddard, Arthur H. Northcutt, Joseph Canon, Fred Brook, Mrs. Clarence Gluth.

In 1953, war housing residence purchased for Sunday school. Rev. Everett W. Groves, pastor. Moved to location, became useful addition to church. Baldwin organ installed 1954-55. In 1959, new parsonage added, Rev. T. Earl Poindexter, pastor.

In 1964, Rev. Martin T. Larson, pastor, first year. Members, 292; church school enrollment, 274. Woman's Society, 84 members, gave $369. Building value $33,500. Parsonage, $20,800.

to turn his hand to many projects not hitherto regarded as part of Christian missions. His attempt to implement his far-sighted statesmanship led to his removal from the superintendency of the mission, but his procedure saved Oregon for the United States of America.

Along with his plan for evangelism Lee saw the urgent necessity for education, improved economic standards, elimination of social and moral evils, and the establishment of law and order under the Government of the United States.

Mountains Rise in the Valley

The stories regarding the Indians' request for the "White Man's Book of Heaven," had led many to erroneous conclusions regarding the supposed eagerness of the children of the forests to accept the Christian way of life. One of the mountainous obstacles to be overcome by the men of the Cross was the moral indolence of those they had come to convert.

This indifference to the better life, with their seasonal habits of moving from place to place, their inherent superstitions, and lack of vocabulary through which the missionaries could communicate the teachings of the Gospel, raised barriers more difficult than the Rocky Mountains.

One of the moral obstacles to be overcome was suggested by Cyrus Shepard [4] almost a year later when he wrote:

"Our establishment is on the East side of the Willamette, about sixty miles above its confluence with the Columbia. There are seven or eight families of settlers within a few miles of us; these are Canadians and Roman Catholics, and have taken native women for their wives. . . ."

The missionaries soon learned that many of these marriages were but temporary, the men discarding their women for others at will.

The Indians, having developed no

FIRST, SEATTLE—1853

First Church, organized in Seattle, December 4, 1853, by Rev. David E. Blaine, had four members, Mr. and Mrs. A. A. Denny, J. H. Nagle, and Catharine Blaine.

First Methodist sermon delivered earlier, by Rev. Benjamin Close, superintendent of Puget Sound District.

Blaine built own home in 1854. First church at Second and Columbia, dedicated, May, 1855. Catharine, Seattle's first school teacher, 1854. Rev. William B. Morse came in 1856. In 1861 and 62, church left to be supplied. In 1862, Rev. Daniel Bagley, Methodist Protestant minister, preached. In 1863, Rev. Nehemiah Doane, pastor, found six members.

A new building, erected at Third and Marion, in 1889, Rev. D. D. Campbell, pastor. Replaced, 1908-10, Rev. W. H. W. Reese, pastor. The sanctuary, Fifth and Marion, cost $205,000, dedicated in 1910. Rev. Anda Wright Leonard pastor 1910-16, elected bishop. Rev. J. Ralph Magee, 1921-29 acquired adjoining lots, became bishop.

Rev. Newton E. Moats, 1939-49, started plans for educational unit. Completed by Rev. Cyrus E. Albertson, occupied, May 6, 1951. Dedicated free of debt, November 30, 1958.

In 1964, Rev. Robert W. Uphoff was pastor for fourth year. Associates were, Rev. Carl McGee and Rev. E. Max Case. Membership 3,460, church school enrollment 1,575. Woman's Society members, 449, gave $2,618.

industrial skills, depended upon hunting, fishing, and a limited supply of roots and herbs for food. The settlers raised vegetables, potatoes, and some grain, but were dependent upon the Hudson's Bay Company for other supplies.

Some of the barriers hindering the work of evangelism included the necessity for building the mission house, and clearing land for farming, which must be done by the missionaries because there was no help to be hired in the valley.

Lee wrote that there was no doctor within sixty miles at a time when all the other missionaries were ill and he was able with difficulty to attend to housekeeping. The Indians were dying off rapidly and Lee lamented the absence of Christian women. He saw clearly that in some areas such women could more effectively point the way to right living than men.

In a letter to Dr. Fisk, Lee wrote that he had asked the mission board to send no more single men to the mission, but, rather, to select men with families, and to send Daniel Lee's "chosen" as soon as possible.

In spite of obstacles the industry of the men was such that 35 acres were put under cultivation in 1835. Crops raised that year lifted the standard of living of the mission family the following winter.

MISSION SCHOOL THOUGHT BEST HOPE

Lee and Shepard saw that the best hope for conversion of the Indians was the mission school, and that their economic stability lay in industrial training for their children. During the first winter Shepard remained at Fort Vancouver to teach the children there. But by early 1835 he began teaching children at the mission school.

Of Shepard's skill and devotion Brosnan said, "The history of his life during the first five years of this period is the history of the first Oregon Indian

---

STEILACOOM CHURCH—1853

Steilacoom was founded by Captain LaFayette Balch, 1851. First Methodist sermon delivered here, 1853, by Rev. Benjamin Close, Presiding Elder, Puget Sound District. Rev. John F. DeVore was first pastor. He had been assigned to Olympia, but Balch and others met his ship at Alki Point, Seattle, and persuaded him to go to Steilacoom. He arrived there, August 23, 1853, organized a Methodist church that day, began soliciting for money and materials immediately.

The building, first Protestant church in Western Washington, was occupied later that year. Land was donated by Balch. DeVore, pastor two years. In 1854 he also served White River. Further appointments were: 1855, supplied; 1856-'57. G. M. Berry; 1858, J. W. Franklin; 1859 (with Puyallup), J. H. B. Royal; 1860 (with Mound Prairie), Christopher Alderson; 1861-'66, does not appear; 1867, H. Patterson; 1868-'69, supplied; 1870-'71, H. Patterson; 1872-'73, S. H. Mann; 1874-'75, C. H. Hoxie. Does not appear after 1875.

Monument commemorating this church was erected in 1908, on the site originally occupied by the building. Marker was erected by the Washington Historical Society, Honorable R. L. McCormick, president, and W. H. Gilstrap, secretary. Rev. D. G. LeSourd, representing Puget Sound Conference, assisted in raising funds.

24

Mission School. Shepard was exceptionally well qualified for his task and was undoubtedly the most successful and consecrated of all the workers associated with Lee's missionary enterprise in Oregon. . . . The five years of service which Shepard gave to the Indian Mission School entitle him to the distinction of being Oregon's first great teacher." He died, January 1, 1840.

The industrial school founded by Lee and Shepard was discontinued and in 1844 the building sold to The Oregon Institute, which Lee also founded. The Institute became Willamette University, the first institution of college rank west of the Rockies.

How apparent victory may lead to defeat is illustrated in the experience of a Cayuse Indian and his family in the school. The man, We-lap-tu-lakt, met Lee on the trail along the Snake River in 1834, and became Lee's admiring friend. Later he entered two sons in the school on the Willamette. He was so impressed that he brought his family to reside near the mission, and entered a third son in the school.

The experience was hailed as a sign that the mission was attracting favorable attention among tribesmen. But victory soon turned to ashes. Two of the man's sons fell ill and died. When the third sickened the father took him with his family and fled the place. This child also died on the way across the mountains.

The terrified parents, full of superstition and fear, blamed the missionaries and the incident served to dampen the enthusiasm for the mission among the Indians for two hundred miles around.

ALCOHOL BROUGHT COMPLICATIONS

Alcohol played a deadly part in contacts between white men and Indians. To combat this evil, the settlers in the community formed a temperance society, February 11, 1836, three settlers signing the pledge that day. In 1837 the society was called upon to take action when the peace of the settlement was threatened by the manufacture of alco-

PORT TOWNSEND—1854

Rev. W. B. Morse, 1954, was first Methodist minister regularly appointed to Port Townsend, although Presiding Elder Benjamin Close had preached there in 1853. By 1858 the board of trustees, Daniel Shaw, Thomas Hartie, Jacob Ebey, had purchased a lot. Trustees who built first church in 1871 were, Nathaniel D. Hill, James J. Harned, and John E. Burns. They purchased the lot April 21. Rev. John F. DeVore was presiding elder of Puget Sound District. Church dedicated July 2, 1871, costing $1,400. Rev. Abraham Laubach was first pastor.

Rev. G. H. Greer, pastor in 1872. In 1876, building completed at cost of $1,200. In 1898, Rev. W. H. Leach, pastor, the church turned around and enlarged. Stained glass windows installed and dedicated December 8, 1900. Rev. E. M. Randall, First Church, Seattle, was preacher.

Church observed its fiftieth anniversary May 25, 1921, Bishop William O. Shepard, preacher. Rev. Clark Cottrell, pastor; and Rev. John M. Canse, district superintendent.

In 1951-59 Rev. Bertrand Robbins remodeled church several times. Under Rev. John Burleson, 1959-63, membership increased. In 1960, a memorial fund was started for new building on different location. The UNA allocated funds for project in 1964. Building to be under way by the 100th anniversary.

holic beverages for sale to Indians and settlers of the area.

Ewing Young and Lawrence Carmichael, from California, began to distill alcoholic beverages for the evil purpose. The distressed missionaries and the officers of the Hudson's Bay Company joined forces to request the offenders to desist. The request was reenforced by the presence of a representative of the Federal Government, William A. Slacum, a friend of the mission. He advised the men to heed the request of the settlers and offered to transport Young to California. Young agreed and the first attempt to engage in the traffic in alcohol in Oregon was thwarted.

Notwithstanding the friendliness with which the Chief Factor of the Hudson's Bay Company treated the missionaries, the laws of the company limited his cooperation. This it was clearly seen would handicap the growth of the mission and limit the freedom of the settlers. Among other restrictions the company willingly lent cattle to the settlers but demanded them back with the increase. Lee and others, dissatisfied with this and other hindrances, organized a company and imported more than 600 cattle from California, distributing them among the settlers at a previously agreed price.

Much of the material supplied by the Company was shipped from England and arrived in unsatisfactory condition. This was true of flour and other perishables.

Since Oregon farms produced satisfactory wheat, Lee built mills to grind flour, and to saw lumber for construction of houses and barns. Thus the restrictions of the Hudson's Bay Company were gradually overcome.

REENFORCEMENTS ARRIVE

As the mission expanded Lee felt the need for more workers and appealed to the mission board for help in the secular department as well as for ministers. The first reenforcement, coming in response to Lee's request, arrived in May, 1837.

PUYALLUP—1854

Puyallup first in conference assignments, 1857, Rev. Jacob Leach, pastor. Possibly Rev. John F. DeVore held services 1854. In 1858, Seattle and Puyallup on same circuit, Rev. Christopher Alderson, pastor. In 1859, Rev. J. H. B. Royal, Steilacoom and Puyallup.

First organization 1882, 27 members received. First pastor, following this event, Rev. W. P. Williams. Trustees: A. L. Barnes, George Elder, Dr. F. S. Williams, William Wilson, B. Avery, Arthur Miller. Pastor's salary fixed at $300 per year. Rev. Albert Atwood, pastor.

First church, on lots donated by Ezra Meeker, built in 1883, Rev. J. E. Leach, pastor. Dedicated, Rev. H. K. Hines. Later Rev. George A. Landen, Rev. B. F. Brooks, Rev. J. W. Dobbs, Rev. W. M. Ludwick, and Rev. Sprague Davis.

In 1889, building enlarged, dedicated by Rev. George Wilding, First Church, Tacoma. Rev. T. J. Massey, pastor. Membership doubled, 1899-02, Rev. W. O. Benadom. Rev. George W. Frame, 1907-11, membership 400, church school, 500. Silver anniversary of church observed. New building dedicated, March 28, 1909. Rev. W. H. W. Reese, First Church, Seattle, preached.

Cornerstone for new building was laid, May 17, 1964.

In 1964, Rev. Randall W. Larson, pastor, fourth year. Members, 1,124. Church school enrollment, 476.

26

Those coming were: Susan Downing, Lynn, Massachusetts, fiancée of Cyrus Shepard; Dr. and Mrs. Elijah White, physician; Mr. and Mrs. Allison Beers, Miss Anna Marie Pittman and Miss Elvira Johnson, teachers.

In the following September newcomers were Rev. and Mrs. David Leslie, Rev. H. K. W. Perkins, and Miss Margaret Smith.

In late 1837 Lee opened a mission at The Dalles, dispatching to the place Daniel Lee and H. K. W. Perkins. There the following year a great revival occurred among the Indians with as many as 1,200 in attendance. Many professed conversion.

A tragic incident occurred that year which served to alienate further some of the Indians from the mission. It had to do with the son of Piu-piu-mox-mox, or The Yellow Serpent, one of the greatest chiefs among the Walla Wallas.

The Chief was a great admirer of Lee and was strongly influenced by him. His son, Elijah, had attended the school at Willamette, and later returned to his home. At the request of a white friend in California the Chief had taken a band of his men, including Elijah, to California to hunt.

While in the South some of the Indians rounded up a herd of cattle, some of which were claimed by white men. In the absence of the Chief the men approached Elijah demanding the return of the cattle. Elijah, it is reported, told them that he had spoken for their return but that his father, being chief, would have to decide. The young man, seeing that the men meant him harm, said, "If I am to die, let me first pray." As he dropped to his knees one of the men shot him dead. The Yellow Serpent gathered his men and returned to Oregon with heavy heart and vengeful spirit. In the disturbances with the Indians seven years later, after the death of the Whitmans at Waiilatpu, Piu-piu-mox-mox was the chief most

CLAQUATO—1858

Claquato first served by Methodist ministers of Mound Prairie and Chehalis Circuits. Land and lumber for Methodist church there donated by Lewis H. Davis, 1858. John Duff Clinger, brother of Mrs. Davis, supervised construction, building doors, window casings. Fourth Methodist church building in Washington. Earlier ones at Steilacoom, Seattle, Olympia.

Historian reported John Harwood, school teacher, first resident pastor at Claquato, moved pupils into building when completed. Harwood evidently a supply. Name does not appear in conference journals. In 1858 Rev. Calvin H. Dray appointed to Chehalis Circuit, Rev. N. S. McAllister to Mound Prairie. In 1859 Rev. W. H. Goddard appointed Chehalis Circuit. No appointment in 1860.

Claquato first appeared among appointments in 1861, Rev. J. S. Douglas, pastor. In 1862 Douglas reported eight members on circuit. Rev. J. H. B. Royal, pastor in 1870; Rev. C. H. Hoxie, 1872-73; Rev. Thomas McGill, 1874-75. In latter year McGill reported 30 members on circuit. Church did not again appear among appointments.

Near-by town of Chehalis, on Northern Pacific Railroad, after 1870, superseded Claquato, and church abandoned after 1875. In 1953 church was restored by Chehalis Post Number Two, American Legion. Was the oldest Methodist Church building still standing in Washington in 1965.

greatly feared by the whites.[5] He was killed while a captive.

First Christian Marriage Solemnized

Lee was distressed by the attitude toward marriage among the settlers and the Indians. With the arrival of Miss Downing, fiancée of Cyrus Shepard, Lee and the missionaries determined to invite the community, including the Indians, to the marriage, set for July 19, 1837.

Before the ceremony, Lee addressed the assembly on the sacredness of marriage, after which the couple was united in the sacred bonds. Then Lee stepped into the audience, and led Anna Marie Pittman to the altar, where Daniel Lee united them in marriage. This surprised all except those participating in the ceremony.

Next, Charles Roe, a settler, was united in marriage to an Indian maiden and then baptized. Immediately afterwards Webly Hauxhurst, the first Methodist convert in Oregon, was baptized and received into the Methodist Episcopal Church. A sermon was followed by the Communion Service.

The congregation was lifted to lofty heights of inspiration, and the Methodist Episcopal Church had that day become a reality in Oregon.

Methodists Sensed Need for Law and Order

One other barrier hindered the establishment of a Christian empire on the Pacific slope under the rule of the United States. In 1818 America and Great Britain entered into an agreement permitting citizens of both countries to exercise equal rights in Oregon. The agreement was renewed for ten years in 1828, and, in 1838, was expected to come up again for review.

Neither country, however, exercised authority in the territory, leaving the actual rule to the Hudson's Bay Company. The company had established

WALLA WALLA, PIONEER—1859 Methodist Church, Walla Walla, organized October, 1859, Rev. G. M. Berry, pastor, Rev. J. H. Wilbur, presiding elder. Building erected, 1860, property donated by County Commissioners. Walla Walla Circuit became Walla Walla District. Rev. J. Harvey Wilbur, presiding elder.

Rev. John Flinn presiding elder pastor at Walla Walla 1861. In 1868 new building costing $10,000 erected.

Church incorporated, 1883. J. H. Wilbur retired, 1882, promoted a second church in East Walla Walla. Built church 1887. Deeded to First Methodist Church. Discontinued in 1893, proceeds used for addition to First Church.

In 1903, new congregation organized in East End, church erected and Rev. Robert J. Reid, pastor. This church in 1918 sold, proceeds applied to Pioneer Church as First had been renamed, after union in 1916. Ground broken, new building, 1917. Dedicated by Bishop Matthew Simpson Hughes, January, 1918.

Austin Pipe Organ installed, 1925 by Ladies Aid Society. Cost, $8,000. Parsonage built 1926. Steps taken to finance educational unit 1944. Site purchased, 1947 for $10,000. In 1952, funds pledged, new unit erected, 1954, costing $230,000. Rev. Albert Wilson, pastor.

In 1964, Rev. David K. Almond, pastor, fourth year. Membership, 1,211. Church school, 670. Woman's Society, 270, gave $1,171. Building value, $355,-500. Parsonage, $24,000. Other, $429,597.

posts at strategic locations throughout the country north of the Columbia. John Jacob Astor's attempt to establish a trading post at Astoria, near the mouth of the Columbia, in 1811 was abandoned in 1815.

In 1825, Dr. McLoughlin moved his headquarters to Vancouver, a hundred miles inland. With trading posts at Walla Walla, Nisqually on Puget Sound, Spokane Falls, Fraiser River, and throughout Canada, this gigantic concern, with headquarters in Great Britain, constituted the only law enforcement agency in all Oregon.

The chief concern of the company was to enforce regulations directly related to its business. Otherwise each man was a law unto himself.

It was into this situation that the missionaries came. The company, through Dr. McLoughlin, extended many courtesies to the missionaries, providing food, equipment, seeds, tools, and transportation, at a price.

This patronizing benevolence alone enabled the missionaries to remain in Oregon. Nevertheless, Lee and his associates early saw that full acceptance of this hospitality would bring the mission and the settlers under permanent control of the company. This was inimicable to the American idea of freedom.

With the declining of Indian population, and the influx of settlers, which came in increasing numbers annually, missionaries and settlers became aware that stable government was essential to the future of Oregon and the Christian mission.

Meanwhile, the work of the mission was expanding. Lee felt that the staff must be augmented. Members of the mission, convinced that only Lee's appearance before the mission board would be sufficient to present the need in a convincing manner, urged him to go East.

Shortly before Lee was ready to start,

WHITE SWAN—1859

Methodist work at White Swan dates to 1859 when Rev. James Harvey Wilbur began to teach on the Yakima Indian Reservation. Church first reported in 1861. First recorded members were: Yakatowit and Delia, his wife; Joe and Susan Stwire, Thomas and Katie Pearne; Joseph and Susan Simcoe; George and Nancy Waters, Coke and Sallie Helm. Pearne and Waters became first ordained Indians to enter Methodist Conference in the Northwest.

First church building at White Swan was erected in 1879. Under Father Wilbur work prospered. In 1880, more than 600 members. After his resignation, the work declined. Rev. James Wilbur Helm became pastor in 1897 and remained until 1915.

In 1937 old building burned and new one erected on adjoining property. Some Indians, disappointed that building not erected on original site, became indifferent. Rev. R. V. B. Dunlap was pastor when new building erected.

In 1950's, under Rev. Harry E. Gardner, four classrooms added, and more in 1963 through gifts in lumber by White Swan Lumber Company.

After Wilbur's time some Methodists entered Shaker movement.

In 1964, Rev. Thomas F. Ludwig was appointed pastor for the second year. Members, 116, church school enrollment, 126. Members of Woman's Society, 34, with gifts of $224.

THESE BISHOPS SERVED NORTHWEST METHODISM DURING PERIODS OF TRANSITION

Bishop W. W. Duncan

Bishop Everett W. Palmer

Bishop S. M. Merrill

Bishop Wallace E. Brown

Bishop C. H. Fowler

Bishop C. W. Martin

Bishop H. H. Kavanaugh

Bishop Titus Lowe

Bishop E. R. Ames

Bishop H. M. DuBose

American citizens among the settlers met at the mission, along with those Canadians who desired to become American citizens, and drew a petition, addressed to Congress, praying that the laws of the United States be extended over Oregon. The petition was to be delivered by Lee to leaders at Washington.

Lee's final decision awaited the approval of his wife of eight months. Her reply to her husband's request for counsel is as important in the history of Oregon as that of Ruth to Naomi in ancient Hebrew history.

With the life of Lee's unborn child stirring within her body, Anna Marie replied:

"I will not take it upon me to advise either way, and I will not put myself in the way of your performance of your duty. If you feel that it is your duty to go, go, for I did not marry you to hinder, but rather to aid you in the performance of your duty."

On the way East Lee visited Dr. Marcus Whitman at Waiilatpu, and Rev. H. H. Spaulding of Lapwai, Idaho. On April 12, 1838, he left Walla Walla, to continue his historic journey to petition the mission board for workers, and Congress for civil law in Oregon.

Lee was accompanied on his eastern journey by five Indian youth. Three were to be placed in school and the others were to serve as sample products of the mission school. June 28, they camped by the waters of Bear River. An entry in his journal at this place will cast light upon Lee's reaction to a message which he would receive only a few weeks later. He wrote:

"This day I am thirty-five years old. I cannot but reflect that I now have arrived at what is called the meridian of life, and that my sun is beginning to decline toward the western horizon. Thirty-five years, and how little have I done to benefit mankind! How long shall I be permitted to labor? Can I expect to see as many more years? No. Well be it so, but let me have grace to improve my remaining days, be they

AUBURN—1860

Church at Auburn had common origin with one at Kent. Rev. D. L. Spaulding began preaching at White River, in 1860, in home of T. M. Alvord. In 1866, log schoolhouse at Slaughter served for religious activities. After Rev. John Flin, held revival in area, first church was built in 1886. Rev. G. F. VanDeVenter, pastor. Rev. Albert Atwood, presiding elder. Auburn on White River Circuit, in 1891, later, a station.

In 1901, parsonage built. Many children converted under Rev. J. M. Weaver. Rev. Harlan R. Stone, pastor, 1922-26, attendance grew, building enlarged.

Ladies Aid organized in 1902, fourteen members. Woman's Home Missionary Society organized in 1926. Many improvements in church building, 1942-45. In 1955, Rev. Myron H. Sharrard, pastor, led building fund drive.

Bell installed in 1886, served 75 years. At times for fire alarm. In 1955, church relocated at East Main between N and O Streets. Building erected here in late 1950's. Rev. John M. Finney, pastor.

In 1964, Rev. Norman R. Lawson, pastor, fourth year. Associates, Rev. Don Glen, in fourth year, and Rev. Paul Graves, first year. Members, 786. Church school enrollment, 544. Woman's Society of Christian Service, members 214. Their gifts $1,433. Church Building valued at $200,000. Parsonage $10,000.

many or few, to the glory of God, and I need have no uneasiness about it. The Judge of all the earth will do right."

The words were written near the summit of the mountains which his spirit already had conquered.

LEE LEARNS OF DEATH OF WIFE AND CHILD

On September 1, Lee was the guest of Rev. and Mrs. Thomas Johnson at the Shawnee Indian Mission, near Westport, Missouri. A messenger from Oregon handed him a bundle of letters, one of which was sealed in black. It informed him that his wife, Anna Marie, and their son of a few days, were dead.

That Lee believed what he had written at Bear River when he said, "The Judge of all the earth will do right," was vouchsafed in his resolution to resist the temptation to return to his empty Oregon home and to continue eastward where his duty clearly lay.

Through Missouri, Illinois, and to New York, Lee lectured about Oregon, its need for missionaries and opportunities for settlers. He presented the claims of the mission to the board and the petition of the settlers to Congress.

Lee was absent from the mission more than two years. Meanwhile he had remarried, taking as his second bride, Miss Lucy Thompson, of Barre, Vermont. So effective was his appeal to the mission board that that organization assigned thirty-one adults including five ministers and their wives. A ship, the Lausanne, was chartered to convey the missionaries and their supplies around Cape Horn to Oregon.

LAUSANNE BEARS REENFORCEMENTS

The company, bound for the Willamette, comprised a total of fifty-one persons. They were: Rev. and Mrs. Jason Lee, of the New England Conference; Rev. and Mrs. J. H. Frost, of the New York Conference, and one child; Rev.

MONTESANO—1860

First Methodist ministers to preach at Montesano: Rev. B. C. Lippincott, N. S. McAllister, 1859. Nehemiah Doane explored area 1859 appointed Rev. J. S. Douglass, pastor. Circuit included Quinault, Oysterville, Old Kamilchie. No parsonage, pastor lived on foot, in saddle, in canoe, spent nights in homes if invited. Building plan started by Rev. A. T. Chapman. Dedicated, 1876, Rev. W. I. Cosper, pastor.

Church formally organized, 1860, Rev. W. J. Franklin, first pastor after organization. Rev. H. C. Rhoades, in 1863, became first school teacher at Montesano. First members included Mrs. William Medcalf, and Mrs. Isaiah Scammon. Church was built, Lower Montesano 1885. New building, erected in 1891, Rev. F. E. Drake, still in use in 1960. Parsonage built, 1885. Epworth League organized in 1890.

Revivals 1915-17 brought many into church. Rev. O. F. Krieger, pastor. New parsonage, 1928, Rev. C. M. Van Marter, pastor. Seventieth anniversary, 1930, Rev. J. M. Canse, pastor. Improvements on church and parsonage in 1942. Rev. Charles Creesey, pastor. Kimball pipe organ installed. Centennial observed, 1960, Rev. Linden B. Jenkins, pastor.

In 1964, Rev. Harold E. Bashor, pastor, fourth year. Members, 472; church school enrollment, 263; Woman's Society, 76, gave, $1,005. Building value, $110,000. Parsonage, $19,500.

and Mrs. Gustavus Hines of the Genesee Conference, and one child; Rev. and Mrs. W. W. Kone, of the North Carolina Conference; Rev. and Mrs. Alvin F. Waller, of the Genesee Conference, and two children; Rev. and Mrs. John P. Richmond, M.D., of the Illinois Conference, and four children; Dr. and Mrs. Ira L. Babcock, New York, and one child; Mr. and Mrs. George Abernethy, New York, and two children; Mr. and Mrs. W. W. Raymond, farmer, New York; Mr. and Mrs. H. B. Brewer, farmer; Mr. and Mrs. L. H. Judson, cabinet maker, and three children; Mr. and Mrs. J. L. Parrish, blacksmith, and three children; Mr. and Mrs. James Olney, carpenter; Mr. and Mrs. Hamilton Campbell, carpenter, and one child; Misses Chloe Aurelia Clark, Maria T. Ware, Elmira Phillips, Almira Phillips, teachers; Miss Orpha Lankton, stewardess; and Thomas Adams, one of the Indian boys Lee took across the continent as an exhibit. The other had died in New York.

The Lausanne sailed from New York October 9, 1839, arriving at Vancouver, June 1, 1840.

With the great reenforcement Lee faced the responsibility of placing a total of nine ministers, eleven men in the secular service, five teachers and a stewardess.

First Methodist Sent to Puget Sound

Although Lee had asked the board for only two additional ministers he was given five. How he deployed these workers is indicative of his vision for the expansion of the mission. They were appointed as follows: Clatsop, near the mouth of the Columbia, J. H. Frost; Nisqually, on Puget Sound, John P. Richmond; Umpqua, Southern Oregon, Gustavus Hines and W. W. Kone; The Dalles, Central Oregon, Daniel Lee and H. W. K. Perkins; Willamette Station, David Leslie; Willamette Falls, Alvin F. Waller.

Other appointments include William Holden Willson, secular department,

WAITSBURG—1860

The church at Waitsburg, organized, 1860 by Rev. George Berry, pastor at Walla Walla. John McGee, A. T. Hard, stewards. Following year Rev. John Flinn, presiding elder, pastor at Walla Walla continued to serve Waitsburg.

First Quarterly Conference on circuit, September 25, 1869. Rev. J. B. Calloway, presiding elder. Small parsonage built in 1870. Rev. J. H. Adams, pastor. Contract let for church building, 1872.

New building dedicated 1873, Rev. W. T. Koontz, pastor. Cost $2,500. Building committee, J. L. Carter, J. Robnett, P. S. George, Henry Bateman. In 1872, Waitsburg Circuit divided, Dayton on new charge.

Waitsburg Circuit, in time, included Union schoolhouse, Huntsville, Coppei schoolhouse, Washington schoolhouse, Dixie, Independence schoolhouse, Yend's schoolhouse, Paul's schoolhouse, Dayton, Spalding schoolhouse, Petit schoolhouse, Cummin's schoolhouse, Touchet schoolhouse, Delta schoolhouse, other points.

First Sunday school, union, so continued until 1886. New parsonage in 1920. Church incorporated, 1928.

In 1956, Conover estate acquired by church for $3,500. Same year, fiftieth anniversary of Brick church celebrated. In 1960, congregation celebrated its 100th anniversary.

In 1964, Rev. Bill L. Bretlinger, pastor, second year. Members, 207, church school enrollment, 119. Woman's Society, 43 members, gave $1,086.

Nisqually; H. B. Brewer, The Dalles, as farmer; Dr. Ira L. Babcock, physician, The Dalles; other mechanics and farmers were to remain at the Central Mission, as was Dr. Elijah White. Chloe Aurelia Clark was assigned to teach at Nisqually; the other teachers and the stewardess were to remain at the Central Station.

Nisqually had been selected by Lee, in 1838, as a site for a mission. The presence of a large population of Indians and a Hudson's Bay trading post induced Lee to select this as the first site in the northern expansion of his work.

Rev. David Leslie and William H. Willson visited the place, arriving April 10, 1839. The latter began construction of a mission house, while Leslie returned to the Willamette almost immediately. The carpenter built the house to the point that it could be occupied and returned to Willamette, there to busy himself until the arrival of the new missionaries.

Willson, having previously traveled the road to Nisqually, apparently acted as guide to the new missionaries. The party, in canoes, floated down the Columbia to the mouth of the Cowlitz River. They found the current in the latter fairly smooth for the first few miles but, after that, so rapid that it required the utmost energies of the boatman. After two days they reached the portage, from which place they were to make the remainder of their journey by land.

They spent the night near the Hudson's Bay farming port, but being surrounded all night by drunken, noisy Indians, and their baggage being exposed, they slept but little. Two days later, July 7, 1840, they started for Puget Sound, using seventeen horses made available by Charles Forrest, manager of the farm. This portion of the journey, over rough roads, required three days.

At Fort Nisqually they were hospitably received by William Kittson, in charge of the station, who provided

---

KENT—1861

First Sunday school at Kent held in schoolhouse, 1861. Rev. David Blaine held services at White River in 1854. Rev. D. L. Spaulding began preaching at Kent, in 1860, in home of T. M. Alvord. Methodist Episcopal Church organized by Rev. Connington Belknap, July, 1865. First members were T. M. Alvord, Peter Saar, R. C. Smith, Jason Clark, and others. White River served with Seattle until 1876. Carrie Alvord Epworth League organized in 1890.

In 1876, Lewis McMillan donated one acre for church and parsonage. Parsonage built there, but church erected, 1883, on another tract donated by J. H. Titus. In 1889, church moved to Central and Meeker Streets. Building here replaced in 1909, by new one dedicated in 1910. Rev. George A. Sheafe, pastor. Pulpit, chairs, Communion table, pews, donated by Irwin T. Alvord, son of T. M. Alvord. Organ installed by Rev. Harry E. Gardner, 1924-28. Church office building was acquired, 1933. Fellowship Hall dedicated in 1954, Rev. Earl W. McAbee, pastor.

New property on Black Diamond Highway, acquired for future, in 1960. Parsonage erected there. Rev. Paul Hamlin, pastor.

In 1964, Rev. Carroll Sprague, pastor. Membership, 941, church school enrollment, 704. Woman's Society members, 132, gave $549. Building valued at $267,-000, parsonage, $32,000.

rooms and hospitality until Willson could make the mission house livable three weeks later.

The Indians surrounding the mission at Nisqually were little more responsive than those at Willamette had been. Yet several events transpired during the life of the mission indicating the contribution the Methodists were making to the life of the Northwest.

More Firsts Occur on Puget Sound

Willson met Miss Chloe Clark for the first time upon her arrival at Vancouver. They were united in marriage at Nisqually, August 16, 1840, by Dr. Richmond. This was the first American marriage in Western Washington.

Eighteen months later, Francis Richmond, son of Dr. and Mrs. John P. Richmond, at Nisqually, was the first American child born in the Puget Sound country. Another son had been born to the Richmonds in New York immediately before they sailed for the Northwest. They named that son Oregon.

Another event in which Dr. Richmond played a prominent role was the first Fourth of July celebration in the Northwest, also occurring at Nisqually.

Notwithstanding their residence in disputed territory the Americans at the fort did not hesitate to show their loyalty to the United States.

They took advantage of the presence of Lieutenant Charles Wilkes, of the United States Navy, on a surveying expedition to stage a Fourth of July celebration with Dr. Richmond as featured speaker. In his address he uttered some prophetic statements:[6]

"We entertain the belief that the whole of this magnificent region of country," he said, "so rich in the bounties of nature, is destined to become a part of the American Republic . . . The time will come when these hills and valleys will be peopled by our enterpris-

CAPITOL HILL—1864

First Methodist Protestant Church organized in 1864, Rev. Daniel Bagley, pastor, had 11 members. First building on Second and Madison. Structure, 1865, cost $3,000. In 1872, an additional story erected to accommodate I. O. G. T. Lodge. New church, in 1883, cost $15,000, but burned in 1889.

Next church, on Third and Pine, cost $44,000, free of debt. For ten years membership declined and property transferred to Board of Missions of the denomination. Congregation moved to 16th Ave. E. and E. John, in 1905, dedicated October 6, 1907. Rev. A. Norman Ward, pastor.

Before 1904, Methodist Protestant churches or Sunday schools had been set up at Georgetown, Columbia, Renton, Ballard, Ravenna, Yesler, Jackson Street, and Green Lake. All these but Ravenna and First Church, had been abandoned before 1939.

Bagley remained pastor until 1885. Succeeding pastors, until 1917 were Rev. S. A. Baker, Rev. H. M. Sexton, Rev. J. H. Skidmore, local Methodist Episcopal preacher; Rev. Clark D. Davis, Rev. H. W. Kellogg, Rev. Frank E. Whitman, Congregational; Rev. T. P. Revelle, Rev. A. N. Ward, Rev. J. M. Gill, Rev. Robert Tyson, and Rev. Leonard B. Smith.

Pastor Smith organized church at Seaview which entered Methodist Union in 1939. In 1964, Rev. Donald L. Swerdfeger was pastor. There were 164 members.

ing countrymen, and when they will contain cities and farms and manufacturing establishments, and when the benefits of home and civil life will be enjoyed by the people . . . We are here also to assist in laying the foundation stones of a great American commonwealth on these Pacific shores."

Five hundred persons, including officers and sailors on Wilkes's ship, British subjects, connected with the Hudson's Bay Company, and four hundred Indians heard Richmond's words.

Richmond held regular services at the station near the fort, explored the surrounding region and visited the Indians. Mrs. Willson proved an effective and faithful teacher and a number of Indian children were enrolled under her care.

RICHMONDS RETURN TO ILLINOIS

Dr. Richmond, because of illness in his family, abandoned the mission and returned to Illinois September 4, 1842. He was born in Middletown, Maryland, August 7, 1811. He studied medicine, graduating from the University of Pennsylvania in 1833. After a short practice of his profession he went to Mississippi, where, in 1836, he was married to Amelia[7] Talley, widow of Rev. Alexander Talley, of the Mississippi Conference of the Methodist Episcopal Church. The same year he united with the Illinois Conference and in 1838 was pastor at Jacksonville, when Jason Lee visited that place. On that occasion he volunteered for the Oregon Mission.

After leaving Oregon, Richmond served churches in Illinois, locating in 1848, having been elected to the State Senate. In 1852 he returned to Mississippi and served a year on the Madison Circuit. Back in Illinois in 1854, he successively served in the House of Representatives, as a Presidential Elector, in the Senate, in the Constitutional Convention, and superintendent of schools of Brown County for eight years. In

GOLDENDALE—1870

Klickitat Circuit was set up in 1869. J. W. Turner, pastor. First class at Goldendale, 1870. Rev. Gustavus Hines. In 1871, Rev. J. H. B. Royal, pastor circuit. Building at Goldendale, erected in 1871. Land donated by John J. Golden. In 1875, new location was purchased from John R. Chatfield. Site still used in 1964. Building erected, 1878. In 1880, membership was 220. Building destroyed by fire, 1888, and immediately rebuilt. In 1904, membership, 230. Building had wing for Epworth League.

In 1910, 260 members, 120 in Sunday school, 86 in Epworth League. Rev. William DeWeese, pastor. In 1920, Rev. Louis Thomas reported two Sunday schools with 317 pupils, and 262 church members. In 1928, Rev. D. A. Storey reported 243 members.

Goldendale originally in Columbia River Conference, The Dalles District. Through rearrangement of charges in 1922, it became part of Puget Sound Conference. In 1929, part of Pacific Northwest Conference.

In 1964, Rev. Robert Gray Hess, pastor fourth year. Members, 453. Church school enrollment, 301. Woman's Society members, 94, gave $696. Building valued at $76,805. Parsonage, $24,500.

Early day preaching places on circuit now discontinued, include Centerville, 1878; Columbia, now Maryhill, 1880's. Horseshoe Bend church still standing, 1958, in disrepair, surrounded by cemetery.

1874 he went to Tyndall, South Dakota, where for one year he was superintendent of the Bonn Homme Mission. He was Post Master at Tyndall in 1884. He died August 28, 1895, in Manitoba, Canada.

A NEW STATE WAS BORN

Meanwhile, events involving Methodists were transpiring south of the Columbia. These had far-reaching effects upon the final outcome of the struggle between Great Britain and the United States for title to the Northwest.

By 1840 the country was astir with hope that Oregon would become a great commonwealth. But the residents of the region were divided in their loyalties. Adults, connected with the mission, and settlers numbered 114 that year. The recently arrived Catholic priests, the Hudson's Bay Company, and most of its former employees declared their allegiance to Great Britain.

A meeting convened at the mission house at Champoeg, February 7, 1841, with Jason Lee presiding, and Gustavus Hines secretary. Plans to establish some form of government were discussed. Another meeting was held in March with little progress made. Finally, May 2, 1843, by a margin of one vote, the group decided for a Provisional Government looking toward eventual American dominance.

Officers of the Provisional Government largely were members of the Methodist Mission. June 3, 1845, George Abernethy, mission steward, was elected first governor of Oregon. In 1849 he was superceded by Governor Joseph Lane, appointed by President James K. Polk, after enactment of a bill establishing Oregon as a Territory.

DISSENSION DIVIDED THE MISSION

Jason Lee, meanwhile, continued to push the work of the mission. He sought to serve the influx of settlers who increased year by year. They were re-

KALAMA—1871

Rev. J. F. DeVore, presiding elder, Puget Sound District, engineered organization of church at Kalama, 1871. First building erected that year, Rev. S. D. Winton, pastor. Church later burned, rebuilt with donated lumber, materials, labor. Rev. A. F. Wilson, pastor.

Second church destroyed by wind, rebuilt in 1894, Rev. W. H. Wilson pastor, at beginning, and Rev. C. C. Pratt, 1895-96. Just as ready for occupancy, it also burned. No insurance but $1,000 debt. Rev. C. B. Seeley, 1897, raised money to pay debt and build fourth church, which was finished under leadership of Rev. O. L. Doane, who completed debt payment in 1899.

In 1927, Rev. A. M. Heard, pastor, fourth church burned, fifth went up, 1928, Rev. Theodore H. Jorgensen, pastor. Building aided by Board of Home Missions, Church Extension. Basement finished, used while remainder completed. That year, membership, 50, church school enrollment, 167. In 1939 church had 66 members, 145 in Sunday school. Rev. J. H. Avery, pastor.

Debt on this building paid in 1943, Rev. Clark Cottrill, pastor.

Congregation scheduled fund raising campaign for new building, 1965.

In 1964, Rev. Donald D. Larson was pastor, second year. Membership, 137. Church school, 252. Thirty members of Woman's Society gave $711. Building valued at $33,000. Parsonage, at $9,000.

placing the Indian population which greatly had decreased. But dissension set in among mission workers. Some had written letters criticising Lee's administration of affairs of the mission. While the Industrial school continued to serve Indians, the numbers were not sufficient to please the most ambitious of Lee's co-workers.

Among the disaffected missionaries were Dr. John P. Richmond, Dr. Elijah White, Rev. W. W. Kone, and Rev. Gustavus Hines. Richmond spent several hours before the mission board after going East. Without Lee's knowledge the Board appointed Rev. George Gary of the Black River Conference, New York, to supercede him as superintendent of the Oregon Mission.

To Lee, it appeared futile to further discuss differences with the Board by mail that required twelve months for a reply. Added to Lee's other burdens had been the death of his second wife, Lucy, March 20, 1842, who left him with a small daughter, Lucy, three weeks of age. Lee felt that the future welfare of the mission required his presence in New York.

In November, 1843, Lee, with his young daughter and Rev. and Mrs. Gustavus Hines, sailed for the Sandwich Islands, hoping there to catch a ship for New York. Mrs. Hines had taken care of Lee's child since her mother's death and Lee had made his home with the couple.

At the Islands Lee learned for the first time that he had been replaced. He was disturbed, but believing it his duty to proceed, determined to go on while Hines, his wife, and Lee's daughter returned to Oregon. A few days later, when the deposed superintendent of the Oregon Mission sailed for the United States by way of Mexico, he gazed for the last time upon his daughter, whom he termed, "My All!"

LEE, VINDICATED, DIED AT 42

In the United States Lee visited Washington to lay before Government

LITTLEROCK—1871

Methodist preaching began at Black River, later Little Rock, in 1870. That year, Rev. H. K. Hines, presiding elder, deeded 80 acres of land for camp meeting site and Methodist Church. Trustees, Augustus Barbee, C. Clark, E. Chapman, A. N. Stearns and William Lemon. Year later, 40 acres sold to Thomas E. Rutledge. Deed signed by G. W. Rutledge, William Eastman, John M. Brewer, trustees of Black River Methodist Episcopal Church.

Early pastors included Rev. J. F. Ward, 1871-73; Rev. C. H. Hoxie, 1873-74; Rev. T. M. Reese, 1874-75. Camp meeting discontinued in 1902. First Sunday school superintendent, Thomas E. Rutledge. His father, William Rutledge, early class leader. First Church erected in 1885. Ladies Aid organized in 1900. First resident pastor, Rev. Charles Myers, 1903-04, also preached at Rochester, Grand Mound, Gate and Mima Prairie.

Building was moved into Little Rock in 1905, parsonage erected across street. Membership of church, 55. Three Sunday schools enrolled 175. Rev. C. F. Bennett, pastor. Later Postal Authorities named the town "Littlerock." In 1920, Littlerock-Tumwater supplied by Rev. J. H. Hicks. In 1939 Rev. Hazeldee Mowry, pastor, 48 members, 75 in Sunday school. In 1960 teamed with Rochester, had 15 members. In 1965 members transferred to Rochester, Rev. Albert VanAndel, pastor.

Officials the urgent need for action regarding Oregon. Later he appeared before the mission board in defense of his administration in Oregon. His statement proved satisfactory to the board which freed him from all blame. Yet it was too late to change orders which had been issued to his successor.

Later Lee visited Wilbraham Academy where he had been a student under Dr. Wilbur Fisk, and, in failing health, returned to his boyhood home at Stanstead, Canada. He departed this life among long-time friends and relatives, March 12, 1845, at the age of 42.

Shortly before Lee's death he sent a letter to Rev. and Mrs. Gustavus Hines to whom he had entrusted the care of his child. The message, written by another, was signed in Lee's own hand. He said:

". . . What shall I say concerning the dear little one? Let her have, if possible, a first rate education, but above all do not neglect her religious education, dear Brother and Sister Hines. I must hold you responsible, under God, to train that child for heaven . . ."

Mr. and Mrs. Hines fulfilled their trust. Lucy, later, Mrs. F. H. Grubbs, was graduated from Willamette University, the institution founded by her father as The Oregon Institute, and later was preceptress there. Her husband was a teacher and gave years of faithful service to education in Oregon.

OREGON COUNTRY BECOMES AMERICAN TERRITORY

Less than two years following Lee's death, the United States and Great Britain concluded a treaty by which England ceded to the United States all the disputed territory south of the forty-ninth parallel. The only remaining undecided boundary question, concerning the line between the mainland and Vancouver Island, was settled by Emperor William of Germany, in 1871.

SOUTH BEND—1871

First Methodist minister, Willapa Valley, Rev. J. S. Douglas, 1871. First pastor, Rev. John N. Dennison, 1871-72. Rev. Ira F. Ward, 1872. In 1875-76, Rev. C. Shepard appointed a committee to erect building, first church in town. Another building in 1889-90, Rev. James Matthews, pastor. Land donated near Cowlitz and Spruce Streets. One thousand dollars subscribed locally. South Bend separated from Oysterville. Rev. Sprague Davis, pastor.

First members: Mrs. Fannie McDonnell, Mrs. Fannie Peoples, Mr. and Mrs. Louis Pedersen. In 1891, F. A. Hazeltine moved to South Bend. He and family active in church more than 70 years. He was owner, publisher South Bend Journal.

Church incorporated, February 28, 1898. Trustees: S. Pitts, F. A. Hazeltine, H. J. Miller, Eugene Peoples, J. H. Turner, J. M. Dennison, F. L. Rice, Mrs. F. A. Hazeltine.

Third church, 1905. Same site used, 1964. Building dedicated, 1912. Bishop Charles W. Smith, officiated. Building remodeled, rededicated, May, 1949, Rev. Paul G. Perkins, pastor. Rev. W. C. Bowman, superintendent, preaching.

In 1961, Charles DeRoos had been member 67 years; wife, Minnie, 61 years. Charles Hammond, 51 years; Mrs. Anna Bond, 50 years.

In 1964, Rev. John W. Martin, pastor, first year. Members, 144; church school, 112. Woman's Society, members 35, gave $8.25.

THROUGH THESE, METHODISM FIRST TOUCHED PUGET SOUND

Nisqually Mission House

NISQUALLY MISSION—William Holden Willson, ship's carpenter, began construction of the Mission house at Nisqually, ten miles north of Olympia on Puget Sound, in April, 1839. In 1840, he was assigned to the secular department at Nisqually, with Dr. John P. Richmond, first Methodist missionary assigned to a charge in the territory of Washington. Richmond performed the first marriage of Americans in the present state of Washington, delivered the oration for the first Fourth of July celebration on the Pacific Coast and his wife gave birth to the first American child born on Puget Sound. Nisqually mission was abandoned in 1842 and Richmond returned to Illinois where Jason Lee first had met him.

William Holden Wilson

Dr. John P. Richmond

Lee's Role in Americanization of Northwest

The role of Jason Lee in the religious, political, and economic development of the Northwest is a matter of undisputed record. Attesting to it are the words of Cornelius J. Brosnan,[8] who felt that the story of the Protestant mission must be interpreted primarily as missions, not political undertakings.

"Consider Lee's visit in 1838 to the East," he said, "with his lectures in eighty-eight cities and towns, including the capital of the nation; his meetings and lectures promoted by a great and influential denomination . . . ; consider Slacum's widely quoted report; consider the Second Petition or Memorial of the Oregonians, framed at Lee's Mission House; the introduction of the Linn Bill; of Cushing's elaborate report embodying two Lee documents, with a publication and distribution of 10,000 copies; consider the fact that Lee's widely attended and published lectures dwelt upon the desirability of the Pacific Coast as a place of settlement and thus assisted in awakening an interest that sent the Peoria Party to Oregon in the spring of 1839, and was a factor in bringing between eight hundred and a thousand settlers, from many states, without previous inter-correspondence of any moment, to a fixed point in the early spring of 1843, with many others in succeeding years pressing after them, all bound for the Willamette Valley; consider the Provisional Government of Oregon and the important part Lee's Mission had in its inception and promotion; consider that experienced politicians saw in the movement for an American Oregon vitality enough to make it an issue in a presidential campaign on the basis of our claims to the territory.—When all these contributions are appreciated one cannot doubt that, though incidental and not primary, the Lee Mission was a significant factor in the settlement of the Oregon boundary controversy."

Thus, in less than twelve years, Lee demonstrated that a man of faith is a match for any mountain.

CHAPTER II

The pace of secular events in Washing-
ton Territory in 1853, and need for
civilizing influence of the Gospel, de-
manded that Methodist leaders on the
Puget Sound be—

Men
of
Action

METHODISM ENTERED WASHINGTON TO STAY

At the 1853 session of the Oregon Conference, Bishop E. R. Ames appointed Rev. Benjamin Close presiding elder of the Puget Sound District, and Rev. William B. Morse, his associate. At that time Methodism had no organized congregation or building in the Territory of Washington which was set off from Oregon that year.

Preaching services had been held occasionally at Vancouver and Cowlitz, by circuit riders residing on the Oregon side of the Columbia. As early as 1852, Rev. William Roberts and Rev. James Harvey Wilbur had visited Olympia and preached there.

Close resided at Olympia where he preached occasionally, visiting and holding services at Steilacoom and Seattle. He delivered the first Protestant sermon on Whidbey Island, April 25, 1853, at the home of Grove Terry near the present Coupeville. He sent Rev. William B. Morse to Whidbey Island and, on recommendation of Bishops E. R. Ames and Beverly Waugh, appointed Rev. John F. DeVore, of the Rock River Conference, to Olympia; and Rev. David E. Blaine, of the Genesee Conference, to Seattle.

Since these men still were in the East and several months would be required for their arrival, Close further surveyed the territory to which he had been assigned.

DeVore, APPOINTED TO OLYMPIA, WENT TO STEILACOOM [2]

Among those who followed Close were men of great force and prompt action who set the pace for early Methodism in the Northwest. The earliest, hardest-hitting, and most vigorous of these was Rev.

John F. DeVore. Close appointed him to Olympia but he went to Steilacoom.

A full appreciation of circumstances that led DeVore to change his appointment will require knowledge of primitive conditions of the country into which he came.

POPULATION GREW NORTH OF COLUMBIA

In 1844, nine years before the advent of DeVore, and two years after Dr. John P. Richmond had abandoned the mission at Nisqually, there were but six Caucasian families, not attached to the Hudson's Bay Company, residing west of the Cascade Mountains in the future state of Washington.[3] They were: James Birnie and George B. Roberts, near Cathlamet, on the Columbia; Captain James Scarborough, across the Columbia from Astoria; Simon Plomondon, Marcel Bernier, and Antonie Gobar, on Cowlitz Prairie. These six, their families, and officers and agents of the Hudson's Bay Company, and Indians were the only persons then residing in Western Washington.

In 1845 John R. Jackson located a claim on Cowlitz Prairie. His home later became the scene of the first court held in the territory. That year George Waunch filed on the Skookumchuck River, near Centralia, but did not move there for a year. In October, 1845, a party led by Colonel Michael T. Simmons settled at the head of Puget Sound, near Olympia. Others in Simmons' group were: James McAllister, David Kindred, Gabriel Jones, George Bush, and their families, and two unmarried men, Samuel Crockett and Jesse Ferguson. This company, totaling 31 individuals, formed the first permanent American Settlement in Western Washington.

Simmons and his companions were vigorous pioneers. Under the leadership of the former, mills to grind flour and saw lumber were erected. In 1850 Simmons sold his interest in the mills to

WOODINVILLE—1871

Building used for first Sunday school at Woodinville, was home of Mrs. Ira Woodin, in 1871. Mrs. Woodin, Mrs. Andrew Hansen, Miss Clara Jacobson, first teachers.

In 1880's Lutheran missionary named Anderson, preached. In 1892, Sunday school moved to Woodinville school. That year, Rev. Alfred Crumley, Bothell, pastor, preached afternoons.

Plan continued until 1902. That year, community church built by donated labor, heated by wood stove and lighted with kerosene. Electricity came, 1910. Land donated by Japanese-American named Yamaka. First full-time minister, Rev. Lorenzo Jean, 1902-03. Others, Rev. S. J. Buck, Rev. William Eldridge, Rev. Richard Oates, Rev. H. W. Mitchener, Rev. H. C. Leavenworth, Rev. A. W. Brown, Rev. B. W. Rinehart, Rev. O. F. Krieger, Rev. A. H. Thompson.

In 1918, building enlarged, entrance changed. Abandoned, in 1957, for new church, and parsonage, 140th Ave., N.E., Rev. Adam Forch, pastor. First service in new building, December 1, 1957. Old parsonage sold, 1960. Rev. Alden R. Graves, pastor.

New parsonage completed by Rev. Donald Forsburg and dedicated June 26, 1961. Rev. Robert A. Uphoff, officiating.

In 1964, Rev. Newton E. Moats appointed second year. Members, 242; church school enrollment, 136. Fifty-five members of Woman's Society gave $986.

NORTHWEST MINISTERS ELECTED TO THE EPISCOPACY BY GENERAL CONFERENCE

Bishop J.
Ralph Magee

Bishop Adna W.
Leonard

SERVING NORTHWEST METHODISM AND ELECTED BY WESTERN JURISDICTIONAL CONFERENCE

Bishop Bruce
R. Baxter

Bishop Gerald
H. Kennedy

Bishop A.
Raymond Grant

Bishop Everett W.
Palmer

Captain Clanrick Crosby, and his partner, and opened a general store on the present site of Olympia.

While Olympia was being reenforced, new settlers were joining those already in other parts of the territory and pushing into new locations. Among these were: Colonel Isaac N. Ebey, Whidbey Island, 1850; Henry C. Wilson, Port Townsend, 1850; Captain William Pattle, Bellingham Bay, 1850; John Vale, North Shore of Willapa Harbor, 1852; B. J. Madison, Dungeness, 1852; C. W. Stuart, Hoquiam, 1853; and others. By 1849, residing north of the Columbia were 304 persons, of whom 189 were American citizens.

Since, following the gold rush in California, the settlers found a ready market for timber products in that state, the population took a sharp rise the following year. By 1850 there were 1,049 residents north of the Columbia. That year a settlement was established near the Cascades on the Washington side of the river above Vancouver.

E. D. Warbass built a hotel at Cowlitz Landing, John Holgate filed a claim on the East side of Elliott Bay, and Olympia was officially named in 1850. By 1853, when Washington became a separate territory, the population had reached 3,963, of which 1,682 were voters.

In 1850 Captain LaFayette Balch, on his brig, George Emery, sailed into the harbor at Olympia with a cargo of speculation goods, hoping to locate there. But since Michael T. Simmons had but recently established his general store and looked with disfavor upon competition, he managed to convey his attitude to Balch who sailed out of the harbor to establish a town of his own.

Balch located at Steilacoom, seven miles north of Nisqually. There he filed on a claim, proceeded to lay out a town site, and let it be known that lots for building homes were for sale at this future metropolis of the Northwest. Aboard Balch's ship was a pre-fabricated house which he set up as a base for operations.

FIRST, MOUNT VERNON—1872

Church at Mount Vernon organized in 1872, with 12 members. Rev. G. H. Greer, Coupeville, organizing minister. Rev. M. J. Luark later became pastor.

Rev. W. B. McMillan, in 1883, did effective work. Trustees in 1888 were: Jaspar Gates, M. T. Phillips, S. C. Washburn. Added next year were J. P. Downs, Zimri Carlton, and F. A. Holeton.

Board of Church Extension provided $250 for first building on lots acquired from Jaspar Gates. Church was dedicated 1890, Rev. Charles McDermoth, pastor. Woman's Foreign Missionary Society organized August 26, 1897. Mrs. E. M. Newman, president. In 1892, Ladies Aid bought a parsonage.

Under Rev. R. L. Wolfe, 1903-04, debt of $440 was paid. Church sold in 1911 and construction started on new building, Rev. H. G. Ward, pastor. Basement ready by 1912, building dedicated, July 9, 1915. Rev. E. H. Todd preaching. Rev. F. H. Baldwin, pastor. The church contributed $2,232 to the Centenary Movement in 1920-21.

In 1957 new location was acquired. Construction on new building began in 1959. First service held August 31, 1960. Building consecrated by Bishop Everett W. Palmer, October 2, 1960. Cost of building $193,000. In 1964 Rev. Fred E. Fox, pastor. Members 612; church school enrollment, 356. Women gave $1,223.

By 1853, Steilacoom, next to Olympia, was the most important town in Washington. Balch was the man who induced John F. DeVore to go to Steilacoom instead of Olympia. It happened in the following manner:

These Laymen Went After a Minister [4]

In early August, 1853, Balch learned that a ship, bound for Olympia, with a Methodist minister aboard, would stop at Alki Point, where Seattle had been founded in 1851. The Captain, with friends, appointed themselves a committee to persuade the minister to change his plans in favor of their town. The committee leaped into a canoe and set out in a race with the ship to Alki Point. The journey on the Sound required two days of hard paddling. But when the ship cast anchor, Balch and his friends were at the landing. He told DeVore that Olympia already had a minister, Presiding Elder Close, that smallpox was epidemic there, and that Steilacoom offered a far greater field for the establishment of a Methodist Church.

DeVore had been licensed to preach by Peter Cartwright and was not without something of that pioneer Methodist's keenness of mind and sense of humor. Deliberately, he drew up a subscription blank and presented it to each of the Steilacoom enthusiasts, calmly inviting him to sign the amount he proposed to contribute for a new church in the home town. Later he circulated the subscription paper among crew and passengers aboard the ship. Being satisfied, he accepted the proposal to go with Balch. History does not record how the minister justified his change of appointment with his presiding elder or the bishop. But he went to Steilacoom.

When DeVore arrived at his new appointment, August 23, 1853, he organized a Methodist Church the first day, and before nightfall was soliciting materials and money for the new build-

TUMWATER—1872

Rev. C. H. Hoxie appointed to Tumwater in 1870. Church organized, 1872, 19 members. Trustees: Nelson Barnes, T. F. Berney, John Dickinson, James Biles. First Quarterly Conference held October 30, 1872. Rev. Herbert Patterson, pastor. Circuit included appointments 20 miles away. Rev. A. C. Fairchild, pastor, Olympia, officiated at organization.

In building church, appeal was made to Captain Clanrick Crosby (uncle of Bing). He said, "I'll give as much as my friend Barnes." Enthusiasm spread and $1,300 raised in one day. Material and labor donated. Building dedicated June 21, 1872, free of debt. Social hall, kitchen, added later. Parsonage was erected in 1872.

In 1884, Rev. A. K. Crawford appointed by Puget Sound Conference.

In the 1950's, kitchen was modernized, rest rooms added, Sunday school rooms and sanctuary, refinished. Under leadership of Rev. H. Gordon Casteel, attendance greatly increased.

For many years this was the home church of Rev. Ebenezer Hopkins who, though retired, continued to travel to schoolhouses and homes in surrounding country leading Sunday schools and preaching.

In 1964, Rev. H. Gordon Casteel was in his fifth year as pastor. Members, 163. Church school enrollment, 165. Woman's Society members, 28, paid $299. Building value $35,000. Parsonage, $15,500.

ing. The edifice, the first church structure north of the Columbia River in Washington, was built that year, and the pastor became known as a man of action.

This reputation followed DeVore throughout his entire ministry in the Conference. For instance, when he was sent to Olympia in 1855, and found the congregation without a church, he built it. He approached Captain Clanrick Crosby for a donation of lumber. Crosby, a man of generosity and humor, had heard of DeVore's prowess. He, in fun, questioned DeVore's ability to do a day's work and promised to donate all the lumber the minister could transport to Olympia in a single day. Early of a morning when the tide was right, DeVore arrived at the mill with a bill of lumber and went to work. By late afternoon he had loaded a raft, and with a favorable tide landed the lumber at Olympia before days-end.

DeVore was prompt and energetic in promoting all facets of church life. During the thirty-five years of his service in the Conference he spent twenty-one in the pastorate, twelve as presiding elder, and two promoting conference agencies.

DeVore's sense of humor never failed him.[5] In 1886 he was appointed presiding elder of the Olympia District. After the appointments had been read, he and Dr. D. G. LeSourd, the other presiding elder, met with Bishop William L. Harris. The Bishop playfully said to DeVore, "We did not appoint you to the district because we thought you were the man for the place, but because there was no one else available." "Yes," replied DeVore, "that was just the way it was in 1872 when we elected you bishop."

After a pastorate in Seattle, DeVore, in 1880, went to Tacoma, a new village on Commencement Bay. There, for six years he pioneered for the Church in new communities and laid foundations for several congregations.

YAKIMA, FIRST CHURCH—1872

Rev. George W. Kennedy was first resident pastor at Yakima in 1872. He served Ahtanum, Tampico, Cowiche, and Wenas. In 1880, Reverend Richard Barrett reorganized the work. Rev. Frank Spaulding served charge while city was being transferred to North Yakima in 1885. In 1888, Rev. John Uren found 20 members. During pastorate church erected at cost of $6,000 and parsonage acquired. Increased membership to 79.

Ladies Aid active as far back as 1885.

Rev. A. H. Henry, 1903-07, erected stone church costing $42,000. New parsonage two years later. Under the pastorate of Rev. W. B. Young, 1922-26, new church built at cost of $140,000. Heavy debt largely paid during pastorate of Rev. J. Edgar Purdy, 1935-41. Final $45,000 wiped out by Rev. Owen J. Beadles, 1954-61. Improvements totaling $20,000 on sanctuary. Also average of 151 members received annually. Benevolences increased from $4,500 to $16,000. The annual budget, from $49,000 to $69,000.

Church expressed interest in strengthening Yakima Methodism, in 1955, by commissioning 28 members to organize new congregation in West Yakima. A gift of $30,000 accompanied them.

In 1964, Rev. J. A. Harding was reappointed for third year. Members, 1,467, church school, 663, and Woman's Society members, 387. Women gave $2,548. Methodist Men, 105.

METHODISM ENTERED SEATTLE

Rev. David E. Blaine and his wife, Catharine, arrived at Alki Point, November 26, 1853, preached the first evening to a congregation of 30, most of whom were men, and on Sunday, December 4, 1853, organized First Methodist Church, the pioneer congregation in Seattle.[6]

November 13, 1851, twenty-four persons, including twelve children, had landed at Alki Point, where Elliott Bay meets Puget Sound, to give Seattle birth. During the following year most of the original group with new reenforcements, moved to the east side of the bay to file claims there. When Blaine and his wife arrived they too crossed to the east shore of the bay to establish the church. They wrote that the town consisted of thirty houses, twenty-six of which had been erected within the past six months.

In early 1854, Catharine became Seattle's first school teacher, and David served for a year as King County Auditor. He reported that there were but 300 white residents in the county at that time.

Meanwhile, David erected a parsonage at Second and Columbia which was occupied in the spring, and, next to it, built a church which was dedicated in May, 1855.

When the Indian Wars of 1856 disrupted life on the Bay, Blaine was transferred to Oregon where he served ten years before returning to New York. In 1883 he returned to Seattle to make his home until his death in 1900.

Rev. William B. Morse, who came to the Sound with Close, served Whidbey Island, Port Townsend, Skagit River, and other points until 1856, at which time he followed Blaine at Seattle. Following a period of service there he located.

The successor of Rev. Benjamin Close as Presiding Elder, was Rev. William Roberts. He had been appointed super-

---

FERN PRAIRIE—1873

First pastor, Fern Prairie, Rev. G. C. Roe, Lewis River Circuit. Class organized, April 21, 1873, Rev. J. H. Allyn, pastor. First church building, 1885, Rev. G. G. Ferguson, pastor. Dedicated that year by Rev. H. K. Hines. Lot donated by Pinkney Blair. Trustees: Pinkney Blair, Thomas Dorman, L. D. Olds. Revivals by Rev. G. G. Ferguson, brought many into church. Continued under Rev. D. M. Ellsworth.

Sunday school organized in 1885, Pinkney Blair, superintendent. Parsonage authorized, May 19, 1887. In 1887, Rev. P. Lewis, local preacher, reported 14 members.

New church erected, 1903, cost $800. Rev. F. P. Post, Fishers Charge, pastor. Building replaced former one, destroyed by fire, and in turn was destroyed by fire, 1924, and replaced.

Fern Prairie on circuit most years, Lewis River, Fishers, and others. In 1905, Rev. M. L. Hardingham, pastor. In 1938, Fern Prairie, with Salmon Creek, Rev. Kenneth Dunkleberger, pastor. Parsonage, costing, $10,000 erected, Rev. Francis Groth, pastor, 1957. Membership, highest point, during this pastorate, 87. In 1958, Fern Prairie alone, Rev. W. S. J. Bleakley, pastor.

By 1960, Fern Prairie, overflowed by Vancouver population, was included among charges of city. In 1964, Rev. Ray H. Northcutt, pastor, 4th year. Members, 65, church school enrollment 76. Building value, $10,500. Parsonage, $13,000.

intendent of the Oregon Mission succeeding Rev. George Gary, in 1847. He served 41 years in Oregon and Washington and was one of the wisest and most skilful leaders and administrators following Jason Lee. He traveled more miles than any other American pioneer preacher except Francis Asbury. Like other early circuit riders in the Northwest, Roberts actually was a circuit walker or paddler, since most of his travels were by foot or canoe, through unmarked trails or dangerous waters.

METHODISM SPREAD THROUGH PUGET SOUND

Beginning in 1856, for three years Rev. John F. DeVore was presiding elder of the Puget Sound District. Under his leadership ministers were appointed to follow settlers into many parts of the territory north of the Columbia. In 1858 charges in Western Washington, scheduled to receive pastors, ranged from Vancouver on the Columbia River to Victoria and Fraser River in British Columbia.

The appointments were: Vancouver, Rev. C. O. Hosford; Cowlitz, Rev. George W. Roork; Olympia, Rev. John W. Miller; Steilacoom, Rev. W. J. Franklin; Seattle-Puyallup, Rev. Christopher Alderson; Whidbey Island-Port Towsend, Rev. H. C. Rhoades; Mound Prairie, Rev. N. S. McAllister; Chehalis, Rev. Calvin H. Dray; Whatcom, to be supplied; Victoria, B. C., to be supplied; Fraser River, B. C., to be supplied. Most of these were heads of circuits with several preaching places attached.

Beginning in 1859, Rev. Nehemiah Doane became presiding elder of the district, serving in that capacity four years. While he was on the district there arrived in Seattle Rev. Daniel Bagley, a Methodist Protestant minister, who had represented his denomination in Oregon for eight years.

When Bagley arrived he exercised a right, extended to all visiting ministers, to hold services in the First Methodist

DAYTON—1874

Methodist church at Dayton, organized, 1874. Trustees: G. W. Miller, J. K. Rainwater, J. M. Hunt, J. H. Kennedy, P. G. Earl. Building committee appointed. Structure costing $3,000 ready for service, March 10, Rev. G. W. Kennedy, pastor, delivering first sermon.

Methodist church first organization chartered in Columbia County, 1876. In 1880, 38 members. Rev. J. D. Flenner, pastor. In 1893-95, Rev. Perry Chandler, pastor. Church remodeled. Two side wings, Epworth League room, choir loft. Rev. Francis A. LaViolette, 1895. There were 190 members, 180 in church school. Church building value $2,250.

In 1910 Rev. A. W. Roberts, pastor. Membership, 113 and 120 in church school.

In 1954, finance campaign raised $43,000, new building. New parsonage, 1957, costing $13,500. Second campaign, 1959, brought $33,000. New educational plant completed and paid for, 1959. Dedicated by district superintendent, Rev. Ac C. Wischmeier, March 27, 1960. Assisting were: Rev. Robert Maulden, Rev. Linden B. Jenkins, and Rev. Marvin E. Jordan, pastor.

Third building campaign, in 1961, netted $28,900 in pledges. New building began March 1, 1962.

In 1964, Rev. Adam S. Forch, Sr., pastor, second year. Members, 261. Church school enrollment, 96. Woman's Society members, 35, gave $309. Building value, $180,500. Parsonage, $13,500.

Episcopal Church, which came to be known as the Little White Church. In 1862 Presiding Elder Doane, unable to find a pastor to serve the congregation, left it to be supplied, and Bagley took over. He was an acceptable and cultured preacher, well liked. Seattle's Methodist Protestants rallied around the new leader and by the end of the year the congregation was flourishing.

METHODIST PROTESTANTISM ESTABLISHED IN SEATTLE

In 1863 Nehemiah Doane was appointed pastor of the church. Bagley suggested that he and Doane take turns preaching, but this Doane refused.[7] Bagley later said that he felt Seattle was not large enough for two congregations, hence his offer. But, being rejected, he took the Methodist Protestant members and began holding services three blocks up Second Avenue. The congregation was organized in 1864, and the new building, known as "The Little Brown Church," was completed in 1865. For a time this congregation was much larger than that at First Methodist Episcopal Church.

Bagley was a man of many interests. It was he who took the leading role in establishing the University of Washington in 1861. As chairman of the board, he was the first administrative head of the school. Later, he pioneered the opening of coal mines in King County. His son, Clarence B. Bagley, was a prominent journalist in the county for many years, and wrote histories of Seattle and King County.

Churches in the Northwest were sorely tried during the Civil War. Rev. Nehemiah Doane, in 1863, found but six members on the roll of First Church, Seattle, after Bagley's followers had left the congregation.

Rev. C. G. Belknap succeeded Doane as presiding elder of the Puget Sound District. The shortage of ministers was so critical that Belknap also served as pastor at Olympia and Grand Mound. The following year he served Grand

NOOKSACK—1874

Methodist preaching at Nooksack dates back to 1874. Rev. A. J. McNemee served community, 1876. Rev. D. G. LeSourd, presiding elder, visited Nooksack Crossing and preached there in 1884. Church organized in 1899, in connection with the church at Sumas. Rev. Isaac Dillon was the first pastor, Rev. T. J. Hazelton, 1903.

First church building purchased from Advent Christian people under Rev. Harry Richardson, 1908. Later they purchased Presbyterian building and that congregation joined Methodists. Rev. J. C. Harrison, pastor, 1910-12, unifying two congregations. New church repaired and painted, and original church rebuilt as an addition to the newly acquired building, providing room for classes and Epworth League. Under Rev. L. C. Schultz, 1914-18, parsonage further improved and, again, under Rev. J. H. Avery in 1920-23. Under Rev. G. C. Squires, 1923-27 further improvements made.

In 1931-37 a full basement was installed by Rev. F. F. Bothby. Rev. A. O. Quall, 1937-42, completed basement, enlarged parsonage. Sunday school sent money to keep two girls in school in Malaya where Rev. and Mrs. Marmaduke Dodsworth were missionaries.

New parsonage was built, 1955, educational unit, 1961.

In 1964 Rev. Murray V. Hyde, pastor. Members, 191; church school enrollment, 188; Woman's Society members, 42, gave $289.

Mound again, in addition to his district duties and, in 1865, was pastor at Seattle and White River.

At the close of the Oregon Conference in 1865, only six charges were named among the appointments to the Puget Sound District. They were: Olympia, Rev. C. C. Stratton; Grand Mound and Chehalis, Rev. H. C. Rhoades; Seattle and White River, Rev. C. G. Belknap; Whidbey Island and Teekalet, Rev. S. H. Todd; Claquato, to be supplied. Vancouver and Cowlitz were on the Willamette District with Rev. William Roberts as presiding elder. Rev. H. K. Hines served Vancouver, and Rev. Herbert Patterson who resided at St. Helens, Oregon, served Cowlitz.

In 1866 Rev. Harvey K. Hines became presiding elder of the district, a position he held four years. In 1870 eight appointments were listed in the minutes, to each of which a pastor was assigned. They were: Olympia, Rev. A. C. Fairchild; Steilacoom, Rev. Herbert Patterson; Seattle, Rev. S. H. Mann; Whidbey Island, Rev. G. H. Greer; Chehalis, Rev. C. H. Hoxie; Claquato, Rev. J. H. B. Royal; Cowlitz, Rev. C. H. Roork; and Vancouver, Rev. T. H. Wood and Rev. Clark Smith. Nine men were appointed to serve these churches besides Rev. John F. DeVore, who, that year, was appointed to a second term as presiding elder of the district.

In 1874, at the end of DeVore's second term, the minutes record five new charges on the district. These were: Skagit, Rev. J. N. Dennison; Tumwater, Rev. T. M. Reese; Dungeness, to be supplied; Oysterville, to be supplied; Lewis River, Rev. Samuel Matthews. Tacoma first appeared among appointments in 1873, but was not mentioned again until 1876, when Rev. Martin Judy was appointed pastor. In 1877 Judy reported 45 members and 77 in the church school. Tacoma was founded in 1868 by General Morton Matthew Mc-Carver. It was incorporated in 1875.

Rev. W. T. Woodward followed De-

NOOKSACK INDIAN MISSION—1874

The first Methodist to preach to the Indians on the Nooksack was Rev. C. M. Tate of the Canadian Church. He held services in the home of Chief Lynden Jim and Chief Johnny in 1874. Rev. A. J. McNemee preached to the Indians in 1876, and in 1880 the tribesmen petitioned the Puget Sound Annual Conference for a resident pastor, promising to build a school. Rev. John A. Tennant built a church for the Indians in the 1880's on land donated by Long Johnny.

In 1899, through a memorial gift by Mrs. M. E. Stickney, the Woman's Home Missionary Society established the Stickney Home and School. F. J. Brown became first superintendent and his wife, instructor.

From 1917 to 1928, Rev. and Mrs. B. V. Bradshaw supervised the work. Under Rev. S. G. Thero, 1929 to 1938, work continued prosperous. From 1938 to 1960 the mission was attached to other preaching places. In 1961-'62 Rev. Marmaduke Dodsworth, retired member of Malay Conference, served mission only. In 1962 Rev. Samuel Carlson pastored the Indians as well as the Caucasian congregation at Nooksack. Dodsworth returned in 1963, continuing until January 1965 when he died. In 1964 the church school enrollment was 82. In 1965 Miss Karen Dodson became pastor.

Vore on the district in 1874, and served one year. When he turned the district over to Rev. A. C. Fairchild in 1875, he had assigned a pastor to each of the thirteen charges listed in the minutes. When Fairchild finished his term four years later, the minutes listed sixteen charges, with thirteen receiving pastors.

Rev. Albert Atwood became presiding elder in 1879, and served four years, after which he pioneered many new charges in the Northwest. In 1902 he published "Glimpses in Pioneer Life on Puget Sound," and in 1907, "The Conquerors," in which he sought to show how Jason Lee, more than any one else, was responsible for retaining American rule over the Northwest.

SETTLERS FLOW TO PUGET SOUND

In the early 1880's settlers were seeking favorable locations on Puget Sound, along the rivers and valleys of Western Washington and the islands of the inland waters. Mills were being established to harvest Washington's magnificent stand of timber, ships were swarming on the Sound, bringing cargoes from across the seas and around Cape Horn, to exchange them for products of farms, forests and mines of the Northwest. Enthusiastic hope for the long-promised railroad to the East was running high.

Thousands of newcomers had been affiliated with churches in their former homes. Among them was a large company of Methodists who were establishing homes in communities where there was no religious influence. Before they could give thought to religion or education, they first must clear land and build homes in the wilderness. Others, with no former religious background, equally were in need of the Gospel.

The days of the pioneer had not ended, rather in much of the area they were just beginning. Because land claims were available in blocks a mile square, early settlers were scattered

---

FIRST, TACOMA—1874

First Methodist preacher, Old Tacoma, Rev. John F. DeVore, 1872. Rev. H. C. Hoxie, assigned, 1874. That year Methodist Church organized, six members. First meeting in tent. Charter members, W. H. Fife, Harriett A. Fife, Isaac Wilson, Melissa Wilson, Minnie Fife, Will J. Fife. First trustees: W. H. Fife, Harriett Fife, Thomas Bendor, David Lister, Elisa Lister. In 1876, Rev. Martin Judy, pastor.

In 1878, church building erected at Seventh and E. In 1892, tabernacle erected at South G. and Ninth Street, cost $5,000. Was used for twenty-four years. Rev. F. B. Cherrington, pastor. In the 1890's, church hindered by debt.

Rev. George C. Wilding, 1888-92 planted Methodism in many parts of city, providing members and leadership for new congregations.

In 1916, Rev. Delmer H. Trimble, pastor, new building erected at South Fifth and K. Streets. Rev. R. H. Schuett, pastor, 1918-22, followed by Rev. H. C. Rhoads, 1922-29.

In 1937-41, Rev. Cyrus E. Albertson, pastor. Church showed signs of sharp growth. Two sessions of church school instituted. Rev. Milton E. Marcy, 1941-51, church observed 75th anniversary. Rev. Clark J. Wood, 1951, was succeeded by Rev. Frank Brown in 1954.

In 1964, Rev. Lawrence J. Linneman, pastor, fourth year. Membership, 1,141, church school, 489. Woman's Society members, 282, gave $3,460. Building value, $1,075,000, parsonage $30,000.

52

over large areas. Roads fit for travel still were far in the future.

Rev. David Gorsuch LeSourd, who for four years was presiding elder, beginning in 1883, left a statement revealing hardships encountered by pioneering preachers of his day.[8]

Dr. LeSourd reported that in 1881 there were many abandoned churches in the Puget Sound country. This he attributed to the disruptions due to the Indian Wars, the most recent, the Chief Joseph's, had closed in 1877.

The size of the district to which LeSourd was appointed in 1883 was described by him as extending from the Cowlitz River on the Columbia, to Sumas and Blaine on the British Columbia Border, a distance of 300 miles by any route one could travel. From the peak of the Cascades to the Pacific Ocean the travel distance was 175 miles.

"On this vast field," LeSourd said, "I had eighteen charges including the Indian and Chinese Missions. Of these, three were unorganized circuits, and two others were left to be supplied. . . . At the beginning of the year there were but eleven church buildings, and some of these, cheap frame structures or log houses. Others were old and out-of-date. Buildings were located at Oysterville, Montesano, Tumwater, Olympia, Tacoma, Seattle, Whidbey Island, Skagit, Dungeness, and California Creek. My farsighted predecessor, Rev. Albert Atwood, had arranged for the erection of seven new churches. These were at: Centralia, Puyallup, White River, Elma, Whatcom, LaConner, and Ferndale."

They Traveled on Dangerous Waters

LeSourd described a revealing incident on his first round of quarterly meetings. The occurrence followed a gathering at Bay Center, on Shoalwater Bay. He said, "On Monday a gale was blowing across the bay, but a brother who had brought his family on Sunday from Oysterville in a 'plunger' decided to return in the afternoon. Rev. Columbus Derrick, the pastor, Brother Hadley,

LA CONNER—1875

In 1875, Dr. J. S. Church saw a stranger sitting on beer keg before the only business house in La Conner, hotel, saloon, general store. The stranger was Rev. J. N. Dennison, assigned to Skagit Circuit. The doctor, a Methodist, took Dennison home, arranged first preaching service in La Conner. First service held in home of Mrs. Louise A. Conner, a Catholic. Church organized in March 1883 with one member. Rev. B. F. VanDeVenter, first pastor. Rev. D. G. LeSourd presiding elder. Ladies Aid organized in 1888.

First building was started in 1883. First resident pastor at LaConner was Rev. B. F. Brooks, in 1884. Five members on the roll at this time. Circuit included Edison and Fidalgo Island, eight preaching points in all. In 1885, Brooks reported 125 members, five Sunday schools. Church building was finished. Rev. E. J. Moore was pastor 1886-87.

In 1892 the Swinomish Indian Reservation was a part of the La Conner circuit. In 1935 the Methodists purchased the building from the Baptists. An educational building was planned for 1963 for the Sunday school. Two Methodist Youth Fellowship groups. In 1964 Rev. Fred Owen appointed pastor for the fourth year. Membership 136, Sunday School enrollment 157. Woman's Society members 28. Women gave $657.

a local preacher, and myself, decided to go with him. We were not far out on the bay when the wind stiffened, the sail came near breaking its stays, and the boat began to leak seriously. While the mother and children crouched in the forepart of the boat, two of us preachers stood on the windward side to keep the craft from turning over, while the third dipped the incoming water with a scoop shovel. Running as close to the wind as possible, we could not make the landing without tacking and in doing this we were in danger of swamping, for the wind had become furious. Finally, to our great joy, we landed at Oysterville."

Discouragements were not always limited to hardships of travel. LeSourd tells of his first visit to the town of Snohomish where he had sent a local preacher to "round up the Methodists." When LeSourd arrived at night the minister was out of town, and no Methodists could be located. Sunday he went to the Presbyterian Church and made his presence known with a hope that he might be invited to preach in the evening. Instead his presence was ignored. He learned later that when the Methodist pastor had preached, there had been an outcry against the "Competition" of another church. The presiding elder concluded, "That was one town where I was not wanted."

A few years later LeSourd was appointed pastor at Snohomish and experienced a profitable ministry there.

Heroes Were at Work

The spirit that rendered effective the preaching of the Gospel in pioneer days is seen in the attitude of Rev. and Mrs. W. B. McMillan,[9] who came from Garrett Bible Institute in 1883 and were assigned by LeSourd to Skagit Circuit. The work extended twenty-five miles along the river. When the presiding elder explained the size of the circuit, Mrs. McMillan said, "My husband will need a horse and buggy for he will not be able to cover that area on foot." Le-

BLAINE—1876

Methodist ministers had visited Semiamoo before 1876. That year Rev. A. J. McNemee was appointed to the Whatcom Circuit of which Semiamoo was head. Other points on circuit were California Creek, Mountain View, Ferndale, Lynden, and Upper Nooksack. Upper Nooksack was fifty walking miles from Semiamoo. He covered the circuit by foot once each month. He boarded among the people, receiving $35 besides $100 mission money.

First service at Blaine held in the home of a Mrs. Kingley. Church apparently already organized. Membership on the circuit in 1877 was 33. There were ten teachers and forty scholars in two Sunday schools.

In 1885 the Semiamoo charge was left to be supplied. In 1893 when Rev. J. W. White was first appointed to Blaine, the church had 70 members, ten teachers and 85 pupils in the Sunday school. In 1910 Rev. C. B. Seeley reported 150 members, church building worth $5,000. There were 20 in the Senior Epworth League. In 1928 Custer and Blaine together.

In 1964 Rev. W. G. Graff appointed second year. There were 96 church members, 53 in the church school, 23 in the Woman's Society of Christian Service. Women gave $491. Church building valued at $33,000 and parsonage at $8,500.

PROMPT ACTION GAVE STEILACOOM A HEAD START

Steilacoom Church

Lafayette Balch

BALCH BRINGS HOME A MINISTER

Captain Lafayette Balch, founder of Steilacoom, as a rival of Olympia, was ambitious to gain prestige for his town. When, in 1853, he learned that Rev. John F. DeVore had been assigned to Olympia and that, on his way to his charge from the East, the minister would pause briefly at Alki Point, Seattle, the Captain gathered a party of his friends, paddled a canoe, a trip requiring two or three days, to the Point to meet the new minister. They told him that Olympia already had a minister, presiding elder Benjamin Close, and that smallpox was epidemic there. They said Steilacoom offered greater opportunities. DeVore, a man of action as well as wisdom, passed a subscription paper among his new friends, asking them to pledge what they would give toward a new church at Steilacoom. Then the passengers and crew of the ship were solicited. Being satisfied with the response, the clergyman resolved to accompany them. He organized a congregation the first day and built that year the first church north of the Columbia River.

Rev. John F. DeVore

Monument
on site
of Steilacoom Church

Sourd explained that such transportation would be out of the question, since the trail traversed terrain where fallen timber and rocks made it almost impossible for a lone horse to travel.

"But," wrote LeSourd, "they bravely went to their field, fitted up the rough board shack, called a parsonage, and there, according to their own statement, spent two of the happiest years of their lives."

Later, McMillan told LeSourd that he often had prayed that God would send him where no other preacher would want to go, but he had no idea, at the time, that God so literally would answer his prayer. During that pastorate McMillan led a revival at Avon which resulted in conversion of thirty persons, nearly all heads of families. "All up and down the river," LeSourd reported, "Methodism was taking root and promised a harvest by and by."

LeSourd tells of his first trip to California Creek in Whatcom County. He tramped fourteen miles through slush and snow with a downpour of rain soaking him from head to foot. Along the way, a kind Methodist woman gave him a cold lunch at noon. When he arrived at the little log church, no one was there. The building was cold and he had no matches. He paced the floor to keep from freezing while waiting for the Official Board. A member finally came and built a fire. While the presiding elder warmed and dried his clothes by the stove he conducted the Quarterly Conference in bare feet.

"This over," LeSourd reported, "the brethren decided that, since it still was raining, we should hold services then and there, instead of in the evening. This meant that the poor, tired presiding elder must preach." But first he donned his soaked coat and attempted to replace his still wet boots, into which his feet refused to enter fully, so he preached standing on his toes, but not from pure exultation and joy.

LeSourd reported another occasion when he and two companions, stranded

COLFAX—1876

First Methodist Church, Colfax, 1876, Rev. M. S. Anderson, organizer. For three years congregation met in Baptist Church, schoolhouse, homes. Pastor paid for lots with personal funds. Church head of circuit. Rev. W. S. Turner, 1879-80, built church. Early members, Mr. and Mrs. Henry Copley, Mr. and Mrs. Henry Ensley, Mr. and Mrs. John G. Potter, Mr. and Mrs. Charles Moys, Mr. and Mrs. Ted Moys.

Ladies Aid, organized, 1895. Woman's Foreign Missionary Society, 1899; Home, 1903. Epworth League, 1899.

In 1910, flood destroyed church, soon rebuilt. Rev. N. M. Jones pastor. Building committee, J. O. Housekeeper, J. P. Hubbard, Ed Armstrong, J. J. Kneale, Benjamin Baker. Building dedicated, 1911. Church, burned, 1920, next year third church dedicated, by Bishop William O. Shepard. District superintendent, Rev. Charles MacCaughey, pastor, Rev. A. A. Callender, Rev. U. F. Hawk, participating.

New parsonage erected, 1928, Rev. H. J. Wood, pastor. Longest pastorate in history of church was that of Rev. E. C. Newham, 1933-40. Rev. Earl McAbee, 1941-44, organized Woman's Society.

In 1942, debt of $5,550 paid. Gift of $1,000 from Mrs. F. A. Nauert.

In 1964, Rev. Chester C. Blair, pastor, second year. Membership, 476, church school enrollment, 187. Woman's Society, members, 76, gave $648. Building value, $120,000. Parsonage, $15,000.

on tideflats out from Stanwood, were compelled to spend a cold snowy night in an open boat, wet and chilled to the bones.

Other serious problems also were faced by men of the Conference. In spite of inflowing populations and prosperity in some of the larger centers, most of the ministers served small and poor congregations. These men were the real heroes of the Cross. One such man was Rev. John Alexander Tennant.[10] He was born in Arkansas, son of a pioneer Methodist minister, in 1830. He studied law, and being dissatisfied with that profession, became a surveyor and came, by way of California, to Washington in 1858. In 1859 he was a member of the Territorial Legislature and later became Indian Agent on the Lummi Reservation in Whatcom County. He married an Indian woman and settled on land allotted to her on the Nooksack River, becoming the first white man to live on the lower part of that stream. He built the finest house in the valley and his farm became the show place of all that country. But he was not a professing Christian. Yet he was a leader in all public improvements in the county supporting the little church and Sunday school at Ferndale.

Tennant was converted at a camp meeting conducted by Presiding Elder Rev. A. C. Fairchild, on the Nooksack, in 1878. His conversion carried an acceptance of a call to the ministry. The promptness with which pioneer presiding elders could act is seen in the fact that the day Tennant was converted he was licensed to preach and appointed pastor at Ferndale. Later he founded the church at Lynden and served as Indian Missionary at Nooksack.

Dr. LeSourd tells of the appointment of Tennant to work in the San Juan Islands in 1885. He and his Indian wife moved to Orcas Island, traveled the parish, preaching to Indians and whites wherever a small congregation could be assembled. He held protracted meetings and many were converted. A class was organized at East Sound. He extended

FERNDALE (UNITED)—1876

The first regularly appointed preacher at Ferndale was Rev. A. J. McNemee, 1876. Ferndale on Whatcom circuit. In 1878 John A. Tennant, who resided there, was converted, volunteered for ministry, appointed to serve the Ferndale charge. Rev. A. C. Fairchild was presiding elder. First full-time pastor was Rev. George Kindred in 1898. First church in Ferndale was erected on the east side of the river with aid from the Board of Church Extension which donated $250. There were 20 members. Rev. Albert Atwood was presiding elder.

By 1891, church had moved to West Ferndale. In 1923, it had moved back to East Ferndale. In 1912-15, under Rev. Jabez C. Harrison, east wing and the basement added. Ground breaking for a new building took place June 18, 1923, with Bishop William O. Shepard presiding, assisted by Rev. Jabez C. Harrison, and Rev. George W. Frame. Under pastorate of Rev. Harry L. Allen basement was excavated and church painted. In 1952, under pastorate of Rev. C. Gene Albertson, the church united with United Church of Christ.

In 1964 Rev. John A. Haygood, appointed pastor for third year. There were 186 members with 122 enrolled in church school. The 52 members of Woman's Society gave $333.

57

the work to Lopez and San Juan Island, and established several preaching places. To reach these he found it necessary to row his boat as much as fifteen miles across rough, cold, and stormy waters, then often to walk six miles over terrain that did not merit the term "roads." For this service the Conference provided $100 missionary support, and he reported offerings amounting to $36. As conference time neared he wrote his presiding elder that he thought he had better be returned the next year, because any other man and his wife would starve on such a field. As for him and his wife, there were plenty of clams to be dug from the beach and they would not suffer. LeSourd, as shrewd presiding elders always have done, sent him back to another year of physical poverty, but richness of soul.

Of similar mold was Rev. J. W. Dobbs,[11] who was transferred from Nebraska in 1884 and assigned to Whatcom. A substantial church had been erected there the previous year and the retiring pastor reported a debt of $100 on the building. Before the new pastor arrived, however, the treasurer discovered that the debt was $1,000. This filled officials with consternation. Feeling they could not meet such an obligation, they resolved to sell the church and abandon the work.

MOSCOW, IDAHO—1876

First Methodist Church, Moscow, Idaho, organized, December 21, 1876, in 12x14 schoolhouse south of town by Rev. M. S. Anderson, pioneer pastor. Charter members, Henry McGregor, W. D. Robbins, Mrs. Libby Robbins, J. W. Hamilton, Frank M. Martin, Alice Duff, Miss Mary Stewart. Shield's Hall first meeting place. First building started, 1883, Rev. Theodore Hoagland, pastor. Sunday school organized 1877. Ladies Aid, 1884. Woman's Home Missionary Society, 1889. Epworth League, 1890. Foreign Missionary Society, 1895. First unit of new building started, 1902. Completed, April 24, 1904, Rev. W. T. Euster, pastor. Debt paid under pastorate of Rev. B. E. Koontz, 1908-11. Church cost, $35,000. Membership, 350. After 1910, membership grew, inspired by revivals under Lowry and Moody, 1912. Membership that year, 641.

Wesley Temple dedicated, June 13, 1923. Rev. Harold O. Perry, pastor. The Wesley Foundation was organized in 1924. Ladies Aid paid last $10,000 of debt, mortgage burned, May 25, 1942, Rev. Owen J. Beadles, pastor.

Kitchen, Epworth Hall, remodeled, 1946-52, Rev. Ernest P. Goulder, pastor. New educational plant completed, costing $100,000 under Rev. Rudolph A. Anderson, 1960-62.

In 1964, Rev. S. Raynor Smith, Jr., pastor, third year. Members, 760. Church school enrollment, 563. Woman's Society members 249, gave $5,434. Value of building, $238,000.

When Dobbs arrived at Whatcom the officials informed him of their decision, saying they could not receive him, advising him to go away. Dobbs kindly and firmly informed the officials that he was there by the authority of the Methodist Episcopal Church and would stay. He did, although his first few weeks were filled with wrangling and threats on the part of certain officials. The women, seeing the rightness of his cause, rallied to his support.

There being no parsonage, Dobbs purchased lots, and, with his own hands, built a home for his family, assuming all costs himself. Before he left the charge, the building was dedicated without debt, every penny having been raised through his own activities.

A New Conference Was Born on Puget Sound

In 1883 members of the Oregon Conference residing in the Territory of Washington, introduced a resolution requesting that the charges lying in the territory west of the Cascade Mountains, be separated from the Oregon Conference to form a new ecclesiastical division to be known as the Puget Sound Annual Conference of the Methodist Episcopal Church. The resolution was adopted and the 1884 General Conference also acted favorably.

August 21, 1884, therefore, the new Conference convened at First Church, Seattle, to begin its independent life, with Bishop C. H. Fowler in the chair. Rev. Isaac Dillon was elected secretary. Fifteen members responded to roll call. They were: Rev. J. F. DeVore, Rev. Nehemiah Doane, Rev. Isaac Dillon, Rev. John Flinn, Rev. Columbus Derrick, Rev. J. N. Dennison, Rev. D. W. Cameron, Rev. Albert Atwood, Rev. D. G. LeSourd, Rev. Frederick Bonn, Rev. G. G. Ferguson, Rev. G. A. Landen, Rev. Andrew Farrell, Rev. B. F. Van-Deventer, and Rev. J. E. Leach. Transferred in were Rev. Andrew Jackson Hanson, Rev. Andrew Farrell, Rev. A. K. Crawford, all from California, Rev. W. I. Cosper, Oregon, and Rev. J. W. Dobbs, Nebraska. Transferred out were Rev. Nehemiah Doane, and Rev. Frederick Bonn to Oregon.

As Western Washington Methodism launched out as an independent Conference a new day had dawned demanding renewed dedication and action. Great events were just ahead. By July 3, 1887, the first Northern Pacific train from the East would arrive at Tacoma. By 1889, Washington, with a population of 239,544, would become a state.

During the thirty years since the first Methodist ministers had been assigned to the new Territory of Washington, more than 1,000,000 persons had migrated across the Rockies to establish homes on the Pacific Coast. By 1889 the

GRACE, MOUNT VERNON—1876

Rev. Eric Shogren, Methodist minister from California, visiting in 1876, was first to preach to Swedish residents at Pleasant Ridge. In 1884 Rev. Andrew Farrell went as pastor. Rev. O. N. Olander organized a congregation, in 1884. Rev. L. Dahlgren became pastor in 1888. First church was dedicated May 20, 1889. The following year a parsonage built by Rev. O. N. Olander.

In 1916, Pleasant Ridge merged with Swedish group at Mount Vernon. The property at Pleasant Ridge was sold for $500. Money used to buy lots in Mount Vernon. Pleasant Ridge building, wrecked and relocated on the new site in town. The cost was $2,750. Rev. S. Moody, Mount Vernon, continued with the congregation after union. He had organized church at Mount Vernon in 1911. First services were held in the Salvation Army Hall and later the Free Methodist Church. The rebuilt church was dedicated September, 1916. Parsonage built under the leadership of Rev. J. A. Willmer, 1918-22.

After Swedish and English conferences merged in 1929, this congregation continued to serve both Swedish and other Americans.

In 1964 Rev. Marvin A. Maddux was appointed for third year. Members, 50; church school enrollment, 69; Woman's Society of Christian Service, 77. Women gave $704.

population of King County would be 40,788; that of Pierce, 27,795, and Spokane, 25,200.

Although some of these advances were still in the future, they were clearly foreseen by that group of Methodist ministers gathered at Seattle First Church, in 1884, to launch a new Methodist Conference upon its course.

Dr. LeSourd reported that in addition to the men already members of the Conference and those transferred in, four others were received on trial. They were: Rev. B. F. Brooks, Rev. W. B. McMillan, Rev. G. R. Osborn, and Rev. J. A. Tennant.

Enthusiasm Sweeps the Conference

"From the beginning Bishop Fowler kept the Conference in a glow of enthusiasm," LeSourd said, "or convulsed with laughter as he played on their feelings, as he used his matchless oratory, his quick wit, or his ready anecdotes. He and all the brethren felt that we were in the beginning of a mighty movement that was to make Puget Sound the center of a vast population, whose Christian forces were to be a great evangelizing agency, not only in all our Northwest, but in Alaska, in the Isles of the sea, and the vast empires beyond."

LeSourd further comments, ". . . The first session of the Puget Sound Conference was a prophecy of the future, hopeful, optimistic, planning large things and brimming over with enthusiasm to bring them to pass. We took hold of our work with a vision of all the races . . . Besides the usual standing committees we appointed others on German, Scandinavian, Indian, and Chinese work. The sum of $150 was raised for the Indian Mission, and $525 subscribed toward the Olympic Collegiate Institute. Brother John Flinn said that the only property he had in the world was an old mare and she was lost, but if we could find her we might apply

---

GRANGEVILLE, IDAHO—1877

Methodist church at Grangeville organized in 1877, by Rev. J. D. Flenner, pastor at Denver, Idaho. First pastor, Rev. W. A. Hall, principal of Columbia River Conference Academy. Rev. A. Maxey, pastor in 1888, led in erecting church building. Church incorporated, 1889. Trustees: W. A. Hall, J. H. Robinson, J. F. McClean, S. R. Church. Church sold 1914.

Congregational church, organized 1899, united with Presbyterian church, in 1903. In 1914, Presbyterian church and Methodist congregations, federated, alternate pastoral leadership.

In 1934, new building started. Committee: L. L. Smith, C. O. Vincent, E. D. Doane, Henry Von Bargen, Mrs. M. L. Ayers, Mrs. E. W. West. Building dedicated, December 9, 1934, Rev. G. P. Keeling, of Kamiah, preaching dedicatory sermon.

Hammond organ installed, 1936, Rev. Nelson C. Pierce, pastor. Gift $500 by Mrs. Mary Coram. Under pastorate Rev. W. O. Bethin, Presbyterian, 1941 branch World Council of Church Women organized. Rev. Harold Black, 1946, received brass cross, candlesticks for altar, gift of Mr. and Mrs. Edwin Nelson, in memory of Mrs. Nelson's mother, Mrs. C. J. Zehner.

In 1952, both denominations agreed that church henceforth be under sponsorship of Methodist Church. Cornerstone for new unit laid, 1952.

In 1964, Rev. William E. Strance, pastor, fourth year. Members, 319.

the proceeds to the collection." The mare was not mentioned again. Twenty-six men received appointments at the close of this Conference. Two districts were established, the Seattle and the Olympia. Dr. LeSourd took the former and Rev. A. J. Hanson, the latter.

During the following ten years Methodism entered many new communities. In 1889 the Conference was divided into three districts. They were: Seattle, Rev. H. D. Drake; Vancouver, Rev. A. J. Hanson; and Tacoma, Rev. H. D. Brown. The following year two other districts were added, Whatcom and Swedish. New presiding elders that year were: Tacoma, Rev. Samuel Moore; Whatcom, Rev. D. G. LeSourd; and Swedish, Rev. Olaf E. Olander; Seattle and Vancouver retained their presiding elders.

The Pastor Was the Key Man

Important as the leadership of the presiding elder may have been, the significant kingdom-building activities of this decade were that of pastors on the field. Dr. LeSourd's revealing biography throws the spotlight on the achievements of some of these men.

One such minister was Rev. G. L. Cuddy, transferred from the Baltimore Conference in 1890, and assigned to Sedro-Woolley, which had been cut off from the Skagit Circuit.

"He showed at once the pluck of a hero," LeSourd wrote. "When he and his cultured wife landed among the stumps and trees of the Skagit Valley he could find but one or two Methodists. Yet he unfurled the Methodist banner and, in spite of lack of means, he built, largely with his own hands and money, a church worth $2,000, and a parsonage worth $500. This was characteristic of all of Brother Cuddy's work throughout his active ministry."

Dr. LeSourd also paid tribute to Rev. A. J. McNemee, a bachelor, one of the most famous pioneers of the period. LeSourd referred to the work of this

ORTING—1877

Methodist preaching services began in Orting, 1877. Church on Puyallup Circuit in 1886. Church was incorporated, Dec. 9, 1889. Trustees, D. D. Wilts, J. R. Chapman, O. C. Hutchins, Gideon Wescott, served as incorporators. Organizing pastor, Rev. John Bretts.

Lots for building purchased May, 1890, contract for church building let to F. Schenck, December, 1891. Rev. J. W. Barger, pastor. Building occupied in fall of that year. Historian stated that it had been open every Sunday since that time, save in case of epidemics. At no time had congregation been without a pastor. Building was enlarged three times to accommodate greater attendance. Women here, as elsewhere, kept church property in good condition, paid deficits, provided leadership in many projects of church. In 1896, South Prairie attached to Orting as one charge. Rev. W. M. Welch, pastor. Arrangement was discontinued but date not mentioned.

In 1916-18, Rev. James E. Milligan became pastor, membership reached 165, church school attendance 175. Ten years later membership, 136, church school enrollment, 151. By 1938 there were 115 members and church school 123.

In 1964, Rev. Donald R. Moller pastor, second year. Membership, 146, church school enrollment, 142. Woman's Society members 50. Group paid $336. Church value $36,500. Parsonage $6,100.

man at Lopez Island, where, with but thirteen members he built a church valued at $1,850, and paid on it $1,650. This was in 1889-90. But the year before this McNemee[12] had been appointed to Dungeness Circuit on the Olympic Peninsula. The field was forty miles long and must be traveled by foot, part of the way along the shore of the Strait of Juan de Fuca.

Port Angeles was on the circuit, and since settlers were moving into the town, McNemee resided there the first six months, after which he moved to Dungeness, the center of the circuit, held a revival, witnessed the conversion of several persons, and built a church.

When at the close of the year, the presiding elder, Rev. W. H. Drake, asked concerning the return of the pastor, McNemee reported that a good mother in Israel, with tears in her eyes, said, "Brother McNemee is a good man and we all love him, but we want you to send us a man who has a wife who can play the organ and teach in the Sunday school."

"That hurt my feelings," said McNemee, "since I had lived six months at Port Angeles with only two dollars on salary. So I moved on to make way for a pastor with a wife and six children." During his ministry McNemee built six churches, one parsonage, finished and dedicated two churches, and repaired six others.

The next pastor to be assigned to Port Angeles, also was unmarried. He was Rev. W. R. Warren,[13] who arrived there in September, 1890. He found no church building, no members, and no place to reside.

In a letter to this writer in 1933, Warren said of his arrival at Port Angeles: "I was invited to stay a day or two with Mr. Nottage and his wife. He was a member of the Infidel Club ... When I told him who I was he said, 'You can stay here overnight, but my old woman will never get meals for men like you.'"

Next morning Warren arose and

STANWOOD—1877

First Methodist preaching services were held at Stanwood in 1877, by Rev. Columbus Derrick. Service held in the home of Mr. and Mrs. F. H. Hancock. The first regular preaching service at schoolhouse, by Rev. B. F. Van De Venter, in 1881. Church organized, 1884, 12 members. In 1890 first church and parsonage were erected. Official board members were D. O. Pearson, F. H. Hancock, George Payne, W. R. Stockbridge, and R. F. McGee. Pastor, Rev. M. C. Van Tyne. Date of dedication, July 27, 1890. First church was lighted by kerosene lamps until 1929 when Rev. Paul R. Campbell had the church wired for electricity. A social hall was added in 1921. Church renovated in 1955 and Wesley Hall built. Rev. Bertrand Robbins served during second World War, remained nine years, infusing new life into the congregation.

Under Rev. Wendell Cone, 1959, church celebrated its 75th anniversary. In May, 1960, ground was broken for a new church building which was occupied in 1961, and consecrated May 4 of that year, by Bishop Everett W. Palmer, Rev. Wendell Cone, pastor.

In 1964 Rev. Robert J. Lyon appointed for second year. Members 302, church school enrollment 133, Woman's Society members, 70. Their gifts, $1,349. Church property value $117,000. Parsonage, $8,500.

started for the village for a bite to eat. His host stopped him at the door, saying, "Come, have a bite, but remember, that's all!" Toward the end of the silent meal Nottage dropped his fork and shouted, "I want you to understand that I am an infidel and don't care a d--- if you are sitting there."

Warren said nothing, but after breakfast took his things and prepared to depart, his host and hostess accompanying him to the door.

"Something said to me, 'pray with this couple before you go,'" Warren reported. "I thought Mt. Baker had rolled over on me, but I got down on my knees. My prayer was ejaculatory, like Rowland Hill's, in that it got to heaven before the Devil got a shot at it . . . When I arose, Mr. Nottage made two quick steps toward me, grabbed my hands, and his salty tears fell on our hands as he said, 'You stay where you are!'"

When Nottage learned that the minister was from Ontario and far from his home, he said, "We will adopt you." Warren consented and they gave him a room.

"Nottage went out among his infidel friends with a halo on his face," said Warren, "and told them of the power of Christ to save, and others were influenced by his testimony."

A church building was erected in Port Angeles, and Warren reported 28 members at the end of the year.

LeSourd, paying tribute to his men, said, ". . . I had reason to rejoice in the faithful service the pastors had rendered, and the success that had crowned our efforts. Four new charges had been organized during my first two years on the district, namely, San Juan Islands, Seattle Circuit, South Tacoma, and Old Tacoma, and Tacoma Scandinavian charge. Revivals had resulted in many conversions and accessions, especially at First Church Seattle, at Puyallup, Bird's School, and at Nooksack Crossing. Fifteen new classes had been formed, as many new Sunday schools had been

COEUR D'ALENE—1879

Methodist preaching began in Coeur d'Alene, Idaho, 1879. First services in Masonic Hall. Church organized that year by Rev. Samuel Driver.

In 1890, all churches in Kootenai County including Coeur d'Alene in Post Falls Circuit. Rev. Lee A. Johnson, pastor. The Ladies Aid organized before 1896, by which time church and parsonage erected. In 1906, church moved, replaced by another. Rev. J. R. Barker, pastor. Building dedicated February 28, 1909, Rev. William H. Fry, pastor. Participating were Rev. E. R. Fulkerson, Rev. Henry Brown, President Fletcher Horton, Willamette University. Many memorials added to warmth of sanctuary.

Mortgage paid June, 1932. October, 1938, Rev. Ralph I. Thomas, pastor, was drowned in Hayden Lake. The parsonage redecorated in 1938 by Ladies Aid, Rev. Willard E. Stanton, pastor. New building dedicated 1958, Rev. Victor Phillips, pastor. Loan of $40,000 from Division of National Missions aided project. Church debt refinanced, in 1958-62, by Rev. Laird Glascock. In 1962, Athol added to the circuit. This church appeared as separate appointment in 1907. There were 40 members and 75 in Sunday school. Rev. S. W. Shirley pastor.

In 1964, Rev. Myron H. Sharrard, pastor third year. Members, 490. Church school enrollment, 287. Woman's Society members, 119. They gave $1,690.

organized, while six new churches or chapels were ready for occupancy."

They Were Humble and Great

A minister of this time whose humility was matched only by the greatness of his heart, was Rev. Andrew Anderson,[14] who became supply pastor at Elma in 1884. He had been a member of the St. Louis Conference since 1871, but came West as a supernumerary and so remained for a year, being restored to effective relationship in 1885. Churches on his circuit included: Elma, Oakville, Satsop, and Ford's Prairie. Later he served the Centralia Circuit, comprising Grand Mound, Bucoda, and Yelm. Other places served were Rochester, Little Rock, and Shelton. These were small charges, but the quality of his life, and the sweetness of his spirit were an inspiration and challenge to all he met. After his death, in 1916, letters of appreciation for his ministry came from great and small among ministers and laymen.

Another man who rendered useful service in rural areas, preaching in schoolhouses and organizing Sunday schools long after retirement, was Rev. Ebenezer Hopkins. He entered the Puget Sound Conference by transfer in 1887 and was assigned to Tumwater. Until his death in 1929, at the age of 87, he traveled his circuit regularly. His was a pioneering ministry and the service rendered was of untold value to residents of rural communities where otherwise there would have been no religious influence.

Upon Hopkins' death his biographer said of him, "His particular delight was the children in the country schools, and to few men is it given to have as wide and extended personal acquaintance with so many people."

The life of this man should prove an inspiration to men privileged to serve in smaller fields in the Northwest.

ELLENSBURG—1879

Ellensburg Circuit appeared in 1885. Rev. G. W. Kennedy first preached there in 1872, in "Robber's Roost" owned by A. J. Splawn. After 1879 part of Kittitas Circuit. In 1884, Rev. Ira Wakefield, pastor. In 1885, Presiding Elder Samuel Gascoigne reported improvements on church, parsonage at Ellensburg, including bell in the tower. That year 40 members were reported on circuit, with four Sunday schools enrolling 120. Rev. Henry Brown became pastor.

In 1886, Ellensburg Circuit had 45 members, two Sunday schools with 85 enrolled. Rev. Henry Moyes, pastor.

First Ladies Aid, 1909, Mrs. J. J. Putnam, president. But the women had been at work there since 1884.

In 1921, a new church dedicated, costing $65,000, part of which had been provided by the Board of Home Missions and Church Extension. Rev. W. B. Young, pastor. Mortgage paid in 1943 under Pastor William Martin. New parsonage acquired in 1949.

A new unit, begun in 1961, included ten Sunday schoolrooms, small chapel, library and offices, cost $115,000. Dedicated in 1962, by Rev. Miller Lovett, pastor. In 1964 church membership, 531; church school enrollment, 319; Woman's Society of Christian Service, 140, who gave $1,219 to local work. Rev. George L. Poor was appointed pastor for third year in 1964.

METHODISM'S EARLIEST PIONEERS IN WASHINGTON

Rev. C. O. Hosford

Rev. David E. Blaine

Rev. John H.
Tennant

Rev. Daniel Bagley

Rev. D. G.
LeSourd

Rev. W. R.
Warren

SOUTHWEST WASHINGTON METHODISM WAS GROWING

During the decade ending in 1893 Methodism steadily was widening its services in Southwest Washington as seen in the number of churches established. The records show that during that period churches in Tacoma had increased from three to ten; along the Columbia River appointments had increased from four to seven; on Willapa Harbor, from two to four; and on Grays Harbor, from three to six.

The fifth decade of Northwest Methodism began in 1894 with five districts, and men assigned to 112 churches. The Districts were: Chehalis, Rev. S. S. Sulliger, presiding elder; New Whatcom, Rev. T. J. Massey; Seattle, Rev. T. B. Ford; Swedish, Rev. O. E. Olander; and Tacoma, Rev. Samuel Moore.

METHODISM ENTERS ALASKA

During this decade Conference members became interested in a Mission to Alaska. In 1900 the Conference sent its first representatives to that country. The missionaries were: Skagway, Rev. M. L. Covington; Douglas City, Rev. N. G. Barton; Ketchikan, Rev. V. Ray Bennett. The following year, Rev. J. Wesley Glink went to Dolmi; Rev. F. A. LaViolette, to Juneau; and Rev. John S. de Mattos to Skagway. This was the beginning of an affiliation between Puget Sound and Alaska that lasted until 1960 when Seattle became an area separated from that of Portland. Alaska remained with the latter area.

The growth of the Puget Sound Conference in the decade ending in 1903, indicated that leaders at the end of the first half Century of Northwest Methodism had no less capacity for action than the founders.

Forty-two new appointments had been added during this decade. One of

ROCKFORD—1879

Rev. M. S. Anderson, first Methodist preacher at Rockford. Small congregation met at home of Mrs. Charles Farnsworth. Church organized that year. Rev. Samuel M. Driver, pastor. Church on Coeur d'Alene Circuit. First building erected, in 1880, on site donated by Charles Farnsworth.

In 1894, church replaced by larger one, dedicated July 17, 1895. Rev. F. W. Utter, pastor. Structure replaced in 1923, dedicated November 25. The Home Mission Board provided $700 aid for building. Rev. Hubert C. Vincent, pastor. At dedication, appeal for $3,028 to cover indebtedness was oversubscribed by $1,635. Loan from Board of Home Missions turned back.

Trustees were, J. E. Cosman, E. C. Frazier, George C. Pratt, W. D. Hamilton, H. D. McDonald, Charles H. Hecht. Rockford Church succeeded Bethel, 1879; Waverly, 1882; and Mount Hope, 1887. Rev. Ruth Lortz only minister who stayed more than three years.

From this church, Henry W. Waltz, Marcus W. Waltz, Victor Waltman, W. C. Armfield, entered Methodist ministry. Betty Eileen Flower, married Dr. Samuel Moffett, Presbyterian medical missionary in Korea. Sister, Jeanne Marie, wife of Presbyterian minister in Washington. Rev. George C. Pratt, entered Pacific Northwest Conference, 1956.

In 1964, Rev. Glenn A. Rudolph, pastor. Members, 113, church school, 125. Woman's Society, 24, gave $773.

those charges was University, Seattle, second largest congregation in the Conference in 1964.

The strength of the Conference at the end of the first half century will be seen in the recital of certain figures. In 1903 the Conference had 11,220 members; 18,373 in Sunday schools, including officers and teachers; value of parsonages, $88,336; and of church buildings, $400,-700; Missionary giving, not including other benevolences, $10,396.

FAITH WAS THE MAINSPRING FOR ACTION

Difficulty of travel over most of the territory had not been solved entirely by the coming of railroads. Witness the case of Rev. Isaac Dillon, one of the great spirits of the period. He was superannuated in 1889 but continued to work among the islands of the Sound. June 6, 1902, he started to row his boat from Port Stanley, seven miles to Newhall, to fill a preaching appointment on Sunday. The next day his boat was found. In it were his traveling bag, his hat, his overcoat and umbrella, but his body was never found. Opposite his name among the honored dead in the Conference minutes, stand the words, "Drowned in Puget Sound."

In a late paper Dillon had written, "I love to go over the restless waters and carry the gospel to the various points among the beautiful islands of the San Juans."

His biographer wrote, "Dr. Dillon was made for action and would go as long as the power of going remained."

Rev. Andrew J. Joslyn became presiding elder of the Tacoma District in 1895, concluding his term in 1901. He retired in 1910 and afterwards made his home at Canby, Oregon. He died of burns resulting from an explosion, December 8, 1920.

Joslyn's final words were verification that the Gospel which men of action had spread throughout Western Washington for a half century still was quick and powerful and sharper than a two-edged sword. He said, "Tell the people that the Gospel that so long I have preached to others does not fail me now."

CHAPTER III

Plight of conquered Indians in Eastern Washington following Indian Wars of the 1850's and complexity of forces shaping the destiny of the Inland Empire, demanded leadership of—

Men of Great Hearts

METHODISM ENTERS A VAST AREA

Six years after Rev. Benjamin Close and Rev. William B. Morse went to Puget Sound in 1853, Rev. James Harvey Wilbur was appointed presiding elder of the Columbia River District.

The area extended from the river's mouth eastward across the Cascades to the summit of the Rockies. East of the mountains it reached from California to the Canadian border. That year, Rev. George M. Berry was appointed to Walla Walla, the first point in Eastern Washington to receive a Methodist pastor.

MEET "FATHER" WILBUR, A GREAT LEADER

In 1860 Wilbur became presiding elder of the Walla Walla District and pastor at Fort Simcoe, on the newly-formed, but still disorganized, Yakima Indian Reservation. During the following twenty-five years, he, as pastor, presiding elder, educational director, and Indian Agent, demonstrated what a great heart could do to level the barriers separating the Indian from the white man and his religion.

Methodism was delayed entry into Eastern Washington by Indian wars that began with the murder of the Whitmans in 1847, and continued intermittently for eleven years.

Further appreciation for the Methodist Mission east of the Cascades will require knowledge of the history of that region during the preceding years. The first white residents of the area were connected with trading posts operated by rival fur companies. A station was built on the Columbia, near the mouth of the Okanogan, by representatives of John Jacob Astor's Pacific Fur Company, in 1811. A few months previously a post was established on the Spokane River by David Thompson, representing the Northwest Fur Company, which, in 1824, merged with the Hudson's Bay Company.[1]

In 1818, Donald McKenzie, representing the Northwest Fur Company, established a trading post at the mouth of the Walla Walla River near the present site of Wallula.

Here, Jason Lee rested briefly in September, 1834. At that time there were no Americans residing east of the Cascades, save a few free trappers.

MARCUS WHITMAN REACHES NORTHWEST IN 1836

The first Americans to settle in this region were Dr. Marcus Whitman and Rev. H. H. Spaulding, who, in 1836, established missions for the American Board of Commissioners for Foreign Missions, at Waiilatpu, near Fort Walla Walla, and at Lapwaii, Idaho.[2] The Whitman massacre, in 1847, ended the mission at Waiilatpu, and the country, for a time, was left to the Indians, and the Hudson's Bay Company.

The home-seeking immigrants, passing through this region by the thousands, during the fifteen years following 1843, were bound for the Willamette or Puget Sound. They tarried here only long enough to rest and procure supplies. Lewis Dawney and Narcisse Raymond took claims near the old Whitman mission in 1852.

In 1853, Governor Isaac Stevens found about 25 old Hudson's Bay Company employees, living with their Indian wives, near old Fort Walla Walla. Brook, Bamford, and Noble then operated a large cattle ranch near Walla Walla.

INDIANS RESENT
THREATENED LOSS OF TERRITORY

Despite the peace efforts of Governor Stevens, in the mid-1850's, the Indians

CENTRAL, SPOKANE—1879

First Methodist Episcopal Church, Spokane, organized, 1879, ten members. Rev. S. G. Havermale did early cultivation. In 1880, Rev. M. S. Anderson, pastor, served six other points.

In 1882, building erected on Sprague Street. Rev. Royal E. Bisbee, pastor. Under Rev. W. C. Gray, 1886-88 brick church erected on Sprague and Bernard. Under Rev. A. C. Wilson, 1888, building sold, congregation moved into tabernacle. Wilson succeeded by Rev. W. A. Shanklin, 1890. Four years later, under Rev. W. W. Van Dusen, congregation again erected sanctuary. Rev. D. W. McInturff completed the building with aid of $9,500 from Board of Home Missions. Certain members withdrew to form Vincent Church. McInturff also withdrew, formed "People's Church." Church, burned in 1905, rebuilt following year. Under Rev. Frederick B. Short Vincent congregation returned, in 1918, and name changed to "Central" Church. In 1923, church had 2,000 members, 1,000 in church school. Ladies Aid 260 members.

In 1941, Rev. Charles MacCaughey, pastor, paid debt. An educational unit built, 1956, Rev. W. Clyde Beecher, pastor. In 1964 Urgent Needs Appeal granted $5,400, loaned $15,000 to lift debt.

In 1964, Rev. James T. Albertson, pastor fifth year. There were 952 members, 242 in church school. Woman's Society, 201; giving $1,688. Building valued at $730,030.

of this area continued resentful of the threatened loss of their territory to the whites, who came in increasing numbers, and began war which ended in 1858. Meanwhile, military authorities ordered all white settlers out of the region.

At the close of the war the order was rescinded and settlers began to reenter.[3] By the end of 1858 Thomas P. Page, James Foster, Charles Russell, J. C. Smith, Christopher Maier, John Singleton, John A. Simms, and Joseph McEvoy had taken claims along the Walla Walla. The following year settlers located along the Touchet River, as far as the present city of Dayton, in Columbia County.

FLOUR AND LUMBER MILLS FIRST INDUSTRIES

John A. Simms built a flour mill near Walla Walla in 1859. Saw mills followed. Merchants and blacksmiths joined other settlers in the vicinity, and the County Commissioners formally named Walla Walla that year.

The discovery of gold in the Nez Perce country hastened the growth of Walla Walla, which was the trading center for the area. In 1861 and 1862, it was reported, up to 25,000 gold-seekers entered the mining territory through that town.

Farmers pressed eastward to take up land, and Lewiston, Idaho, was platted in 1862. In 1864 farmers discovered that wheat could be grown successfully on upland areas. This opened a source of wealth far exceeding that of all the gold taken from the mines of Idaho. In 1866 flour was first shipped from the region. Congress approved the establishment of the Territory of Idaho, March 2, 1863.

Thus Methodism entered Eastern Washington within a year following the first settlers. George Berry had been received into the Baltimore Conference in 1852. In 1855 he served on an Oregon Conference Committee dealing with the Conditions of the Indians. He went to Steilacoom in 1856 and that year was a

CHENEY—1880

Methodist church at Cheney, born in butcher shop, in 1880. Rev. D. G. Strong, presiding elder, first preached there November 25 that year. Rev. Theodore Hoagland, pastor, held first service, December 28, with two women in attendance.

Charter members were Mr. and Mrs. John C. Tyler. First prayer meeting held at home of Job Robbins, March, 1881. Site for building, selected by Presiding Elder D. G. Strong, cost $100. In 1882, Rev. D. G. Strong, pastor, found 9 members.

Ladies Aid, organized and went to work. Building 20x36 was completed in 1881, valued at $450. Parsonage purchased, 1891.

Second building, costing $4,000, erected in 1889. Dedicated, December 1889, Rev. M. H. Marvin, pastor, and Rev. Volney C. Evers. Ladies Aid carpeted building and painted interior. In 1900 another church building erected. Building remodeled, 1908.

In 1911, Dr. N. D. Showalter, president State Normal, Cheney, induced Andrew Carnegie to donate pipe organ. Methodists federated with Congregational church, 1928. Lasted 34 years. Federation dissolved, April 2, 1961. A new parsonage was dedicated, May 3, that year. Eight members were received, bringing total to 80.

In 1964, Rev. Howard S. Pitts became pastor. Membership, 152. Church school, 99. Woman's Society members, 43. They paid $887.

member of the committee which took first steps to organize the Olympia Collegiate Institute. In 1858 he served as chaplain in the United States Army at Steilacoom. After two years at Walla Walla, he went to Corvallis, Oregon, and did not again serve within the territory covered by this history.

WILBUR ADDS NEW DIMENSIONS TO METHODIST WORK

The arrival of James Harvey Wilbur,[4] affectionately known as "Father," added a new dimension to Methodist work in Eastern Washington. His greathearted attitude toward his brethren in the ministry, the laymen, the Indians, and even lawbreakers, was so irresistible that he set a standard for the Christian ministry seldom equaled and never excelled in the history of Northwest Methodism.

The 1860 journal of the Oregon Conference makes no mention of Wilbur's activities in Eastern Washington save those supplied by brief statistics. But undoubtedly he explored the entire territory assigned to him.

Several reports indicate that Wilbur visited Fort Simcoe in 1859. Since Colville, in Northeastern Washington, was included in the appointments in 1860, it is likely that he visited that point. In 1860 he was appointed presiding elder of the Walla Walla District and pastor at Fort Simcoe. He taught in the Indian school until 1864 when he was appointed Indian Agent by the Federal Government.

Judge E. V. Kuykendall,[5] who, as a boy, resided at Fort Simcoe in the 1870's, has given insight into the spirit and method of Wilbur's approach to his work. His father was a physician attached to the Agency, and the son had free run of the place.

According to Kuykendall the condition of the Indians in Eastern Washington was deplorable. They had been thoroughly defeated in the war, their

FIRST, CENTRALIA—1881

First Methodist preaching at Centerville, by student from Willamette University, 1860. First pastor, Rev. W. P. Williams, also Willamette. In 1881, 46 members, church valued at $400. Rev. George R. Osborn, pastor, 1883.

Land for church, donated by George Washington, Negro. Building, dedicated, 1884, by Rev. H. K. Hines.

Cornerstone laid for new building, May 31, 1903, Bishop Earl Cranston, officiating. Edifice dedicated, January 10, 1904, Bishop John W. Hamilton. Rev. J. W. Miller, pastor.

Pipe organ installed through efforts of Dr. Paul Sweet, 1931, Rev. Philip H. Raymond, pastor.

Mrs. J. B. Frye, first president of Ladies Aid. Woman's Foreign Missionary Society, Mrs. Nellie Muck; Home Missionary Society, Mrs. Frank Clark.

Rev. G. W. Frame, 1916-20, led service in memory of departed soldiers of war. May 9, 1945, Rev. Erle Howell conducted service honoring men of church in service of Country.

J. L. Baker, Eugene Simmons, each superintendent of Sunday school 31 years. John Raught, treasurer, and head usher, half century.

New building, dedicated April, 1960, Rev. Bruce Parker, pastor. Former pastors, Rev. R. A. Anderson, Rev. Charles T. Hatten, Rev. S. Raynor Smith, promoted building.

In 1964, Rev. Clinton A. Aiton, pastor, fourth year. Members, 724, church school, 509. Woman's Society, 166.

lands had been taken, and they had not received compensation promised by the Government. Many of their men had been killed and their horses, chief source of wealth, largely destroyed.

The Indians had been ordered onto the reservation, but many of them sullenly refused to obey. They could not understand why the lands over which their fathers, for generations, had roved in freedom was declared to be no longer theirs. With this attitude, Wilbur was not unsympathetic, yet he knew that the best interests of all concerned would be served through rigid enforcement of the law.

CHIEF MOSES, FAMOUS INDIAN LEADER, MEETS WILBUR

A leader among the tribes of the Grand Coulee was Chief Moses, for whom Moses Coulee and Moses Lake are named. He rebelled against attempts to bring him and his people onto the reservation with other tribes which often had been their enemies.

One of Wilbur's first acts as Agent was to invite Moses to council. The Chief came, robed in finest regalia. The agent patiently explained the purpose of the Government to give every family land, with seeds and farm implements, and to teach them how to produce food from the soil. He offered to make Moses chief of police on the reservation.

When these two men faced each other there was born a mutual trust and friendship that never was broken. Wilbur proved that a greathearted attitude toward a former enemy was more powerful than the rifle to break down barriers of enmity and distrust.

Wilbur was born at Lowville, Lewis County, New York, September 11, 1811. He united with the Black River Conference in 1832, and came to Oregon in company with William Roberts, superintendent of the Oregon Mission, in 1847. These two greathearted men took advantage of a stopover in San Francisco to deliver the first Methodist sermon and organize the first Methodist

GARFIELD—1881

First Methodist pastor, Garfield, Rev. W. J. White, 1881. With Palouse, where pastor lived. Schoolhouse, built, 1882, used by all denominations, including Methodists. In 1885, Methodists used Baptist Church. Rev. T. C. Hoagland, pastor. In 1888 Rev. F. L. Young, pastor, organized church, erected building. Next year, Rev. G. E. Wilcox first resident pastor.

In 1912, old church replaced by new brick veneer building, costing $11,000. Rev. Charles W. Monson, pastor. Dedicated by Bishop R. J. Cooke. Building committee, J. H. Vannice, Charles W. McCall, S. J. Scott, Jonas A. Crumbaker. Mortgage burned, 1926. Two charter members present, Mrs. R. C. Bellus, Mrs. Lewis C. Love.

Rev. Otho McKinley Love, entered ministry from Garfield, 1925, serving Jessie Lee Home, Seward, Alaska.

In 1927, parsonage partly burned. Church acquired new building at distance from church, was used 25 years. From 1949 to 1957 no resident pastor. Church erected modern parsonage next door to church. John E. Miller donated property for parsonage. Later, Miller acquired deed to other land near church, presented it to congregation to complete needed space for many activities.

In 1964, Rev. Jerry F. Smith, pastor, second year. Members, 119. Church school enrollment, 113. Woman's Society members, 76, gave $648. Value of church property, $91,600. Parsonage, $17,000.

church and Sunday school in California before proceeding northward.

Wilbur's first assignment was the Oregon Institute at Salem. He pioneered work in Portland and served the Umpqua Academy in Southern Oregon. As a teacher and Indian missionary, he rates the greatest in Methodism.

CANNON SUMMONS PEOPLE TO FIRST SERVICE IN OLYMPIA

Wilbur and Roberts, in 1852, conducted the first Methodist service in Olympia. His method of assembling the settlers was as unique as his approach to other problems. A cannon had been set up at the village center to give warning in case of Indian attack. The minister arranged to have the cannon fired shortly before the hour of service. The population hurriedly gathered, relieved to find that instead of an Indian war, the ministers wished to invite them to join an attack on sin.

Wilbur has been described as above six feet, two inches in height, thick chested, strong and handsome, in a manly fashion, possessing a voice to match his physical strength. His personality combined fearlessness, exceeding tenderness, and a firmness that dominated other wills.

A writer tells how Wilbur handled two youths who disturbed a camp meeting he was conducting in Oregon. The youth had ignored Wilbur's warning to desist. While the clergyman led a hymn, they became so boisterous that Wilbur left the pulpit, marched down the aisle, singing in stentorian tones. He approached the boys who had not been aware of his nearness. Still singing, he knocked the boys' heads together with stunning force. When satisfied the lesson had been imparted, he marched back and took his place without missing a note. There was no more disturbance.

FIRST CHURCH,
LEWISTON, IDAHO—1881

First Methodist Church, Lewiston, Idaho, organized 1881. First appeared among appointments 1876, Rev. G. W. Shaffer, pastor. Rev. H. B. Lane preached there, 1875.

Rev. E. C. Rigby organized society in 1879, soon turned work over to his brother, Rev. Jessie W. Rigby, who found three members, Mrs. J. W. Poe and daughters, Rena and Sadie. This pastor, in 1881, set up a permanent organization. Additional charter members: Mrs. Miller, Mrs. Strong, Mrs. Thompson, Mrs. Seeds, Mr. Wright, and Mr. Strong.

In 1882, Rev. Levi Tarr, pastor and president Lewiston Collegiate Institute.

Women organized before 1883. Woman's Missionary Society, 1882.

Land for Lewiston Institute, donated by Rev. J. H. Wilbur. Cornerstone of new church laid, May 8, 1884.

New building, erected 1907 costing $100,000. Rev. W. T. Euster, pastor. Rev. Robert J. Reid, Rev. Charles MacCaughey. Rev. Julius C. Harvy completed building. Debt finally paid, 1943.

Pipe organ costing $3,400 was installed 1910-11. Rev. Clifford W. Williams, pastor. In 1918-20, debt reduced to $2,500. Rev. Henry T. Greene, pastor. Rev. E. A. Wolfe, 1925-29, received 370.

In 1964, Rev. Bruce B. Groseclose, pastor, fifth year. Membership, 700, church school, 366. Woman's Society, 112 gave $2,667. Value of building, $255,000. Parsonage, $16,150.

WILBUR QUICK TO CONDEMN, QUICK TO FORGIVE

Wilbur was strong in his condemnation of wrongdoing, yet quick to relent at signs of repentance. He refused to tolerate intoxicants on the reservation. An incident of 1884 will illustrate the greatness of his attitude toward a fellow minister accused of indulgence in alcohol.

Rev. S. M. Driver, who had been transferred as a probationer from the Oregon Conference in 1880 was accused in open conference. Wilbur moved that he be given a chance to speak. Driver confessed, begging for mercy. Wilbur's motion that the man be given another chance was carried. Father Wilbur tenderly took Driver under his wing, and, from that day, the two were closest friends, and the erstwhile offender rendered effective service as long as he lived.

Wilbur continued, until 1882, with the Agency, with the exception of the year 1870 when the Army took over at Simcoe. At that time, Northwest Methodists joined a national protest against leaving the welfare of the Indians in the hands of the Military. At the end of the year the minister again was appointed to the Agency, where he remained until his request for retirement was accepted.

CENTENARY, SPOKANE—1881

Union Park Methodist Episcopal Church, Spokane, organized in 1881 with 13 members. Rev. W. T. Euster cultivated field. Ground donated and first building erected in 1890. Rev. Royal E. Bisbee, advisor. Later, church struggled with partial pastoral service, incomplete building, heavy debt, through depression of 1890's. In 1893, 28 members.

In 1904, new parsonage built, wing added to church. Rev. M. R. Brown, pastor. In 1910, Rev. John J. Law, pastor. The congregation united by 1911, 243 members. Full basement completed in 1910-11 and in 1912, addition was built. Under pastorate of Rev. George Parrish, 1921, new building started. Bishop William O. Shepard presided at cornerstone laying May 27, 1923. Building cost $60,000. Fourteen thousand donated by Centenary fund. Name changed to Centenary because of this aid.

Church remodeled, some debts paid, and others refinanced under Rev. Ernest Winfield, 1932-33. Rev. J. Homer Magee, 1933-36, Rev. Robert Mauldin, 1936-41, and Rev. E. Clifford Newham, 1941-46, refunded debts, paid some obligations. Freeway took church in 1954, another erected, costing $160,000. Pipe organ installed in 1955.

In 1964 Rev. Wendell Cone pastor, fourth year. Membership, 265, church school enrollment, 239. Woman's Society members 85. Paid $722. Church valued at $174,000, parsonage at $20,000.

After his retirement from the Indian service, Wilbur continued active in the Conference until his death in 1887.

The year Wilbur became presiding elder of the Walla Walla District, five charges were announced east of the Cascades. They were: Walla Walla, Rev. G. M. Berry; The Dalles and Cascades, Rev. John Flinn; Klickitat and Wasco, Rev. W. D. Nichols; Colville, to be supplied; and Simcoe Indian Reserve, Rev. J. H. Wilbur.

In 1861 Rev. John Flinn became presiding elder and Gustavus Hines was assigned to Oro Fino, Idaho. The latter place was the scene of extensive gold discoveries. Flinn served the district four years, during the difficult period of the Civil War, when ministers were not

74

available. At the beginning of his last year only two other pastors were appointed to serve eight charges. Points receiving ministers were: Idaho City, Rev. C. S. Kingsley; The Dalles, Rev. B. C. Lippincott; and Cascades, Rev. John Flinn. Walla Walla, Lewiston, Colville, Umatilla, and the Grand Ronde-Powder River charges were left vacant.

Flinn was succeeded on the Walla Walla District by Rev. W. S. Lewis, who died during the year. Of ten charges on the district that year only two received pastors. They were: Grand Ronde and Powder River, Rev. Z. B. Ellsworth; and The Dalles, Rev. I. D. Driver. That year the Yakima District with Rev. James H. Wilbur, presiding elder, appeared. All five charges were left to be supplied save Simcoe where Wilbur was pastor.

Two Ministers Serve Six Circuits

When Rev. Isaac Dillon became presiding elder of the Walla Walla District in 1866 he found only two ministers appointed by his predecessor to serve six charges. Rev. J. D. Deardorf went to Walla Walla, and Rev. John Tindall to The Dalles. Umatilla and Birch Creek, La Grande and Powder River, Cascades and Canyon City were left to be supplied. Two years later when Dillon turned the district over to his successor, Rev. J. B. Calloway, six of the eight charges were given pastors.

In 1868 the country included in the Walla Dalla District was overrun by miners and settlers. The veteran of the Oregon Mission, Rev. William Roberts, made his services available to the Idaho Mission, where he remained three years, laying foundations for churches which later would flourish.

At the end of two years on the Walla Walla District, J. B. Calloway appointed pastors to eight of nine charges.

"Father" Wilbur Presents Two Indians to Conference

The year 1869 was one of triumph for

AVON—1882

Methodist services first held at Avon in the homes of individuals in 1882. Rev. B. F. Van De Venter, preaching. The church was organized in 1884 with 21 charter members. That year plans laid for building which was completed three years later. Rev. W. B. McMillan, pastor. Lot donated by Arthur H. Skaling; ancestors were great friends of John Wesley in England. At a meeting November 1, 1884, $330 donated. Building dedicated free of debt, 1887 having cost $750. Shakes for the roof were cut by A. E. Flagg and James McCain. Skaling drew the plans for the church. In 1920 the church was moved from its original location on the river to its 1964 site.

An organ was given to the church by Mrs. Paul Eubanks, a charter member. The first organist was Mrs. Bessie Dicks who came to Avon in 1882 as a charter member. Twenty-eight ministers served this church during its first 75 years. A new parsonage built in 1929 was valued, in 1964, at $10,000. Value of the church building, $37,000.

In 1964 Rev. R. Clinton McGaffe was appointed for the second year. Church members, 139; church school enrollment, 147; Woman's Society of Christian Service enrollment, 42. Women paid $480.

HE INTRODUCED METHODISM IN THE INLAND EMPIRE

Rev. James Harvey Wilbur

Rev. James Harvey Wilbur, presiding elder of the Columbia River District, and Pastor George M. Berry, organized at Walla Walla, in October, 1859, the First Methodist Church on Washington soil, east of the Cascades. Wilbur was missionary and Indian Agent at Fort Simcoe for 23 years.

The church at Satus, on the Yakima Indian Reservation, is the only building erected by Rev. James Harvey Wilbur, still standing. Later, it became the place of worship of a group of Indian Shakers.

Commandant's Quarters
Fort Simcoe

Guard House at
Fort Simcoe

Father Wilbur for his painstaking efforts on the reservation. That year he presented two Indians for admission on trial in the Conference. They were Thomas Pearne and George Waters, who had been hand-picked and trained. Pearne was assigned to Simcoe and Waters to the Simcoe Circuit. They were the first Indians to be admitted to a Methodist Annual Conference. They served effectively throughout the remainder of their lives.

H. K. Hines Ranks With Greathearted Men

Rev. Harvey K. Hines, who became presiding elder of Walla Walla District in 1870, ranks at the top level among the greathearted men who served in the Inland Empire. He was admitted into the Genesee Conference in 1848, and transferred to Oregon in 1853. In 1859 he became presiding elder of the Willamette District. In 1866 he traveled the Puget Sound District. After being transferred to the Idaho Conference he was elected to the General Conference in 1892. He was eight years editor of the Pacific Christian Advocate, and honored by election to many national committees of the Church.

Hines was author of A Missionary History of the Pacific Northwest. He traveled over the Northwest by steamboat, 75,000 miles, stage 5,000 miles, and private conveyance 100,000 miles, a total of 180,000 miles.[6]

A New Conference
East of the Cascades

In 1872 General Conference approved a resolution from the Oregon Conference, proposing to set up an independent Annual Conference east of the Cascade Mountains. Accordingly, the presiding bishop, Jesse T. Peck, in 1873, read appointments to three districts in the newly formed East Oregon and Washington Conference. The name, in 1876, was changed to "The Columbia River Annual Conference." Bishop Peck read 23 appointments to territory in

OAK HARBOR—1882

Exact date of first preaching service at Oak Harbor not known. Rev. George A. Landen, in his unpublished autobiography, said it was one of the three appointments on the Whidbey Island Circuit, when he went there in September, 1882. Rev. W. B. McMillan served the circuit in 1887. Apparently the church was not organized until some years later.

Rev. J. M. Hixon, Crescent Circuit, held services over a store building at Oak Harbor, in 1909. In 1910, Rev. F. S. Pearson, superintendent of Olympia District, said the Sunday school there was more prosperous than the one at Crescent.

Oak Harbor, with Crescent, first appeared in conference appointments in 1910. Rev. C. H. Baldwin, pastor. Following year a Ladies Aid building was erected costing $1,000.

In 1916 Rev. B. N. Galbraith was appointed to Oak Harbor where he remained 20 years. Under his leadership a church building costing $12,000 was started, in 1920, and dedicated by Bishop W. O. Shepard, June 5, 1921. In 1920, the Olympia District was dissolved and Whidbey Island Churches transferred to the Bellingham District, under Rev. J. M. Canse, superintendent.

In 1964, Pastor Calvin W. Moore reported 438 church members; church school enrollment of 403; Woman's Society of Christian Service, members, 65, paid $715.

77

which, fourteen years before, only two had existed. These were: Walla Walla District, Rev. H. K. Hines, presiding elder; Walla Walla, Rev. S. G. Havermale; Dayton, Rev. H. B. Lane; Colfax, to be supplied; Pendleton, Rev. O. B. Brewer; Grand Ronde, to be supplied; Eagle Creek, Rev. F. Elliott; Waitsburg, Rev. W. T. Koontz; Snake River, to be supplied; Weston, Rev. H. C. Jenkins; La Grande, Rev. G. W. Adams; Baker City, Rev. L. A. Powell; Chaplain United States Army, Rev. J. O. Raynor.

The Dalles District, Rev. H. Caldwell, presiding elder; The Dalles, Rev. J. S. Vandersal; Ochoco, to be supplied; Yainax, Rev. James Harer; Canyon City, Rev. A. J. Joslyn; Wasco, to be supplied; Klamath, to be supplied; Goose Lake, to be supplied; Klickitat, Rev. Hugh Caldwell; Yakima, Rev. George W. Kennedy.

Indian Mission District, Rev. J. H. Wilbur, presiding elder; Simcoe, J. H. Wilbur, and Rev. Thomas Pearne; Siletz, Rev. W. C. Chattin; Chehalis, to be supplied; Missionary at large, Rev. George Waters.

Two of the charges announced on the Indian Missionary District were not within the bounds of the Conference, and several others were not within the area included in this volume.

DAVENPORT—1882

Methodist Episcopal Church at Davenport, organized, 1882, with eight members. Trustees were, J. W. Earles, George Oman, J. P. Lawrence, J. F. West, George Oswalt, Charles Buck, A. P. Oliver. Rev. M. S. Anderson was the organizing pastor. He was followed, in 1882, by Rev. L. J. Whitcom. Later by Rev. N. E. Parsons and Rev. J. H. Shepard, in 1885.

The Ladies Aid was organized at an early date. First church building was erected in 1892 and the parsonage, same year.

A revival in 1908 added 65 to church rolls. A new church building was erected in 1916, and dedicated, same year. Rev. Fred E. White, was pastor. Rev. W. H. W. Reese, Tacoma, delivered the sermon. Between 1918 and 1926 the German Congregation merged with the English-speaking congregation. Rev. A. F. Kroneman was pastor 1926-36.

In 1953, a new parsonage, costing $20,000, was erected. Rev. James E. Doak was pastor. An oil burning furnace was installed, in 1956. Rev. George A. Odgers and Rev. Paul Brown entered the Methodist ministry from this church.

In 1963, Rev. Joseph L. Woodford, pastor fourth year. There were 194 members, 132 in Sunday school and 60 members of Woman's Society of Christian Service gave $834. Value of church building, $103,750. Parsonage, $31,000.

G. W. KENNEDY HAD DOG-CAT FIGHT DURING SERVICE

Rev. George W. Kennedy, who appeared this year as pastor at Yakima, had been assigned to that charge the preceding year. He came from Illinois with his parents by wagon train in 1853, and settled in Southern Oregon. He united with the Oregon Conference in 1871. That year he continued to teach school near Waiilatpu, but in 1872, was sent to Yakima Circuit.[7]

Kennedy wrote a volume, "The Pioneer Campfire," in which he related incidents occurring on the way to Oregon, and those encountered during more than a half century in the ministry. One of the amusing anecdotes related in Kennedy's book concerns an incident which occurred at a Quarterly Meeting, conducted at Ahtanum, by presiding elder, Rev. H. K. Hines, in 1872.

The meeting was held in a schoolhouse and Dr. Hines was preaching. Kennedy wrote, "A dog from one of the homes had followed in, and lay down near the stand. But while we were hoping for good behavior on the part of the canine, lo, a cat appeared. True to his instincts, the dog made a dash for the cat, and the cat jumped on the desk, and next leaped through the window, smashing the glass to smithers. The dog turned toward the door and went yelping out to chase the cat. Referring to it afterwards, Dr. Hines said that was the most 'dogmatical' and 'categorical' discourse he had ever preached in his life."

WASHINGTON'S FIRST RAILROAD, WALLA WALLA-WALLULA

At about this time the first railroad in Washington was completed from Wallula to Walla Walla. This greatly decreased freight and passenger rates from Walla Walla to the Columbia River.

During the fourteen years since Methodism first entered Eastern Washington, the number of members had grown to 930, Sunday school enrollment to 600. Five church buildings worth $8,400 had been acquired. Four parsonages were valued at $1,900. This was the material strength of Eastern Oregon and Washington Conference when it was born. Yet its strength was not to be measured by numbers nor monetary values, but rather by the greatness of the hearts of its leaders. In this it was rich—and strong.

When the new Conference convened for its first session at Walla Walla, July 30, 1874, Bishop S. M. Merrill was in the chair. Only twelve names were listed as members. They were: Rev. J. H. Wilbur, Rev. Harvey K. Hines, Rev. Hugh Caldwell, Rev. S. G. Havermale,

FERN HILL, TACOMA—1882

Fern Hill, Tacoma, organized, 1882 by Rev. W. P. Williams. First members were: Mr. and Mrs. George W. Byrd, William Wilson, Angus Wilson, Mary Wilson, Susan Wilson, Mrs. Isabella Given, H. S. Patten.

First Sunday school organized, 1880, Byrd Schoolhouse. Mrs. Byrd and Mrs. C. J. S. Greer, first leaders. First trustees of church: George W. Byrd, William Wilson, T. R. Wilson. In 1887, Rev. George A. Landen received 36.

Ladies Aid organized June 7, 1891. Mrs. Cynthia Meador, president. In 1903, Rev. Horace Williston repaired roof, foundation.

For first building 1887, George W. Byrd, donated lot. Parsonage built, 1890. Rev. T. C. McMullen, pastor. In 1903-04, Rev. J. M. Wilder, received 40 members, improved building. New parish house dedicated, June 13, 1926. Rev. Olin M. Graham, pastor.

Rev. Byron C. Gallaher pastor, observed fiftieth anniversary. Further improvements in 1948-51, Rev. Wayne D. Griffen, pastor. In 1956, ceiling of sanctuary painted. Rev. Don Baldwin.

In 1959, new site acquired for church building. Contract let 1960. Rev. Adam S. Forch, pastor. Building fund campaign 1961 brought $51,132 pledges. Building complete 1964.

In 1964, Rev. Wilfred L. Johnson pastor second year. There were 357 members, 278 in church school and 55 in Woman's Society. Women gave $789.

Rev. H. B. Lane, Rev. S. S. Vandersal, Rev. J. Harper, Rev. George W. Kennedy, Rev. J. O. Raynor, Rev. Andrew J. Joslyn, Rev. Thomas Pearne, and Rev. George Waters. Five probationers were listed: Rev. W. T. Koontz, Rev. G. W. Adams, Rev. E. R. Horner, Rev. N. Barnes, and Rev. A. Eades.

Into the hands of these seventeen men was committed the task of evangelizing the vast Inland Empire. Among them were veterans like Wilbur and Hines, seasoned by a quarter century of pioneering. Others like Havermale, Koontz, Waters, Pearne, Joslyn, Lane, Harner, and Kennedy, were at the threshold of fruitful ministries, which, under God, would raise the banner of Methodism in every community in that vast region.

Rev. S. G. Havermale, in 1874, as chairman of the committee on State of the Work, presented a report that revealed insight and dedication worthy of the tasks before the Conference. In it he lamented that the time required to travel over the circuits left too little for study and pastoral service.

Some needs listed by Havermale, were: "more men, strong men, whose hearts and hands are in the work; more liberal contributions on the part of the people." He concluded, "By the help of God we mean to hold these outposts till reenforcements come."

PULLMAN—1882

Methodist Church, Pullman, organized, 1882. Twenty charter members. Rev. C. M. Bryan, Moscow, preacher. Charles and Josephus Moore donated lots for church and D. S. McKenzie, lots for parsonage. John Laymon hauled first load of lumber from Sullivan Mill, Moscow mountains. Building erected 1882.

First parsonage, 1889, Rev. C. E. Gibson, pastor. Articles of Incorporation filed August 8, 1888. Signed by J. H. Malone, W. J. White, George W. Reed. First Quarterly Conference, November 29, 1890. Rev. Henry Rasmus, presiding elder. L. N. B. Anderson, pastor. Church property ordered sold, money used for new building. Church Extension Board loaned $500 on condition that church be named, "Simpson Memorial," building completed, 1892, parsonage, 1902. Matthew H. Marvin, pastor.

New building started, June, 1908, completed January, 1909. Dedicated by Bishop Edwin H. Hughes. Wesley Foundation started 1920-23, Rev. John G. Law, pastor. Debt paid, mortgage burned, 1926, parsonage built, 1929, Rev. Norman McCay, pastor. Rev. Alden R. Graves, 1943, launched plan to enlarge Wesley Foundation.

Wesley Foundation building erected, 1952. New church, costing $156,418 was erected in 1958. Rev. Donald M. Fife, pastor.

In 1964, Rev. William G. Burney, pastor, first year. Members, 584.

SPOKANE DISTRICT ORGANIZED IN 1883

Rev. W. S. Turner, who served as presiding elder of the Walla Walla District from 1881 to 1884, completed the first decade of independence of the Conference. Rev. G. C. Roe served The Dalles District from 1881 to 1883. Both men exercised leadership in expanding the outreach of the Conference. In 1883 the Spokane District was organized with Rev. M. S. Anderson presiding elder.

END OF A DECADE OF INDEPENDENCE

The Conference closed its first decade with 47 members and six probationers. These were appointed to 71 charges on five districts. In addition the following were appointed to special assignments: Rev. J. H. Wilbur, educational agent and missionary at large; Rev. W. A. Hall, president of Columbia River Conference Academy; Rev. I. C. Hall, president Spokane Falls College; Rev. H. K. Hines, editor Pacific Christian Advocate; Rev. Hugh Duncan and Rev. R. A. Dall, members of Montana Mission; Rev. E. Smith, missionary to Utah; Rev. G. M. Irwin, president Blue Mountain University.

There were 2,732 members and 718 probationers. Sixty-four Sunday schools showed an enrollment of 3,843. Contributions for pastoral support, $30,036. Thirty-five church buildings were valued at $69,800, while 27 parsonages were reported to be worth $19,380. Thus in ten years church membership had increased threefold, Sunday school membership, sixfold, value of church property, eightfold, and worth of parsonages, more than tenfold.

Something of the struggle to achieve these gains being put forth by ministers of the Gospel, was revealed in 1884 in certain requests presented to the Board of Missions through the Annual Conference. Take, for example, the statement of Rev. M. S. Anderson, presiding elder of the Spokane District. He stated that six years earlier only one minister served the territory then included on his district. At the time of the request there were twelve ministers and he said that there was more work than fifteen could do. "The appropriation is small at each charge," Anderson said, "while some charges are left to be supplied with little or no assistance whatever.

"To continue on each of these charges," Anderson said, "the appointments already served, is all that any

---

GARDEN STREET, BELLINGHAM
1883

First Methodist Church, Bellingham, organized, 1883 with seven charter members. Rev. B. A. Hill, local preacher, first pastor. Trinity Church, organized at Sehome, 1891. First full-time pastor Rev. B. F. Van De Venter, followed later by Rev. J. W. Dobbs. In 1912, Trinity Church erected new building on Garden and Magnolia streets. In 1917, First and Trinity united, took name, "Garden Street" Church. Pastor, Rev. George C. King.

Rev. Thomas Elliot, pastor in 1919, led members to accept union. Rev. Jabez C. Harrison, 1920-26 led congregation to consciousness of its place in community. Rev. Charles McCaughey, 1926-29 led militant fight for temperance, law, and order. Rev. Thomas Jeffrey, 1933-35, a scholarly preacher. Church celebrated diamond jubilee, 1948. Trustees were V. E. Hughes, Fred Swihart, Earl Fralick, Robert Hyldahl, Ray Hawk, Mrs. J. Tiffany, E. J. Baldwin, Louis Jones, and Mrs. L. Niedhammer. The pastor, Rev. Don Swerdfeger. Woman's Society president, Mrs. Waldo Altman. Church school superintendent, Arthur Wilkinson. Lay Leader, Ray I. Wise. The church raised $33,396 for diamond jubilee fund, built new parsonage, $20,600. Ted Palmer chairman Diamond Jubilee Committee. In 1964, Rev. Joe Walker appointed second year. Members 1,303. Church school enrollment, 696. Woman's Society membership 335.

pastor can do, and often more than he can do well. But new towns and settlements are springing up within the bounds of every circuit. Some of these are becoming points of influence. They want the Gospel. The interests of Methodism demand that it be provided for them. But to serve them the pastor must discontinue as many other places and the fruit of the past labor be lost."

Anderson went on to say that these twelve charges should be divided into fifteen. Such a division he declared would require an additional appropriation of $700.

"Beyond this occupied field," Anderson continued, "we have five large counties, some with a population of probably 400, others 800, or more, and not a preacher nor a dollar in this part of our work."

The presiding elder concluded that to serve these new fields and divide the charges already opened would require eight new men with a total additional appropriation of $1,850.

NEED OF IDAHO CHURCHES EMPHASIZED

Other districts presented similar appeals. Consider the report of Rev. W. S. Turner of the Walla Walla District. He said, "Grangeville Circuit comprises the valley known as Camas Prairie. The extent of the valley is about 20 by 25 miles, and it contains a population of 1,600. There are two villages, Mt. Idaho, the county seat, and Grangeville. Mt. Idaho has a population of about 400 and Grangeville, the same. One preacher is all there is among these 1,600 people. Mt. Idaho has no preaching except when a transient visitor happens there. Grangeville has regular preaching by Brother W. A. Hall, principal of our academy there. The remaining population of the valley are wholly destitute of preaching or pastoral care. We cannot support a man here without missionary help."

The presiding elder concluded, "We need $300 of missionary money to meet

---

CASTLE ROCK—1883

Castle Rock, as a preaching place, was on Cowlitz Circuit, in 1883. Services in cabins, log schoolhouse. First circuit rider, Rev. T. B. Reese, followed, in 1884, by Rev. John Laity. First resident pastor, Rev. W. T. Zenor, 1887-90. Church organized, 1890, Rev. M. A. Covington. Building dedicated, October, 1891, still standing in 1964. Rev. C. C. Stratton, president Portland University, officiated. Cost of building, $1,775. Board of Church Extension donated $250. Loaned $300. Balance, $500 raised on day of dedication.

Officials, 1890-91: Mrs. Eliza Mitchner, Mrs. Mary White, Mrs. Ella Linn, T. W. Wooley, J. Carnine, Felix Miller, E. J. Searles, G. F. White, C. F. Atkins, Wilson Estey. By 1964, 37 ministers had served church. One conference member, Rev. Murray Hyde grew up in this congregation.

Notable, among ministers of this church, is service of Rev. Martin Scarbo, who, in 1964, was appointed for the sixteenth year. When he became pastor in 1949, there were 143 members and 238 in church school. Building was valued at $12,000, and parsonage at $4,000. In 1964, membership was 248, church school enrollment, 248. Woman's Society of Christian service, with 100 members, contributed $1,185 to local funds. Church building value $56,000, and parsonage $8,500. Total budget was $18,614.

the absolute wants of this field. Five new points are open to us."

Rev. S. Gascoigne said, "The Dalles District is a vast mission field. Within its bounds are more than fifty organized school districts where the Gospel has never been proclaimed. From many of these fields is heard the Macedonian cry, and we are unable to meet their pressing wants.

"The extension of the Northern Pacific Railroad, and other lines, through the district, has brought in an immigration numbering thousands. They are pioneers and very poor, often lacking the necessities of life, while they are subduing the wilderness. They are hungering for the Gospel, yet are able to pay but little for its support."

Shouts of Victory Heard in 1886

Cries for help were mingled with shouts of victory. This is seen in Gascoigne's report in 1886. He told the Conference, "Brethren, this year the Lord has given us the victory! We have obtained the help of God! We have had protracted meetings in all the appointments, attended with great power. On many of the charges the membership has been more than doubled by the reception of new converts. During the year three elegant churches have been built and dedicated free from debt. We have built and paid for two new parsonages. We have done well on payments on old indebtedness. Two other churches, Echo and Hood River are in process of erection."

In that far-off day, seemingly, payment on ministerial support was not a criterion for judging victory. Witness the statement of Gascoigne which followed. He said, "Our people will give if the claims are properly presented. Ministerial support has been poor, very poor, yet neither the pastors nor their families have murmured. Indeed, Bishop, you have before you the most self-denying and heroic company of Methodist preachers to be found on the continent."

COSMOPOLIS—1883

Rev. S. D. Lougheed first Methodist assigned to Harboro, 1883. Circuit included Cosmopolis, Aberdeen, Hoquiam, Cape Flattery. Principal preaching place, Cosmopolis. A year later, 20 members, two Sunday schools, 40 enrolled. In 1884, Rev. J. H. Stuntz served Aberdeen and Cosmopolis. In 1885, Rev. Charles McDermoth, Aberdeen Circuit, resided at Cosmopolis. In 1886, 36 members, two Sunday schools, 36. In 1890, Rev. W. I. Cosper, Cosmopolis and Wynooche, 22 members, no Sunday school.

In 1900, Rev. D. S. Jones, 24 members, one church, 120 in Sunday school. In 1911, Rev. E. E. Simmons, supply, 50 members, 80 in Sunday school. Church building, value $2,000. Parsonage, $1,000.

In 1918, Rev. Erle Howell, succeeded Rev. N. V. Moore who reported 37 members, 127 in Sunday school.

In 1913, Oregon and Washington Railroad constructed tracks along street in front of church. Congregation complained, railroad settled for $1,100. Church bought lots, but continued on location for lack of funds to build. In 1920, Presbyterian church and manse purchased, renovated, used 43 years. Replaced by portables, 1964, through aid of Urgent Needs Appeal. Mrs. Hortense Anabel, pastor.

In 1964, left to be supplied. Members, 122, church school enrollment, 69. Woman's Society members, 25, gave $1,175.

83

Truly, then, as now, victory of a Methodist ministry was measured by his ability to live within his income.

During the years when foundations for future civilizations were being laid in the Inland Empire by Methodist ministers and their families, sacrifice was their daily bread. Presiding elder, Rev. N. E. Parsons, in his report to the Conference in 1887, revealed his sensitive appreciation for such self-denial. "Pilot Rock," he said, "has been served by Rev. R. Barrett. He and his family have endured a year of sacrifice. The circuit has but a small membership. Financially they are poor. Crops have been almost a failure for two years. A new church was built last year that taxed them to the utmost. The missionary appropriation was only $50 for a family of five. But their faith and trust was in God. He sent aid to them through the Woman's Home Missionary Society, and kept them from suffering."

LAYMEN FACED CROP FAILURES AND POVERTY

The mention of crop failure and poverty on the part of laymen and their families is significant. It is a reminder that suffering and sacrifice on the part of pastors and their families often was matched by that of the people. Undoubtedly it was the willingness of the pastor to suffer with his flock that won for Methodism its place of leadership in the Northwest.

To some of these pioneer preachers with family problems, economic pressure often proved too much to endure. Occasionally one dropped out hoping to improve his lot through other pursuits.

Such a man was Rev. Sanford Luther Burrill, who united with the Columbia River Conference in 1876. Because of family needs he took the supernumerary relation after three years at Weston, Oregon. During the ensuing sixteen years he preached occasionally while engaged in farming or business. But the urge to be back in full time service never forsook him.

GERMAN CHURCHES—1883

German Methodism began to take root in the Northwest in 1883, Walla Walla being the first church organized. With the discontinuance of the German Conference as a separate entity, in 1928, the following churches became a part of the Pacific Northwest Annual Conference:

Connell, Washington, Rev. G. A. Maag; Bethel, at Ridgefield, Washington, Rev. G. S. Roeder; Ritzville, Washington, Rev. George J. Kleinbach; Rocklyn-Davenport, Rev. H. B. Mann; Rosalia, Rev. A. F. Hilmer; Spokane, Rev. E. J. Aschenbrenner; Walla Walla, Rev. J. A. Beck.

Rev. A. F. Cramer was the district superintendent of the German churches in this area at the time of the merger. Rev. F. H. Luecke was field secretary for the conference pension fund. Following 1928 the membership of most of these churches became absorbed in the English-speaking congregations.

In 1892, the minutes of the North Pacific German Mission Conference listed congregations at Centralia, Chehalis, Fairhaven, Whatcom, Harrington, Seattle, Snohomish, Spokane Circuit, and Tacoma. These evidently had dropped by the wayside during the intervening years. German congregations, like other language groups, suffered from the loss of their youth who usually united with English-speaking churches.

Dates of organization of some of these groups not available.

84

Burrill's son, Robert, wrote a biography of his father in which he related the relief the family felt, in 1895, when presiding elder, Rev. G. M. Booth, of the Spokane District, persuaded him to reenter the ministry. During the next six years he served Sprague, Prosser, and Toppenish. Failing health compelled him to take the supernumerary relation in 1901 and retire in 1907.

OUTSTANDING SERVICE BY EARLY LEADERS

Despite sacrifices and discouragements some men continued year after year, glorifying every appointment by the radiance of their spirit. Such a man was Rev. William T. Koontz,[8] who was received on trial in the Oregon Conference in 1871. His first assignment was Waitsburg, which became a part of the East Oregon and Washington Conference in 1873. Automatically he became a member of the Columbia River Conference.

Typical of work done by Koontz, is that described by Rev. W. C. Gray, presiding elder of the Spokane District in 1890.

"As an organizer and builder of churches," Gray wrote, "Brother Koontz, of Sprague, takes the lead. He built two churches last year and organized two circuits out of one. This year he built another church, and his official board asks that a station and circuit be made of the Sprague work, and pledge a support. Sprague petitions and insists that he return next year as pastor of that station.

"I have a whole county on my district which is calling for Brother Koontz to come and organize. I think he ought to go, backed by missionary money, and if he does, I should not be surprised to see him come to Conference with a district organized and a request that he be appointed presiding elder. The church built this year is called Koontz Chapel."

GERMAN METHODIST,
WALLA WALLA—1883

The German Methodist Church, Walla Walla, born of inspiration of Rev. James Harvey Wilbur, who in 1882, saw need for Methodist work among German population. Rev. Frederick Bonn, presiding elder of German Methodist work appointed Rev. William Esslinger to organize church at Walla Walla. After building was erected, 1885, Mr. Esslinger returned East. Church, erected on land donated by Rev. James H. Wilbur who promised to donate money to complete church after members had given all they could.

Esslinger, followed by Rev. John Hager who was succeeded by Rev. Albert Koenecke. In 1888, Rev. Joseph Hepp, discouraged, ready to disband mission. Under Rev. J. G. Noering, 1891-95, membership increased.

In 1900, Rev. C. A. Wentsch, pastor, served four years. Membership grew, congregation talked of new building. In 1906-08, Rev. H. F. Lange, increased congregation, new church planned. Rev. F. H. Lueke, presiding elder.

Building committee, Gustav Schmukel, Conrad Diettrich, John Stoller, William Pfeiffer, Jacob Fieker. Church dedicated, Christmas, 1908.

Rev. J. C. Mueller, 1916-24, during first World War, German speaking people suffered hardship.

In 1929, Rev. George Kleinbach became pastor, serving 17 years. At end of ministry, October 13, 1946, church closed, property sold.

SOME METHODIST
FIRSTS IN EASTERN WASHINGTON

First
Walla Walla Church

Pioneer Church
Walla Walla

PIONEER CHURCH IN INLAND EMPIRE

Pioneer Church, Walla Walla, is sucessor to the First Church, organized by Rev. James Harvey Wilbur and Rev. George M. Berry, October 18, 1859, the first Methodist Church on Washington soil east of the Cascades. Wilbur Church was organized in 1903. In 1917 these two congregations were merged to form Pioneer Church. The sanctuary was erected at that time. The Educational unit was constructed in 1954.

Where Spokane Methodists
First Worshiped

Rev. S. G. Havermale

DAYTON CHURCH FACED SERIOUS PROBLEMS

A series of unfortunate incidents which held the congregation at Dayton in turmoil for years is related here to illustrate some of the frustrations often faced by congregations. The town, in the 1880's, was a prosperous community of 2,000 inhabitants. It had a devoted congregation of loyal and sacrificial Christians. Some of its misfortunes are suggested in the following:

In 1886 Rev. H. K. Hines said, "Dayton has had another unhappy year. The supply from the East made good promises but never came. Late in the year, I advertised for a man, and Brother J. F. Naugle responded. He has been holding good congregations." Suddenly, Hines reported, Naugle's wife died and he took her body East for interment. He wrote that he had decided to enter Boston Theological Institute and would be no longer available.

"Dayton must have help. This is a pivotal point," Hines concluded.

The presiding elder again reported in 1887. "Dayton charge has had another year of sore trial and affliction. A young man of more than ordinary ability, was their pastor and the society was well pleased with his appointment. During the year he showed signs of discontentment and, finally, about the first of July, he left the work; not, however, until his conduct became so impudent as to cause public comment. The Conference cannot afford to run any risk in the coming appointment at Dayton."

In 1888 the presiding elder commented upon the struggle endured during the year by the new pastor at Dayton. But, in 1889, he reported, "Dayton has had another year of peculiar history. It was left to be supplied, and after considerable correspondence, I secured the services of Rev. E. H. Fleisher, of the Northwest Kansas Conference, a man of rare ability as a Methodist preacher. He was just the man for

POMEROY—1883

Pomeroy first appeared in conference appointments in 1883, Pomeroy Circuit. Rev. W. T. Koontz, pastor. First Sunday school organized by Mrs. G. S. Heaton, before 1883.

First church built by Rev. W. T. Koontz, 1883. Moved in 1895, during pastorate of Rev. T. H. Fertig. Building burned about 1918, Rev. F. N. Morton, pastor. Services held in Baptist church until April 6, 1924, when new church dedicated. New parsonage occupied, 1920. Church building began 1921. Cost of church $22,500 cash, donated labor, materials.

Among faithful workers mentioned by Rev. F. N. Morton, were, C. W. Fitzsimmons, Jeffrey Williams, James Oliver, Asbury Oliver, Amos Bartlow, Mark Fitzsimmons, R. W. G. Mast.

In 1954, church completely remodeled, rededicated, April 4. Rev. Lloyd Alden, pastor. Parsonage moved, December, 1954, new educational unit planned.

First stake marking corner of new unit driven by Matt Killingsworth, chairman of trustees, May 1, 1955. Clarence Miller, local carpenter supervised construction. First used by Sunday school, December 18, 1955. Building shared with public school, first months, pending construction of a new school building.

In 1964, Rev. Everett L. Groves, pastor, first year. Members, 470. Church school, 259. Woman's Society, 84 members, contributed $95. Value of building, $186,087. Parsonage, $12,000.

the place, but his dear companion, who was ailing when they came, grew rapidly worse and he was compelled to return with her to the states, that she might die among her people."

In 1890 Dayton appeared to be happy, since no mention was made of the place by the presiding elder. In 1891, however, another blow fell. August 18, the parsonage was destroyed by fire and the church damaged. Less than two weeks later, the church began to build a new parsonage.

Further evidence of ministerial sacrifice is seen in a report entered in the conference journal of 1886. "On the Walla Walla District, we have eleven preaching stations," said the report. "The aggregate salary, including house rent, was $3,809. The average to the pastor was $346, or 95 cents per day. In a family of five that would be nineteen cents per day for each person. This makes no allowance for travel, books, periodicals, medical attention, nor other expenses."

YES, THERE WAS HUMOR AT TIMES

In face of these conditions, ministers often took time to banter each other. An example is found in the report of Rev. N. E. Parsons, of the Walla Walla District in 1887. "Brother Brown came to the work prostrated," he said, "but the mountain air, with the love of his people, has so restored and invigorated him that he feels (to use his own expression) as STRONG as the presiding elder of the Lewiston District." To understand the veiled humor of this remark one must remember that the presiding elder referred to was Rev. D. G. Strong.

Reports during this decade often throw interesting sidelights upon changing attitudes toward established methods of procedure. To illustrate, take a report by this man Strong, who commented with doubts, upon the effectiveness of what had been called revivals. He said, "If evangelists are a sine que

---

QUEEN ANNE—1883

James Frankland was first church school superintendent of Battery Street Church, organized in 1883, with 45 members, from First Church, residing in Bell Town. First Board of Trustees were, David T. Denny, B. L. Northrup, J. L. Payne, Andrew Uren, F. L. Johnson, William Hughes, J. H. Northrup.

First pastor, Rev. Louis Albert Banks, 1884-86, left church to attend theological school.

In 1905, church followed members to Queen Anne Hill, locating on Fifth Ave., W. Name changed to "Queen Anne Methodist Episcopal Church." Lots purchased, February, 1905. Contract let for parsonage, June 6. Rev. H. O. McGill, pastor. Congregation housed in temporary tabernacle for first service. Cornerstone of church laid June 11, Rev. A. B. Leonard of Board of Foreign Missions presiding. Building dedicated, March 26, 1906. Bishop David H. Moore officiated. The sum of $4,225 raised. Cost $14,000.

In 1950, church, under Rev. Wilbur M. Snyder, embarked upon major renovation. Remodeling of exterior completed under Rev. Charles Fisher, of sanctuary and church school facilities, under Rev. M. Chester Morgan, 1962.

In 1964, Rev. Robert F. Waller was appointed for second year. Membership, 515. Church school enrollment, 331. Members of Woman's Society, 124. They gave $1,274. Church valued at $244,500. Parsonage, $10,500.

non to a revival let us have them, but we believe that the agency for the healthiest revival is the pastor, but the pastor must be a good man, full of faith and the Holy Ghost."

SALOONS AND LAWBREAKERS DIDN'T LIKE HIM

A remark throwing light upon the character and personality of a pastor came from Rev. N. E. Parsons of the Spokane District. It concerned Rev. R. C. Moter, who had been sent to Moscow, Idaho, after Conference the previous year. He said, "This has been a very prosperous year. Indeed, under such a leader it is hard for a place or church not to be prosperous. The saloon men and lawbreakers haven't much love for him."

Moter, concerning whom Parsons spoke, was transferred from the Arkansas Conference in 1888. After serving part of a year at Moscow, he successively served Colfax, Prairie City, John Day, Oregon, Athena, Oregon, and Davenport, Washington. Later he was five years presiding elder of the Dalles District, beginning in 1891.[9]

In 1890, presiding elder, W. S. Gray, began his description of the Columbia District with a humorous salute to one of his charges. He said, "The district begins at the point where has been concentrated the optical attention of the universe—Pasco." The remark probably was inspired by the fact that the transcontinental line of the Northern Pacific, enroute to Seattle from Spokane, detoured 100 miles out of the way to include Pasco. Later, the presiding elder remarked that he had allowed Pasco $10 for that year's missionary support, and observed that the pastor took the money and agreed to open the work.

SECOND DECADE COLUMBIA RIVER CONFERENCE SHOWS GROWTH

When the Columbia River Conference concluded the second decade of its history in 1893, its minutes listed 71 members and eleven probationers. Seven

ZION, ROCKLYN—1883

Zion Methodist Episcopal Church, was organized among German-speaking Americans at Rocklyn, in 1883. First service conducted in home of Mr. and Mrs. Goetlieb Mielke, by laymen. For six years, this home was place of worship. First pastor, Rev. Adam Buehler, in 1884, started first campmeeting, near Harrington, that year. He organized German missions at Rosalia, and Ritzville.

First church, erected in 1889, under pastorate of Rev. J. George Maelring, dedicated that fall, by Rev. George Hartung, Portland presiding elder. In 1896 some members withdrew to organize German Evangelical Church, two miles south. Later, this church closed, members joined Harrington Evangelical Church.

In 1905 Zion's building was replaced, dedicated October 22, 1905. Rev. H. F. Lange, presiding elder, in charge. Parsonage built in 1910. Church repaired, re-decorated, painted, in 1947. Mrs. J. Dean King, pastor.

In 1958, congregation observed its 75th anniversary. When German Methodism united with English speaking groups, in 1929, this congregation ceased to be language church.

In 1964, Rev. Lawrence E. Yates, Presbyterian minister had served six years. Members, 32, church school 50.

Historian commented, "A cross stands in front of church to remind all who pass by that sin still may be forgiven."

members were superannuated, 11 supernumerary, three in school, and one a missionary in Brazil. Thus, to fill 76 listed appointments, including presiding elders, there were but 54 available ministers. Nineteen charges were left vacant.

MEN OF HIGH CALIBER LED THE CHURCH

Among five men who played a prominent role in guiding the Conference through the later years of its third decade, was Rev. Robert Warner,[10] who served six years on The Dalles District, beginning in 1896. During forty-eight years as a Methodist minister, Warner served Alba, Columbus, Yakima, Ellensburg, Pendleton, Wilbur at Walla Walla, Sand Point, Moscow, and Wenatchee. He served as superintendent of the Spokane Deaconess Hospital from 1921 to the end of his ministry.

Warner was a member of the General Conference in 1908, 1912, 1916, and 1924. He was a member of the Board of Home Missions and Church Extension of the general church for a quadrennium.

In 1898, Rev. C. E. Gibson[11] was appointed presiding elder of the Moscow District by Bishop C. C. McCabe. He entered the Columbia River Conference in 1888, and served St. Paul's Church, Spokane; First Church, Yakima; and Central Church, Portland. He was three times presiding elder, serving Moscow, Walla Walla, and Spokane Districts. In 1910, he was a delegate to the Missionary Conference at Chicago, and to General Conference in 1912.

Bishop McCabe also appointed Rev. Matthew H. Marvin[12] to the Walla Walla District. He entered the Columbia River Conference in 1888. His appointments included Cheney, Rockford, Latah, Pullman, Spokane, and Ellensburg. He served the Walla Walla District four years. Later he ministered to churches at Walla Walla, Waitsburg and Sunnyside, and one year as financial

---

OCEAN PARK—1883

Ocean Park Methodist church grew from Ocean Park Campmeeting Association, organized 1883, owning 250 acres of land. Methodist preaching services on peninsula dates to 1871, when Rev. John F. DeVore, presiding elder of Puget Sound District, sent Rev. John N. Dennison to Oysterville from which place he served other communities, including Ocean Park. Articles of Incorporation filed, June 10, 1914. Trustees: Martha Hadley, Mrs. Emma Mathews, L. L. Bush, H. E. Campbell, Vio Bitley. Later other communities were served by Ocean Park pastors. Oysterville, Ilwaco, Chinook at one time or another were among them. After 1937 known as Ocean Beach Parish.

Later Ilwaco merged with another denomination. Bell in Ocean Park tower first in church at Oysterville, 1872. Ministers with longest service at Ocean Park: Rev. C. H. Cowdy, 1911, six years; Rev. Henry Albright, 1923, six years; Rev. Robert E. Thomas, 1938; Rev. Harold E. Dixon, 1939, eleven years; Rev. Erling Bergen, 1950, nine years.

Rev. Harold E. Dixon firmly established Ocean Park Camp, and Rev. Erling Bergen continued repairing grounds, buildings of camp, church. In 1964, Rev. J. Fred Stilwell, pastor, second year. Members 51, church school, 44. Woman's Society members 43, gave $789. This church placed first paid order for history, "METHODISM IN THE NORTHWEST."

secretary of the Deaconess Hospital at Spokane, Washington.

Because of Marvin's deep sympathy with the common man he became patron saint of like-minded men of the Conference. In 1921 he became a member of the Industrial Welfare Commission of the State of Washington. In this position he sought to bring about better working conditions for laborers, especially working girls. He was three years Chaplain at Moran School for Boys on Bainbridge Island.

Another presiding elder appointed by Bishop McCabe[13] was Henry Brown, who served six years on the Spokane District. Afterwards he went to First Church, Walla Walla, in 1904. He transferred from the Northwest Iowa Conference to the Columbia River Conference in 1885. Here he served Ellensburg, Pendleton, The Dalles, and Jefferson Street Church, Spokane. In 1893 he edited the Columbia Christian Advocate, later going to Lewiston, Idaho. Other appointments include Goldendale, Post Falls, Grace Church, Spokane, and corresponding secretary of the Conference.

An effective leader of those days was Rev. Olin W. Mintzer,[14] who was presiding elder of the Republic Missionary District for six years, beginning in 1902. During his term of office he increased the number of appointments on his district from 20 to 46.

GREAT PROGRESS IN FIRST 44 YEARS

Results of the initial 44 years of Methodism in Eastern Washington and Northern Idaho cannot be committed to type. Nor can statistics reveal the influence of such a movement on the souls of men. Yet figures can indicate progress.

Whereas, in 1859, only a few settlers were established in Eastern Washington and Northern Idaho, by 1903, villages, towns, and cities were scattered throughout the Inland Empire, and were to be found in all inhabitable portions of the territory. Fully 150,000 persons resided in this area.

In 1903 there were 126 charges, some

SNOHOMISH—1883

David Sexton was first superintendent of Sunday school at Snohomish. The point first appeared in minutes, 1883, left to be supplied. First pastor, Rev. W. H. Johnson, preached at Pilchuch, Larimer schoolhouse, Lowell, Parker schoolhouse, Eby's Slough, Marysville, Fall City, Snoqualmie, Tualco, Cherry Valley.

First meetings, Masonic Hall. Twenty members. Rev. H. B. Porter, pastor in 1884. Church building dedicated July 26, 1885. Methodist Church Extension Society granted $250 and loaned $250. A bell mounted in 1887.

In 1887, under spell of promised railroad, membership doubled. First train came 1888. A parsonage erected in 1893, Rev. F. E. Drake, pastor. Under Rev. David G. LeSourd, 1893-94, many converts added. Under Rev. R. L. Fahs the debt was paid. Under ministry of Rev. G. B. Sheafe, 1901-03 the membership reached 165. In 1910, Rev. Richard Oates, building moved one block, basement installed.

During first World War, Presbyterians and Methodists shared pastor, Rev. F. L. Moore. The following year, Rev. W. T. Randolph continued arrangement. Rev. D. A. Storey, 1919-23 paid debt of $1,150. Improvements under Rev. Robert B. Shaw, 1940, cost $1,340. In 1954, Rev. Paul Perkins, installed new organ.

In 1964 Rev. S. Christian Thele, members 370, church school 215, Woman's Society 62. Women paid $600.

with two or more preaching places. There were 85 conference members and 24 probationers. Four were in school, eight supernumerary, and 16 superannuated. Thus, 83 ministers were available to fill 130 places, including presiding elders. Yet the minutes listed only 21 vacant charges. Twenty-two were supplied by local preachers, or retired men.

That year there were 10,805 members, 178 Sunday schools with 14,792 enrolled; 149 churches valued at $345,750; 82 parsonages worth $21,567, and pastoral support, $69,490.

Meager as these figures may appear, sixty years later, they indicate the direction in which those greathearted men were leading.

Chapter IV

Northwest Methodism, for first six decades of twentieth century, continued to win notable victories through the dedicated service of—

Great Hearts in Action

Six Decades of Expansion, Consolidation and Entrenchment Surveyed

The six decades following 1903 witnessed vast changes in the Northwest. Growing populations, transitions in industry, and congestion in urban areas, placed demands upon Methodist leaders testing their greatness of heart and capacity for effective action.

Expansion Demands Strong Leadership

As Methodism moved forward, rate of progress depended upon the strength of personal leadership. This was recognized in the report of Rev. Henry Brown, presiding elder of the Spokane District, in 1904. He called the roll of men on his district and burst into verse:

> "The world wants men—largehearted men;
> "Men who shall join its chorus and prolong
> "The psalm of labor and the psalm of love."

The presiding elder struck the keynote for the following decades of Northwest Methodism. His description of the kind of men required for the Christian task was no mere fantasy. It applied to men already working on his district. He cited one of them.

"Our pastor on the Endicott circuit," he said, "Roy D. Hadley, has done a work of which any pastor might be proud. Quietly, and trusting in God for wisdom and strength, he began the labors of the year; carefully and prayerfully he surveyed the field and laid his plans; with large faith, inflexible purpose and untiring zeal, he moved forward through the long months of a strenuous campaign, and now he comes here without any blowing of trumpets and modestly reports two churches built, completed, and costing from $1,400 to $1,800 each, with the furniture and all provided for."

How a church that had decided to die was kept alive by a dedicated pastor and his wife, illustrates the theme of this chapter. The place was Wallace, Idaho, and the minister, Rev. Charles MacCaughey;[1] but the story was not recorded until 33 years later, when MacCaughey wrote:

"We went to Wallace in the fall of 1906. The district superintendent told us that the membership was small but united! He was right. The membership consisted of Mr. and Mrs. Smith and they were united. It also consisted of Mrs. Proebsting, and they were all untied, on one thing, that they did not want a preacher, and that they would not have one.

"Mrs. Smith and Mrs. Proebsting met us at the train. They took us to the Smith home and fed us. Then they broke the news very gently that we were not to stay, but must go back. They said that they had tried over and over to keep the church going, but they had come to the end of their rope. They could not run a church without congregations and money, and both of these were absent. The last preacher, Brother Carpenter, and a mighty good man, had gone in the middle of the year, and what was the use of crucifying another man?

"Now there is one good thing about the Methodist Church. It puts you out on a raft in the middle of the ocean, and you always stay no matter how undesirable the raft may be. You stay, not because you are a hero, nor because you love the raft, but because the ocean is deep and cold.

"We decided to stay. The good women said they could not promise us any definite salary, but there was an eight-room parsonage, and we could

SWEDISH CHURCHES—1883

First Swedish church in Northwest, at Seattle in 1883. Rev. Andrew Farrell, pastor. Cedar Home, 1888, Rev. Andrew Farrell. Pleasant Ridge organized in 1884 by Rev. Eric Shogren, first pastor. Rev. Andrew Farrell also served this church about this time. Church at Skagit City organized in 1887, Rev. O. E. Olander, pastor. Mount Vernon, organized by Rev. K. O. Berglund in 1911. Church at Field, Washington, organized in 1912 by Rev. John Johnson, first pastor. Churches at Everett and Edmonds appeared among appointments but soon were discontinued. The Fremont Church in Seattle was organized in 1902 by Rev. E. G. Falk, first pastor. The church at Tacoma was organized in 1890 by Rev. A. Peterson. A church at Olympia at this time was short-lived.

Churches were announced at Nora and Albion, Idaho in the '80's but soon disappeared. The church at South Bend was short-lived. The church at Spokane was organized in 1894 by Rev. Bernt Howe. The church at Venersborg, Washington was organized by Rev. John Ovall in 1909. The one at Vancouver, Washington was organized in 1911 by Rev. John Ovall. Most of these churches were soon absorbed in English speaking congregations after Swedish Methodism, as a separate entity, dissolved in 1928.

rent rooms, and the church would pay us what they could.

SOMETIMES A CONGREGATION OF SIX OR SEVEN

"In all that town, counting Methodists, Baptists, Congregationalists, and Episcopalians, there could not have been more than 75 church members. For our first six months we never had a congregation of more than 25 and often it was six or seven. The Congregational Church, however, was running a very popular service, and had as their pastor, Rev. J. D. Neilan, who has ever remained one of my most constant friends.

"Mr. Neilan did a great thing. He was well liked and was getting a good salary, but he entered with me into a campaign for decency in Wallace, that broke him socially and financially. I remember the afternoon that we knelt in his study and pledged ourselves to God, that, come what might, we would never cease until we had hit gambling and vice in that town as hard a blow as we could strike.

"The loveliest thing of all was the great gang of young men and women who rallied to us and built themselves around the church. We had wonderful times. Those kids would come to the parsonage and cook meals and sing and have the most glorious times. Some of them fell in love with each other and we married them."

Insight into the inner dimensions of a pastor of this time is found in a report of Rev. O. W. Mintzer, superintendent of the Republic Missionary District, in 1908. He said, "Cheney, and Pastor W. E. Thompson, are a glad surprise. A few years ago it was small and struggling, supported partly by missionary funds. Now, Sunday school, 235; pastor's class, largest outside of Seattle; thirty-one conversions, seventy in Epworth League; membership, strong and commanding; church and parsonage enlarged at a cost of $8,500, of which $5,000 is paid in already; a new church organized, built and dedicated at

FIRST, ABERDEEN—1884

First Church, Aberdeen, organized, 1884, Rev. S. D. Lougheed, pastor. In 1886, 11 members, Rev. Charles McDermoth, pastor Aberdeen Circuit. First services in abandoned saloon. Samuel Benn donated lots. Church dedicated by Rev. H. D. Brown, 1887. Church Extension Society gave $500, Ladies Aid, $250. Balance, $3,000 raised on dedication day.

Trustees, 1887: J. C. Pearson, E. H. Emery, B. F. Doty, A. D. Wood, L. J. Weatherwax. Rev. A. J. Joslyn, 1893, experienced finance problems. In 1907 Rev. Francis A. LaViolette, pastor, new location. Parsonage erected, 1909, Rev. B. F. Brooks, pastor. Church covered, dining room completed. Services there, 1910. Rev. J. T. McQueen, 1911-12. Incomplete church dedicated. Rev. Everett M. Hill, 1916-19 completed church. Debt was concern for 25 years. Pipe organ installed by Rev. L. C. Hicks, 1935-38. Mortgage burned by Rev. R. A. Anderson, 1940-45.

Chimes installed by Rev. Roy Jenkins, 1948-50, also new furnace for parsonage. Church re-done inside.

Improvements continued under Rev. Elmer Beckman, Rev. Harold Black. In 1960-63, Rev. Floyd E. Green started new building campaign. Plans continued under Rev. Howard Yoder, 1963.

In 1964, Rev. Howard W. Yoder, pastor, second year. Members, 493; Sunday school, 274. Woman's Society members, 120, contributed $1,660. Building value $205,000, parsonage $11,000.

95

Meadow Lake, four miles out; Cheney will advance salary for the coming year several hundred dollars."

PRESIDING ELDERS SET THE PACE

Although the pastor is the key to expansion and growth, in Methodism the pace must be set by the district leader. During the years following 1903 presiding elders and district superintendents in the Northwest, exhibited a leadership which brought the Church to the end of the period with many achievements to its credit.

Growth of the Conference was indicated in the report of Rev. U. F. Hawk, of the Spokane District, in 1910. Twenty-three of the 37 charges on his district had been opened during his term of office. Sixteen original charges had been given to other districts.

After the 1908 General Conference, presiding elders became district superintendents. Four such leaders were appointed to districts by Bishop Charles W. Smith, in 1911: Rev. Bracken E. Koontz, Coeur d'Alene District; Rev. C. A. Hodshire, Columbia District; Rev. Harold O. Perry, The Dalles District; and Rev. Andrew Warner, Walla Walla District.

ASOTIN—1884

Land donated to Asotin Methodist Episcopal Church, 1884, by Theodore M. C. Schank, and William H. Reed. Trustees: M. B. Mitchell, F. A. Curtis, T. G. Bean, William Farrish, S. F. Bennett, N. Ausman. Church incorporated October, 1885.

Parsonage built before 1888 and church before 1890. Church Extension Society granted $250 for building. Addition built after 1892. Parsonage remodeled, renovated often.

Asotin first appeared in 1882, Rev. J. W. Rigby, pastor. Rev. Henry W. Waltz followed, 1884. Rev. Zebulon K. Henizman, pastor in 1887. Rev. Jonathan Swaine, appointed in 1890. Asotin on Spokane District.

Rev. Paul Little, 1909, first kept complete records of members, baptisms. Succeeding pastors: Rev. J. S. Bell, 1913; Rev. O. W. Mintzer, 1916; Rev. William Gornall, 1918; Rev. J. G. Carrick, 1919; Rev. F. F. Boothby, 1923; Rev. S. E. Hornibrook, 1926. Church reported 85 members, 148 in Sunday school, 12 members Epworth League. There were 21 junior members of League. The Woman's Foreign Missionary Society gave $132.

In 1938 Rev. J. D. Llewellen reported 100 members, 217 in church school. Rev. Ralph Bolick, 1940.

In 1964, Rev. Errol K. Stevens, pastor, second year, membership, 139; church school enrollment, 162. Woman's Society members, 40, gave $981. Building value, $19,200. Parsonage $4,000.

In 1917, Koontz reported to the Conference that the membership had grown from 1,360 to 4,325; benevolences, from $4,303, to $8,248; Sunday school enrollment from 2,201 to 6,827. Pastors and people had built ten new churches and six parsonages, costing $40,000.

EASTERN WASHINGTON EXPANSION CONTINUES

The second decade of this period was a time of expansion. The world had been made "safe for democracy" and the hearts of Methodists were sensitive to the cry of human need everywhere. Both Columbia River and Puget Sound entered wholeheartedly into the Centenary Movement. Giving for the cause in the Columbia River Conference was indicated in the following figures taken from Conference minutes. In 1918 Disciplinary Benevolence giving was $39,371, but in 1919 it leaped to $65,934, and in 1920 to $101,479. Although collections showed a decline in the following years, the Centenary was the greatest missionary event among Northwest Methodists to that time.

Two Conferences Consolidated in 1929

In response to a trend toward consolidation, all charges of the Columbia River Conference located in Oregon, except Freewater and Milton, were shifted to the Oregon Conference, in 1922. A resolution calling for union between the Columbia River and Puget Sound Conference, introduced in 1927, was approved by the General Conference, and became effective in 1929.

In 1928 the Conference was manned by 77 effective elders, 11 undergraduates, and 15 supplies. Also listed were 131 preaching places attached to 118 charges, with 23,173 members.

Expansion in Western Washington

While Methodist leaders were expanding the work in Eastern Washington, from 1904, their brethren on the West side were busy in a similar enterprise.

Whidbey Island Pastor Uses His Wit

Rev. George A. Landen, presiding elder and district superintendent for 20 years, came to the Conference in 1882. In his autobiography, he tells of an incident which transpired on the way to his first assignment on Whidbey Island. It reveals something of the necessity for pioneer ministers to use their wits in winning the confidence of settlers.

A farmer took Landen in his wagon from Oak Harbor to the home of the Izetts, a distance of four miles. The farmer was eager to know the business of the newcomer, but Landen evaded

BAY CENTER—1884

Methodist Church at Bay Center dates to 1884, when first appeared in conference appointments. Rev. J. E. Leach, pastor. Preaching services held there earlier by ministers from Oysterville and Willapa Circuit, who undoubtedly visited place from time to time.

In 1885, Bay Center Circuit, served by Rev. J. E. Leach. Following year, Bay Center teamed with Oysterville served by Rev. James Matthews until conference, 1891. That year he was followed by Rev. D. M. Ellsworth.

Congregation continued to share pastors with other churches until, in 1912, Rev. C. H. Cowdy served church alone. In 1913, church with Willapa, Rev. E. B. Reese, pastor. During years, 1928-38 church did not appear among the appointments. Probably hidden on circuit with other churches.

In 1950, Bay Center teamed with South Bend, both left to be supplied. In 1951, Rev. Fred Owen and his wife Sophie, reported for the church that there were 38 members, with 68 in Sunday school. In 1960, Bay Center was teamed with South Bend, Spruce, and Walter. Bay Center had 41 members, 46 in Sunday school. Rev. Bernard E. Mott, pastor, first year.

In 1964, Rev. John W. Martin, pastor, first year. Members, 30; church school, 37. Woman's Society with 12 members gave $558.

his questions. "When finally he could stand it no longer," Landen reported, "he bluntly asked what was my business. I replied frankly that I was a Methodist preacher sent to take charge of the circuit. 'Humph!' the man reacted, 'If you are no better than most of the preachers they have sent here lately you might as well go back to your Kentucky home.' 'Well,' I replied, 'I am not to be the judge of that.' I invited him to come out to the schoolhouse where I was to preach in the morning and hear for himself. 'Well,' he said, 'you will starve here.'

"Then I met him by saying, 'Have you anything to eat at your house?' 'Sure,' he said.

"'If I come your way, will you give me a meal?' I asked.

"'Certainly,' he replied. 'You will always be welcome at our home.' Then I said, 'As long as you and the rest of the farmers around here have something to eat, I am not going to starve.' I had many a good meal at his home and found rest in a comfortable bed many a night."

CONFERENCE REPORTS REFLECT CHURCH GROWTH

Growth during this period was evidenced in conference reports. In 1905 ten churches had made payments on debts, eighteen new edifices and parsonages had been completed. Thirty had improved buildings and parsonages. One new congregation had been organized, and membership had increased from 12,233 to 13,326. Missionary giving had increased $1,191.

Rev. B. F. Brooks reported that membership on the Tacoma District, was up by fifty percent, and overall giving had skyrocketed by 118 percent. On the Bellingham District alone 22 parsonages and churches had been improved.

In 1908, Rev. W. S. Harrington of the Seattle District reported progress during the six years of his tenure in office. The number of charges on the district had increased by seven in spite of several

FIRST, CAMAS—1884

First Methodist sermon at Camas at home of Mr. and Mrs. Brelsford, 1883. Rev. F. M. Robertson, preacher. Class organized, 1884, five members, Mr. and Mrs. D. L. Russell, Mr. and Mrs. Brelsford and daughter, Viola. Rev. G. G. Ferguson, Lewis River Circuit.

Lot donated by D. H. Stearns. Rev. A. Marshion, followed by Rev. W. H. Drake, 1887-88, and Rev. T. W. Butler, 1888. Union Sunday school started in 1883, in home of William McMaster, first superintendent.

First church building began, 1889, Rev. T. W. Butler. Dedicated in 1891, Rev. F. M. Pickles. Methodist Sunday school started, 1892, Rev. James Matthews, pastor, and Mrs. Dunbar, superintendent. Following year Sunday school had 30 members.

Pews, furnace installed, 1911, Rev. H. L. Townsend, pastor. Basement in 1916, Rev. D. A. Storey. By 1920, Sunday school enrollment was 200. New parsonage acquired 1925, Rev. C. E. Todd, pastor. In 1940, Rev. George L. Poor, parsonage remodeled, Sunday school attendance increased by 262. Rev. Elmer Beckman, 1946-48, lots purchased. Funds for new church started. New building, 1949-50, Rev. Robert Shaw, pastor. Interior of church finished, furnished, 1952, Rev. W. W. Pearson.

In 1964, Rev. L. Marshall Campbell, pastor, first year. Members, 402; church school enrollment, 250. Building value, $140,000. Parsonage, $22,000.

having been taken away. Value of church property had leaped from $126,450 to $400,600. Pastoral support from $17,000 to $40,000, and payments for missions and church extension had increased 100 percent.

HARRINGTON GIVES SEATTLE CREDIT FOR GROWTH

"These advances," Harrington said, "have been made possible by the rapid growth of Seattle, the loyalty and liberality of our members, and by the wisdom, ability and devotion of our excellent corps of pastors."

NORTHWEST TRANSPORTATION STILL DIFFICULT *//9296*

Steamboats, railroads, and automobiles did not end transportation difficulties for Northwest itinerants. Witness the incident reported by Rev. F. S. Pearson as late as 1909.[3] He said he had visited every church on his district at least four times and missed but one appointment. "We were caught in a storm while in the waters of the Strait," he said. "Our steamer was covered by tons of frozen spray, and enveloped in snow, and tossed by fierce winds and waves. For these reasons we failed to make our appointment."

The year 1910 saw national headliners among evangelists employed on the Bellingham District. Among them were: William A. (Billy) Sunday, Osborn, the "Drummer" Evangelist, F. A. Enslow, of Chicago, and Dan Shannon, the "Cyclone" Evangelist. Few members were received, but the general uplift was reported good.

A new sanctuary costing $205,000, with furnishings, had been dedicated at First Church, Seattle, where Rev. W. H. W. Reese was pastor. Superintendent, Rev. Joseph P. Marlatt, announced that with 1,700 members this was one of the great congregations in all Methodism.

Superintendents took note of all important happenings on their districts. In 1914, Rev. G. A. Landen reported the

FIRST, CHEHALIS—1884

Methodist church organized at Chehalis in 1884, 30 members. Church on circuit, served by Rev. D. W. Cameron, Olympia. First building, costing $2,500 dedicated, April 18, 1886. Parsonage in 1889.

Previously, however, Methodists had preached and built a church at nearby Claquato as early as 1858, on ground donated by Lewis Davis. In 1879, Saundersville, was renamed Chehalis.

Church raised and full basement constructed, 1905. Church completed in 1923, costing $60,000. Rev. A. J. McKenzie, pastor, who died in December, 1922, shortly before congregation entered the new building.

Church celebrated its 75th anniversary, in 1957, Rev. Walter S. Gleiser, pastor. Bishop A. Raymond Grant delivered anniversary sermon. On December 6, that year a home-coming day was observed with a service honoring members of 25, and 50 years.

Following second world war, Mr. and Mrs. C. E. Sonnemann and Mr. and Mrs. Leonard Sonnemann, donated chimes as memorial to five young men who gave lives in service of Country. Longest pastorate in history of church, that of Rev. Walter S. Gleiser, who served from 1953 to 1964.

In 1964, Rev. Harold C. Williams, pastor, first year. Membership was 800, church school enrollment, 395. Woman's Society members, 167. They gave $818. Building value, $140,000. Parsonage, $27,500.

LEADERS AT BEGINNING OF THE SECOND HALF CENTURY

Garden Street Church, Bellingham

EARLY METHODISM ON BELLINGHAM BAY

First Methodist Church Bellingham was organized, 1883, with seven charter members, Rev. B. A. Hill, local preacher, first pastor. Trinity Church, organized at Sehome, in 1891. First full-time pastor, Rev. B. F. Van DeVenter. In 1912 Trinity Church erected a new building on Garden and Magnolia. In 1917 First and Trinity united to become Garden Street Church. Rev. George C. King, first pastor.

Rev. O. W. Mintzer

Rev. George A. Landen

death of Mrs. A. Robertson, wife of the pastor at Friday Harbor, who was injured through a fall while packing to move to a new assignment. He also told of the death of the eight-year-old son of Rev. and Mrs. George F. Pollock, a child who had been an invalid for seven years. That year infants had been born in the homes of Rev. G. C. Squires, Rev. J. C. Harrison, Rev. J. R. Sasnett, Rev. G. F. Pollock, Rev. E. V. Bronson, Rev. D. A. Storey, and Rev. R. C. Hartley, all on the Bellingham District.

A Northwest Pastor Becomes Bishop

At the close of the 1910 session of the Conference, Rev. Adna Wright Leonard was appointed to the pulpit of First Methodist Church, Seattle. Six years later he was elected to the Episcopacy.[4]

The Seattle pulpit, vacated by Bishop Leonard, was filled by Rev. J. E. Crowther, who wrote and produced Methodism's pageant, "The Wayfarer," at the Centenary Celebration at Columbus, Ohio, in 1919.

Revival Fires Burn in Unlikely Place

In 1916, Bishop Matthew Simpson Hughes appointed Rev. Jabez C. Harrison to the Olympia District. Three years later, Harrison reported a unique experience in which he had participated at Blyn, a small community on the Olympic Peninsula. He had assisted the pastor, Rev. Allen M. Frederick, in revival services. At the end of the meeting, he had baptized ten children and 22 adults, and received 49 persons into the church.

The unusual feature was the various nationalities represented. Included were a Clallam Indian Grandmother, and several of her sons and daughters whose father was a Chilean. There were twelve Portuguese, a Frenchman, a Russian, and two Italians, together with others with various strains of American blood.

Harrison said with enthusiasm,

ELMA—1884

Elma first served by Methodist minister around 1860. In 1863-68, Rev. H. C. Rhoades served the circuit including Elma. Rev. H. B. Lane, 1868-70, was followed 1870, by Rev. C. H. Hoxie. First regular supply pastor, Rev. Andrew Anderson, 1884. A church, with parsonage next door, built, 1895.

Meantime, Rev. Charles E. Cunningham served circuit in 1890. Rev. F. S. Pearson, in 1900, reported 110 members, three Sunday schools, enrolling 200. In 1910, Rev. J. W. Frescoln, reported 186 members, 300 in Sunday school and building valued at $3,500. In 1920, Rev. R. V. B. Dunlap, second year at Elma-Malone, reported 156 members, two Sunday schools with 205 enrolled.

Rev. F. A. Ecker, 1922-26, traded for a new parsonage. In 1938 there were three congregations, Elma, Malone, and McCleary. Rev. G. Edward Knight reported 153 members, and 296 enrolled, three Sunday schools. Additional remodeling was done by Rev. Lloyd N. Alden in 1939-44.

In 1964, Rev. Herbert G. Luscomb, pastor, fourth year. Members, 243. Church school enrollment, 137. Woman's Society of Christian Service, 55 members, gave $736. Building valued at $27,000. Parsonage, $10,000.

This church, in mid-Chehalis Valley, held up the Methodist variety of the gospel for more than 100 years. Continued to carry Christian banner.

"When the Christianity of Jesus Christ has had its full opportunity we shall have scenes like this all over the earth."

Everywhere ministers were taking joy in their work. At the close of his first year on the Bellingham District, in 1922, Rev. George W. Frame commented with enthusiasm upon the fellowship of Methodists. He said, "I have come to appreciate as never before, the polity, purpose, and unprecedented opportunity of the great Church which we serve, and the joy of fellowship and teamwork with the brethren of the district. There is an immense amount of enjoyment in just living and being sacrificial co-laborers with the good God."

Rev. Byron H. Wilson came from Southern California in 1924 to succeed Rev. George A. Landen on the Seattle District. Three years later he appraised certain churches on the district as follows: "Bothell has one foot in the city and one in the country. Des Moines is one of our most important fields to hold and to keep. Port Orchard some day will fail to recognize itself. Soon Renton will be one of our strongest charges."

Growth in church membership of these charges will indicate how clearly Wilson peered into the future. Figures for 1963 showed Bothell had advanced from 198 to 762; Des Moines, from 74 to 901; Port Orchard, from 96 to 437; and Renton, from 164 to 1,054.

More churchly edifices were springing up. When the new building for University Temple was dedicated in 1927, under the pastorate of Rev. James E. Crowther, Rev. John W. Caughlin was planning the new Trinity Church at Ballard, which was designed to meet all the needs of the congregation. It was occupied in 1930.

PUGET SOUND CONFERENCE HOLDS LAST SESSION IN 1928

The final session of the Puget Sound Conference convened at Epworth Church, Tacoma, in 1928. A new build-

---

LYNDEN—1884

Rev. George R. Osborn was among earliest preachers at Lynden. Services held in log schoolhouse. Later, Rev. John Flinn preached there. The church was organized in 1884. Rev. John Tennant became first resident pastor, 1887. H. A. Jordan gave land for church built under Tennant, in 1887, dedicated October 7, 1888, by Rev. T. J. Massey, presiding elder, assisted by pastor and Rev. John Flinn.

First parsonage, built in 1898, cost $50. First addition to church building, completed in 1907, Rev. A. J. Whitfield, pastor, and dedicated October 18.

Basement installed in 1925-28. Rev. D. A. Storey, pastor. Parsonage costing $5,000 built in 1929. Rev. T. A. Graham, pastor. Final payment by Ladies Aid in 1937. Sanctuary was lengthened in 1949, Rev. Paul R. Campbell, pastor. New chancel and other additions cost $17,000. A bequest of $5,000 by Mrs. Ana Richbaw inspired improvements. In 1955 an electric organ purchased. Rev. Floyd E. Wells, pastor, and replaced by another in 1962 by Rev. James N. Updyke. Plans were laid in 1960 for a new building to cost $180,000.

In 1964 Rev. Marvin E. Jordan was appointed for the second year. Membership was 307. Sunday school enrollment 287, Woman's Society of Christian Service, 42. They gave $289.

ing there had been erected under the leadership of Rev. Raymond S. Reese.

Bishop Titus Lowe presided as he entered upon a twelve-year period of leadership of the Portland Area. At the closing session he read appointments to 161 charges, with ten others to be supplied. Conference membership including probationers, was 205. Pastors during the preceding year had received $232,070 in salaries, compared with $86,243 in 1904. Church membership had leaped from 12,000 to 28,000, and value of church property from $449,085 to $2,492,000. Missionary giving had climbed from $8,000 to $35,000.

A Decade of Trends Toward Union

Union[5] between the two Conferences in the Northwest in 1929, was symptomatic of what was going on church-wide. Heretofore, division had been the watchword. Since 1853, Columbia River, Puget Sound, and Idaho, formerly in one Conference, had been separated from Oregon.

In the 1920's talk of union between Methodism's major bodies carried with it thoughts of union between Conferences. Washington and Northern Idaho Methodism was prepared for the move and consolidation of Northwest Methodism seemed logical.

Facilitating this move were several factors. Among them, removal of travel barriers, and closer cooperation between East and West Washington. Harbingers of the trend had been the shift to Oregon of The Dalles District, and the later return of Swedish and German churches to the English-speaking Conference.

With a consciousness of its historical heritage the united Conference began to plan a Jason Lee Centennial for 1934.[6]

MEAD—1884

Methodist preaching began in Mead Community by Rev. Mark Waltz, 1884. Pastor, Rev. M. S. Anderson, of Peone, followed, preached occasionally in 1885. Mead settlement taking shape as town. Rev. A. J. Loomis, 1888-90 organized Methodist Church at Mead, 1890, and Mr. and Mrs. Theodore Cushing donated an organ that year.

Ladies Aid, organized in 1902, began working for building. Edifice, costing $1,800, in donated labor and materials, was dedicated, October 28, 1904, by Rev. Bracken E. Koontz, Hillyard Church.

Between 1905 and 1909, churches were built at Peone, Pleasant Prairie, Greenbluff, Foothills, on circuit with Mead. Peone church abandoned, 1920.

Mead congregation, in 1939, added an abandoned Congregational church to their plant for educational purposes. Under pastorate of Rev. Robert B. Rathbun, 1954, church attendance increased from 20 to 180, and members to 150. In 1956, Wesleyan Center opened. Two years later old building burned. Wesleyan Center used for church. This building had been an abandoned tavern. In 1964 Urgent Needs Appeal funds were allocated for building in a more favorable location, scheduled for erection in 1965.

In 1964, Rev. Ronald C. Kurtz pastor second year. Members, 131, church school enrollment, 170. Thirty members of Woman's Society gave $401.

ANOTHER MEMBER CONTRIBUTED TO THE EPISCOPACY

Rev. J. Ralph Magee, who was transferred to First Church, Seattle, in 1921, was elected to the episcopacy in 1932.

NORTHWEST METHODISM WINS OVER DEPRESSION

The years following union between the two Conferences were marked by the depression of the 1930's. This experience brought decreases in every statistical column. First signs of recovery came in 1934 when Conference membership showed an increase of 770. Church school attendance continued downward and did not rise until 1946.

As the Conference slowly emerged from the depression a spirit of moderate optimism prevailed. In 1935 salaries had increased and other finances were advancing. Church building campaigns had been conducted at Kelso, Aberdeen, Eatonville, Port Angeles, Cashmere, Okanogan; Fowler, Spokane; Chewelah; Mason, Tacoma; and Grace, Seattle. Several parsonages had been built during the year.

The cabinet that year challenged the pastors to lead their churches into deepening spiritual experiences. Rev. Harold O. Perry, speaking for the cabinet, pointed out the fallacy of the notion that persons could be won to Christ just by being nice to them. "If Jesus represents what God is like," he said, "His message is universal and His life mandatory."

ADVANCING CIVILIZATION BROUGHT PROBLEMS

The report of Rev. Paul H. Ashby, of the Spokane District, in 1937, laid emphasis upon the complexity of the work in the Northwest in post pioneer times. He said, "Fast automobiles, paved roads, consolidated schools, closing of crossroads stores, and similar developments, have had great influence on rural life. Maintaining an open country church still is a problem. We have

NORWEGIAN-DANISH CONGREGATIONS—1884

The first session of Western Norwegian-Danish Annual Conference assembled at Moscow, Idaho, 1888. Bishop W. X. Ninde presiding, Rev. J. L. Ericksen, secretary.

Norwegian-Danish congregations in Washington and Northern Idaho appeared in following order: Tacoma, 1884, Rev. C. J. Larsen; Moscow, Idaho, 1885, Rev. C. J. Larsen; Blaine, Idaho, 1886, Rev. C. J. Larsen. First Norwegian-Danish, Seattle, 1889, Rev. C. J. Larsen. Port Townsend, 1889, Rev. J. S. Anderson. Spokane, 1889, Rev. C. J. Larsen. Rockford, Washington, 1889, Rev. J. C. Paulsen; South Bend, 1890, Rev. Carl Erickson. Aberdeen, Washington, 1892, Rev. H. S. Waaler; Fairhaven, Bellingham, 1890, Rev. C. J. Larsen; New Whatcom, 1899, Rev. O. Heggen. These two congregations, united in 1923, became Gladstone Street church. Served by Mrs. O. T. Field, 1938-52. LaCentre, 1891, Rev. C. N. Hauge. Everett, 1892, Rev. P. M. Ellefsen.

Churches were organized at Wilmer, Troy, and Bear Creek, Idaho, 1902, Rev. Carl Eriksen. These churches soon were discontinued. Cove, Washington, Rev. C. August Petersen, 1905. Fragaria and Olalla churches were organized, 1921, Rev. F. A. Scarvie.

Final session of Western Norwegian-Danish conference convened at San Francisco, California, 1939, Bishop James C. Baker presiding.

opened four of them this year. Their day will come again."

Aldersgate Bicentennial Observed in 1938

In 1937 the Conference looked forward to a celebration of the bicentennial of Aldersgate. The next year some churches dramatized the history of Methodism to emphasize need for an Aldersgate experience. A rising tide of spiritual devotion was observed that year. As evidence, superintendents took note of increases in giving as well as building and repairs.

On the Vancouver District Rev. Ernest Harold noted opening of several churches closed during the depression. Rev. J. M. Adams reported more than 600 new members on the Walla Walla District.

This was the last year of the Methodist Episcopal Church. The final event of consolidating three Methodist bodies in the territory was to be consummated at the next session of the Conference.

Methodism Again Was United

The annual Conference session which united Northwest Methodism convened at Garden Street Church, Bellingham, June 14-18, 1939. Bishop Wallace E. Brown presided, and Rev. Frederick L. Pedersen was secretary. All congregations of the three major Methodist bodies in Washington and Northern Idaho were included in the merger.

Methodist Protestantism Adds Strength

After the First Methodist Protestant Church had been founded in Seattle by Rev. Daniel Bagley, other congregations of that denomination followed. By 1904, preaching places, or Sunday schools were reported at Renton, Georgetown, Columbia, Ballard, Ravenna, Yesler, Jackson Street and Green Lake.[7]

All but three of these congregations had been discontinued before the 1939

SEDRO WOOLEY—1884

Sedro Wooley founded as two rival towns, across cow path from each other. Later gave up rivalry and became one.

Methodist preachers followed first settlers in 1850's, but no church organized until 1884. First service was held in the Van Fleet Schoolhouse. Class, organized in the home of David Batey continued to meet there for two years. Rev. W. B. McMillan was organizing pastor. There were thirteen members.

Church was incorporated under Rev. G. L. Cuddy, pastor in 1891. He appointed building committee of which he was member. Others on committee were David Batey, J. Y. Terry, Lewis Kirby.

Trustees were, Hiram Hammer, Lewis Kirby, David Batey, R. H. Young, C. F. Bingham, C. H. McChesney, Rev. George L. Cuddy, John Y. Terry, A. A. Tozier. Building was dedicated October 21, 1894. Rev. T. J. Massy presiding elder, was assisted by Rev. D. G. LeSourd, Rev. T. J. Loy, Rev. L. E. Wornam, and Rev. Charles McDermoth.

Ladies Aid was organized before the church was built. Woman's Home Missionary Society and Woman's Foreign Missionary Society, before 1939.

In 1964, Rev. Joseph O. Patterson was pastor. Membership, 234, Sunday school enrollment, 200. Woman's Society of Christian Service, 62. They gave $205. There were 20 enrolled in Methodist Men.

union. Ravenna Church, north of the University of Washington, Seaview, in West Seattle, and First Methodist Protestant Church, brought the strength of thriving congregations into the union.

Southern Methodism Enters the Fellowship

The Methodist Episcopal Church, South, first entered the Northwest in 1858. Dr. Orcenath Fisher was the first presiding elder. The first session of the Columbia Annual Conference of that body convened at Corvallis, Oregon, in 1866, with Bishop H. H. Kavanaugh presiding, and Rev. W. A. Finley, secretary. The East Columbia Annual Conference appeared in 1892, in which year the session was held at Palouse, Washington, with Bishop W. W. Duncan in the chair, and Rev. J. W. Compton, secretary. The name again was changed to The Northwest Annual Conference, in 1918 when the Columbia, East Columbia and Montana Conferences merged. The session was held that year at Milton, Oregon. Bishop H. M. DuBose presided, and Rev. H. M. Law was secretary.

Southern Methodism contributed six congregations, 565 members and 523 Sunday school pupils, to the 1939 merger. These churches were Corbin Park, Spokane; and Marvin Memorial, Walla Walla, in Washington. Those in Idaho were Juliaetta, Lapwai Indian Mission, Leland and Cavendish. Rev. W. Raymond Wilder was pastor at Corbin Park; Rev. E. J. Maxwell, at Lapwai, assisted by Rev. Stephen Reuben, Indian, supply; and Rev. J. E. Walbeck, Leland-Cavendish. Four other points appearing in the 1939 minutes were, Arrow, Sweetwater, Bethel and Troy. No statistical report for these places ever appeared, and by 1964, they long since had ceased to be included among appointments. Marvin Memorial lost its identity in 1955 when it merged with Grace to become the United Methodist Church, Walla Walla. Southern Methodist congregations, discontinued

---

VASHON—1884

First Methodist services at Vashon held in grove, in 1884. Church organized with 17 members. Several were members First Church, Seattle. Rev. Albert Atwood, organizer. Rev. F. Ailward, first pastor who served Colby and Bethel in Kitsap County.

Church built of logs, donated labor, was first place of worship on island. Rev. John N. Dennison, First Church Seattle, delivered dedication sermon. Rev. David E. Blaine, founder First Church, Seattle, assisted. Friends in Tacoma donated stove. First Church, Seattle donated lumber to finish interior.

Church was popular from start. Children thrilled to attend. Parents punished children by keeping them away from Sunday school.

In 1885 Vashon became independent. Rev. Enoch Dudley, pastor. Under Rev. W. H. Leach, 1892, church experienced growth. New church dedicated in 1908, under Rev. G. H. Wold. Other pastors of period were, Rev. James E. Milligan, and Rev. John H. Berringer. From 1920-25 Methodists and Presbyterians federated. Methodists found it difficult to recover after withdrawing.

Log church razed in 1948, for safety. New parsonage, 1951. Mortgage paid, 1960.

In 1964, Rev. Fred Rarden assigned for fourth year. Membership 120, church school 83, Woman's Society members 34. They gave $369.

106

before the merger, had been at Oaksdale, Kenwood, South Spokane and Palouse, Washington, and Lewiston, Idaho.

Besides ministers already named, the merger brought into the Conference Rev. P. D. Hartman, effective elder, and Rev. J. H. Dills, Rev. H. S. Shangle, and Rev. G. H. Gibbs, retired elders.

From the Methodist Protestant Church came Rev. Wilbur M. Snyder and Rev. W. H. Hodges, effective elders.

Personal Lay Evangelism Takes Hold in the Northwest

Northwest Methodists began experimenting with personal lay evangelism on a Conference-wide scale, in 1941. At that time, Rev. Guy Black led a campaign for the Portland Area. Training sessions were held in Tacoma, from which ministers fanned out to lead their laymen in local church campaigns.

As a result increases in accessions on confession of faith were reported throughout the Conference. Seattle-Tacoma District received 1,606 new members, and 947 were added to churches on the Puget Sound District. On the Spokane District one church increased its membership by 53 percent, and Walla Walla District gained 717 members.

Similar Conference-wide efforts continued at intervals for a decade. In 1950 more than 300 ministers and laymen on the Puget Sound District called on 3,000 prospects and won 1,000. That year, heart-warming experiences by laymen, visiting from house-to-house, were reported from all districts. At Aberdeen, on the Vancouver District, Rev. J. S. Cleland, retired, entered the new Central Park area to establish a church. Through house-to-house visitation he won 175 members, of which 163 came on profession of faith.

By the end of the decade this plan for winning men had become accepted procedure by Northwest Methodists.

WINLOCK—1884

Rev. J. W. Patterson organized first church at Winlock April 1, 1884. Charter members included Mr. and Mrs. William J. Byham, Mr. and Mrs. Levi Rose, Mr. and Mrs. Henry Metz, Mrs. A. J. Rhodes. Henry Metz was elected superintendent of Sunday school, organized that year.

Winlock was served by a local preacher, Rev. David Mather, through 1886.

Lot for church building bought from Jack Nealy, November 15, 1887. Church, parsonage completed next year.

In 1894, Conference Home Missionary Society erected orphanage at Winlock. Rev. W. H. Wilson, superintendent. Closed in 1900.

In 1906, new location was purchased. Owner of mill offered to pay moving expenses because church was so close to his mill that it often caught on fire. In 1914, parsonage burned, soon rebuilt. Rev. Raymond S. Reese, pastor.

In 1921, church at Toledo closed, membership transferred to Winlock. In 1929, Napavine church closed, united with Winlock.

In 1945, Virgil Harkins set up $5,000 trust fund for new church. By 1956, $600 had been added. New sanctuary completed, 1964.

In 1964, Rev. Edgar Lee Starr, Jr., pastor, third year. Membership 237. Church school enrollment, 117. Woman's Society, 30, gave $670. Building value, $68,000. Parsonage, $8,500.

AMERICA ENTERS SECOND WORLD WAR

American entry into the world conflict in 1941 shifted the pattern of church procedures. In 1942, Rev. Norman McCay reported that Vancouver's population had leaped from 30,000 to 100,000. Families moved so often that pastors could not follow them. He cited the need for three new pastors in that city.

Vancouver Methodists were working with Council of Churches leaders in an endeavor to meet the emergency. One outcome of united efforts was the new church at McLoughlin Heights under Methodist auspices.

WAR ECONOMY CHANGES PATTERN OF LIFE

Rev. Frederick L. Pedersen, superintendent of the Walla Walla District, said, "Work hours have been changed, living patterns have been upset, homes have been broken and moved, associations of people in organizations have been blasted, purposes and goals for living have been challenged. Along with this great fact must go another—the Church has the Gospel which will bring peace on earth and good will among men!"

The influx of persons was accompanied by an acute shortage of pastors, many of whom had entered the armed forces. Yet this was a period of skyrocketing ministerial salaries and payments on debts. Building and improvements were forbidden because of war rationing of materials.

This was the period of Special Opportunity funds, raised to enable the church to move into new fields as rapidly as workers could be found. In some places women were pressed into service. Rev. Carl K. Mahoney employed Miss Helen Pabis and Miss Laura Butler to pioneer among newcomers and assist pastors in acute situations in Seattle.

BOTHELL—1885

Rev. Albert Atwood held first service in the Bothell area, in November, 1885. Church organized that same year, with 16 members. First trustees were, George Bothell, John J. Harvey, George Burdick, Frank W. Spear, W. G. Young, and G. W. Clark.

In 1890 Rev. George R. Osborn died while serving church. First resident pastor, Rev. Alfred Crumley, 1892-94, also preached at Woodinville, three miles away. A unit of first building erected in 1889-90 with aid of $500 donation by Board of Church Extension. Lots donated by David Bothell family. Church incorporated October 1, 1910.

Rev. J. H. Beall, 1926-30, erected educational unit. Church painted under leadership of Rev. Elwyn H. Scheyer, 1937-44.

In 1954, Misses Merle and Erna Olin donated two lots for new church site. Trustees purchased other adjoining land, making four acres. Ground broken in September, 1957. Building which won national award for beauty of design, was erected. Last service in old building, May 4, 1958. Rev. J. Warne Sanders, pastor.

Rev. S. Raynor Smith, Junior, pastor in 1960. Wife died following year. In 1964, Rev. J. Allen Justad appointed third year. Members, 869, church school enrollment, 687. Woman's Society members, 110. They gave $1,411.

Northwest Methodism Enters Crusade for Christ

The Conference, in 1945, joined the church-wide Crusade for Christ. Everywhere congregations oversubscribed their quotas toward the $25,000,000 nation-wide goal to rebuild Methodist institutions in war-torn countries. Following hostilities the Conference launched a thrust to occupy territory assigned by Council of Churches in growing suburbs and new communities. New congregations born out of this effort were in Seattle, Everett, Tacoma, Bremerton, Olympia, Vancouver, and Spokane.

Conference Council Organized in 1952

A further step in the entrenchment program was the establishment of the Interboard Council in 1952. Through this agency all boards and commissions came to channel their activities, under the general leadership of an executive secretary, who also was director of adult work for the Conference. Rev. Elwyn H. Scheyer was first to hold this position. Associated with him were directors of youth and children's work.

This plan was altered in 1958 when the agency became known as the Conference Council. Rev. Oscar M. Adam became executive secretary in charge of program, with associates in charge of departmental services. Rev. Francis M. Kinch became executive secretary of administration.

Entrenchment Techniques Strengthen Local Churches

Campaigns designed to strengthen the local church conducted during the 1950's, included an attempt to enlist tithers. On Palm Sunday, 1952, 1,439 persons pledged themselves to tithe. The Advance for Christ, also promoted during this time, increased giving by $50,000 in five years. Through the Area

COTTONWOOD, IDAHO—1885

Methodist services in Cottonwood, Idaho, began 1885. Rev. Luella M. Smith, Grangeville Methodist Church, held services in hall on Main Street. In 1893, lots received from J. S. Rhoades and began building. Rev. F. L. Buzzell, pastor at Grangeville. Probably served Cottonwood. Three churches, 58 members on circuit. In 1896, Rev. Thomas D. Gregory, pastor.

Cottonwood first among appointments, 1900. Rev. J. E. Daniels, first year. Returning pastor, Rev. C. H. Miller reported no members or finance. In 1901, Rev. J. B. Bucholz, supply. Rev. J. E. Daniels reported 43 members, 52 in church school, one church building valued at $1,250. In 1904, 39 members, 50 in church school, according to report by Rev. J. E. Daniels. In 1907, Rev. G. A. Pease appointed pastor, thirty-two members.

In 1928, there were 142 members, left to be supplied. In 1938, Rev. C. W. Groth reported 101 members and 43 in Sunday school.

New building erected in 1953, opened for worship, May 31. Rev. Ludwig Eskildsen, pastor. Dedicated May 5, 1957, Rev. J. Earl Lake, pastor. Membership, 108, and 74 in church school.

In 1964, Rev. Mack E. Farmer, pastor, second year. Church membership 75, church school 86. Twelve members of Woman's Society, gave $536. Building value, $7,880. Parsonage $5,600.

Forward Movement, launched in 1952, conference leaders sought $575,000. Pledges reached $485,850, and subscribers paid $169,229 the first year. New churches, struggling congregations, Wesley Gardens, and the College of Puget Sound, benefitted by this effort. This program was followed by the Spiritual Life Mission emphasizing family devotions, Bible reading, and tithing.

Through these efforts the Church was mustering its forces, and entrenching itself for new thrusts aimed at Christianizing all of society. Areas of special interest included social, economic, and moral fields.

COLUMBIA BASIN CHALLENGE ACCEPTED BY METHODISTS

Opening for sale of the first section of 1,000,000 acres of newly irrigated land in the Columbia River Basin, in 1952, presented a new challenge to Northwest Methodists. The State Council of Churches allocated certain areas to the Methodists. Sites speedily occupied were Moses Lake, Highlands, Kennewick; Burbank and Riverview at Pasco. Several churches in this area which had slumbered in virtual stagnation for decades, suddenly came alive with new members and interest.

EAST MILL PLAIN—1886

First Sunday school, East Mill Plain, Harmony schoolhouse, 1886. George A. Whipple, superintendent. First preaching service, May 23, that year, Rev. G. G. Ferguson, LaCamas. Church organized that year, 9 members. They were: Mr. and Mrs. George Whipple, Mr. and Mrs. George Peebles, Mr. and Mrs. S. S. Cook, Mrs. Hiram Stamp, Mr. and Mrs. Crisp. Five ministers that followed resided, LaCamas. Parsonage built 1892.

Work started, Harmony Church, 1892, dedicated, July 30, 1893. Rev. C. C. Stratton preached.

Class organized between Mill Plain and Fisher's Landing, 1891, 13 members, called Epworth Church, built sanctuary. March 17, 1921, merged with Harmony, became East Mill Plain. Rev. B. G. Clemins, pastor, 1920-25.

In 1921, Harmony building moved to location of Epworth, used for Sunday school. Fiftieth anniversary of church observed, 1936, Rev. C. H. Cowdy, pastor. Annex remodeled, 1936-42, Rev. T. H. Jorgensen, pastor. Further remodeled, 1942-45, Rev. Howard P. Buck, pastor. More remodeling during pastorates of Rev. Claude Brown, 1945-48, Rev. Harry Walling, 1948-58.

In 1964, Rev. Marion Koth, pastor, third year. Members, 135, church school, 107. Woman's Society membership, 19, gave $372. Value of building, $20,000. Parsonage, $6,500. Ten former members, became ministers, six missionaries.

Some churches took note of the 100th anniversary of the entry of Methodism in Puget Sound in 1953.[8] Most ministers, however, were busy pursuing the Forward Movement and Spiritual Life missions.

First Church, Seattle, under the leadership of Rev. Cyrus E. Albertson, pastor, spent six weeks in celebration of its 100th anniversary. On Centennial Sunday, 126 new members were received into First Church.

On the Walla Walla District, Rev. Joseph H. Beall reported that 14 congregations had built new edifices, repaired old ones, or erected parsonages. The anniversary found in Seattle and Tacoma, 22,158 members, succeeding the four pioneers who had become

TYPICAL RURAL CHURCHES IN EASTERN WASHINGTON & IDAHO

Church at Lacrosse

SOME RURAL CHURCHES STILL PROSPER

While good roads, consolidated schools, closing of crossroads general stores, have resulted in abandonment of many rural churches in this part of Washington and Idaho, some continue to serve and prosper.

The Grangeville, Idaho Church

Church at
Finley, Washington

The Methodist Episcopal
Church South at
Juliaetta, Idaho

charter members of First Church, Seattle, 100 years earlier. In the entire Conference were 74,056 Methodists, fruit of the first 100 years.

No one was satisfied. Leaders set new and higher goals for the years ahead. Lyle, on the Vancouver District, had the first resident pastor in its long history. Rev. Wendell Cone began to operate a mobile chapel to reach hitherto neglected populations on the Olympic Peninsula. The film, depicting the life of John Wesley, widely shown in the Conference, created consciousness of the debt Northwest Methodists owe to John Wesley.

The 1950's brought unprecedented membership, attendance and financial giving to Northwest Methodism. With more means available many churches increased their staffs. Congregations, which fifteen years earlier could, with difficulty, support a pastor, now employed directors of education, as well as associate pastors. Secretaries to handle clerical work became the rule.

CHANGING ECONOMY FORCES CHURCHES TO CLOSE

Prosperity, however, did not visit all congregations within the Conference. Many were abandoned. Varying circumstances entered into such closing. Wallville, in Pacific County, is an example. In the 1920's, this community supported a church with 83 members and paid a salary of more than $1,500. By 1939, the community no longer existed. Its one industry, a saw mill, had been dismantled and its residents had departed.

Several churches in Rainier Valley,[9] Seattle, were operating in the 1920's, but by 1940, were abandoned. Madison Street Church, Seattle, had 165 members in 1928. Population shifts led to its abandonment in 1935. Asbury Church, in the populous Fremont area, reported 400 members in 1943, and was closed in 1944. Such experiences called for a second look at Methodism's urban strategy.

SOUTH COLBY—1886

Methodists began at Colby, 1886. Leaders of the Sunday school that year, Mrs. Anspauch, Mr. and Mrs. Thomas Harding, and Mrs. Joseph S. Grout. First preaching by Rev. G. R. Osborne, in 1887. Followed, 1890, by Benjamin Freeland, local preacher, dentist. Rev. F. S. Pearson, 1892, Rev. A. J. McNemee, 1905-09.

Building erected at near-by Bethel in 1891 by Rev. Albert Atwood. Services at Colby continued in schoolhouse, and later, Seventh Day Adventist church. In 1905, Colby, with 7 members, became a separate charge, Rev. J. W. White, pastor. Rev. A. M. Marsh, seven months later, conducted revivals, added members. In 1907, parsonage erected, by Rev. A. J. McNemee.

For years, following 1930, Colby attached to Port Orchard, Rev. Arthur Morton, Rev. John R. Butler, Rev. T. L. Blaisdell, pastor. In 1944, Rev. John Mathone, pastor, church experienced revival. New building erected in 1948, Rev. Mark Freeman, pastor. A new parsonage, in 1952, Rev. John Freeman, pastor. Members 112, Church School 194.

In 1955, $18,500 pledged to complete church building. Conference added $3,000, and in 1957, church opened for services.

In 1964, Rev. Ralph Butler, pastor, sixth year. Membership, 146, church school enrollment 130. Woman's Society membership 50, gave $1,159. Church value $55,000; parsonage, $10,500.

A New Episcopal Area Receives Bishop

The year 1960 brought far-reaching changes to Northwest Methodism. That year the Conference became a separate Episcopal Area. Dr. Everett W. Palmer, pastor at First Church, Glendale, California, was elected bishop and assigned to the Seattle Area.

Conference leaders, that year, laid emphasis upon recruitment for Christian services. They recalled that the Northwest never had provided its own ministerial leadership. The day had come, not only to recruit ministers, but workers in all lines of Christian endeavor. This year the Conference authorized a Commission on Christian Social Concerns for the local church. Included were former boards and committees on temperance, social service, world peace and race.

The Conference took a new look at the ecumenical frontier and gave consideration to an expanding fellowship.

Group Ministry and Larger Parish Plans Appear

Districts announced experiments with two types of service to smaller churches. The first, known as group ministry, provided for the pooling of experiences by pastors of a number of adjacent churches, with one minister acting as chairman. The larger Parish plan provided for a pastor to head a staff of ministers, serving a group of congregations. On the Walla Walla District the former plan was in effect with Clearwater, Orofino, Peck, Cavendish, Cottonwood, Nezperce, Culdesac, Lapwai, Kendrick, Juliaetta, Pierce, and Headquarters, cooperating.

Church School Decline Gives Leaders Concern

Leaders expressed concern in 1961, for the downward trend in church school attendance. Meanwhile, church membership showed an increase of 8,975. The Conference Board of Education proposed a major thrust aimed at

CORBIN PARK, SPOKANE—1886

Corbin Park Methodist Episcopal Church, South, was started in 1886. Rev. J. W. Compton bought lots for $600. Later sold for $1,700 and, with profits, bought better site.

In 1889, Rev. R. B. Swift, pastor, preached in hired hall, bought lot on Sprague Avenue, organized Hargrove Church, built sanctuary, started mission school in Forest Park, which later became Corbin Park.

Forest Park Mission Chapel built in 1899. First pastor, Rev. A. L. Thoroughman, appointed in 1900. By end of year there were 65 members. Rev. John Dills, in 1902, united competing congregations. Cornerstone laid, September, 1903, on Park Avenue for building to house newly united congregation. Bishop H. C. Merrill dedicated church, September 4, 1904. Parsonage erected in 1907. Rev. R. K. Triplett, pastor.

In 1922-23, building improved, and reconsecrated. Rev. C. A. Rexroot, pastor. Debt paid, 1930, Rev. P. D. Hartman, pastor. 1939, church renamed "Corbin Park." Rev. W. Raymond Wilder, pastor.

Church languished after war with youth gone and abandonment was considered. But realizing people in neighborhood needed service, congregation decided to continue.

In 1964, Rev. Homer Sexton was pastor, third year. Members, 133, church school 103. Building valued at $48,000, parsonage, $10,500.

113

training educational leadership in new methods of instruction.

The district superintendents, in a composite report, lamented the lack of progress within the cities. It was noted that the Conference had occupied less than half of the locations assigned to Methodists by Council of Churches. Lack of funds to purchase sites was blamed for this failure. It was hoped, however, that six churches could be organized during the year to come.

Northwest Methodists Won Victories to the End

During the 111 years ending in 1964, Methodist ministers had been sent to 745 points in the Northwest. Yet, at the close of the period there were but 286 pastoral charges in the area. More than 400 places to which Methodist ministers once had been sent no longer were being served by the Church. Nevertheless, Methodist strength in the region was not to be discounted.

World Service giving that year was $446,355, an all-time high. Church members in the Conference totaled 97,782. More than 10,000 of these were in the 33 congregations which had come into being since 1943. This impressive total in itself bore evidence that great-hearted Methodists, through concerted action, still were winning victories for Christ and His Church.

CHAPTER V

Men of
Forest
and Plain

*The work of "Father" J. H. Wilbur
among the Yakimas marks him as Methodism's greatest missionary to—*

(Methodist Missions to Northwest Indians reviewed)

METHODISM'S FIRST OBJECTIVE

When the Methodist Church first sent missionaries to the Northwest the one objective was conversion of the Indians.

There were few others to convert. When Rev. Jason Lee crossed the Rocky Mountains, in 1834, there already were in the region no more than fifty non-Indian residents. A few roving hunters and trappers, four Hudson's Bay trading posts, with white staffs, and possibly twenty retired former employes of the company, who had settled on the land with their Indian wives, were the sole Caucasian residents in the Northwest.[1]

No utterance of Methodist Missionary Society, or Lee, indicated any other purpose than conversion of the Indians.

Yet, a singular change occurred. In less than ten years, conversion of the Indians faded into a side line and came almost to be obscured by the aim to bring the newly arrived white settlers under the influence of the Gospel.

Nevertheless, the passion to bring the saving influence of Christ to men of forest and plain never wholly died.

INDIANS IN ALL PARTS OF NORTHWEST

When Methodists first entered the present State of Washington, sixty-four Indian tribes lived in the region. Forty-five of these occupied the area west of the Cascades and nineteen were found in the region east.

Presumably the greater number of small tribes west was due to difficulties of travel and communication through dense jungles extending from mountain top to ocean. Forests forced the Indians to concentrate along streams, lakes, sound, and sea. Although, over trails, they penetrated forests and crossed mountains, the favorite mode of transportation was the canoe, fashioned from giant trunks of red cedar. In these they pushed up rivers, crossed lakes, navigated the Sound, and braved the Pacific. Principal items of food were fish, game, roots, and berries.

East of the Cascades the Indian's favorite means of transportation was on horseback. Lush grass, covering the area, provided forage for great numbers of these animals. An Indian's wealth was counted in terms of horses. The men were expert riders and speedily could cover great distances. Aside from carrying heavy burdens the horse also provided food in extreme emergencies.

Other sources of food were fish, game, roots, and berries, east, as well as west. The Indian's mode of life largely was dictated by need for food, in pursuit of which he regularly migrated to forest, and mountains. Many tribesmen annually visited the Rocky Mountain area to procure buffalo meat for winter use. Also, they shifted residence with the seasons to find pasture for horses.

KELSO—1887

Kelso first appeared in Conference minutes in 1887, Rev. E. L. Hughes, pastor. Parsonage built that year. Rev. F. M. Pickles, 1888, planned church. Freeport on circuit.

New church dedicated July 24, 1892, Rev. J. I. Smith, pastor. Sermon by Rev. A. J. Hanson, presiding elder. In 1890's Catlin, Ostrander on Kelso Circuit. Church at Ostrander built, 1894, Rev. G. G. Ferguson, pastor. Dedicated by Rev. S. S. Sulliger, presiding elder. Church at Catlin, formerly Freeport, built in 1892, Rev. C. P. Stayton, pastor.

Debt, Kelso church paid 1898-01, Rev. C. E. Fulmer, pastor. In 1908, Catlin annexed by Kelso, churches merged. Rev. N. M. Temple, pastor. Church used as emergency hospital for influenza patients in 1918. Rev. O. F. Krieger, pastor.

New church erected 1927-'29, Rev. C. D. Rarey, pastor. Rev. L. C. Hicks, 1932, espoused Liberty Party, ran for governor, defeated. Church opened doors to flood victims, 1933. Fire destroyed church, 1937-45. Rev. Harold Bashor, pastor. Church rebuilt. First service, 1939, Bishop Titus Lowe, preaching. Mortgage burned six years later. Electric organ, 1952. Rev. Carroll H. Sprague, pastor.

In 1964, Rev. Ludvig Eskildsen, pastor, seventh year. Members, 575; church school, 414. Woman's Society, 136, paid $1,105. Building value, $150,-000. Parsonage, $35,000.

Arts and crafts employed east and west were limited to manufacture of articles needed in the Indian's way of life. Spears, nets, boats, shelters, mats, baskets, and articles of clothing were fashioned according to need.

With the coming of fur traders the Indians learned to use guns, knives, blankets, and cooking utensils which they acquired through barter for furs, fish, and game.

LONG LIST OF TRIBES IN WASHINGTON

Principal tribes east of the Cascades were: Nez Perce, Cayuse, Yakima, Spokane, Coeur d'Alene, Colville, Kalispel, Kittitas, Okanogan, Sanpoil, Walla Walla, and Wenatchi. West the tribes first encountered by whites were: Clakamas, Cowlitz, Chinook, Chehalis, Nisqually, Duwamish, Kathlamet, Klallam, Makah, Nooksack, Puyallup, Quinault, Quillayute, Samish, Semiahmoo, Skagit, Snoqualmie, Suquamish, and others.

Apparently there is no accurate record of numbers of original inhabitants. Rev. and Mrs. David Blaine,[2] in 1853, estimated that about 150 Indians resided on Elliott Bay. East of the mountains, more than 2,500 assembled at Walla Walla in 1855 to meet Governor Isaac Stevens to discuss the treaty which resulted in their removal from their lands. The habit of moving from place to place, and gathering at different times, in large numbers, probably was the source of over-estimation of populations.

INDIANS HAD THEIR OWN RELIGION

Contrary to widespread notions, the religion of the Indians included a clear-cut conviction that God had created for them the earth and its products—game, fish, herbs, berries, and all items needful for life.[3] Their religious ceremonies were expressions of gratitude to the Creator for these gifts.

Indians held strict standards of honor, recognizing property rights of fellow-tribesmen, as well as those of other groups. Rights to hunting and fishing locations were religiously respected, although owners of such privileges were generous in making them available on loan to others. It was a point of an Indian's honor to keep his promise. These attitudes led him to look with suspicion and fear upon the white man's tendency to appropriate his land without payment, or at other times to break his promise.

The Hudson's Bay Company, with its limited number of posts, had shown no disposition to occupy large areas of Indian land.[4] The few former employees of the company, who settled on the land, had identified themselves with the Indians by taking their women for wives.

MARYSVILLE—1887

Marysville's first regularly appointed pastor, Rev. A. J. McNemee, took charge of the Snohomish Circuit in 1887. The church had 13 members. Circuit large and travel difficult. In absence of pastor, John Spencer, local preacher supplied. He lived four miles up River making trip in rowboat. E. L. Chesney, a bachelor, aided him.

In 1889, Rev. W. H. Johnson became pastor. He was followed, in 1890, by Rev. John Moles who served five months. Marysville became a station in 1890 with Rev. John Flinn, pastor. He was followed by Rev. W. C. Hockett, who built first church, costing $3,000, doing carpenter work himself.

Early prayer meetings held in home of Mrs. E. Munson. Articles of Incorporation filed January 28, 1892. There were 14 members. In 1892 Marysville combined with Stanwood, Rev. J. W. Patterson pastor. Church waned in 1893-95, Sunday school closed. Under Rev. George W. Frame, 1895-98, work prospered. After 1898 Marysville became a separate charge. The debt on the building was paid by Rev. J. D. Dimick, 1898-1900. Membership doubled under Rev. Paul H. Ashby, 1911-13.

In 1964 Rev. Lloyd A. Doty was appointed for the sixth year. Membership 476, church school enrollment 462, members Woman's Society of Christian Service 168. Women gave $614.

117

The Catholic missionaries who built simple, but neat stations, and devoted themselves to teaching and serving, had not encouraged settlers to occupy the land. With these the Indians lived in peace.

On the contrary, Dr. Marcus Whitman at Waiilatpu, and the Methodists at The Dalles, to whom at first the Indians were friendly, soon found their attitudes changed. When the Indians at Waiilatpu saw products of the soil being sold to white settlers who threatened to take more of their land, they began to harbor resentment born of fear of loss of their most precious possession.

White missionaries promised the Indians a new faith that would do much for them. The Indians interpreted this promise as applying to health, and the hereafter. But when the only daughter of the Whitman's drowned,[5] the event struck a blow at the Indian's faith in the power of the white man's religion. Later, when red men near the mission began to die in numbers from a malady, hitherto unknown among them, resentment mounted. They believed the white men had used sorcery.

Similar experiences were encountered at Willamette, The Dalles, and other parts of the Northwest. Words of suspicion and fear were spread abroad.

At Waiilatpu, the Indians attacked the mission, Nov. 29, 1847, murdering the Whitmans and twelve associates. The Methodists at The Dalles were similarly threatened. The Cayuse War followed, and the death of many Indian warriors at the hands of white men did not lessen suspicion against the newcomers.

INDIANS BITTERLY OPPOSED TO STEVENS' TREATIES

When Washington became a territory, and Governor Isaac Stevens began to conclude treaties with the Indians, their resentment grew to white heat.[6] They felt they were being forced to give up their land. Some chiefs refused to en-

---

WATERVILLE—1887

Waterville first appeared as an appointment with Grand Coulee, in 1887. Rev. T. W. Atkinson, pastor. In 1888, Rev. H. F. Williams reported 25 members. A year later, 37 members, church valued at $1,500.

In 1890, church on Columbia District, 40 members, parsonage value $400, church $2,000. In 1895, 154 members, four Sunday schools, 120 enrolled on circuit. Rev. M. R. Brown, pastor.

In 1900, Rev. F. B. Utter reported 92 members, one Sunday school, 70 enrolled. In 1910, there were 96 members and 140 in Sunday school. In 1929, Rev. Waldo W. Pearson, reported 48 full members and 56 non-resident, with 80 in Sunday school. The next year congregation federated with Baptist Church. There were 48 full members and 56 non-resident. Waterville placed on Puget Sound District in 1931. Next year, left to be supplied.

In 1935 Rev. G. R. Kincaid said there were 45 full members, 25 non-resident, with 135 enrolled in Sunday school. Rev. Dwight G. Bennett, in 1936, reported 39 full members, 15 non-resident.

In 1964, Rev. William J. Brooks, Baptist pastor, reported 43 members and 134 in Sunday school.

Waterville was a pioneer congregation in the North Columbia. Its pastors assisted in organizing congregations at Chelan, Wenatchee, and other points.

dorse the agreement. Others signed with reluctance, feeling they had no alternative.

Many refused to move onto the reservations, convinced the price offered for their land was inadequate. Thus the Indian Wars of 1855-58. Details of that conflict may be found in secular histories. These facts are recounted here that the reader may more clearly understand the handicap this Indian psychology placed upon Methodists who offered their religion.

METHODIST MISSIONARIES NOT FIRST IN NORTHWEST

Methodist missionaries in Washington were preceded, not only by Marcus Whitman, but by Catholics as well. Fathers Francis Norbert Blanchet[7] and Modesto Demers arrived at Vancouver, Saturday, November 24, 1838. The next day they celebrated the first Catholic Mass in present Western Washington. December 16 they arrived at Cowlitz Prairie where they established the Mission which still stands.

Catholics also visited Nisqually and performed religious rites before the arrival of Dr. John P. Richmond. During the summer of 1839, while William Holden Willson was constructing the mission building to be occupied by Richmond, a year later, Father Demers spent several days at Nisqually, where he baptized a number of children and two adults, besides performing a marriage ceremony.

Blanchet took over the Willamette Catholic Mission in 1839 and assigned Demers to Cowlitz. In 1840, Blanchet established a mission on Whidbey Island. That year Demers visited the upper Columbia, spending time at Walla Walla, Colville, and Okanogan. Father Peter J. de Smet was already among the Flatheads farther east, and Demers communicated with him.

Catholics continued to come. In 1841 Fathers Anthony Langlois and B. Z. Bolduc were added, the former, to St. Paul on the Willamette, and the latter

ST. PAUL'S, SPOKANE—1887

St. Paul's Church, Spokane, was organized, October 9, 1887, as Jefferson Street Church. Rev. N. E. Parsons, presiding elder. Rev. R. E. Bisbee, pastor. Charter member, H. N. Muzzy, donated lots. Building cost $3,300. Soon, 68 members, free of debt. Rev. W. H. Fry, 1900-05, building doubled in size, pipe organ installed. Rev. E. M. Hill, 1907-10, new location, basement built, changed name to St. Paul's. New building dedicated, April 5, 1914, Rev. U. F. Hawk, pastor.

St. Paul's merged with Epworth, 1951. Church remodeled, redecorated, Rev. Ernest F. Harold, pastor, 1940-49. Chancel divided, John B. Hazen Memorial pipe organ installed. Church school facilities remodeled, 1949-59, Rev. E. J. Aschenbrenner, pastor.

Church celebrated 75th Anniversary, October 7, 8, 9th, 1962. Featured speakers, Bishop Everett W. Palmer, Bishop A. Raymond Grant, Rev. Edward J. Aschenbrenner. Rev. A. R. Perrino, pastor. Hamilton Hardin, Lay Leader; Frank Cockrell, Official Board chairman. Leaders: Aaron Sheldon, Men's Club; Lee Pennell, Adult Fellowship; Jean Merriwether, MYF; Mrs. Dan DeWitt, church school; Mrs. E. G. Peters, Woman's Society.

In 1964, Rev. Lloyd F. Holloway, pastor, second year. Membership, 876; church school, enrollment 634. Woman's Society, members, 162, gave $731. Building value, $324,140. Parsonage $16,000.

to Cowlitz. Father F. M. Blanchet became in turn, Vicar-General, Bishop, and Archbishop, of Oregon. His brother, Father A. M. A. Blanchet, later was appointed Bishop of Nisqually, and Demers became Bishop of Vancouver Island.

In 1847, twelve years before Methodists entered Eastern Washington, and five years ahead of DeVore at Steilacoom, the Catholic Ecclesiastical Province of Oregon numbered three Bishops, 14 Jesuit Fathers, four Oblate Fathers, 13 secular priests, 13 sisters, and two houses of education.

Sixty years later the historian, Clinton Snowden, said, "The Catholic missionaries acquired and retained over the native population west of the Rocky Mountains, a far more perfect control than the Protestant missionaries were ever able to secure."

Twelve years before Rev. James Harvey Wilbur first visited the Yakima Reservation, St. Joseph's Mission had been established on the Ahtanum by Father Jean Charles Pandosy.

WILBUR BEGINS TO TEACH AT SIMCOE

Rev. James Harvey Wilbur's first work at Simcoe was as teacher.[8] He arranged for pupils to reside in dormitories provided by the Agency. Since most of the parents were destitute, he also provided food and clothing from Government funds allowed for that purpose. He required each pupil to do a certain amount of manual labor in addition to class work. Mrs. Wilbur also taught in the school and worked with women of the Reservation.

Wilbur's highmindedness and efficiency did not shield him from opposition by politicians. In 1862, B. F. Kendall, superintendent of Indian Affairs for Washington Territory, wrote William F. Dodge, Commissioner of Indian Affairs at Washington, D. C., that he had removed Wilbur from his position as superintendent of teaching.

BAY VIEW—1888

Incorporation papers for Bay View church filed August, 1888. The first trustees were W. J. McKenna, John W. Martin, B. L. Inman, J. W. Bradley, T. B. Elliott. First building erected that year. Rev. J. W. White, pastor. Congregation occupied same building 76 years. Church first supplied from LaConner, then Anacortes. Ladies Aid organized in 1889. Rev. E. J. Moore, pastor at LaConner pioneered church prior to 1888.

In 1905 Rev. R. M. Schoonmaker pastor Bay View, also served Allen. In 1918 with LaConner, Rev. C. E. Sanders, pastor. There were 26 members, 31 in Sunday school. In 1925, Bay View with Edison. Rev. J. D. Bird pastor. In 1929, 37 in Sunday school. There were nine members of church. In 1956, with Blanchard and Samish, Rev. Donald P. Sondal pastor. There were eleven members and eleven in Sunday school. In 1960, church did not appear among appointments but had been teamed with Samish previous year. Rev. M. M. Lehmann reported 21 members, 28 in Sunday school. Twelve women in Woman's Society, and church building was valued at $13,000. In 1964 Rev. R. Clinton McGaffee was in second year. There were 54 members and 28 in Sunday school. Church building was valued at $5,000 and there was no parsonage.

Charges included his alleged extravagance in providing help to the Indian pupils, including presents which it was claimed were to bribe them to attend Sunday school and worship services. He also charged that on a previous occasion, Wilbur had sided with the resident agent, Dr. R. H. Lansdale, in defying the authority of the superintendent when attempting to discharge his duty. He said, "Wilbur had usurped the authority of the Agent and seemed determined that no employee should be allowed to continue on the reservation who entertained religious views differing from those entertained by himself."

Kendall reported that Wilbur's request to remain on the reservation as a minister appointed by the Oregon Conference of the Methodist Episcopal Church, also was refused.

This dismissal, however, did not settle the matter. Soon Wilbur was back as head of the school. When, in 1864, he was appointed Agent, he wrote the Commissioner of Indian Affairs that his predecessor had wasted the allowances provided by the Government, and that the Indians believed much of it had been appropriated by the former agent to his own use. Under Wilbur affairs began to move smoothly, a new experience on the five-year-old reservation.

Wilbur sought to teach the usual branches of learning to his pupils and also to instruct them in the arts of farming, carpentry, milling, and woodsmanship. To every family, willing to make use of them, he offered land, seeds, implements, and instruction in their use. Flour and lumber mills were erected and workmen taught to operate them. From lumber thus produced the residents were taught to construct their own houses.

PROBLEMS MULTIPLIED FOR WILBUR

As agent on the reservation Wilbur's problems were multiplied. Fourteen tribes had been assigned to the reservation but many refused to move. Chief Kamiakin,[9] of the Yakimas, resisted

---

GRAYS RIVER—1888

The first Sunday school at Grays River, on lower Columbia, was organized December 13, 1888. Later it met in the Fairview schoolhouse, which became the Art Badger home. Mrs. Emerson was the first church school superintendent. First preaching service took place in 1877. Rev. Mr. Watson was the first preacher. The church was organized in 1888. The trustees were Thad Barr, J. W. Lawrence, Jesse Baker, H. O. Lamb, and Thomas A. Foss. The organizing pastor was Rev. T. H. Stimson and the church was on the Olympia district. The Woman's Foreign Missionary Society was organized August 3, 1888 with 14 members. Mrs. Jessie Barr was the first leader. First church erected 1894 costing $1,200. Rev. A. J. McNemee, pastor.

The church was moved in 1912 to a site on the river near Barr's home.

A new building was erected in 1962 costing $34,000. Rev. John Freeman, pastor. Chairman of the trustees in 1962 was T. S. Barr. In 1964 Rev. John Freeman still pastor. There were 42 members and 52 in the church school. Mrs. Raymond Badger was church school superintendent. Mrs. Don Church was president of the Woman's Society of Christian Service which had an enrollment of 14. The women gave $864 that year.

EARLY METHODIST MISSIONS AMONG THE INDIANS

The Church at Lapwai

Chief Moses

METHODISM ENTERS LAPWAI

The Lapwai Mission was established in 1836 by Rev. Henry Spaulding, a Presbyterian. About 1910, some of the Indians there, appealed to the presiding elder of the Methodist Episcopal Church, South, requesting membership in that denomination. They were advised to remain loyal to their mother denomination. Two months later they appealed again saying, "If you do not receive us we will unite with some other denomination." Sixty were thus received. A building was erected which, later, was burned. The building shown here was erected in the 1920's, to serve descendants of the converts of Rev. Henry Spaulding.

Rev. George
Waters

Cowlitz Mission

Rev. J. H.
Dills

every effort to induce him to resume leadership of his people on the reservation. In his place Joe Stwire was elected head chief and was known as White Swan. He was a Methodist and often attended sessions of the Annual Conference.

Problems arising and strength of Wilbur's rule were pointed out by Judge E. V. Kuykendall.

"The Government punished rebellious tribes by removing them to new surroundings," he said. "Thus causing severe nostalgia and melancholia due to homesickness. A band of over 500 incorrigible Paiutes and Bannocks were brought to Fort Simcoe in 1878. Soldiers were kept there for several months, until it was thought the Indians were settled and in a peaceful mood. After the soldiers left, however, the Indians became homesick and restless. Among the Paiutes was a chief, whom the soldiers had nicknamed Paddy. He was very humble while the soldiers were there, but after their departure he became belligerent, even advocating violence against the whites. Father Wilbur summoned him to a council. He came with several warriors in war paint and gaudy feathers.

"The council was held under a spreading oak in Father Wilbur's front yard. The warriors were seated on the ground. I was an interested spectator from our front yard near by. Father Wilbur called upon Chief Paddy for an explanation of his attitude. He arose and began speaking, and seemed to lash himself into a state of fury.

"As Paddy became louder and more inflammatory, he began to make threats. Father Wilbur cautioned him to be calm and reasonable, and to cease his threatening remarks. The tirade grew louder and more belligerent. Father Wilbur stepped quickly to his side, ran his powerful right hand under the heavy braid of hair hanging down Paddy's back, clamped his fingers over the back of the Chief's head, and marched him through the circle of warriors to the jail,

PORT ANGELES—1888

In 1888 Rev. A. J. McNemee of Dungeness Circuit, resided six months at Port Angeles. In 1890 Rev. W. R. Warren found no congregation. He organized church with nine members, October that year. First trustees were Lafayette Henderson, A. R. Chitwood, Charles Elry. Lots for building purchased on First and Peabody. Prayer meetings in home of A. H. Nottage, Warren's first convert. In 1891 a building costing $900 had been erected, with $250 debt.

Building enlarged in 1901 by Rev. George W. Frame. Bell for tower given by G. M. Lauridsen. A building costing $53,000 erected in 1929, used for first time, October 20, that year, dedicated May 4, 1930, at Seventh and Laurel. In 1928, congregation united in worship in service with Lincoln Memorial Congregational Church. Property and pastor to be Methodist. Pastor, Rev. Erle Howell. Chairman trustees, Frank Dustman. Chairman building committee, Orville L. Harris. Parsonage purchased by Rev. Oscar M. Adam, in 1953. Addition costing $100,000 housing Sunday school, office, parlors completed, Rev. Lloyd Holloway, in 1961. In 1952 chimes dedicated in memory of O. L. Harris. Rev. Raymond Wilder, pastor.

In 1964 Rev. Robert R. Rings appointed for the second year. Membership, 664; Sunday school enrollment, 316; Woman's Society members, 164; gave $822.

or 'skookum house,' near by, and locked him up. He ordered Paddy's men to remain seated until he came back. They were so astounded that they scarcely moved until he returned. He then told them to go back home and behave themselves. 'If I hear any more such talk,' he said, 'I'll throw the last one of you in jail and keep you there until you come to your senses.' They departed quietly. Paddy soon became repentant and begged to be released, promising to quiet down and be good. He kept his promise and there was no further trouble.

"In all his contact with the Indians Father Wilbur never carried a weapon of any sort, and was never injured. They had faith in his fairness and were awed by his utter fearlessness."

COMMITTEE REPORTS REVEAL CONFERENCE ATTITUDES

During this time committee reports to the Annual Conference sessions revealed the attitude of Methodists toward the Indians. In 1855 the Oregon Conference provided for the Skagit Indian Mission in Western Washington, but left it without a pastor. The following year Nisqually and Chehalis Indian Mission was listed among charges, but like Skagit, was left to be supplied.

DREW MEMORIAL, PORT ORCHARD—1888

Drew Memorial Methodist Church, Port Orchard, organized in 1888. Town then known as Sidney. It was part of Vashon Circuit. Congregation met in various halls. In 1891, Rev. John Jensen served Bethel also as part of circuit.

Articles of Incorporation adopted, March 21, 1894. Rev. T. B. Ford, presiding elder. Rev. Fred S. Pearson, pastor. Trustees: A. W. Robinson, D. J. Davis, W. A. Stark, T. W. Taylor, Elmer Shaffer, J. B. Finch, Minnie Shaffer, Judith Phillips, Eva Curtis. First church building costing $1,000 was dedicated July 22, 1894. In 1929, fire destroyed Drew Memorial building, piano and organ only being saved. New building went up on different site, Sidney and Kitsap Streets.

The fiftieth anniversary was celebrated in 1938, Rev. Haven Martin, pastor. In 1942, Port Orchard again became a station with Rev. Carroll Sprague, pastor. In 1957 new building was acquired for Sunday school, $10,000 being expended to make it usable. Under Rev. Wayne Griffen, in late 1950's three morning services started. In 1960, the narthex built by aid of Rev. Karl Ekaas and laymen.

In 1964, Rev. Harvey DeVries, pastor, fourth year. Members 454. Church school enrollment, 292. Woman's Society members 78. They gave $900. Value of church building, $38,000. Parsonage, $13,800.

That year the Conference acted favorably upon a resolution presented by the committee, recommending that the presiding bishop appoint a missionary to each of the Indian Reserves as soon as practicable. The resolution further expressed confidence that the policy of the Federal Government toward the Indians afforded great hopes in efforts to Christianize them. But no appointment was made.

Three years later the Conference again resolved, "We will ever hold ourselves ready to go forward as Providence shall open the way, and labor for the salvation of the Indians."

In 1861 the Conference endorsed a resolution asking the Federal Government to appoint strictly moral men to head Indian Reserves in Oregon and Washington Territories. Meanwhile, Wilbur was the only man Northwest Methodists had at work among the Indians.

Three years later still, the Conference expressed deep concern by resolving that its members do all within their power to strengthen the Government in carrying out its plans on behalf of the Indians.

While the Conference was thus passing resolutions, Wilbur was producing results at Simcoe. In 1866 he reported 161 Indian and 13 white members of the Methodist Church there. For the first time White Swan appeared among the appointments on the reservation. The Conference called attention to the presence of thousands of Indians within its bounds, inviting men to volunteer as preachers and teachers.

A year later, Rev. A. C. Fairchild was appointed to work with Wilbur, but he stayed only one year. In 1868, Simcoe had 194 Indian members, two local preachers, and two houses of worship. The committee reported that only at Yakima did the Conference have work among the Indians. At that place fifty had professed faith during the year and native teachers were at work in Sunday schools.

When Father Wilbur presented Rev. Thomas Pearne and Rev. George Waters to the Conference for admission on trial in 1869, Chief White Swan, the brother of Waters, appeared to tell of the great spiritual needs of his people. The following year the reservation was placed under the charge of the Army and Wilbur was displaced, leaving Pearne and Waters solely responsible for interests of the Church.

When Wilbur returned as pastor and Indian Agent in 1871, he found his two proteges faithfully carrying on the work. That year Waters and Pearne were ordained deacons. The Conference paid tribute to the Government for its policies, but scored its failure to execute its plans, stating that the Agency should

TRINITY, RITZVILLE—1888

Rev. W. T. Koontz held first Methodist service at Ritzville, in 1888, in a schoolhouse. He organized church in November of that year, with nine members.

Ground breaking ceremonies for first building occurred, April 29, 1889. Building dedicated, August 4, same year. Rev. W. C. Grey, presiding elder, delivered the sermon. Debt paid in full, 1897. Improvements made in 1892, 1896, and 1901. New auditorium and full basement added in 1917.

Building was sold to Seventh Day Adventists, in 1947. Methodists occupied new building, April 9, 1950. Bishop Gerald H. Kennedy officiated. Rev. Clifford Knight, 1943-50, was pastor. He was followed by Rev. Alfred Carter.

A German Methodist Episcopal Church had been organized at Ritzville in 1887. First church was built in 1891-95, and their first pastor was Rev. H. F. Michel. Another German church in the community served for some years, but, in 1906, these groups were united as one congregation. Rev. Karl Jahn, was pastor.

In 1934, this congregation united with the English-speaking Trinity Methodist Church at Ritzville.

In 1964, Rev. James Updike, pastor for second year. Membership, 383, church school, 150. Seventy-nine members of Woman's Society of Christian Service gave $416. The church building was estimated at $173,500 and parsonage at $16,500.

be in the hands of Christian men. It was charged that money appropriated for education during the previous year had not served the cause intended, but had been spent for political purposes.

The next year there were 400 members of the church on the reservation. There were two ordained deacons and six licensed exhorters. George Waters had held a revival among the Nez Perces at Lapwai with 146 converts. Thus activities on the Yakima Reservation continued to move steadily forward until Wilbur retired.

Efforts to Reach Indians Broaden

The passing years found some Methodists employed in other Indian fields in Washington. In 1867, Rev. W. C. Chatten, a member of the Conference, was superintendent of the Indian school at Quinault Reservation on the Pacific Coast. In 1874 the committee reported three Indian Reservations intrusted to the care of the Methodist Episcopal Church. Two were in Western Washington.

The Agent at Quinault, G. A. Henry, an exhorter in the Methodist Church, reported that "Religious progress had been slow, although morally and in other ways the Indians showed much promise. Religious services were held each Sunday in English and Chinook. Services were largely attended by Indians who were well behaved."

Neah Bay, on the Strait of Juan de Fuca, had been assigned to the Methodist Church, and Rev. A. C. Huntington, a Congregational minister, was agent. A resolution stated, "We should establish in each reservation as thoroughly organized Christian Mission of which we are capable. In doing this we must have Methodists to do the work, and Methodist ministers clothed with Divine authority to preach the Word among them."

Similar statements of purpose continued for years. In 1878 the committee reported that the Congregational min-

---

ROSALIA—1888

German Methodism began in Rosalia in 1888 when Presiding Elder Geo. Hartung, began holding services in homes. English services began 1908 when Rev. Roy O. Hadley began services in a hall.

First church erected under leadership of Rev. George Bucholz. Land donated by Miss Barbara Horlacher. First building in Rosalia, in 1899, Rev. W. J. Herwig, pastor. Dedicated, June 3, 1900. Was enlarged under ministry of Rev. D. E. Carter, 1937-47, and Rev. C. A. Wentsch.

In 1909, the Casper Brothers Memorial Methodist Episcopal Church, erected under Rev. D. M. Helmick. In 1917, Congregational Church and English Methodist Church federated. In 1936, the Federated congregation and the German Church federated to become the Rosalia Methodist Church.

In 1958, new building costing $70,000 erected. Rev. Chester Blair, pastor. Walter Feldman was chairman of board of Trustees and Carl Solbrack, chairman of building committee. Mrs. John Peterschick, president Woman's Society, Mrs. Fritz Allert, church school superintendent. All church furniture, including sanctuary lights, were memorials or gifts.

In 1964, Rev. G. Edward Knight pastor, second year. Membership, 317, church school enrollment, 208. Woman's Society members, 73. They gave $818. Church building valued at $135,000. Parsonage, $11,000.

ister at Neah Bay had been removed from the Agency and that his successor, not a Methodist, had made no provision for religious services. G. A. Henry at Quinault, had been replaced by Colonel Oliver Wood, who had made no report to the Conference.

These words appeared in the report in 1880: "The Government has placed five reservations within the bounds of the Conference under the supervision of the Methodist Episcopal Church. We evidently are expected to nominate persons for the office of agent who are good business men and strictly honest. We should nominate none but those who are strictly pious and who will heartily cooperate with our church in all its efforts to civilize and Christianize these unfortunate people. Every reservation under our supervision ought to be organized into a Methodist Mission. The agent and all the employees should be consistent members and in hearty sympathy with the Methodist Episcopal Church. There should be a minister on every reservation to preach the gospel, visit the sick, pray with them in their lonely cabins, and bury the dead."

SUCCESSFUL WORK AMONG THE NOOKSACKS

In 1882 work was under way at Nooksack, in Northwest Washington, where there were "200 souls, 80 of which were members of the Methodist Church." These Indians had "refused to go to the Lummi Reservation because they disliked the reservation business and refused to be under the supervision of the Jesuits," a report stated. This was the first mention of Methodist work on the Nooksack.

The Indians had built a little chapel and wanted a teacher. The Conference Missionary Committee was asked for $250 to pay salary and a like amount for traveling expenses for an instructor. The next year the teacher had been found and money appropriated. The Indians had promised to care for the building.

TRINITY—1888

Trinity Church, Ballard, began, 1888, when Rev. E. S. Stockwell founded Gilman Park Church. First services held in tent where Carnegie Library later stood. Building inspired, in 1903, by a gift of land from L. C. Gilman.

In 1903, Bayview Church organized, and, in 1905, Ballard Park came into being. Foote Memorial, in 1907, later Calvary. Sixty-second Street Church organized later. Joined Calvary and Gilman Park, in 1925, to form Trinity under leadership of Rev. John W. Caughlin, and Rev. Gertrude L. Apel. Congregation began to plan edifice adequate to needs of Ballard. In 1929, construction began on new building at W. 65th and 22nd Ave., N.W.

Building included educational unit, recreation hall, Gothic chapel. Cost, $153,000, dedicated March 30, 1930.

Rev. E. J. Huston, 1931-34, reduced debt through $5,000 gift from Board of Church Extension. Rev. Alexander Bennett, 1938, with district cooperation raised funds to further satisfy creditors. Final payment to Board of Home Missions made in 1946, under Rev. Harry E. Gardner.

Under Rev. Rudolph Anderson, in 1958-60, parsonage was acquired. Rev. Olin E. Parrett, 1962, acquired a parsonage for associate pastor, and made many improvements and repairs. Membership, in 1964, was 834, church school enrollment 653. Woman's Society, 133.

CANADIAN FIRST METHODIST MISSIONARY ON NOOKSACK

The first Methodist minister to visit the Nooksack Indians came from Canada.[10] He found the Indians adherents of the Catholic faith, missionaries of which had been among them for some time. The Canadian minister was Rev. C. M. Tate, who left a record of his work with the mission. According to this account, previous to the year 1874, an Indian called Peter, from Nooksack, was employed by George Chadsey, a Sumas farmer. Peter occasionally attended the Methodist Church at Sumas and became interested. He fell victim to tuberculosis and returned to his home to die. In September, 1874, his brother-in-law, Long Johnny, went in quest of the Canadian Methodist missionary, to bring consolation to the dying man. Tate, who recently had been transferred from Port Simpson, on the Alaskan border, returned with Long Johnny. He conducted the first Methodist service among the Nooksack Indians, in an old slab shanty near Everson. There the dying man was being nursed by his sister.

Much of the night was spent in singing and prayer, in which the sick man heartily joined. Tate held another service for the Indians the following morning and then went to call on white persons in the neighborhood.

Rev. T. L. Woodward was presiding elder of the Puget Sound District at that time, but evidently knew nothing of the opening of this work.

FIRST REVIVAL SERVICE FOR INDIANS AT LYNDEN

Two young Indians from LaConner, William George and Jimmy Adams, in 1875, attended the camp meeting at Chilliwack, in Canada, and were converted. On their return they stopped at Lynden and held services at the home of Lynden Jim, chief of the Nooksack Tribe, one of the first Indian converts on the Nooksack River.

SHELTON—1888

Shelton first appeared on Oakland circuit in 1885. Rev. Gordon Henry, pastor. Sunday school was organized in 1888, with Miss Clara Ansorge, superintendent. First preaching services held in home of Mrs. Jane Morrow. In 1886, Rev. W. H. Johnson of Kitsap County supplied circuit. In 1877, circuit became known as Shelton. Rev. G. F. Meade, pastor.

In 1886 Rev. W. H. Johnson acquired a lot at Second and Cota Streets, gift of Mr. and Mrs. David Shelton. Through local subscriptions of $500 and $250 gift from Church Extension Society, church building erected and dedicated, May, 1890. Rev. C. E. Luce, pastor. The following year there were 87 members in Sunday school. Church incorporated in 1892. In 1892-94, Rev. J. N. P. Hickerson baptized 66 members and paid debt of $147.

Rev. Forrest Tibbits, 1932-36, made many improvements on building. Rev. Robert Mauldon, 1941-44, continued improvements and Rev. Wayne Wright, 1947-49 erected an addition.

In 1964, Rev. Horace H. Mounts, pastor, second year. Members, 654, church school enrollment, 602. Woman's Society membership, 136, giving $771. Church building value, $116,500. Parsonage, $16,000.

When Shelton church was established the only connection with the outside world was by boat. In 1964, freeway connected it with Olympia.

Some white persons, fearing the Indians did not know what they were doing, sent for Tate, who found a revival in progress. Tate was accompanied by Captain John, head chief of the Chilliwack Tribe, and a local preacher who ministered to members of his tribe on both sides of the line. Four preaching appointments were arranged, two for whites and two for Indians. Every three weeks the Canadian minister came to preach. Services for Indians were held at the homes of Chief Lynden Jim and Chief Johnny. Land for the first church in Lynden, to be used by both whites and Indians, was donated by H. A. Judson, who, with his wife and daughter, became members of the Methodist Church in 1875.

Rev. A. J. McNemee,[11] of the Puget Sound District, took over the work on the Nooksack in 1876. He had been appointed to the Whatcom Circuit with headquarters at Blaine, fifty travel-miles by foot from Lynden. Since no mention of Indian work on this circuit appears in the minutes, it may be that McNemee's involvement in the Nooksack Indian service was unexpected by the authorities. Later, in an autobiography, McNemee said, "The best time of my life was when I was trying to preach to those poor Indians. They seemed to appreciate my work and, like a lot of children, had confidence in what I said to them."

The year the Puget Sound Conference became independent from Oregon, presiding elder, Rev. D. G. LeSourd, reported that the Indian school at Nooksack had been successful. Mrs. Hill, the teacher, began with only four or five pupils, which number increased to 23. Friends of the enterprise were encouraged by interest shown by parents and children. Indians were acquiring homes and rapidly adopting civilized modes of life. He said their highest ideal of a Christian was a Methodist.

Ten years later the Committee reported that the Nooksack Mission was the only work among the Indians in the Conference. It was under the charge of

SUMNER—1888

First Methodist Church, Sumner organized 1888, 11 members. In the 1850's and '60's, pastors from Steilacoom. Puyallup occasionally held services. In 1888, church became station. Rev. Sprague Davis, pastor.

First building, 313 Washington Street, later used by Free Methodist Church. Church cost $2,500 and lots $400. In 1904, Rev. Horace Williston, pastor, another building purchased, moved beside church, enlarged and used for parsonage. Property, with house, adjoining church to north, was purchased, 1913, Rev. F. S. Pearson, pastor. In 1916, church observed 25th anniversary, claiming 217 members. July 9, 1922, Rev. George F. Hopkins, pastor, ground broken for new church. Building dedicated, April 8, 1923, by Bishop William O. Shepard. Cost, $37,500.

Debt a burden. Church school fluctuated in attendance. Between 1942 and 1949 more than $12,000 of indebtedness was paid. Mortgage burned, December 12, 1949, Rev. Harry E. Gardner, pastor. Front of sanctuary changed, 1959, under leadership of Rev. Tracy Manley. Seventy-fifth anniversary, celebrated 1963, Rev. Edward McClurg.

In 1964, Rev. Edward McClurg, pastor, third year. Members, 445, church school enrollment, 262. Woman's Society of Christian Service, members, 105, paid to local expense, $570. Building value, $125,000. Parsonage, $17,000.

Through years church tower of strength in community.

MISSION AND INDIAN LEADERS IN INLAND EMPIRE

Rev. E. J.
Conner
and Wife

Rev. Stephen
Reuben

Rev. W. C.
Chattin

The Lapwai church, under Southern Methodist sponsorship, was served mostly by Indian pastors. Among presiding elders and other leaders having to do with the mission were Rev. P. D. Hartman and Rev. H. S. Shangle.

Chief Lynden Jim

Rev. H. S.
Shangle

Rev. P. D.
Hartman

Rev. A. H. Marsh, who held services once in two weeks. The Stickney Home, operated by the Woman's Home Missionary Society, was housed in a building worth $5,000, located on 25 acres of land. Mr. and Mrs. James Stark manned the school.

The longest pastorate on the Nooksack was that of Rev. B. V. Bradshaw, who served twelve years, beginning in 1917. Under his ministry, work was opened at the Tulalip Indian school near Marysville. Sunday school and Epworth League were prosperous until the Government closed the school in 1932.

Rev. S. G. Thero followed Bradshaw in 1929 and served nine years. Rev. Marmaduke Dodsworth, a retired missionary to Malaya, was assigned to this work in 1954 and served five years, in connection with Sumas, a white congregation. After an absence of one year, he returned to serve the Indian work alone for two years.

Dodsworth later reported that with the exception of two years under his ministry, the Indian Mission had been attached to another church. "The arrangement," he said, "has never been successful, as the pastor could not give adequate attention to the work among the Nooksacks."

When Dodsworth first took over the work, there was no Sunday school. He started one on Saturdays since he and his wife had to be at Sumas church on Sunday mornings. In 1961 the school was held at 10 o'clock on Sunday and thus continued under the ministry of Rev. Samuel Carlson, appointed in 1962.

Dodsworth, in 1962, wrote, "The mission is a challenge and an opportunity as well as the responsibility of the Methodist Church. Rev. C. M. Tate held a special service among these people and converted them to the Methodist way, back in 1874. Cannot we in this day of motor cars do the same?"

CHELAN—1889

First Union Sunday school at Chelan started August 11, 1889. Chris Robinson, superintendent. Met in small building jointly occupied with day school. Methodist Church was organized March 29, 1891. Articles of Incorporation filed May 17, 1893. First trustees, H. A. Graham, W. S. McPherron, D. J. Switzer, A. F. Nichols, J. M. Snow. Rev. G. M. Booth, presiding elder. Rev. L. M. Hayworth, Waterville, first pastor.

First Woman's organization, known as Union Aid, dates to 1890. Mrs. C. C. Campbell was president. First building, erected for a school, was jointly occupied by the Methodist Church, and the Union Sunday school. Union Aid bought 110 chairs and a bell.

First Methodist Sunday school organized at Lakeside in 1894. W. W. Emerson was superintendent and Mrs. Emerson organist. Methodist Aid, as Dorcas Society, organized January 5, 1895, with 51 members. Mrs. S. H. Wooden, president.

First Methodist Church building erected in 1896 at cost of $250 cash and donated labor. New building erected in 1953 and dedicated in 1958. Rev. J. J. Ellington, pastor. Committee, Kenneth Kingman, Art Garton, James Reed, Art Freese, Wallace J. Miller, L. L. Harn.

Pastor in 1964, Roger K. Johnson. Members, 470; Sunday school, 215; Woman's Society of Christian Service, 105. Their gifts were $549.

WORK AMONG THE YAKIMAS SHOWS RESULTS

Father Wilbur, describing results of work on the Yakima Reservation in 1877, said, "Many of the good results are apparent in their personal cleanliness, their dress, houses, schools, and churches. This class of Indians are exerting a salutary influence upon the Yakima Nation, and teaching them in language they cannot misunderstand, the advantage they have gained in abandoning their roving habits, making themselves farms and homes, enriching themselves with stock and products of the soil.

"The practical working of the Yakima Agency convinces us that with good land, such as white men settle upon, with good practical business and Christian men as agents and employers, and a small appropriation of money to purchase seeds and tools to help them to get a start, all the Indians of the nation may be made self-supporting."

Six hundred and twenty-seven members and probationers were reported at Simcoe in 1878. The following year Wilbur returned to the Government $8,000 of the money allotted for agency operation. One hundred and fifty-five probationers from among the newly-arrived Paiutes and Bannocks were added in 1879.

The year Wilbur retired there were 520 members and probationers on the rolls at Simcoe. Yet, two years after Wilbur left the Agency the outlook was less promising. The work had suffered a sharp decline and members and probationers had dwindled to less than half the previous numbers.

"Our Indian brethren have been left almost entirely to themselves without presence or help of a minister among them," it was reported.

A year later, the presiding elder, Rev. Samuel Gascoigne, reported that Rev. James C. Teeter had served the Indians faithfully and that a revival had resulted in the conversion of 100 who had united

DES MOINES—1889

First Methodist Sunday school in Des Moines, held in home of F. A. Blasher, June 12, 1888. Frank Finnell first superintendent. First preaching in Blasher home, 1888. Rev. M. Sampson, Tacoma, preached, 1889. Church organized, 1891, by Rev. T. J. Massey, 19 members.

Ladies Aid organized, 1891, Epworth League, in 1893. Rev. S. S. Guiler, pastor, 1893-94, followed by Rev. Robert Hatfield, Tacoma, local preacher.

First building at 219 St., Sixth Ave., So., Rev. A. S. Gregg, pastor, 1897. Rev. R. W. Paul, 1903-05, erected new building at Ninth Ave., So. and So. 223 St., by volunteer labor. Piano donated by Mrs. Clara Storey, 1920. Rev. George Abbott, pastor. Debt cleared in 1928, Rev. D. A. Storey.

Building fund launched, 1937-45, by Rev. C. E. Miller. New sanctuary erected and, in 1947, Hammond organ installed, under pastorate of Rev. Earl Poindexter. Two morning services started 1954. Under pastorate of Rev. Ernest P. Goulder, new building including educational unit and sanctuary, erected. Conference loaned $25,000 and Board of National Missions granted $3,000. A bank loan of $75,000 completed financing.

In 1964, Rev. Rudolph A. Anderson appointed third year. Church membership, 1,061, church school enrollment, 743. Woman's Society members, 381. They gave $1,260. New parsonage, in 1963.

with the church. Again in 1887 the same elder said that Rev. G. C. Roe had enjoyed a good year. Yet, in five years the membership had declined to 150.

When Rev. J. W. Helm was appointed to Simcoe in 1897, he found 90 members, and 18 years later he reported 45. By 1926 membership had dropped to 13.

About this time white persons residing near White Swan, where the Indians' church was then located, began to worship with the Indians. Rev. John McNees, in 1928, reported 130 members of the church, and Rev. R. V. P. Dunlap, a decade later, reported 140. In 1964 membership was 116, 40% of which were Indians.

INDIAN WORK ELSEWHERE FARES NO BETTER

Elsewhere Indian work fared no better. The first report of Methodist work at Nespelem, on the Colville Reservation, appeared in 1914. Rev. A. A. McGinnis, who had been serving there, reported 12 members. The work was left without a pastor that year, but in 1916, Rev. J. H. S. Hollman was appointed. At the end of the year he reported 17 members. In 1928 Rev. R. T. Holland reported 13 members. After a decade Rev. C. A. Burris said there were 35 members and in 1963 when Rev. Laird V. Glasscock was appointed to Nespelem and Grand Coulee, there were 45.

It was at Nespelem that Chief Joseph, greatest of Nez Perce warriors, spent his last years. After his defeat by General Oliver O. Howard he was taken to Oklahoma where he was very unhappy. General Howard succeeded in arranging for his transfer to the Colville Reservation where he died in 1904. His monument, given by James J. Hill, stands in the Nez Perce Cemetery, north of the town.

It was concerning work on the Colville Reservation that, in 1937, Superintendent Paul H. Ashby, of the Spokane District, apologized, "We have been about as successful as John Wesley and

---

HARTLINE—1889

Eighteen members joined Hartline Methodist Sunday school at its first meeting, July 28, 1889. Mr. Dyke was first superintendent. School met in homes until 1891, and then in abandoned shack. Occasional preaching services began in 1891. Rev. G. H. Muller, minister. First members were Mrs. Jacob Farley and Mrs. Margaret Barnby, 1891. Services held at Coley school. Church served by pastors from Wilbur in early days.

In 1900 members were reenforced by a colony of Welch Methodists who provided strong leadership. First resident pastor was Rev. R. A. Gailey in 1901. The first church was built by him.

During influenza epidemic in 1918 church was used as hospital.

In 1918 Rev. G. E. Heineck led in erection of brick church. Destroyed by fire in 1933. Basement and insurance used to rebuild same year.

From 1923 to 1947 Almira and Hartline were a circuit. After 1947 Hartline independent. In 1959 a pipe organ was presented by Mr. and Mrs. D. F. Jolly. Basement finished in 1961.

Church celebrated its 70th anniversary, December 31, 1961. Bishop Everett W. Palmer delivered sermon. In 1964, Mrs. William Martin appointed for second year. Members 74, Church school, 61, Woman's Society of Christian Service, 24, gave to local work, $543.

Jason Lee in Indian missions."

This was humor raising its head above pathos and tragedy.

Responsibility for the Indian mission at Lapwai, Idaho, came to the Conference in 1939 when the southern church entered Methodist union. In 1964 the pastor, Rev. James H. Thompson, reported 75 members here.

FAITHFUL MINISTERS MET WITH SUCCESS

Statistics of church membership do not tell the whole story of success of Indian missions. The influence of faithful ministers through the years, leadership of dedicated government agents and teachers, and the examples set by residents in adjacent white communities, have wrought profound changes in the life and habits of these first Americans.

The Yakima Nation is an example. When Father Wilbur returned to the Agency in 1871, he said, "If I fail to give moral character to an Indian I can give him nothing that does him permanent good. If I can succeed in giving him moral character, then he no longer needs the gifts of Government."

RANDLE—1889

Methodist Church at Randle grew from Vance-Osborn Circuit of 1889. Charter members included Mr. and Mrs. James Randle, Mary Randle, Matthew Randle, Mr. and Mrs. C. T. Siler, Mrs. Lou Siler Owens, Mrs. John L. Davis, William Davis. First pastor, Rev. Jasper N. Taylor, also he preached at Vance and Mossyrock. Rev. William Rule, 1893-96, preached in homes of vicinity. First log church, 1894, built by people. First Sunday school superintendent, John L. Davis who also was superintendent of Baptist Sunday school where his wife was member.

Rev. W. J. Rule brought Alfred Whitfield out of discouraged retirement, 1894 to become effective preacher.

In 1900, Rev. E. L. Bower, pastor. Ladies Aid organized 1902. In 1907 Mrs. Mary McMahan, president. Vance Circuit included, Mossyrock, Mayfield, Salkum, Fuller. There were 57 members.

In 1908 Rev. O. R. Anderson pastor Morton and Vance. Other appointments discontinued. Congregation moved to Randle 1910, Rev. D. A. Storey, pastor. New church dedicated, 1912, Rev. T. E. Elliott, district superintendent.

Parsonage at Randle erected, 1912, Rev. R. B. Parcel, pastor. Randle alone after 1911. In 1923, basement built, Rev. C. C. James, pastor.

In 1964, Rev. James A. Mott, first year. Members, 75; church school 84. Women gave $784. Building value $17,500. Parsonage, $7,500.

A criterion for measuring character on the part of the Indian is his ability to earn his living through cultivation of the soil. This method of livelihood practically was unknown among Northwest Indians when the whites first found them.

Chief Kamiakin was first to introduce irrigation into the region. He had learned about it from the Oblate priests who founded St. Joseph's Mission at Ahtanum. Letters of Father Wilbur contain frequent references to this method of land improvement. In 1880 he wrote, "At least ten miles of ditches have been dug." [12]

Since that time irrigation has become well established on the reservation. In 1962, for instance, 138,000 acres were under irrigation, producing crops the value of which was $21,000,000.

The reservation owns timber in the mountains valued at $67,000,000. Between 1943 and 1962 timber cut on a sustained yield basis was valued at more than $19,000,000.[13] This money less administrative costs belongs to the Indians and is used to promote tribal projects.

After 1922, when Agency headquarters was moved to Toppenish, Government schools were closed and Indian children absorbed in public schools.

Local government is by a Reservation Tribal Council consisting of fourteen members representing the original treaty tribes. Members of the body are elected at General Councils. Power to transact all tribal business, except that expressly reserved, was delegated to the Council in 1944.

The tribe has its own code of laws regulating conduct between its members on the reservation. Ten major crimes are handled by the Department of Justice through Federal Courts. The Indian bureau at Washington gradually has turned more and more power to Tribal Council, County, and State authorities.

According to the democratic concept the power of a people to govern themselves is a sign of moral character. The Yakima Nation has proved its capacity for self-government. But, if, after a century of Christianizing influence, Indian character still shows signs of weakness, cannot the same be said of the character of white men who have experienced 1900 years of such influence?

<table>
<tr><td>The presence in the Northwest of language groups from Europe and Asia inspired Methodists to render notable service to—</td><td>Men of Many Tongues and Nations</td></tr>
</table>

(Methodists Serve Language Groups in the Northwest)

FROM EAST AND WEST THEY CAME

With the great influx of immigrants into the Northwest in the late nineteenth and early twentieth centuries, came men from Europe and the Orient, each speaking his own language.

To greathearted Northwest Methodists, these men of many tongues and nations presented a challenge to be taken in stride. They believed that the Christian Evangel should be offered to men of every race.

THE CHINESE CAME FIRST

The first experiments in language work were among the Chinese. The earliest reference to the presence here of these Orientals in the journal of the Oregon Conference appeared in a brief note attached to the treasurer's report in 1855. Less is told than one would like to know. Apparently, a group of Chinese had become acquainted with the young daughters of Rev. T. F. Royal, principal of Umpquah Academy, and, as an expression of admiration, had given them fourteen dollars to buy candy. The children, already missionaries at heart, showed their gratitude by giving the money to the conference treasurer, requesting that it be used for the China Mission, presumably, work in China sponsored by the General Board of Missions. The note confirms the presence of Chinese in Oregon at that early day.

With the advent of public works and railroad building in the 1870's and '80's, infiltration of Chinese was accelerated. The first mention of missions among them in Washington appeared in the conference journal in 1880. Rev. John F. DeVore, pastor of First Church, Seattle, reported that a class among these Orientals had been organized in connection with his church during the previous year.

That year a Chinese chapel in Seattle had 15 members and 57 in attendance during the year. Mrs. Belle Thomas, assisted by others, had conducted a night school, free of charge, for three years. The mission board in New York was asked for $2,500 for Chinese work in the Conference. Yet the mission was left without a pastor, because no one was available for the work.

In 1881 the mission conducted a weekly school with two classes in Bible and one in English. Prayer meeting was held Friday night and ten new persons had enrolled on a recent evening. Mrs. Thomas and Mrs. H. E. Parkhurst were leaders. Seventy-nine individuals had attended that year.

The following year 111 had attended the school and there was one church member and 12 probationers. Several of the latter had moved away, some to return to China. Members of the group desired a pastor of their own nationality and would pay $100 toward his support. The mission at Portland had made a similar request, promising a like amount of support. The Conference expressed the hope that the mission board would appropriate $1,400 to employ a minister who would divide his time between Portland and Seattle.

Twenty thousand Chinese were reported in Oregon, Washington and Idaho in 1882. The California Conference was asked to take over the Chinese work, and permit its assistant Chinese missionary, Rev. Andrew Jackson Hanson, to take charge. An appropriation of $2,500 was asked of the Board of Missions.

At the end of another year the mission under Hanson had prospered. Missions were active in Portland, Salem, and Seattle. Two hundred and seventy persons had been instructed. Hanson had elected to transfer to the Puget Sound Conference and the Chinese project was to be sponsored by that body. He also

GRACE, SEATTLE—1889

Grace, Seattle, began in 1889, with J. S. Taylor, Sunday school superintendent. First preacher, Rev. H. H. Mahaffie, held meetings at 24th and Jackson. Church incorporated, June 6, 1890, with 7 members. Trustees were J. S. Taylor, L. J. Jones, T. C. Tallman, R. M. Schoonmaker.

In 1890, Rev. H. D. Brown, pastor. Group named Jackson Street Church, located at 28th Ave., So. and Jackson. New site purchased at So. 30th and King Street, cost $4,500, opened June 7, 1891. Consecrated by Bishop C. H. Fowler.

In 1891, Rev. W. B. McMillan, found debt $6,500. Women gave $500, Board of Church Extension loaned $3,000, David T. Denny cancelled $1,400 bill, debt paid. Building improved in 1892 by Rev. T. W. Butler who added 100 members. Parsonage built in 1897, Rev. W. H. Selleck. Rev. Robert C. Glass freed church of debt in 1902.

Rev. E. Raymond Attebery, 1925-45. Parish Center consecrated in 1929, by Bishop Titus Lowe. In 1945, Rev. John Finney began fund for new building. Completed by Rev. James E. Milligan, 1952. Debt paid, 1956, under Rev. Wayne D. Griffen.

In 1964, Rev. Robert F. Vahey, pastor for third year. Membership, 238, church school enrollment, 91. Woman's Society members, 50. Building valued at $140,000.

wished to continue in English work. In 1885 he was appointed presiding elder of the Olympia District while superintending the Chinese mission. Rev. Chan Hon Fan became assistant superintendent of work among the Orientals in Oregon and Washington.

ANTI-CHINESE RIOTS BREAK FORTH

Sentiment against Chinese in the Northwest smoldered for years. As early as 1878, Rev. William Roberts reported to the Oregon Conference that of the 150,000 Chinese in the United States, most of them were on the Pacific Coast. Portland was the residence of from 1,500 to 2,000. Twelve years earlier, a Chinese Sunday school had been organized by Rev. J. F. Jones at Taylor Street Church, Portland. Roberts recommended that missions for these Orientals be organized wherever possible.

The following year Roberts, with Rev. Isaac Dillon and Rev. J. H. Acton, reported on the agitation. While they considered it very serious, it was based upon greatly exaggerated forebodings of danger from these immigrants from Asia. The committee members believed that much of the agitation was due to the desire of politicians to capitalize upon public prejudice to gain votes.

Thus, the committee championed the Chinese cause at a time when to do so was very unpopular. Roberts again volunteered to serve as a missionary to these abused strangers.

The agitation against the Orientals burst into flame in Washington in 1885.[1] All Orientals were driven from Tacoma, and most of them from Seattle. In Tacoma, law enforcement officers were in league with the agitators. But in Seattle, Sheriff John H. McGraw determined to give equal protection to all. He deputized and armed several hundred citizens whom he employed to protect the Asiatics. While most Chinese in Seattle chose to leave under pressure,

SNOQUALMIE—1889

First Sunday school at Snoqualmie, in 1889, held under large tree on Meadowbrook farm. Rev. A. J. McNemee, Squawk Circuit, preached in community in 1885.

Meadowbrook Farm, large producer of hops. In 1889, circuit rider moved through hop rows inviting workers to church service under tree where Sunday school met. In bad weather services held in tent. Organ kept in Mount Si Hotel to prevent keys sticking with dampness. Preacher was Rev. Mr. Curtis, name not in conference journals.

Methodist Church organized, 1890, Rev. R. M. Schoonmaker, first pastor. Charter members included, Mr. and Mrs. Robert Terhune, Mr. and Mrs. Will McCloud, A. F. Kinsey, Mr. and Mrs. E. J. Kinsey, D. R. Kinsey, John Carr, Mrs. O'Dell.

Ladies Aid early on job, helping pay for doors, windows, and the bell, installed in 1893. Old church sold in 1924, under pastorate of Rev. Joseph H. Beall, and new edifice erected. In 1939, church was burned and immediately rebuilt. Mrs. W. W. Warren donated a rose window in memory of her husband.

In 1959, under leadership of Rev. Myron H. Sharrard, building was dedicated and educational unit added.

In 1964, Rev. Howard P. Buck, appointed for third year. Members, 364; church school, 320. Woman's Society numbering 114, gave $192.

the few who chose to remain were protected. Otherwise, all would have been driven away.

Apparently, Methodists took no concerted action concerning the riots. Only two references in the journal of 1886 indicate that the Conference was aware of them. That year Rev. A. J. Hanson, presiding elder of the Olympia District and superintendent of the Chinese Mission, said of the mission in Portland, "Despite the excitement of a dreadful agitation, its church life has been steadily maintained." He said nothing of the Seattle work.

The other reference to the agitation came from Rev. D. G. LeSourd, presiding elder of the Seattle District. He indicated that the agitation to expel the Asiatics disturbed the church and seriously involved Pastor Lewis Albert Banks of Battery Street Church. He said the minister took a bold stand for the law and constitutional rights of all and remained unmoved at his post, until, according to previous arrangements, he departed for Boston Theological School.

Secular historians, however, give details of the agitation, and Snowden tells what happened to Banks. The minister, a volunteer among Sheriff McGraw's deputies, was in the band, including State Militia, who defended a group of Chinese against a threatening mob, February 8, 1886. At one point, to protect themselves from the onslaught of rioters, Sheriff's men fired several shots, killing one man and wounding others.

The law violators immediately evoked the law, charging several of the Sheriff's men, including Banks, with murder. The men were arrested, but not imprisoned, because at that moment, Governor Watson C. Squire announced a proclamation of martial law by President Grover Cleveland. After the agitation had subsided the men again were arrested but never brought to trial.

Seattle's historian, Clarence D. Bagley,[2] himself a Methodist and a member of the Sheriff's volunteers, described

---

EPWORTH, TACOMA—1889

Epworth Church, Tacoma, organized, December 24, 1889. Rev. George C. Wilding, pastor First Church, leading. Rev. R. H. Massey, pastor. First Sunday school, A. J. Collins, supt.

Church incorporated, December 28, 1890, John N. Berry, Charles Collins, Cyrus Metzger, trustees. September, 1890, Rev. J. W. Maxwell, pastor, received 42 members, first year.

Ladies Aid active early. Woman's Foreign Missionary Society, organized 1891. Mrs. R. J. Scott, president. First building dedicated, 1889 by Rev. George C. Wilding. Parsonage built, 1891. Church Extension Society loaned $500. Under Rev. P. H. Bodkin, 1891-92, revival brought 100 into the church. Rev. D. G. LeSourd, 1895-03, erected new church.

Rev. Edward H. Todd, pastor, 1903, enlarged chancel, installed two windows. Ladies Aid paid last $500. Rev. A. B. Chapin, 1905-06, received 109 members. Rev. W. H. W. Reese, 1914-17, built gymnasium. Epworth Heights lodge built, 1920-23, Rev. Andrew Warner, pastor. Rev. Everett M. Hill, 1923, started new building fund. Building erected under pastorate of Rev. Raymond S. Reese, 1924-28.

In 1964, Rev. LaVerne E. Tooley, pastor, fifth year. Members, 450. Church school, 359. Woman's Society members, 100, contributed $944. Church valued at $276,000. Parsonage, $33,000.

Twenty-five members of this church entered the ministry.

EARLY METHODIST LANGUAGE LEADERS
IN THE NORTHWEST

Rev. George
Hartung

Blaine, Idaho
Norwegian-Danish
Church

Rev. Frederick
Bonn

Rev. C. Aug
Peterson

Rev. E. J. Nanthrup

Rev. Francis A. Scarvie

Rev. O. A.
Olander

Rev. Francis
Ahnlund

Rev. Andrew
Farrell

the scene but omitted the reference to Banks. He listed the names of persons enrolled in the defending group. Among them were such Methodists as Edwin S. Meaney, David J. Denny, Junior, and Charles Kinnear, who at least had Methodist leanings.

Apparently this closed the experiment with Chinese missions in the Northwest. The only mention of this work after 1886 appeared in the minutes of the Conference in 1892 when it was reported that 1,000 Chinese resided within the bounds of the Conference. The committee asked for an appropriation of $500 to serve them, to be administered by the presiding elder of the Seattle District. In later years Chinese work on the Pacific Coast was in the hands of a mission conference, administered from California.

EVANGELISM AMONG SWEDISH IMMIGRANTS MEETS WITH SUCCESS

The first Swede to reside on Puget Sound was John P. Fryberg, who came in 1857, remaining here until the end of his life. His brother, who came shortly after his arrival, died in Interbay, in Seattle, in 1912.

Most of the Swedes who came in great numbers in the 1880's were Lutherans who soon organized churches of that faith. Yet some had been Methodist in the eastern part of the United States and responded favorably to efforts of Northwest ministers who sought them out.

FIRST SWEDISH MISSION IN WASHINGTON ESTABLISHED IN 1883

The first Methodist work among Swedish residents of Washington began at Seattle, in 1883.[3] In 1884, Rev. Andrew Farrell was appointed to take over that work, and Rev. C. J. Larson was appointed to Tacoma in 1885. The following year the Columbia River Scandinavian Mission was announced at Skamokawa, but left without a minister. In 1877 the conference Committee on Swedish Work asked for language ministers to take the Gospel to first genera-

WILD ROSE—1889

First religious services in Wild Rose in 1884. Held in homes, Jessie Howell, Henry Reiper, Joe Torbert. In 1885, schoolhouse was used. Church organized, 1889, by Rev. Milton S. Anderson, Hazard, Washington.

Land for first building acquired, 1892, and building erected next year with donated materials, labor. Church sat in middle of prairie as symbol of Christian faith.

People came from far and near by wagon, buggy, carriage, horseback, afoot. But they came, through snow, mud, rain, summer's dust.

There being no parsonage, the people lodged the minister when he came to preach, and sometimes he stayed several days. In 1908, church struck by lightning and burned. But the pulpit and pews were saved. Pews, repainted, still served in 1964. Historian said, "New church was bigger and finer, but no more appreciated and loved by the people."

Ladies Aid purchased an old schoolhouse for $50, moved it to church for additional room. Rev. L. N. B. Anderson, pastor in 1914 when building erected.

In 1964, Rev. Carl B. Beal pastor, first year. Membership, 23, church school enrollment, 94.

Historian observed, "This church has had its struggles and difficulties, but today, stands at the center of the prairie, as a Christian monument."

tion Swedish residents. Rev. L. Dahlgren was sent to the Skagit River Church in 1888.

By 1890, a Swedish District had been organized with Rev. Olaff E. Olander presiding elder. Appointments included: Des Moines, Fremont, Hood's Canal, Pleasant Ridge; Portland, Oregon; Port Townsend, Seattle, Spokane Falls, South Bend, Willapa, Tacoma, Whatcom, and Fairhaven. This was an ambitious program since but two ministers were available. Rev. O. E. Olander was to serve Pleasant Ridge and Rev. Nicholas G. Nelson, Seattle.

Bear Creek, Idaho, and Spokane had been added to the district by 1891. Other charges opened in succeeding years were: Guy, 1899; Nora-Albion, Idaho, 1901; Cedarhome, and Everett, 1902; Edmonds and Olympia in 1903.

Rev. Andrew Farrell, presiding elder of the Swedish District in 1907, reported membership on his district had increased twenty per cent during the year. He also reported "a united company of preachers, with confidence restored and a good outlook."

PACIFIC SWEDISH MISSION CONFERENCE GETS UNDER WAY

ALDERSGATE, SOUTH BELLINGHAM—1890

First preaching service in South Bellingham, known as Fairhaven, took place under Rev. G. C. Boswell in 1889. In November of that year church organized with 58 charter members. Sunday school was organized the following year. Rev. G. C. Boswell, an ordained deacon of Seattle, supplied the congregation until 1890. Rev. W. H. Drake of Seattle was the presiding elder. The first woman's group was organized in 1891. The first building, dedicated July 27, 1890, cost $7,500. Rev. F. W. Loy pastor that year. Following were such men as Rev. W. B. McMillan, Rev. Charles McDermoth, Rev. F. H. Chamberlain, Rev. Fred S. Wright, Rev. J. N. Dennison, and others.

A parsonage was erected adjacent to the church in 1906. Methodist Youth Fellowship, Woman's Society of Christian Service, Methodist Men, church school, Boy Scouts of America, were maintained through the years.

In 1962, under leadership of Rev. Ritchie D. Ocheltree, Sr., lots were purchased at 15th and Larrabee with view to relocating the building. In 1964 the name was changed from First Methodist Church, Bellingham to Aldersgate Methodist Church. Rev. John R. Qualley was appointed pastor for the first year. Church membership, 139; church school enrollment, 140. Woman's Society of Christian Service membership, 25. They donated $219.

Swedish work in the Conference became a part of the Pacific Swedish Mission Conference in 1908. The organization of this new body was effected at Oakland, California, September 2-6 of that year. Bishop Henry W. Warren was in the chair and Rev. G. A. Warner was secretary; Rev. G. E. Kallsted, treasurer; and Rev. K. O. Berglund, statistician. The final session of this Conference convened at Los Angeles, September 19-23, 1928, with Bishop Charles W. Burns, presiding. Rev. J. N. Burdell was secretary; Rev. J. H. Levedahl, treasurer, and Rev. K. O. Berglund, statistician. Berglund served as statistician every year during the history of the Conference with the exception of 1921, when he was relieved by Rev. C. J. Wells. The Conference was dissolved in 1928, permitting congregations and pastors to unite with the English-speaking Conference where they were located.

At the last session of the Pacific Swedish Mission Conference the following men were appointed to churches in Washington and Idaho; Superintendent of the Swedish District and pastor of First Swedish Church, Seattle, Rev. Francis Ahnlund; Cedarhome, Rev. K. O. Berglund; Spokane, Rev. G. Harry Nelson; Spokane Circuit, Rev. J. A. Willman; and Venersborg, Rev. Eric Nelson.

Swedish Methodists, both pastors and laymen, were earnest, devoted Christians, deeply loyal to the Methodist Church. They also loved their Annual Conference and gave it up with reluctance. In their day they made great contributions to Northwest Methodism, but their numbers steadily diminished because of the tendency of their children to unite with English-speaking congregations. Literally, this Conference, like those of other language groups, saved its life by losing it.

The emotional attachment to their Conference and the reluctance with which members faced its inevitable dissolution was pictured in a paragraph of the historical statement in the 1928 journal. The historian said:

"It was a solemn moment when the recommendation to dissolve was introduced. Never before in twenty years had the Conference faced such a momentous question. If the recommendation was adopted it would make an end to our Conference organization, and also, to a great extent, sever the intimate relation the brethren had so long enjoyed. After serious consideration, it was unanimously voted to dissolve—all for and none against the resolution. Never shall that great moment be forgotten. No heart was untouched. Yet there was no sign of misunderstanding. All went harmoniously, every brother fully realizing what it meant, and acting in perfect good faith."

ANACORTES, FIRST—1890

First Sunday school in Anacortes began in 1890. W. V. Wells was superintendent. Rev. W. W. Mallery first Methodist preacher in 1890. Services held in skeleton framework covered with canvas. Church organized July 28, 1890 with 27 charter members. Trustees, W. A. McLean, W. V. Wells, G. K. Heath, Dr. J. D. Wetzell, Austin Dudley, Frank W. Spear, J. W. Moore. Rev. D. G. LeSourd was presiding elder of the Whatcom District. Amos Bowman loaned a house for meetings and gave a lot for church building, begun in 1892. Building remained unfinished for ten years. A troublesome debt discouraged congregation. Under Rev. Rial Benjamin, 1902, adjustments were made with creditors and the church completed by aid of a loan from the Board of Missions.

The original tower of the church was 110 ft. which was lowered for safety in 1934. In 1940, under Rev. Decatur N. Lacy, the fiftieth anniversary of the church was celebrated. A new entryway opened, chancel divided, new pews and an electric organ installed. The building committee included Harry D. Jackson, R. T. Tucker, and Herbert Dexter.

In 1964 Rev. Carl Richardson Boyd was appointed pastor for the fourth year. Members 344, church school enrollment 214, Woman's Society of Christian Service 60. They gave $1,000,

143

Among the Swedish brethren, there were sizable laymen, such as P. M. Paulson, president of the Laymen's Association. In a farewell address to his brethren, he said, "Let us be faithful in our church attendance. Let us remember our obligation to God, to the church, and to our fellowmen, home and foreign missions. Let us pray much and pray well.

"May we all appreciate and support the entire program of our bishop, district superintendent, and our pastors, remembering that 'in unity there is strength.'

"Above everything else, let us be Christians in the fullest sense of that mighty word. Only by being true Christians can we be good Methodists, but we are Christians in the first place, and Methodists in the second place. Only in Christ are we saved."

METHODISTS SERVED GERMAN AMERICANS

The pioneer leader of Northwest German Methodism was Rev. Frederick Bonn. He had a hand in the organization of most of the early German language churches in the area. He was admitted into the Oregon Conference in 1880, and thenceforth gave himself to evangelize Germans in his territory.

The first Methodist leader to sense the need of Germans in Walla Walla was Father James Harvey Wilbur, the great heart whose sympathies were as deep and broad as human need. He became acquainted with the German settlers in that district, and assembled several families who wanted a church. It was through his suggestion that Bonn sprang into action, organized the congregation and sent Rev. William Esslinger to be its pastor in 1883. The church building to house the congregation was erected largely through the efforts of Wilbur who made substantial contributions from his own funds.

In 1883 Rev. William Roberts reported to the Oregon Conference that

DEER PARK—1890

First Methodist preaching at Deer Park, in 1890, by Rev. M. S. Anderson. Church first mentioned in record in 1904, was on Wild Rose Circuit. That year parsonage was erected, and following year, church became a station with resident pastor, Rev. Herbert P. Ide. School building acquired for church worship. Debt paid on parsonage that year.

Ladies Aid organized in 1906. Mrs. Dolly Ross was first president. In 1910 Mr. and Mrs. Peter J. Kelly donated land for new building. In June, services held in unfinished fellowship hall. Between 1911 and 1915, congregation grew. A. G. Craig Sunday school superintendent. In 1918, Williams Valley Church disbanded, members joined Deer Park.

In 1926, Mrs. William Hoskins, wife of pastor, partially departmentalized Sunday school. In 1936, the charge was again placed with Wild Rose for pastoral service. Under leadership of Rev. Ruth Lortz, and her associate, Miss Lucille Sprengle, sanctuary was refurnished and, under Rev. C. H. Cowdy, 1946-50, the basement was finished for Sunday school.

In 1964, Rev. Carl Beal pastor, third year. Members, 157, church school enrollment, 137. Fifty-three members of Woman's Society gave $294. Two former members of this church entered the ministry and one went as medical missionary to Africa.

Bonn had left Portland the preceding fall to work on Puget Sound, on the promise of authorities to provide support for two German preachers for Washington. The promise had been fulfilled, a church had been erected at Tacoma, and lots for a building purchased at Seattle. Meanwhile, Bonn was preaching at Olympia and other points with German-speaking congregations in view. The General Board of Missions had been requested to grant $2,500 to aid the work.

A German church was organized at Spokane in 1883,[4] and one at Rockford in 1885. In the latter year the Puget Sound Conference pledged support to the German work within its bounds. In 1888 German missions in the area became a part of the North Pacific German Mission. In 1892 the name was changed to North Pacific German Mission Conference, and it became the Pacific German Annual Conference in 1905.

Under this banner the German work in the Northwest continued to serve until, in 1929, ministers and congregations became a part of English-speaking work. By that time the language phase of Methodist service almost had run its course, and eventually most of the congregations merged with near-by English-speaking churches.

Besides places already named in Washington and Northern Idaho, German Methodism, during its history, served Centralia, Cheney, Colfax, Connell, Dayton, Edwall, Everett, Fairhaven, Harrington, Kent, LaCamas, Lind, Lewiston, Idaho; Moscow, Idaho; Odessa, Rathdrum, Idaho; Ridgefield, Ritzville, Rocklyn, Rosalia, Spokane, and Spokane Circuit.

German ministers, retired or effective, residing in Washington and Idaho in 1928 were: Rev. A. J. Aschenbruenner, Rev. J. A. Beck, Rev. F. W. Bucholz, Rev. L. Gaiser, Rev. Joseph Hepp, Rev. A. F. Hilmer, Rev. George Kleinbach, Rev. H. F. Lange, Rev. G. A. Maag, Rev. H. B. Mann, Rev. G. S. Roeder, and Rev. A. J. Weigle.

FIRST, HOQUIAM—1890

First service in boom-town, Hoquiam, 1890. Harbor Land Company donated two lots, condition that Methodist Church, costing $3,500, be started in sixty days. June 3, contract let. Trustees, Seth Warren, George W. France, H. O. Lamb, J. W. Hull, George E. Watson. Church extension Society granted $250, loaned $500. Rev. A. L. Walker, pastor. Boom broke, people departed, membership dropped to nine. Never more than 40 until 1900. Church saved by heroic efforts of Rev. E. V. Claypool, Rev. T. E. Elliott, Rev. Charles Revelle, Rev. J. W. Satterthwaite, Rev. W. O. Benedom, Rev. E. L. Benedict, Rev. O. H. McGill, sacrificial congregation. During period, $2,996 paid on debt.

Chief force in church, group of women, Mrs. Emily Morgan, Mrs. E. France, Mrs. H. B. Watson. In 1907, pipe organ costing $2,400 installed. Rev. E. L. Benedict. In 1912, basement added, church enlarged. Rev. O. H. McGill, pastor.

Under pastorate, Rev. W. W. Switzer, 1917-20, further improvements made. Under Rev. Paul H. Ashby, 1920-23, membership grew. Church rebuilt inside and out, 1948-58, Rev. Lloyd N. Alden, and Rev. Bruce G. Parker, pastors. Church school unit consecrated November 8, 1964.

In 1964, Rev. Fred O. Hunt, pastor, second year. Members, 275, church school enrollment, 365. Woman's Society members, 77, gave $645.

First World War years brought many trials to the German-speaking congregations. Persons speaking that language were branded spies. Even though young American citizens from their homes were serving in the Armed Forces of the United States, parents often were suspect. Thus pastors and people found it difficult to carry on. Yet they never wavered in their faith in God, their Church, and the privilege of American citizenship.

Service rendered by these congregations is typified in a paragraph in the history of the Walla Walla congregation. The historian, Robert Wentsch, said, "We can well be proud of the influence and service it has rendered to the community. Among the young people who have received Christian instruction in the church there are ministers, doctors, dentists, contractors, business men, farmers, lawyers, as well as men filling responsible government positions. All are good citizens of our United States of America. May those memories remain sweet within our hearts."

Sons of Norway Contribute Much

The first Sons of Norway to settle in the State of Washington landed at Oak Harbor, on Whidbey Island, in 1847. The first Norwegian Lutheran Church was established at Stanwood in 1876. At first the arrival of these hardy Norsemen was slow, but as the years passed the volume increased. By 1960 there were in King County, alone, more than 10,000 Norwegians of the first and second generations. Thousands of the members of later generations had ceased to be identified with the Norwegian community through Americanization and intermarriage.

The contribution to American life made by these residents is seen in the fact that in Seattle they are engaged in almost every kind of enterprise. The Norwegians are noted for their honesty. A Seattle pastor said, "Traditionally, the

KELLOGG, IDAHO (UNITED)—1890

First preaching service of record, in Kellogg, Idaho was in 1887, by a minister by the name of Lorne, probably from Montana. In 1890-94, Rev. W. J. White traveled circuit without aid of missionary compensation first two years. He rebuked sin, Sabbath desecration, and intemperance. Was respected, but no church organized. In 1894, Rev. J. W. Craig of the Methodist Episcopal Church, South, visited Kellogg.

Wardner and Kellogg served by Rev. W. H. Selleck in 1895. Following year, trustees of newly organized church, bought a lot and small building which became parsonage. Church building began, August, 1896, first used at Thanksgiving, that year.

In 1917, Kellogg appeared in appointments, had new building. In 1930, Methodists united with Congregational group, were incorporated as a federated church, in 1932. In 1955, Methodist property sold and lots purchased for new building. In 1957, congregation became "The United Church." Building completed 1960, valuation, $65,000.

Plan of union provides for service alternately by ministers representing cooperating denominations. Members retain original church affiliation.

In 1964, Rev. Robert H. McPherson of United Church of Christ serving second year. Methodist members, 228, church school enrollment, 188. Twenty members of the Methodist Woman's Society of Christian Service, gave $540.

146

Norwegian is scrupulously honest. He hesitates to commit himself to any proposal he is not sure he can fulfill. His word is his bond."

The same pastor also said, "Norwegian churchmen are uniformly orthodox. Our people are conservative in doctrine, informed, and constant."

DANES CONTRIBUTE HONOR AND RELIABILITY

Danish residents of the Northwest come out of a similar background of honor and reliability. A Danish pastor said, "In Denmark a contract between two individuals is not put into writing. The parties simply clasp hands, and the fulfillment of the compact becomes a matter of honor."

Danes are industrious. In the Northwest they are found in most lines of activities. They also have a deep sense of loyalty. An attractive characteristic is the fact that although they never cease to love the land that gave them birth, they take out citizenship papers as soon as the law allows. Thus they show their loyalty to the land that has given new opportunities. These traits are carried over into their religious experiences.

It is not known when Danes first came to Washington, but some were in the state in the 1880's. Among them were Mr. and Mrs. M. J. Lehman, whose daughter, Mrs. Arthur Ellsworth, early became a Methodist.

The first Norwegian—Danish Methodist congregation in the Northwest was organized at Tacoma in 1884, by that ubiquitous Methodist presiding elder, pastor and missionary, Rev. C. J. Larsen.[5] This man was intimately associated with Norwegian-Danish Methodism on the Pacific Coast. When he died in 1934, Rev. W. W. Youngson, a long-time pastor and district superintendent in the Oregon Conference, said of him: "Moving to Oakland, California, in 1878, with his bride, he came under the min-

---

KENDRICK, IDAHO—1890

Kendrick, Idaho first appeared among appointments, 1890. Rev. F. B. Utter, pastor. In 1891, there were 87 members and 148 in three Sunday schools. Two church buildings were worth $2,000. In 1895, Rev. C. B. Bell, pastor, built parsonage.

Stewards at time, Mrs. J. Gardner, Mrs. N. E. Walker. Recording Steward, H. D. Stanton. Communion steward, Mrs. N. B. Long. Trustees: N. B. Long, E. H. Dammerell, N. E. Walker, H. D. Stanton, J. Gardner. Ladies Aid Society instructed to elect three of their members to act as parsonage committee.

Hospital committee, Mrs. George Wayland, Mrs. Bramblet, Mrs. John Brown, Mrs. E. H. Dammerell, Mrs. N. E. Walker.

In 1905, Kendrick supplied by Rev. George Pease. There were 28 members and 66 in church school. By 1919, Rev. M. L. Anderson, pastor. There were 75 full members on circuit and 142 in two church schools. Nine years later, Rev. Lester E. Taber, pastor, reported 86 members in two churches, with 120 in one Sunday school.

In 1939, Kendrick with American Ridge, Rev. W. S. T. Gray, pastor. There were 56 full members and 96 in one Sunday school.

In 1964, Rev. David A. Zaske, pastor, first year. Members, 117, church school, 139. Forty-five members of Woman's Society gave $442. Value of church, $6,600. Parsonage, $2,000.

EVIDENCE OF CHRISTIAN LEADERSHIP
IN JAPANESE SERVICE

Highland Park Church
Spokane

Rev. U. G. Murphy

First Japanese Church in Northwest was organized at Spokane in 1902. The Seattle congregation dates to 1904, that at Tacoma to 1907, and at Wapato to 1927. These churches and their pastors entered the Pacific Northwest Annual Conference in 1964, upon disbanding of the Pacific Japanese Mission Conference.

Blaine Memorial Church,
Seattle

istry of the talented Dr. Guard. Called of God, he began to preach among the Scandinavian people. Thus began the ministry that led Dr. and Mrs. Larsen over California, Oregon, Washington, Idaho, and Montana, and to a wonderful pioneer ministry in Alaska. He was an evangelist, organizer, and builder of churches. His human sympathy knew no bounds. His life was unselfish and sacrificial.

"He ranged the Pacific Northwest with unbounded enthusiasm. He took this great Oregon country on his heart—its vast possibilities, and Methodism's opportunities. He knew the preachers. His intuition was sound. His observation keen. His sympathetic heart, compelling."

In 1889, Larsen organized the church at Seattle, and another at Spokane. Rev. J. S. Anderson organized a congregation at Port Townsend that year.

The Norwegian-Danish work was organized into a Mission Conference in 1888 at Moscow, Idaho, with Bishop W. X. Ninde, presiding. Rev. J. L. Ericksen was secretary. In 1895 it became the Western Norwegian-Danish Annual Conference. This session met at Astoria, Oregon, with Bishop Thomas Bowman presiding, and Rev. F. Hermans secretary.

When the Conference was dissolved in 1937, congregations in Washington and Idaho were located at: Spokane, Aberdeen, Cove, South Bend, Tacoma, Rockford, Seattle, Bellingham, Everett, LaCenter, Fragaria, and Moscow, Idaho.

Rev. Martin T. Larson, editor of the Memorial Journal of the Conference, published in 1944, introduced his volume with these words:

"The story of Norwegian-Danish Methodism of the Pacific Coast is worthy of a distinctive place in the history of American Methodism. Without it much spiritual value and influence would be lost. Numerically Norwegian-Danish Methodism never was strong, but there is a wider aspect and a deeper significance of this branch of Method-

---

LELAND, IDAHO—1890

First member, Methodist Episcopal Church, South, Leland, Idaho, Mrs. Hannah M. Daugherty. Six months later, Amanda Ward and Alice Johnson, united. First church built on land given by W. W. Johnson. Parsonage acquired two years later.

Methodist Episcopal Church appointed Rev. J. B. Barker to Leland, 1894. In 1895 Rev. G. E. Wilcox, pastor. That year Leland had 71 members, one building. Congregation disbanded after 1911.

In 1900, "Campbellites" held special meetings, some Methodists united with that group.

Parsonage of Methodist Episcopal Church, South, built before 1895. In 1933, old building wrecked, materials used to improve parsonage, new building. Kitchen, bath added.

In 1946 parsonage no longer occupied, was rented. Wrecked, 1962.

Between 1890 and 1962, no members were added to this church during 29 years. Seventeen added in 1891, twenty in 1893, twenty-five in 1900, seventy-seven in 1922, none the following year. Forty-four were added in 1933 and seven the following year. None were added during 1941-45. By 1962 only eight more had been added. None joined between 1948 and 1961.

In 1964, Rev. Daniel P. Smith, pastor, third year, Leland, Peck, Cavendish circuit. Membership 49. Seven members of Woman's Society raised $514. Building value, $9,000.

149

ism, which can never be expressed by the statistical tables. Besides, it must be kept in mind that the Norwegian and Danish people came from countries of smaller population, having an established State church of the Lutheran Confession, which, although staid and formal in its ways, impelled respect and authority. Methodism, with its warm message and great zeal to win souls for Christ, which so markedly distinguished its early existence, appealed to the Norsemen. This, coupled with the knowledge of religion, which formed an important part of the instruction in the public and higher schools of the old countries, produced excellent church members. Thousands of Norwegians and Danes were influenced by the Methodist meetings, even if only a minor part of these actually joined the church. Its influence extended so far that things peculiar to Methodism, as that of kneeling in prayer, testimonies and lay preaching, were adopted in large measure by the Lutherans."

In this same memorial journal, Rev. M. L. Olson, writing of the influence of the Norwegian-Danish work, called attention to the fact that in most Sunday schools of this group, attendance often exceeded church membership. This was not generally true, he pointed out, in English speaking congregations.

Olson further stated, "No doubt hundreds of souls would have continued in their sins but for Western Norwegian-Danish Methodism. Bishop Nicholson, in 1928, when presiding at our conference at Oakland, said, 'I doubt whether the people of these churches would have been won for Christ, had not the foreign language been the instrument.'"

Olson concluded, "The whole part will never be written; holy aspirations, lofty purposes, self-sacrifices, invisible victories, and kindly ministries unheralded and unsung by men. Can these be indexed in figures or leave their imprint on cold type? No! So this little story only gives a fragmentary picture."

OAKVILLE—1890

Articles of Incorporation for Oakville Church, filed November, 1890. Several Methodists had arrived at settlement in 1872-73. Among them, James R. Harris, Mrs. Delia Newton, Henry Barker, Olive P. Brewer, W. T. Paul, Mr. and Mrs. E. R. Newell, Augustus Balch, Rev. Andrew Anderson.

These Methodists built church, dedicated it free of debt, March 9, 1890. Articles of Incorporation, that year, signed by: E. P. Newell, James P. Harris, Dexter Newton, William T. Paul, Oliver P. Brewer, Jacob Fitz, George D. Harris.

Church enlarged, renovated, 1926, Rev. Lloyd Burke, pastor. Committee: H. W. Paul, C. L. Vaughn, A. J. Carpenter, W. J. Lemmon, Ralph Ross. Ladies Aid, Sunshine Club, Victory Club, gave cooperation. The annex was dedicated by Bishop William O. Shepard, and District Superintendent, James T. McQueen, March 18, 1928.

Dexter Newton had then been member of Official Board fifty years. Cradle Roll was organized, with Mrs. J. T. McArthur, superintendent in 1940. Parsonage burned in 1941, Rev. Henry Driver, pastor. Soon rebuilt with aid of churches of district.

Improvements on buildings and grounds under Rev. James S. Randle. In 1964, Miss Ruth M. Lortz, pastor, fourth year. Members, 97; church school enrollment, 84. Woman's Society members 33, gave $428. Building value, $19,658. Parsonage, $5,200.

Methodists Served Finnish Citizens

The vanguard of Finnish nationals began to trickle into the Northwest in the late 1800's. They began to arrive in numbers in the early part of the twentieth century. By 1920 there was a large concentration on Grays Harbor. In 1922 a mission was established at Aberdeen, under the leadership of Rev. E. A. Hart,[6] who served as an associate pastor of First Church. Hart continued to lead this mission for thirteen years. In 1934 he reported 58 members, but the following year the work was discontinued.

Finland is said to be the most completely Lutheran country in the world, ninety-five per cent of its residents being Lutherans. Some neglect their church while others are won to other denominations, but most never shift their ecclesiastical loyalty.

Methodist experiment with Finnish missions in the Northwest cannot be said to have been attended with great success, although its outreach was greater than numbers indicate. The influence and sincere efforts of a great brotherly heart can know no end.

Methodism Appealed to Filipinos

Northwest Methodism's sole work among Filipinos was begun in Seattle by Rev. and Mrs. T. Walter Bundy in 1926. The purpose of the initial organization was Christian fellowship, church membership not being indicated. The Bundys had spent several years in the Philippine Islands as missionaries, returning in 1924.

For several years this Christian Fellowship held regular sessions in the Blaine Room of First Church, meeting Sunday afternoons. Later, a Sunday school was organized, with Mrs. Bundy leading, assisted by members of the group. In the early 1940's meetings were held in the evacuated Japanese church, but the group returned to First

PARKLAND—1890

Methodist Sunday school organized Parkland, 1890. Early leaders were: Alvin Soule, Mrs. Fannie Penn, Mrs. Alice Holmes. Same year, Rev. Fred S. Pearson, Fern Hill pastor, began preaching.

In 1900, the first building was erected on lots donated by William Wilson. First building erected across from Parkland schoolhouse. Rev. Horace Williston, pastor. William Wilson made pulpit with aid of other laymen.

In 1924, Rev. Joel Vigus, pastor, church enlarged. Basement excavated, cost $4,000. Two years later, same pastor, new church constructed. Church celebrated 38th anniversary, 1928, Rev. M. S. Jamieson, pastor. There were 100 in church school, Woman's Foreign Missionary Society active.

While Rev. William F. Andrews, pastor, 1953-56, Methodist men were organized and portable Sunday school unit built. In 1955, goal of $40,000 set for new building. In 1957, church acquired army chapel from Fort Lewis for $60. It was moved to location and used for nucleus of new building. Under Rev. Donald Northdurft, 1957, the congregation entered building which was consecrated, December 8, that year, by Bishop A. Raymond Grant.

In 1964, Rev. Arthur Campbell, pastor, fourth year. Membership, 459. Church school enrollment 377. Woman's Society of Christian Service members, 97. Gave $727. Building valued at $138,350. Parsonage at $31,650.

Church in 1944. In 1945, Bundy gave up direction of the meetings, and Bishop J. C. Baker appointed Rev. Grandino Baaoa, lay pastor. An attempt to bring the Sunday school into that of First Church only partially was successful.

After this experiment Filipino leaders, encouraged by Caucasian advisors, began to anticipate a church of their own. In 1947, through cooperation of Rev. Newton E. Moats, pastor of First Church; Rev. Carl K. Mahoney, superintendent of the Seattle-Tacoma District, Bishop Bruce R. Baxter, and the Board of Missions, these devoted Christians took possession of a building of their own.

At the dedication service, members of the group took leading roles. One sang a solo, another officiated at the piano, and still another presented the building to the bishop for dedication. A Filipino woman reported for the Woman's Society of Christian Service, and a member of the group reported on finances. It was evident that Filipinos were assuming responsibilities and sharing privileges that may never have fallen to them in a large Caucasian congregation.

Following the dedication of the church, Rev. Pio Daba, a Filipino, was appointed pastor. He served until 1952, when he was succeeded by Rev. D. F. Gonzalo, who still was with the congregation in 1965.

This congregation, known as the Fellowship Methodist Church, had 54 members in 1964. Yet it has performed a unique service among the 3,000 members of the Filipino Community in Seattle. Its Christian Fellowship activities have attracted hundreds of persons each year. Many, coming under this influence during a brief stay in Seattle, write from various parts of the world to pay testimony to the spiritual values received while in the city. Typical of such testimonies are the following:

"The Filipino Christian Fellowship is like my school and home which have opened my eyes and thoughts to new and better things of life. It gives me a

---

PASCO—1890

Methodist church at Pasco organized, 1890, Rev. S. N. Dayton, pastor. Building completed that year. Rev. Henry Moyes, pastor, in 1893, had three members: Mrs. Robert Gerry, Mrs. J. Coleman, A. A. Bacheler.

Pasco first mentioned among appointments, 1895, Rev. Jacob Geizentanner, pastor. In 1896, he reported $888 salary, 26 members, 40 in Sunday school, building valued at $1,200. In 1904, Rev. E. L. Tuttle, Kennewick, preached monthly. There were seven members. Rev. A. A. Metcalf, 1906, increased membership to twelve.

In 1910-11, Rev. O. A. Hammond, pastor, received 50, increased membership to 94. In 1919, new property converted into church, Rev. M. M. Eaton, pastor. Trustees: F. M. Cole, W. K. Cox, Dan E. Smith, W. W. Hales, George L. Marsh, Bernard Reinkens, H. B. Jensen, Charles Marvin, Charles Walls. Sunday school superintendent, Charles C. Marvin; Ladies Aid president, Mrs. George Marsh.

New parsonage erected, 1940, Rev. R. A. Partee, pastor. New church consecrated, 1948. Rev. Charles T. Hatten. Membership reached 979 in 1950, Rev. Rudolph A. Anderson, pastor. In 1960, church sponsored Riverview Church, Rev. Randall Larson, pastor.

In 1964, Rev. John Finney, Jr., pastor, fourth year. Membership 831. Church school, 411. Woman's Society, members, 133, gave $574. Value of building $158,000. Parsonage, $20,850.

LEADERS OF THE FILIPINO MISSION IN AREA

Rev. and Mrs. T. W. Bundy

Rev. D. F. Gonzalo

Whitney Memorial
Japanese Church,
Tacoma

Rev. J. George
Kleinbach

chance to live fairly with friends as a result of my daily acknowledgment of God as my Father."

The author of this testimony, Ambrosio Monta, wrote from the Philippine Islands where he was serving in the Bureau of Education at Masinlock, Zambales.

Maxine Gonong, a co-ed at the University of California, wrote: "The Filipino Christian Fellowship services have increased my knowledge of the Bible a great deal. One of the best activities that the organization has fostered is the teaching of the Bible. Such study has drawn me nearer to the fellowship."

NEGROES ENTER NORTHWEST METHODIST CHURCHES

First efforts to serve Negroes in Seattle were reported by Rev. W. S. Harrington, superintendent of the Seattle District, in 1908. He said, "A new charge, christened, 'St. Paul's' has been born during the year. This colored child starts off with a good degree of vigor, and, under the pastoral care of Rev. James N. Wallace, promises to become strong and vigorous. Bishops Moore and Warren took great care in the selection of a pastor, and Brother Wallace is proving to be the right man in the right place."

A year later, Rev. J. P. Marlatt, then superintendent, had the following to say, "It became clear in the early part of the year that our colored church, St. Paul's, could not sustain its pastor, and with the concurrence of the Conference Board of Home Missions and Church Extension, and the consent of Bishop E. H. Hughes, it was agreed that Rev. J. N. Wallace should be transferred to the Lincoln Conference, and the church has been without a pastor ever since. There is no immediate prospect of doing very much with it, as the colored population is very limited, and they already have two churches among them."

That year St. Paul's was left to be supplied and thereafter disappeared

SKAMOKAWA—1890

First preaching service at Skamokawa, at Colwell mill, August, 1890. Rev. E. L. Hughes, preaching. Trustees, 1890, A. J. Montgomery, H. S. Payne, G. D. Fletcher, H. N. Price, S. A. Howe. Land donated by owners of Colwell Mill. First building constructed, 1893-94, Rev. John Flinn, pastor.

Ladies Aid organized October 22, 1889, in home of Mrs. Price.

The old church was destroyed by fire, January, 1954—two children lost their lives. Thomas C. Hall, a layman was supplying. New building erected 1954-55, consecrated, April 1956. Rev. Melvin M. Finkbeiner, district superintendent, preaching. A new parsonage, 1957.

Until 1964, twenty-nine ministers served this church. Two hundred and seventy-eight persons had been baptized, 125 couples married. The new church was dedicated October 5, 1958, by Bishop A. Raymond Grant. Rev. Will Richards, pastor.

The minister remaining at Skamokawa shortest time, Rev. A. Demoy, serving, February 1, to April 24, 1901. The minister with longest record of service, Rev. W. B. Lamb, local preacher, serving from 1928 to 1944.

In 1964, Rev. John B. Freeman, pastor, fifth year, also serving Grays River. Membership, 102, church school enrollment, 112. Woman's Society of Christian Service, membership, 15, paying $928 to local cause. Building value, $33,000. Parsonage $15,400.

from the conference records. This was the end of the first trial.

Another attempt to promote a Negro Methodist Congregation was made during the Second World War. In 1944, it was reported that Rev. Theodore Walters had been appointed pastor of the Washington Street Church, to meet in the evacuated Japanese sanctuary. He was returned for the second year. No mention of the church appeared in the Conference records in 1945. Walters, however, was continued on trial in the studies of the second year, and left without appointment to attend school, which apparently he failed to do. In 1946 he was discontinued.

At the beginning of the second world war Seattle had more than 5,000 Negroes. By 1950 the number stood at 27,000, and continued to grow. These Americans also flowed into Vancouver, Tacoma, Spokane, and other communities.

Negroes were freely received into Caucasian churches of their choice. Yet, at first, they reluctantly were admitted into some church organizations. In Seattle, Negroes tended to congregate in the Madrona and Northern Mt. Baker districts. Until about 1930 this was a fashionable residential area. But as minority groups entered, Caucasians moved away. By 1960 the white population was a minority group.

In this area was Grace Methodist Church, which had been organized as an all-white congregation in 1889. By 1940 the membership stood at 345. Its leading members were business and professional men who supported the church liberally with time, talent, devotion, and money.

The first infiltration of minority groups into the church were Japanese and Chinese, principally the former. After the return of the Japanese from relocation camps, following the Second World War, the tempo of this infiltration was increased. By 1950 these groups were active in various departments of the church, including the

ST. PAUL'S, TACOMA—1890

Services leading to organization, St. Paul's Church, Tacoma, held in tent, Rev. B. F. Brooks, 1890. Tent pitched at South 40th and L Streets. Church organized, April 12, 1890. Trustees, E. V. Benham, A. Kuykendall, J. E. Hill, W. W. Allen, G. C. Britton. Articles of Incorporation, drawn April 19, that year.

The 23 members of congregation worshiped in tent until tabernacle erected. Latter was rented to the Protestant Episcopal Church Sunday afternoons.

A site at South 43rd and L Streets acquired in 1891, building erected, costing $1,200. Rev. B. F. Brooks in four years received 72 members. Rev. Horace Williston, 1894-99, built youth work, organized choir. Rev. George W. Frame, 1902-07, received 98 members, dedicated new building, 1905.

Parsonage erected in 1908, Rev. C. E. Todd, pastor. Indebtedness paid under leadership of Rev. W. B. Marsh, 1908-13. Pipe organ installed, Rev. J E. Milligan pastor, 1917-23. Rev. Paul Ashby led in building new unit, 1923-25. Building repaired, grounds beautified, parsonage remodeled and lodge built at Epworth Heights under Rev. Frank Goodnough, 1932-39. Rev. W. E. Callahan saw membership growth and church school attendance climb, 1942-47.

In 1964, Rev. Nolan B. McClurg, pastor, eighth year. Members, 476. Church school 307. Woman's Society 100 members, paid $866. Building value, $162,000. Parsonage, $21,500.

155

church school, the Woman's Society and youth fellowship program.

As Negroes came in numbers, whites moved out and the former quickly became a majority group, working in all departments. By 1960 the congregation was well on the way to becoming segregated, and mission funds were required to keep the church operating.

In 1963 Rev. Robert Vahey was appointed pastor. He was able to stem the tide for a time. In 1964 the church reported 240 members of which 30 percent were Caucasian, the others, mostly Negro.

On the east side of Tacoma is another Grace Methodist Church with a history dating back to 1903. Unlike its Seattle counterpart, this congregation is located in a community of laboring residents, in the lower economic brackets, yet, substantial, dependable, and loyal churchmen. Its membership was 113 in 1940. With the Second World War the complexion of this community likewise began to change. By 1964 eight Negroes and three American Indians were among the 63 members of the church. Rev. Fred Hertzog was pastor.

SOME JAPANESE-AMERICANS BECOME METHODISTS

Japanese first began to arrive in the Northwest in the 1880's. Methodist attempts to serve them began in Portland, Oregon, in 1893. First services were conducted by a Japanese local Methodist preacher, Rev. Teikichi Kawada. After establishing the church in Portland, he returned to Japan, where he became a well-known preacher and leader.

It was from the Portland Church that Methodism reached out to Japanese in Washington. Genhichi Tsuruta, from that church, organized a congregation at Spokane in 1902. Two years later he founded the church in Seattle. Three years after the founding of the Seattle church, that congregation sent one of its members, Seeichi Higashida, a local preacher, to Tacoma where his preaching aroused sufficient interest to warrant

TEKOA—FARMINGTON—1890, 1895

Church at Tekoa organized, 1890, by Rev. Matthew H. Marvin. Services held in Congregational Church until 1894, Rev. William DeWeese, pastor, 1893-94. First building erected under pastorate of Rev. R. M. Moore, 1898. Dedicated free of debt.

Farmington, 1895, on circuit with Garfield, Rev. T. H. Fertig, pastor. There were 38 members. Church building valued at $800. In 1905, Tekoa and Farmington, together, 123 members, 279 in Sunday schools.

In 1915, Farmington alone, Rev. H. C. Clark, pastor. Tekoa served by Rev. E. E. Evans. Farmington had 172 members, 173 in Sunday school. Rev. J. W. Poolton, pastor. In 1938, Farmington with Tensed, reported, 38 members. Rev. E. J. Smith, pastor. In 1964, Farmington and Tekoa reported 61 members, 87 in church school.

In 1936 Epworth League, Tekoa installed window, dedicated to Rev. M. H. Marvin. Rev. Elmer Beckman pastor.

Fiftieth anniversary Tekoa church, celebrated in 1940, with Bishop Bruce R. Baxter delivering sermon. Rev. Joseph M. Adams district superintendent. Rev. Paul Perkins, pastor. A new building consecrated, March 25, 1951. Chairman of trustees at time was Dr. W. E. Abegglen. Chairman of building committee, F. W. Pratt.

In 1964, Rev. Raymond B. Huddleston, pastor, second year. Members, 175, church school 236. Church building $75,000.

a church. Accordingly, Rev. Toraichi Seto organized a church there in 1907.

Higashida became a member of the Seattle congregation in 1907, later attended the College of Puget Sound in Tacoma, and for almost sixty years was a pillar of the Seattle congregation. In 1964 he still was a respected elder statesman in that congregation.

Methodism was established among Japanese in Wapato, in the Yakima Valley, by a woman. Mrs. Aya Okuda, an evangelist, in 1927, held a series of services there which resulted in a number of conversions and the establishment of the church.

Northwest Japanese Methodist congregations early became a part of the Pacific Japanese Mission Conference, with episcopal administration from California. Pursuant to an enabling act by the General Conference in 1960, the four Japanese congregations in Washington state became a part of the Pacific Northwest Conference in June, 1964. Ministers coming into the Conference with the merger were: Rev. J. C. Kono, Rev. Harry H. Murakami, Rev. Shigeo Shimada, Rev. Robert M. Yamashita, and Rev. Wesley N. Yamaka.

Apart from the influence of Japanese ministers, one of the strongest forces among these Americans of Japanese origin was that of Rev. Ulysses Grant Murphy, a former Methodist Protestant missionary to Japan. For almost a half century he was pastor, friend, and counsellor to many thousands of Japanese residents in the Northwest. As an unofficial Methodist ambassador, he organized Bible study groups, advised youth concerning plans for higher education, preached the Gospel in homes where there were no churches, and, in later years, counselled hundreds of Japanese war brides entering this country with American husbands.

Murphy first came to Seattle in 1892 as a home missionary of the Methodist Protestant Church. For a year he preached at Columbia City and near-by

BURLINGTON—1891

First Methodist church in Burlington organized in 1891. Building completed January 29, 1893, had been two years in building. Rev. Charles McDermoth, pastor. William McKay and T. G. Wilson, leading laymen. First Sunday school secretary, Mrs. Alice Koch Cressey. President of Trustees, 1894, Daniel Neeley.

Church on circuit served by visiting ministers. In 1901, Rev. S. S. Guiler lived at Avon, preached at Burlington. Rev. J. W. Kearn first to reside in new parsonage built in 1904. Followed, 1905, by Rev. T. F. Allen. Church re-built, 1907, Rev. E. J. Smith, pastor. Dedicated, July 28, by Bishop D. H. Moore, Rev. Spencer S. Sulliger, presiding elder. In 1954, board started new parsonage, replacing old one, in use fifty years. Building dedicated March 4, 1956, costing $18,000, free of debt. Rev. J. Ray Neiser, pastor, 1954-62. In 1957, improvements made on grounds, outside of building, extensive improvements inside. Cost was above $1,000, not including much donated labor.

This church, during the years, has emphasized the Methodist doctrine of holiness of life. A close fellowship between members has been characteristic of this congregation.

In 1964, James E. Doak, pastor, third year. Membership, 244; church school enrollment, 241. Woman's Society, members, 70, giving $317. Building value, $40,000, parsonage, $18,500.

Renton, as well as several other points in the area.

In 1893 the mission board sent Murphy to Japan, as a teacher to train Christian leaders. Because of ill health he and his wife returned to America in 1908. After a year on a California farm, and five years in the pastorate, he returned to Seattle, hoping to head off a rising tide of anti-Japanese sentiment then sweeping the country.

Murphy's first contacts with Northwest Japanese were through Christian members of the Japanese communities. He found his experience as a missionary an advantage because he could speak their language. Soon he was visiting regularly 60 communities in Idaho, Oregon, Washington, Montana, and Wyoming. Besides conducting services he acted as unofficial counsellor. He assisted hundreds of Japanese to adjust to the American environment.

Some of the children Murphy taught became prominent leaders in their communities and churches all over America and in Japan. When Japanese were evacuated from coastal areas during the war he lost all his congregations on the Coast, but kept in touch with many who never returned.

In 1953 Murphy's friends arranged for him to revisit Japan. Upon his return the State Department summoned him to Washington, D. C., for a conference.

In 1960 Murphy's friends in Seattle staged what they called a silver tea, and presented him a substantial purse. That same year the Japanese Government, through its Consul-General in Seattle, cited him, along with former Seattle Mayor, William F. Devin, and Genji Mihara, president of the Seattle Japanese Community, for distinguished service to Japanese-Americans.

Murphy, born in Maryland, August 26, 1869, was in 1964, at the age of 95, as active and enthusiastic as ever about his work with his Japanese-American friends. He too, contributed immeasurably to Northwest Methodism's service to men of many tongues and nations.

Sacrifice for missions at home and Christian Evangelism abroad identify Northwest Methodists as—

Men of World Outlook

THE MISSIONARY MOTIVE BROUGHT METHODISTS TO THE NORTHWEST

It was the world outlook which, in the beginning, prompted Rev. Jason Lee, his companions, and successors, to come to the Pacific Northwest to share the Gospel. The vision grew out of a deep devotion to Christ, a conviction that men were lost without Him, and a spirit of sacrifice that rendered them willing to endure the inevitable hardships involved in such an undertaking.[1]

THE SPIRIT THAT MAKES A MISSIONARY

The missionary spirit was a two-edged sword that cut inwardly and outwardly. It impelled consecrated men and women to dedicate their lives to the soul-saving tasks where they found themselves, and also to keep ever in mind that there were other sheep in folds beyond their immediate settlements, and across the seas.

From the beginning every Christian worker in the Northwest was a missionary. The Methodist Church pioneered the Christian mission in most communities of Washington and Idaho. The "Circuit Rider," who here usually traveled on foot, followed the pioneer settlers into every corner of the Far Northwest. While ensuing years saw great changes in conditions under which churchmen worked, the field remained essentially missionary in mid-twentieth century.

In 1964 the percentage of church members to total population in the Northwest was lowest in Continental United States. Whereas that percentage, nation-wide, was more than sixty, in the states of Washington and Idaho, it was little in excess of thirty.[2] Northwest leaders found it frustrating that more than one-half the Methodists

159

who moved to the region dropped out of church altogether. The reply most frequently given in response to the invitation to transfer membership, was, "I worked so hard in the church back East that I intend to take a little vacation." In more than fifty per cent of the cases this "vacation" was for life.

Uncertainty of length of residence played an important role in this drop-out. A case in point was the woman who answered questions on a visitor's card in First Church, Seattle, in 1947. She said she was a temporary resident, but admitted she had lived in the city 37 years.

THE PRICE OF VICTORY MUST BE PAID IN ADVANCE

If a man's investment of his life were a criterion by which to judge his outlook the pioneer missionaries of the Northwest were men of world-wide vision.

The perils faced by the harbingers of Christian civilization on the North Pacific Coast were similar to those described by the Apostle Paul. In those early days every minister stood on his own merits. His acceptance or rejection by those he would serve depended upon the manner in which he acquitted himself in his relation to other men.

> ### FIRST, EVERETT—1891
>
> Prior to 1891, Everett Methodists were served from Marysville. That year Rev. A. H. Marsh, Marysville, organized a church with 9 members. They were, Mr. and Mrs. John Spencer, Mr. and Mrs. G. W. Swalwell, Mr. and Mrs. W. G. Swalwell, Mr. and Mrs. Robert Swalwell, and Walter F. Swalwell. Services began in the real estate office of W. G. Swalwell whose unfinished home later became temporary place of worship.
>
> Rev. B. B. Davis finished the year and, in 1892, Rev. Horace Williston became pastor. Rev. D. G. LeSourd, district superintendent. Trustees, A. Folsom, H. S. Wright, C. W. Miley, W. W. Black, E. J. Pittman, M. M. Smith, W. G. Bickelhaupt, W. F. Swalwell, and A. M. Soper. Ladies Aid President, Mrs. Effie J. Swalwell.
>
> Wesley Hall, costing $800, erected in 1892 at 2815 Maple Street. Church edifice started November 1900, at Broadway and Wall, cost, $13,000. Lecture room opened September 1, 1901, Rev. E. M. Randle, First Church, Seattle, delivered the sermon. Building dedicated 1902 by Rev. J. R. Lovejoy.
>
> In 1963 new building completed, Rev. Harold C. Williams, pastor. Pastor, Rev. Paul E. Peterson, 1964. Members, 888; church school enrollment, 345. Paid on World Service and Conference Benevolences, $3,648. Woman's Society of Christian Service, membership 216, paid $1,433 to district and conference.

Upon his first appearance every man was met by an appraising eye. Some were taunted, but not always in an unfriendly manner. Some met these tests of manhood in such way as always to win the day.

Such a man was Rev. John F. DeVore. His reputation for victories in such contests was widespread. It is said that in November, 1853, he was visiting near Nisqually when his attention was called to a flock of fine turkeys owned by his host. The minister was told that if he could catch one of the birds he could have it. Not accustomed to let such a challenge go unaccepted, the clergyman took off his coat and caught the finest bird of the flock.

Two years later, when DeVore was

160

pastor at Olympia, his search for funds to complete the church there led him to Mound Prairie, twenty miles away. He found the James men with a crew in the harvest field cradling grain. When he told James of his mission, he was informed that if he would take the cradle and cut a swath around the field he would be given a dollar for each man present.

DeVore, it was reported, counting the men, concluded that the promised reward was worth the effort. He took the cradle and swept around the field with the capability of an expert. He collected.

Rev. and Mrs. David E. Blaine[3] reported many hardships endured in getting the first church established on Elliott Bay. In a letter in January, 1854, Catharine described some of these and, inadvertently, revealed the spirit in which they were met. She said, "Our one room is so open that we can look out through the cracks on either side. It freezes not six feet from the little stove when we have as much fire as we can get into it. You would rightly infer that we are not very comfortable, but we console ourselves with the thought that this will not last long, indeed it is getting warmer already."

One of the most difficult features of the pioneer work was that of travel.[4] In this connection, Rev. D. G. LeSourd, presiding elder of the Puget Sound District in 1883, tells of an attempt to reach Dungeness. On Friday he walked from Port Townsend to Port Discovery, a distance of some seventeen miles, arriving there after dark, taking lodging in a rooming house. The Indian boat engaged to take him to Dungeness the next day, failed to clear the harbor because of lack of wind.

Landing, the missionary walked along the beach until he came to Sequim Bay, which projected five miles inland. As the tide rose he found it impossible to progress along the beach so he climbed the bluff, thirty-five feet high. Aloft, he found the underbrush so dense that progress was impossible. Again he de-

ROCHESTER—1891

Rochester first appeared among appointments with Gate City in 1891, to be supplied. Following year, as Rochester Circuit, to be supplied. Rev. J. N. McDonald reported having received $140 in salary previous year, 16 members, 35 in Sunday school. Church organized previous year. In 1894, Rochester Circuit, 26 members, no church building. In 1896 Little Rock and Rochester served by Rev. Andrew Anderson.

In 1915, Rochester with Oakville, Rev. F. W. P. Camp, pastor. In 1912, old building moved, burned in 1924. Old two-room school building moved to church site, remodeled, used for church. Rev. T. J. Hazelton, pastor. In 1930, annex added, Rev. C. L. Vaughn.

More Sunday school space was added, 1950, Rev. Austin R. Rugger, pastor. Building burned in 1959. Churches of conference gave aid. New building dedicated August 28, 1960. Rev. Albert Richardson, pastor. Building debt free, save for loan for furnishings. In 1960, Rochester was "Together-all-family-church."

There were two Sunday school teachers for every class, school growing. In 1964, Little Rock, Rochester, became combined congregation with services held at Rochester.

In 1964, Rev. Albert E. Van Andel, pastor, fifth year. Members, 127; church school enrollment 297. Woman's Society, 35 members, gave $862. Value of building, $61,100.

scended to the beach and walked a few hundred yards before again finding his way blocked.

"Once more I ascended the bluff by clinging to a fallen fir tree whose roots held where it had grown, leaving the top hanging downward. I would place an arm around this, throw my valise as high as I could and, digging the toes of my boots into the bank, climb foot by foot till I reached the top. Soon I found my way hedged by thickets as before. I even got down on hands and knees and tried to crawl through the tangle, but failing in this, I slid down the cliff into the water. Climbing over stumps and old logs, I waded along the wall of clay on my left, my coat tail floating in the water.

"After going two or three miles in this way, I found a dry and wider margin on which to walk. But night was coming down and it was beginning to rain. I could not possibly compass the head of the bay by night. What I should do I knew not, for I was wet, physically exhausted and had no matches to kindle a fire. To remain out all night in that chill atmosphere was to risk perishing. Happily for me I had arrived opposite a house on the other side, three-quarters of a mile away."

SATSOP—1891

Roseville Sunday school organized, Sherwood schoolhouse, January 18, 1891. J. H. Brewer, superintendent. Epworth League, 1894, January 1896, became Satsop Sunday school. Rev. L. J. Covington, pastor.

All ministers free to preach. Rev. Eben Sherwood, Christian minister, father of Floyd, often filled pulpit.

Building committee appointed Dec. 18, 1897. Members were: George Maris, G. C. Morgan, J. H. Brewer, J. F. Foxwell, C. W. Heath; Rev. C. C. Pratt, pastor. Church dedicated, July 31, 1898 debt free. Gift Board of Missions.

Satsop on Elma Circuit. Parsonage at Satsop built in 1905, by committee, Lizzie Foxwell, Mrs. A. W. Parrish, Mrs. Effie Fuller. Ladies Aid organized, 1905, Lizzie Foxwell, president.

Additional lots acquired in 1907. In 1950 Albert Glenn, who grew up in church, began agitation for addition. Plan fostered by Rev. Charles Creesev. Rev. J. D. Llewellen, Rev. John W. Kuller. In 1957 Quarterly conference authorized building. Committee: Gene Wheeler, Buford Goeres, Roy Hazel, Elmer Hoskins, Rand Wood, Miles Fuller, Joe Johnson. Roy Hazel directed construction. Building cost $7,023, balance $10.98, 1958, Rev. John Kuller, pastor.

In 1964, Rev. H. Grant Harvey, pastor Satsop-McCleary. Members, 79; church school enrollment, 75. Woman's Society, 23, gave $606. Building value, $35,000.

LeSourd called loudly and, being heard, by the owners of the house, was rescued. After a night of hospitality in this home, he resumed his journey the following morning. Walking along the beach twelve miles he reached Dungeness at noon, where he was to preach at 11. He found the local preacher in the pulpit searching desperately for a text. LeSourd said, "Of course the presiding elder must preach, and preach he did, twice that day. What I went through that Saturday and Sunday may account for some of my early gray hairs."

In 1883 Rev. S. D. Loughead was appointed to Harboro Circuit. Presiding Elder LeSourd, in his report the following year, left much to be said because of his desire to be brief. He reported:

THESE MISSIONARIES REPRESENTED
PACIFIC NORTHWEST IN WORLD FIELDS

Mr. and Mrs.
Charles A. Irle

Mrs. Willene Whiteley
Powell

Rev. and Mrs. Mark Freeman

Miss L. Marie Corner

Rev. and Mrs. Linden
B. Jenkins

"This new circuit embraces the counties immediately tributary to Grays Harbor. It is a promising field in which Cosmopolis, Aberdeen, and other towns are rapidly springing up. The membership on this charge has been somewhat demoralized, owing to the irregular method of supplying appointments during the last half of the year. Brother Loughead reports that he has been active on some part of his work all the time and that he has explored the country north toward Cape Flattery, finding fruitful soil for Methodism."

After 80 years, it appears the kindly presiding elder should have given more consideration to the reasons for the irregular method of meeting appointments on this circuit. Rev. S. D. Loughead had been appointed to a territory larger than that of Connecticut and Rhode Island combined. Cape Flattery was 150 miles from Cosmopolis, head of the circuit, and could be reached only on foot, traveling for more than 75 miles along the shore of the Pacific Ocean and with seven major rivers to be crossed enroute. Trails were a novelty and the most primitive roads a quarter century in the future.

Some of these men, with humor, looked back upon these hardships as mere incidents in the task of building Christian civilization in the Northwest. For instance, Rev. A. J. Mc-Nemee,[5] in retirement, used to entertain the conference with tales of narrow escapes. Of one incident he wrote: "While on the Dungeness Circuit, I regularly walked from Port Angeles, seventeen miles by the beach to Dungeness. One day when I came to Morse Creek, I found the water too high to cross in the usual place. Several hundred yards upstream I found a log that promised a way to cross. But, in the middle of the swollen stream, my foot slipped and I plunged into the water. As I proceeded along the beach in dripping clothes, I came to a place where the water was so near the bluff that I had to wait two hours for the tide to recede. I sat upon an old log and occupied myself think-

---

NORTH BROADWAY—1891

Haven Methodist Episcopal Church was organized in 1891. After 1896, church would have been abandoned but for Grandma Dwyer, who was pastor, janitor, and church school leader. In 1898, Rev. J. M. Dennison reported 35 members, no furnace, no furniture, and a Sunday school of 40. He finished church first year and paid mortgage second.

First building was erected at Harvard and John Street, by Rev. E. D. White. Under Rev. E. E. Morris, 1909-11, building re-located at Broadway and East Lynn St.

Under pastorate of Rev. Walter Torbet, 1941-44, building was renovated, debts paid, salary raised, and 50th anniversary observed. Membership reached 126, church school enrollment, 167. Under Rev. John Henry Soltman, 1944-46, the building was carpeted, furnaces installed in church and parsonage.

Kitchens in church and parsonage, remodeled under Rev. Darrell Iwerks, 1947-51. Rev. J. C. Snowden, 1954-56, led in continuing remodeling and repairing. Rev. L. Wayne Bond, later, further remodeled and repaired. Under Rev. G. Hurst Paul, 1958-62, salary raised to $3,600. Members, 80.

In 1964, Rev. Gene Allen Ernst was appointed for second year. There were 104 members, and 52 in Sunday school. Woman's Society, with 35 members, gave $490. Church property worth $45,000 and parsonage, $13,000.

ing of the emoluments of the pioneer preacher on Puget Sound. At length I found consolation in the thought, that at least I could maintain my ministerial dignity."

They Paid With Their Own Lives

The most appalling price paid by many of these pioneer missionaries was the loss of their own lives or those of members of their families.

Some fell victim to tuberculosis, resulting from exposure and privation. One of these was Rev. M. S. McAllister, who died in 1862, age 30. Of him it was said, "As a gospel minister he took high rank, he was known for untiring industry, fervent piety, ardent zeal, diligence in study and rapid improvement. Impelled by a strong desire to save souls he was often led to labor beyond his strength to bring them to Christ. Had his life been spared his prospects for eminent usefulness and high position in the ministry were very flattering."

By 1902 four other young ministers had died, ages from 28 to 35. From 1889 to 1903 seven young women, wives of pastors, died from age 21 to 32. But equally touching was the death of 31 parsonage children during the twenty-year period from 1889 to 1909. Most of these were less than five and two were over twenty. Other ministers, in broken health, were forced to give up work. A few, unable to endure the pressure, gave up the ministry.

Among those who continued there was never a word of complaint. A sentence in a letter by Catharine Blaine to relatives in New York, expressed the attitude of those early soldiers of the Cross. She said, "Before we came we did not know how hard it would be, but even if we had, we would have come anyway."

The pioneer settlers were no better off than the ministers who served them. Most of the settlers had disposed

SOUTH PARK—1891

Earliest Sunday school in South Park area conducted by Rev. E. S. Stockwell, visiting from house to house, reading Bible, offering prayer. The church, organized, 1892, named "Shaw Memorial Methodist Episcopal Church," because of gift of $500 from Miss Susan Shaw, Portland, Maine, in memory of brother killed in Civil War.

Building dedicated in 1900, Rev. Rowland Hughes, pastor. Building, 814 Southern, torn down in 1911 and new one erected at 8th So. and Trenton. Name changed to South Park Methodist Church, 1953.

Because a freeway ran through property, congregation acquired new structure at 10th Ave., So. and So. Cloverdale, in 1958. First service held June 15, and building dedicated, November 30, under ministry of Rev. D. L. Rothweiler.

This congregation, south of Duwamish River, the only Methodist Church in vicinity, rendered, for seventy years, great service to the local community. Many community gatherings were held in the building.

In 1964, congregation was attached to Grace Methodist Church and served by Rev. Robert F. Vahey, who was appointed to Grace for the third year. Membership 71, church school enrollment, 103. Seventeen members of Woman's Society of Christian Service, gave $377 to local work. Building valued at $39,000; parsonage, $11,000.

of all their belongings save what they could bring in wagons.[6] Many were forced to abandon along the way much of that with which they started. Many left children, wives, or husbands buried along the Oregon Trail. Arriving, most, if not all, their money was gone. Food supplies were exhausted. Thus, destitute at the end of the trail, the settlers must hew their future homes from the wilderness.

Those who tarried east of the Cascades found themselves on arid lands without available timber with which to build.

Families found it necessary to continue to live in their wagons until places could be put together for dwellings. West of the mountains this always was a log house, with a door closed by some kind of fabric, and small windows covered in the same way. The one room served for sleeping, living, cooking, and eating.

In Western Washington, one family, more fortunate than others, found a one-room shack which had been abandoned with roof covering but one half of it. It was late fall and rains had set in. Cooking was done in the half without a roof, and eating and sleeping took place in the space covered by a shelter.

A descendant of the party of brave men, women, and children, who, settling at Alki Point in November, 1851, gave Seattle birth, painted a vivid picture of family reactions.[7]

According to this account, it was raining when the party was left on the beach. Baggage was dragged to a level above high tide and left there with the women and children while the men looked for a place to spend the night. The crude cabin built for them was without a roof. When the men returned they found the women and children huddled amidst the brush—weeping.

Multiply these and worse experiences by 100,000 families and one can feel the sense of desolation, and loneliness, that filled the hearts of the vast multitudes of settlers who crowded the Northwest during the half century following 1834.

Thus one gains more sympathy for those Hebrews in the Wilderness of Sinai, who wept for the flesh pots of Egypt.

After building the home, land must be cleared for the plow. For most settlers some years passed before money was available for more than the necessities of life.

Beginning with the California gold rush, sale for timber, so abundant in Western Washington, provided a means of ready cash for many residents, but those who spent time cutting timber usually were delayed in getting their farms under way. Meantime, meager food, exposure, and other privations imposed great hazards. All needed, and most welcomed, the inspiration brought by the Christian ministers, but few were able to contribute to the support of the church.

Under these conditions the missionaries labored on, gaining a little here, and a little there, until at length a great empire was won for Christian civilization.

WORLD INVOLVEMENT A PART OF THE CHRISTIAN SPIRIT

Notwithstanding the concern of the missionaries with the immediate tasks of sustaining themselves and sharing the bread of life with the settlers, the outward thrust of the two-edged sword of the Christian spirit never dulled.

The Oregon Conference early established a custom of celebrating the anniversary of the missionary cause at each annual session. In 1855, Rev. John Flinn, who delivered the address, attributed the difficulties of the Christian mission to the depravity of the unrenewed heart. Flinn was followed by Rev. H. K. Hines, who painted in glowing terms, the future triumphs of the cause when every member of the church should be a missionary laborer.

These addresses were followed by an appeal for money to support missions by Rev. J. H. Wilbur. The offering totaled $36.80 in cash, and pledges in

SULTAN—1891

Methodism at Sultan dates from 1891, when Rev. Jerry McKean, pastor at Monroe, began services. The road often was impassable. At such times, John Kager, a local preacher, supplied pulpit.

First sanctuary, on land donated by Joshua Mummey, constructed by Abe and John Kager. In 1904, bell mounted in the tower, called residents to worship and announced death of fellow citizens.

About 1903, churches organized at Goldbar and Startup, were served from Sultan. Later, building at Startup, sold to Seventh Day Adventists. Methodist congregation formed nucleus of Baptist church. Building at Goldbar occupied by Open Bible Standard Church.

First pastors at Sultan, lived in church basement, often inundated in winter. Old-time resident remembers rescuing pastor's children from flood. In 1932, new parsonage erected above danger. In 1954 new sanctuary built at Sultan, old one became fellowship hall. In 1954, First Presbyterian church, Index, became Community Methodist Church. Rev. Everett M. Ritchie, pastor. John Burleson and Rev. Thomas Ludwig renovated building.

In 1964 Rev. Jesse Modahl was appointed second year. There were 147 members at Sultan, 32 at Index. Church school enrollment 145, Index, 30. Woman's Society of Christian Service enrollment at Sultan, 43; Index, 12. Women contributed $100.

the amount of $230. Contributions considered worthy to be included in the secretary's report were: From Francis Fletcher, an early convert in Yamhill County under the labors of the missionaries, $100 for the mission in Japan; from Brother Staats, converted two months before Conference, $25 for the same object. The reporter concluded, "All went away feeling that it is good to join in the work of sending the gospel to all the world."

NEED FOR MISSIONARY SUPPORT EMPHASIZED

In the resolution on support of the ministry for this same year is found a statement that sets forth the conditions which placed Oregon in the status of missionary territory. The statement was, "In view of the many embarrassments clustering around the financial department of our church in Oregon and Washington Territories, arising from the sparseness of the population, opposition to the church, and destitution of necessary means of support, as well as in view of the rising importance of our field of labor, most of which is, in reality, a missionary ground, we hereby respectfully ask and urge the missionary board, to make an appropriation of at least $8,000 for the ensuing year to meet the needs of the preachers on the destitute portions of the work."

HOME MISSIONARIES SUPPORTED FOREIGN MISSIONS

Those leaders of the church were not only concerned for the support of the missionaries within their own Conference, but were determined that the world outlook should not be dimmed. To the end that the missionary spirit should continue to reach outward, the Conference, in 1859, adopted a resolution requiring the presiding elders to arrange with preachers on every charge to hold a missionary anniversary.

In proof that the cause of missions was serious business with the Conference, a resolution also was passed pro-

---

SUMAS—1891

Methodists of Canada and United States were active at Sumas in the 1870's. Sumas Methodist Episcopal church was incorporated February 18, 1891. Trustees were, Peter Saar, John M. Saar, B. A. McBurney, J. L. Fry, A. H. Wright. Rev. J. W. Patterson, pastor.

Rev. C. C. Culmer followed in 1891. With a loan of $500, from Board of Church Extension, a contract to erect the church building was let to J. L. Fry, member board of trustees. An understanding historian said, "The work on the building was done with love and skill." A parsonage built on adjacent lot in 1904. Rev. G. H. Ward, pastor. He was followed in September by Rev. J. H. Kevan. Building went up in Block 14 of Johnson's Third Addition to the town of Sumas.

In 1963 new Wurlitzer organ installed, the bequest of Mrs. Minnie O. Gargett, with aid of contributions of others. Trustees that year, Albert Piro, Glenn Jordan, Arthur J. Moe, Roger Humphreys, Lorren Coleman, Arthur J. Humphreys. Rev. Mack E. Farmer pastor that year. The church was served with Blaine, but in 1964 became independent. In 1964 Rev. Stanley R. Kuntz became pastor. Church members, 72; church school enrollment, 72; Woman's Society of Christian Service, 36. They contributed $459.

FIVE AREAS WERE SERVED BY
THESE MISSION LEADERS

Rev. W. O. Pflaum

Rev. Clyde J. Hall

Rev. and Mrs. Marmaduke Dodsworth

Miss Mary Bedell

Rev. Leon Strunk

viding that at the next annual conference session, failure of a pastor to have taken a missionary offering would be a bar to the passage of his character. The date for receiving the missionary offering was fixed for May.

The Conference that year, anticipating that one of its members might go to Japan as a missionary, recommended Rev. L. T. Woodward as a man eminently qualified to be the first Methodist missionary to be sent to that land. The Conference, first to make a contribution to missions in Japan, had given $1,000. Rising on the tide of enthusiasm, engendered by that fact, the body recommended the establishment of such a mission and urged the appointment of its candidate.

The Conference also pledged that in the event the collections should fail of the promised $1,000, its members would make up the deficiency. Going further it was resolved to raise an additional sum of $2,050 for missions.

Woodward did not go to Japan but remained to render effective service both in Oregon and Washington Territories.

CHURCH EXTENSION SOCIETY WELCOMED

The newly formed Church Extension Society was first recognized and welcomed by the Oregon Conference in 1867. The purpose of the society was said to be to promote the cause by aiding with building of houses of worship throughout the United States and its Territories by grants or loans. Such aid should be granted only to those churches which would, after the aid, be unencumbered save obligations to the Society. The Conference resolved to take collections for this cause in all principal appointments.

The missionary program was an ongoing concern of Northwest Methodists. Attesting to this fact were frequent reports. In 1869, Rev. L. T. Woodward,

ASBURY, TACOMA—1891

First Methodist preacher in South Tacoma, Rev. Horace Williston, 1890. Organized Asbury Church, October, 1891. Incorporated in 1895, Rev. R. Z. Fahs, pastor. Trustees, A. J. Richardson, S. H. Mason, F. Suitor, R. A. Scott, A. Harris. Presiding elder was Rev. Samuel Moore. Epworth League organized in 1892.

First building begun 1891, dedicated, June, 1892, Rev. E. E. Morris, pastor. Rev. Samuel Moore officiated. Church moved to South 50th and Puget Sound Avenue, under Rev. G. L. Cuddy, 1896-03. In 1910 a revival added 25 members.

Between 1915 and 1940, church was rebuilt, lodge at Epworth Heights was acquired, a dramatic club, men's brotherhood, junior and intermediate Leagues were organized. Debt refinanced, and paid.

Pastors during period were Rev. R. V. B. Dunlap, Rev. George F. Pollock, Rev. Truman Blaisdell, Rev. W. M. Dews, Rev. Rudolph A. Anderson.

Between 1940-62 educational hall erected, and a new building dedicated by Bishop A. Raymond Grant, and debt paid. Pastors during this period were Rev. Frank Haley, Rev. Harry L. Allen, Rev. Don Lamka, Rev. Robert Albertson, Rev. Blaine Hammond.

In 1964, Rev. Herbert Eugene Miller, pastor, third year. Members 669, church school enrollment, 342. Woman's Society members, 117, paid $739. Rev. Lloyd Doty and Rev. Neil Richardson entered ministry from this church.

treasurer of the Conference Missionary Society, reported total receipts for the year to be $1,162.57, with an additional donation of $13 for the mission in Japan. In 1870 total receipts were $1,239.15.

The Conference, meanwhile, lost no time in availing itself of aid from the Board of Church Extension. In 1872 the society had recommended the following amounts for churches within its bounds: Mansfield, loan $1,000; Waitsburg, loan $200; and donation $100; Empire City, loan $100, and donation $100; Canyonville, loan $100, and donation $150; Dines Chapel, donation $150; Oysterville, donation $300; Steilacoom donation $150. The total was $1,650. Applications from Grants Pass and Kirbyville Circuits had been placed on file.

A year later the report showed that the parent board had approved donations of $650, and loans of $750, a total of $1,400. The society reported that during the year, a total of $1,500 had been allocated to the Conference on condition that the body would raise $1,000 for the parent society.

The period that followed was one of financial struggle. Some examples of shortages were: In 1877, total raised for Extension Society, $110.80; in 1878, $119.50; in 1880, $108.30. During the latter year the Missionary Society had donated $1,370 to supplement the salaries of ministers in the Conference.

CHURCH EXTENSION SOCIETY AIDS EASTERN OREGON AND WASHINGTON

The East Oregon and Washington Conference, at the beginning of its separate existence, reported that the Missionary Society had granted aid to supplement salaries in the amount of $2,500, and that collections by the Conference equaled $208.12. The Church Extension Society had appropriated $1,500 to assist churches in the Conference on the condition that it raise $200. The condition had been met.

The following places within the Puget Sound District were, in 1876, considered

MASON, TACOMA—1891

Mason Church, Tacoma, was organized in 1891. Rev. George C. Wilding, First Church, requested 24 of his First Church members to organize a church in the North end of the city. A new church dedicated April, that year. First regular pastor was Rev. Charles C. Fulmer. Previously city missionary, Rev. Horace Williston, had done ground work.

First parsonage erected, 1904. Rev. George A. Landen, pastor. New building, North 28 and Madison Streets, erected 1911. Rev. F. L. Baldwin, pastor. In 1924, community building added, Rev. John G. Law, pastor. Sixtieth anniversary observed, 1951, Rev. J. Henry Ernst, pastor, 1945-61. Membership grew to more than 1,700. Half million dollar building erected.

Mason became leading church in Tacoma. In 1961, Rev. John C. Soltman, pastor. In 1964, he reported 1,926 church members, 1,363 in Sunday school, 202 in Woman's Society. Women gave $2,792. Building valued at $868,900 and parsonage at $22,800.

Howard Gregory, church historian, life-long member, in 1964, paid tribute to W. P. Hopping who for more than 40 years was outstanding man in this congregation. Gregory's father, Edwin Gregory, ranked second. Mason was fortunate for years in the number of strong men who gave strength and influence to work of church.

mission stations and granted aid; Puget Sound District, $250; Olympia, $75; Tacoma, $50; Whidbey Island, $50; Whatcom, $75; Dungeness, $50; Mound Prairie, $100; Chehalis, $100; Oysterville, $100; Cowlitz, $50; Lewis River, $57.

By 1889 the Columbia River Conference had entered into more prosperous times. The treasurer reported an over payment of $10 on an $1,800 assessment to the Board of Missions. For the Church Extension Society there had been paid an excess of $12.95 on an assessment of $400. The Church Extension Society had appropriated the sum of $1,750 to aid conference churches.

As collections grew and the Conferences expanded appropriations from the parent boards also increased. For example, in 1887 missionary maintenance appropriation to the Columbia River Conference was $6,260. This same year the committee on missionary needs submitted a report revealing conditions faced at that time. "The number of points it is absolutely necessary for our church to occupy, are now rapidly increasing in our territory. Immigrants are coming to us in great numbers, forming new settlements, but generally are unable for the first two or three years to do much, if anything, for the support of the gospel. Probably not less than twenty new points ought this year to be occupied, but it would be impossible to occupy them, if we had the men to supply them, without a large increase in money to assist in the support of the men."

The committee expressed the opinion that the General Committee ought to appropriate at least $7,500 to aid the Conference in this work.

Differences of opinion regarding rights of the Conference to determine what churches were to receive such aid, arose at that early time. In 1888 the Columbia River Conference approved a resolution requesting the General Conference to so amend the constitution of the Church Extension Society as to per-

THORNTON—1891

First church school at Thornton, Washington, was held in schoolhouse, in 1891. Mr. and Mrs. John Weltman, leaders. Articles of Incorporation were filed February 21, 1898. Trustees were L. L. Holt, E. R. Smith, G. M. Witter, E. S. Mars. The organizing pastor, Rev. C. E. Gibson. In 1912, church had 52 members. In 1928, there were 40 members, and 125 in Sunday school. Church building and parsonage were valued at $1,000 each. Rev. William Daniels, pastor. In 1938, there were 30 members with 49 in church school. Rev. J. E. Williams, pastor.

In 1953, Rev. Charles Fisher, pastor. This church was completely renovated and remodeled at cost of $17,000 with 4,000 hours of donated labor. The project was completed under Rev. Chester C. Blair, 1953.

Remodeling committee, Ralph Heming, chairman; Mrs. Margaret Wells, John Hester, Gene Eastep, Elmer Huntley, Mrs. Dale Curtis, Dale Peringer, Mrs. Cliff Tollet, Cliff Tollet, John Weitman, and Sam Hester.

Forty ministers had served this church by 1964. For years Thornton was a station, but later was served by pastors from Rosalia.

In 1964, Rev. G. Edward Knight was assigned for the second year. There were 85 members, and church school enrollment of 52. The building was valued at $34,000.

mit that body to make appropriations allowing the Conference to decide where money should be applied.

That Northwest Methodists were not being neglected by the parent Board of Church Extension was revealed in 1896 when it was reported that that area, in 30 years, had received from the parent board, $54,250, and paid in return the sum of $6,951. The situation was made more complex by the fact that 31 charges in the Conference, having received loans from the parent society, had failed to pay principal or interest.

Missionary needs of the Northwest continued great. The Columbia River committee on missionary needs, in 1902, said that a section of North Central Washington comprising eight counties and an area of 20,231 square miles and 10,583 inhabitants, should be occupied at once. The sum of $2,000 was requested of the church extension board to permit entry into this field.

Three years later it was reported that among the churches indebted to the Board of Church Extension, five were in arrears not only on principal, but interest as well. Total due on principal was $1,440, and on interest, $1,418.62.

Impatience at the lag in missionary giving crept into the report of Rev. H. O. Perry, secretary of the Committee on Home Missions and Church Extension. He made due notation of the fact that Home Missions and Church Extension had been combined in one board, and further said that there was "No greater home missionary field than this and no greater need for new churches. We must draw the attention of the parent society to this new field in the Northwest, but with less than fifty cents per member given for Home Missions and Church Extension, we are unworthy of their attention."

GIG HARBOR—1892

Methodism organized, Gig Harbor, November 18, 1892. Leader in organization, Mrs. Sarah Franklin, wife of Robert I. Franklin. Franklins donated reed organ. Other pioneers were Mr. and Mrs. W. S. Peacock, Mr. and Mrs. A. E. Johnson, Mr. and Mrs. S. J. Teachman, Mr. and Mrs. Morris Iliss, Mr. and Mrs. Joshua Young, Mr. and Mrs. Henry Cundiff, Mr. and Mrs. John Carlson, Dr. and Mrs. O. R. Rust, Mrs. Amanda Hammerlund, Mrs. Harry Rowley, Mrs. G. Curtiss.

Church organized at Artondale, 1912, merged with Gig Harbor in 1930's, Rev. S. V. Warren, pastor, both congregations.

After 1900, Gig Harbor Church torn down and rebuilt on new site. Building erected, 1917. Agnes Sund, 14, was superintendent Sunday school.

In 1947, Rev. John B. Magee, professor at College of Puget Sound, became pastor and served 11 years. New addition to the building was erected and dedicated, November 17, 1957, by Bishop A. Raymond Grant. That year church celebrated sixty-fifth anniversary. In 1963, property adjacent to church purchased and congregation ready for further expansion. Rev. Kenneth Peterson, pastor.

In 1964, Rev. Bruce Forman, pastor, for second year. Membership, 237. Church school enrollment 194. Woman's Society membership 30. They gave $598. Church building valued at $92,950.

Churches Receiving Aid Honor Bound to Pay

The Columbia River Conference, in 1908, laid down some ethical principles to govern churches who had borrowed money from the Board. A resolution said, "It is very evident from the standpoint of religion and business that when a church accepts a loan from the Board of Home Missions and Church Extension, it is under the same obligation to pay the interest as it comes due as though it had been due to a bank or money lender."

Western Washington Continued a Mission Field

West of the Cascade Mountains, also, missionary needs were greater than the supply of men or money. In 1884 the Puget Sound Conference committee on missionary needs reported that of the 30,000 square miles in the Conference, much had not been occupied by Methodists, because of lack of means to enter new fields.

The following year the body adopted a constitution for its missionary society, and in 1886 the committee reported, "Twenty preachers added to this Conference today, would hardly supply the demands for the gospel on these new and older fields the church is trying to occupy."

At this time, one hears again from the Puget Sound country the report of problems faced by settlers. "Such is the cost of coming to this country," the committee said, "so limited are the means of the majority of those who do come, and so heavy the expense of rendering these timbered valleys remuneratively productive, that for many years to come the people themselves, willing as they are on the whole to aid in the support of the Gospel, will be unable to furnish their ministers a comfortable maintenance."

No wonder, therefore, that the committee in 1887 laid down the following requirements for men who would successfully serve in the Northwest. "We

PE ELL—1892

First building erected for Pe Ell church, on land donated by S. C. Wheeler, 1892. Parsonage built same year. First services held in the home of Mrs. William Hendricks. First congregation reported Baptist. But in time majority were Methodists.

Women organized in 1897. Bought bell and carpet for church. Kitchen and Sunday schoolrooms added in 1921. Ladies Aid bought 24 chairs, purchased piano, 1922. Rev. Andrew Monroe, pastor. Parsonage burned in 1928, not rebuilt. Church redecorated inside and out, 1930. Rev. J. C. Lawrence, pastor. Improvements continued under pastorate of Rev. James S. Randle, 1947-50.

Sunday school paid for tile and piano for building purchased from school district, 1955. New building provided adequate space for worship and educational pursuits. Methodist Youth Fellowship, purchased candleholders for altar. Purchase of new building, spearheaded by Rev. W. C. Bowman, district superintendent, Rev. R. Campbell, pastor.

Rev. Evald Leps, 1955, laid carpet, and altar tile. Organ given by Mrs. Myrah Shandy. Office was added to church in 1956. Ladies tailored draperies for sanctuary, 1958. Mortgages paid in full, April 19, 1962.

In 1964, Rev. Edgar Lee Starr, pastor, third year. Members, 64; church school enrollment 156. Woman's Society members 30, gave $360. Church building value, $20,000.

need more men," the reported stated, "men called of God to preach the gospel; young men of culture, and full of faith and the Holy Ghost, grit and grace enough for hard work. There is ample room in our Conference for twenty such men, and we need them now."

PUGET SOUND METHODISTS SUPPORT SEAMAN'S MISSION

In 1891 the Puget Sound Conference manifested interest in a new kind of missionary enterprise, that of ministering to the many hundreds of seamen annually entering the ports of Western Washington. The Seaman's Bethel Mission, evidently independent, was considered one of the responsibilities of the Conference. Missions were reported at Tacoma, Seattle, Port Townsend, Portland, and Astoria. In 1894 it was reported that the Conference had received in aid the sum of $4.50 for every dollar contributed by that body to the Board of Church Extension. And the next year the committee deplored the change in policy of the Board which permitted it to grant aid to churches costing more than $10,000, saying the policy encouraged extravagance. Up to November 1, 1896, 105 churches had received donations totalling $21,375, and loans of $31,950.

SPECIAL EFFORT TO RAISE FUNDS SPONSORED

At the turn of the century the Puget Sound Conference organized the Twentieth Century Commission for the purpose of raising, within its bounds, money to fund debts. The next year it was reported that $63,904 had been realized from the effort and that some debts had been paid on churches in each district.

The Centenary movement of 1919 and the following years was a natural outcome of a deep missionary passion throughout the denomination. In the Pacific Northwest it was oversubscribed because Methodists of this area were acutely aware of the urgency of the missionary cause.

SAND POINT—1893

First Sunday school in Sand Point, Idaho, held in deserted saloon, in 1893. Mrs. Anna B. Nesbett and Mrs. L. D. Farman, first leaders. Rev. G. C. Stull, presiding elder, Montana, among the first Methodist ministers to preach here. Rev. William Hoskins, June 1897, preached three months. Rev. A. H. Morton, Montana, first pastor.

He organized church with ten members, Mrs. J. H. Nesbett, Mrs. L. D. Farman, Mrs. John LeHuguet, and daughters Josephine, and Pearl, Mrs. J. R. Law, and daughter, Gertrude, Mrs. John Redmond, Mrs. Daisy Ridley.

In 1900, Sand Point transferred to Columbia River Conference. First church building converted schoolhouse purchased for $500, half of which came from Board of Church Extension, in 1901. Mrs. Farman, chairman first building committee. There were 27 members, church building valued at $800, and parsonage valued at $400. In 1905, new church erected on site given by Mr. and Mrs. Farman.

Rev. William Hoskins, delivered first Thanksgiving sermon heard in Sand Point, in 1903. On 60th anniversary, 1961, Rev. Carl H. McGee, pastor, dramatized the work of the pastor in brochure presented to all members of the congregation.

In 1964, Rev. Richard H. N. Yost appointed for third year. Membership, 500, church school enrollment, 177. Woman's Society membership, 66. Women gave $1,160.

175

Within the Puget Sound and Columbia River Conferences, new churches were aided that otherwise might have been compelled to wait many years for help. Also new fields of service were opened as a result.

MISSIONARIES SENT TO LOGGING CAMP

West of the Cascades an unusual project made possible by Centenary funds, work among loggers and lumbermen, was started in 1920 by the appointment of Rev. R. C. Hartley, superintendent.

The following year Hartley reported that within the bounds of the Conference there were more than 900 logging camps, employing more than 22,000. He had visited camps in 11 counties and given regular service to some. In line of duty he visited three hospitals, making 1,528 calls on the ill. The Epworth League at Aberdeen, under the leadership of Tessie Wilmoth, had given cooperation in hospital visitation. Rev. George N. Magwood had been employed to work among men of 11 camps, and Rev. Harry E. Greening was stationed at Raymond, on Willapa Harbor, to serve in that area. Rev. Harry L. Wolfe was serving camps near Darrington, and Pastor A. C. Baar, of Hamilton, had increased attendance at his church services by personal visitation in the near-by camps. This work continued into the mid-1930's.

Missionary work among migrant workers, principally in Central Washington, was done through cooperation with the Council of Churches. The Church contributed regularly to this enterprise.

MINERS RECEIVED THE GOSPEL

The Centenary movement promoted a missionary enterprise among the miners at Wilkeson, on the slopes of Mount Rainier, near Tacoma.

To this work, the Conference, in cooperation with the Woman's Home Missionary Society, sent Rev. and Mrs. Thomas J. Gambill, in 1921. At the time

---

TRACYTON—1893

Methodist ministers first held services at Tracyton in 1893. A Sunday school started by M. E. Johnson, in 1889. First, a Lutheran minister by name of Jensen, and Baptist clergyman name of Johnson, both of Sidney, served the group.

In 1893, the Methodists started Sunday school and were served by elderly minister by name of Luce, who was followed shortly by Rev. Mr. Anderson, who crowded the schoolhouse. In 1907-08 Silverdale and Tracyton shared pastors. Rev. H. R. Merrill, in charge. Building started that year.

Church incorporated, 1909, with H. P. Hansen, J. P. Hansen, Martin Jacobsen, W. H. Hazard, J. P. Riddell, signing papers.

In 1946, church bought parsonage looking to time it would be independent. Two years later, hope was realized when Rev. Thomas C. Slate became their very own minister. This gave morale a great boost and all went to work. Progress was rapid. Educational unit was erected, costing $20,000, paid in 100 weeks. Sunday school grew. Before new unit complete old building purchased to supplement it.

New building used by public library. This proved good public relations.

In 1964, Rev. Robert G. Calkins, pastor, second year. Membership, 108, church school enrollment, 119. Woman's Society, 24, paid $405. Church value, $45,000. Parsonage, $18,000.

the miners had been on strike for five months, and continued two years longer. The contest began at Wilkeson and spread to all parts of the country. It was one of the bitterest struggles in the history of American mining.

Gambill reported that because of undernourishment the children suffered many ailments, mothers were distracted because of worry, miners were ill-tempered, and mine operators were indignant.

The Gambills began with the children. Through aid of the Woman's Home Missionary Society clothing was provided. Children were taken to dentists, physicians and surgeons for treatment. Young people were assembled for Christian services and other activities.

The Methodist minister was welcomed into the Union Councils both local and District. Time and again he was invited to sit in the offices with presidents of the two largest coal producing firms on the Coast to set forth the Christian ideals of mutual respect and consideration on the part of employers and employees.

A little church and a club house were erected and a parsonage built for the pastor and his family. Although this was a community where ninety percent of the population were Catholics, the Methodist minister gained the respect of all. At least one young man entered the ministry from Wilkeson and many others found their way to college and fields of usefulness. All this was because the world outlook of Northwest Methodists began with the need closest at hand. The Board of Home Missions and Church Extension donated $5,000 for the project.

CENTENARY SAVED CHURCH IN SPOKANE

East of the mountains Centenary funds were used to inject new life and hope into many churches and to establish others. It saved the life of Centenary Church in Spokane. The congregation faced an embarrassing indebtedness of $20,000. Dr. D. D. For-

---

ANATONE—1894

Anatone first appeared with Paradise, 1894. Methodists had preached there for years. Early pastors: Rev. John Williams, Rev. John LeCornu, Rev. Jesse W. Rigby, Rev. W. E. Armfield. Rev. S. E. Emerson supplied 1894.

First building on lot donated by L. K. Brown. In 1899 Church Extension Society granted $250 for building. Trustees: David Morgan, H. B. Day, J. S. Chapman, E. M. Clemens and Alice McIntosh. Mrs. Anna West first Sunday school superintendent.

In 1904-06, church moved to lots deeded by J. W. Clemens. In 1907, Rev. E. J. Snell, first resident minister. W. H. Luther first lay delegate to conference, 1907. Circuit included Pine Grove, Fir Grove, Kelly, Montgomery, Weissenfels Ridge.

Parsonage erected, 1908, Rev. Lafayette Davis, first occupant. Rev. J. H. Artz, pastor, 1909-10. Church membership grew from 90 to 123, church school from 44 to 90 under Rev. C. A. Pickering. Room added to church building, costing $600. Rev. Everett M. Filbert, 1927, instructed the children.

Church and parsonage burned, 1951, both rebuilt. Church Extension granted $1,500. Dedicated, 1952. Rev. Harry Chatterton, pastor. Byron H. Brown, chairman trustees.

In 1964, Rev. John W. Simmons, supplying second year. Church membership, 72, church school, 49. Woman's Society, members, 49, giving $579. Church value, $45,100. Parsonage, $16,100.

sythe, executive secretary of the Board of Home Missions, proposed to the Conference to donate $10,000, provided the balance could be raised locally. The proposal was accepted and the church relieved from debt.

The year before the merger of the Puget Sound and Columbia River Conferences, the former gave for missions $54,571; specials, $4,973; Woman's Missionary Societies, $32,147; and Conference Benevolences, $50,094; a grand total of $141,785. The following year the Pacific Northwest Conference apportioned the following amounts for institutional benevolences: Wesley Foundation and Northwest Training School, $16,000 each, and Kimball School of Theology, $3,500.

CONFERENCE STRESSES MISSIONARY CULTIVATION

Still stressing the importance of home missions, the Conference, in 1933, recommended that each pastor preach on Home Missions and Church Extension at least once in every three months. It was voted to allocate for home missions 37.25 percent of total World Service giving for the coming year.

At the tenth annual session of the Pacific Northwest Conference the committee on home missions deplored the fact that so many Methodist churches were being abandoned in communities with greater populations than ever before, and petitioned the parent board for more support to weak churches. Missionary funds for maintenance during the year just closed had been $10,764.25.

METHODISM SERVED IN MILITARY CAMPS

After the outbreak of the Second World War in Europe, when the United States began to mobilize its forces in anticipation of involvement, Northwest Methodists organized services for the Army Camps and other concentrations of military personnel. In 1943, Rev. Fred Isaacson, who had been appointed by

---

ARLINGTON—1894

Arlington first appeared in 1894, Rev. G. L. Cuddy, pastor. First Sunday school met in Haller City schoolhouse. Cuddy followed, in 1895, by Rev. George W. Frame, Marysville. Services held in Free Methodist Church.

Church organized in 1895, with eight charter members. They were Robert Maxwell, Mary Maxwell, Cynthia Blair, Harvey and Lettie Marsh, Evelyn R. Lovell, Melinda Winnie; and A. L. Blair. Organizing pastor, Rev. George W. Frame. Rev. T. J. Massey, presiding elder.

First Ladies Aid organized, 1899. First parsonage built same year, costing $180. First church building erected in 1898, dedicated without debt. Isaac Dillon was pastor. There were thirty-four members.

Church was burned January 23, 1927. Erection of new church began in 1928, Rev. Earl E. Reisner, pastor; completed, 1938, Rev. Frank R. Gillett, pastor. Building cost $35,000. C. L. Marsh, chairman of Board of Trustees. Debt funded under Rev. J. C. Hofstetter, mortgage burned in 1952. New parsonage built in 1954.

In 1963, Rev. Rollin E. Stierwalt, pastor. There were 185 members and 136 in church school. Church school superintendent, Mrs. Larry Munizza. President of Woman's Society of Christian Service, Mrs. A. J. Edson. There were 45 members of Woman's Society and Wesleyan Service Guild combined. They gave $1,318.

the Conference to head this work, reported his activities as follows: "The Methodist Service Fellowship has been at work in the three camps near Tacoma, McChord Field, Fort Lewis, and Camp Murray. The aim has been to carry the work of the church to the camps, and to bring into the church the army personnel and talent that reciprocal service might be rendered. Gospel teams of young people, singers, and musicians, Bible class teachers, speakers, and church literature have been brought out to the camps. Special groups of singers and entertainers have been brought from the camps to the church, and home contacts have been made for soldiers on overnight leave."

The Work of the City Missionary Unions

Something of the workings of the Methodist Unions within the Conference, was described by Rev. C. K. Mahoney, superintendent of the Seattle-Tacoma District in 1943. He said, "This district is perhaps unique in Methodism in that it is composed of two City Missionary Societies, which together comprise all the charges of the district except one. These two societies are incorporated under the laws of the State of Washington. They buy, sell, and hold property including some of the churches. The Seattle Society owns the Deaconess Settlement in Seattle, and the Tacoma Society holds title to the Wilkeson property."

A similar society operated on the Spokane District. There missionary institutes were used, as a means of stirring up within the minds of the people, greater concern for the cause. In 1945 the superintendent of the Spokane District, for example, reported that four missionary institutes had been held on his district during the year. They were held at St. Paul's Church, Spokane; Cashmere, Okanogan, and Pateros.

How the Conference, during and following the war years of the 1940's, pressed relentlessly for more and more support for the missionary cause, is seen

CHINOOK—1894

First Methodist Sunday school was organized at Chinook in 1894, probably meeting in private home. First preaching service in 1894 by Rev. John F. Ford. "Father" Hadley organized first class and acted as pastor. Church organized January 6, 1896, 14 charter members. Trustees November 1, 1895, C. C. Bundy, J. R. Hall, W. A. Ford, Fritz Johansen, and J. T. Jerow. Organizing pastor, Rev. R. A. Atkins. Articles of Incorporation dated January 6, 1896.

Village drunks helped erect first building in 1906. It cost $400. Pastor was Rev. E. B. Reese, followed by Rev. M. R. Phillips.

Dan Williams served as church treasurer for twenty years. It is reported that when funds were inadequate he paid the bills himself. He passed away in 1945. In 1929 Rev. Henry Albright, pastor, also served Ocean Park.

In 1940 Rev. Harold E. Dixon served Ocean Park Parish.

In 1960 Rev. Jack Caldwell also served Ocean Park. There were 12 in the Woman's Society who gave $466. The church building was valued at $3,400 and the parsonage at $2,875.

In 1964, Rev. J. Fred Stilwell was pastor, second year. There were 14 members of the church and no Sunday school. President of the Woman's Society of Christian Service was Mrs. William Litschke.

179

SOME NORTHWEST METHODIST DEACONESSES SERVING IN VARIOUS FIELDS

Miss Helen Marie Kraut, R.N.

Miss Eva N. Burch

Miss Eunice Allen

Mrs. Alberta Kinch Lundin

Miss Leila Dingle

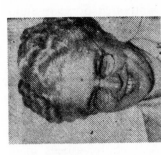

Miss Annette Kiehlbauch

Miss Lucile Sprengle

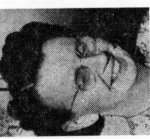

Miss Bessie Pease

Miss Charlotte Howland

in goals set for several years: For World Service and Conference Benevolences goals were fixed as follows: In 1943, $101,715; 1945, $115,319; 1950, $158,009. Total goals for the year beginning in 1960, were $365,000, and for 1963 the goal was $466,000.

NORTHWEST METHODISTS SERVE ABROAD

A number of ministers of the Pacific Northwest have matched offerings in money with their lives to serve the cause of Christ in missionary fields abroad. While the exact number of such men is not available, some of them still were on the fields in 1964, and others, retired, resided within the bounds of the Conference. Among them is Rev. William O. Pflaum, who first united with the Puget Sound Conference in 1907, going to Chile in 1913. There he was head of a school training young people for Christian service, and superintendent of a hospital. He returned to the United States in 1931, transferring back to the Pacific Northwest Conference. He retired in 1944, and since 1952, has resided at Wesley Gardens, Conference retirement home.

Rev. John S. Herrick went to Bolivia as a missionary from the Northwest in 1917. He retired in 1959 and transferred into the Pacific Northwest Conference in 1961.

Rev. T. Walter Bundy first united with the Conference in 1916, served in the Philippine Islands, 1919-'24, and since that time served in the Pacific Northwest until his retirement in 1957.

Rev. Linden B. Jenkins was a teacher under the Board of Missions in Malaysia more than twenty years. He united with the Pacific Northwest Conference in 1947 and retired in 1963.

Rev. Francis M. Kinch united with the Oregon Conference in 1921, and served as a missionary in South America from 1926 to 1934. He returned to Oregon in 1934, and united with the Pacific Northwest Conference in 1937.

MABTON—1894

First preaching service at Mabton in 1894. Probably Rev. R. C. Moter, presiding elder, or Rev. J. W. Rigsby of Bickelton. Methodist Episcopal Church organized that year. Number of charter members unknown. In 1894 Pastor Rigsby reported two Sunday schools with 65 members on circuit. Some probably were at Mabton. First resident pastor was Rev. M. L. Wilson in 1908.

The first Methodist building, on Reservation Road, was shared for a time with Presbyterians. Public school also occupied building. Among early ministers were Rev. William E. Ragen and Rev. B. J. Hoadley.

A later building was erected in 1911 under Rev. Miner C. Newell. Church, first served from Bickelton, became independent in 1948, Rev. John E. Besant, pastor.

Mrs. Arthur King, cradle roll superintendent for years, succeeded by her daughter-in-law, Mrs. Norman King. Together, more than 40 years. A. T. Carlson, treasurer from 1909, succeeded, in 1929, by his wife who still was serving in 1959—fifty years together.

Pastor Ruth Lortz, 1949-50, fitted garage for wood-working and invited boys of neighborhood to use it.

Rev. Oren Walters appointed first year in 1964. Members of church, 90, Sunday school, 164. Members of Woman's Society of Christian Service, 40. They gave $207.

He retired in 1964, becoming counselor to the retired brethren.

Rev. Donald F. Ebright, united with the Kansas Conference in 1932, served as missionary in India from 1945 to 1957, transferred to the Pacific Northwest Conference, and in 1958, served as first president of Alaska University for one year. He became associated with Meals for Millions Foundation, Los Angeles, in 1959.

Rev. Leon E. Strunk united with the Pacific Northwest Conference in 1955, and in 1958 went to Brazil as a missionary.

Rev. Howard W. Yoder first united with the New York Conference in 1925. He went to Peru in 1930; to Bolivia in 1949, and came to the Pacific Northwest Conference in 1963.

Rev. Marmaduke Dodsworth united with the Puget Sound Conference in 1917; went as missionary to Malaya in 1920, retired in 1955, and returned to the Northwest, but retained his membership in the Malayan Conference. He died in 1965.

This chapter relates unbelievable hardships faced by Methodist preachers traveling to posts in the Northwest afoot and by ship, canoe, horse—a thrilling story of—

Men of the Itinerancy

Pioneer Methodist ministers in the Northwest, more than in any other part of America, were men of the itinerancy. Yet, travel here was more perilous than elsewhere. Difficulties encountered were described in 1897 by Rev. H. K. Hines,[1] who himself had traveled 180,000 miles through this area.

Hines spoke concerning members of the mission staff who received assignments to serve in the Northwest, in 1840.

"Their mode of conveyance was the canoe, its pathway the mightiest river's flood, the dashing torrent's foam, or anon the swinging surf that beat upon the ocean's shore," he said.

"MOST UNCERTAIN, PRECARIOUS, LABORIOUS ITINERANCY"

"This was the most uncertain, precarious, laborious itinerancy a Methodist preacher ever attempted," he continued. "Now dashing down foaming and eddying cascades, where the wrong scant of an Indian's paddle-blade by a single inch would shoot the canoe like a catapult against some beetling crag or submerged rock; now wading up the ice-cold stream and wearily tugging at the cordel-rope for hours to make a single mile, or now pulling at the paddle hour after hour to cross miles of river or bay against winds and tides was the most real and least ideal of any itinerancy ever attempted.

"Nightfalls found no house or home; only a camp under a fir tree, or under the lea of some great basaltic cliff. No gathered congregation, large or small, would welcome the weary itinerant to the cheer of a hand-shake or the restful influence of a worshipful song and Christian communion; only the still, awful quietude of mighty forests, or the

183

PIONEER SADDLEBAGS AND WASHINGTON'S
TWO EARLIEST METHODIST CHURCHES

SADDLEBAGS

Rev. Hubert Vincent

The Satus Church

The Claquato Church

more awful solitude of the mighty plain," Hines said with authority.

Such perils of transportation faced every Methodist minister after his arrival here. Yet, to get here, he must overcome equal dangers on the long trek from the East.

The first missionaries came to the Northwest by the overland route, across the great plains, over the unmarked mountains, and down their dangerous slopes. Rivers must be crossed, often at loss of life. Hazardous gorges must be traversed. Often wagons must be disassembled and, with ropes, let down lofty precipices, piece by piece. Livestock must be coaxed to descend frightening crags. Many of them were killed in such attempts, while wagons and equipment sometimes were dropped and destroyed.

AMBUSH BY INDIANS A CONSTANT THREAT

Ambush by Indians was a constant threat, and prospect of illness haunted every company. The years, 1852 and 1853, came to be known as the "cholera years," during which deaths occurred almost daily in every train. Some entire families were wiped out.

Many of these prospective settlers were Methodists. Notable among them was the family of Rev. Andrew J. Joslyn,[2] whose parents brought him, a child of seven, over the trail in 1850. Later, Joslyn was a Methodist minister in the Northwest from 1870 until 1920.

Joslyn related an experience encountered while crossing the mountains. His family found a man in Burnt River Canyon with three children, the oldest, about ten years of age, and the youngest a baby. The mother was dead and they had lost all their animals but one ox. It was impossible for them to go on and the father was desperate. A collection was taken and another ox bought. That enabled him to continue his journey.

Many equally pathetic instances have been recorded. In one case, a little girl, all of whose family were dead, was left

MONROE—1894

Rev. E. B. Reese, circuit rider, organized first Sunday school at Monroe, in Austin's livery barn, in 1894. First church members were Amelia Austin, Andrew Braaten, Addie Hayes, Maria Johnson, Frances Regan.

Rev. O. L. Doane and Rev. Meade L. Cunningham, circuit riders served Monroe before 1900.

In 1900 Rev. A. H. Marsh became full-time pastor. The first church, a frame building with a bell tower was completed in 1896. A new brick building costing $20,000 was dedicated by Bishop William O. Shepard in December 1924 under the leadership of Rev. E. D. White. Rev. George W. Frame was district superintendent. Later the church acquired a Wurlitzer amplified reed organ and a set of Maas chimes.

Later improvements in the sanctuary include aisle and chancel carpeting, cathedral lanterns, and public address system. A divided chancel also was installed. Under leadership of Rev. Forrest D. Tibbitts, 1955-62 membership increased 21 percent.

In 1964 Rev. Harold O. Perry was appointed for the second year. There were 310 church members; church school enrollment, 173 ; Woman's Society membership, 77. Women gave $704. Church property value $113,800. Parsonage $21,000. Other property $17,500.

From this church came Rev. Harold Bashor, who was twice district superintendent in the conference.

to drive the ox team through to the Willamette with no adult help. The Joslyn party was floating down the Columbia River near their destination when they were forced by an approaching storm to land and make camp not far from Vancouver.

MOTHER HOLDING DEAD CHILD ON RAFT

"It grew dark," Joslyn said, "and began to rain soon after we got the fire started. A party of strangers, making this last stage of their long journey on a raft of their own construction, soon came to shore. We helped them to land. A woman handed Mother her baby to hold while she procured some necessary articles from the raft. As soon as Mother received it she said to my sister, 'The baby is dead and its poor mother does not know it.' The infant had died in its mother's arms while she was watching the struggles of the rowers to reach the shore and save themselves from the river and the storm."

The only alternate route was by ship around Cape Horn, along the Pacific Coast to the mouth of the Columbia River or into Puget Sound through the entrance to the Strait of Juan de Fuca at Cape Flattery. Dangers encountered on this route were described by Caroline C. Leighton,[3] who from 1865 to 1881, traveled over all this territory from San Francisco to the Canadian border, with her husband, an employee of the United States Geodetic Survey.

Mrs. Leighton vividly pictured the difficulties of early travel involving the bar of the Columbia, the "Big Bend" country in Central Washington, and the entrance to the Strait of Juan de Fuca.

The passage of the bar at the mouth of the Columbia was described. "The most interesting part of the journey was the passage of the Columbia," she said. "The bar at the mouth is a great hindrance to its free navigation, and vessels were often detained for days and even weeks waiting for a favorable opportunity to cross. We waited five

PROSSER—1894

The Methodist Episcopal Church was organized at Prosser in 1894. In 1895, Pastor Henry Moys reported 51 members of church and 86 in Sunday school. The first meeting place was Prosser schoolhouse. Other points on the circuit were, Kiona (Benton City), Pasco, Kennewick, Mabton, and Sunnyside. In 1895 Prosser and Zillah became a circuit.

The first trustees were, William Knowles, Mr. Sampson, Joe Ponti, Mr. Marryman, and Thomas Dingle. Methodists built their church and parsonage on corner of Sheridan and Sixth Street, mostly with volunteer labor. It was dedicated free of debt, November 13, 1898. Rev. Sanford L. Burrell, pastor.

In 1919 building sold for a funeral home and, in 1922, a new building was started at Sixth and Prosser Avenue. Dedicated July 20, 1930. Rev. O. L. Anthony, pastor. Sermon by Rev. J. Ralph Magee, superintendent Seattle District. Board of Home Missions loaned $5,500. Third parsonage was purchased in 1953 for $14,000.

Rev. Chester Morgan, in 1947, became first unmarried pastor of the church. He was married to Catherine Cooney in November of that year. In 1964, Rev. Tracy W. Manley was appointed for the third year. Members, 424; Sunday school enrollment, 189; Woman's Society, 96, with gifts of $584.

186

days outside in the fog hearing all the time the deep solemn warning of the breakers to keep off. Our steadfast captain as long as he could see nothing refused to go on knowing well the risk. In all that time the fog never once lifted so that he could get the horizon line.

FIVE DAYS TO CROSS COLUMBIA BAR

"At the end of the fifth day he entered in triumph with a clear view of the river, the grandest sight I have ever seen," Mrs. Leighton related. "The passengers seemed hardly to dare to breathe till we were over the bar. Some of them had witnessed a frightful wreck there a few years before when after similar waiting in the fog for nearly a week a vessel attempted to enter the river and struck the bar. She was seen for two days from Astoria but the water was so rough no lifeboat could reach her. The passengers embarked on rafts but were swept off by the sea."

When Rev. Jason Lee, with his daughter, Lucy, and Rev. and Mrs. Gustavus Hines, started on his last trip to New York, the dangers of this bar delayed his exit more than a month. The above description explains the reason why. John Jacob Astor's ship, The Tonquin, manned by Captain Thorn, lost eight men here, in 1811, while attempting to cross the bar to establish Astoria as a trading post.

Mrs. Leighton described a narrow gorge in the Columbia through which a steamboat on which she traveled attempted to pass on a trip to Colville. "The most remarkable part of the river is where it is compressed to one-sixth of its width in passing through a mountain gorge three-quarters of a mile long," she said. "The current is so strong there that it takes from four to six hours for the steamer to struggle up against it and only one minute to come down. . . . When we reached this canyon our real difficulties began. We attempted to enter it in the afternoon but met with an

WALLACE—BURKE, IDAHO—1894

Methodist preaching services began in the Wallace, Burke, Gem area, in 1894. Rev. W. H. Selleck first pastor was followed by Rev. M. R. Brown February 1897. Lots for church acquired at Wallace, November, 1897, and building costing $2,150, dedicated, October 21, 1900. First parsonage completed in 1901. Rev. H. W. Mobbs, pastor. New pipe organ costing $1,700 installed at Wallace, 1906-08, Rev. Charles MacCaughey pastor.

During the pastorate of Rev. Charles MacCaughey, it was said that Wallace changed from a wide-open town to a modern city. He joined with the Congregational pastor in drive to eliminate gambling and vice. Group of youth rallied to lay foundation of church.

In 1927, Rev. W. M. Martin, pastor, entrance to the church was changed. Fiftieth anniversary was observed in 1944. Rev. Everett M. Filbert, pastor. Bishop Bruce R. Baxter delivered sermon.

Best attendance in history of church registered under Rev. Kenneth Lawson, 1960-63. Fred Levering, historian, joined church in 1909. By 1960 had been Superintendent of the Sunday school 25 years, member of Annual Conference twelve years, and member of the Jurisdictional Conference at San Francisco.

In 1964, Rev. Franklin A. Nash was pastor, first year. Members, 161, church school, 144. Twelve members of Woman's Society gave $31.

187

accident which delayed us until the next morning. Meanwhile the river began to rise. It goes up very rapidly—fifty, sixty, I believe, even seventy feet some times. We waited twelve days in the woods for it to subside.

"Everybody grew very impatient and, at length, one night the captain said he would try it the next morning. . . . A heavy rain came on lasting all night so that it seemed rather desperate to attempt to go through it if the river was too high the night before. I could hardly believe it when I heard the engineer getting up the steam to start. . . .

PASSAGE THROUGH GORGE FULL OF THRILLS AND DANGER

"As soon as we went on board the boat . . . a violent thunder storm came on, lightning, hail, and rain, and a pine tree, crashing down, fell across the bow of the boat. . . . There were most evident signs of disapproval all about us, the sky, a perfect gloom, and the river continually replenishing its resources from the pouring rain and strengthening itself against us. When we steamed up to the entrance of the canyon the boat was fastened by three lines to the shore, and the men took out a cable 600 feet in length which they carried along the steep, slippery rocks and fastened to a great tree. One of them rolled down fifty feet into the water, was caught by his companions before he was whirled away.

"The men then returned to the boat, let on all the steam, and began to wind up the cable on the capstan. With the utmost power of men and steam it was sometimes impossible to see any progress. Finally, however, that line was wound up and the boat was again secured to the bank and the cable put out the second time. This part of the passage was still more difficult, and after the line was arranged two men were left on shore with grappling irons to keep it off the rocks, a great, fine looking one who appeared equal to any emergency and a

NEZ PERCE—1895

Nez Perce, Idaho, first appeared in minutes, 1897, Rev. J. E. Williams was appointed for third year. On circuit were three churches, combined membership 75. Three church buildings valued at $1,500.

In 1898, Rev. Jacob F. Sargent, pastor. Following year circuit left to be supplied. Rev. James Greenslade, appointed, 1900, evidently Nez Perce alone, for but one church value, $500, 42 members.

Rev. Roy D. Osterhaut pastor, 1904. In 1905, point combined with Cottonwood to form circuit, left to be supplied. The next year Rev. W. G. Light supplied the circuit and was followed in 1907 by W. H. Zeller. During the years until 1928 successive pastors were: Rev. F. R. Spaulding, Rev. T. H. Fertig, Rev. Mark Pike, Rev. J. A. Hoffman, Rev. Trevor Orton. In 1928, left to be supplied.

In 1938, point was again with Cottonwood, Rev. Claude W. Groth, pastor. That year there were 64 members and 49 in church school. Church building valued at $4,000, parsonage, $1,500. In 1950, with Cottonwood, Rev. Reah H. Dougherty, pastor. There were 81 church members, 81 in church school.

In 1964, Rev. Mack E. Farmer, pastor, second year. Members 103, church school enrollment, 75. Woman's Society, 39, gave $595. Church building value, $10,000. Parsonage, $3,000.

188

little one with sandy hair and a lobster-colored face and neck. . . .

"As we drew near we saw that the line had caught on something beneath the surface of the water so that they could not extricate it. The little man toiled vigorously, standing in the water nearly up to his head, feebly seconded by the big one, on the rocks. It seemed as if the line would part from the strain or the boat strike the next moment.

"The mate shouted and gesticulated to them but no voice could be heard above the raging water and they either could not understand his motions, or could not do as they were directed. The boat bore directly down upon them. Presently it seemed evident to us that the little man must sacrifice himself for the steamer. . . . He stopped a second, then flung back his cap and threw himself under the boiling water.

"Up came the rope to the surface, but the man was gone. Instantly, after, he scrambled up the bank and the great magnificent man did nothing but clutch him on the back when he was safely out. We had then wound up about two-thirds of the cable. Immediately after this remarkable occurrence, the great heavy line came wholly up out of the water. A bolt flew out of the capstan which was a signal for the men who were at work on it to spring out of the way.

"The captain shouted, 'Cut the rope.' But at that instant the iron capstan was torn out of its deck and jumped overboard with the cable attached to it. I felt thankful for it for I knew it was the only thing which could put an end to our presumptuous attempt. I felt this rope would be a great snare to us in case of accident. Three of our four rudders were broken, but the remaining one enabled us to get into the eddy that carried us to a little cove where we stopped to repair damages sufficiently to come down the river. So we turned back defeated."

HILLYARD, SPOKANE—1895

Methodist church was organized at Hillyard, Spokane, in 1895. Parsonage built in 1898, Rev. W. B. Eakin, pastor. Under his pastorate, 1899-04, small chapel built, and church erected in 1900. Mrs. M. R. Brown, wife of pastor, organized Ladies Aid in 1895. Mrs. H. R. Stevens and Mrs. Dennison were charter members.

Rev. George Gable, pastor in 1900, reported 171 members in three churches. There were five church schools with 250 enrolled. In 1911, Rev. C. A. Hodshire reported 280 members on circuit. There were 206 members in Hillyard Church, in 1928 and 237 in church school. Church then valued at $10,000. Ten years later, Rev. E. G. Ernst was pastor and he reported 315 members with 152 in Sunday school.

In 1950, Rev. Enoch E. Willman was pastor. He reported 183 members and 150 in church school. Church building valued at $15,000 and parsonage at $4,000.

Hillyard was built in a community whose residents were railway employees. During the peak of railway transportation the church prospered accordingly. When railroad business slumped so did the membership of this church.

In 1964, Rev. James Thuirer was appointed, first year. Membership, 168. Church school enrollment, 60. Woman's Society members, 37, giving $594. Church valued at $28,000, parsonage at $13,600.

Passing Cape Flattery Full of Danger

The exit from the Strait of Juan de Fuca was described by Mrs. Leighton. "Passing Cape Flattery is a great event of the voyage," she said. "It is always rough there. Our captain had been sailing on this route for fifteen years, but he said he had never seen a worse sea than we encountered. We expected to sail on the water but our vessel drove through it. . . . Every time we tried to round the point great waves advanced against us, so powerful and defiant looking that I could only shut my eyes when they drew near. It did not seem as if I made a prayer but as I was myself a prayer only a winged cry. I knew then what it meant to die. I felt that I fled from the angry sea and reached in an instant serene heights above the storm.

"Finally, as a result of all these desperate efforts, in which we recognized no gain, the captain announced that we had made the point but we could get no farther until the wind changed. And while we still felt the fury of the contrary sea it was hard to recognize that we had much to be grateful for. We saw one beautiful sight though, a vessel going home, helped by the wind that hindered us. It was at night and the lights struck up on her dark sails and made them look like wings as she flew over the water. What bliss it seemed to be nearing home and all things in her favor."

Mrs. Leighton continued, "The water drove us from the deck. The vessel plunged head foremost and reeled from side to side with terrible groaning and straining. If we attempted to move we were violently thrown in one direction or another and finally found that all we could do was to lie still on the cabin floor holding fast to anything stationary that we could reach. We could hear the water sweeping over the deck above us and several times it poured down in great sheets upon us. We ventured to ask the captain what he was attempting

WENATCHEE—1895

Wenatchee's first Sunday school organized, July 1, 1895, seven members. J. O. Smith, first superintendent. The church organized April 16, 1895, with 12 members, by Rev. M. R. Brown, of Waterville.

Rev. Bracken E. Koontz, in 1895, became pastor of Waterville Circuit with ten appointments. Rev. B. L. Hicks, his associate, was assigned to Wenatchee and became resident pastor.

First building, in 1896, Chelan Avenue and Orondo Street. In 1900-03 Rev. B. F. Utter built the parsonage with his own hands. Church and Sunday school membership doubled. Rev. L. R. Kufus, following Utter, led town in moral reform.

In 1907, new church building, costing, $4,500, dedicated free of debt, by Rev. D. L. Rader, editor, Pacific Christian Advocate. Wesley Chapel was built under Rev. Robert Warner, 1917-21.

Under Rev. Joseph H. Beall, 1940-47, building fund reached $78,000. Fund continued by Rev. Willard E. Stanton, reached $122,000 in 1950. Under Rev. James T. Albertson, 1950-60, new building costing $500,000 was erected. Donations of labor equalled $80,000. First service, July 27, 1954. Dedicated, April 8, 1956, by Bishop A. Raymond Grant. New parsonage acquired in 1956.

In 1964, Rev. G. Richard Tuttle appointed for fifth year. Members, 1,423, church school enrollment, 1,036. Woman's Society members, 307, with gifts of $1,541.

to do. 'Get out to sea,' he said, 'out of the reach of storms of the land.'

" 'That is brave sailing,' I thought, though I would not have gone if I could have helped it. We struggled on in this way for a day and a night and then he said we were beyond the region of storms from land."

COLUMBIA—OLYMPIA TRIP SLOW, DANGEROUS

Mrs. Leighton described another journey from the Columbia to Olympia by land. She said, "We saw along the Cowlitz Valley marks of the havoc and devastation caused by the floods of last winter. The wild mountain stream had swept away many familiar landmarks since we were last there, in fact had abandoned its bed and taken a new channel. . . . Where we had quietly slumbered is now the bed of the stream.

"We mourned over the little place at Monticello where for eight years a nice garden with rows of trim currant bushes had gladdened the eyes of travelers and the neat inn kept by a cheery old Methodist minister had given them hospitable welcome—not a vestige of the place now remaining. Civilization is so little advanced in that region that few men would have the heart or the means to set out a garden."

During the thirty-two years following the appointment of Rev. Benjamin Close to the Puget Sound Missionary District, in 1853, all territory in Washington, west of the Cascades, was in one presiding elder's district. It was more than 300 miles north and south and 175 miles travel distance from the summit of the Cascades to the sea.[4]

FIFTY-MILE WALK WAS COMMON FOR PREACHER

Often a minister was appointed to a parish 150 miles in length and it was not unusual for him to walk 50 miles to get from one preaching point to another.

During the early part of this period

REDMOND—1896

Methodism erected its first church in Redmond in 1896. Congregational Sunday school had been organized in 1888, with R. Cottrill, superintendent. Building known as "Perrogo Church," erected earlier.

Trustees of the Methodist Church were, Robert Roberts, Cassius M. Whitehead, J. G. Anderson, James Stricker, P. Thayer. Early out-of-town pastors were, Rev. Thomas Houlston, lay preacher from Gilman Park, Seattle; Rev. William Bowman, Rev. J. W. Walker, retired.

In 1926, church was moved to N. E. 80th Street. Rev. Ralph W. D. Brown, pastor. He led in enlarging the building to make room for the Epworth League. Remodeled structure was dedicated by Bishop William O. Shepard, in 1928. Rev. William E. Callahan was pastor at time. Rev. Waldo W. Pierson, was pastor, 1933-36. Under his leadership, church advanced, parsonage built without debt. Rev. Harry L. Allen, 1938-44, was first to serve the congregation for six years. He paid church debt and added two rooms to parsonage. Under Rev. Revelle Roach, 1944-49, membership doubled. Rev. Robert L. Lyons, 1953-59, added the educational unit and under Rev. Peter Misner, 1959-64, the sanctuary was completed.

In 1964, Rev. Frank Jackson appointed. Membership was 358, church school enrollment, 203. Woman's Society of Christian Service, 80. They gave $1,292.

travel between Eastern and Western Washington was along the Columbia River, where The Dalles threatened the life of every traveler. Cargoes must be portaged around the falls, requiring the aid of other persons.

Concerning this journey, Rev. H. K. Hines[1] said, "In addition to this the Indians residing at that location were reported as very hostile and the old voyagers of the Northwest Company and of the Hudson's Bay Company were always compelled to bear their burdens in one hand while they held their rifles in the other for instant use, as they went to and fro on errands of barter."

Hines further said, "The strongest expeditions were sometimes defeated and it required all the skill and bravery of such daring and disciplined mountaineers as Ross, McDougall, McClellan, or McCay to insure a safe passage through the robber bands of Wishram. Dr. McLoughlin himself said to Mr. Lee, 'Before you came to the country we could not send a boat past The Dalles without an armed guard of sixty men. Now we go up singly and no one is robbed.'"

COLUMBIA IN MID-WINTER VERY DANGEROUS

Rev. H. K. Hines quoted excerpts from the diary of Rev. Jason Lee describing a journey up the Columbia in mid-winter. Lee wrote, "We frequently passed through patches of snow and broken ice which greatly retarded our speed. The breeze increased to a gale which rendered our condition perilous. The river soon became dreadfully agitated and our situation became more and more serious. The wind was on our quarter, and, with our blanket-sail which we had rigged early in the day we were able to drive before the waves except when we were retarded by the islands of floating snow and ice. To land was impossible.

"By laying as closely to the wind as possible we could just clear the rugged

192

points of ice which had formed out from the shore, and the rocky bluffs which arose in aweful sublimity over our heads. In this perilous condition, by exerting ourselves to the utmost we could just keep before the waves so as to prevent their breaking over our quarter. . . . We soon encountered a dense mass of snow and ice. The waves began to break over our boat, and the man at the stern sung out lustily, 'Pull away!' as our only hope of safety. We saw a mountain wave coming, but could not escape it entirely. It broke over our quarter and nearly engulfed the man at the helm, and left a great quantity of water thick with snow and ice in our canoe. Fortunately we were soon through the snow and able to clear a point of rock where we were in imminent danger of being dashed upon. Beyond this the waves were not so high, and we passed on until near dark before we could find a place where we could land and encamp for the night.

"The snow was twelve inches deep," Lee continued, "which we removed with our paddles, and made a fire, and with some difficulty procured wood enough for the night. After supper the Indians talked over our danger. The man in the stern of the canoe said if he had been afraid of the water when it dashed upon him and not looked well to the canoe, it would have been upset and all plunged into the river. Perhaps the Indians could have gained the shore but for that I was too heavily clothed and would soon have gone down. . . . But I was fully composed and able to stay myself entirely on the Lord. But I see he has more work, or more sufferings, for me. Well, all I ask is to be able to fulfill my day."

MISSIONARY TRAVEL ON WILLAMETTE BY CANOE

Travel by Methodist missionaries along the Willamette also was by canoe. The falls at Oregon City imperiled the life of all travelers passing that way. Men on shore with strong ropes must let the canoe down the rapids. In 1842,

Rev. Jason Lee[1] and some companions all but lost their lives at this place. In 1843, four Methodist missionaries and two Indians did lose their lives there. The missionaries were Cornelius Rogers, his wife, the eldest daughter of Rev. David Leslie, her sister Aurelia, and W. W. Raymond.

Rev. Jacob Mills,[5] pioneer missionary in Montana, described a journey through Idaho at the turn of the century. "One day I had the beginning of a seventy-mile drive to make. A friendly man who was going the same way offered to accompany me. During the whole of that first day the snow fell. . . . There were no homes or houses where we could have a meal, a bed, or any domestic comfort. Hot coffee, flapjacks, fat bacon, and some canned stuffs were the acceptable bill of fare. Supper over . . . we turned in, wrapping up in blankets and nestling under an overhanging arch formed by the top of a small tree and a high rock. But we quietly stretched ourselves on the bed, and patiently snored till the morrow. When arising we found the ground frozen. . . . We enjoyed to the fullest extent the coffee and other bracing viands.

"Then on we went, all day, repeating the same experience again next evening. This all to make appointments, and see that the work goes on."

Rev. D. G. LeSourd,[4] presiding elder of the Puget Sound District, described an experience on the Nooksack River in 1885, when travel from the Upper to the Lower Nooksack either was by foot or canoe. LeSourd's group chose the latter.

"It was after the camp meeting was over, that we three preachers took passage with nine Indians including four children in a large river canoe," he said. "It was the time of the June floods and the river was running bank full. Our boat, rushing at great speed, struck a submerged log that lay across the channel."

Then follows a thrilling account of an unforgettable experience that could have cost lives.

TRINITY, SEQUIM—1897

Sequim first appeared among appointments, in 1897. Rev. L. M. Hawthorn, pastor. Next year there were 36 members, 75 in Sunday school. Left to be supplied. A church building valued at $1,200 reported.

Rev. A. J. McNemee, appointed in 1905, remained two years. There were 58 members, 96 in Sunday school. Two years later, Rev. C. F. Bennett found 40 church members and 89 in Sunday school. In 1915 Rev. F. F. Frisbe reported 36 members, 70 in Sunday school.

Rev. J. M. Amundson became pastor in 1925, took pledges for new building. When not reappointed, in 1928, became Presbyterian minister, organized church of that denomination at Sequim.

Rev. D. S. McGuire, in 1928, found 104 members, 303 in Sunday school. Church building erected, in 1929, at cost of $20,000. In 1938, when Rev. W. G. R. Dan became pastor, there were 200 members, 150 in Sunday school. Building valued at $21,500.

After 1960 members Blyn church were counted with those at Sequim, which after 1951 held title to the Blyn property. Trinity paid to Board of Home Missions and Church Extension the loan held against property.

In 1964 Rev. Vincent S. Hart, Junior, was pastor. Members, 256; church school enrollment 186. Woman's Society members, 76. They gave $2,000.

194

Dr. LeSourd's Canoe Party Wrecked on Log

"In spite of efforts to ward off danger the boat upset carrying all down with a whirlpool under the log, saving one Indian woman who leaped from the boat and landed safe with her babe, waist deep in the jam of logs." LeSourd said, "Brother J. W. Dobbs, Chief Lynden Jim, and myself went down in the suck of the whirlpool ten or fifteen feet where we were at the mercy of the current. But lifting our hearts in prayer, God heard and answered. When I was almost suffocated. . . . I came to the surface and, trying to swim ashore, found all my strength gone and simply floated till I clutched a limb and held on till Lynden Jim came to my rescue and held me up till I could stand on my feet.

"All the others made their escape save one Indian girl, the granddaughter of Lynden Jim, who was drowned. We went on foot to Lynden leaving our hats, overcoats, valises in the river and were thankful to be received into the homes of generous friends who did all they could for our comfort."

The Methodist itinerants who traveled over these rough trails were men powerful of body and stout of spirit and their travels were for one purpose. Rev. G. W. Kennedy,[6] a Methodist minister who served in Eastern Oregon and Washington from 1872-1924 repeated the experience related to him by a man who had been a cowboy, "God in his goodness sent a little preacher down to that country," the man said. "One day we saw a man riding across the prairies singing 'Jesus Lover of My Soul.' He came to the ranch, got down and said, 'Boys I want you to put my pony up and feed him. I am a Methodist circuit rider and have come out here to stay with you.' I looked at him and loved him, but I was afraid to get close to him. My heart would not beat right. I was afraid to ride his horse to water for fear it would fall down and kill me. Brother, his horse was religious. His saddlebags

AMERICAN RIDGE, IDAHO—1898

Methodist church, at American Ridge, erected in 1898. Rev. C. D. Bell, pastor. Rev. W. W. Van Dusen was presiding elder. Money donated by Methodists, Presbyterians, United Brethren, Dunkards. Trustees: Harry Belheart, Joe Davidson, E. W. Jessup.

Pastor Bell did most of the hauling, from the Peterson saw mill near Tory. Among several carpenters who donated labor were Mr. Utter and Mr. Duthie. Building enclosed by harvest time, when all hands went to the fields to work, Pastor Bell with them.

By end of harvest the Annual Conference had appointed Mr. Bell to Leland, Rev. C. E. Gibson, presiding elder, Rev. E. A. Thomas becoming pastor. Bell, a carpenter, came back to help finish the building.

Rev. P. A. Cool, pastor First Church, Spokane, delivered sermon at dedication in late fall. Church was free of debt, costing $1,200 and was available for use by various denominations whose adherents had contributed to its erection.

American Ridge first appeared among appointments in Pacific Northwest Conference in 1932. Rev. E. J. Smith, pastor, first year. In 1938 Rev. W. S. T. Gray, pastor. There was one church building, seven members and no church school. It last appeared among appointments in 1941. In 1944 the historian reported the building still standing, in good condition.

195

would put you under conviction. When we sat down to eat and went to help ourselves as usual, he said, 'Wait men, I'm going to ask a blessing.'

"Everything was still as death," the man continued. "When he turned loose my mind went back to my boyhood when I heard the old father ask a blessing at home.

METHODIST ITINERANT PREACHERS FACED REAL HARDSHIPS

"The boys began to eat and before they were through he said, 'Now men, don't leave here until we have prayers.' I was afraid to go. After supper he took his Bible and sat down and read a chapter with a good deal of Hell in it. He read as long as he wanted to. He was boss of the devil. He got down on his knees and prayed just as loud as a man could. He shook us over the pit. I saw billows of Hell. My heart went awful fast. Then it would seem to stop dead. It seemed like I was going to die. He told God about everything we had ever done, all the stealing, lying, fighting, and cursing. When prayers were over we were just barely able to walk out but we got out as quickly as possible.

"The next morning the preacher asked the blessing again and said, 'Don't you boys go out until we have had prayers, then I will have to leave you, but I will be back in about a month.' After breakfast he prayed until it nearly broke our hearts and then he got on his pony and rode away. About a month rolled around and we got sort of anxious to see the man again. He came again and acted about as he had the other time, but some of us didn't do just as we did before.

"When he was through with the evening prayer I went out with the boys and told them that prayer had been down on my nerves for a month. I couldn't beat it any longer, that I would quit then and there the blasphemous life I was living. Then I went into the bushes and told it all to God. I tell you, before the next day dawned I was a changed man. Many a faithful pastor

CLARKSTON—1898

Methodist Church, Concord (now Clarkston), January 8, 1898. Rev. Henry Brown, Lewiston, preached there, 1896. Building erected 1899, occupied 1900. Board of Church Extension loaned $250, granted $250. Cost $1,250.

In 1900, name Concord changed to Clarkston. First offering plates were corn poppers covered with cloth.

Four ministers first year: Rev. Jacob F. Sargent, Rev. M. S. Anderson, Rev. T. C. Craig, Rev. R. D. Osterhaut, 1899. Rev. W. B. Eakin 1900-04.

J. S. Beard, P. F. Wolford, F. W. Dustan, trustees. F. W. Dustan first Sunday school superintendent. Mrs. Louis Chaflin first president Ladies Aid; Miss Laura Wood, president Epworth League.

New basement, 1911, Rev. H. L. Beightol, pastor. In 1920, furnace replaced, cost, $2,282.75. Three-floor addition, 1945-52, Rev. E. G. Ranton.

New building begun, September 20, 1959, Rev. Guy Roberts, pastor. Rev. Ac 'C. Wischmeier district superintendent. Baptists purchased old building. First service new building, October 2, 1960, Rev. G. Edward Knight, pastor. Church consecrated, January 1961, Bishop Everett W. Palmer, preaching. By 1962 congregation felt need for educational unit in near future. Cost of building $98,000 plus donated labor. In 1964, Rev. Kenneth W. Country-man, pastor, second year. Members, 489. Church school, 373. Woman's Society members, 116, gave $1,081.

196

found the stars for his crown out there among the roughest of men.' "

ONE HUNDRED-FIFTY MILES, HORSE AND BUGGY, TO REACH FIRST CONFERENCE

Kennedy, whose first appointment was to the Yakima Circuit in 1872, described the journey he and his bride made following his marriage, July 31, 1879, to Miss Bell Small of Baker City. On Saturday morning he and his bride started for the Annual Conference to be held at Walla Walla one hundred and fifty miles away. The journey was by horse and buggy. They spent a few days at a camp meeting at Grand Ronde Valley, where he preached and helped the pastor, Rev. G. W. Granis. They then proceeded toward Walla Walla over the Blue Mountains. When they arrived at Bingham Springs Halfway Place, they stopped for the night. "There was some kind of 'fandango' going on," Kennedy said, "and the good proprietor could give us only a bed on the floor, on buffalo robes with a pair of blankets. We were tired and glad to get that, but oh, that noise put two days together without sleep." The next day they drove forty miles over the high mountains and, on arrival, he preached the opening sermon of the conference session. "This was a succession of practical experiences most surely for a bride of five days," he said.

In 1852, the only road in the Territory of Washington was that from Warbassport on the Cowlitz to Olympia[7] and this was scarcely passable for wagons, especially in the winter. There was a sort of trail from Olympia to Fort Nisqually with a ferry across the river at Packwood's place.

The ferry was unreliable. The river here, at high water, was about two hundred feet wide and the current always swift and dangerous. The settlers had once or twice built a flimsy bridge across it, but their work invariably was washed away by the first high water, or made useless by changes in the river.

BREMERTON, FIRST CHURCH—1899

First Church Bremerton organized June, 1899, thirty members. Trustees: F. Coder, D. J. Davis, S. H. West, Lucy L. Smith, Asa H. Coder, W. J. Bolinger, A. V. Coder. Organizing pastor, Rev. M. S. Anderson. Rev. A. J. Joslyn, presiding elder. Articles of Incorporation filed, 1900.

Building, Fifth and Pacific, costing $5,000, for William McKinley Memorial Methodist Episcopal Church, dedicated December 7, 1902. Rev. W. S. Harrington, presiding elder, Seattle District, delivered sermon. Members, 48.

In 1910, building enlarged, Rev. R. L. Wolfe, pastor. In 1918, church used for emergency hospital, influenza victims. That year, Rev. Francis A. La-Violett, pastor, led in erecting new building with aid of Centenary funds.

Twenty-fifth anniversary, observed, 1927, Rev. Alexander G. Bennett, pastor. Rev. B. F. Brooks, former pastor delivered sermon. Rev. Roy L. Sprague, pastor, observed 30th anniversary, 1932. Mortgage, burned in 1942, Rev. Martindale Woods, pastor.

In 1962, action was taken to relocate. Rev. Albert H. Wilson, pastor. Church building sold and building erected on Marine Drive and Bertha Avenue. Congregation pledged $81,000.

In 1964, Rev. Kenneth W. Peterson, pastor, second year. Members, 752. Church school enrollment, 469. Woman's Society members, 166, gave, $2,260. Building value $428,323. Parsonage, $17,500.

Chief Factor Douglas of the Hudson's Bay Company nearly lost his life there in the early fifties.

In December, 1852, a subscription was taken for improving the road up the Cowlitz, and the county commissioners authorized a new road to be let out from Yelm to McCallister's place near the mouth of the Nisqually. They planned another from Steilacoom to Duwamish, which was urgently demanded by the people of Seattle in order to give them access to the metropolis and communication by land to the world outside.

ROAD CROSSING CASCADES OF VITAL IMPORTANCE

Settlers on the Sound felt it most important to build a road across the Cascades which would permit the immigrant trains to come direct from Walla Walla to Seattle. Until such a road could be provided travelers must continue to go down the Columbia to The Dalles, and thence by raft and portage around the Cascades to Portland. Thus, they first reached the Willamette for which many of them had started originally and where many others remained, who would otherwise have come to the Sound.

Dexter Horton, a Methodist Protestant, who later became one of Seattle's leading financiers, was a member of the expedition which, in 1855, decided upon the wagon route across the Cascades.

Local travel remained difficult. For example when Rev. Jerry McKean was appointed, in 1891, to serve the church at Sultan in Snohomish County, he lived at Monroe making his way to Sultan on horseback. The road between the two places was a rough slashing through the dense timber, and often was impassable in winter. At such times John Kager, a local preacher, filled the pulpit. He lived at Startup, and the road was said to be worse than that between Sultan and Monroe, but he walked, often accompanied by his children, sometime

---

CUSTER—1898

First Methodist sermon at Custer probably delivered by Rev. J. W. Patterson of Ferndale in the Custer schoolhouse in 1898. Church incorporated June 24, 1903. Trustees were J. H. Kirkpatrick, Sherman Johnson, David Hintz, Ed Brown, and William Creasey. In 1905, Ed Brown donated ground for a building. Church and parsonage complete by 1908. Rev. J. H. Berringer was pastor. In 1907 the pews were sawed by Fred Jeffers from timber which came from the farm of Glen Rogers, member of the church. An electric organ was given by Will Hawkins in honor of his deceased wife, Josephine. A lighted cross was donated by Dr. Carl Hyles. In 1956 Dr. Hyles donated a home to be used as a parsonage. Rev. O. J. Rorabach was pastor. This property dedicated in 1956. The mortgage was paid under Rev. John Methone.

In 1964 the congregation celebrated their 60th anniversary. In 1950 and '55 Rev. Thomas H. Roddey did external remodelling of the church. Electric chimes were installed by Rev. Dennis DeVore in 1947. In 1964 Rev. Jessie L. Tooley was pastor. There were 96 members of the church, 69 in the church school, and 24 members of the Woman's Society of Christian Service. This group gave $522.

returning at night for the evening service. After the railroad began
operating in 1892 all pedestrians walked the railroad track which
had at least no mud holes.

KING COUNTY TRAVEL IN 1885 VERY DIFFICULT

Rev. A. J. McNemee[8] described the difficulty of travel in King
County. "When I took charge of the Squawk Mission September 18,
1885," he said, "we had at Seattle two preachers, Rev. John M. Dennison of First Church, and Rev. L. A. Banks at Battery Street. Rev.
John Flinn had White River Circuit and my appointment included
nearly all the rest of King County to the Snohomish County line. It
took me three weeks to go around the circuit afoot as there were
scarcely any roads, only a sled road or a pack trail and often only a
blazed path, sometimes not even that, to follow. Often when going
down the Snoqualmie River bottoms I followed the bear trails in
preference to crawling through the brush."

McNemee described the building of a church on this circuit. "I
spent four weeks burning down the big fir trees and clearing the logs
and brush on this one acre of land for the church," he said. "Some of
these trees were four to seven feet thick.
On the subscription paper for the
church I had pledged in cash $12.50, in
lumber $60, and in labor $100. I had
applied to our Board of Church Extension, for a donation of $150 which
money was not received until long after
the church was built.

"Kean's mill where I was to get the
lumber was three miles above Falls City
on the Snoqualmie River," McNemee
continued. "When George Stevenson
and I went after the lumber we had to
spend three days rafting other lumber
before we could get it. At daylight one
morning we got our raft ready, and
started down the river. Mr. Kean, an
experienced river pilot, offered us his
help. As he and George got on the raft

CONNELL—1899

Methodism in Connell pioneered by
Germans. Rev. Adam Buehler, German
Methodist, at Paradise Flats, organized
first church, 1899. First building later
became chicken coop. In 1900 Buehler's
new home used for worship. In 1901,
new school building used. Church incorporated, 1901. Rev. J. W. Beckley
pastor.

New building erected, 1908, Rev. C. H.
Waltersdorf, pastor. Dedicated 1909,
Rev. H. Haueisen, pastor.

In 1901, German Methodism organized
in Connell. In 1906, moved. Pastor
Paradise Center served Connell.

English speaking Methodists organized, Connell, 1904, Rev. Ely Fly, pastor, erected building, used until 1949.

In 1905, Rev. J. F. Cook, pastor,
served Eltopia, Mesa, Kahlotus, Pasco.

In 1924, German church, Paradise,
merged with congregation in town. In
1936, German and English congregations united, used English building.
Rev. E. J. Smith, pastor.

In 1940, Rev. Myron H. Sharrard,
pastor, plans laid for new building.
Started 1947, Rev. Waldo W. Pierson,
pastor. Committee: Herman Kleind-
worth, Clarence Finkbeiner, Norman
Wirth, Mrs. Wesley Kliphardt, Mrs.
Ellen Kelsey. Building opened, April 3,
1949, Bishop Kennedy, preaching.

In 1964, Rev. Darrell L. Iwerks, pastor, fifth year. Membership, 223, church
school, 186. Woman's Society members
48. Value church building, $126,000.
Parsonage, $22,000.

they at once lashed themselves to it with ropes. When I asked them the reason they pointed to the seething whirlpool just below the mill and said there was danger of being washed overboard. At first I thought they were trying to play a joke on me. I was to steer the raft and being a good swimmer I concluded to take the chance.

"When we reached the whirlpool we were tossed around like a chip on the water and we went around several times before I could steer the raft into an eddy. It having sunk in the water, we were left standing knee deep on a raft with ten thousand feet of lumber. After hard work we reached the channel and the current took us swiftly down the river.

RAFTING LUMBER ON SNOQUALMIE RIVER DANGEROUS

"After we had gone half a mile, Mr. Kean said we were over the worst of it and he left us. Afterwards the raft struck a big boulder and we were hung up in the middle of the river. The only thing we could do was sit on that raft, the rain falling in torrents, waiting for the river to rise and float us off. This was on Thanksgiving Day, 1885, but there was no dinner for us that day. After two hours the raft floated and as there was a freshet and strong current in the river we soon reached the landing in Falls City. About 2:00 P.M. George said he had been away for four days and wanted to go home and see his family so he left me to carry the lumber up the slippery bank or lose it, lest the freshet should carry it away. Ben Bailey helped me for one and a half hours. It was dark before the last of the lumber was carried above the high water. Of all hard days of work I thought that was the worst. I had been out in the storm since daylight and had had nothing to eat, but I was thankful that we had saved the lumber."

Similar conditions of travel handicapped Methodist ministers in Northern Idaho. The historian of the church at

LAPWAI, IDAHO—1898

Mission at Lapwai, Idaho, organized by Rev. Henry Spaulding, Presbyterian, associate of Dr. Marcus Whitman, 1836. In 1898, Methodist Episcopal Church assigned Rev. George Waters to serve community. Later, Methodists and Presbyterians agreed, Methodists to withdraw from Lapwai, Presbyterians from Yakima Indian Reservation.

About 1910, group of Lapwai Indians appealed to presiding elder, Methodist Episcopal Church, South, to accept them into Methodist church. Indians advised to remain loyal to denomination. Later they returned, saying, "If you do not receive us into the Methodist Church, we will unite with some other Protestant denomination."

Sixty Indians were received into the Methodist church. Building erected at time, destroyed by fire in early 1920's. Replaced by building still used, 1964. With Methodist union, 1939, Lapwai entered Pacific Northwest Conference, Walla Walla District. Rev. S. J. Maxwell, pastor. In 1940, Rev. Stephen J. Reubin, pastor. There were 100 members, 75 in church school. Church valued at $2,400. In 1950 there were 71 members and 118 in church school. That year 22 members of Woman's Society gave $326.

In 1964, Lapwai was attached to Orofino and served by Rev. James H. Thompson, fourth year. Membership, 76, church school enrollment, 75. Woman's Society, members, 21, giving $150. Building valued at $18,000.

200

THESE ITINERANT PASTORS TRAVELED THOUSANDS OF MILES

Rev. William Roberts

Rev. William J. Rule

NORTHWEST'S GREATEST CIRCUIT RIDER

Rev. William Roberts came to Oregon in 1847, to succeed Rev. George Gary, as superintendent of the Oregon Mission. Later, as presiding elder, pastor, and missionary to the Indians and Chinese, he traveled more than 200,000 miles, a record equaled by no other American circuit rider, save Francis Asbury.

Rev. Andrew J. Joslyn

Rev. Harry Chappell

Coeur d'Alene reported that most of the ministers there, in the early days, were circuit riders serving Post Falls, Harrison, Rathdrum, and sometimes Hayden Lake as well as Coeur d'Alene. This was true of Rev. T. G. Hodgson who in the 1890's served the charge for eight years. His granddaughter by marriage, Mrs. Tom Miller, states she believed that he sometimes preached at St. Mary's. His regular circuit, somewhat over eighty miles, was covered with horse and buggy. When he went to St. Mary's, another forty miles was added to his route.

Travel on the Sound by canoe, even with Indian guides, was not always safe. Catharine Blaine, in 1854,[9] wrote relatives that Captain Barstow, and Colonel George N. McConaha, speaker of the Legislature, coming down from Olympia in a canoe manned by six Indians, were overtaken by a violent squall which upset the canoe, drowning the white men and two Indians.

Rev. David E. Blaine walked to appointments outside of Seattle. June 26, 1854, Catharine wrote home, "Yesterday Mr. Blaine went up the river to preach. He has an appointment five miles up, once in three weeks. He walks up and back and the road is such a one as you old country folks never dreamed of calling a road. Stumps, logs, holes, and hills so that a walk of ten miles over it and two sermons, together with the care of the Sunday school, is no very small day's work, and yet, I have never heard him complain of feeling Mondayish."

On August 6, 1865, Rev. David Blaine wrote his parents from Oregon City describing his trip to that place from Seattle. "You will learn before receiving this that I left my good wife at home three weeks ago last Thursday to attend Conference. It has been a grievous affliction to me to endure this separation, but to Katey, who has been alone, it has probably been much more so. But I had not the means to pay both our expenses to Oregon and our arrangements at

RAYMOND CIRCUIT—
1898, 1912, 1915

Three churches on Vancouver District, often included in Raymond Circuit, include Willapa, which first appeared in 1898, Rev. E. C. Parker, pastor. There were thirty-one members and 70 in Sunday school. East Raymond first appeared in 1912, teamed with Lebam, Rev. George Abbott, pastor. Church building was worth $1,200, thirty in the Sunday school and 16 members, in 1913. Menlo appeared in 1915. In 1916, with Lebam, a total of 33 members. In 1922 again teamed with Lebam, Rev. W. T. Beatty, pastor. In 1939 East Raymond, Old Willapa teamed together, Rev. Clark M. Smith, pastor. He also served Lebam and Menlo. In 1950, East Raymond, Old Willapa, Raymond served by Rev. Harry E. Gardner. In 1960, East Raymond, Menlo, Willapa, served by Rev. Kenneth B. MacLagan. Parish had 305 members. There were 58 in Woman's Society. They gave $531. In 1964 Rev. John Larsson, in third year. He reported 313 members in five organized churches. There were 325 enrolled in five church schools. There were 58 enrolled in Woman's Society of Christian Service groups on this parish and the women gave $607 that year. Church buildings on the parish were valued at $125,650, while the parsonage was valued at $11,705.

202

home seem to make it necessary that she remain or someone else.

DAVID BLAINE DESCRIBES HIS TRIP TO CONFERENCE

"You may wish a short account of my journey hither," Blaine said. "Brother Morse and myself purchased a canoe in partnership and came as far as Olympia in that. From Olympia we came on foot some sixty miles to the Cowlitz Landing carrying our saddlebags. Made this distance in two days. We might have had a horse for $10 but we thought walking nearly as easy as riding, besides we could not have earned $10 so easy in any other way. We came down the Cowlitz in a canoe for $4 to Monticello at the mouth of the river. We came to Portland in a steamer for $5. From Portland to Oregon City in a steamer for nothing."

Something of the reaction of a wife when her husband was away on the Sound in a canoe was expressed by Catharine Blaine September 16, 1855. She said, "Mr. Blaine came home a week ago last Friday, and last Tuesday started off again. He is now attending a camp meeting held twenty miles south of Olympia. It was to close tomorrow, so I cannot expect Mr. Blaine back again before the middle of this week, and very likely he will not be here before the last.

CATHARINE BLAINE DESCRIBES PROBLEMS OF PREACHER'S WIFE

"It will depend somewhat on the weather, and what opportunity he may have to come from Olympia. There was no one from here went with him. He had his arrangements all made to go alone in his canoe contrary to the advice of almost everybody, and in opposition to my remonstrances. I thought it would be not only exceedingly fatiguing but decidedly unsafe, but he insisted there is no danger at this season of the year.

"Providentially, however, a vessel came along that was going to Olympia and he went in her, taking his canoe to

SEABOLD—1899

Church work at Seabold, Bainbridge Island, started in 1899, when women organized a Ladies Aid. In 1908, group decided to organize a church. Since Lutherans were predominant, it was agreed to operate under Lutheran banner, attached to no denomination.

Thirty-three members signed registration books. Articles of Incorporation adopted, June 9, 1909. First church required two years to build. N. Kline, construction foreman, and boys from school spent afternoons molding cement blocks for basement. Benches and windows purchased from Lutheran Church in Seattle.

Church dedicated, 1910, C. J. Carlson reelected president of Board.

In 1955, congregation decided to affiliate with denomination. They consulted Council of Churches and were assigned to Methodists. In 1956, Methodists began to lead. Rev. Clark J. Wood, district superintendent, appointed Rev. William O. Pflaum, retired. Afterwards, Rev. Don Cramer, student at University of Puget Sound, and Rev. John Haygood, recently graduated from theological seminary, served. In 1960, Rev. Justin Morrill, pastor. In 1962, church building moved to new location one block down street, enlarged and renovated.

Rev. Justin I. Morrill was reappointed for fifth year, in 1964. Church had 117 members, with church school enrollment, 170. Woman's Society of Christian Service with 35 members, gave $650.

return in if he has no other chance. I rather hope if he does venture out alone in it he will get just a little ducking, not enough to hurt him any but teach him a lesson of prudence."

These conditions did not change overnight nor did the coming of railroads bring immediate relief to the Northwest Methodist itinerant. As late as 1892, Rev. T. B. Ford,[10] presiding elder of the Seattle District, half in humor remarked of the pastor serving the Snoqualmie Circuit, "Brother Schoonmaker, a hard worker and a good walker (for he rides a circuit he must walk), has labored earnestly, enduring hardness as a good soldier, and had success at Snoqualmie."

CHAPTER IX

Northwest Methodists were determined to dispel ignorance. Through elementary schools, Sunday schools, Bible study, good literature and church publications they sought enlightenment. A challenging story of—

Men of Learning

Northwest Methodists First Set Up Schools

From the earliest days Methodist leaders in the Northwest worked with determination to bring enlightenment to minds and hearts of men through education.[1]

The first step of Oregon Methodists to evangelize the Indians was to set up schools for the children. It was for that purpose that Rev. Jason Lee brought Cyrus Shepard to Oregon. Likewise, when Lee sent Dr. John P. Richmond to head the Nisqually Indian mission, the minister and his family were accompanied by the first Methodist teacher in Washington, Miss Chloe Aurelia Clark.

Schools were important in the minds of settlers. Witness a letter by Rev. David Blaine,[2] who wrote a little more than a week after arriving on Elliott Bay: "I suppose Catharine will take the school here for the next three months at about $65 per month. A subscription was started yesterday. One man who has only two children to send has signed for $100."

On August 4, 1854, Catharine[2] wrote to her sister, Seraphina, "Here the children have no school now, but during the three months I taught them, they seemed to feel how great the privilege they were permitted to enjoy was, and every moment was improved. They felt it to be a great punishment to be kept from school and if asked which they would rather do, play or go to school, how quickly they would reply, 'go to school.'"

This keen interest in elementary education was Conference wide. Two years after Methodism entered Washington Territory to stay,

205

the Oregon Annual Conference declared the position of the Church on education: "Knowledge is essential to individual and national prosperity, enterprise, and freedom; to the spread and perpetuity of civilization; to the continuance and increase of facilities for human progress, happiness, and power; yet none of these can be obtained by education or knowledge unless accompanied by 'the fear of the Lord which is the beginning of wisdom.'"

The Quarterly Conference of the church at Walla Walla, held in October, 1860, resolved: ". . . that in the judgment of this Quarterly Conference, measures should be taken at the earliest practicable period for the erection of such academic building and the commencement of a school in this valley, as the educational requirements of the Church and community demand." This brave resolution came from a Quarterly Conference, financial reports to which reflected dire poverty. Offerings during the past quarter were $23 for the pastor and $2 for missions.

While it is not known that such a school grew out of this resolution, it is certain that the valley was not long without an elementary school. On September 30, 1865, the Quarterly Conference voted to hold the next meeting at Moore's schoolhouse.

The Oregon Conference, in 1866, set forth the Methodist attitude toward the public school. "We regard the common school system as one of the best safeguards of American citizenship, and rejoice in the general spread of knowledge by its means," the statement declared. "While we should deprecate any diversion of the common school to sectarian purposes, yet, regarding the Bible as the source of civil and religious liberty, we trust it will continue to be read in all our schools without note or comment."

WASHOUGAL—1899

First Methodist pastor at Columbia, later Washougal, was Rev. E. C. Parker, 1899. The following year he reported 14 members and 46 in two Sunday schools, church valued at $500. In 1908, Rev. George A. Landen, presiding elder, reported modest chapel at Washougal, erected during previous year, valued at $925.

In 1909, Rev. E. J. Huston, pastor. Parsonage built by A. A. Hathaway, furnished by women of church. Evidently parsonage not property of the church because, five years later, Rev. V. A. Spicker reported the old church had been converted into a parsonage. Rev. R. B. Parcel, 1918-24 served a term as mayor of Washougal.

In 1919, Hannah E. Tewksbury, of Pennsylvania, gave $300, through Division Church Extension, as memorial to her uncle, Eugene D. Tewksbury.

In 1931, Washougal had 125 members, and average church school attendance, 140. In 1940, Rev. Kenneth Dunkelberger served Washougal and Salmon Creek. In 1944, Rev. Howard P. Buck lived at East Mill Plain and served Washougal. In 1953-55, Rev. Joe Walker, pastor, placed emphasis on social issues. Some conservatives, objecting left the church.

In 1964, Rev. J. Dean Stout, pastor, fourth year. Membership, 133; church school enrollment, 141. Woman's Society, members, 36, gave $314. Church value, $45,000. Parsonage, $6,500.

SUNDAY SCHOOLS THE MEANS OF SPREADING RELIGIOUS KNOWLEDGE

Northwest Methodism soon abandoned the attempt to operate elemen-

206

tary schools, believing that this work could be done more adequately by the state. But, in the beginning, the Church seized upon the Sunday school as the most effective means of spreading that religious knowledge considered essential to spiritual growth and Christian citizenship.

A resolution adopted by the Oregon Conference in 1855 declared, "We are more than ever convinced that our Sunday school enterprise should call forth our most earnest prayers, and persevering zeal for the promotion of its objects." Members of the Conference pledged to present to the people the claims of the Sunday School Union of the Church and to take up collections for the same.

A year later the committee recommended that the Conference members pledge to organize Sunday schools where two or more persons could be assembled for that purpose. The Conference also was committed to encourage all adults under the care of the churches to attend Sunday school.

Small Beginnings in the Sunday Schools

In 1855 in all Oregon and Washington there were reported to be 58 Methodist schools, an increase of 24 over the previous year. There were 351 officers and teachers, an increase of 165. The 1,389 pupils enrolled represented an increase of 538. There were 6,246 books in Sunday school libraries, an increase of 3,693. The number of Bible classes had increased to 19 from 10 the year before. The 113 conversions through the Sunday school was an increase of 92 above the previous year.

Those early Sunday schools faced problems that sound strangely contemporary. In 1857 the Conference resolved that parents should be urged to lead as well as send their children to Sunday school. The following year the conversion of 75 children through the

---

CONCONULLY—1900

Conconully first appeared among appointments of conference in 1900. Rev. A. W. Trine, supplying for first year. The following year he reported 75 members on circuit, four Sunday schools with 100 enrolled. In 1903 Trine reported 46 members on circuit, two Sunday schools with 100 enrolled. One church building was valued at $3,300.

Rev. I. V. Parker, supply, in 1904. In 1905 A. W. Trine was pastor again. Rev. J. F. Redfern was pastor in 1907, and A. S. Redfern served circuit in 1908. In 1910 Rev. J. J. Pacey found 70 members, two Sunday schools, with 125 enrolled. The church building was worth $3,500. In 1914 Rev. C. W. Geisler began a three year pastorate. In 1918 Rev. J. W. Downs found 60 members in two churches.

In 1923 Rev. Harry Fleisher became supply. In 1926 Rev. John Moede began four year pastorate. In 1930 Rev. C. W. Groth found three congregations, 35 members. In 1940 there were 17 members and 70 in church school, Rev. Walter Pierson, supply. In 1950 Rev. Benjamin Peters made no statistical report.

In the late 1950's the church was not listed among the appointments. But in 1965 Rev. Paul F. Ashbrook was appointed to serve this place along with Omak and Nespelem.

SERVING THE YOUNG PEOPLE OF THE PACIFIC NORTHWEST

Lazy F. Ranch

Rev. J. H. B. Royal

SUMMER CAMPS INSPIRE YOUTH

Summer camping for youth began east and west in Washington, early in the twentieth century, soon becoming integral part of the training program of the church. Thousands of Youth have had vision broadened and spiritual life deepened.

Beulah Park
Norwegian-Danish Camp
Vashon Island

Rev. E. M. Randall

Epworth Heights

Sunday schools, placed the seal of divine approval upon the movement.

"The Sunday schools have been called the cradle of religion, the nursery of the church," said the committee in 1858. "In our children are the future members, stewards, leaders, exhorters, ministers, editors, authors, and bishops."

Some ministers of that early day strongly advocated the Sunday school cause in season and out. Rev. J. H. B. Royal [3] was one of these. An incident illustrating his zeal and its outcome transpired when he was pastor at Steilacoom in 1859. Some of the officers and men at Fort Steilacoom frequently attended church. In a sermon Royal emphasized the importance of the Sunday school. At the close of the service Colonel Silas C. Casey, Commandant of the post, came forward and said, "After making such an excellent address you ought to receive $100 for the Sunday school work." Lieutenant H. M. Roberts, of the United States Engineering Corps, standing by, said: "My first impulse was to give twenty-five cents, and I gave it, but that was not enough; allow me to give five dollars more."

The next day a note was received from Lieutenant Roberts, saying: "I called at your home last night. Not finding you, I take this means of sending you another five dollars for Sunday school work."

A few months thereafter a second note was received which read:

"Dear Mr. Royal: After leaving you I sailed for San Francisco. While on the ocean I thought of your address, and decided that when I went into winter quarters I would organize a Sunday school among the children of the fort, and have a Bible class for the adults.

"I have written the editor of the Pacific Christian Advocate offering to give five dollars to every Sunday school which could be organized this year. Many schools have been started as the result of this offer, so that your address has already brought more than $100."

The Conference in 1861, resolved to

LIBERTY—1900

First Sunday school at Liberty organized 1900. First Methodist preaching service in 1902. Both in Liberty schoolhouse. Church organized in 1903. Trustees were Ralph Masson, H. Gomer, J. H. Wallace. Organizing pastors were Rev. B. J. Hoadley of Sunnyside Methodist Episcopal Church and Rev. H. E. Blackmon of the Brethren Church of Walla Walla.

One Bible teacher, a German, will long be remembered because at close of each session he called his group to prayer with the words, "Let us bray."

This church was for many years part of a circuit including Sunnyside. Rev. G. W. Booth was presiding elder The Dalles District.

First Ladies Aid organized 1904 with forty members. Lumber for the first building came from Tacoma and was hauled eight miles from Alfalfa by teams. The building near the Liberty schoolhouse cost $1,800. It was erected in 1921. Rev. William Parrot, Presbyterian minister, was pastor. All trustees were Presbyterian. Building bought from Presbyterians in 1952. J. S. Bell was Sunday school superintendent, and Rev. Harry Gardener, pastor.

In 1964 on circuit with Buena, Rev. W. B. Asp appointed pastor for the second year. Members numbered 93; church school enrollment 69; church school superintendent, Mrs. Earl Slagg. Woman's Society of Christian Service enrollment 20.

require its members, when answering roll call, to state whether or not they had fulfilled the provisions of the Discipline regarding the instruction of children.

In 1865 there were 67 schools in the Oregon Conference, with 434 officers and teachers, and 3,628 scholars. In 1874 the Conference recommended greater attention to the circulation of Sunday school publications and the establishment of Sunday school libraries. The 85 schools reported in 1878 represented a decrease of 14 from the previous year. There were six less officers and teachers, but 224 more scholars, the total number of which was 4,642.

A report of Rev. N. E. Parsons, presiding elder of the Walla Walla District in 1887, revealed that conflicting interests had created difficulties for those who would promote strictly Methodist schools. He said: "The Union Sunday School incubus has dwarfed our life and stayed our progress in many places, but thanks be to God we have set up our banners in every charge and circuit on the district." It was about this time that similar problems were suggested in a report from the committee on Sunday schools, which urged: "Wherever practicable let Methodist Episcopal Sunday Schools be organized and fully equipped with our own literature."

The 1890 Columbia River Conference report showed progress in the number of persons receiving Christian instruction through the Sunday school. There were 89 schools, 842 teachers and officers, and 5,616 pupils. Fourteen years later the Conference had 186 schools, 1,758 officers and teachers, with an enrollment of 14,453.

West of the mountains similar progress was indicated. In 1893 the Puget Sound Conference reported 155 schools, with 10,051 pupils enrolled. The committee enthusiastically declared, "The Sunday school is one of the chief sources of growth of the Church, and one of the mightiest agencies both in conserving and propagating the doctrines of the

LIND—1900

Methodist Church at Lind was organized in 1900 by Rev. S. Smith of Delight Circuit. Five charter members were, C. W. Hammond, Mr. and Mrs. D. E. Crawford, Mr. and Mrs. F. L. Ulm.

Rev. A. J. Gould, pastor, Delight Circuit, in 1901, led in construction of first church building. Trustees, C. W. Hammond, F. L. Middleton, F. E. Crawford, J. J. Merriman, Day Imus. Church dedicated, December that year.

Gould left before end of year, was followed by Rev. J. H. Martin, later by Rev. J. S. Bell.

Fund raising for new building began in 1946, Rev. Robert Hicks, pastor. Structure completed under pastorate, Rev. William H. Ritchie, 1947-61. Committee, Mrs. C. H. Brittenham, Mr. and Mrs. J. L. Hays, Mr. and Mrs. Dan Lyle, John Miller, Mr. and Mrs. E. C. Phillips, Mr. and Mrs. R. H. Phillips, Mr. and Mrs. John Shimek, and Mrs. Edward Wahl. North wing added to church, in 1955-56.

Thirty ministers have served this congregation since its organization. Longest pastorate, that of Rev. W. H. Ritchie, fourteen years. From the charge he became superintendent, Walla Walla District.

In 1964, Rev. Roger K. Johnson, pastor. Membership, 242, church school enrollment, 162. Sixty members, Woman's Society of Christian Service raised $430. Church building valued at $120,000 and parsonage at $13,500.

Church." It was further urged that the Methodist Catechism be taught diligently in the schools, and that Methodist literature alone be used.

A new type of promotional strategy was introduced in Puget Sound Conference in 1903 when Rev. John Lutas was appointed by the bishop to be Sunday school secretary for the Conference. His duties were to cooperate with the secretary of the Sunday School Union, a Methodist organization, in all matters relating to Sunday school interests.

In 1908 Rev. C. B. Sears was appointed Sunday school missionary, a position he held until 1914.

Northwest Methodists early availed themselves of the graded lessons which were authorized by the General Conference in 1908. As early as 1909, the committee recommended that Sunday school workers make use of the teacher-training courses prepared by the board.

In 1914 Rev. J. M. Weaver succeeded Sears as Sunday school missionary, and the following year reported that he had organized 17 new schools, and reorganized another. He had assisted 18 schools with free literature for three months, had done preliminary work in organizing 17 schools and held revival meetings in eight places. Seventeen persons had been converted in the meetings and Sunday school institutes had been held on each district in the Conference.

Weaver reported in 1918 that he had spent five months of the year promoting evangelism and organizing teacher training and Bible classes. Thirty-six of the former had been set up and 27 of the latter. He stressed that evangelism and leadership training should head the list of Sunday school objectives during the coming year.

When Rev. J. Edgar Purdy succeeded Weaver in 1924, he took the title of Director of Christian Education and placed major emphasis upon strengthening local church school programs and organization to enable them to meet

OROFINO, IDAHO—1900

First Methodist preacher at "Oro Fino" Rev. Gustavus Hines who spent the year, 1861-62 there as a missionary among miners. First Methodist Sunday school, Orofino, 1900. Leaders, Mr. and Mrs. Ellis Small and Mr. and Mrs. S. A. Dunlap. Met in Moody Hall. First minister, Mr. Thornquist. Church organized, December 17, 1901. Rev. Charles E. Gibson, presiding elder. Articles of Incorporation filed; trustees, J. M. Merrill, H. Noble, O. A. Anderson.

Ground for building donated by C. C. Fuller, S. A. Dunlap, and William Shriver, leaders in building church, completed, 1904. Church occupied new location, 1910. Old building sold, $1,250. In new building, 1912. Rev. J. H. Hart, pastor. Loan, $250 by Division of Church Extension, 1910, in 1914, $200, in 1923, $500, in 1928, grant of $500. Again another, 1950.

Building erected, 1912, destroyed by fire, 1938. New building completed in a year, Rev. George W. Cooper, pastor, 1934-43. Orofino always part of a circuit, though usually central point. Other points, Cavendish, Pierce, Headquarters.

Educational unit completed in 1956, Rev. L. Marshall Campbell, pastor. Cost of structure, $28,000. Debt remaining, $6,200. Membership at time, 250.

In 1964, Rev. James H. Thompson, pastor fourth year. Membership 279. Church school, 234. Woman's Society, members, 21, gave $150. Church value $18,000.

requirements of standard Sunday schools. In 1928 his services were extended to the Columbia River Conference and thereafter his time was limited to organization and promotion on district or conference level.

Rev. Andrew Warner succeeded Purdy in 1930. When he gave up the work three years later he was not immediately replaced. Miss Bertha Pease later became director of Christian Education and youth work for the Conference and served until 1945 when Rev. Elwyn H. Scheyer became executive secretary of the Conference Board of Education.

In 1929 when the Puget Sound and Columbia River Conferences merged the number of Sunday schools involved in the union was 335, with 5,852 officers and teachers, and 47,872 persons enrolled.

Ten years later when Methodist union was effected the Pacific Northwest Conference of the Methodist Church reported 312 schools, with 5,136 officers and teachers and 49,378 enrolled. By 1963 the enrollment had climbed to 62,584, with 7,317 officers and teachers in 289 schools.

FIRST, BONNERS FERRY—1901

Bonners Ferry first appeared in 1902. Left to be supplied. In 1903, had 78 members, 180 in Sunday school. Rev. J. M. Eastland reported.

First Methodist preaching service held in Knight's of Pythias Hall, 1897. Church organized in 1901. Construction began on first building at Bonners Ferry, December, 1905. Edifice dedicated, November 13, 1910. The building suffered flood damage in 1948, was moved back onto foundations and used until 1957. It was located on Oak Street, in the lower part of town.

In 1948 Rev. Ralph M. Walsh reported 278 members and 113 in Sunday school. Rev. Neils A. Christiansen was appointed for the second year in 1950. In 1957, Rev. Bernard E. Mott, accepted supply, was appointed for the second year. There were 267 members and 288 in Sunday school.

In 1957, congregation erected new building costing $150,000, on the corner of Denver and Lincoln Streets. The debt was $45,000. C. A. Newell was chairman of the building committee.

In 1964 Rev. M. Wesley Arms was pastor for second year. There were 365 members and 252 in Sunday school. The 72 members of Woman's Society of Christian Service gave $795 to local work. Church property valued at $163,000, and parsonage, $18,649.

EPWORTH LEAGUE UNITES METHODIST YOUTH

Prior to 1890 Methodist youth work, outside the Sunday school, was carried on by various independent organizations, differing in name and plan throughout the denomination. When the Epworth League came into existence as the official organization for Methodist youth, Northwest leaders welcomed the new movement and soon it was in operation in churches on both sides of the mountains.

The first indication that the Columbia River Conference had taken official notice of the League appeared in the journal for 1892. With mingled confidence and skepticism, the committee reported: "The spontaneous origin and remarkable growth of this youngest daughter of Methodism seems to indicate that it is a child of Providence and that it meets a felt want. With its lofty aim there seems much to hope for and little to fear from this additional wheel in the machinery of Methodism."

In 1908 the Columbia River Conference noted that the first Epworth League Institute had been held in 1906, that there were three in 1907 and six in 1908. Hope was expressed that one could be established in the Northwest.

The following year the committee expressed regret at the presence of too many old persons in the League. The belief was voiced that persons over thirty should be in the League only to give advice and encouragement, and should not take much time in the meetings. It was emphatically stated that the League was for young persons under 25. It was further urged that an institute be held in or near Spokane in 1910.

The Spokane District conducted an institute at Liberty Lake, in 1911. Registration was 185. In August the hope was expressed that a Conference institute might be scheduled for 1912. This hope was fulfilled and the attendance was 186. In 1913 there were 225 present.

In 1913 Lake Chelan was the site of an institute with 146 attending. The first institute at Coeur d'Alene, Idaho, was held in 1917. But in 1919 it was cancelled for the year. Gatherings at Chelan and Richland attracted an attendance of more than 300. Other institutes, set up by this Conference from time to time, served their day.

In the Puget Sound Conference Epworth Leagues got off to a good start. In 1904 Rev. Edwin M. Randall, president of the University of Puget Sound, was elected General Secretary of the Epworth League.

The Puget Sound Conference Board of Epworth League was established in 1907. The following year the conference-wide organization met at Tacoma.

LANGLEY—1901

First class at Langley, organized August 11, 1901, had 14 members. E. D. Spooner was class leader and Rev. W. F. Doty first pastor in 1902. First service held in schoolhouse. Little progress at Langley until Rev. A. J. McNemee became pastor in 1909. First day he located desirable church site. The first Sunday he took offering for lamps for new church, second Sunday for hymnals. On the third, he announced he was ready for donation of lots. Two were given, next to the one he had selected. He sold one, purchased lot of his choice. He applied to Board of Church Extension for $200, took subscriptions and began construction two months after arrival. Six months later building costing $1800 complete free of debt. Two years later, bell purchased for $40. Albert Melson and Martin Mortinson hoisted bell in place.

Basement completed in 1938. Inside finished, with insulation and wallboard in 1946. Later, pews were finished with Woman's Society of Christian Service providing material. Additions made in 1948. Roof reshingled, 1950, Rev. Harold Slocum, pastor. In 1964, Rev. Frank Goodnough appointed. Membership 227. Church school enrollment 101, Woman's Society of Christian Service members 46. Their gifts $3,000. Church valued at $30,000. Parsonage $14,000.

The Annual Conference, meeting at the same place, appointed a committee to investigate the possibilities of establishing a permanent site for the conference sessions.

A year later the committee reported that the Sound Trustee Company, holding large interests at Redondo Beach, on Puget Sound, had offered to deed to the Conference certain land for a permanent meeting place, and to contribute for a building, ten percent of monies realized from sale of lots on the tract by or to conference members.

In September, 1912, the Tacoma District Epworth League, held an institute on the Redondo site. The following year a conference-wide institute was held on Bainbridge Island. In 1914 the first conference institute was held at Epworth Heights, on land donated by the Sound Trustee Company. This site was used for institute and summer camping until about 1959. At that time the site was surrounded by permanent residents and had become a part of Interurban Seattle-Tacoma. The location was sold and the proceeds used to purchase a new conference location.

Other Puget Sound Conference Institutes were at Ocean Park, Discovery Bay, Samish Island and Deception Pass. The Norwegian-Danish brethren operated an institute at Beulah Park, on Vashon Island, for twenty years beginning in 1920.

For more than twenty years the trend in the Conference was toward district institutes, planned and supervised under district leadership. But after the early 1950's, the trend was toward bringing the district camps under Conference control, directed by the Conference Council. Lazy F. Ranch, near Ellensburg, was the first site procured under the new plan.

THE BIBLE WAS BASIS FOR MORALITY AND SAFEGUARD TO PERSONAL LIBERTY

Northwest Methodists have been great believers in the Bible. After the church became permanently established

---

MORTON—1901

Morton visited by Rev. Edwin L. Bower fortnightly 1900, 1901. First members reported, 1901: Mrs. Tom Hopgood, Mrs. Hiram Chapman. George and Mary Engle, Robert and Nellie Pickens, John Linder, Grace and Mae Temple.

Rev. O. R. Anderson, 1907-10, a carpenter built church. Rev. D. A. Storey, 1910-11, single, roomed at Hopgood Hotel. In 1912, church on Tacoma District, served by Rev. C. D. Miller. In 1912-13, H. E. Chapman Sunday school superintendent, Mrs. Chapman president Ladies Aid, Mrs. A. J. Weeks president Epworth League. In 1914, parsonage acquired, Rev. F. C. Thompson, pastor. In 1915, parsonage moved, new floors, other improvements. In 1917, Sunday school reached attendance of 200, 46 united with church. Changes made in sanctuary 1929, Rev. C. E. Preston, pastor. In 1934-40, Rev. O. S. Whitesides installed stained glass windows, altar, lectern, pulpit, baptismal font, erected parsonage with chapel. Woman's Society of Christian Service organized, 1940, Rev. Donald Baldwin, pastor. Improvements continued. Rev. Harry Chatterton, 1955-57, led in purchase of new building, costing $5,000. Fiftieth anniversary celebrated, 1957, Educational building. Complete, 1960.

In 1964, Rev. Samuel A. Carlson, supplying second year. Membership 172, church school 246. Woman's Society members 28, gave $625. Building value, $59,591. Parsonage, $10,500.

Rev. M. J. Purdue

Rev. Reah Dougherty

Rev. J. M. Weaver

Rev. Oscar M. Adam

Rev. Andrew Warner

Mrs. Bertha Pease Hartsell

THESE EXECUTIVES SERVED CONFERENCE EDUCATIONAL INTERESTS

Rev. J. Edgar Purdy

Mrs. Gerie Brown

Rev. C. B. Sears

Rev. Elwin Scheyer

in Washington Territory, and before the Puget Sound Conference became independent, the Oregon Conference spoke for Washington Methodism. It was under these circumstances that in 1855, the committee on the Bible Cause reported that one of the conference members, Rev. I. C. Phillips, was agent of the Bible Society. The committee said, "The demand for the Bible is very great. About one family in three of the inhabitants of the territory is destitute of the Bible. Among the many reasons why the Bible should be put into the hands of every human being is that it is the only basis of all true morality, the safeguard of personal liberty, and of republican equality, the foundation of all true philanthropy, and the true ground of all popular education. It is emphatically the word of God and comes to us requiring at our hands its own dissemination."

Methodists of Washington continued through the years to keep the importance of the Bible ever before conference members and their converts. Accordingly, in 1856, the Conference pledged support of the Bible Society in the spread of the Book, and agreed to comply with the disciplinary requirements that offerings be taken for the cause.

The year the Columbia River Conference was separated from Oregon, the committee reaffirmed the traditional Methodist attitude toward the Bible. It was said, "We regard the Bible Cause as one of vast importance to us in this new Conference, as it is everywhere."

In 1875 canvassing agents for the Bible Cause in Oregon and Washington had traveled 9,753 miles, visited 10,653 families, given 460 free Bibles to destitute families, and sold 1,560 copies of Old or New Testaments, valued at $1,241.31.

A report to the Puget Sound Conference in 1911 showed that the American Bible Society, in Nevada, Oregon, Washington, Idaho, and California, had 26 Bible missionaries who had sold over 56,000 Bibles and New Testaments in

UNIVERSITY TEMPLE—1901

University Methodist Temple began in 1892. First service held at Payee's Hotel on Lake Union at Sixth Ave. N. E. Group organized as Methodist Episcopal Church in 1901, by Rev. Rial Benjamin, Methodist Evangelistic Union. Assisting were Rev. A. E. Burrows, Asbury Church, Rev. Edwin M. Randall, First Church.

Ladies Aid, organized forthwith, played important role in progress of church. Rev. William H. Leach, city missionary, 1903, led in erecting building 28x50 at East 42d and Brooklyn. Edifice, valued at $25,000, built with aid of $3,000 from Church Extension Society, $1,000 from Evangelistic Union, dedicated, April 28, 1907, by Rev. H. C. Jennings. Parsonage erected by Rev. John M. Canse, 1910-14.

Church enlarged, renovated, under Rev. A. H. Lathrop. Site at 15th N. E., E. 43rd, donated by Board of Home Missions during ministry of Rev. Arch Tremayne, 1919-23.

October 16, 1927, sanctuary, costing $350,000 dedicated on this site; Rev. James E. Crowther. Debt paid in 1947 with conference cooperation. Educational unit, costing $500,000, completed in 1956, consecrated by Bishop A. Raymond Grant. Rev. Cecil Ristow was pastor. New parsonages were acquired in 1961 by Rev. Lynn Corson.

In 1964, Rev. Lynn Corson appointed, fifth year. Rev. Edwin Towle, first. Church valued at $1,000,000. Parsonages $40,000.

53 languages among foreigners, logging and mining camps, and the frontier.

Further witness to the importance placed upon the Bible by the church is seen in the fact that every school established by Northwest Methodism has offered courses in Bible.

METHODISTS EMPHASIZED THE PRINTED WORD

Traditional Methodist emphasis on reading as a means of learning early came to the fore in the Northwest. A favorite method of spreading Methodist beliefs was the tract. For decades the committee on the Tract Cause kept this issue before every conference session.

In 1855 the committee expressed joy in the success of the cause within the Conference during the preceding year. "We ought to feel it a duty," the committee exhorted, "to engage, with increasing zeal, in the circulation of these publications, until from the East to the West, from the North to the South we are supplied with salutary and sanctified literature, whose tendency it will be to elevate and purify the public sentiment and taste, rather than to degrade and corrupt the public morals."

The committee appraised certain popular publications then in circulation, warning against their pernicious effects upon faith and public morals. It was recommended that the Conference take action to secure a tract depository in Oregon and appoint a colporteur to travel through the land circulating such literature as Methodists believed would be in keeping with Christian teachings.

A year later the committee repeated the call for action. "There still exists," the group said, "the same imperative necessity for prompt, united, and vigorous action as in former times; there is the same obligation to furnish the people with instruction and knowledge; the same destitution, in respect to religious books; the same tendency to supply

BRIDGEPORT—1902

Bridgeport first appeared in 1902, but to be supplied. In 1903, Sunday school had 51 members. First preaching service at home of Boyd Teeter. In 1903, Rev. W. E. Beach reported 39 members and ministerial budget, $150.

First church building dedicated in 1906, costing $1,500. The Junior League, in 1911, purchased piano for church, costing $75. Basement enlarged in 1914, by volunteer labor. Twelve Sunday school classes paid for windows. First Woman's Missionary Society in 1915.

In 1950, the beginning of the near-by Chief Joseph Dam project brought many workers, and the church undertook to erect a new building to house overflowing church and Sunday school attendance. Rev. John B. Coan, pastor. The congregation pledged $10,000, and the Division of Church Extension was asked to grant $5,000. Difficulties in architectural plans and financing caused delays. By 1953 Sunday school enrollment was 350. After the dam was completed most of the newcomers departed, and church and Sunday school attendance receded.

In 1964, church membership was 135, and Sunday school enrollment, 167. There were 22 members of the Woman's Society of Christian Service and Wesleyan Service Guild. Church building valued at $60,834, parsonage at $11,222, debt, $1,840. Rev. Raymond L. Poindexter was pastor.

their place with either the vile, the worthless, the skeptical, or at least, the Christless literature of the Age."

Rev. William Royal, in 1857, was appointed agent for the tract cause. The following year a complaint arose regarding the distribution and sale of literature at camp meetings. The committee replied that this was a part of the duty of the agent, provided he did not engage in such activity on the Sabbath or while religious services were in session.

COLUMBIA RIVER CONFERENCE COMMITTED TO THE PRINTED WORD

The Columbia River Conference was born committed to the spread of the printed page. The year of its birth the committee said, "while Satan is flooding the land with literature of most dangerous tendencies, we will use our best endeavors to supplant it with these precious leaves, which are for the healing of the nations."

Thus it is clear that to whatever those pioneer Christian leaders put their hands they pursued it with enthusiasm. For a half century the distribution of tracts was one of the prime concerns of Methodists in Washington and Northern Idaho. As the years passed, however, circulation of books gradually came to receive major emphasis. Yet the Church has not ceased to turn out tracts on many subjects to further its interests, purposes, and goals.

GRACE, EVERETT—1902

A Methodist Sunday school was organized in the north part of Everett, in 1902. Rev. I. R. Lovejoy, pastor of First Church, officiated. The school met in the home of Mr. and Mrs. W. W. Miller. In 1904 Summit Avenue Methodist Episcopal Church organized, by Rev. M. A. Casey of First Church. In charge was Charles A. Robertson, local preacher of First Church. The women organized early were busy in 1904. A lot for the first building was donated by W. T. Swalwell. The Riverside branch of the Ladies Aid of First Church purchased land and building materials. Congregation incorporated in 1909 as Grace Methodist Episcopal Church, Rev. W. G. R. Dann, pastor. The parsonage was built under Rev. W. W. Switzer, 1911-13. Building erected in 1923, under Rev. C. E. Sanders, was dedicated October 21. Rev. Edward H. Todd, delivered sermon. District Superintendent was Rev. George W. Frame. Board of Home Missions and Church Extension granted $5,000.

In 1943, Wilson Chapel was built in memory of George H. Wilson. Dedicated in 1952 while Rev. Jack M. Tuell was pastor. In 1953 organ installed, Rev. C. Ellsworth Wilson was pastor. In 1964 Rev. Donald Corner pastor. Church members, 137, and 128 in Sunday school. The Woman's Society enrolled 38 and gave $769.

NORTHWEST METHODISTS DESIRED THEIR OWN PUBLICATION

Along with the circulation of the Bible, tracts and books, Northwest Methodists found great joy in their own publication, The Pacific Christian Advocate. The desire to inform all its members of activities, beliefs, programs, and goals of the church, was a part of the heritage of the Methodist Mission.

About the time Methodism entered Washington territory, Oregon Conference leaders were laying plans for a publication to enlighten the Church on all matters Methodistic. In the Oregon Conference journal for 1855 appears a reference to "The New Paper," planned for the Conference. The committee expressed conviction of the profound need for such, and pledged cooperation in circulating it.

The following year Conference members resolved to use their utmost efforts to increase the subscription lists of the Pacific Christian Advocate to 2,000 by January 1, 1857. A year later the committee again stressed the needs of the paper, and pledged to endeavor to increase subscriptions. The group agreed that each pastor would be held responsible for collecting all subscriptions sent in by him.

Financial difficulties confronted the Advocate. In 1859 the indebtedness of the paper was $2,816. Past-due subscriptions aggregated $4,417. Yet, it was said collections would cost more than could be realized from the effort.

The question faced by the Conference was, "Did they want a paper or not?" If not, present procedure would accomplish their purpose. If they wanted a vigorous paper, as a potent agent in the suppression of vice and the extension of the great principles of righteousness in these ends of the earth, the pastors should exercise themselves in collecting delinquent subscriptions and soliciting new ones.

The next year the committee on the Advocate declared: "We desire to see it live," and asked the editor, Rev. Thomas H. Pearne, to give each pastor a list of delinquent subscribers on his charge for collection.

When the nation was engaged in Civil War, in 1861, the Conference said the paper was indispensable and commended Editor Pearne upon his fearless stand on the great crisis agitating the nation and threatening its very existence.

During the following years, had it not been for the desperate sense of its im-

KENNEWICK—1902

First Methodist services, Kennewick, 1902, Rev. J. J. Calloway, Kiona, preaching. Organized community Sunday school, W. C. Warren, superintendent. Church October 8, 1902, five members. Rev. E. H. Rubicam, pastor. Ladies Aid Society organized, Nov. 20, 1902. Mrs. Mary Cox, president. First resident pastor, Rev. A. N. Sanford, 1904.

Building campaign for $2,000 launched, November, 1904. Church erected that year, valuation $3,000. Later, basement and side rooms added, with donation of $500 from Division Church Extension. Dedicated free of debt, February 11, 1906. President J. H. Coleman, Willamette University, officiated, assisted by Rev. Walton Skipworth, presiding elder.

New church building constructed, 1920-22, Rev. J. E. Strevey, pastor. Dedicated June 1, 1923, Rev. A. A. Callender, pastor. Debt, $40,000 finally paid, 1944. Pastors leading in final payments, Rev. Robert LaMott, Rev. John B. Coan.

Pipe organ installed, 1946, dedicated, 55th anniversary of church, March 23, 1957. Educational unit consecrated October 26, 1958. Rev. Kenneth H. Underwood, pastor.

In 1964, Rev. Robert W. Hicks, pastor, third year. Membership, 1015, church school, 502. Woman's Society, 149 members gave, $792. Building value, $426,000. Parsonage, $28,000. Grants and loans from Division of Church Extension during years aggregated $19,311.

THESE SERVED THE CAUSE OF EDUCATION

Rev.
Edward Laird
Mills

W. W.
Woods

Rev. Francis Kinch

Discovery Bay Institute
Olympic Peninsula

portance and the fierce determination to maintain it, the paper would have been permitted to die. In 1864 Rev. H. C. Benson succeeded Rev. Thomas Pearne as editor. Three years later, after a decade of service, the committee praised the paper for its value but mourned the lack of circulation. Subscriptions totalled 1,512 of which 200 were received in Portland, home of the paper. Pastors agreed to begin collections for the paper as soon as they returned to their homes from the conference session. Appreciation was expressed for the manner in which Editor Benson was conducting the paper.

Columbia River Supported the Paper

The year the Columbia River Conference was born, it espoused the paper with vigor. It resolved, "That we adopt the Pacific Christian Advocate as our own conference organ." The committee also stated, "Identified with the Pacific Christian Advocate from the beginning, we desire to hold our identification with it to the end. It has been ours, we desire it still to remain ours."

Such a statement from a new Conference must have given heart to the editor, sitting, as he was, by the bedside of his child so financially ill that the doctors had given it but a fifty-fifty chance for survival.

This diagnosis was pronounced by the Oregon Conference the same year. After explaining that the paper could do no better than pay its current expenses for the coming year if it were out of debt, a forlorn hope, the committee said; "In any event the paper must live. We need it; we need to have a medium of communication between our preachers and people. We need a paper from which we can constantly learn what is going on in our widely separated fields of labor. We need some means by which we can inform each other, and thus be the better able to help each other in our work. We need the paper to inform the rest of the world that we live in a

RENTON—1902

Renton first appeared among Methodist appointments in 1903, attached to Rainier Beach. Circuit was supplied by Rev. F. H. Calder. Rev. Roland Hughes was pastor in 1904. That year Renton and Rainier Beach reported a total of 50 members, with 125 in Sunday schools. In 1910 there were 83 church members and 158 in Sunday school. In 1920, Rev. F. G. Willey reported 133 members and 194 in Sunday school.

Some records show church organized in 1902 with 25 members. In 1901, F. J. Hilliker advanced $300 to purchase site on Williams Street. The building was completed, April, 1903, dedicated free of debt, September, 1904. In 1911, new church erected, Second and Mill.

Rev. Lawrence Linneman, 1956-61, launched building plan culminating in new building, costing $150,000, on Windsor Hills. New church occupied in 1958. An $80,000 educational unit added later.

Rev. Earl Dean became pastor in 1961, Rev. Charles E. Gruenwald, associate. Under this leadership church expanded service to Renton.

In 1964, there were fifteen circles in Woman's Society of Christian Service, with 200 members. They gave $770. Membership, 950, church school enrollment, 560. The church sponsored Boy Scouts, Girl Scouts, a men's bowling team. Building valued at $387,000 and parsonage at $38,500.

goodly land where there is room to spare and where Christian people may find social advantages as well as fields of labor denied them elsewhere. It is indispensable."

The paper lived. In 1879, the committee reported that under the management of Rev. Abraham Laubach financial affairs of the Advocate were in better condition than ever. It had been financially self-supporting through the year and had reduced its indebtedness. Circulation was 2,000, but only 1,200 of these were in the patronizing territory.

The paper continued to serve, inspire, and instruct. For eight years, 1868-'76 Rev. Isaac Dillon was editor. He was succeeded by Rev. J. H. Acton who served four years. At the expiration of his term of service assets of the paper were reported to be $3,784 and liabilities $2,833. Total subscriptions numbered 1,004. The preceding May the General Conference had turned ownership of the paper back to the Conferences and donated $2,500 to cover arrears to the end of the current year.

For the following eight years, Rev. H. K. Hines was editor of the paper. At its 1888 session the Puget Sound Conference resolved that "We remember as a brother in the Lord, the retiring editor, Dr. H. K. Hines, and assure him that we esteem him very highly. We also request the bishop to appoint Rev. A. J. Hanson business manager of the Advocate." The Conference also welcomed the new editor, Rev. W. S. Harrington, who entered upon a four-year term with the paper.

Rev. A. N. Fisher succeeded Harrington in 1892. When he was succeeded by Rev. D. L. Rader in 1904, the committee reported that the new editor had said that 10,000 subscriptions would make the paper entirely self-supporting. He was commended for his attempt to make the paper distinctly religious and spiritually helpful. In 1910, the last year Rader was editor, the subscription list

GREEN LAKE—1902

First Methodist Sunday school at Green Lake held in a tent on site later occupied by church. First church school superintendent, Mrs. F. H. Weiant. Rev. T. E. McMillen had preached in the community in March, 1895, in the I. O. G. T. Hall. A church organized 1895 with 13 charter members. Graduating from tent, later meeting held in homes of C. J. Eddy and George Collins.

The first building for the church was started May 24, 1903, by Rev. Rial Benjamin, pastor. Men, women and children gathered native stones, found in abundance, to erect the building. Because of its unusual appearance and size, neighbors called building "Benjamin's White Elephant." In 1910, building was remodeled, enlarged, and basement finished. Andrew Carnegie gave $1,200 for pipe organ.

In 1950 new parsonage erected, Rev. A. P. Aiton, pastor. In 1954, Rev. Earl Dean, pastor, many improvements made, including converting furnace from coal to oil. In 1959-60, the building was remodeled at cost of $65,000. Rev. Earl Dean, pastor.

The church sponsored Boy Scouts, Girl Scouts, and various other community projects.

In 1964, Rev. Wayne D. Griffen was appointed for fourth year. There were 506 members, 247 in church school, 142 in Woman's Society, which gave $1,741.

had grown to 8,000 and it was hoped that the 10,000 mark might be reached by the end of the quadrennium.

Robert H. Hughes, a layman, became editor in 1911 and held the position until succeeded by Rev. Edward Laird Mills in 1920. Mills edited the Pacific Edition of the Christian Advocate until the General Conference of 1940 unified all editions and authorized a general paper to be edited and published in Chicago. Rev. Roy L. Smith became editor and continued until succeeded by Rev. T. Otto Nall in 1952.

Thus, through the years, from the beginning, Methodists of the Northwest sought to promote learning among their children, youth, and mature members by all means available. The aim always was to develop citizenship for a Christian Civilization in this region.

CHAPTER X

Determination to maintain Christian con-
tent in secondary and higher education
was early evidenced among Northwest
Methodist leaders. How early efforts
failed but perseverance won are dra-
matically presented in—

Men of Higher Education

(A Hundred Years of Methodist Adventures in Higher Education)

THE CHURCH BEGAN DREAMING EARLY

Following closely upon establishment of elementary schools, Northwest Methodists began early to dream of secondary and higher education. Long before the Church came to Washington and Idaho, leaders had laid foundations for advanced education in Oregon. Among such institutions in that state were Santiam and Umpquah academies, Portland Academy and Female Seminary, Oregon City Seminary, the Oregon Institute, predecessor of Willamette University, and others.

The felt need for advanced training of youth on Puget Sound was expressed as early as 1856. That year the Committee on Education of the Oregon Conference announced that the time had come for a more liberal provision for "the education of both sexes in the higher branches of literature and science."

Following through on this conviction, the Committee on Education, in 1856,[1] said, "The Memorial from persons proposing to establish an institution of learning in Washington Territory, under the patronage of the Conference, has been duly considered, and we recommend the conference to approve of the establishment of such an institution, to be called 'The Puget Sound Institute,' located at Olympia, and request the following persons: viz.:—Hon. D. R. Bigelow, G. M. Berry, W. S. Parsons, Hon. A. A. Denny, Hon. A. S. Abernethy, James Biles, T. F. Berry, J. S. Smith, William Wright, W. D. Van Buren, Dr. R. H. Lansdale, J. F. DeVore, to take the necessary steps to become incorporated as a Board of Trustees, to select a favorable site, during the year, and make a report to this body, at its next session."

In 1857 the Committee on Education reported that the Puget Sound Wesleyan Institute had passed through the first year of its existence, "and presents 'clear papers,' with a most hopeful and promising 'balance sheet.' We gather the following facts from the report of the trustees: A charter has been obtained, and a board of trustees organized, under it. Rev. Isaac Dillon, who has been serving the school, during its initial year, has been elected Principal, and his reappointment to that post is desired.

"Rev. J. F. DeVore is the Agent, and his conference appointment as such, is sought. A donation of ten acres of land, adjoining Olympia, has been made to the Institution by Hon. D. R. Bigelow."

METHODIST SCHOOLS MUST BE RELIGIOUS IN INFLUENCE

A report on institutions of learning set forth the policy of Methodist schools. "While there is no sectarian inculcation, either by precept or otherwise," it was said, "while the most entire catholicity is exhibited, they are at the same time religious in their influence, and conservative of morals, as well as promotive of mental development. The discipline of the schools is in all instances, such as should meet the decided approval of every parent and guardian who seeks the real welfare of his children or wards."

In 1859, Rev. B. C. Lippincott became principal of the Puget Sound Collegiate Institute and served two years, being reappointed in 1860, but no further reference to the school appears in the minutes.[2]

EAST OF CASCADES AMBITIOUS PROGRAM ADOPTED

Methodists east of the Cascades turned their attention to higher education, adopting a program more ambitious than that of their Puget Sound brethren.

The Eastern Oregon and Washington Conference, in 1874, accepted sponsorship for Blue Mountain University at

---

HIGHLAND PARK JAPANESE, SPOKANE—1902

Highland Park Japanese Methodist Church, Spokane, organized, December 3, 1902, by Rev. Genhichi Tsuruta. Seven charter members. Sunday school first organized September 12, 1915, in early home of Klondike Kate, on Howard and Third. Mrs. Seijiro Uemura, first superintendent.

Women organized, 1918, with six members. Mrs. Seijiro Uemura, president. In 1935 congregation purchased First Swedish Methodist building. Rev. Shigeo Taraba, pastor. Cost of building, $5,000. New building completed, 1958, cost $100,000. Rev. Shigeo Shamada, pastor. George Numata, chairman trustees. Building dedicated debt free, May 16, 1965 by Bishop Everett W. Palmer.

Edifice located on 19 acres of wasteland costing 2,865 dollars, less than a mile from city center. Members of church landscaped Japanese-style rock garden worth $50,000. Japanese-style Hexagon House of Prayer in church garden. Church and grounds show place for Spokane, was featured in Together Pictorial, April, 1959, and Methodist Americana, November same year. Visitors come from all over United States.

In 1964, 330 members, 257 in church school. Mrs. Richard Sakai, superintendent. English Woman's Society of Christian Service enrolled 40. Mrs. Harry Honda, president. Japanese group enrolled 72 with Mrs. H. Nishifue, president. Women gave $368. Rev. Shigeo Shamada, pastor since 1950.

225

La Grande, Oregon. The next year the committee reported that brick had been burned for the first building and declared there ought to be more schools for the education of students above the common grades.

Three years later the Conference agreed to establish an educational institution in Idaho. In 1879 the Columbia River Conference Academy, at Grangeville, had been operating for six months with an average attendance of 35.

West of the Cascades, in 1867, the Oregon Conference received a proposal to sponsor Vancouver Academy.[3] A committee appointed to investigate, the next year, recommended that the proposal be accepted. For the next three years the academy apparently prospered under the principalship of Clark Smith, who resigned because of ill health in 1871, and was succeeded by E. W. Curtis.

In 1875 the Academy had been closed for the year. Two years later the committee suggested that the Conference follow a policy of fewer schools with better support, and asked that the Vancouver building be sold and the land kept for future use.

METHODIST MINISTERS INVOLVED IN EDUCATION

CALVARY, TACOMA—1902

First Sunday school at Bismark, Tacoma, started in 1902 by Rev. James E. Milligan. Church organized under leadership of Rev. W. M. Welch, August 8, 1904. Eight charter members were, Mr. and Mrs. C. Miller, Mr. and Mrs. G. B. French, Mrs. Clara Harader, Mrs. Janie Parrott, Mrs. William Sellers, Mrs. Mollie Davis.

Epworth League oganized February 6, 1906, Junior League in 1908. Ladies Aid was organized in 1904. Mrs. C. E. Miller. president. Queen Esther's organized in 1913 under leadership of Mrs. H. K. Kline, wife of pastor. Lots for first building at Bismark donated by C. C. Miller, same site in use in 1964. Building dedicated December 18, 1904 by Bishop David H. Moore. Rev. B. F. Brooks, presiding elder and Rev. F. L. Tuttle, pastor. Parsonage completed in 1908. Rev. O. L. Kendal, pastor.

Epworth League room and basement added, 1909, Rev. W. O. Pflaum, pastor. In 1915 additional lots purchased, Rev. T. H. Jorgensen, pastor. Other additions, new rooms, furnace, through the years, under Rev. T. A. Graham. Fiitietn anniversary observed, 1955 under Rev. Percy E. Pike.

In 1964, Rev. Elmer J. Church, pastor first year. Membership 201. Church school enrollment, 211. Woman's Society of Christian Service membership 56, giving $516. Church value $45,000, parsonage at $16,000.

Some Methodist ministers were involved in state education. Witness the case of Rev. J. L. Powell, a member of the Oregon Conference, who, in 1881, was appointed to the presidency of the University of Washington Territory. A year later he was granted location by the Conference.[4]

Rev. G. M. Irwin, member of the Columbia River Conference, was successively president of Blue Mountain University, superintendent of Public Schools in Oregon and Alaska.

In 1882 Methodists of Eastern Washington brought twin schools into being. Lewiston Collegiate Institute, Lewiston, Idaho, saw the light of day about the same time that Spokane College, at Spokane Falls, was born. Rev. Levi Tarr,

226

pastor of the Lewiston Church, was president of the Idaho school, and Rev. Royal E. Bisbee[5] was elected president of the institution at Spokane Falls. In 1886 Spokane College had 115 students, and its property was valued at $23,000.

The Lewiston institution had experienced embarrassing financial conditions, but in 1887, following graduation of its first college student, it took the name, "Wilbur College." It was worth $15,000.

The committee on education, in face of these conditions, bravely declared, "The first question is not, 'Where can we obtain the cheapest education?' nor 'simply the highest educational finish,' but, 'Where can our children obtain a Christian education?'"

There was no report from the Academy at Grangeville, in 1888, but property held by Spokane College was reported to be valued at $97,647.68. The college at Lewiston had not been in operation, and debts were listed at $5,150, with assets of $500. The Academy at Grangeville, in 1889, had resumed operation and had secured the services of Rev. Wellington Bowser of the South India Conference, as principal. Spokane College reported assets of $529,034 and endowment subscriptions and trust deeds worth $42,000. Its students numbered 169. The committee reported that question had been raised regarding title to the Spokane College, but that the matter had been investigated and the title found to be clear beyond question.

IMPROPER TITLE COST CONFERENCE HALF MILLION

Wilbur College at Lewiston was not mentioned in 1890, but the schools at Grangeville and Spokane were said to be prosperous. One year later, however, the title to the real estate of Spokane College was reported in jeopardy. The commission representing the Conference had interviewed the original donor seeking to persuade him to receive back part of the property in exchange for a

CHEWELAH—1903

First Methodist sermon in Chewelah, delivered 1903, by Rev. Thomas C. Iliff, Salt Lake City. Church organized, 1904. Mrs. George McCrea, class leader. First Pastor, Rev. C. J. St. Hill. First services in Woodman Hall. Rev. J. E. Herrington, second pastor. He organized Sunday school in 1905, Mrs. McCrea, superintendent. Ladies Aid organized that year with Mrs. A. M. Basterday, president. Epworth League started, 1906.

In 1907, F. C. Williams, G. H. McCrea, W. I. Eichmeyer acquired lots for church and parsonage. These started under Rev. Harry F. Pemberton, 1908. First trustees were, George McCrea, F. C. Williams, W. L. Eichmeyer, W. H. Carder, Duncan Rule. Tower finished during pastorate of Rev. A. F. Kronneman. Pews installed and back of parsonage sided. The church and parsonage repainted in 1913, Rev. O. E. Faulkner, pastor. League room finished and porch added to parsonage.

Rev. Gertrude L. Apel, 1923-26, erected recreational hall. Hall remodeled in 1956 under leadership of Rev. Roy Kuhns. Rev. Fred Riehle led congregation to add kitchen, dining room, rest rooms, study, in 1957-60. Rev. Ray Poindexter, 1960-62 led in completing the nursery.

In 1964, Rev. Charles W. Johnson, appointed third year. Members 165, church school enrollment, 93. Woman's Society members, 31. They gave $1,564. Church value, $38,000, parsonage, $11,000.

clear title to that portion of the land on which the buildings stood.

The board of trustees of the College, in secret session, had arranged to deed the school to a group known as "The Union University Movement." Their right to do so was challenged and the Conference voted to demand complete accounting and delivery of the property.

The commission sent to serve the ultimatum reported that their demands had been ignored and that legal advice in Spokane discouraged further attempts to recover the school.

Thus a half million dollars worth of college property slipped through the hands of the Conference because land had been accepted without proper title.

In 1893 the Grangeville school proposed that the Columbia River Conference take over its assets and pay its debts. But this was not done. No report of this school was presented to the Conference thereafter and the same was true of Wilbur College at Lewiston.

But the Conference was not ready to give up. In 1895 the body adopted a resolution proposing that an educational institution be established within the Conference and that all propositions for such should be subject to ratification by that body.

In 1896, Rev. F. A. LaViolette, chairman of the committee on education, recommended that Rev. John S. Anderson be approved as receiver for Blue Mountain University. This marked the end of another Methodist adventure in higher education. The Columbia River Conference entered the twentieth century without such an institution within its boundaries.

PUGET SOUND ALSO EXPERIENCES EDUCATIONAL DIFFICULTIES

The Puget Sound Conference accepted a new school, the Olympia Collegiate Institute, in 1883. With enthusiasm and optimism, the next year the body adopted a resolution, "We will commit ourselves at once and heartily

CHIMACUM—1903

Chimacum first appeared in conference minutes in 1903. That year, new parsonage had been built at Chimacum on the Irondale and Hadlock Circuit. New church erected at Hadlock in 1906, value $2,000. In 1909, a church was dedicated at Chimacum, valued at $2500, free of debt. Rev. H. C. Leavenworth was pastor. Hadlock was reorganized in 1917, with 24 members, and continued a part of the Chimacum Circuit. In 1951, Rev. Wendell Cone began mobile ministry in Jefferson and Clallam counties, making his headquarters at Chimacum. Blyn, Irondale, Hadlock were other points on the circuit.

Rev. Harold Slocum, pastor of circuit in 1954, continued mobile ministry. District superintendent instructed him to reorganize the church at Hadlock and operate it as a unit with Chimacum. Two congregations reincorporated as one, in 1955. Woman's Society groups became one in 1958, under pastorate of Rev. George L. Poor. Social and other activities were divided between Hadlock and Chimacum.

In 1964 Rev. Ritchie D. Ocheltree II was appointed pastor for third year. The charge had 173 members, 162 in the church school. Woman's Society of Christian Service, 31. They gave $514. Methodist Youth Fellowship 32 members. Church property was valued at $73,000. Parsonage valued at $20,500.

228

to the purpose and policy of building up within the bounds of the Conference an institution of learning which, by example and facilities and able administration, will command the respect and patronage of Methodist people within the territory." A committee to administer the school was appointed. Members were: Rev. D. G. LeSourd, Rev. John F. DeVore, Rev. A. J. Hanson, Rev. F. M. Robertson, Rev. J. A. Ward, J. S. McMillin, W. H. Fry, D. W. Taylor, and David Lister.

The committee, in 1884, reported that the building and grounds were valued at $5,000, and enrollment the previous year had been 43. Principal, Rev. A. K. Crawford, had resigned and the school was in need of a new head. The instructors during the preceding year had taught at great sacrifice.

The Board of Trade at Port Townsend, in 1886, offered a bonus to the Conference to encourage the location of the new university at that place. The Conference determined to accept the offer provided conditions were met that year. Rev. D. G. LeSourd, Rev. John N. Dennison, and Rev. Abraham Laubach were appointed a committee to complete arrangements with the Port Townsend group.

A year later the Port Townsend Board of Trade asserted it had met the conditions, but the committee reported otherwise, and both parties were relieved from the contract.[6]

TACOMA MAKES OFFER TO ESTABLISH UNIVERSITY

With enthusiasm for higher education unabated, in a supplementary report, the committee resolved, "Believing as much as ever, that in the near future such an institution of learning should exist within the bounds and under the patronage of the Puget Sound Annual Conference we name as parties who should have full power to act for us, the three bishops of the church resident at Minneapolis, Denver, and San Francisco, together with our four brethren of the Conference: Rev. John F. De-

EATONVILLE—1903

Eatonville first appeared among conference appointments, 1903. In 1905, Rev. Francis A. Ecker, first pastor. Already a parsonage valued at $475, erected on ground donated by Mrs. Jane Osborne Van Eaton. There were 14 members. In 1906, 20 members, Kapowsen added to circuit. In 1907, Rev. A. M. Brown, pastor, receiving $100, parsonage. In 1912, Rev. G. L. Cuddy, found three members. Eatonville, purchased unfinished building from Christian Church, with the aid of $250 from Board of Home Missions. Church dedicated, value $2,000. Membership twenty-five. Ladies Aid helped with labor.

Church enlarged, cost of $3,400, dedicated May 5-7, 1922. Rev. William O. Shepard officiated, Rev. Harry E. Gardner, pastor. Mrs. T. S. Galbraith gave chairs for kindergarten.

Remembered as Sunday school superintendents: Mrs. J. R. Morris, D. A. Jackson, Mrs. J. W. Reynolds, wife of pastor.

Congregation called "Community Church" because it sought to serve the community. City library in the church for time, funerals and weddings always free. High point in membership of church, 1955, under Rev. J. W. Reynolds, 161. After mill burned membership decreased.

In 1964, Rev. Alfred S. Palmer, second year. Members 113, church school enrollment 117. Thirty-eight members of Woman's Society gave $500. Church value, $22,000. Parsonage, $13,000.

Vore, Rev. F. W. Loy, Rev. Isaac Dillon, and Rev. D. G. LeSourd." The Conference pledged itself to be bound by any agreement they might enter into, as long as the order remained unrescinded.

That year the Conference received an offer to establish the university at Tacoma. It was also reported that Olympia Collegiate Institute had enjoyed a good year.

In 1889 it was reported that Rev. T. J. Massey, financial agent for the University, had accomplished all that circumstances permitted. Total assets of the new school were $190,000. In 1890 the Puget Sound University had completed its building, organized its faculty, and had opened its halls for students on September 15. The new president, Rev. F. B. Cherrington, was welcomed into the Conference. Rev. Samuel Moore was appointed financial agent, and a board of trustees confirmed.

In 1893 the University had enjoyed a year of "signal success." The student body of 17, four years earlier, had grown to 225. Among valuable endowment and other gifts contributed to the University in 1896, was a liberal personal gift from Rev. John F. Goucher, which had made possible the opening of a branch Academy at Montesano.[7]

This new Academy, in 1897, reported 138 students, but soon passed from the scene.

In 1898 a plan of consolidation between Portland University and that of Puget Sound was favorably considered. But, because of legal obstacles, the Tacoma institution withdrew from the plan.

UNIVERSITY OF PUGET SOUND ADOPTED AS NEW NAME

The trustees of Puget Sound University, in 1903, voted to discontinue operation of the school, an action which placed the school wholly in the hands of the Conference. Rev. E. M. Randall, pastor of First Church, Seattle, was elected president, and the name of the

HUGHES MEMORIAL, EDMONDS—1903

A Sunday school organized at Edmonds, 1884, at home of Wellington Smith, first superintendent. In 1895, Free Methodists took charge. Swedish Methodist Sunday school organized in 1903, and English-speaking congregation first appearing in 1904, was organized, 1908 with 17 charter members.

That year, Rev. C. B. Sears held services in Swedish Methodist Episcopal Church. In 1909, Rev. Charles Eaton received 50 members. In 1915, Ladies Aid organized by Mrs. S. G. Jones.

Abandoned Swedish church was acquired by payment of assessments and mortgage, in 1918. Following year, Rev. C. E. Preston, appointed and, in 1920, he began to sponsor a new building to be memorial to Bishop Matthew Simpson Hughes who died at Easter time that year. Bishop William O. Shepard gave the movement full support. Building erected. Old church moved.

During pastorate of Rev. J. H. Berringer, 1928-33, old church repaired and painted as home of "Mountaineers" sponsored by pastor. Under Rev. Henry Haines, 1943-50, church grew. Rev. Raymond Proudfoot, 1950, started campaign for building at new location. Completed under Rev. Robert Hicks, 1958-62.

In 1964, Rev. David L. Aasen, third year, Rev. M. Chester Morgan, associate, second year. Members, 1,310, church school, 1,138. Woman's Society, 189, gave $1,625.

school changed to University of Puget Sound. New courses were added.

The Conference at its next session, was told that the school had enjoyed a successful year. Randall had resigned from the presidency, and Rev. Joseph E. Williams had succeeded him.

Gratifying reports of the condition of the University came from the president in 1905. The Conference adopted a recommendation that the sum of twenty-five cents per member be apportioned to the churches for the support of the school.

The work of President Williams was highly endorsed at the 1906 session of the Conference, and the committee praised the successful labors of Rev. Edward H. Todd, corresponding secretary. Net enrollment that year was 322. Good will and interest prevailed among students. There had been progress in current expenses, but the books had kept about even because of increase in cost.

University Is "Permanently" Established

The committee, in 1907, expressed faith that the University was to be permanent. "We feel that room for doubt no longer remains," the committee said, "regarding the providential location and permanency of this institution of higher education."

Looking toward the future, the committee announced the need for an endowment of a half million dollars. President Williams had resigned, and Professor L. L. Benbow, recently elected vice president, was to be in charge the following year. By the next year Benbow had become president. New members on the faculty and the retention of Rev. E. H. Todd as corresponding secretary, rendered the outlook for the school most hopeful.

Between 1907 and 1909 attendance climbed from 385 to 544. The trustees, the latter year, had issued $20,000 in seven per cent bonds to pay indebtedness. A mortgage had been placed on the west third of the campus containing the

MAGNOLIA—1903

First Methodist church service, at Interbay, held in abandoned hotel in 1903. A Reverend Mr. Murphy, preacher, according to report. Bethel Methodist Episcopal Church incorporated July 5, 1904. In 1906, ten members reported. Organizing pastor was Rev. James M. Dennison. First lot acquired by church was at 16th Av. W. and W. Dravus St. A tent housed first congregation.

A gift of $100 from Church Extension Society inspired congregation to build, in 1907. Rev. J. C. Kallgren, pastor. Lot sold and new ones acquired at 22d and W. Dravus. In 1906, Bethel and Sixty-second St. Church, Ballard, were served by one pastor.

Under Rev. James Badcon, 1915-22, Bethel experienced "Finest years." High point in Sunday school attendance came in 1920 when 150 were enrolled. Four young men have entered the ministry from church.

In 1959, name changed to "Magnolia Methodist Church," plans made to shift location. In 1963, with aid of U. N. A. funds, lots purchased on 34th Av. West, between Armour and Barrett. Services began in Magnolia Y. M. C. A. at that time. Ladies Aid and Woman's Society were active from beginning.

In 1964, Rev. Richard Nye became pastor. Members 88, church school enrollment 89. Woman's Society members, 23. They gave $583.

231

gymnasium, to secure bonds, to retire which no funds were in sight.

Rev. J. C. Zeller, new president of the University in 1909, it was be-lieved, "was a man sent of God to lead on the road to success. Rev. E. H. Todd had severed his relation to the university. The year 1910 brought glowing reports of advances in the school. The committee, speaking highly of Zeller, said, "We now have in this institution a school with a faculty second to none in the Northwest. Registration this year will be thirty to forty per cent greater than last."

A year later Zeller again received high commendation. Total at-tendance for the year was 498, with 102 enrolled in the College of Liberal Arts, an increase of ninety per cent during the past two years. A psychological laboratory and clinic, a department of education, and a course in Sunday school training had been opened that year. More than $3,000 had been taken in share funds subscriptions the past three months. Yet the committee said, "The financial situation is so critical, the competition among the schools of the state so keen, and the im-portance of the school to our Methodism so great that a failure on the part of the Conference to provide more money for maintenance would be a calamity."

MORAN—1903

Moran first appeared in 1903, Rev. B. T. Willis pastor. There were 43 mem-bers. In 1905 Rev. J. C. Kirkman, pas-tor, 42 members, 80 in Sunday school. In 1914 Rev. John Evans was in his second year. There were 45 members, 100 in the Sunday school, church build-ing was valued at $1,000.

In 1928 Rev. William Gornall was pastor. There were 84 members, 108 in Sunday school. One building worth $6,000, parsonage valued at $2,500. In 1935, Moran was with Mica, Rev. Thomas C. McFeron, pastor. In 1939 Moran was teamed with Manito of Spokane. Rev. Edwin D. Rounds, pas-tor. It was with Valley Chapel in 1950. Mrs. Royce Cydrus was in her third year. There were 43 members and 108 in the Sunday school. In 1960, Rev. F. H. Cronkite was in his first year. There were 23 members and 116 in the Sunday school.

In 1964, Rev. Kenneth Lawson, sup-ply, was in his first year. He was killed in an accident soon after confer-ence and Rev. Rarden Vergin, pastor at Liberty Park, completed the year. There were 44 members of the church and 66 in the Sunday school. The church building was valued at $38,000 and a parsonage valued at $13,000.

Continued success was reported, in 1912, under the leadership of President Zeller. Attendance for the year had been 415. A law school had been authorized in June.

First Endowment Gift a Challenge to University

In the spring a gift of $50,000 had been offered by James J. Hill on condi-tion that $250,000 be raised for endow-ment. Plans already had been laid for a financial campaign in the fall. The com-mittee said, "If the endowment is to be secured it means the enthusiastic en-dorsement of this Conference and the re-turning of every member to his charge with the determination of making the interests of the University paramount during the coming year. Pledges already received amounted to $75,000.

Evidently no one was willing to admit that an unpaid debt eventually would bring a day of reckoning. Even in 1913, when the school faced its greatest crisis, the committee on education only hinted at danger. The report declared the school had just opened its new year with the largest enrollment in its history. But President Zeller had resigned, and the commitee launched into a plea that the University was needed in the Northwest.

It was left for Edward L. Blaine, president of the board of trustees, to tell the Conference how critical the situation really was. He said, "In making this report I have tried to be neither pessimistic nor optimistic. But to place before you the facts. If the situation is either encouraging or discouraging, the cause must be found in the facts."

Blaine went on to say, "The past year has been one of struggle. The present chaotic monetary condition has rendered the task of financing the University especially difficult. This is augmented by the failure of some of our churches to meet amounts asked of them. That we have been able to come to the end of the year with the school running is due to the self-sacrificing loyalty of faculty and the forbearance of our creditors. Even with these concessions we have been able to meet the salaries of our faculty for little more than one-half of the year. Plans have been made to reduce expenses for next year, but such reductions will not meet demands unless more of our churches meet the apportionments of fifty cents per member."

With true Christian honor Blaine went on, "I find it hard to square our present condition and plans for the immediate future with my own ideas of honesty and integrity. I am tempted to say that unless the demands for a denominational school in this section is sufficient to insure the support and permanency of the school, it would better be discontinued. We cannot insist that our teach-

OROVILLE—1903

Rev. O. W. Mintzer, in 1902, was first Methodist to preach in Oroville. First Sunday school was organized by Rev. A. W. Trine, a pastor at Conconnully, April 26, 1903. First Superintendent, Robert Thompson.

Church organized in 1907 with Robert Thompson, Ira W. Follis, W. R. Rash, E. B. Crinnell, trustees. First meetings held in old schoolhouse, but abandoned store was appropriated for sanctuary, parsonage and church school.

Robert Thompson, in 1907, placed in charge of congregation. Dr. O. P. House donated lots for church site and, with a loan of $400 from Board of Church Extension, the cornerstone was laid August 20, 1908. Two adjoining lots acquired for parsonage. In 1908 Mrs. Thompson became pastor. The building was consecrated November, 1909. Ladies Aid assumed church debt in 1910.

In 1919 a former saloon was purchased and moved to church lots for primary department. Building, repaired in 1930, expansion program started in 1941, and fourth enlargement made in 1945.

In 1939, Mrs. Fred Gorst became first president of Woman's Society of Christian Service. In 1964, Rev. Clyde P. Bachman became pastor for the fourth year. Members, 178, church school enrollment, 190. Forty-six in Woman's Society, their gifts, $420. Methodist men, 15.

233

ers instruct our pupils in the principles of honesty when we have shown ourselves dishonest in meeting our obligations to them.

"We should have at once at least $10,000 to meet pressing obligations created in the maintenance of the school, and not as the result of any extravagance, and an effort be made to relieve the school from the present burden of debt."

University Highly Regarded in Educational Field

Then in a more optimistic note, Blaine went on, "The University has never held so high a place among the educational institutions of our section. The class of work done has never been better. The personnel of the student body has never been of so high a character. The opportunities for service have never been more numerous. With the probable withdrawal of Whitworth College from Tacoma, it seems that our claim for support from our people, both from within and without Tacoma, has never been more just."

Blaine's report stirred the Conference to the depths. Some members preferred to show their honesty by discontinuing the institution. Others believed that honesty involved meeting obligations, not only to creditors but to oncoming generations of youth. The Conference was called in special evening session. Impassioned pleas for discontinuance were matched by urgent calls for ministers and laymen to support the school in a manner worthy of Methodist pioneers.

Leonard Sounds Clarion Call for College

The fate of the university continued to hang in balance until long after midnight. Then Rev. Adna W. Leonard took the floor, and, in a plea that shall never be forgotten, sounded a clarion call for the Conference to do the thing God wanted done. The vote that followed favored continuing the school. Rev. Edward H. Todd, vice president of Wil-

---

RAINIER BEACH—1903

Rev. F. H. Calder, pastor of Church at Renton, began first Methodist preaching service at Rainier Beach, in Lake Side Hall, in 1903. The minister organized the church that same year with 53 members. First church building erected, 1904 under the ministry, first pastor, Rev. John R. Ball, who took charge in 1903. The first parsonage went up in 1909 with pastor, Rev. E. V. Smith, supervising construction. Under Rev. R. C. Hartley, 1915-17, basement completed. In 1929-32, Rev. Frank E. Goodnough, pastor, further additions, pastor's study completed.

Original building located on lots 16-17, Block 53, Rainier Beach. In 1937-43, Rev. J. H. Berringer paid assessments. In 1950-51, Methodist Union of Seattle gave $400 to keep church open.

In 1953, National Board of Missions gave $2,597; conference, $10,000; and loan, same amount. New building erected and conference loan paid by 1959. Another, of $75,000 from the National Board of Missions, was reduced by one-half, 1957. Building consecrated, May 4, 1958. Rev. Milton Andrews was pastor. Dr. Louis E. Braile, chairman building committee.

In 1964, Rev. George A. Cummings reappointed for fourth year. Membership was 386, church school enrollment, 251, and Woman's Society of Christian Service membership, 50. Women paid $480. Church building was valued at $114,100.

NORTHWEST'S CENTER OF HIGHER EDUCATION

Rev. Edward H. Todd

Rev. F. B.
Cherrington

The attempts of Northwest Methodists to establish institutions of Higher Education, resulting in the University of Puget Sound, is one of the thrilling chapters of service rendered to the Area by the church.

In 1914 name of University of Puget Sound was changed to College of Puget Sound, and again, 1960, the name became University of Puget Sound as scope of work justified.

Edward L.
Blaine

C. H. Jones Hall

Rev. R. Franklin
Thompson

lamette University, was elected, without consultation, to become president.

UNIVERSITY BECOMES A COLLEGE

During the first year of Todd's administration, the name of the school once more was changed. It became The College of Puget Sound. But its troubles were not over. Financial support remained difficult.

E. L. Blaine, in 1914, reported some of the difficulties. He said, "The action of the State Board of Education in striking our normal department from the accredited normal schools of the state, caused some anxiety, but due to the zeal of President Todd, this action has been rescinded and we are now rated as an accredited school."

Blaine continued, "The endowment campaign has lagged, due to reasons beyond the control of your trustees. But we have reports that during the past week, members of the Commercial Club of Tacoma have committed themselves to raise $100,000 for endowment of the college. Whether we shall be able to meet the conditions of James J. Hill by the fixed time remains to be seen. If he will consider this a subscription, we are less than $50,000 short of the mark."

Then with debt threatening the life of the College, Blaine concluded, "Committing the affairs of the College into your hands, for careful and prayerful consideration, we ourselves stand ready to carry out your bidding."

A FINAL TRY FOR ENDOWMENT

In September, 1915, the Conference had not raised the amount of money needed to meet Hill's requirement. The body resolved that the time between adjournment and October 1 would be set apart to organize personal campaigns to secure the $65,000 still needed to complete the quarter million endowment and pay certain indebtedness.

RAVENNA—1903

Ravenna Methodist Protestant Church, organized in 1903, six members. First school met at East 57th and 26th N. E., same year. Herbert Mackie was superintendent. Rev. T. P. Revelle, pastor of First Methodist Protestant Church, first preacher. Congregation met in Yesler Sunday school building. First pastor, Rev. H. T. Gould, was succeeded by Rev. H. J. Hartsell, December, 1903.

Building destroyed by fire in 1911, immediately was rebuilt on 33rd Ave. N. E. and E. 56th St. Rev. S. C. Benninger, pastor.

In 1920, new parsonage erected. Ground broken for new sanctuary in 1922, Rev. George W. Beck, pastor. Dedicated, May, 1923. Rev. T. H. Lewis, president of Methodist Protestant Church, and Rev. C. H. Beck, president of Board of Missions of the church, officiated at dedication. Only three Methodist Protestant Churches west of Mississippi were in Seattle.

Under pastorate of Rev. W. L. Hoffman, following 1924, membership reached 300 and church school, 400.

While Rev. W. H. Hodges was pastor, 1931-44, unification was achieved between Methodist denominations. Under pastorate of Rev. D. L. Rothweiler, 1946-54, pipe organ installed. Membership continued growth.

In 1964, Rev. Lewis R. Martin appointed for sixth year. Members, 322, church school enrollment, 214. Woman's Society of Christian Service, 86. They gave $534.

236

The campaign was successful and, in 1916, Rev. James E. Crowther, chairman of the committee on education, reported that Hill had paid the $50,000 pledged and over $25,000 additional had been collected. More than $175,000 was in the form of interest-bearing notes.

COLLEGE RESOLVED TO PAY AS IT GOES

The trustees reported in 1917 that the expenses of the College had been supplied through the income and that there had been paid on subscriptions, during the year, $34,947, making a total of $109,947.05 in invested endowment. Enrollment in the College of Liberal Arts that year was eighty-nine per cent greater than two years earlier. E. S. Collins had offered to pay $5,000 to start a $30,000 endowment fund for the Department of Religion. This department already had been started by placing Rev. Ira A. Morton at its head.

TODD'S LEADERSHIP RECEIVES HIGH PRAISE

The committee expressed appreciation for the wise leadership of President Todd, and said, "He is attaining an increasingly commanding place in the commonwealth of Washington. The College has had a successful year academically and financially. It has received Class A rating from our Board of Education and diplomas are received without discount at Columbia University."

Twelve thousand dollars had been received as endowment for the department of religion.

PIERCE COUNTY TOPS HALF MILLION

The Conference in 1919 pledged itself to conduct an intensive campaign in the churches for $500,000, if Pierce County and Tacoma would secure bona fide pledges for a like amount. A year later the campaign in Tacoma was reported successful with $547,000 pledged.

"It now remains for the Puget Sound Annual Conference," it was resolved,

ST. JOHN—1903

First Methodists in St. John were Mr. and Mrs. Jess Lockhart, who moved there from South Bend, Washington, in 1894. Lockhart visited Quarterly Conference at Thornton, inviting presiding elder to send preacher. In response, Rev. Trevor Orton was sent in 1903. Church organized in October, with seven members. They were Mr. and Mrs. M. S. Oaks, Mr. and Mrs. James Doran, N. S. Ridenour, Mr. and Mrs. J. A. Lockhart. Later, 19 others.

In 1918, Methodists federated with Congregational church. Rev. R. F. Hawk, pastor.

Ladies Aid, organized in 1903. Mrs. J. M. McDonald, president. Church building, started in 1905. Rev. Charles MacCaughey went in September. Church building dedicated December 3. Parsonage built by Rev. C. A. Smith, 1908. Sanctuary remodeled, in 1937, under pastorate of Rev. J. Earl Secord.

Abandoned Free Methodist Church building acquired, in 1944, under Rev. John Moede, pastor. New building dedicated May 8, 1954, Bishop A. Raymond Grant. Rev. Albert E. VanAndel, pastor. Junior choir started by Rev. James Doak, 1956. Rev. Donald Benedict, 1961, organized two Methodist Youth Fellowship groups.

In 1964, Rev. David W. Biles became pastor for first year. Membership, 124; church school enrollment, 118. Woman's Society members, 21, gave $537. Building valued at $85,000. Parsonage $21,500, "to match the achievement of Pierce County by raising $500,000. We, therefore, here and now pledge ourselves to secure the $500,000 before we assemble in annual conference one year hence."

COLUMBIA RIVER TO THE RESCUE

In 1920 E. L. Blaine paid tribute to the Columbia River Conference for its contributions. He said, "The action of the Columbia River Conference in 1913 by which all moneys received from educational collections north of the southern boundary of Washington, should go to the College of Puget Sound, has been an ever-increasing factor in the success of the school."

A NEW SITE FOR THE COLLEGE

At that session of the Annual Conference Blaine announced that the trustees had acquired a new site of 40 acres only a short distance from the present location. The trustees would proceed with the improvement of this tract and the erection of building as fast as funds were collected.

"Notwithstanding the history of the past," Blaine said, "our eyes are to the front, and we are convinced that unless steady and decisive forward strides are made in the next few years we shall then face a situation nearly as critical as the one in 1913."

A year later, Rev. J. Ralph Magee, chairman of the committee on education, reported that more than $500,000 had been pledged to match a similar amount underwritten in Tacoma and Pierce County. "We have written promises, therefore," Magee said, "of more than $1,000,000 for equipment and endowment."

NEW ENDOWMENT CHALLENGE
"NO TASK FOR COWARDS"

No sooner had the General Education Board of the Rockefeller Foundation

GRACE CHURCH, TACOMA—1903

Grace Church, Tacoma first appeared in 1903. Rev. H. H. Newman, pastor. In 1904, church had 37 members, 110 in Sunday school, one church building worth $1200. In 1912, Rev. S. G. Jones pastor, 87 members, 233 in Sunday school. Church building, valued at $3,750, parsonage worth $2,000. In 1919, there were 37 members, 100 in Sunday school, Rev. Vincent Stearns, pastor. Ten years later Rev. Joel Vigus, pastor. There were 45 members and 150 in Sunday school.

In 1940 Rev. O. E. Faulkner, in third year. There were 100 members and 91 in Sunday school. In 1950 Rev. Don H. Glenn was supplying for the first year. One hundred seventeen members, and 74 in the Sunday school. In 1960 Grace Church was left to be supplied. Rev. J. Smith pastor the previous year reported 90 members and 93 in Sunday school. There were 42 women in the Woman's Society of Christian Service who gave $216. In 1964 Rev. Fred W. Hertzog was in his fourth year as pastor. Membership was reported to be 63, church school enrollment 112. Twenty-six members of the Woman's Society of Christian Service had given $671. The building was valued at $21,000 and the parsonage at $8,100.

heard of the success of this campaign, than the organization sent another challenge to the Conference. The offer was for $250,000 as a gift provided Northwest Methodists would match the sum by January 1, 1923.

The committee on education announced, "This is no task for cowards, nor even for the faint-hearted. But having put our hands to the plow we cannot turn back. The way seems a little dark, because of economic conditions, but progress is in advance. As a Conference, therefore, we shall gladly keep the doors of our churches open for President Todd and his co-laborers to proceed with a still hunt among our people in an attempt to meet the flattering offer."

In 1922 Blaine, in optimistic mood, declared the past year had been the most successful in the history of the College. The promise was for an attendance to tax the capacity of present buildings.

Blaine again paid tribute to the brethren of Eastern Washington and Idaho. He said, "The Columbia River Conference has opened its doors to our workers, believing that $150,000 would be a fair amount to raise within its bounds. The amount thus raised will help to offset the shrinkage of pledges on this side of the mountains. This is evidence of the connectionalism that is our church, and the fact that we are but one body of Christians the world around."

A Building on the New Site

Victory again was announced for the college in 1923. The committee said, "Last year this Conference authorized a financial campaign for the College for $250,000 to meet a challenge for a like amount from the General Education Board. We report an over-subscription on December 7, 1922. God has led us and raised up friends for us. On May 23, 1923, Mrs. Frank M. Jones, of Tacoma, pledged $180,000 to provide for the erection of the first building. It is now under construction and is to be known

TWISP—1903

Sunday school first organized in Twisp in 1903. J. F. Crockett, superintendent 12 years. Cooperated with Methow Valley Sunday School Association. First Methodist minister was Rev. A. W. Trine, followed four months later by Rev. J. C. Beach.

Church organized and Articles of Incorporation filed January, 1904. Trustees were: E. F. Johnson, J. F. Crockett, and James Watson. Rev. B. F. Utter, organizing minister.

The first Ladies Aid in Twisp organized in 1903, with Mrs. Ella Couch, president. First church building, 18 x 30 feet, erected in 1905, with aid from Board of Church Extension. In 1910 building enlarged, and in 1923, again remodeled under pastorate of Rev. Gertrude L. Apel.

In 1928-30, Ladies Aid paid $350 on church debt, leaving remainder of $550. In 1932 the Board of Home Missions granted $250, and Ladies Aid assumed balance. The interior of the church was finished in 1944.

In 1964, Rev. Robert Dabritz was reappointed for seventh year. Members, 111, church school enrollment, 70, and Woman's Society members, 26. Women paid $664.

Historian of the Methow Valley churches described the work of faithful ministers and laymen, over period of sixty years, indicating devoted and sacrificial service to members and community. Isolation is no barrier to the spirit of Christ.

as C. H. Jones Hall, in honor of her deceased husband." The new plant was to be ready for occupancy by September, 1924.

THE COLLEGE FREED FROM DEBT

In 1925 three buildings had been erected and were in use. The new Science Hall was under construction. By the sale of property and collections of subscriptions, the College would be freed from debt by October 1. The College was in the same class as tax-supported institutions of higher learning of the state. This was indicated by its membership in the Northwest Association of Secondary and Higher Institutions of Learning.

The student body, it was predicted, probably would tax present facilities before new buildings and equipment could be provided. The near future would witness the erection of at least one more academic building and a dormitory, to cost at least $40,000, for girls coming from outside Tacoma.

Collections during succeeding years did not meet expectations. By 1926 only $100,000 had been collected from the General Education Board. Although nearly $700,000 was in the invested fund, collections had not kept pace with expiration of pledges. The people were urged to increase benevolence to the College to provide adequate buildings and maintenance.

COLLEGE CONTINUES TO REGISTER GROWTH

The College continued to register growth and enrollment. A year later the question of faculty and physical equipment presented a serious problem. The committee commended the president and board of trustees for the policy of expanding only as visible resources warranted it, and urged rigid adherence to this plan. "We desire to register the fixed policy of the Annual Conference," the committee said, "to maintain control

---

CLARK FORK-HOPE—1904-1907

Lots deeded to Methodist Episcopal Church, Clark Fork, Idaho, by John Nagle, in 1904. Building completed, September, 1905.

For years church was on circuit with Hope, Idaho, where Methodism began in 1907, with seven charter members, W. F. Sharoi, C. Hopperstead, Pheba A. Olson, were directors. Rev. George A. Wells, first pastor, March 5, 1908, started parsonage. Rev. A. H. Morton, pastor, 1910. Church property sold, Sunday school lagged. Rev. O. E. Falkner, superintendent of public school reorganized Sunday school with seven members. Number grew to 42, in 1911.

Rev. R. C. Moter, 1910-13, continued school. In 1913, Rev. William Daniel served Hope and Clark Fork. In 1938 Hope was not listed. Appeared again in 1941, with Mrs. Mary Groves, pastor. Under her leadership church prospered. Under her pastorate and that of successor, Rev. Robert Rathbun, improvements made on churches at Hope and Clark Fork. Historian asserted, the ideal of this church remains to hold up the standard of scriptural holiness as proclaimed by John Wesley.

In 1964, Rev. Merritt R. Metcalf, assigned to these churches, second year. Members at Hope, 26; church school, 53. Eleven members of Woman's Society gave $97. Clark Fork membership, 48; church school, 91. Woman's Society, 22. They gave $826.

240

of the College, and so direct its affairs that the social and religious life of our students may continue in the highest and finest traditions of our Methodism."

The College continued to grow. In 1928, increased enrollment demanded an augmented faculty, physical equipment, and buildings. The board of education stated, "No sooner is our fine new science hall completed, than the demand for additional housing facilities arises."

It was reported that the conditions laid down, in past years, by the Rockefeller Foundation, still had not been met. College officials were authorized to employ necessary help to solicit and collect money.

The Pacific Northwest Annual Conference, in 1929, was told that there had been no progress in securing funds toward settlement with the General Education Board. That agency had agreed to wait until June 1, 1930. "The Conference must not record failure in meeting that challenge," it was resolved. "This institution was founded in sacrifice by the fathers. It can only be maintained in the same way. We therefore pledge the board of trustees and Dr. Todd the hearty and loyal support of this Conference in securing the balance of $155,000 of the pledge of the General Education Board, and in the placing of $150,000 back of the department of Religious Education."

The College had not been able to concentrate all its efforts in matching the offer of the Rockefeller Foundation. Other urgent needs required sums even larger than that demanded to meet the Rockefeller offer, so that while much money was raised, little of it could be applied on the endowment matching fund.

FINANCIAL PROBLEMS BECOME MORE COMPLEX

The Conference, in 1930, was told that the final date fixed by the General Education Board was December 31, 1930. There remained still $135,000 to be claimed. To get this, it was said, the

NORTH BELLINGHAM—1904

North Bellingham Congregational Church, organized September 11, 1904 and Sunday services shared by ministers of Congregational and Methodist Episcopal Churches at Ferndale. May 30, 1915 seventeen members requested formation of community church. Sixteen members and eight associate members formed first congregation. Arthur Rogers chairman, Mrs. Sarah Smith secretary.

Rev. J. C. Harrison, pastor at Ferndale M. E. Church served as first minister. A resolution in 1915 favored Methodist Church. Dr. J. M. Canse, district superintendent, July 4, 1915, received those desiring to become members of the Methodist Church. Henry J. Smith, W. C. Harley, and G. E. Thompson signed the first incorporation papers.

Twenty-five ministers served since that time. They were Jabez C. Harrison, J. M. Hixon, W. M. Rutledge, J. W. Moles. L. H. Miller, Charles B. Sears, H. L. Allen, H. A. McPheeters, R. B. Parcel, J. R. Norton, Dow deLong, A. W. Smith, Elwyn H. Scheyer, W. Paul Fulmer, Lloyd A. Doty, W. H. Forsythe, Henry R. Cross, R. S. McCulloch, L. C. Schultz, Harlan R. Stone, Paul G. Perkins, John W. Kuller, Joseph O. Patterson, John Mathone, Jessie L. Tooley. In 1964 Jessie L. Tooley was pastor. There were 88 members, 105 in church school. Seventeen members of Woman's Society had given $100. Building valued at $15,000. There was no parsonage.

241

balance of the debt of $80,000 on the science hall must be paid. The College had presented this matter to the citizens of Tacoma and Pierce County.

The College had well organized plans for the development of a department of religious education. A man was employed for the department but it was necessary to have three. To attain this end the College proposed the raising of an additional $150,000 to endow three chairs. A Methodist layman had pledged $50,000 of this amount on condition that the other $100,000 be given by other Christian people. A total approximating $350,000, therefore, was the goal for collections.

The 1931 session of the Annual Conference convened in mid-depression days. It was reported that total enrollment at the college during the past twelve months was 1,252. The school had lived within its income, and the budget was balanced for the coming year, but money to match the General Education Board had not been forthcoming. It was said that the challenge was made for the purpose of increasing endowment which would increase supporting income. It was necessary to collect approximately $175,000 more, before September 30, 1931, in order to receive the Board's unpaid balance.

CARLTON—METHOW—1904

Carlton and Methow were not among appointments in 1964. But records show that Rev. B. F. Utter preached occasionally at Methow in 1904. Church school organized at Carlton soon after town began in 1906. In 1910 Sunday school at Methow was functioning under superintendency of Mr. Green. School cooperated with Methow Valley Sunday School Association. Rev. Ralph Thomas, pastor at Winthrop-Twisp, preached regularly at Methow in 1923-24. Conference records do not show an organized Methodist Church there.

Methodist church organized at Carlton prior to 1925. In 1932 there were 13 members. That year, Rev. John McNees held services every Sunday afternoon in the brick school. When church building completed in 1945 there were 68 members.

May 30, 1948, church building washed down Methow River, not replaced. Following year attempt made to combine Carlton and Twisp. Members took turns transporting children to Twisp for Sunday school, church. In 1949, people bought used school bus for purpose. Bus discontinued in 1952.

Woman's Society of Christian Service continued until 1953, in brick schoolhouse before giving up. In 1963, there was a non-Methodist Sunday school at Carlton.

Although Methodist Church no longer served communities, many persons continued grateful for memory of Methodist ministrations there.

At its June session in 1932, the Conference was told that the college had reached full settlement with the General Education Board. The achievement, December 13, 1931, was an outstanding event in the history of the College. A gift of $150,000 from the Leonard Howarth estate, had made possible this achievement. Along with it, E. S. Collins paid his pledge for the endowment of the chair of English Bible, and others paid their subscriptions.

That one victory demanded another was forcefully illustrated in the statement that on February 18, 1932, this notable victory was celebrated together with the inauguration of Founders and Patron's Day. At the celebration College officials announced the desire to increase holdings to $5,000,000 by 1936. A plan was adopted to reach this goal.

COLLEGE WINS RECOGNITION IN DEBATE

The College during this time was winning recognition for scholarship and forensic skill. The girl's debate team of the College had won first place on the Pacific Coast, in 1933, and the men's team had won second place in debate and in oratory. Fifty-two colleges were represented at the meet. Puget Sound graduates had taken high rank among graduate institutions of the country.

Although the College closed its 1933 year with a deficit of $7,000, it still was outstanding among colleges throughout the country. To overcome this deficit every pulpit of the Conference was to be open to representatives of the College.

COLLEGE PASSES HALF CENTURY MARK

In June, 1938, President Todd reported that the College had celebrated its fiftieth anniversary. The celebration had three phases. It honored the memories of past founders and patrons; demonstrated progress in the field of liberal arts; and featured announcement of the raising of the fiftieth anniversary fund. Total enrollment in the College the previous year was 1,225. Todd said, "We are now more solicitous to improve the quality rather than the quantity of our work."

A year later Todd reported that $825,000 had been spent on the College plant with its sole indebtedness the $15,000 on the new residence hall for women.

In 1940 the fine arts faculty and curriculum had been improved in the first year of a four-year project set up by the grant of $35,000 by the Carnegie Foundation. The teaching staff had grown to 45, with ten additional fellows and assistants. A new residence hall for women was complete. The regular student body approximated 700 and enroll-

DARRINGTON—1904

Methodism started in Darrington with a Sunday school in schoolhouse in 1904. In 1913-14 Frank L. Bloxham was superintendent. The first preaching service held in 1904, Rev. A. B. Towne delivering the sermon.

The church was organized in 1905. In 1907 there were 16 members. The women were organized about 1906. They were very active and actually kept the church alive.

The first Epworth League was organized in 1909 by N. C. Rhoades, principal of the Darrington School. The first building was erected, largely through the labor of Rev. A. B. Towne, Charlie Burns, and an unnamed workman. The first parsonage was built in 1914. First electric lights installed in 1926. The first building located on Seeman Street was moved in 1928. Rev. Paul Campbell, 1925 organized Boy Scouts. From 1929 to 1944 the church on circuit with Arlington. Rev. J. C. Hofstetter, in 1937, built tables for dining room. Mrs. Mel Carter first president of Woman's Society of Christian Service in 1954. An electric organ was installed, 1957 under the pastorate of Rev. Gregory Zimmer.

In 1964 Rev. Rollin E. Stierwalt was pastor. There were 60 church members, 65 in Sunday school; 18 in Woman's Society of Christian Service, gave $250.

ment in summer and other classes brought the total to about 1,100.

College Is Methodist Agent to Mold Leaders

The board of education reported to the 1941 session of the Conference that the College was Methodism's instrument to mold business, social, professional, industrial, and religious leaders. The roll of the Conference, it was said, testified to College leadership. Of 291 members, over twenty per cent either attended or accepted degrees from the College. Of the members on trial nearly fifty-four per cent had like relations. Positive leadership also had been rendered by laymen who had been connected with the College. Enrollment for the year was 581 men and 487 women. Regular day-class enrollment numbered 719. Degrees conferred in June that year numbered 96. Teaching staff was 64 of which 44 were full-time instructors. On Wednesday morning each week, a required worship service, including a sermon by a local minister, was conducted largely by students.

Dr. R. Franklin Thompson Succeeds to Presidency

In 1942 Dr. Edward H. Todd was commended upon having completed 29 years as president of the college. It was announced that by his request, he would retire July 31. During his presidency the College had acquired an adequate site, secured endowment, obtained regional and national leadership, national accreditation, grown in size of student body and faculty, and contributed Christian leadership to the churches and the communities of the Northwest. Dr. R. Franklin Thompson was welcomed to the presidency succeeding Dr. Todd.

In 1944 President Thompson reported, "We are proud of the religious leadership and statesmanship the College renders. Many of our students and faculty are in places of leadership in Methodism. We believe firmly in the

EPHRATA—1904

Rev. H. O. Perry delivered the first Methodist sermon at Ephrata in "The Old School House Church," in 1904. In 1905 the congregation numbered 33, and Sunday school 50. Pastor received $60. The property was deeded to the church in 1909.

In 1922 the original Court House was purchased for $1,000. Rev. J. E. Bovey was pastor.

In 1930 the congregation merged with the Presbyterians to form the Union Church, but in 1942, the group became the Community Methodist Church. Two years later, the building was remodeled and moved back from "C" Street and away from First Street.

On a Sunday in 1944 the congregation paid down $4,000 and pledged $8,000 more for building. Parsonage acquired in 1944. Building dedicated March 11, 1945, by Bishop Bruce R. Baxter.

Federal Bureau of Reclamation established headquarters here in 1950's. Church experienced rapid growth. In 1955 money pledged to erect new educational building, completed in 1958, Rev. Fred E. Fox, pastor. Building dedicated March 16, 1961 by Bishop Everett W. Palmer. Campaign immediately begun to finance second unit, completed in 1963.

Members, 648, in 1964. Church school enrollment, 622; Woman's Society of Christian Service, 70 members, gave $515. Rev. Robert Ortmeyer was appointed pastor in 1964.

church supported college. The close relationship which the College has with the conference is a constant inspiration. The fact that most of the churches have taken the college day offering is a great aid."

COLLEGE AND CONFERENCE INTERDEPENDENT

Again in 1944, Dr. Thompson said, "The life of the College has always been largely dependent upon the Conference. Twice in its history this Conference has met in special evening sessions, to decide the fate of the College of Puget Sound. Out of this Methodist heritage your College grew, and true to this heritage it will remain. Each senior this year stated that not only was the atmosphere of the College one in which the spiritual life was strengthened, but each had felt his own life made spiritually stronger. In our last survey one student in 16 had definitely decided to become a religious leader. This is a fine record when the national average in church related colleges is one in every 70, and in state schools, one in every 7,121."

MINISTERS CAN HELP THE COLLEGE

President Thompson, in 1946, stressed the need to create good will. "A minister took ten minutes to speak to a non-churchman about leaving a bequest to a church-related college," he said. "Recently, when the will was probated, the College received $200,000."

COLLEGE MEETS CHALLENGE OF POST-WAR ERA

The period immediately following the second world war saw a great influx of students at the College. Dr. Thompson, in 1947, said, "The past academic year has been a trying one. We have grown from 400 during the war to nearly 1,600. This year has seen the building of the men's dormitory, housing 122. It has seen the coming of three temporary government buildings which will provide for 560 additional students. Our

LACROSSE—1904

Church at Lacrosse organized 1904. Prior to that Rev. J. C. Kirkman, pastor at Endicott had preached. First church organized in 1904. "LaCross" first appeared among appointments, 1905. Rev. M. L. Anderson, supplying. Next year Rev. W. L. Bradley, pastor. No churches, 35 members, two schools, 35 enrolled on circuit.

In 1915, Rev. Charles L. Creesey, pastor. Two churches, 50 members, two Sunday schools with 159 enrolled. Two church buildings were valued at $4,000. In 1920, Rev. James Opie, pastor, new church dedicated, by Bishop William O. Shepard. In 1921 there were 92 members on roll, 332 in Sunday school, church building valued at $37,500. Parsonage at $3,500.

Ladies Aid was organized in 1904, Mrs. Mary Grewell one of the earliest presidents, was reelected, from time to time, for years. Epworth League first organized in 1912. The congregation celebrated its fiftieth anniversary in 1954, Rev. Paul Hamlin, pastor. There were 229 full members and 177 in Sunday school. Building valued at $68,000 and parsonage at $6,000. Baldwin electric organ installed June 29, 1956.

In 1964, Rev. J. Ray Neiser, pastor third year. Name appeared as Lacrosse. Membership, 232. Church school enrollment, 125. Woman's Society, 24 gave $349. Value of church building, $79,000. Parsonage $24,500.

245

faculty has increased over one hundred per cent in the last year. It includes nine ordained ministers. We now have 26 student ministers studying at the college. Ordained and licensed ministerial students, holding charges, are granted one-half tuition, as are the sons and daughters of all ministers. This averages a college rebate of approximately $3,000 each year."

In 1950 the College of Puget Sound was third largest in Methodism, not counting the great universities. The Conference at that time gave an average of thirteen cents per member for the support of the College, against the fifty cents per member set as the goal by the General Conference.

In 1951 the College experienced the uncertainties of the undeclared Korean War. The president reported that the school had suffered the most severe year in several generations. "The problems of student life," Dr. Thompson said, "are the same as those found in your congregations. The morale of young men has seldom been at such low ebb. Uncertainty concerning the draft law, the confusion in high places, have all given rise to problems greater than before. The College of Puget Sound has felt these problems most keenly, but they have not been nearly so severe as on most campuses."

AIR FORCE UNIT PLANNED FOR COLLEGE

That year the College planned an Air Force unit on the campus. Concerning it, President Thompson said, "There has been much misinformation regarding Air Force units at the College. In the first place the College is free to discontinue the unit when it wishes. It chooses the officers, most of whom are Methodists, and all are churchminded."

By 1952 the College still was operating without a deficit, considered excellent, when 59 other Methodist colleges had a total deficit of $1,570,000. President Thompson expressed gratitude to those who had made this record possible.

LYLE—1904

First Sunday school in Lyle, 1904. First church on Community plan. Entered first building, 1911-12. Organized as a Methodist congregation in 1918. First pastor was Rev. C. L. Lowther. Rev. W. B. Lamb began in 1925.

Trustees Community Church, 1912: Louis Christianson, George Snyder, L. H. Lawson. Property transferred to Methodists, 1948, although authorized in 1938. Louis Christianson, sole surviving trustee, signed quit claim deed.

Lyle, for years was served by pastors of other churches or local preachers. First resident pastor, Rev. Claude Groth, 1952-54. First parsonage owned by congregation acquired in 1953. Trustees were Bryal Clark, Olaf Baker, Les Bond, A. S. Johnson, Russell Niblack, Ralph Pitman.

Women organized, May 15, 1922 as Balch Ladies Aid, with 7 members. Rev. W. B. Lamb served 1923-25, followed by Rev. R. C. Young, White Salmon. In 1953, Rev. Leonard J. Ruff reported 27 members, 148 in Sunday school. Women organized, according to Conference plan, Woman's Society of Christian Service. They numbered, 25, gave $193. At that time church building value $10,000 and parsonage, $5,000.

In 1964, Rev. Everett M. Ritchey, pastor first year, at Lyle and D. J. Trailer Camp. Members 54, church school enrollment 67. Woman's Society members, 20, gave $131. Building value, $16,600. Parsonage, $6,200. Paid pastor $2,100.

College Returns to Name University of Puget Sound

By 1960 the College again had become The University of Puget Sound. The work of the Methodist student movement on the campus had been strengthened. A director of student life, had been added to the faculty, and a deepened awareness of the opportunity for service had confronted students in their daily activities. The committee concluded its report, "We can be proud of the fine academic standard of our Methodist University of Puget Sound."

In 1963 total assets of the university stood at $13,962,068.80, a gain of $365,309.73 over the previous year. This was a gain of 466% since Dr. Thompson became president.

Unable to Accept All Applications

The number of high school seniors inquiring annually about entry into the freshman class was alarming, because of the large number that must be turned away for lack of facilities. In 1963 more than 5,500 inquiries were received. Thirteen hundred applied for admission, but only 805 could be accepted. Only 522 actually were enrolled as bona fide freshmen. The other 283 did not enter because they were involved in multiple applications and went to the schools first accepting them.

This inability to accept so many who wish to come reduced the number of inquiries. In 1964 more than 2,000 such communications were received, but only 700 could be accepted.

"This," said President Thompson, "illustrates how severe is the need for more room. A new science building is imperative. The Howarth Hall was planned for a student body of 600, but we now have more than four times that number. The proposed new science hall would care for an additional student body of 900.[8] This would greatly lift current pressure."

MEDICAL LAKE FEDERATED—1904

Medical Lake first appeared in 1904. In 1905, supplied by Rev. C. B. Reese. There were 51 members and 60 in Sunday school. Two buildings were worth $2,400. In 1908 Rev. Charles Elrey, pastor. In 1910 Rev. D. L. Clark, pastor. In 1913 the church was teamed with Meadow Lake. Rev. T. H. Fertig in first year. In 1914 with Meadow Lake and supplied by Rev. William Martin. There were 27 members and 59 in Sunday school. One building was valued at $2,000.

In 1928 it was left to be supplied, 45 members and 45 in Sunday school. One building was valued at $2,000 and the parsonage at $1,000. In 1939 again with Cheney (Federated), Rev. Orville Dennis was supplying for fourth year. In 1950 Mrs. J. T. Bennett was in her second year. No members reported. In 1960 Rev. James Y. Horton in first year reported 112 members and 213 in Sunday school. There were 44 members of the Woman's Society of Christian Service. In 1964 Rev. Charles B. Billups, Jr., minister of the United Christian Church, pastor. There were 98 members, 167 in Sunday school. There were 55 members of Woman's Society of Christian Service. There was one parsonage valued at $16,000.

While the University of Puget Sound enjoyed greater financial security than in any time in its history, the urgency for expansion was greater than ever. As the student body grew so did the need for more endowment, buildings, and faculty. The most dangerous thing that could happen to the school would be to cease to grow.

Yet, to permit the University to cease to expand, with need, was farthest from the thoughts of President Thompson and the Board of Trustees. As evidence, Dr. Thompson, in October 1964, said, "There are eight new buildings on the architects' drawing board of the University of Puget Sound: The Charles McIntyre Memorial Hall, which will house the School of Business Administration and Economics; three men's dormitories; three buildings in the new Science Complex, which will be started in 1965; and the new William W. Kilworth Memorial Chapel, which is to be constructed within the next three years on the campus."

Northwest Methodism Follows Its Students to State Schools

The Wesley Foundation movement arose in Methodism to undergird with religious training Methodist students in state institutions. The first step toward its promotion in the Northwest was taken in 1919 when Rev. Thomas J. Gambill was appointed student pastor at University Methodist Church, Seattle.

In 1921 Gambill was succeeded by Rev. Stanley G. Logan, who was named associate pastor. That year the conference committee on education recommended, the appointment of a commission to study the situation and gather information concerning the establishment of a Wesley Foundation, and report to the next Annual Conference specific suggestions as to the type of service to be rendered and the organization needed.

The committee appointed was composed of the following: Resident bishop,

NEWPORT FEDERATED—1904

Newport first appeared along with Priest River, Idaho in 1904. Rev. L. N. B. Anderson, pastor. There were 78 members, church valued at $2,200, 180 in Sunday school. In 1905 Rev. A. H. Morton was pastor. With Priest River and Priest Rapids there were 100 members and 50 in Sunday schools. In 1914 Rev. Frank Spaulding, pastor. Ninety-seven members, 197 in Sunday school. One building was worth $3,700. In 1928 Rev. John R. Butler, pastor. Eighty-nine members and 160 in Sunday school. In 1939 Rev. Laird V. Glascock, reported 132 members and 161 in Sunday school. Church building valued at $5,000, parsonage, $1200. In 1950 Rev. Gene Ford, supply, 149 members and 142 in Sunday school. In 1960 Rev. Ruth M. Lortz reported 136 members, 123 in Sunday school. There were 40 in the Woman's Society of Christian Service, and they gave $996.

This church which was federated with the United Christian Church was served in 1964 by Rev. Charles A. Pobanz of that denomination. He was in his third year. Reported 118 members and 90 in the Sunday school. Forty in the Woman's Society of Christian Service, and they gave $50. Building was valued at $2,000 and the parsonage at $6500.

district superintendents, president of the College of Puget Sound, the student pastor, one layman from University Church, Seattle, and one minister, and one layman from each district. The following year this committee asked to be continued for further study. It recommended that a committee of five be empowered to direct the work as their study and judgment should indicate. The committee was given authority to appeal for funds to complete construction and furnish the property known as Wesley House.

A year later it was reported that two houses adjacent to University Church had been purchased with Centenary funds and had been united to form one house. Construction of the building was in progress. Two hundred and seventeen of the 700 Methodist students at the university had been organized as the Wesley Club. Much was being done to meet the social and religious needs of the young people. About thirty were preparing for full time service in the church.

HUNDREDS OF METHODIST YOUTH HELPED

In 1926 the committee reported that hundreds of Methodist young people were receiving encouragement and counsel from the institution, under the direction of Rev. Stanley G. Logan. The following year it was said that 1,000 students at the University of Washington were Methodists.

In 1929 Logan was succeeded by Rev. J. Randolph Sasnett. The committee recommended the correlation of the work at the University with that on the campuses of other state institutions of higher learning in Washington and Idaho. It also was recommended that henceforth the work be directed by a conference Wesley Foundation Executive Committee.

WESLEY FOUNDATIONS AT THREE COLLEGES

In 1932 foundations were operating at Seattle, Pullman, and Moscow, Idaho. It

---

BLAINE MEMORIAL—1904

Blaine Memorial Church, among Japanese Americans, in Seattle, held first Sunday school in private home, 1904. Mrs. Genhichi Tsuruta was first church school superintendent. First preaching service was held that year with Rev. Genhichi Tsuruta preaching. The service was held on Main Street February 11. Church had been organized January 28 of that year with eight charter members. The church was a part of the Pacific Japanese Mission. The district superintendent was Rev. Herbert Johnson.

The first woman's group, organized in 1905 with twelve members. First church building, erected in 1912, made possible by donations from Japanese all over the United States. First building was at 1306 S. Washington Street. Cost was $25,000.

New building, erected in 1962, cost $350,000. Rev. Jubei C. Kono, pastor. Rev. Wesley Yamaka served Nisei congregation. Eddie Shimomura chairman of Board of Trustees.

In 1964 Rev. Jubei C. Kono pastor, Isei congregation, Rev. Harry Murakami of Nisei group. There were 614 members of the church, 411 in the Sunday school. Mrs. Margaret Yamagimachi superintendent of church school, Mrs. Masako Kanatomi, president of Woman's Society which enrolled eighty members. They had given $600.

This bilingual church remained 99% of Japanese ancestry from first to fourth generation.

was noted that leaders at these places had inaugurated programs providing for regular collegiate credit for courses in Bible and religious education, and the University of Idaho, and Washington State College, granted full scholastic recognition to instructors and courses.

Methodist student registration at state institutions continued to grow so that by 1937 it was said to be 1,240 at Seattle, with similar growth apparent elsewhere. A full time worker at Pullman was recommended along with better facilities for carrying on the work. The Campus Christian Council at the University of Washington had instituted a religious emphasis week on the campus once each quarter. Fifteen Christian scholars were assured for a week on the campus the following winter.

By 1943 a Wesley Foundation unit had been introduced at the State College of Education at Ellensburg. By 1964 such work also was in full swing at Bellingham, Cheney, and Lewiston, Idaho.

Thus Methodists of the Northwest gave evidence, not only of determination to provide higher education for youth in church-related schools, but to follow their young people with Christian surroundings into state-supported schools of higher education as well.

Northwest Methodist Laymen brought high Christian ideals for more than a century to education, church, business, and political life—thus proving themselves to be—

Men of Loyalty

NORTHWEST PROGRESS OWES MUCH TO METHODIST MEN

Ministers have not made all the sacrifices, performed all the deeds of heroism, nor possessed all the spiritual power that laid foundations for Christian civilization in the Northwest. Every achievement of a minister has been matched by outstanding civic service by laymen of the Church.

This was recognized from the beginning. Rev. Jason Lee, realizing that a minister was not all-sufficient, brought laymen to assist in the Oregon Mission. Soon after the mission was established on the Willamette, he asked for more laymen as farmers, carpenters, business managers, teachers, and advisors in matters pertaining to spiritual objectives of the mission.

LAYMAN BUILT FIRST MISSION HOUSE IN WASHINGTON

When Lee established the first mission in Washington, he entrusted the construction of the mission house into the hands of a layman, William Holden Willson. It was a group of laymen, led by Captain LaFayette Balch, that persuaded Rev. John F. DeVore, to go to Steilacoom, rather than Olympia, to establish the first church in the Puget Sound country. These same laymen assisted with money, materials, labor, and counsel, that Steilacoom might have the first Protestant house of worship north of the Columbia River.

It was through the encouragement and dedication of Arthur A. Denny, charter member of First Methodist Church, that Rev. David E. Blaine was able to establish Methodism in Seattle. A layman, Grove Terry, opened his home on Whidbey Island where Rev.

251

Benjamin Close delivered the first Methodist sermon in that isolated region.

Judge D. R. Bigelow, a layman, used his influence to support the church at Olympia for a full generation. The record of the First Quarterly Conference held in Eastern Washington contains the names of several laymen, who by their presence, announced to a pagan society that they wanted something better than they had.

This Quarterly Conference[1] with Rev. James Harvey Wilbur in the chair, was held at Walla Walla, October 11, 1859. The presiding elder wrote a note on the opening page of the record in which he described life in the community before the coming of the Methodists.

LAYMEN CHANGED SOCIAL TREND IN WALLA WALLA

"The society was what we have generally found on the Coast before religious influence has been brought to bear," Wilbur wrote. "Horse racing on the Sabbath, and drinking and gambling at all times in most places met the eye of the visitor.

"Indians and whites were mixing and mingling and it was not difficult to find white men that were as much lower than the Indians, as their advantages were above." The population of the circuit was estimated at about fifteen hundred.

Out of this society and into the First Methodist Church at Walla Walla, stepped several men whose influence would change the trend of civilization throughout the Inland Empire.

G. M. Gitus, William B. Kelly, John Moore, and A. B. Roberts were elected stewards.

A similar story could be recited of the founding of almost every Methodist Society in the Northwest. The records of Methodist achievements here during the one hundred and thirty years of its service, gives no occasion to discount the influence and contributions of dedicated and loyal Methodist laymen.

BETHANY, TACOMA—1904

Bethany Church, Tacoma, organized, 1904, by Rev. George Frame, pastor St. Paul's Church, and Rev. James Clulow, city missionary. Rev. J. S. Reed, pastor in 1907, preached in hall, 59th and Thompson.

Building, 56th and I Streets, dedicated, December, 1904, Rev. J. P. Marlatt preaching sermon. New church at So. 56th and Thompson, 1911, dedicated, December. Rev. James E. Milligan, pastor. Building started by Rev. J. W. Blackwell, 1910.

Parsonage built by Rev. Francis A. Ecker, clubhouse by Rev. Ed. Gebert, 1920-22. Rev. E. J. Huston, 1922-29, built plant at South 57th and South Park Avenue, including church, clubhouse, parsonage.

Debt crisis was settled October 1, 1937, through four-fold effort—Savings and Loan cancelled $6,000 of interest, members paid all they could, churches on district came to the aid of the church, and the Board of Home Missions and Church Extension loaned $7,500. Thus debt of $26,000 was reduced to $10,000. Rev. Erle Howell, pastor 1935-39.

Debt to Home Missions paid under Rev. Ernest Barber, 1939-43. Electric organ installed 1951-56, Rev. Harry Coates, pastor. Sanctuary was remodeled in 1960's.

In 1964, Rev. Lloyd N. Alden, pastor, first year. Members, 379, church school, 250. Woman's Society members, 98, paid $1,083. Church building value, $95,000. Parsonage, $15,000.

In Annual and General Conferences

The importance of loyal laymen in church councils early was recognized by the Oregon Conference. In 1858 that body adopted a resolution inviting laymen to participate in its deliberations. It proposed that the stewards convention of each district choose annually three laymen to attend the sessions of the Annual Conference, serve on committees, and vote on all questions relating to the financial, educational, and benevolent operations of the Church.

That this resolution became immediately effective is seen in the fact that the following year the Puget Sound District was represented in the Annual Conference by William Rutledge and Alfred Hall. The Columbia River District, which included Vancouver and other charges on the Washington side of the Columbia, was represented by Alexander S. Abernethy, brother of Oregon's first governor.

Laymen Were Early Given Positions of Responsibility

Laymen early were given places of responsibility for conference institutions. In 1865 several laymen were listed as trustees of Willamette University. Rev. J. H. Wilbur, Agent and Pastor at Fort Simcoe, was careful to select Christian laymen for his associates. Dr. George Kuykendall, a layman, not only was agency physician, but for a time, superintendent of the Sunday school.

Some ministers took a dim view of admitting laymen to the Annual Conference, nevertheless their presence there proved a cause of spiritual resurgence. No group of ministers could fail to feel the warming of the heart by such a message as that presented to the Oregon Conference in 1875.

"We love the cause of Christ and the institutions of Methodism," the laymen said. "In the wisdom of our divine Master, through lay representation, vast

WOODLAND PARK—1904

W. Merwin Tomlinson, first superintendent of West Green Lake Sunday school, 1909. Rev. W. W. Batcheller had been preaching in area since 1904. First services held in homes and, in 1905, in Harms Hall. In 1906 the name changed to Woodland Park Church. Congregation organized in 1904, had 36 members, in 1906.

Cottage, acquired in 1906, 73rd and Fremont Avenue, used for Sunday school. Site at 72d and Greenwood, acquired in 1908, Rev. M. P. Elden, pastor. In 1917, parsonage purchased, Rev. A. W. Brown, pastor. Under Rev. Raymond S. Reese, 1919-24, site at 78th and Greenwood acquired. First unit under construction, April 1922.

Estimated that completed church, seating 642, and 600 in church school would cost $40,000. First unit, dedicated June 17, 1923, cost $30,000. Debt of $7,000 paid under leadership of Rev. H. C. Kohr, 1942.

Plans for new sanctuary begun by Rev. John M. Finney, 1945, were carried out, in 1950, by Rev. Harold C. Williams, consecrated, 1952, under Rev. Donald Swerdfeger. Church seated 300, valued at $196,000 in 1964. Under Rev. Rhea Dougherty, off-street parking provided in 1957.

In 1964, Rev. Owen J. Beadles appointed for third year. Members, 640. Church school, 635, and 135 members of Woman's Society gave $402.

power has been drawn from the laity, and added to the executive councils of the church. Therefore, we offer profound gratitude to Almighty God that we thus stand united in this grand and glorious work.

"Ours, brethren of the ministry, is a precious privilege of sharing with you, to some extent, in this glorious work."

The message continued to assure the clergy that the laymen cheerfully accepted the division of labor and prayerfully assumed their share of the responsibilities.

"Our aims are one," the laymen said. "Our hopes are one, our work is one, differing only in the measure of execution."

Three years later the laymen of Columbia River greeted their ministers, "The laity of the church look to you, our brethren, under God, as their guide in Christian life, and feel their obligation to follow you, as you follow Christ. We are acquainted with the general purity of your lives, with the devotion, the self-denial, and consecration that marks your work. We remember how earnestly you have labored, how fervently you have prayed for our salvation and for the salvation of our children and friends. And we give you our most hearty thanks."

Few words could have been so well calculated to inspire a group of ministers to resolve to become more effective servants of Christ and His Church.

Laymen did not give up hope for representation in the General Conference. In 1894 laymen of the Columbia River Conference again asked that body to use its influence with the General Conference to admit laymen in equal numbers with ministers. Their request was eventually granted.

METHODIST BROTHERHOODS WERE RECOGNIZED

A new men's organization was recognized by the Columbia River Conference in 1908. The Methodist Brotherhood was said to be a society for men in the Methodist Episcopal Church. Its

---

SUMMIT—1904

First Methodist Sunday school, at Summit, organized January 3, 1904, in log house belonging to Alonzo Long. Date of church not clear. Epworth League organized, February 10, 1905. In 1906-07, organization of the church at near-by Midland, took most of Summit's members. These congregations served together from 1906 to 1909 when Summit became separate charge. Rev. O. R. Davids, pastor.

In 1903, Thomas Slade deeded property to the church, work began on building. Rev. William M. Welch, pastor. The church enclosed, 1904.

In 1914-17, Rev. Arthur Stearns, pastor, church, remodeled, enlarged, dedicated free of debt, 1916. Rev. Lloyd A. Burk, 1921-23, moved parsonage, erected Sunday school and social hall. In 1923, Summit and Calvary, Tacoma, on same charge, Rev. Ira J. McFarland, pastor. Rev. Harley J. Wood, pastor, 1937-43, part time Summit, Grace, together.

Summit operated Daily Vacation Bible School, 1948, with Rev. John Butler pastor, and his daughter, Laura in charge. Property purchased for parsonage 1958, old one used for Sunday school purposes. A pipe organ was installed in 1958-60 under Rev. Floyd Cronkhite.

In 1964, Rev. Douglas C. Mitchell, pastor, fifth year. Members, 287, church school, 236. Woman's Society members, 50, paying $1,575 to local expense. Building valued at $109,900. Parsonage $10,000.

254

THESE LAYMEN PROVED THEIR LOYALTY TO METHODISM

Captain
Lafayette Balch

Gordon Clinton

Rufus
Woods

Arthur E.
Cox

Judge Daniel
R. Bigelow

Ralph J.
Bennett

Logan H. Roberts

J. C. "Cliff" Haley

Chapin D.
Foster

Alexander
Smith
Abernethy

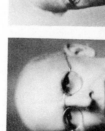

Seth
Morford

object was to associate the men of the church and congregation more closely together in religious, social, missionary, humanitarian, and reform work. It was the outcome of efforts on the part of many church leaders to unify the different men's societies. The following year the Committee on Brotherhoods recommended that the group be given a place on the Conference program.

The Layman's Association was organized in Spokane in 1910, with thirty men present. The same year the Conference spoke with praise of the men's organization, saying, "We rejoice in the fact that the Methodist Brotherhood has become such a power in our Church. The Brotherhood in earnest will impress any community of the supreme importance of the Church in the Christian life."

The Puget Sound Conference organized the Layman's Association in 1906. Thomas S. Lippy was elected president and the following year he expressed the hope that laymen could be of help in raising minister's salaries to a living level, and assume responsibility for increasing missionary giving.

With the Union of Methodism came the Lay Leader. On some districts these leaders soon were at work. In 1941, Superintendent of the Walla Walla District, Joseph M. Adams, reported a Lay Leader in every charge. In some instances the leaders were helping their pastors to get acquainted with the needs of the communities. "C. W. Booth, Lay Leader at Nez Perce," he said, "knows how to get the pastor out to where the farm life is hidden among the hedges. Pastor C. A. Brown is the man to rise to such a challenge and has organized a class at Central Ridge, for a dozen or more folk. Roy Murray, at Lacrosse, meets twice a month with his men and leads them in church activities. Dayton men prepare and serve an annual dinner, and present a unique program which attracts the attention of the whole community."

ALLEN—1905

First Sunday school at Allen held in the schoolhouse, 1905, by Rev. R. M. Schoonmaker. Church was organized 1906. Among charter members were John W. Martins, Mrs. Benjamin F. Thomas, David Essarys, Alonzo Long, Mr. and Mrs. Henry, Mr. and Mrs. William McRae, Mr. and Mrs. Berger, Mr. and Mrs. Geesamen, Melville Watkinson, Mr. and Mrs. Bixby, Mrs. Will Carver, Mr. and Mrs. Egbert.

Church with Bayview 1906-18; Avon 1919-27; again with Bayview 'till 1947. First building, begun in spring of 1914, completed by September and dedicated January 15, 1915 free of debt. Cost $1500, with gift of $250 from Board of Church Extension. Rev. George F. Pollock, pastor.

Rev. A. O. Quall was pastor 1918 to 1922. The church merged with Burlington from 1930 to 1938. In 1938 Rev. Will Richards resumed services at Allen.

In 1943-44 Mrs. Gertrude Dealy was pastor. Membership increased from 16 to 93. In 1947-48 new parsonage was erected. During this period pastors were Rev. John Mathone and Rev. John Kuller. From 1948 Allen was on the Blanchard charge. In 1964 Rev. C. H. Lund appointed pastor for fifth year. Members 244. Sunday school enrollment 163. Woman's Society of Christian Service members 45. Women paid $739.

District Lay Educational Meeting Planned

That same year, Charles A. Robbins, Conference Lay Leader, and Chapin D. Foster, secretary of the conference committee on Lay Activities, reported a plan to conduct educational meetings on all districts and send literature to inform lay leaders of their duties in the local church. Again in 1943 these men reported that the promised meetings had been held for two years and would be continued. The use of teams of lay speakers was urged.

At the end of twelve years of lay activities, Robbins and Foster again reported that enough had been accomplished to show that more could be done. During the past year, it was reported that at Conference, district, and subdistrict rallies, emphasis had been laid upon stewardship, and Lay Leaders had pressed the matter of Methodist Men's Groups.

After twenty years of Lay Activities, Merrill Stover, Conference Lay Leader, reported that during the Conference sessions a meeting had sought to orient new lay members of the Conference and to introduce nominees for election to General Conference. A meeting at Lazy F. Ranch in September had sought to train Lay Leaders for their tasks.

Stover set forth a six-fold program for the ensuing year. The men would continue to charter Men's Clubs, reactivate inactive members and win new ones, emphasize Men's Scholarship funds for the University of Puget Sound, promote stewardship, hold fall board meetings at Lazy F. and help local clubs to organize and find programs.

Methodist Men Spread the Leaven of Faith in All Activities

Northwest Methodist Laymen, through more than a century, have been active in all areas of civic and community life. It would be impossible to list the many avenues of service through

BELLINGHAM, EUREKA—1905

Eureka Methodist Church was organized in September 1905, nine charter members. Rev. J. W. Flesher organizing minister. Service held in home of Mr. and Mrs. Adin E. Mark. First regular pastor was Rev. F. A. Guiler, 1907. Church building dedicated December 15 that year. Rev. S. S. Sulliger presiding elder and Rev. D. L. Rader, editor Pacific Christian Advocate participated. Building located on Undine and Alabama Streets, was known as "The Tabernacle," later used as Boy Scout hall.

In 1924 the social hall was converted into parsonage. In 1944 name of church was changed to Eureka Methodist Episcopal Church. In 1951 the old church was moved back on lot to be used for social purposes. A new kitchen and a fireplace room were added to the enjoyment of the congregation.

Congregation merged with Garden Street church in 1962. This experience proved a trial to old-time members of the church. History was compiled by two daughters of Mr. and Mrs. A. E. Mark, charter members of the church. The daughters were Hannah Mark Murray and Margaret Mark Romigh, both members of the church for fifty years. The first Epworth League was organized by the Rev. Roy Owens who also conducted a Bible class.

257

which these men have spread the leaven of their faith. They have served as educators, members of school boards, Boy Scout leaders, City Councilmen, County Commissioners, Legislators on state and national levels, Judges, Governors, and spearheaded many types of movements seeking the public good.

METHODIST LAYMEN ACTIVE IN COMMUNITY LIFE

The best one could hope to do here would be to cite examples of service rendered by Methodist men, who, in community life, have manifested that Christian spirit and those moral standards which have tended to lift Northwest society.

George Abernethy, already cited, came West to manage the secular department of the Oregon Mission under Jason Lee. His leadership in public affairs merited his election as first Governor of Oregon Territory. William Holden Willson, mission carpenter, studied the rudiments of medicine and came to be known as "Doctor Willson." He managed the sale of Methodist property at Salem, disposing of the entire townsite for the church. Interested in politics, he was present at Champoeg where Oregon Territorial Government was organized, and his continuing interest in all affairs effecting public welfare won for him a place as a most respected citizen.

Among those whose activities were restricted to Washington, was Arthur A. Denny,[2] founder of Seattle. He was first to stake a claim in the downtown portion of the city, was successful in business, and promoted the welfare of city and state.

Denny was a member of the first Territorial Legislature, serving nine years. In 1861 he accepted an appointment by President Lincoln as registrar of the United States Land Office at Olympia. In this position, and as Legislator, he used his influence to aid Rev. Daniel Bagley to establish the University at Seattle against opposition of competing

BLANCHARD—1905

The first Methodist Sunday school in Blanchard began February 26, 1905 in a schoolhouse. A. J. Lawson first superintendent. First Methodist preaching services held 1904. First regular pastor was Rev. H. C. Carter who, in 1911, was pastor at Avon. There were 20 charter members of the church. First building was erected in 1911. Terry Coble donated a lot and made first subscription. A. J. Lawson also made a subscription and within 24 hours $800 was pledged. Work began in July.

September 3, 1911 Rev. G. A. Landen, presiding elder of the Bellingham District, dedicated the church debt free. Mission board gave $200.

Rev. J. Randolph Sasnett, pastor 1912 was followed by Rev. J. L. Grandy who served two years. The trustees when the church was erected were A. J. Lawson, Terry Coble, H. Bettner. The stewards were Mrs. A. J. Lawson, Mrs. Terry Coble, Mrs. H. Bettner. 1944 to 1947 Rev. Thomas C. Slate pastor of Grace Church, Mt. Vernon, served Blanchard. Although membership declined congregation determined to provide Sunday school, grateful for those who went before.

In 1964 Rev. Clarence H. Lund was pastor. There were 47 church members, 43 church school pupils, 20 members of the Woman's Society of Christian Service, who gave $100.

towns. Without Denny's support the University would have failed.

Denny was a prime mover in the effort to separate Washington from Oregon, as a surveyor plotted the Seattle townsite, and was a lieutenant in the army of volunteers stationed at Duwamish during the Indian War. After resigning from the position in the Land Office at Olympia he was elected to Congress, where he continued to use his influence for Washington.

Layman Gave First Ten Acres for Territorial University

Denny gave ten acres of land for the site of the Territorial University. He was a partner with Dexter Horton in the first bank, and was Seattle's first Post Master. Clarence Bagley credited Denny's personality with the rise of Seattle from a little sawmill town to a position among the great cities of the world. David E. Blaine, who spent his first two weeks in Seattle in Denny's house, said, "Everything good in this town dates back to Mr. Denny."

Seattle's first banker and capitalist was Dexter Horton,[3] a Methodist who arrived on Elliott Bay in 1853, accompanied by Thomas Mercer. He was without funds upon arrival and in debt to Mercer for bringing him here from Oregon. He went to work in Yesler's mill, and later, he and his wife cooked for nine months at another mill at Port Gamble. With money saved from this venture he entered the mercantile business, and in 1870 opened the first private bank in Washington. It became a State Bank in 1887.

Following the great Seattle fire in 1889, Horton inspired courage in the hearts of fellow residents by immediately beginning to rebuild his home and business block.

Horton was a member of First Methodist Protestant Church and, for ten years, superintendent of the Sunday school and a lifelong leader in the congregation. He was a member of the

---

BUENA—1905

Sunday school, occupying Springdale school, organized in 1905. Later the leaders erected their own community building. By 1908 two classes were taught by Mrs. J. S. Knight and John Woodall. Latter soon succeeded by S. D. Jacobs. That year Rev. J. M. Huggins, pastor at Toppenish, held first church services in community building. In June, 1909, Methodist Church organized with 13 members. Congregation served from Toppenish and later Liberty.

First trustees were: Edd Hatch, William Silvers, Joel Bliss, S. D. Jacobs, John Barrack. Rev. Walton Skipworth was presiding elder in 1909.

Ladies Aid was active by 1913. That year name changed to George A. Hall Memorial Methodist Church, honoring a man who had obtained a grant of $75 from the Board of Home Missions. Changed at his request.

Building moved to Buena that year and improvements added. Rev. C. C. Curry, of Toppenish, was pastor. Other pastors during early years were: Rev. F. R. Spaulding, Rev. A. A. Callender, Rev. J. O. Johnson.

In 1964, Pastor W. B. Asp reported 92 members of church, 62 in Sunday school, 20 in Woman's Society of Christian Service, which gave $100 to conference funds. Church had paid pastor $1,640, and World Service and Conference Benevolences $511. Liberty was the other point on circuit.

expedition, which in 1855, decided upon the location of a wagon road across the Cascade Mountains. His was a benevolent spirit and many a man, in temporary want, was indebted to him for aid. He became a capitalist, but never lost contact with the people.

METHODIST LAYMAN HELPED ESTABLISH DIGNITY OF COURTS

The man who did most in the early days to establish the dignity and authority of Washington courts was Judge Joseph R. Lewis,[4] Chief Justice of the Territorial Supreme Court from 1875 to 1879. He first came to the Territory as Associate Justice in 1872 and was stationed at Walla Walla. He found courts held in disrespect by criminals and often dominated by unprincipled attorneys. It was soon clear that Judge Lewis would tolerate no such attitudes. He demanded respect and got it. It was through his efforts that justice in Washington came to be held in highest esteem.

For four years following 1879 Judge Lewis engaged in general practice of law in Seattle. He was a member of First Methodist Church, and was chairman of the building committee which erected the edifice at Third Avenue and Marion Street, in 1889.

CASHMERE—1905

The Cashmere Church was organized March 24, 1905, with 60 members. Rev. Fred Cooper, organizing pastor. Rev. O. W. Mintzer, presiding elder. First meeting in G. A. R. Hall. Rev. L. N. B. Anderson, first appointed pastor. Articles of Incorporation filed November 28, 1905.

Parsonage built in 1906. Church building, 35 by 54, first used that year. Building dedicated May 9, 1909. Offering taken to erect Sunday school and Epworth League addition to building.

In 1911, Ladies Aid, Woman's Foreign Missionary Society, Woman's Home Missionary Society and Men's Brotherhood all were active in the church.

Under pastorate of Rev. John S. Bell, began drive for new building in 1922. Edifice dedicated in 1928. Rev. F. E. Stidd was pastor. The debt, which had burdened the church during the depression, was lifted in great Day of Joy celebration May 15-16, 1943.

A Hammond Organ was dedicated in 1946 as a memorial to four war casualties from the congregation. A new parsonage was dedicated in 1957, and Chimes as a memorial to Mr. and Mrs. J. L. Padfield, were dedicated the same year. Church membership in 1964, 303; Sunday school, 238 ; Woman's Society of Christian Service, 70. Their gifts to conference, $839. Pastor in 1964, Rev. John W. McCollum.

The Judge was one of a committee of fifteen that effected the Public School System of Seattle. He was a member of the Territorial Legislature in 1885. He played a leading role in the establishment of the First National Bank in Yakima, and was its president until November, 1889. He was one of the founders of the Dexter Horton State Bank, and an early stockholder. He was a member of the Seattle Charter Commission and served with distinction in drafting the article on Public Works in the plan for Seattle's City Government.

LAYMAN BROUGHT FIRST WAGON TO SEATTLE

Thomas Mercer[5] was a charter member of Seattle's First Methodist Protestant Church. He was born in Ohio, March 11, 1813, and crossed the plains to Oregon in 1852. He arrived in Seattle in 1853, bringing the first wagon to the town. He took a claim on the western shores of Lake Union where he made his home as long as he lived. Before coming to Seattle he had been active in the Antislavery movement and this interest continued through the Civil War years. It was he who first suggested the name of Lake Union and Lake Washington.

Mercer was active in all public enterprises and began early to work for the Lake Union Canal which he did not live to see. He supported churches, Y.M.C.A., orphanages, and public and private charities. As Seattle's population increased, land values grew and Mercer became wealthy. Through the depression of the 1890's, however, he forfeited much of his possessions.

During the Indian War following 1855, many buildings in Seattle, not protected by guards, were destroyed. Yet some of Mercer's buildings were spared. An Indian later said this was because they thought Mercer might want them later. Historians think the buildings were spared because Thomas Mercer had always dealt with the Indians with the same forthright honesty with which he dealt with other men.

Mercer was Probate Judge in King County, but refused to seek re-election for another term.

A Seattle attorney who espoused the cause of Prohibition was Charles Jorgan Smith,[6] a native of Norway who arrived in the city in 1889. He worked with the Woman's Christian Temperance Union, and was instrumental in having prohibition written into the law of the State of Washington.

In 1897 Smith was successful in securing passage of various laws beneficial to the fishing industry. He and his wife were members of the Methodist Episcopal Church.

Governor Ernest Lister[7] was a member of the Methodist Church in Tacoma,

COLVILLE—1905

Rev. James Harvey Wilbur visited Colville in 1860. Congregation dates its beginnings from 1905. That year, 33 charter members formed a church. Meetings in various homes and Odd Fellows hall. Started to build at Main and Sixth, in 1907. New pastor, Rev. H. A. Sheldon, disapproved location, selected new one. First service in new building, February 16, 1908. Trustees, W. D. Hanna, J. A. Tilton, J. J. English, J. M. Scroggs, W. J. Cornwall.

Under leadership of Rev. George Wells, 1909, main building erected, dedicated, January 12, 1912. Rev. J. S. Bell, pastor. Debt paid, 1918.

Church federated with Congregational body, 1929-30, under pastorate of Rev. M. M. Eaton. The four ministers during the federation were, Rev. Everett Hunt, Rev. Chester Blair, Rev. Arthur S. Ford, Rev. Don Baldwin. The Federation was dissolved, 1950, each congregation resuming own services.

First official meeting of Methodist group, April 16, 1950, elected trustees, Guy Markham, Chester Hills, Mrs. J. J. English, Verne Stebbins, Romona and Harold Kohlstedt. Later Mrs. Delbert Scoles and Sid Zoodsma were added. Mrs. Guy Markham was church school superintendent.

In 1964, Rev. Robert L. Irwin pastor for second year. Members, 349, church school enrollment 251. Woman's Society members, 82, gave $419. Building valued at $34,200, and parsonage at $13,623,

to which city he came with his family in 1884. After graduation from Business College he engaged with his father in Iron Works. He became interested in politics during the first campaign of William Jennings Bryan for the presidency. In recognition of his service to the party he was appointed chairman of the Board of Control, having charge of the State Reformatory and other penal institutions as well as the State Hospital for the Insane. He held this position until 1903.

Lister, in 1909, was elected member of the committee to revise the charter of Tacoma, on which he did effective work in framing the instrument under which the city adopted a commission form of government. He was nominated for Congress in 1909. Although not elected, he carried his county, thus showing political strength. He was elected Governor in 1912, serving in that office until his untimely death in 1919. During his term of office the Peace Portal at Blaine was erected.

Building and construction in Tacoma and Southwest Washington was advanced by Joseph Brierly Hawthorne,[8] of Tacoma. He attended the Methodist Church although it is not clear that he was a member. As a contractor he built many miles of steam and electric railroads, among which were Pacific Traction Company in Tacoma, and a branch of the Oregon and Washington Road from Centralia to the mines. He was elected to the City Council of Tacoma in 1904, 1906, and 1908. During these years he secured a number of changes in the management of public affairs beneficial to taxpayers.

MILTON—1905

First Sunday school, Milton, 1905, met in building on Third Street.

Church organized October, 1905, 13 members. They were: Mr. and Mrs. A. Reeves, Mr. and Mrs. E. T. Short, Mr. and Mrs. William Kleopell, Mr. and Mrs. C. Buffington, Mr. and Mrs. C. E. Kinney, Misses Edith, Elsie, and Ethel Waters.

Articles of Incorporation signed July 12, 1906 by A. Reeves, Thomas S. Short, Jr., C. E. Kinney, William Kleopell, E. T. Short. Presiding elder, Rev. B. F. Brooks.

Organizing pastor, Rev. William O. Pflaum. Outstanding student pastors were: Samuel DuPertius, Homer Moore, C. Warren Jones, Thomas Sway..e, others.

Church building dedicated Easter, 1907. Mortgage $3,000, burned, 1912, Rev. Homer Moore, pastor.

Mrs. Luella M. Wilhelm, pastor, 1929-39, parsonage acquired, and Silver Jubilee observed. Plans for new church laid under pastorate of Rev. Don H. Glenn, 1943-50. Cornerstone laid, 1954, Rev. Pierce Roberts, pastor. Dedicated April 4, that year. Rev. William O. Pflaum, first pastor, delivered sermon. Rev. Owen J. Beadles, district superintendent. Rev. William O. Pflaum delivered the sermon, 1956 at Golden anniversary. Rev. E. Gardner, pastor.

In 1964, Rev. Jack E. Wright, Jr., pastor, fourth year. Members, 196. Church school, 194. Woman's Society 45, gave $350. Building value $65,000.

LAYMEN CARRIED CHRISTIAN IDEALS INTO PUBLIC ENTERPRISES

Christian ideals of the Methodist flavor were carried into many public enterprises in Spokane by James Calvin Cunningham,[9] who arrived in that city in 1889, and became interested in real estate and insurance. He assisted in the organization of the Union Trust Com-

262

pany of Spokane. He successfully promoted many other business enterprises, but his first love was service of civic and community importance.

Cunningham was a member of the Board of Education of his home city, and active in its Chamber of Commerce. He always took an interest in religious and charitable enterprises. He was a founder of the Young Men's Christian Association, assisting in directing its building project. He served on its Board of Directors and Finance Committee. He was one of the organizers and procured the charter for the Maria Beard Deaconess Home and Hospital and president of the Board of Trustees. He was secretary of the Board of Trustees of First Methodist Church for sixteen years. He also was a trustee of the Deaconess Pension Fund, a national organization established in 1909.

Methodist Layman Chairman of Constitutional Convention

Alexander Smith Abernethy,[10] among laymen first to sit officially in the Oregon Annual Conference, was a brother of George Abernethy, first Governor of Oregon. He took a land claim in Cowlitz County near Oak Point on the Columbia about 1846. He built the first sawmill on the river in 1848 and also operated a grist mill. He was elected to the Territorial Legislature in 1854 and again in 1856. He was active in organizing the Republican Party in Washington and opposed Governor Isaac Stevens in declaring martial law over a dispute during the Indian War of the mid-1850's. He was chairman of the Washington Constitutional Convention and was elected to serve in several county posts.

Laymen Active as College Trustees

Laymen of the Conference were as active and interested in higher education as the ministers. Witness Dr. Edward H. Todd's[11] list of 223 persons who served as members of the Board of Trustees of the College of Puget

RAYMOND—1905

The first Methodist church at Raymond was organized January 1, 1905. Rev. W. E. Cox, pastor. First church building was dedicated January 5, 1905, Rev. G. A. Landen, presiding elder, with Rev. D. L. Rader, editor Pacific Christian Advocate, preaching. First parsonage completed in 1906. Institutional Hall, in 1909.

Building was partly destroyed by fire in 1911. The rebuilt and enlarged edifice was rededicated December 3, that year. Rev. Adna W. Leonard, pastor First Church, Seattle, officiated. Rev. J. M. Weaver, pastor. New parsonage was acquired in 1924. Rev. William Park, pastor. New brick edifice was dedicated May 16, 1926. Rev. E. H. Todd, officiating, Rev. George F. Hopkins, pastor. Lois Rhodes Memorial Cross was dedicated by Bishop Bruce R. Baxter, April 12, 1942. Rev. Daniel E. Taylor, pastor. Mortgage burned, April 16, 1944, Rev. R. Franklin Thompson, College of Puget Sound, officiating.

Attending the fifteenth anniversary celebration at Raymond in 1955 were, Rev. Duane E. Carter, Rev. E. R. Kaemmer, Rev. A. W. Brown, Rev. W. E. Stanton and Rev. W. E. Cox, first pastor, fifty years earlier. Rev. Austin C. Rugger, pastor.

In 1964, Rev. John A. Larsson, third year. Members, 313, church school enrollment, 315. Woman's Society members, 58, gave $607. Building value, $125,650. Parsonage $11,705.

THESE LAYMEN HELPED BUILD CHRISTIAN CITIZENSHIP

Harry E. Wilson

Hon. Joseph R. Lewis

A. A. Denny

Eugene C. Simmons

Arthur S. Cory

Harry L. Brown

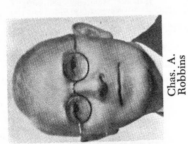

Chas. A. Robbins

James C. Cunningham

Robert J. Genins

Ray I. Wise

Sound from its founding until 1946. Of these 94 were ministers, four were housewives, and 125 business and professional men. These were the men, who, in an unbroken line of loyalty, endured hardships, sacrifice and despair, that the College might live.

Dr. Todd expressed for himself and for the Conference deepest gratitude for each of these, and singled out five for special mention. Heading this list was Edward L. Blaine,[12] son of Rev. David E. Blaine, founder of First Church, Seattle. He was born in Oregon in 1862, and educated in New York. He returned to Seattle in 1890, was successful in various business enterprises, but is better known for his contribution to public welfare.

Blaine served on the Civil Service Commission of Seattle from 1896 to 1899. He was elected to the City Council in 1910, serving several terms. He was among the men who established the Seattle Good Will Industries, and was a trustee of First Methodist Church and Seattle Seaman's Friend Society.

Perhaps the greatest service rendered by Blaine was to the cause of higher education, through membership on the Board of Trustees of the College of Puget Sound from 1905 to 1945. For thirty-seven years of this time he was president of the board.

Dr. Todd who worked with him twenty-nine years said, "He has been a loyal and effective co-worker and has been a leader through the administration of each president. His advice and counsel has been wise and constructive. His service to the college has been invaluable."

To no other man does Northwest Methodism owe so much for the progress of higher education in the Conference as to Edward L. Blaine.

Alfred Lister[12] was a member of the Board of Trustees of the College from 1902 to 1942. He was a Tacoma Banker, founder and staunch supporter of Trinity Methodist Church, and leader in

LIBERTY PARK, SPOKANE—1905

Liberty Park Methodist Church, Spokane organized 1905, 14 members. Rev. W. S. Turner, pastor. Charter members: Father Turner, Mrs. Potter, Mrs. J. W. Robinson, Mr. and Mrs. Evan Walser, Mrs. Nellie Bowers, Mr. and Mrs. William Nichols, Mr. and Mrs. U. G. Allen, Mr. and Mrs. W. A. Brown, Mr. and Mrs. Leonard Starr.

Ladies Aid organized before church. Mrs. Weger, early president, willed church $500.

To purchase lots in 1907, Rev. W. S. Turner gave his life's savings, $600. By fall a bungalow was completed. Brick building erected in 1912, dedicated by Rev. T. D. Moore, pastor, still occupied in 1958. Leonard Starr presented pulpit to church, 1912.

During depression of 1930's, Rev. E. C. Newham, Rev. Fred Pedersen and Rev. J. Henry Ernst, served two churches. New parsonage erected 1937-41, Rev. J. Henry Ernst, pastor. Under pastorate of Rev. Harry E. Coates, drive to pay debt resulted in overpayment of $266.

Under Rev. Merritt W. Faulkner, 1945-51 choir robes purchased and an organ installed. Under Rev. Ritchie D. Ocheltree, Sr. money pledged for addition to building. Under Rev. Robert R. Rings, 1953, addition begun and completed 1958, cost, $60,000.

Rev. Rarden W. Vergin, pastor, third year 1964. Members, 352. Church school 153. Women, 91, gave $754.

financial circles of Tacoma for decades. He was the brother of Governor Ernest Lister.

When Lister retired from the Board of Trustees of the College, Dix H. Rowland, a colleague, paid him the following tribute: "He filled the office of secretary for 11 years and treasurer for 21 years. In every campaign for the College he has been an enthusiastic leader and giver. He has believed intensely in the mission of the College, and has shown it by his works. The gratifying manner in which our mortgage investments withstood the depression, was due in no small measure to his wise counsel in making such investments."

For many years Dix H. Rowland [12] was attorney for the college corporation. He was a member of First Methodist Church, Tacoma, and was elected to the Board of Trustees for the College in 1912. He served as secretary, treasurer, and was a member of the Finance Committee as well as the Executive Committee. He was a man of loyalty, wise attorney, and dedicated layman, whose services to the College cannot be estimated.

Another man singled out by Dr. Todd for special praise was Charles A. Robbins,[12] his close co-worker for twenty-six years. He became Bursar for the College in 1916, and remained in that position until after Dr. Todd's retirement. Of him the retiring president said, "He is a man not only of financial acumen, but the soul of honor and integrity. He became the 'watch dog' of the treasury."

Before coming to the College Robbins had been a missionary teacher in South America. For many years he was Lay Leader of the Pacific Northwest Conference, and chairman of the Conference Board of Home Missions and Church Extension. He was elected to the General Conference many times and served on boards and commissions of that body.

The Methodist layman who gave more money to the college than any other was

---

ADDY—FOOTHILLS—1906, 1927

Addy first appeared among appointments in 1906. There were 37 members, 100 in Sunday school. In 1908, Rev. H. F. Pemberton, pastor. Church building valued at $1200. In 1909, teamed with Arden. Rev. Paul Gardner, supply. In 1914 Rev. F. J. Osborne, pastor. Three Sunday schools enrolled 100. In 1928 Rev. A. F. Peterson supply. There were 24 members and 103 in Sunday school. In 1939 Rev. Chester C. Blair, pastor. Addy and Valley reported fifty in Sunday school, one church valued at $3,000, parsonage at $1500.

In 1959 the Annual Conference authorized sale of building, lien held by Board of Missions satisfied.

Church at Foothills first appeared in 1927. Rev. S. E. Taft, pastor. In 1937 Rev. Ernest W. Denning supplying. In 1939 Rev. John Finkbeiner, pastor also served Greenacres. Combined membership of two churches 121, 75 in the Sunday school. In 1950 church left to be supplied. There were 18 members and 88 in the Sunday school. In 1959 the Annual Conference authorized that church be abandoned and building sold. After the satisfaction of a lien of $200 held by the Board of National Missions the remainder of the proceeds from the sale was to be used for church extension on Spokane District.

E. S. Collins,[12] an Ostrander lumberman. He became a member of the Board of Trustees of the College in 1903, serving until his death in 1934.

Dr. Todd paid tribute to Collins as follows: "He was one of those self-made men who came to the Pacific Northwest and made a niche for himself. He looked upon himself as a trustee of his holdings and gave liberally to the Church and its institutions. Of all those who gave to the college, he took the lead. He is to be credited with having given one-tenth of the money raised during the years of intensive campaigning. He must be recognized as the financial founder of the College of Puget Sound."

The retiring president also singled out Harry L. Brown,[12] well known Tacoma business man and member of Mason Methodist Church. Todd said, "He came to the new president of 1913 with inspiration which was priceless. It was not merely a welcome, but an assurance of confidence and financial help. Mr. Brown has been a loyal supporter and counselor. He became a member of the Board of Trustees in 1919 and has been its vice president for years."

THIS LAYMAN PROMOTED THE WRITING OF THIS HISTORY

The man who did more than any other to bring about the writing of this History of Northwest Methodism, is Chapin D. Foster, who became president of the Historical Society of the Pacific Northwest Conference in 1956. He brought to the head of the society a long series of experiences and service to public welfare as well as the Church, which especially qualified him to appreciate the need and guide the project.

Foster was born in Minnesota and, for a time, worked in the editorial department of a Minneapolis newspaper. In 1908 he came to Tacoma and worked for several months in the editorial department of the Tacoma News. By the

BENTON CITY—1906

Church at Benton City, 1906, organized at Kiona, across river. Methodists served community before 1900. Rev. J. J. Calloway, resided at Pasco 1900. Followed by Rev. E. H. Rubicam 1901 who erected first church. Land donated by W. A. and C. O. Kelso.

Articles of Incorporation, church at Kiona, filed June 8, 1905. Trustees: W. A. Kelso, W. C. Warren, C. H. Spencer. Building completed, 1906. Church undermined by flood, rescued, moved, used for 50 years.

In 1914 Benton City began to grow. Federation of Methodists and Presbyterians lasted few years. By 1930, Benton City Sunday school enrolled 100, met in small church. Mrs. Arthur Johnson, president Ladies Aid, borrowed money, enlarged building.

Rev. C. W. Geisler, pastor, lived in shack, until three room parsonage erected. In 1945, Rev. George Nafus, pastor, church painted, remodeled, aided by Division of Church Extension.

With population growing, in 1946, church building planned. Church Extension gave $1,000. Sale of Endicott parsonage brought $5,236, sale of old building, $8,000. New building started. Rev. Edwin B. Towle, pastor 1949-53. Church membership, 185, church school, 235. Building value $45,000. Rev. Louis V. Martin, pastor 1953-59.

In 1964, Rev. John Earl Lake, pastor, fourth year. Membership, 300; church school, 190. Woman's Society, members, 47, gave $298.

end of the year he returned to his native state, but his experiences in Washington had spoiled him for life in the mid-west. By 1911 he had acquired the Grandview Herald in the Yakima Valley.

In 1924 he became proprietor of the Chehalis Advocate in Lewis County, which he published for twenty years. During his 33 years in the newspaper business he refused steadfastly to accept advertisements for tobacco or alcoholic beverages.

In 1944 Foster became Executive Secretary of the Washington State Historical Society and moved to Tacoma.

Foster gave much time to his local church. He was superintendent of the Sunday school at Grandview and at Chehalis, and a teacher of classes in both churches. For 15 years he represented the church at Chehalis in the Annual Conference and for an equal time was reserve member of the Annual Conference from First Methodist Church, Tacoma. He was elected to General Conference in 1936 and served four quadrenniums, besides membership in the Uniting Conference in 1939. For four years he was a member of the General Conference Board of Temperance and eight years on the General Board of Publication. He was District Lay Leader and secretary of the Conference Layman's Association. For twelve years he was president of the Methodist Missionary Union of Tacoma.

Foster took keen interest in projects of benefit to community and state. For seven years he was president of the Southwest Washington Fair Association. During this period he was instrumental in passage of a state law providing state aid to fairs.

Because of his interest in nation-wide publicity for his state, Foster, in 1936, was given letters of introduction to twenty State Governors by Governor Clarence Martin, providing interviews with them in the interest of their cooperation in a publicity campaign.

Some of the other activities in which Foster was involved include: Pacific

---

SIMPSON AVENUE, HOQUIAM—1906

Simpson Avenue Church founded March 28, 1906. First Church, Hoquiam purchased lots. Rev. Alfred Bates organized Sunday school. Church organized 1908. Following year, First Church deeded land to congregation and purchased adjoining lot.

Church incorporated 1908. Trustees, M. H. Omshee, J. T. Beech, I. G. Waldron. Parsonage completed in 1910. Building costing $2,600, started. Rev. H. J. Harding, supply, served church, 1922-29, erecting new parsonage.

During 1930's depression years, congregation served from First Church. Pastors this period, Rev. Everett M. Hill, 1932-34; Rev. J. Homer Magee, 1936-39; Rev. Vern A. Spicker, 1939-41.

In early 1920's, church experienced rapid changes in pastoral leadership. Rv. C. C. Harris, 1918-19 stayed one year. Followed by Rev. E. O. Harris, whose health failed in the middle of year, forced his resignation. Rev. J. F. Smith, 1920, stayed less than year. Rev. M. R. Brown, retired, died at the end of two months of service. Rev. E. W. Anacher, 1921-22 remained year and ten months. A young man with extreme Pentecostal leanings, disrupted, divided congregation.

The leadership of Rev. H. J. Harding in 1922-29 stabilized the situation.

In late 1930's and early 1940's membership sagged and, since the church was less than two miles from First Church, congregation merged with that group, 1942.

Coast Director of Public Relations for American Forest Products Industries; organizer and president, Washington Fairs Association, four years; President Chamber of Commerce at Grandview and Chehalis; President Chehalis Rotary Club; President Lewis County Concert Association; active member Lewis County Grange 15 years; Trustee University of Puget Sound 23 years; member of State Unemployment Commission under Governor Roland H. Hartley; President Washington Newspaper Publishers Association; Vice President American Association of State and Local History; Organizer first Northwest History Conference; and Vice President Washington State Chamber of Commerce.

While Executive Secretary of the Washington Historical Society, Foster headed the Washington Territorial Centennial in 1953. When he became President of the Conference Historical Society, three years later, he began to work for a published history of Northwest Methodism. His first move was to enlist cooperation of pastors in writing a history of each local church for Conference Society Archives. This he felt would be necessary as source material for a history of the Conference. Eight years and 800 letters later, in 1964, he reported that all local histories save a half dozen, were in.

He played the leading role in securing for McNeil Island Penitentiary a chapel costing $100,000 which was dedicated in 1965.

A layman who gave his life to the cause of Christ through the local church for more than sixty years of the twentieth century was Harry E. Wilson. Soon after his arrival in Seattle in 1901, he began to teach in First Methodist Church school. In 1911 he was elected superintendent, and, in 1917, became full-time director of Christian education, a position he held for twenty-five years.

Wilson, a lawyer, dedicated his training and talents to Christian education. He was first in the Northwest to employ

KAHLOTUS—1906

First Methodist meetings, Kahlotus, 1906. Small building erected with help of grant from Division of Church Extension. Early promoters, Mr. and Mrs. Orin Herron, John and Ed Montgomery, Mr. and Mrs. William Richmond, Mr. and Mrs. E. J. Gilleland, Roy McCall.

Church served irregularly by visiting ministers. Mr. and Mrs. Redd were prominent in Sunday school. Mrs. A. F. Pillsbury, also devoted.

To build church Mrs. Monroe, owner of restaurant, made trips among employed to collect part money for church before spent for intoxicants. Before 1916, building burned, with insurance another erected.

Changes due to war, 1917-18 depleted population, church encountered difficult days. In 1931, Mr. and Mrs. Carl Johnson, teachers, proved great help with Sunday school. In 1934-41, Lind, Kahlotus together. Rev. R. C. Jacobs, pastor. From 1942-49, Connell, Hatton, Kahlotus together, Rev. M. H. Sharrard, Rev. G. W. Trial, Rev. F. L. Lowther, Rev. Waldo W. Pierson, pastors. From 1950, to 1962 Kahlotus alone. In 1962, Rev. Darwin E. Secord, pastor.

In 1958, new sanctuary constructed, Rev. Lovell Phillips, pastor. Former building converted into parish hall, Sunday school facilities.

In 1964, Rev. Frederick B. Riehle, pastor, second year. Members, 87. Church school 89. Woman's Society, 16 members gave $173. Building value, $62,600. Parsonage, $9,000.

audio-visual aids in the church and became an authority in this field. As a student of Christian art he excelled as an interpreter of the great masters. He equalled the best in the Northwest as a teacher of the Bible.

When Wilson retired from full-time service with the church in 1942 at the age of 72, he continued as a full-time volunteer worker, teaching the Bible, interpreting Christian art, leading junior church, promoting audio-visual aids. In 1961 he was cited for sixty years of service through the church school. He formally retired a second time in 1965, at the age of 95, disclosing his plan to visit the Holy Land to witness scenes he so often had described to his students.

Another outstanding Christian layman who has made valuable contributions to Northwest Methodism is Dr. Arthur S. Cory of Chehalis. His entire married life of 62 years has been spent in that city. No member of that church has been more active—Sunday School teacher many years, Honorary Lay Leader for life, member Annual Conference, delegate to General Conference 1920; "greeter" morning service for many years; member city Board of Education three terms and State Legislature eight terms; organizer Lewis Co. Savings & Loan Ass'n and its president 1922-62. He and Mrs. Cory have made many trips to all parts of the world, followed by substantial gifts to foreign mission fields; Governor Pacific Northwest District Kiwanis International. Active in many phases of Christian work in the Northwest.

These Are Not All Who Contributed to Northwest Progress

Sincerity and gratitude require that it be stressed here that, over a hundred and thirty years, many thousands of other Methodist laymen have served church, community, and state, with devotion, dedication, and loyalty, equalling that of those whose names appear here. Indeed the men named in this chapter could not have made this impact upon Northwest Society, without the loyalty and devotion of thousands of other laymen who of necessity must remain unnamed.

Further, it is freely and humbly admitted that Methodism is but one of the great Christian bodies whose combined impact upon the Northwest has laid foundations for the degree of Christian civilization currently enjoyed.

Women have been at heart of Northwest Methodism—earning money for ministers' salaries and debts, promoting Home and Foreign Missions, offering inspiration and setting goals for moral achievement as—

Women of Dedication

METHODIST WOMEN HAVE SET THE PACE FOR A CENTURY

How the finer sensibilities of Northwest Methodist Women, from the beginning, pointed the way to higher standards of life, is set forth in a letter written by Catharine Blaine[1] after Seattle's first church building was opened in 1855.

THIS LETTER PRETTY ROUGH ON MEN

Catharine reported how men of the town profaned the church by tracking into it heavy clay from the streets. Further indignity was heaped upon the holy edifice when some men from the town, heavy users of tobacco, disdainfully expectorated upon the sacred floor. The minister's wife, in deep humiliation, took mop, pail, and suds and cleaned the sanctuary with her own hands. When neighbor women learned what Catharine had done they joined her.

In 1953, the women of the Seattle church, celebrating their centennial, and seeking information about their early history, discovered this letter. Capitalizing upon it, they declared Catharine to be the first representative of the Ladies Aid [2] in Seattle.

The role of women in early Northwest Methodism is further illustrated in a report by Mrs. Alice Simmons, woman's historian for the church at Ellensburg.

When the cornerstone for the church there was laid, the men brought a 1,200-pound bell from The Dalles, Oregon, by wagon train. "The women of the church paid for it," Mrs. Simmons wrote, "and were rewarded by the bell's sweet tones on Sundays." [3]

But thousands of Northwest Methodist women were moved with a

271

dedication more far-reaching than housekeeping. They made that important business a point of departure for the performance of deeds of love and mercy, aimed at saving body, mind, and spirit of God's children everywhere.

It all began in the dedicated hearts of Methodist women who pioneered with their husbands in the Northwest. While organization forms changed with the years, women's activities centered about local church, home and foreign missions.

DEDICATED WOMEN WORK FOR THE LOCAL CHURCH

The earliest work of women in the local church was not formally organized. An individual, like Catharine Blaine, seeing a need, proceeded to meet it. Often a group would band together to perform a service without thought of organization.

Gradually, these women came to elect officers and hold stated meetings to plan their activities. This procedure took place in many local churches before a name for their organization was adopted.

From evidence in their own records there were Ladies Aid Societies at work in the Northwest in the late 1880's, but minutes of the Puget Sound Annual Conference did not refer to them until well into the twentieth century. In the Columbia River Conference, however, they were recognized much earlier. The first direct reference to the group in Puget Sound came in the report of Rev. Thomas E. Elliott, superintendent of the Vancouver District, in 1919. This body was mentioned with the Missionary Societies. He said, "The best work on the district is being done by the Woman's Home and Foreign Missionary Societies and the Ladies Aid. The women in many of the smaller charges are the backbone thereof. If it were not for the women on the district who, in many charges, are the only stewards that can be had, we would have to close the churches. Under the

FOWLER, SPOKANE—1906

Fowler Church, Spokane, was organized in 1906, by Rev. Andrew Monroe. He was followed by Rev. F. H. Fertig, 1908-10. During this pastorate the building was started with donated labor. Ladies Aid took a concession at the Spokane Fair which they continued for several years. They purchased stained glass windows. Mrs. Amelia B. Fowler, widow of a Methodist minister, Philadelphia, contributed $1,800 and the church named in her honor.

In 1953, Rev. Roy Jenkins, pastor, Corinthian Hall was started for church school purposes. A kitchen was included and much of the work done by volunteer labor. In 1961, basement was finished to provide more classrooms. In 1963, work began to remodel and refinish the sanctuary and build new social hall. This was completed in November, 1964. Rev. James A. Moore, pastor. This minister who entered the conference in 1931, has shown an aptitude for undertaking difficult project and remaining on the scene until the task was complete. He still was pastor in 1964, after nine years.

There were 844 members of the church, 428 in church school. Woman's Society of Christian Service had 132 members, who gave $1,242. The building was valued at $90,000 and parsonage at $5,000. There was no debt.

most discouraging circumstances they labor on for God and foreign lands."

It was not until 1929 that the Pacific Northwest Conference recognized the importance of the Ladies Aid Societies by including their financial report in the statistical tables of the journal. These dedicated women, during the preceding year, had contributed the tidy sum of $136,110 to the work of the Church.

SCOPE OF WORK LIMITED ONLY BY NEED

The scope of the work of the Ladies Aid was limited only by the needs of their churches and communities. Some of these activities are suggested in reports of women's historians of local churches.[4] An example is that of the church at Everett.

"In 1900," the historian said, "the women of Everett organized the Ladies Aid to assist in the growth of a small Methodist group. During the first world war a company of young women met at the church to sew for the Red Cross."

The historian at Ellensburg wrote, "In 1919, the trustees applied to the home board for help in building a new church. This was granted and a building costing $65,000 was dedicated in 1921. In 1923 the Aid started serving dinners at the fair grounds, in a tent, to pay off the mortgage."

The Ladies Aid at Twisp, in the Methow Valley, was organized in 1903. To raise money each woman took turns serving a complete dinner in her home on meeting days and charged for it. At other times each member would earn a dollar and, at a meeting with husbands present, relate to the group how the money was earned. Funds thus raised were used to keep the church open.

WE WONDER HOW MANY MEALS PREPARED

At the Crown Hill Methodist Church in Seattle, the Ladies Aid was organ-

HAYS PARK, SPOKANE—1906

First Methodist Sunday school at Hays Park, Spokane, April 1, 1906, met at home of Mr. and Mrs. George Barker. First prayer meeting held month earlier, March 6, in home of Mr. and Mrs. E. R. Graham. Church organized March, 1906, Rev. Trevor Orton, pastor. District superintendent was Rev. U. F. Hawk. Ladies Aid organized April 23, that year, at home of Mrs. H. W. Warren.

First church building, donated and moved to location, still in use in 1962, although enlarged by additions. The parsonage built in 1907. Basement excavated and building reroofed, 1910.

In 1938, plans laid to enlarge church. Rev. Hubert C. Vincent, pastor. Plans completed, building dedicated, May 28, 1939. Mortgage burned March 8, 1942, Rev. Frank Haley, pastor. Ground broken for new parsonage, February 25, 1951, and occupied August 5, 1951, Rev. Melvin Finkbeiner, pastor. Ground purchased for educational addition, April 19, 1957. Rev. Everett W. Groves, pastor. Structure occupied, September 11, 1960, Rev. H. G. Luscombe was pastor. Old parsonage removed in 1960 and ground leveled for parking.

In 1964, Rev. Harlan D. Jones was appointed fourth year. Church members, 252, church school enrollment, 156. Woman's Society membership 61. They gave $324. Value of church building, $89,250. Parsonage, $15,300.

ized soon after the establishment of the congregation in 1913. To serve meals in the basement for church programs and financial projects, the women cooked on a "temperamental" range. Before every meal the pipes must be taken down, cleaned, and set up again. Money was scarce and fuel was not always available. Therefore, members of the group brought boxes of kindling and other fuel, to keep fires going. There being no janitor, the women gathered once in two weeks to clean, scrub, and dust the building.

The ladies of First Church, Seattle, in 1877, earned $900 by sponsoring an excursion for San Francisco residents, to Seattle and Victoria, British Columbia. After the 1906 earthquake at San Francisco, the Seattle women repaid, in a measure, their California neighbors by assembling clothing and medical supplies for their relief. They prepared 480 garments, 200 packages of bandages, and a twenty-box supply of "lint" for sufferers. Circle I donated a furnished house for this activity besides sending $273 for general aid.

QUILT STARTS FUNDS FOR NEW EPWORTH CHURCH

At Epworth Church, Tacoma, the Ladies Aid, in 1893, started a quilt, with 64 blocks and 384 names, which was completed two years later. Money raised was used to help build the new church. Three years afterwards these women paid the final $500 on the mortgage.

Members of the Society of Anatone, in 1906, attended meetings under trying circumstances. Some walked, others came in buggies, and a number rode horseback. One woman, it is remembered, trudged two miles to each meeting, without permitting rain or snow to prevent her attendance.

At Colfax, in 1895, the newly organized Ladies Aid stated the objectives to be, "To raise funds for the church and parsonage, help the needy and in every way work for the best interests of church

SPOKANE VALLEY—1906

Spokane Valley Methodist Church resulted from uniting Opportunity, 1906, Dishman, 1910. Former began with Sunday school in schoolhouse. First building erected 1911, by Rev. U. F. Hawk.

Early ministers at Dishman after 1910: Rev. A. McClintock, Rev. John C. Snowden, Rev. Thomas Lawson. From 1912 church on circuit with Opportunity. Rev. M. R. Brown, pastor.

First building erected in 1912. Dishman and Opportunity merged, 1939, erected church building. Rev. Harry L. Slick, pastor. Board of Home Missions and Church Extension gave aid, through loan. This was paid and church dedicated, 1946, by Bishop Bruce R. Baxter.

New parsonage erected, 1947, costing $16,000. Rev. Everett M. Filbert pastor. Hammond organ, installed and two morning services started, 1949. Educational unit erected in 1954-55, with $5,000 from Forward Movement funds, and loan of $27,000 by Board of Home Missions. Consecrated by Rev. Richard Decker, October 1956. Building chairman, Forest S. Peters. Pastors during period were: Rev. Kenneth Countryman, 1953-55, Rev. H. Eugene Miller, 1955-57.

New sanctuary consecrated, September 24, 1961, by Bishop Everett W. Palmer. Rev. David K. Almond, pastor.

In 1964, Rev. D. G. Northdurft appointed, fourth year. Members, 925, church school, 413. Woman's Society, 140 members, gave $729. Church building valued $341,070. Parsonage, $16,500.

NORTHWEST PIONEERS IN METHODIST WOMEN'S WORK

Mrs. David
Lawson

Mrs. F. W.
Pratt

Mrs. John P.
Richmond

Atlantic Street
Center

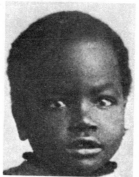

Negro girl,
Diana

Mrs. David
E. Blaine

Mrs. Francis A.
Scarvie

Miss Anna M.
Cady

Miss Ruth
Fogle

and congregation." These objectives were achieved with devotion. The Ladies Aid at Cottonwood, Idaho, was in business as early as 1907. A member, recalling those days, said, "We are not up front but have been and still are working behind the lines, and have been a real factor in keeping a church in Cottonwood."

Thus the story goes for Ladies Aid Societies in every church, and they still were a vital force in 1939, when, with missionary groups, they contributed their strength to the Woman's Society of Christian Service.

WOMEN WORKED FOR OVERSEAS MISSIONS [5]

The Eastern Oregon and Washington Conference first recognized the Woman's Foreign Missionary Society in 1875, in a report signed by Rev. S. G. Havermale and Rev. S. S. Vandersal. They spoke of this group as the strongest of the organizations of the Church, and took satisfaction in noting the steady growth manifested in this department, and the abiding hold the society had on the great heart of the Methodist Episcopal Church. "While yet in its youth," the report said, "the church is in possession of the most satisfying evidence of its adaptation and power to supplement her great missionary enterprise in foreign and home fields." The report further recommended that every church organize a foreign missionary society among its women.

The Oregon Conference first included the report of the Woman's Foreign Missionary Society in its statistical tables in 1876. The women reported $11.50 raised. The following year they had paid $17.85. On another occasion the Oregon Conference was told that this society "In the hands of an all wise God, is a powerful instrument in the great work of peace and good will to man."

From this small beginning these dedicated women have steadily increased in numbers, influence and power.

EAST VANCOUVER—1906

East Vancouver Church, first known as Irvington, was served by Rev. Ezra Hayes, 1906-07. First Sunday school, in Harmony schoolhouse that year, Mrs. Paul S. Adams, superintendent.

Church incorporated, February 6, 1908, by: Alpha B. Hathaway, John A. Hogden, George W. Lamka. Church, started March 27, and dedicated April 30, 1908. Rev. Clarence True Wilson, officiating. Rev. Edward H. Todd, preached in evening. In 1910, Sunday school attendance, 158; Rev. John H. Berringer, pastor. New parsonage 1910.

In 1943-44, annex built, Rev. Ac C. Wischmeier, pastor. Trustees: George D. Lamka, Tom Brown, Dwight Skinner. Annex dedicated, February 25, 1944. Bishop Bruce R. Baxter, officiated. Building aided by Board of Home Missions and Church Extension.

A Methodist Men's Club was organized, 1946 with six men. Rev. Lloyd N. Alden, pastor. Church was raised, improved, 1953, with aid of $8962, Area Forward Movement Funds. New parsonage, erected, 1953, Rev. M. Chester Morgan, pastor. Cost, $14,500. Former parsonage converted for church school. Electronic organ, installed 1955 and following year, fiftieth anniversary celebrated.

In 1964, Rev. William E. Callahan, pastor, second year. Members, 738. Church school enrollment, 325. Woman's Society membership 109, gave $318. Building value, $159,000. Parsonage $16,100.

FOREIGN MISSIONARY SOCIETY RECOGNIZED BY GENERAL CONFERENCE

A decade later, 1887, the Columbia River Conference indicated that the Woman's Foreign Missionary group had been officially recognized by the General Conference.

As Northwest Methodism entered the twentieth century these women steadily gained prowess and ability to produce funds for their work. In 1904 they had raised $1,804.

In the year ending 1923 the church-wide Woman's Foreign Missionary Society had raised $2,500,000, and had 700 missionaries in the field. The Columbia River group was supporting a missionary in China, two in South America, one in Korea, and one in India. Six years later these women contributed the sum of $9,471, a decrease of $993 below the previous year.

West of the Cascades the Puget Sound Conference, in 1890, recognized the place women had won for themselves in the councils of the church. A day was set for members to vote on the question of admitting women to the General Conference. Date for balloting was fixed for November 20.

In 1928 these women of Puget Sound gave through the conference treasury the sum of $18,962. Ten years later the society of the Pacific Northwest Conference gave $19,333. This was the only item under Disciplinary Benevolences showing an increase over the preceding year.

CONFERENCE WOMEN WORKED FOR HOME MISSIONS

The first mention of the Woman's Home Missionary Society in the Columbia River Conference came in 1887. The Society had been formally recognized by the General Conference, and it was resolved to encourage it in each local church. The following year a committee highly commended the

WHITE BIRD—1906, WINONA—1919

White Bird, Idaho, first appeared, 1906. Left to be supplied. Six years later, left to be supplied. Evidently attached to other churches. In 1919, W. T. Gamble, pastor. Charge on Moscow District. In 1922, left to be supplied. In 1929, with Idaho County Mission, Rev. Everett M. Filbert, pastor. At time of Methodist Union, attached to Grangeville Circuit, Rev. Nelson C. Pierce, pastor. There were 19 members of church and 39 in church school. A church building was valued at $500 and parsonage at $300.

In 1950 White Bird was still with Grangeville, which latter had become federated. Rev. LaVerne Tooley was in his second year as pastor. There were 28 members and 46 in church school.

In 1964, still with Grangeville, Rev. William E. Strance, pastor, fourth year.

Winona, first appeared in minutes with Thornton. Rev. J. J. Matney, was pastor, first year. In 1938, it was with Endicott, and Benge. Rev. Ralph Bolick, pastor. In 1950, Winona was with La-Crosse. There were 17 members and 51 in church school. Last appeared among appointments, 1958. Rev. Ronald K. Johnson, pastor. There were 18 members, 37 enrolled in church school, and 13 members of Woman's Society, giving $125. A church building was valued at $4,000.

group. It was said, "The Society is growing in favor very rapidly under the efficient management of Mrs. D. G. Strong. They have collected $160.65 for all purposes." Cost of supplies and aid to thirteen needy preachers and their families amounted to $52.50. In 1890 they had earned a total of $559, and in 1904 they had contributed $481.

In 1895 these women of Puget Sound established the Stickney Home and School for Indian children at Nooksack. The following year it was reported that the school was directed by J. R. Stark who had personal charge of the industrial department. Miss Alice C. Stark led the day school. Enrollment was 21, and average attendance 15. Mrs. Stark was matron of the home, superintending the boarding and clothing of the children. She gave them lessons in housekeeping and sewing.

HOME FOR ORPHANS ESTABLISHED IN ALASKA

The Home Missionary women, in cooperation with the National Society, established The Jessie Lee Home for orphans in Alaska around the turn of the century. In 1960 all work in Alaska was assigned to the Portland Area of the church, yet women of the Pacific Northwest Conference continued to take deep interest in the home and school for Indians and Eskimos in the Far North.

Other work done by the Woman's Home Missionary Society is indicated in reports from individual groups. At Colfax, for instance, the women gave substantial aid to families of needy pastors within the Conference and other pioneers wherever found. At Cashmere the Society gave its earnings through the conference office to be used at the discretion of the state and national officers.

DEACONESSES APPEAR IN THE CONFERENCE IN 1896

The presence of deaconesses in the Columbia River Conference was first recognized in 1896, when a committee

---

KENNYDALE—1907

In 1907, a group of Christian people in Kennydale decided to organize a Methodist Church. There were 15 members. A building was erected and district superintendent Rev. W. S. Harrington appointed Rev. T. L. Dyer, pastor.

First building cost $1,200, replaced by new one, 1912. It seated 125 and basement provided space for Sunday school and social gatherings. Rev. Daniel Earl served Kennydale and Bryn Mawr. Pastors lived outside Kennydale. In 1923, Rev. W. S. Garner came to reside there and congregation acquired a parsonage. Later, Rev. B. W. Haggerty, Rev. A. W. Luce, Rev. C. N. Chelledan occupied the parsonage.

Under the pastorate of Rev. Clyde Walker, 1944, building repaired, later, destroyed by fire, but soon replaced. Congregation, meanwhile, met in school and barracks. Rev. John W. Caughlin was pastor-adviser. Because of war, two years required to complete construction. Building entered in 1946. With aid of Board of Home Missions and Church Extension, finally finished, under pastors that followed. These included Rev. Ernest Barber, Rev. Paul Brown, Rev. Edwin Rode, Rev. Henry Cross, Rev. John Freeman, Rev. Gregory Zimmer.

In 1964, Rev. John K. Burleson was pastor. Membership, 166, church school enrollment, 211. Woman's Society of Christian Service, 24. They gave $215.

278

paid tribute to the work of this group in the entire church and spoke with appreciation of the Maria Beard Deaconess Home in Spokane. The fine work of the deaconess board and the excellent character of the deaconesses were commended. The Deaconess Home and Hospital was under the care of Miss Mary J. Comstock; the Old People's Home was under the management of Miss Mary J. Curnick, and the rest home directed by Miss Clara A. Brown. The committee said, "There is no question in the minds of ministers and laity as to the value of deaconess work in its various forms."

Deaconess achievements came into the limelight in Western Washington in 1900 when the Deaconess Board of the Puget Sound Conference reported a home in Seattle with two deaconesses employed. Miss Cora Adron had served twelve months as superintendent, and Miss Ada Burbank had served as visiting deaconess since July. The visiting deaconesses had made more than 1,800 calls. The superintendent had delivered sixteen addresses on the work, and taught Sunday school classes thirty-six times, with an attendance of 300. For the needy $35 had been expended. A successful girl's class and one for mothers had functioned well.

The Deaconess Board of the Puget Sound Conference sponsored several projects. Among these were Seattle General Hospital, Deaconess Settlement of Seattle; Community House, Tacoma, and Deaconess Orphanage at Everett.

The Children's Home at Everett functioned as an orphanage until, in 1962, the institution adopted new objectives and became a clinic for the study and treatment of children with emotional disturbances.

An institution which was strictly educational in nature is included here because it was entirely sponsored by the Conference through the Deaconess Board. To Miss Bertha A. Black,[6] a deaconess and long-time instructor in the Deaconess Training School, goes credit

LEAVENWORTH—1907

Leavenworth first mentioned in conference journal in 1893. Left to be supplied. In 1904-06 served as part of Cashmere Circuit, but not organized. First Methodist organization there was Sunday school in 1907. Five teachers and 40 pupils. Used old building on 8th Street. First superintendent, O. B. Norrell.

Presiding Elder G. M. Booth probably preached there in 1893. Church organized in 1907 with 20 members. Trustees, T. M. Brender, Charles Albright, James Edwards, A. M. McKenzie, J. H. DeBord. Presiding Elder, Rev. O. W. Mintzer. Rev. Melvin Rumohr was first pastor. He found nine saloons open day and night in the railroad town. His first greeting was, "I'm sorry for you. You'd better go back. Nobody goes to church here. You'll starve." He stayed and proved his advisor wrong.

First woman's society, 1908. Mrs. Nellie Maston, president. First building, begun in May, 1908, dedicated June 10, 1909, cost $1,750. Basement finished in 1912. Rev. Edward H. Todd delivered opening sermon.

New building, erected in 1948, cost $85,000. Rev. LaVerne E. Tooley was pastor. Rev. Ritchie D. Ocheltree, in first year in 1964. Members, 267, church school enrollment, 141. Members Woman's Society of Christian Service, 25. They contributed $325. From 1904 to 1964 served by 31 pastors.

for the details included in the following information regarding it.

Deaconess Training School Proves Valuable

Like all other Methodist institutions of the Northwest, this School was started by a dedicated person with an idea. Miss Elizabeth Jones, a deaconess attached to the staff of First Methodist Church, Seattle, entertained the conviction that the Conference needed facilities to train its own young women for Christian service. Because of her belief the School was opened in 1905 under the name, "Seattle Bible Training School for Deaconesses, Missionaries, and Other Christian Workers." Miss Jones, in addition to her duties at First Church, acted for a time as first head of the school. Later, Miss Annie Marie Cady, a deaconess, became the first full-time superintendent, continuing until 1915. Succeeding Miss Cady were: Miss Mary B. Sweet, 1915-18; Miss Anna B. Carpenter, 1918-20; and Miss Ruth A. Fogle, 1920-34. The school was closed for financial reasons when Miss Fogle retired.

During the thirty years the school functioned it graduated 181 students. Twenty of these became missionaries, serving in India, China, Korea, Japan, Malaya, The Philippines, Mexico, Central America and Africa. The first of these was Miss Louise Godfrey who went to India.

Among other graduates, 90 became deaconesses, serving as teachers in Methodist schools, nurses, chaplains and official workers in Methodist hospitals. Others served as pastors of churches, deaconess heads and assistants in children's homes and schools, including the orphanage at Everett. In 1964 there were 12 retired deaconesses residing within the bounds of the Conference.

The Woman's Society of Christian Service Emerges

Women of the Northwest, like those throughout the Church, united their forces in one organization known as the

PACIFIC—1907

Methodist Episcopal Church, Pacific organized by group of laymen, 1907. They were William Miller, George F. Filer, C. G. Simmons, Morgan Lasley, M. A. Brown, R. E. Blackman. First Sunday school superintendent a Mr. Lore, father of Mrs. Mark Hedman, long-time member, church school leader.

Lots for first church donated by C. D. and Bessie O. Hillman. With aid of grant of $250 from Board of Home Missions a church was built and dedicated September 6, 1907. Used for school purposes first winter. Rev. Harry Allen preached first sermon, as pastor, October 26, 1908.

Dining room added, church painted by Ladies Aid, 1937. Rev. O. A. Faulkner, pastor. Parsonage built, 1920, Rev. C. C. James, pastor. Church steeple destroyed by lightning, September 12, 1940.

Church observed fiftieth anniversary, October 27, 1957. Rev. Raymond Brown, pastor. Woman's Society, then had two circles. Church choir, Methodist Youth Fellowship in operation. Congregation installed electric organ in memory of Mrs. Nora Hedman, 1959. All paid at time of installation. Rev. Jeff Smith, student pastor from College of Puget Sound.

In 1964, Rev. William D. Ellington, pastor third year. Members, 128, church school enrollment, 15. Woman's Society of Christian service paid $100. Church valued at $14,500. Parsonage at $14,500.

Woman's Society of Christian Service, following Methodist Union in 1939. The change was so radical, however, that some months elapsed before some local groups actually merged. First it was necessary to wait full instructions from the national organization. Even after full details were available to every local group, time was required to get under way by those most nearly ready. In many cases old habits and attachments to former groups were so strong that women were reluctant to merge their forces.

More churches had Ladies Aids than Missionary groups, and there were more Foreign than Home Missionary Societies. In no case was the personnel in any two societies identical. Nevertheless, the Woman's Society of Christian Service was born full of enthusiasm, and this spirit increased year after year. In 1963 the historian for the women of a small church wrote of the spirit of rebellion that in 1940 was in the hearts of some of her group. But she closed her report with the triumphant words, "We now are delighted to be members of the largest woman's organization in the world!"

United Methodist Women Went to Work[7]

The enthusiasm with which Methodist women went to work is seen in reports by district superintendents and state officers of the Society. For instance, in 1941, Rev. Joseph M. Adams, superintendent of the Walla Walla District, reported Woman's Societies of Christian Service in most of the churches of his district. Fifty-nine presidents reported a combined membership of 2,882. Yakima First Church had 254; Pioneer, Walla Walla, 188; Moscow, Idaho, 154; Pullman, 130; Grace, Walla Walla, and Clarkston each had 105; and Kennewick, 100. Fifty-seven societies had raised $17,534.

Rev. Walter S. Gleiser, superintendent of the Spokane District reported that the conference convention of the women

RIDGEFIELD-SARA—1907

Ridgefield first appeared among appointments, 1907. Rev. Ezra Hays, supply, second year. In 1908, there were 44 members, three churches, 105 in three Sunday schools.

First Sunday school superintendent, Sara, David Converse. Wife charter member Ladies Aid, that year. George Buker, built first church at Sara assisted by Claude Carpenter. Charles Hinchcliff gave $2,000 and memorial plaque, erected in his memory.

In 1960, Ridgefield sanctuary enlarged, new roof on church, organ purchased, all bills paid.

Congregation of German Methodists at Ridgefield, in 1891, united with English speaking brethren, 1929.

In 1910, English speaking congregation at Ridgefield was on circuit with Pioneer, Rev. Evan E. Evans, pastor. There were 41 members, 75 in Sunday school. In 1916, Ridgefield served alone, Rev. H. O. Cooper, pastor. There were 62 members and 74 in Sunday school. In 1928, there were 59 members; 116 in Sunday school. In 1938, this church was served alone by Rev. L. C. Bennett, 49 members, and 128 in Sunday school. In 1945, teamed with Bethel, and ten years later, alone, 72 members, 166 in Sunday school.

In 1964, Rev. Edward F. Altes, pastor, second year. Members, 143; church school enrollment, 150. Woman's Society, 35, giving $742. Building value, $12,900. Parsonage, $6,500.

had met on his district at Wenatchee, that a district meeting had been held at Almira, and sub-district gatherings at Cashmere and Spokane. Societies on his district having raised more than $2,000 each were Central and St. Paul, Spokane. Wenatchee and Spokane Valley were crowding the $1,000 mark. Rosalia, a smaller church, had the remarkable membership of 99.

"The women are eagerly adjusting to the new organization and form one of the invaluable forces of our Church," Gleiser reported.

That year the Puget Sound District reported a membership of 2,500 women.

Classic Tribute Paid to Work of Women

Charles McCaughey, Superintendent of Seattle-Tacoma District, whose reports always sparkled, paid a classic tribute to the new woman's organization on his district.

"Let us now praise famous women," he said, "and The Woman's Society of Christian Service. The Lord manifested in them great glory, even His mighty power from the beginning; such as did the work of ten men; women renowned for their cooking, giving no orders to their pastors, but always paying deficits. Such as found out gorgeous recipes and set them down in writing. Lo, these set banquets to which men flock. They eat abundantly, paying half what the food costs, and wipe their mouths saying, 'We served the Lord.' Such men shall perish as though they had never been, but the memorial of these women shall stand forever."

Reporting for the Vancouver District that year, Rev. Norman McCay said his district had 31 organized Woman's Societies of Christian Service, with 1,793 members; seven Wesleyan Service Guilds, with 108 members; ten young women and girls groups with 137 members; eighteen children's leagues, and 19 spiritual life leaders. Total giving

---

RIVERTON—1907

First meeting looking toward Methodist Church at Riverton, held October 24, 1907, at McCay's Hall. Church incorporated, November 1, 1907. Rev. Cyrus L. Gilbert, first pastor. He served Sunnydale, five miles away, held early service at latter point, walked to Riverton for morning service, back to Sunnydale for other service, and back to Riverton in the evening.

The Ladies Aid, organized in 1907, pledged $500 toward first building, kept happily busy and inspired others. In 1910, they kalsomined church, installed carpet around pulpit.

Ground broken for the first church early in 1908, and building was completed in April, 1909. Volunteer labor, Ladies Aid serving meals.

In 1932, Rev. F. A. Ecker, pastor, congregation celebrated twenty-fifth anniversary. Basement was excavated in 1948. In 1962, Wesley Church, organized in 1890, merged with Riverton. In 1955, plans made for new facilities. New location selected on Military Road. Additions to this property purchased in 1962. Church then owned two full blocks. With property valued at $50,000, and $20,000 cash, church expected to launch building shortly.

Rev. Harold Cribb was pastor in 1964, and Rev. C. W. Thompson, associate. Members, 505, church school enrollment, 285. Woman's Society of Christian Service, 80. They gave $452.

through the conference treasurer was $3,712; and for the local church activities, $12,731. The week of prayer offering was $90. There were 107 subscriptions to World Outlook and 264 to Methodist Woman.

That same year the Woman's Society reported that by October, 1939, there were 106 charter societies, and by the end of 1941 there were 202. Signing the charter roll had been 6,221 women and by the end of 1941 the number had grown to 10,796. Among those were 960 new members who had never belonged to any group of women in the church before.

New Activities Program Is Launched[8]

The Department of Christian Social Relations and Local Church Activities was a new departure. This group planned and directed activities and services suggested by community conditions and had general oversight of the work formerly done by the Ladies Aid Society. At Bremerton this department instituted a new service. In that city, where population suddenly had leaped from 3,500 to more than 30,000 in three years, the department had set up a friendship center, in cooperation with the Bremerton Council of Churches, where defense workers and naval personnel found opportunity to become acquainted with other newcomers to the city. The department also stressed cooperation with the women of the Council of Churches throughout the Conference.

During the previous year an interfaith luncheon had been staged in Seattle, where Jewish, Catholic, and Protestant women had enjoyed mutual fellowship. Mrs. Jennie Fulton, of Seattle, a member of the Advisory Committee of the National Board of the Woman's Society of Christian Service, spoke for Protestant women.

Through mission study classes the women were forging ahead in creating the missionary spirit among their mem-

RONALD—1907

Sunday school, organized in Ronald schoolhouse, January 27, 1907, was beginning of Ronald Methodist Church. Hanson Firth, Congregationalist, was the superintendent of the Sunday school, started as branch of the denomination. In 1908, it became union school, and, in 1909, congregation decided to be Methodist. Rev. Carl J. Kallgren, city missionary, organized church, February, 1909, 14 members.

George F. Nash, superintendent of Sunday school, Hanson Firth, choir director. Ladies Aid organized, 1909, Mrs. Ellen Harschman, president. In 1912 the ladies raised funds for parsonage. First building erected, 1909, 175th and Linden. Board of Church Extension donated $400.

Church renovated under leadership of Rev. K. L. Haga, 1921-22, and all debts paid. Rev. F. L. Baldwin, 1924, started congregation planning for new church on Aurora and 180th. Chairman of building committee was J. U. Cassel. Building dedicated in 1925 by Bishop William O. Shepard. Rev. Byron H. Wilson, district superintendent. In 1941, Rev. Waldo Pierson, pastor, paid the debt.

Under pastorate of Rev. Darrell Berg, 1951-59, membership grew from 189 to 951. The budget, from $12,000 to $53,000. An associate pastor employed for education. New building completed.

In 1964, Rev. Merritt W. Faulkner was pastor. Members, 818, church school enrollment, 620. Woman's Society members, 110, gave $640.

bers. The group had pledged $2,500 to the Tacoma Community House; $850 to the community house at Wilkeson; and $900 to the Japanese Mission in Spokane. The missionary pledge for the previous year had been $28,500, but payments on it had fallen short. Nevertheless, the faith of the women had led them to pledge $30,000 for the year to end in 1943.

Wesleyan Service Guild Aids Employed Women

The Wesleyan Service Guild was described as an attempt to give every employed woman in the church opportunities for fellowship, service, and spiritual growth similar to that afforded to other women. Nineteen such guilds were reported throughout the conference, with 339 members. They had raised $660 for missionary work beside that paid for local church activities. This report was presented by Mrs. David J. Lawson, first conference president of the Woman's Society of Christian Service.

The society continued to grow in numbers, in giving and spiritual service. In 1943 Mrs. Carl K. Mahoney, conference president, reported that the pledge of $30,000 had been paid. The women were paying the salaries of 11 missionaries. A year later Mrs. Mahoney reported 233 societies in the Conference with 11,420 members. The group had become responsible for a missionary, Miss Mary McCall, of Seattle, who was a public health nurse at Bareilley, India.

Mrs. Jennie Fulton, conference president in 1946, reported 1,384 women had been enrolled in mission study classes during the year and that membership had reached 12,358.

Mrs. C. H. Christopher, president in 1950, reported 244 societies in the Conference, but still there were churches without woman's organizations. Forty churches had Wesleyan Service Guilds. The membership of the Society had reached 16,100 and the women had sent

SILVERDALE—1907

First Methodist pastor, Silverdale was Rev. R. W. Carr, 1905. Early meetings held in schoolhouse. Church organized, March, 1907. First pastor, Rev. H. P. Waldron, also served Tracyton on Dyes Inlet. In 1908, Rev. H. R. Merrill served the circuit. Salary at Silverdale fixed at $310, Tracyton to give pastor Sunday offerings which seldom paid expenses. Pastor covered circuit on horse or walked, regardless of weather.

Lots for church building acquired October, 1907 for $450, borrowed from James Dingman. From 1930-35 Rev. Mary McKee served Silverdale, made many improvements in old building. Her salary climbed to $1200.

In 1957, new site for parsonage and building, acquired by congregation. Rev. J. Philip Porter, pastor. Construction began, March, 1960, under Rev. Paul G. Perkins. Building was opened for worship in August, 1963. Building cost $130,000. Debt, $80,000. Third crusade for building funds began January 14, 1964. Consecrated by Bishop Everett W. Palmer, June 19, 1964. Rev. Ac C. Wischmeier, district superintendent. Sanctuary seating 215, social unit, kitchen, crib nursery, toddlers nursery rooms, kindergarten, were included in the new building.

In 1964, Rev. Paul G. Perkins, pastor, fifth year. Membership, 225. Church school enrollment, 349. Woman's Society, 39. Women paid $1,459. Value of building, $150,000. Parsonage, $15,000.

THESE PROMOTED NORTHWEST WOMEN'S WORK

Mrs. Thomas
Swayze

Tacoma Community
House

Mrs. H. C.
Christopher

Mrs. R. K. Smith

Rev. Ruth Lortz

Mrs. George
Sandstrom and
Tsuguo Ikeda

Mrs.
John Eby

more than $62,000 to the Division of Missions. Two years later Mrs. Christopher reported the payment of $68,740 by the women on their missionary projects. She said the group had assumed the salaries of most of the missionaries who had gone out from the Conference and were still on the fields.

A new missionary, Miss Willene Whiteley, had been commissioned the preceding spring, but before sailing she had been married to Rev. Lyle Powell, commissioned at the same time, and the two had gone to India under the Board of World Missions.

Fine Record for First Twenty Years

At the end of twenty years of the history of the Woman's Society of Christian Service, Mrs. R. K. Smith, conference president, reported that the former Deaconess Settlement of Seattle, now the Atlantic Street Center, had changed its program in keeping with the needs of the community and times. Through a grant it was specializing with maladjusted youth. The Japanese mission at Spokane, long sponsored by the women, had become the Highland Park Church and, by its own request, was self-supporting. The Tacoma Community House had celebrated fifty years of service. During the year the women had accepted the support of two new missionaries, Laura Lee Brown, who had gone to Brazil, and Winnifred Sanberg in Nepal. Leila Dingle of the Philippines, a long-time missionary of the society, had come home and Mary Bedell, who went to China in 1918, had retired to reside at Wesley Gardens.

In 1963 Mrs. John Eby, president, reported that the women had paid $90,000 to missions during the preceding year. They had celebrated 75 years of Deaconess work in The Methodist Church. The sum of $300,000 had been granted the Atlantic Street Center by the National Institute of Mental Health for a five-year research study of the be-

---

GREENACRES, SPOKANE—1907

First Methodist services in Greenacres community held in schoolhouse. Church was organized in 1907 and soon thereafter Ladies Aid was born. The Woman's Home and Foreign Missionary Societies followed.

President, Ladies Aid, Mrs. Nipple. First project, raising funds to build church. Aid pledged $550 for the building. In year money in hand and membership doubled.

J. Green Long donated lots for first building, 1907. Structure went up in 1908. It was burned, however, following completion, and women started raising funds for another. This was dedicated December 15 that year. Rev. Henry Brown, pastor.

Parsonage erected in 1922. Basement of church completed and church schoolroom added in 1926. New Methodist Hymnals were added in 1935.

Pastors serving this church include Rev. Robert Thompson, Rev. E. J. Mason, Rev. Will Daniels, Rev. Dave Clark, Rev. Samuel E. Taft, Rev. Robert Maulden, Rev. Frank W. Lowther, Rev. Byron Gallaher, Rev. Mark Freeman, Rev. C. E. Estabrook, Rev. Milton DeArmand, Rev. Darrell Iwerks, Rev. John Finkbeiner, Jr., Rev. Erling Bergin, Rev. William Burke, Rev. Arthur Campbell, Rev. Lewis Ray, Rev. Richard H. N. Yost.

In 1964, Rev. Robert Dibble was pastor, third year. Members, 157, church school enrollment, 126. Woman's Society members, 20. They gave $442.

haviour problems of a selected group of seventh grade boys. The women had provided $11,000 toward an additional building to be used in a similar study of girls.

WOMEN NEVER RESTED ON THEIR LAURELS

Never resting on their laurels, these dedicated women announced that they had assumed the expense of a woman on the Walla Walla District to work with the Clearwater Group Ministry project. A major portion of the support was to be provided by supplemental giving.

Illustrating what a group of faithful women can do for a Church and an entire community is the experience of Rainier Beach.[9] This congregation came into being in 1903, and, for forty years, served an important community in Southeast Seattle. However, during the second World War it suffered a decline so that by 1947 its active membership had dropped to forty.

That year the Conference appointed Rev. George Gable, a retired member of another Conference, to supply the charge. What happened during the ensuing years is told by woman's historian, Mrs. Ada Hanscom.

"The church was at the point of disbanding," Mrs. Hanscom said, "when Rev. George Gable conducted his first service in June. The only persons present were four women, Mrs. H. Sheldon, Mrs. William McClinchey, Mrs. Jennie Sandberg, and Mrs. Margaret Clark.

"To this small group of women the Gables drew others, and in a short time a few men had been induced to join them. In two years plans were laid for a new church building. To those four women, in attendance that Sunday morning, must go much credit for the continued existence of the church. Had they not been there the church more than likely would have been closed."

This did not end the story at Rainier Beach. In 1958 the congregation conse-

LE SOURD, TACOMA—1907

Le Sourd, sponsored by Epworth Church, 1907. First meetings in unfinished house on newly acquired property. Fred Baxter first Sunday school superintendent. Rev. W. W. Schenk pastor, Epworth.

Church, organized November, 1907, 15 members. Named for Rev. D. G. Le Sourd, former pastor Epworth. September, 1908, 65 in church school. Year later, 75, with 35 members of church. In 1909, Rev. T. C. Newby, pastor.

Ladies Aid organized, 1912, Mrs. Lechner, president. In 1916, lots acquired at North 12th and Stevens Streets. Building started November, that year, Rev. Harry E. Gardner, pastor; consecrated, 1917, free of debt, 1918. In 1925, portable room and small kitchen.

Rev. G. P. Headly, College of Puget Sound, pastor 1925, won many youth. In following years, additions made to accommodate growing attendance. Epworth League organized in 1930, Woman's Foreign Missionary Society, 1928.

By 1952 land acquired for new building. Solicitation for funds followed. Ground broken for new plant, April 3, 1955. With Home Missions, and grants from Area Forward Movement, First Church Seattle, Mason, Tacoma, building consecrated, September, 1956, Bishop A. Raymond Grant. New organ added, 1957, and parsonage acquired.

In 1964, Rev. H. Robert Morton, pastor, third year. Members, 238, church school, 132. Woman's Society, 64 members, gave $1,953.

crated a new sanctuary costing $90,000. The mortgage was burned in 1962 with all indebtedness paid. That enthusiastic congregation turned immediately to the erection of additional space to accommodate its growing church school. In 1963 the church had 401 members.

"In all this," Mrs. Hanscom said modestly, "the women had an active part, and they will continue to work for God and His church at Rainier Beach."

Mrs. Arthur S. Cory, First Methodist Church, Chehalis, Washington, is an example of the kind of woman whose dedication inspired and enriched the lives of other women throughout the Northwest. She, with her husband, went to Chehalis as a bride in 1904. Soon after her arrival she became a member of the choir, and later responded to the plea of a group of seventh-grade girls to become their teacher.

From that day Christian education and missions became Mrs. Cory's first love and dedication. Unrelated activities were left to others. For 53 years the children and their needs claimed her. For eighteen years she was superintendent of the primary department, enlisting the aid of topflight women of the church as assistants.

Mrs. Cory placed emphasis upon knowledge of the Bible, and presented hundreds of copies of the Book to members of her classes who completed assigned memory work. Many of her former pupils, grown to manhood and womanhood, continued to treasure the books, identifying them with the church and their teacher.

For fifteen years Mrs. Cory served as conference secretary of the Children's Missionary Department of the Woman's Society of Christian Service. Prior to that time she was an officer in the Woman's Home Missionary Society, assuming the responsibility for payment of the conference pledge year after year.

In 1957, Mrs. Cory was honored by her church as its Mother of the Year. In 1965, though retired from active participation, she maintained a keen interest in the church school.

CHAPTER XIII

In championing the cause of the weak, helpless, oppressed, ill and aged, Northwest Methodists from the beginning were—

Men of Compassion

METHODISTS CHAMPION THE CAUSE OF THE WEAK

The compassionate spirit, characteristic of Methodists everywhere, led those of the Northwest early to identify themselves with the weak, defenseless and needy.

Methodism was introduced into Washington at a time when the issue of slavery was at white heat. The first pronouncement of the Conference on the issue came in 1855,[1] when the committee on slavery said it would not be possible to find words strong enough to express abhorrence of the system of American slavery. "Its fearful aggregate of evil embraces nearly every vice found in society," the committee said. "This is true in the actual circle of its presence. It paralyzes the strong arm of enterprise, blunts the moral sense, stifles the kindlings of sympathy, dries up the springs of benevolence, empoisons the fountains of thought and feeling, perverts the judgment and sears the conscience."

Two years later the Conference adopted a resolution saying, "The system never originated in a pure benevolence nor disposition to promote human happiness. Christianity can never sanction it. Therefore the members of the Conference cannot be expected to look with favor upon attempts to cherish or extend slavery."

In 1859, with the Civil War two years in the future, the General Conference was petitioned to urge all annual conferences in slaveholding states faithfully to administer the Discipline concerning slavery. The General Conference also was asked to exhort all members having to do with the great evil to guard the marriage and parental relations of their slaves, and to teach them to read the Word of

289

God. The General Rule on Slavery condemned all sinful slave holding.

In the midst of the Civil War, the Conference, in 1864, advocated an amendment to the Constitution that would wipe out slavery forever in the country, and, in 1866, expressed gratitude to God for preserving the nation as one. It concluded, "It also is a matter for thanksgiving to God that He has judged, condemned, and forever destroyed the great embodiment of crime and guilt, human slavery."

CONFERENCE SETS UP FREEDMAN'S AID SOCIETY

When the Methodist Episcopal Church set up the Freedmen's Aid Society, after the war, to evangelize and educate former slaves, the Oregon Conference threw its weight behind that venture. In 1873 the conference committee said, "The cause of freed men is one which has really enlisted our sympathy in the shape of dollars and cents." During the year the Methodists had contributed $64 to the cause.

The Conference further promised its moral and pecuniary support. In 1876 it was said that the object of the movement was the religious and intellectual training of many thousands, who, without this service, must remain in ignorance and moral darkness. The Church was likened to the Good Samaritan who saw the slaves robbed and wounded, and had compassion upon them.

The next year the Conference resolved to consider the Freedmen's Aid Society one of the important enterprises of the Church and pledged to it hearty and generous support.

The Eastern Oregon and Washington Conference began early to champion the cause of freed men, when, in 1875, the body exhorted the people to support it. The pastoral address to the Conference the following year said the work of the society was essential to the success of Methodist efforts to promote the welfare of this portion of the American people.

A year later, a report to the Columbia

WHITNEY MEMORIAL, JAPANESE, TACOMA—1907

First Methodist preacher to Japanese at Tacoma was Rev. Seichi Higashida, a local preacher from Seattle Japanese Church. He began September 22, 1907. Movement started among Japanese students attending night school at the Central Methodist Episcopal Church. Higashida was a student at the College of Puget Sound. A member of this class was Toraichi Seto who continued with that congregation more than fifty years.

In 1909, Rev. Fusao Sakaijawa became first full-time pastor. In 1911 a woman's group was organized with Mrs. Akiye Yashida, first president.

Sunday school class for Nisei students started in 1914 by Rev. Saburo Nomi, assisted by Umanosuke Tomita and Jotaro Mori.

A troop of Japanese Boy Scouts, sponsored by the church in 1928, was organized by Albert Whitney. In his honor the church became "Whitney Memorial."

The first church building was erected between 1925 and 1929 under the inspiration of Rev. S. Izaki, pastor. Building dedicated in 1929. In 1936 congregation was host to the Annual Conference. Rev. Otoe So was pastor. In 1957 the church celebrated its fiftieth anniversary. Rev. Alpha Takagi was pastor.

This church became a part of the Pacific Northwest Annual Conference in 1964. Rev. Robert M. Yamashita, pastor.

NORTHWEST PIONEERS IN COMPASSIONATE SERVICE

Wesley Gardens—Wesley Terrace

Rev. Stanley G.
Logan

NEW DEVELOPMENT IN CARE FOR THE AGED

Northwest Methodists first set up hospitals in the late 1890's. But to Rev. Stanley G. Logan, goes credit for first dreaming the dream of modern retirement homes, and pioneering the establishment of Wesley Gardens at Des Moines, 1952. Wesley Terrace followed a decade later on adjoining site. Rockwood Manor at Spokane and Bayview Manor at Seattle were occupied in 1960, the latter sponsored by First Church, Seattle.

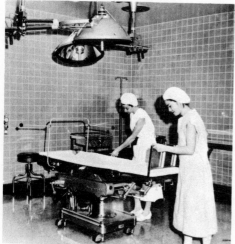

Rev. Willard E.
Stanton

Central Washington
Deaconess Hospital
Wenatchee

River Conference, signed by Sanford Burrell, stated, "The freed men of the South are destined, at no distant date, to become a large and important part of our population. Whether they shall be an element of strength or weakness to our government depends largely upon the help they receive from the North."

The refrain urging support for the Freedmen's Aid Society was taken up by the Puget Sound Conference, a committee of which, in 1885, said, "Two hundred thousand colored Brethren of the South belong to the Methodist Episcopal Church. Fifteen hundred preachers and teachers are at work among them."

Northwest interest in the Negro never waned, although it added other objectives for the race with the passing of the years.

The Sanitary Commission Commended for War Work

During the Civil War the compassionate heart of Northwest Methodists turned to the condition of men in the armed forces. A note in the Oregon Conference Journal in 1864 is revealing. It said, "The Government does all in its power to make its heroes comfortable. Surgeons, hospitals and medical ministries are provided as abundantly as ever accompanied an army on the march. Yet when a great battle occurs and 40,000 wounded and dead are upon the battle field in a single day's fighting, the ordinary military appliances fail to render assistance in due time, and hence, many valuable lives are lost. In order to meet this demand, the Sanitary Commission was organized by patriotic citizens and accepted by the Government. It poured its treasures and its comforts into the lap of an heroic manhood, with its agents to apply them, and thus, snatched from the soldier's grave thousands of its noble citizens, returning them to the broken lines."

The Conference pledged its support to this cause and prayed God's blessing upon the agency.

PATEROS—1908

Rev. J. C. Beach was first pastor of the Methodist Church at Pateros, which he organized in the fall of 1908, with 17 charter members. The church grew out of a Union Sunday School which had been organized in 1903. Charter members were, Mr. and Mrs. William Burgess, Mrs. Martha Cooper, Mr. and Mrs. Alfred Dicus, Miss Mary Eustus, Mr. and Mrs. J. W. Mansfield, Mr. and Mrs. D. W. Sanderson, Miss Grace Sanderson, Miss Beatrice Sanderson, Miss Clara Sanderson, Miss Gladys Sanderson, Mr. and Mrs. C. J. Steiner, and Mrs. N. J. Ward.

Mrs. Charles T. Borg organized the Ladies Aid Society in 1910 with six charter members. By 1921 there were sixty members.

The first building was completed and dedicated in 1914. Rev. P. C. Money was pastor. The Epworth League was started before the church was organized, by C. J. Steiner. The Men's Fellowship was organized in 1950, with Harold Terpening, first president. Rev. Walter Sloan was pastor. Twenty-seven ministers have served this congregation since its organization.

In 1964, Rev. Paul W. McConnell was appointed for the third year. Membership was 157, church school enrollment, 151, and Woman's Society of Christian Service, 50. Their gifts totalled $588. Value of church property, $44,250. Parsonage, $7,935.

Moral and spiritual ministry to the men in the Armed Forces of the United States also became a concern of Northwest Methodists. Therefore, when Congress, in 1891, proposed a bill to provide chaplains for men in uniform the Columbia River Conference approved the measure and urged the presiding elders of all districts to present this matter to their representatives in Congress.

CHAPLAINS URGED FOR THE PENITENTIARY

The interest of the Conference in providing chaplains also turned in the direction of penal institutions. Accordingly, in 1902, Columbia River Methodists were told that although sanitary conditions and police regulations at the State Penitentiary at Walla Walla were commendable, and the local ministers took turns in conducting Sunday services there, this did not fully meet the spiritual needs of the 656 inmates of the institution. A memorial to the Legislature urging that body to appoint a Chaplain was adopted.

The following year it was reported that while the Legislature favored the proposal, the Constitution prohibited appropriation of money for such a cause. In response the Conference proposed an amendment to the Constitution which was enacted by the Legislature and approved by the voters in the fall election. In 1905 the Legislature provided for the chaplaincy at the penitentiary and a member of the Conference, Rev. John LeCornu, was appointed to the position by the Governor, in June, 1905. In 1910 the Conference was informed that a chapel had been erected at the penitentiary at a cost of $25,000.

HOSPITALS ESTABLISHED UNDER CONFERENCE SPONSORSHIP

Compassion for the ill and suffering led Northwest Methodists to establish hospitals. In 1887 the Committee on Hospitals reported that there was a movement afoot to establish a hospital

SPANAWAY—1908

Spanaway Church, incorporated November 24, 1908. Rev. James T. McQueen organizing pastor. Rev. James E. Milligan succeeded, serving one year. Original church building erected at South 162d and Pacific Avenue, 1908. In 1915, Spanaway and Fern Hill together on circuit, Rev. J. H. Berringer, pastor. Later church teamed with Parkland. From 1921-33, Rev. Allen M. Fredericks, Rev. Joel Vigus, Rev. Forrest Tibbetts, Rev. W. J. Scott, Rev. A. L. Cook, Rev. Frances Camp, and Rev. Orville Weeks served congregation.

In 1943-45, Rev. Bessie Pease and Miss Annette Kiehlbaugh, deaconesses, carried on Sunday school.

In 1945, Rev. Louis V. Martin built parsonage with gift of $850 from Board of Home Missions.

In 1946, 115 in Sunday school and 105 in church. Congregation served by Rev. Arthur Campbell 1949-50. Church redecorated 1955. Rev. William F. Andrews pastor. Church moved to South 163rd St. April 15, 1956. Church separate charge, 1956, Rev. J. C. Snowden pastor. Parsonage built 1957-62, Rev. George Nafus, pastor. Ground broke for sanctuary September, 1963. Project received loan of $2,000 from Urgent Needs Appeal funds.

In 1964, Rev. Alan F. Nubling, supply, in first year. Members, 177, church school enrollment, 158. Woman's Society members 25, gave $52.00. Building valued at $93,820. Parsonage $15,285.

in the Northwest sponsored by the three conferences. The report was presented to the Columbia River and Puget Sound Conferences. A committee was appointed to cooperate. During the year the movement progressed to the point that in 1888 the institution had been located in Portland, housed in a rented structure pending construction of a permanent one. The new building would cost $75,000. By 1891 the modern hospital had been completed and was lighted with electricity and equipped with all modern appliances. The first bed had been endowed by a member of the Puget Sound Conference, Rev. W. S. Harrington. Interest of Washington Methodists in the Portland hospital waned as institutions of like nature sprang up in their midst.

Thought of a hospital in the Columbia River Conference was first mentioned in 1891 when a committee, appointed the previous year, reported that the Portland hospital was flourishing and asked the General Conference to appoint a committee to study the possibility of locating hospitals throughout the land.

In 1900 the Puget Sound Conference Deaconess Association took over the Seattle General Hospital which had been operating on First Avenue since 1893. The institution was prosperous and a permanent home, erected by Mr. and Mrs. Thomas Lippy at a cost of $30,000, was to be ready for occupancy in a few weeks.

WHITE SALMON—1908

Methodism organized at White Salmon, 1908. Rev. H. C. Clark organizing pastor. Church, in Columbia River Conference until 1922, transferred to Puget Sound, 1924. First church, erected in 1910, used until 1956. Basement excavated, furnished, in 1916. Gravel used to mix concrete. Pastor, Rev. E. T. Reid, 1913-14. Rev. F. R. Jackson, served the following year.

When grade school burned, 1923, church offered use of building, which was accepted, until new school complete in 1924.

In early years White Salmon was residence of pastors serving, Appleton, Lyle, Mt. Broad, Husum. Because of increasing population, in 1951, Rev. George P. George, pastor, dropped other points, giving full time to White Salmon. Husum turned over to Church of God. Membership steadily grew following 1945. Church purchased adjoining property, 1954, with view to erecting additional space. For this purpose $40,000 was pledged, in 1954, and building started, same year. Church schoolrooms ready for occupancy first. Church planned to remodel old building and change inside. New addition was consecrated, March 17, 1957. Church looked forward to completion of sanctuary.

In 1964, Rev. Alfred J. Waln, pastor, second year. Membership 244, church school enrollment, 217. Woman's Society, 46 members gave, $200. Church building value $95,712. Parsonage, $7,228.

In 1912 the Seattle General Hospital showed a most gratifying state of affairs, it was reported. Receipts for the year were $3,720 above expenses. More than $6,000 of charity work had been rendered, operations numbered 1,443, and the mortality rate was very low. The training school had enrolled 51 student nurses and the property was valued at a quarter million dollars.

In 1924 Thomas Lippy had deeded to the Hospital Association full title to the property with the proviso that the board pay to him or his wife the sum of $500 per month for life. The Deaconess Board had transferred title to the hospital to the Annual Conference. In 1925 it was reported that in the 25 years since the Methodists began to operate the hospital, 75,000 patients had been treated. No discrimination had been made as to native or non-resident, rich or poor, white or black.

Beginning in 1923 the hospital fell steadily behind financially. In 1929 an effort was made to reinvigorate it. Rev. L. G. Reynolds was brought in to head the institution and lead in a financial campaign to erect a new and more spacious building on a new site. Depression days had set in and the campaign was unsuccessful. A further vain attempt was made a year later. In 1934 the hospital passed into other hands and Methodism ceased to own an institution for the care of the ill in Western Washington.

Efforts of Eastern Washington Methodists to establish hospitals were more rewarding. In 1898 Rev. M. H. Marvin, chairman of the committee on the Deaconess Home reported that the Marie Beard Deaconess Hospital and Home at Spokane had enjoyed a year of prosperity. It was the gift of Mr. and Mrs. P. F. O'Neill, and had cared for 132 patients during the year, one-half of whom received free treatment.

The Central Washington Deaconess Hospital was first reported to the Conference in 1915. It had been incorporated and was housed in a building which, seven years earlier, had cost $17,000 and presently was valued at $25,000. In 1923 a new building for the Hospital costing $135,000 had been dedicated. Four years later it had received for services $55,000 with expenses running $5,000 less. That year the Deaconess Hospital at Spokane had treated 5,000 patients, doubling its volume of business in the past five years.

The Hospital at Wenatchee, in 1930, asked permission to build a new wing costing $48,000 and acquire equipment to cost $60,000 more. At that time the Walla Walla General Hospital was

---

BRYN MAWR—1909

Articles of Incorporation for Bryn Mawr Church, filed September 2, 1909. Four charter members were: Albert Cole, Mrs. Robert L. East, Mrs. Ray Wilson, and Mrs. N. E. Wilson.

Rev. Roy L. Sprague, first pastor, 1910, started fund to purchase building site. Rev. Daniel Earl, pastor, 1914, acquired two lots, erected parsonage. Rev. R. L. Wolfe, 1915, sold parsonage, acquired two lots at 85th So. and So. 115th St. Trustees were, Albert Cole, R. L. East. Board of Home Missions granted $100 for building. First unit built in 1915. Four church members, 36 in Sunday school.

In 1923, sanctuary added with aid of $200 from Board of Home Missions. By 1945 Rev. John R. Butler, pastor, there were 92 members and 143 in Sunday school.

Building committee appointed, 1955, Joe Schulz, Frank White, Wes Storey, Ray Beyer, Homer Latta, John Gleason, Mrs. P. C. Woodstock, Ted Wilson. Ground broken for new building, April, 1957. Rev. Frank Jackson, pastor. Loans from Division of Church Extension, of $30,000, gift of $2,000 from First Methodist Church, and $1,000 from Seattle Methodist Union, made building possible. Consecrated, October, 1957.

In 1964, Rev. K. W. Larrison, pastor. Members, 249, Sunday school enrollment, 411, Woman's Society members, 46, gave $844.

METHODISTS SERVE THROUGH HOSPITALS—HOMES

Spokane Deaconess
Hospital

Rev. Clark J.
Wood

Rockwood Manor

Rev. Cyrus E.
Albertson

Bayview Manor,
Seattle

offered to the Conference, and Rev. Robert Warner, head of the Spokane institution, was appointed to investigate. The offer was rejected. The Wenatchee Hospital reported it was struggling with deficient financial income. The bonding company had cancelled $3,000 of interest, reduced interest rates from six to four per cent and the Hospital was to pay $300 per month on the contract. This would liquidate the debt in eleven years.

In 1950 the Hospital in Spokane erected new additions costing more than $1,316,000. During the preceding year it had cared for 10,332 patients and 2,123 infants had been born within its walls. Gross income had been $1,135,779. In 1955 the Hospital at Wenatchee had cared for more than 10,000 patients.

In 1960 the United States Government donated the Kadlack Hospital at Richland to the Conference Board of Hospitals and Homes. During the first year the institution cared for 1,091 patients and delivered 799 infants.

The Hospital at Spokane, in 1963, occupied a new multimillion dollar building. It had run at near-capacity all year. The Kadlack Hospital had established a nursing scholarship foundation. The Hospital at Wenatchee was enjoying a new facility which had cost $780,000 housing surgery, X-ray, physical therapy and laundry.

Thus, east of the Cascades, the Conference operated three successful hospitals while there was none on the west side.

RETIREMENT HOMES ARE ESTABLISHED

The first attempt of Northwest Methodists to provide retirement homes was foretold in a resolution adopted in 1899, endorsing the idea of homes for elderly persons. The following year such a home had been opened under deaconess care in Spokane. Eight homeless women had been received. During the following forty years little was said of such institu-

---

FINLEY—1909

Methodist church at Finley incorporated June 18, 1909. Acquired title to lots for building, March 31, 1910. Paid by Ladies Aid Society. Old schoolhouse costing $300 moved to site. Repaired at cost of $1,735. Church Extension society granted $250. Building dedicated, April 23, 1910.

Methodist ministers had preached at Finley as early as 1904. Rev. S. L. Tuttle, Kennewick, first to preach. Rev. H. J. Wood, in 1905, Rev. L. N. B. Anderson in 1908. First full time pastor, Rev. H. N. Rounds, 1909. Remained until death, 1912. Rev. J. D. Bird, pastor, 1913-14. Thirteen united with church. Parsonage erected 1918, Rev. A. A. Callender, pastor. Other additions and improvements through years. Rest rooms and other additions completed in 1954, costing $1,300. Funds provided by Federal Government as result of closing Hover Church by construction of McNary Dam on Columbia River.

Church extensively revamped in 1954, new Spinet model Hammond organ installed. In 1957 furnace blew up, smoked the basement classrooms, insurance firm paid for clean-up.

In 1955, trustees: Jake Adams, president; M. F. Riek, secretary; Earl F. Myers, treasurer.

In 1964, Rev. Thomas Ray Martin, pastor, fourth year. Membership 85, church school 135. Woman's Society, members, 18, gave $329. Church building value, $15,000. Parsonage, $10,500.

tions except in occasional mention of Deaconess Hospital, Spokane.

During the Second World War the issue arose again. In 1944 the Conference appointed a committee to take steps looking toward such an establishment. In 1945 Rev. Stanley G. Logan, chairman of the committee, reported that no site had been chosen. The institution would be called "Wesley Gardens," and Logan was appointed executive secretary of the new home.

A year later, Logan reported that much promotional work had been done directed toward three basic goals. Wesley Gardens was to be made known throughout the Conference, a site was to be selected and a study made throughout the country to assemble facts relating to methods of operating such a home. The Board of Trustees had taken an option on 32 acres of unidentified land. Later the site was revealed as located at Des Moines, overlooking Puget Sound.

In 1948 Logan reported that the financial campaign to provide funds for the home had been retarded due to attempts of the Conference to raise pension funds for its retired members.

Much time had been spent laying out the grounds, the executive secretary reported in 1949. Rather than wait for funds to build the first residence hall the trustees had decided to start with the erection of cottages on the site. These would go up on land belonging to the Gardens, at the expense of the prospective residents, and would belong to the corporation for resale when no longer needed by the original builder. The first such cottage was built for and by the Logans. A total of 38 had been erected by 1964.

A campaign authorized in 1950, to raise $350,000 for the Home was postponed because most of the churches still were struggling with the pension campaign. The following year Logan reported that it would be necessary to extend the eligibility requirements for prospective residents and resort to a system of founder's fees to finance con-

GRANDVIEW—1909

Rev. William E. Regan, pastor, The Methodist Episcopal Church of Mabton, organized the first Sunday school at Grandview in 1909. Charles Moulton first superintendent. Rev. W. L. Wilson, of Mabton, organized the church there later that year. Simultaneously the Ladies Aid came into being with 8 members. Mrs. A. E. Lowe, president.

Church building, begun in 1909, was dedicated July 17, 1910, by Rev. Edward H. Todd, corresponding secretary of University of Puget Sound.

Carl Bunch elected first president of Epworth League in 1911. There were 35 members. That year the church had 81 members and church school 155. Rev. J. E. Williams, pastor.

The first parsonage was built by Rev. H. J. Wood in 1912. Mrs. Wood was first president of Woman's Foreign Missionary Society. Wesleyan Hall was built in 1922. Rev. Orland A. Scott, pastor.

March 18, 1957, authorization was given for new sanctuary, which was consecrated by Rev. William E. Callahan, Junior, superintendent of Columbia River District, December 1, 1958. A new addition was completed in 1964.

In 1964 there were 427 members of the church, 202 in Sunday school and 77 in Woman's Society of Christian Service. Rev. Charles R. Davenport was reappointed for the fourth year in 1964.

struction of the first unit. The system proved satisfactory and ground was broken for the first unit in May of the following year.

By 1954 the unit was almost ready for occupancy and 80% of the cost had been provided through founder's fees. Some friends had purchased memorial rooms without intending to occupy them. This would provide for certain residents who were unable to pay founder's fees.

Rev. William Park, first resident at the Gardens, moved into his apartment in June, 1954. By the end of the year 94 rooms were occupied and 70 applicants were on the waiting list.

Rev. Willard E. Stanton, who became superintendent of the home in 1954, reported the following year that among retired residents at the Gardens were six ministers, a teacher, four missionaries, a deaconess, a seminary teacher, two or three college teachers, and many other interesting persons. Monthly charges for board, room, cleaning, laundry, and nursing care was to be based upon actual cost.

The trustees authorized an addition in 1956 and it was completed the following year, providing 142 new units, kitchen, dining room, social hall, more hobby shops, and a thirty-bed infirmary. Thousands of dollars of free work was being done each year.

Beginning in 1960 Wesley Gardens Corporation erected Wesley Terrace, an entirely separate building across the street, north of the original home. It was ready for occupancy in December, 1961, with accommodations for 285 persons. More than 200 already were occupying their apartments by 1962. The new plant had cost more than $4,000,000 and had an indebtedness of $2,500,000. Payments on indebtedness were being met regularly for the entire Gardens project. Free services were being tendered to certain residents. Twelve had been admitted without admission fee, sixteen had been admitted at reduced costs and 19 were paying less than the standard

LEBAM—1909

In 1909, two women at Lebam leading Sunday school in Joe Gibson's building. Desiring better location, appealed to community. Four men responded: George Drymon, James Dickey, George Basham, Joe Goodell, enlisted interest of community, solicited lumber and supplies. Henry Bunker gave land, mill supplied lumber, men volunteered labor.

Ladies of community, with box socials raised money to buy materials. When building walls up and roof on structure, money and materials were exhausted. No doors, windows, furniture for inside. Project halted. Rev. S. S. Sulliger, presiding elder Methodist Church, hearing of the difficulty, offered aid, provided people would unite with Methodist Episcopal Church.

Objective in organizing church and Sunday school was to offset social conditions in the little logging town. Week ends were a time of carousal, when loggers came in from near-by camps and spent their money in saloons, making the village scene of riotous living.

Rev. Walter M. Dews, 1909-10, was first Methodist minister assigned. During following years, Lebam was on circuits. In 1962, it was with Pe Ell, Rev. Merritt R. Metcalf, pastor. In 1963 with Raymond, Rev. J. A. Larsson, pastor. In 1964 Lebam does not appear in the minutes, but was with Raymond Parish, Larsson, in third year.

rate per month. Thus, forty-seven persons were being subsidized.

Rockwood Manor at Spokane, in 1959, began construction of a residence for retired persons. Part of the cost had been provided through founder's fees and the balance, $2,872,500 had been borrowed through an F.H.A. loan.

Bayview Manor, in Seattle, was completed in 1961 and received the first of more than 250 residents in April. It was erected under the sponsorship of First Methodist Church, Seattle, on a lot willed to the church, with specifications that it be used for some type of home. It cost more than $4,000,000 and first funds were provided by founder's fees. During this period similar retirement homes were projected for Bremerton, Wenatchee, and Yakima. But it was discovered that, with other denominations in the field with similar projects, the area was already saturated. The other attempts at establishing homes were abandoned.

In 1964 the Conference had within its bounds four retirement homes with an investment of around $14,000,000 and about 1,000 residents.

MANSFIELD—1909

Mansfield was first mentioned in 1909. Next year there were 72 members, with 60 in Sunday school. Rev. J. B. Smith, supply. Mrs. Jennie Mayfield, president of woman's organization. Building erected in 1910. Grant of $250 and loan of $250 from Board of Home Missions. Building, valued at $1,700, was dedicated July 17, 1910. Debt was less than $600. Parsonage value $500.

Pastor Smith had organized two classes and established four preaching places. Rev. Charles Snowden became pastor in 1912. In 1914 there were 55 members in Epworth League, and 40 in Junior League.

New pews were installed in 1947 and work begun on basement class rooms. Improvements costing $500 made in 1951. In 1954 the church cooperated with the Christian congregation in Daily Vacation Bible School.

In 1959 talked of uniting with the Christian Church, but idea dropped in 1960. That year the Woman's Society of Christian Service dissolved in favor of a new fellowship. At Easter, 1961, more than half the congregation withdrew to affiliate with a Community Church. That year Rev. E. V. Smith became pastor. Church reported 54 members which dropped to 24 in 1962, after which Mansfield did not appear among conference appointments. On Columbia River District.

CONFERENCE CONCERNED WITH HOMELESS CHILDREN

The compassion of Washington and Northern Idaho Methodists was not limited to projects wholly sponsored by the Conference. They were also interested in the plight of homeless children. When in 1896 the Washington Children's Home Society, a private charity, affiliated with a nation-wide association, began work in the state, Methodists were interested.

In 1905 a conference report stated that the society had cared for and placed in homes, more than 600 children. Two hundred and eighty-four had been received during the past year. The Conference approved a plan to unite all denominations in this child-saving work.

The year following Rev. M. A. Covington, a member of the Columbia River Conference, was appointed agent for the society. In the Puget Sound Conference the committee on Special Charities took note of the work of the society and pledged support. It was explained that it was not the plan of the society to operate as an institution but to bring homeless children and childless homes together. Many of the children already placed had gone into Methodist homes and some into the homes of ministers of the Conference.

A report to the Puget Sound Conference in 1910 indicated that the Children's Home Society had been compelled to change its mode of operation somewhat. Rev. H. D. Brown a member of the Conference, and head of the society, had addressed the body speaking especially of the industrial training home for children under the care of the society at Port Orchard. The Conference promised to assist the society in making its work known throughout the state.

A year later it was explained that the work was undenominational, and classed as a general Christian charity. "It is the way in which the church is helping the fatherless and the widow in their affliction and trying to carry out the divine plan of placing the solitary in families," it was said.

Through the years several ministers of the Conference served as special agents of the Washington Children's Home Society, giving full time to the promotion of the cause. Besides those already mentioned the list included the following: Rev. M. A. Covington, Rev. C. S. Revelle, Rev. C. C. Pratt, Rev. E. S. Chappell, Rev. George A. Sheafe, Rev. H. C. Leavenworth, and Rev. J. H. Carter. Northwest Methodists did not lose their interest in homeless children when the Federal Government provided funds for Aid to Dependent Children after 1933. The society continued to serve as before, although the need for general solicitation for funds was reduced.

MONITOR—1909

First Methodist preaching service held in Monitor in 1909, in the school building. In April of that year, trustees, F. M. Roys and F. N. Taylor, began a series of purchases to provide site for church building. First land bought from B. M. Chapman who later deeded other property to church. Board of Home Missions and Church Extension granted $250 in 1909, specifying church title be Simpson Memorial Methodist Episcopal Church, if possible. Church incorporated, January 3, 1910, as Monitor Methodist Episcopal Church.

First church erected in 1911. Congregation worshiped in basement until structure complete. Parsonage, first on property of F. N. Taylor, moved to church site, 1917. Remodeled by Rev. John D. Moede in 1923.

State Highway Commission, in 1950, condemned property for highway. Paid Church $28,000 for land. Permitted buildings to be moved, parsonage to new site, but church building sold for $1,500. Relocated on 5-acre tract on West side of Wenatchee River. Building erected in 1950, cost $30,000. Rev. Raymond L. Pilcher was pastor.

In 1964 church membership was 100, church school enrollment, 76. Members of Woman's Society of Christian Service, 30. They contributed $243. Church property valued at $61,000. Rev. Donald L. Russell, pastor here and East Wenatchee, in 1964.

Methodists Sponsor First Goodwill Industries in Washington

Among other expressions of the compassionate heart of Northwest Methodists was the organization of Goodwill Industries within the bounds of the Conference. In Tacoma, the first unit in Washington was organized, January 8, 1922. By the next session of the Annual Conference in September, it was reported that the volume of business since January had been more than $5,000. One hundred and fifty disabled persons had been employed, as many as 27 at one time. These persons had received in wages $1,877, offering them a chance and not charity.

Many homes, threatened with disintegration, had been saved, many conversions had taken place. Twenty-five hundred bags had been distributed and plans laid for 10,000 to be placed throughout Tacoma and vicinity.

Goodwill Industries came to Seattle in 1923 with Rev. Abraham Vereide as superintendent. This institution served under the auspices of the Methodist Church until depression days led to its being turned over to interdenominational direction. Goodwill was introduced on Grays Harbor in the late 1920's and in Spokane in 1929.

In 1960 Goodwill Industries within the Conference received income aggregating $3,194,000 and paid out in wages $1,318,000 to 1,698 persons, thus keeping them off public assistance.

In Seattle, 904 persons received $795,059. In Spokane 228 persons received $245,387. Tacoma was spending $350,000 to renovate and improve its old buildings. In 1964 Goodwill Industries operated in Seattle, Tacoma, Spokane, Walla Walla, and Aberdeen. Besides these places, stores were located at Kent, Everett, Yakima, Pasco, Kennewick, and Richland.[2]

Thus the compassion of Northwest Methodism has flowed forth in many directions, giving evidence that the spirit of Christ still dominates the heart of the Church.

The year 1965 saw the completion of a modern building for the Goodwill Industries at Tacoma, to cost more than $300,000. Thus was fulfilled the dream of Rev. H. W. Michener, founder of Goodwill Industries in Tacoma and superintendent of that institution for more than 20 years.

CHAPTER XIV

Through advocating cooperation in Labor-Industrial Relations, fraternity between Races and peaceful solutions to International Problems, Northwest Methodists have proved themselves—

Men of Brotherhood

CONFERENCE ADVOCATES UNIVERSAL BROTHERHOOD

Methodists of the Northwest have marched with every column seeking to promote brotherhood. In movements to further better relations beween individuals, groups, and nations, conference leaders have carried the banner of understanding. Although some pronouncements may have been out of step with reality, it cannot be questioned that these churchmen were motivated by a sincere desire to build a Christian world.

BROTHERHOOD IS GOAL IN LABOR AND INDUSTRY

The first evidence of deep concern for better labor-industrial relations appeared in the report of the Puget Sound Conference Committee on Social Service in 1909. The year previously the General Conference had issued its "Social Creed." The committee, declaring its conviction that the Federation for Social Service had a clear message on the gospel of labor and brotherhood, expressed its hearty commendation, urging ministers and laymen to use its courses of study.

On the committee to study industrial and labor relations were such laymen as E. L. Blaine, N. D. Pollom, W. S. Ward, T. H. Starks, and O. P. Callahan. Ministers were Rev. C. A. Bowen, Rev. Richard Oates, Rev. James T. McQueen, Rev. W. H. H. Forsyth, and Rev. J. P. Reid.

An outcome of the new interest in social service was the appointment of Rev. O. H. McGill as industrial evangelist. In 1915 he was secretary of the Committee on Social Service and as such had visited logging camps and mills in twelve counties. He had held conferences at coal mines at Issaquah, Black Diamond, Ravensdale and Tono. He

303

had delivered 160 sermons in churches and elsewhere. He had assisted men to find employment, visited and spoken at labor meetings, preached and encouraged the principles of cooperation between labor and industry, and assisted in the organization of cooperative shingle mills.

The industrial evangelist, in 1921, had given his entire time to the promotion of the cooperative movement among workers of the state.

In 1924 the Committee on Social Service became more biting in its pronouncements. It said, "It is not possible to humanize industry until the world recognizes that human rights must be prior to property rights. Humanity is not a battleground but a family. Acquisitive society must yield to the cooperative commonwealth."

Columbia River Takes the Banner in Behalf of Labor

The Columbia River Conference began its championship of the cause of labor by making a mild statement in a resolution issued in 1912. It expressed sympathy with the efforts of the laboring people of the state to secure an adequate minimum compensation law, to banish child labor and properly protect the rights of women compelled to toil away from their homes.

The following year the Conference expressed its willingness to continue the exchange of fraternal delegates with the State Federation of Labor.

The Pacific Northwest Conference, in 1929, adopted the report of the Social Service Commission, which said, "We firmly accept for ourselves the principles enunciated in the 'Social Creed of the Churches,' embedded in the Discipline," [1] and urged all ministers to read the paragraph to their congregations on the Sunday preceding Labor Day.

During the depression years of the 1930's the cause of labor became more insistent and the Conference pronouncements more drastic. The Social Service Committee, in 1931, defined what it

---

OKANOGAN—1909

Methodism entered Okanogan in 1909. Church organized March 16, that year, with 10 members. Trustees, J. C. Wallace, A. M. Stark, E. R. Copple. Roy I. Snider, local preacher, first class leader. Thursday evening cottage prayer meetings began immediately.

First services held in a rented hall. In 1910 a frame building was constructed on lots purchased from Mrs. A. H. Kahlow for $300. The church, costing $650, located on Northwest corner of Third and Tyee Streets.

Ladies Aid earned money to buy lumber. Captain Bureau sawed it at cost, E. R. Copple hauled it with a team of horses, J. C. Wallace surfaced it, and other men helped contractor C. O. Dodd with construction. The women served meals.

Rev. J. W. Wright, in 1912, well known opponent of liquor traffic, made his influence effective. He was respected and feared by saloon men.

A new building, costing $20,000, was started in 1920 with assistance from Board of Church Extension, under leadership of Rev. Owen J. Beadles. It was dedicated April 3, 1921 by Bishop William O. Shepard. A parsonage was acquired in 1941, and improvements added to building in 1958.

Pastor in 1964, Rev. Alex Poobus. Members, 210, and church school enrollment, 71. Woman's Society members, 40. They contributed $251.

304

called the basic cause of periodic unemployment. "We create material goods faster than they are consumed," it was said. "When manufacturers are compelled to stop, laborers who create consumption become unemployed and dependent upon charity. Industrial production and profits are increasing faster than we are learning to distribute them justly." The Committee called upon Methodist laymen to conduct their business in accordance with the principles of Jesus, placing brotherhood and human values before material profits. It also recommended reduction of the hours of labor.

The Committee, in 1933, boldly championed an economic program calling for common ownership of natural resources and the means of production that human needs may be satisfied. It advocated economic opportunity for all who work.

Committee Urges Enactment of Compulsory Unemployment Insurance

A year later the Committee urged that the United States no longer delay enactment of some form of compulsory unemployment insurance and old age pensions and declared in favor of the child labor amendment then before the nation.

These pronouncements came during the depression and immediately following the year in which voters of America overwhelmingly had enthroned the New Deal.

The year prior to Methodist Union found the Conference friendly toward both labor and industry. The Committee recognized the democratic principle of collective bargaining, as applying equally to labor and employer, and the right of each group to organize for its corporate welfare and future. The different groups of organized labor were urged to work together for their mutual good, and the Conference viewed with concern the tendency to conflict between organized labor and the farmer.

ORCHARDS—1909

Orchards first appeared among conference appointments in 1909. Rev. E. J. Bates, pastor. It was teamed with La-Camas. The two churches reported sixty-five members, 130 in Sunday school. Building valued at $8500, parsonage at $600.

In 1919, Rev. Henry Albright was pastor. There were 108 members, 103 in Sunday school, 24 in the Epworth League. In 1928, Mrs. J. H. Porter was supply, fifth year. There were 51 in Sunday school and 40 members of the church. In 1940 Orchards was left to be supplied. There were 71 members and 122 in Sunday school. In 1950 Orchards was teamed with Salmon Creek, and Rev. Charles E. Dockstader was pastor, second year. There were 34 members and 69 in Sunday school. Woman's Society of Christian Service reported 15 members and they had given $100 toward the local work. In 1960 Rev. Jessie L. Tooley was pastor for fifth year. There were 143 members, 123 in Sunday school, 37 women had given $600.

In 1964 Rev. Loval R. Phillips was pastor for second year. There were 164 members and 109 in the church school. Thirty-five members of Woman's Society of Christian Service had given $580. The church building was valued at $38,000, parsonage at $16,000.

305

With Europe on the verge of war in 1939, the Conference reaffirmed the historic stand of the church that capital and labor should face their problems in the spirit of Christ, and advocated the nationalization of the munitions industry.

In 1942 the Conference reaffirmed its adherence to the policy of reasonable hours of labor, just wages, fair working conditions, one day's rest in seven, employment security and the policy of collective bargaining.

Following the Second World War, with most of the objectives advocated by the Conference firmly embedded in the social and economic structure of American life, the Conference turned its interest in brotherhood in other directions.

METHODISTS AMONG FIRST IN DRIVE FOR PEACE

The first indication that the brotherly conscience of Northwest Methodism embraced the cause of peace came in a report to the Columbia River Conference in 1890. The body responded to a resolution submitted by the Presbyterian General Assembly recommending a peaceful solution to international misunderstandings. The Conference, endorsing the resolution, said, "The principles of the Christian Religion are the only ones, that, in our view, can effect a salutary peace and put an end to war. A rational and wise arbitration can accomplish more for the peace and safety of nations than the sword."

Twenty years passed before either conference uttered other pronouncements relating to peace. In 1910, the Puget Sound Conference joined the Swedish[2] brethren in expressing its approval of efforts at peace and disapproved the enormous sums annually spent by armies and navies of the world.

Apparently the First World War came and went without evoking any strong disapproval of war. Ten years after America's entry into the conflict the

PECK, CAVENDISH, IDAHO—1909

Methodist church, Peck, Idaho first appeared in minutes, 1909. Rev. J. C. Bucholz, pastor. Had 25 members, no Sunday school. Pastor received $150 on salary.

In 1911, Rev. A. M. Lambert, pastor. Received $400 salary. Twelve members reported. Church worth $1,000. Had paid $642, building and improvements.

In 1928, Peck and Southwick, together, had 90 members. Paid $525 plus house valued at $120. Rev. V. A. Spicker, pastor. In 1938, with Orofino, Rev. George Cooper, pastor, 5th year. There were 58 members, one Sunday school, 91 enrolled. One church building worth $1,300, parsonage, $1,200.

In 1950, Rev. G. Edward Knight, pastor, second year. There were 36 members, 105 in church school. Woman's Society, 13. Building value, $2,500. Parsonage, value $2,000.

In 1964, Rev. Daniel P. Smith, pastor third year, members, 43, church school enrollment, 64.

Cavendish evidently came into Pacific Northwest Conference through union with the Methodist Episcopal Church, South. First appeared, 1939, Rev. J. E. Walbeck, pastor, with Leland. There were 17 members, 20 in Sunday school. One church building, valued at $2,500.

In 1964, with Leland and Peck, Rev. Daniel P. Smith, pastor. Members, 40, church school enrollment, 32. Woman's Society, 14 members, raised $114. Church building value, $3,400. Parsonage, $7,825.

Social Service Committee noted a reluctance among Christian people to face and cope with the major sins against human life, war, racial discrimination, and injustice. These were said to be the major causes of concern in society. It was said that the major job of the minister was to "Christianize the mind of society in its outlook on war."

The Committee on World Peace, in 1929, stated, "This is a day of amazing progress toward world peace, not as a sentimental reform, but as an economic necessity. Forces that unite mankind are taking precedence over forces that divide the human family. The nations are becoming increasingly interdependent." The committee went on to cite the culture, economic and scientific developments, which, it declared, "All override the boundaries of nationality."

Bishop Titus Lowe, presiding over the first session of the Pacific Northwest Conference that year, calling attention to the book, "All Quiet on the Western Front," said the book would cure the reader of love for war.

Yet, at that time unseen resentments at past injustices of war already were rankling in human hearts. Mussolini was in Italy shaking the sword at humanity, desire for conquest was taking possession of the heart of Japan, and Hitler was planning his revenge upon mankind.

War issues from the heart and pious pronouncements do not provide a sure bulwark against it.

NORTHWEST METHODISTS ADOPT STRONG ATTITUDE AGAINST WAR

Northwest Methodists, however, continued declarations regarding world tranquillity. In 1930, Rev. E. Ray Attebery, secretary of the Social Service Committee, for example, expressed the belief that progressive limitation of armament by agreement among nations was the logical and natural step in the process of delivering the world from the curse of internal anarchy.

On another occasion the General Con-

SELAH—1909

A Union Sunday school started at Selah before 1909, also a Union Ladies Aid, which sponsored the Methodist Episcopal Church, in 1909. Mrs. C. B. Crockett, first president of Ladies Aid. The Epworth League also was organized in 1909.

First church building, costing $7,292, completed and ready for use in 1910. The parsonage was constructed in 1913. Rev. J. E. Mountain helped with organization and Rev. C. Springer, retired, guided the church through financing and erecting the building. Rev. J. K. Craig became first resident pastor in 1911.

A new building for the congregation entered the planning stage in 1951, under Rev. Blaine Hammond. Mr. and Mrs. W. B. Dowdy gave two acres of land and two others were purchased.

Rev. Ralph Richardson, in 1956, began the building. Old church sold and congregation housed in Masonic Lodge. Ground broken, September 27, 1957. In June, 1958, congregation occupied the unfinished structure and began vain struggle with debt payments and psychology of unfinished building. In 1963 Urgent Needs Appeal, loaned church $26,500. Building completed and refinanced, and new era began.

In 1964, Rev. Edgar C. Hirsh became pastor. Membership, 546, church school enrollment, 400. Woman's Society, 87. They gave $1714 to local work. Building value $170,000.

ference was asked to petition the Federal Government to grant to conscientious objectors of the Methodist Church the same consideration granted members of the Society of Friends. This session of the Conference disapproved the compulsory feature of military training in colleges, and urged the entrance of America into the World Court. It pledged President Herbert Hoover support in efforts to reduce armaments through international agreements.

In 1934 war was declared to be sin, and, not only unnecessary but futile and suicidal. "No Christian should engage in war for any purpose or give it his sanction or approval," the committee said.

Recommended as aids to prevent future wars were: A statement by the United States Government specifying terms upon which it would be willing to join the League of Nations; Ratification of the World Court Protocol; and International control of trade in arms. It was recommended that the United States take the leadership among the nations in an energetic move for reduction of armaments, and maintain our army and navy on a peacetime basis. It was further recommended that the Government annually appropriate, for the use of a Department of Peace, a sum equal to five percent of our annual appropriations for war.

The committee deplored the invasion of Chinese territory by the Japanese and the martial movement of Mussolini against Ethiopia.

With the United States at war in 1942 the Committee urged the necessity to maintain church services and assemblies. "We affirm the principle of loyalty to God against any other allegiance. Out of the ranks of men with conscience have our powers of democracy come," it was said.

The Committee said that the spirit of revenge and retaliation is contrary to the moral order and that cooperation between nations is essential to a just and durable peace. "The United States has responsibility to bring international

MANITO, SPOKANE—1909

A combination Methodist and Baptist Sunday school, organized in Manito area, Spokane, 1906, in schoolhouse. Since Methodists outnumbered Baptists, group mutually agreed to organize a Methodist church. In 1909 Methodist church started with 39 charter members.

Pastoral cultivation had been done by Rev. J. C. Kirkman, pastor at Moran. Organizing pastor was Rev. W. E. Armfield. Rev. J. C. Lawrence, 1909.

Epworth League organized, January 23, 1910, Benton McClure president. Ladies Aid started 1910. Woman's Foreign Missionary Society, 1917.

First building, 1910, was completed in two months. The growing congregation, in 1924 entered a new $60,000 sanctuary. Rev. Ernest F. Harold, pastor. A. P. Moore, C. W. Randall, J. Hancock, building committee.

Under the ministry of Rev. James Moore, 1942-43, debt erased, gymnasium and dining hall remodeled.

The Rev. Eugene Muench, 1951-59 stayed longer than any other pastor. Membership showed rapid growth, reaching more than 700. An educational unit was occupied in 1959, consecrated January 17, 1960 by Bishop A. Raymond Grant. Edward Carter chairman building committee. Rev. Robert Ortmeyer, pastor.

In 1964, Rev. Paul E. Hamlin appointed first year. Members, 811, church school, 434. Woman's Society 118. They gave $1,519. Building value $365,910. Parsonage, $15,500.

THESE METHODISTS PRACTICED BROTHERHOOD

Rev. M. A.
Covington

Rev. Paul E. Hamlin
and Mosobalaje Dyawaye
and Min Ku Cheong

Rev. Daniel E.
Taylor

Rev. Wesley Yamaka

Grace Church,
Seattle

Rev. Louis Albert
Banks

relations into conformity with the moral law," it said, and also expressed faith "That the purpose of God in history eventually will be realized."

Conference Committee Concerned Over Russian Relations

The year after the war ended the Committee called upon the Government to release conscientious objectors as fast as men were released from military service. It also expressed concern over the relations between the United States and Russia, and honestly admitted, "We do not profess to know the answer. We are opposed to appeasement, we are equally opposed to steps which will involve us in war with her. We are convinced that within these limits peaceful solutions can be evolved."

That year a report signed by Rev. Robert Shaw called for Congressional action requesting the President of the United States to invite governments of all nations to send representatives to a conference which will be charged with the single duty of achieving world disarmament on land, sea, and air.

In 1950 the Committee on World Peace said, "We call upon the Christian Church to take its stand upon the teachings of its founder, Jesus, who repudiated the use of violence and taught in practice the power of love." Governments were asked to cease manufacture of A-Bombs and H-Bombs. It also declared "War between the United States and Russia is not inevitable."

The outlawry of nuclear weapons was advocated in a resolution adopted in 1959, which conceded that this must be achieved universally and simultaneously by all countries under the United Nations supervision.

Brotherhood Practiced Toward Retired Employees

The need to support retired ministers was early acknowledged, but for

---

METZGER, SPOKANE—1909

The Harris C. Metzger Memorial Methodist Episcopal Church organized in Spokane, July 11, 1909. Rev. Andrew Monroe, pastor. In September Rev. J. L. Hess appointed by Annual Conference. Rev. U. F. Hawk, presiding elder, acquired lots. Building erected, named for man who gave $300.

Rev. W. E. Armfield, pastor, 1910 proceeded to organize all departments of church. Ladies Aid born with 40 members. Epworth League, 46. Junior League, 48. Men's Brotherhood 42, Boys Club 111, Sunday school, 11 classes. There were 196 members of church.

Under the pastorate of Rev. Bracken E. Koontz, 1919-21, larger church and basement, begun, but unfinished. Rev. Robert W. Maulden, 1925-29, led congregation to complete, floor basement. Under leadership of Rev. Hubert C. Vincent, 1939, church remodeled and wing added, dedicated, March 17, 1940. Bishop James H. Straughn preaching.

Rev. Orin D. Watson, pastor 1956, remodeled kitchen, church attendance doubled. Thirty-four members received and 28 baptized. Following year new gas furnace installed. Between 1953 and 1957 church membership declined. The new members received under Pastor Watson turned the tide of confidence and faith.

In 1964, Rev. Wayne R. Schaub appointed, second year. Members, 153, church school, 125, Woman's Society, with 24 members, $119. Building value, $20,000. Parsonage, $7,150.

decades, offerings for them were too meager to be of practical help. In 1893 the Columbia River Conference fixed the last Sunday in December as the time to receive the annual offering for retired ministers. The offering was to be taken separately from the presentation of any other cause. Seventy-five percent was to be used for the annuity fund and the remainder for necessitous cases. Annuity claims for retired ministers was set at ten dollars per year, and, for widows, one-half that amount. Each effective minister was expected to contribute at least five dollars each year to the fund.

The conference stewards in 1897 reported receipts for retired ministers amounting to $1,154.50, which was divided between twelve annuitants. Each received from $25 to $212. An amount equal to two percent of each pastor's salary was assessed against the churches for retired ministers.

Deficiencies continued. In 1901 the claims of annuitants was $4,250, but only $1,486 had been collected.

In 1904 came the first suggestion of an endowment for the fund in the Puget Sound Conference. The next year 19 claimants received a total of $2,224.25. In 1906, 22 claimants received a total of $2,100. That year a special commission in the Columbia River Conference reported a proposed constitution for the Conference Claimants Endowment Association. The same year the Puget Sound Conference authorized the formation of the Conference Claimants Society. Rev. Charles McDermoth was appointed agent and requested to provide a plan of organization to be presented at the next session of the Conference. Articles of Incorporation for the Preacher's Aid Society were adopted the next year.

In 1918 the Puget Sound Conference set a goal of $250,000 for endowment for its retired ministers and set the year for the campaign for 1920. In 1922, endowment secretary, Rev. W. H. Baker, reported that he had received less than

---

TIBBETTS—1909

Tibbetts Methodist Church, organized, 1909, by Rev. Paul H. Ashby on first appointment. There were 50 members in 1910. In 1911, 90 members, 107 in church school, and building valued at $3,100. A parsonage had been completed free of debt. Mrs. Ella Spangle, president Board of Stewards.

The building erected on land donated by Mary Emma Tibbetts on condition that church be called "Tibbetts Memorial Methodist Episcopal Church." In 1915, sanctuary rebuilt with complete basement. In 1920 congregation purchased north lot for future use. In 1923 erected modern parsonage there. South lot was acquired 1925 for similar reason at sheriff's sale. This gave Tibbetts half-block land.

The church, altered through years was at length deemed inadequate for future growth. Annex added on south lot in 1929 and, in 1942, under Rev. Elmer Beckman, mortgage was paid. In 1951, Rev. LeRoy Walker planned to finance educational unit. Concluded the following year by Rev. Francis M. Kinch and completed, in 1955.

In 1958, Rev. Troy Strong, led congregation in erecting sanctuary, completed 1960.

In 1964, Rev. Donald M. Fife, pastor. There were 771 members, 393 in church school and 158 members in Woman's Society, gave, $2,176. Building valued at $361,000.

$21,000 in notes and pledges for the fund, and urged that the campaign be carried out immediately after the conference session. Still money was slow coming in. The next year the fund had increased by $25,000. In 1925 the Conference authorized the raising of $800,000 to enable it to enter the Reserve Pension Plan.

In 1928, Rev. George Hopkins, executive secretary of the Board of Conference Claimants, announced that income from endowment had been $31,971.

The Columbia River Conference launched an endowment campaign in 1926, with a goal of $225,000, and set the starting time for 1927. In 1929 the Preacher's Aid Society discontinued receiving members in favor of the Conference Claimants Board.

The Board of Conference Claimants, in 1938, began transferring funds to the General Board of Pensions at Chicago. Rev. Roy L. Sprague, executive secretary, proposed that the Conference adopt a goal of $500,000 for pensions. Ninety-nine retired ministers and a like number of widows shared in the distribution of $102,331, that year.

The Board of Conference Claimants, in 1945, was authorized to raise $300,000 for endowment. In 1947, executive secretary, Rev. Paul H. Ashby, reported that the campaign was ready, and the following year he said that $272,245 had been pledged, with $132,766 in cash. This was sufficient, he said, to place the Conference in the four-fold Reserve Pension Plan. Entrants were to pay into the fund an amount equal to two percent of their salaries. Full-time accepted supply pastors were included.

The contract with the Board of Pensions had increased to $505,000, of which $451,363 had been paid by 1951. Unpaid subscriptions totaled $53,000. Two years later the entire sum had been paid to the Board. In 1957 the Conference signed a contract with the Board for a total of $3,016,252, with interest at three percent. The contract was

YELM—1909

Sunday school organized, Yelm, in 1850's, in home of James Longmire. Earliest Methodist ministers remembered, Rev. John F. DeVore, Rev. Ebenezer Hopkins, Rev. B. F. Brooks. Near-by Eureka, had Methodist class in 1899. McKenna Methodists were active in 1901.

First church at Yelm was community congregation, 1908. To build church group solicited money, served dinners, had happy time, enthusiasm high. When church was almost ready for occupancy, money exhausted, so were laborers. Building stood unoccupied and unusable.

In 1909, Rev. J. W. Blackwell, pastor Methodist Church, Eureka, began holding services. People gave up non-denominational idea, proposed a Methodist church, if that denomination would accept, complete church, build parsonage. Through a donation of $250 from Methodist Board of Church Extension, new heart in congregation, building and parsonage completed.

During years, primary room, dining room, kitchen, added. An educational hall and youth center, built with aid of $4,000 from Board of Home Missions and Church Extension, in 1920's. Debt paid, 1943, Rev. Hunter McCain, pastor. Sanctuary was rebuilt, dedicated, 1948. Rev. Will Richards, pastor.

In 1948, Rev. L. Philip Porter, pastor, fifth year. Members, 238. Church school enrollment, 233. Woman's Society members, 51, gave $276. Church value, $52,700. Parsonage, $10,500.

scheduled to run 30 years. Annuities to pensioners was frozen at $40 per year with the possibility of greater payments if annual income to the Board justified it. In 1963 the Conference began paying at the rate of $43 per service year.

Thus, after more than seventy years of struggle, the Conference at last had achieved a goal far in advance of its original dream.

CONFERENCE CHAMPIONS CAUSE OF CIVIL RIGHTS

Early Northwest Methodists did not always regard members of other races as brothers. Many references in the writings of such men as Rev. H. K. Hines indicate that he looked upon the Indians as a degraded people. The letters of Catharine and Rev. David Blaine contained statements indicating that, to them, the Indians were inferior.

Mrs. Blaine, especially, may be excused somewhat for the harshness of her judgment of the Indians on Elliott Bay, when it is remembered that some of the women had indeed been degraded by white men. Catharine held these men in contempt equalling that with which she regarded their victims. Nevertheless, there is no evidence that the Blaines made any effort to reach the Indians with the Gospel.

There are occasional hints in the records left by Rev. J. H. Wilbur, that sometimes he thought of these people for whose salvation he so faithfully labored, as backward.

Regard for other races, Indians, Japanese, Chinese, Negroes, as brothers, was a slow development among Northwest Methodists. Yet, that members of other races were children of God and subject to His saving grace was never doubted.

Christian concern that members of other races should be treated as brothers was not highly developed among the earliest of church leaders in this territory.

McCLEARY—1910

First services in McCleary in 1910. Rev. Andrew Anderson among earliest visiting preachers. Ladies Aid organized 1909. Mrs. Henry McCleary, president. First resident pastor, Rev. R. H. Reed, 1911-13. Mrs. A. W. Teagle organized first Sunday school class. Articles of Incorporation adopted, in 1917, Rev. L. D. Cook, pastor. Trustees, Leonard McCleary, A. W. Teagle, George Townsend, James Harlan, F. R. Lanning. Building deeded to Methodist Church by Henry McCleary. New building planned in 1922, site acquired, 1924. Henry McCleary pledged $5,000, women, $1,000. Building went up 1924-25. Rev. R. A. Gailey, pastor. Women purchased piano for church, hot water tank for parsonage. Church completed in 1926, cost $20,000. Dedicated, April 11, 1926. J. W. Reynolds, followed Gailey in 1927. Church without a pastor, several years. Sunday schoolrooms added, 1954-56, Rev. S. Christian Thele, pastor. Parsonage painted, 1957-59, Rev. Alex Poobus, pastor. Improvements included choir loft, pulpit, altar. Junior choir, organized by Mrs. Poobus. Memorial fund established, pipe organ installed.

McCleary Methodists celebrated fiftieth anniversary, 1960. Rev. Linden B. Jenkins preached December 4th, Bishop Everett W. Palmer December 11. In 1964, Rev. C. Grant Harvey, pastor, second year. Members 79, church school enrollment 89. Woman's Society 44, gave $1,100. Building value, $40,000. Parsonage, $5,000.

Aside from the insistence that Indians receive humane treatment and the benefits of the Gospel, the earliest intercession for another race had to do with the Chinese. This action of the Columbia River Conference appeared in the minutes of 1893 when the body memorialized the United States Senate and House of Representatives to repeal the Geary law which discriminated against Chinese entering the country. The law which required each Chinese to keep in his possession a certificate attesting to his right to be here and indorsed by a white citizen, was declared by the Conference to be unfair.

Racial Discrimination Called a Major Sin

Little notice was taken of racial issues, as such, until, in 1927, the Puget Sound Conference Commission on Social Service spoke of racial discrimination as one of the major sins against human life. In 1942 a statement was made by the Committee on Social Service which said, "All citizens of alien parentage should have full opportunity to exercise their rights of citizenship." In the same resolution it was declared, "There should be freedom of worship, speech, and scientific inquiry. Security from want and oppression should not be limited by race, color, or creed."

A statement issued in 1955 evidently expressed the consensus of opinion of the Conference. "We affirm the recommendation of the last General Conference that opportunity be given, without discrimination or segregation for full participation in all activities of the church by interracial and international groups that make up our Methodist fellowship. That there be equality of accommodations at national and international meetings of the Church, that the institutions of the local churches, colleges, universities, theological schools and homes, carefully restudy their practices and policies, as relate to race, making certain that these policies and practices are Christian." The Confer-

---

VALLEY—1910

The church at Valley first appeared in 1910, teamed with Chewelah. Rev. A. F. Kroneman was in first year. In 1911 there were 85 members on circuit. In 1913, Rev. O. A. Faulkner was pastor. The two churches had 42 members and 340 in the Sunday school. Two buildings were valued at $4800. From 1923-28 Rev. Gertrude Apel pastor. There were 112 members on the charge and 298 in the Sunday school.

In 1930 Valley was served by Rev. William Park, membership reported with Chewelah. In 1935, church was with Addy and Chewelah, Rev. Dwight G. Bennett, pastor. In 1939 with Deer Park, Wild Rose, Rev. Ruth M. Lortz pastor. Valley and Addy together reported 48 members, 50 in Sunday school. In 1950 Valley was with Chewelah, Rev. Ronald K. Johnson, pastor. Valley alone had 98 members, 97 in Sunday school. There were fifteen in the Woman's Society of Christian Service who had given $200. In 1960 Valley teamed with Chewelah. Rev. Fred Riehle in third year. In 1964 Rev. Charles W. Johnson was in third year. There were 115 members and 52 in church school. One church was valued at $15,000.

ence also recommended that all Methodist churches employ members of staff on the basis of character and qualifications without racial discrimination.

In 1960 the Conference approved a proposal committing itself and its members to work to end discrimination wherever found, including churches and institutions. It was resolved that the churches and members make a serious examination of their own attitudes and practices regarding racial equality and fellowship, and seek to bring practices into conformity with Christian ideals. It also went on record as favoring the state law against discrimination including private as well as public housing. It declared for the end of discrimination in cemeteries and all business including real estate offices.

CENTRALIA ARMISTICE DAY TRAGEDY SHOCKS NORTHWEST

Certain members of the Conference undoubtedly were motivated by the spirit of brotherhood when they persuaded the Conference to set up a committee to investigate the Centralia Armistice Day tragedy, in which several men were killed, resulting in commitment of seven men to the penitentiary for life. Proponents of the investigation contended that the men found guilty of the murder had acted in self-defense when they fired upon members of the American Legion near their hall in 1919.

The members of the International Workers of the World, who were sentenced to prison, had been tried in the Superior Court of Grays Harbor County and found guilty. Many members of the Conference, including citizens of Centralia, felt that the court had found justly, and believed that the committee and the Conference should leave the matter there.

However, in 1930, the committee announced that The Federal Council of the Churches of Christ in America, the National Catholic Welfare Conference, and the Central Council of Jewish

---

WINTHROP—1910

First Sunday school in Methow Valley began at Silver, in 1887, in the home of Mr. and Mrs. Samuel Metcalf. Mrs. Metcalf, superintendent. The first Sunday school in Winthrop was organized before 1906 and met in the school building. First Preacher, Rev. W. E. Beach.

The Methodist Church was organized in Winthrop by Rev. O. W. Mintzer, September 18, 1910, eleven members. Rev. Fred M. Greenstreet, first resident pastor.

First church building started June, 1912, and usable in September of that year. It was in the town of Heckendorn, later part of Winthrop. Rev. James Taylor became pastor in 1912. The first parsonage acquired, September 19, 1919. Church overhauled in 1936.

A new building was erected in 1958, and a new educational unit, started in 1962, completed in 1963.

Winthrop has been the residence of the pastors serving the Methow Valley most of the time since work began there. Winthrop owns the parsonage and Twisp pays ten dollars per month rent.

In 1964, Rev. Robert Dabritz was appointed pastor for the seventh year. There were 120 members of the church, 77 in Sunday school, and 41 members of the Woman's Society of Christian Service. Women contributed $435 to local work.

315

Rabbis, had promised to aid in the investigation. DeWitt Wykoff of the Department of Research and Education of the Federal Council had spent two months on the field and had returned to New York to prepare his report.

The committee reported in 1932 that some of its members had appeared before the State Parole Board at each of its quarterly meetings, and that Eugene Barnet and O. C. Bland had been released on parole. One of the men died in prison and the remaining four eventually were released on parole.

Thus is presented an abridged record of attempts of Northwest Methodists to promote the cause of Christian brotherhood.

CHAPTER XV

What Northwest Methodists believed
and how they harnessed this faith to
achieve spiritual purposes is clearly
stated in this chapter on—

Men of Faith and Purpose

NORTHWEST METHODISTS BELIEVED IN THEIR MISSION

Methodist leaders who established and guided the Church in Washington and Idaho, during the first century, believed in their mission and were dedicated to its fulfillment.

From the time of Rev. Jason Lee there were differences of opinion regarding methods and procedures,[1] but always agreement that Christian civilization must be moral and spiritual.

At first glance the pioneer Methodists saw moral and social practices which they deemed incompatible with the Christian way of life. Drunkenness, gambling, Sabbath desecration, violations against the sanctity of home, constituted the way of life in every place.

When Methodist leaders first arrived they found battle lines already drawn. Promptly they girded themselves for the conflict which still raged more than a century later.

A METHODIST IS NO FRIEND OF ALCOHOL

Methodist leaders in the Northwest have ever been true to their inherited conviction that beverage alcohol is the enemy of society, and that neither individual nor state can consort with it without sin.

By 1856 liquor already had become a political issue. That year, the Conference expressed conviction that it was grossly inconsistent with the character of a Christian to lend his influence to promote to office men favoring the use of ardent spirits as a beverage.

Furthermore the members of that Conference favored prohibition. They memorialized the Legislatures of their respective territories to prohibit the sale of intoxicating liquors. Two years later the Conference resolved to seek to lead members of the church to make personal pledges to abstain from all intoxicating drinks. The body also enjoined every minister who used tobacco to cease such practice.

A year later the Committee reported that intemperance still was ravaging the West. But it was felt that the cause of temperance was growing. Attention was called to the number of petitions, in the hands of the committee, praying Legislatures to alter the laws permitting granting of licenses to sell intoxicating liquor.

In 1861 the Conference declared that the cause and principles of temperance ought more frequently to be explained to the people. Conference members pledged themselves to give special instruction to children on the subject.

The battle raged throughout the Civil War. In 1867 the Conference became more specific about its grounds for opposing the traffic in beverage alcohol. It said, "It destroys the tenderest ties of social life, prostrates all that is great, and blights what is good in humanity. It is the cause of unmitigated political, social, and moral evil, and should not have the support of law. Because it betrays the man of honor into infamy, the man of virtue into a sinner, it is not only the enemy of morality and mental and moral improvement, but a most frequent cause of Sabbath desecration, profanity, licentiousness, suffering, pauperism, degradation and death. We do not regard any man competent to fill any office of trust or honor, who is not, in addition to other qualifications, a thorough, practical temperance man."

Through all the years Methodists held to the conviction that any condition fraught with such dire capacity to blight the individual and curse society, was the concern of all of society. It should not be left to the church to fight the battle against it alone. It was with this in mind that the Conference, in 1879, declared, "We are fully convinced of the wisdom and absolute need of total legal prohibi-

BLYN—1911

Methodism first appeared in Blyn, December 1911. Meeting held in Blyn Hall. Later, services in Michigan School, then back to hall.

First Sunday school superintendent was George Gedelman. James Stewart was Secretary, P. B. Gedelman, Mrs. George Gedelman, and Mrs. Reuben McKinney, were teachers.

In 1916, Rev. Charles McLaughlin, Trinity Church, Sequim, began holding services, and Rev. J. M. Weaver, Conference Sunday School superintendent, reorganized the school under Methodist banner. In 1917 Rev. A. M. Frederick, pastor at Blyn and Dungeness. Church was reorganized with 19 members.

In 1919, Rev. Jabez C. Harrison, superintendent of the Olympia District held special evangelistic meetings, and received 48 members.

In 1920, congregation again attached to Sequim, and interest of members lagged. In 1925, many were inactive.

In 1931, Rev. Harry E. Greening began preaching services. Next year state highway took site and building moved to another location. Blyn again attached to Sequim, and Rev. B. H. Hart, pastor.

Next 20 years church met irregularly, and Sunday school lagged. Rev. Wendell Cone reorganized the church and school in 1952. Woman's Society organized in 1953. Rev. Fletcher Forster, of Sequim began preaching services.

After 1960, statistics were reported with Sequim.

318

tion." The report was signed by L. J. Powell, Joseph Hoberg, N. Clark.

As the Church waged war against legalized alcohol, allies appeared. The Woman's Christian Temperance Union and the Anti-Saloon League came into action to strengthen the cause of temperance. The Columbia River Conference, in 1876, recognized the potent influence of women in temperance reform and welcomed the action of the 150,000 of these workers who petitioned Congress for national legislation against the manufacture and sale of distilled and fermented liquors.

WOMAN SUFFRAGE RANKS AS ISSUE WITH PROHIBITION

In 1888 the work of women suggested to the Columbia River Conference a new strategy, that of woman suffrage as a means of voting the traffic out of existence. The ministers resolved, "We cannot break the fetters of the nation with a shackled ballot. The whole cannot be free while a part is bound." From that time votes for women became an issue ranking with prohibition.

Certain Methodist leaders performed spectacular feats in defense of temperance. Rev. James Harvey Wilbur, Indian Agent at Fort Simcoe, used his authority to keep the traffic off the reservation. His attitude and tactics are illustrated in the following:[2]

A certain lawless man set up a stand near the reservation to dispense alcoholic beverage to all comers. Wilbur appealed to the sheriff who declined to act on the ground that the man was dangerous. When Wilbur minimized the danger the sheriff offered to deputize him to deal with the man. The minister accepted.

Later the Indian Agent and a helper, mounted on horses and leading a third, paused near the offensive place. Leaving the assistant and extra horse concealed, the Agent rode alone to the premises. The man was in the act of

FELIDA—1911

The church at Felida first appeared among the appointments on Vancouver District in 1911. Rev. J. H. Geoghegen was pastor in his first year. In 1912 he reported 49 members, 46 in the Sunday school, and 25 in the Epworth League. There was one building valued at $700 and no parsonage. In 1919 Rev. F. E. Reddick, was pastor. He reported 165 in the Sunday school but no membership. Felida teamed with Salmon Creek and Sarah in 1929. Report showed 235 enrolled in the two Sunday schools and 125 church members. In 1940 there were 60 enrolled in the Sunday school and 63 full members. In 1950 Rev. D. E. Carter was in his fourth year as retired supply pastor. There were 39 members and 60 in the Sunday school.

In 1960 Felida was supplied by W. S. J. Bleakley in his second year. There were 43 members. There were ten women in the Woman's Society who gave $180 and the building was valued at $9,000, the parsonage at $1,000. There were 33 enrolled in the Sunday school.

In 1961 the annual conference declared the church abandoned and the building sold. The proceeds of the sale to be applied for church extension on Vancouver District.

319

taking a drink, but when he saw Wilbur and suspected his mission, he took a shotgun from its rack and placed it muzzle outward across the counter, and began to curse and berate the clergyman.

When, a few minutes later, the man reached for another drink, Wilbur seized the opportunity to knock him down, and the two clinched. After a struggle Wilbur won. The helper, with the extra horse, was called, the prisoner was tied hand and foot and taken to the guardhouse near the agent's residence. During the next days Wilbur personally took bread and water to his prisoner, each time giving fatherly advice to his man, calling him to repentance.

In time this procedure bore fruit, the man repented and promised to reform. He kept his promise. Some years later, when Wilbur was in Palouse on business he met the man again, a respected farmer and church member who told him he was married and had a happy family.

Temperance Committee Wages Fight Against Liquor Traffic

Year after year the Committee on Temperance came forward with some new attack against the liquor traffic. In 1891 the committee said, "The flag of this republic waves over two institutions that are utterly dissimilar, and between which there rages an irrepressible conflict. One is the American home, the other the American saloon. The home is a blessing, the saloon a curse. The home is of God, the saloon is of the Devil. The home points towards Paradise, the saloon towards Perdition. On the side of the home are the virtuous and good, on the side of the saloon are the vicious and bad. On the side of the home are the churches and Sunday schools, on the side of the saloon are the Liquor Dealer's Association, the Personal Liberty League, and many of the leading secular papers, the corrupt politicians, and the purchasable vote. On which side is the American flag?"

In 1903 the Conference called for scientific temperance instruction in

FIRCREST, TACOMA—1912

First Methodist services Fircrest, 1909. Rev. Joel Vigus, Rev. DeWitt Franklin, Rev. J. L. Kendall first preachers. Rev. C. B. Sears, promoted Sunday school, 1910. Rev. J. T. McQueen, 1911-12 preached in tent on land donated by Major Bowes.

Church without pastor from 1925-44. Mr. and Mrs. W. Freeman kept Sunday school open. In 1944, Methodists resumed services. In 1946, Rev. Elmer E. Beckman, pastor, paid indebtedness on parsonage. Boy Scouts started by Rev. K. N. Ekaas, in 1947. Also Cub Scouts. Under Rev. Robert Huston, 1948, room scarce, Sunday school held in parked cars of teachers. Name of church changed to Fircrest, 1946.

In 1949, new church building constructed. Rev. Owen J. Beadles, district superintendent. In 1951, $1,000 received from Board of Home Missions. In 1953 volunteers roofed church. Rev. Donald Utterback, pastor. Dr. and Mrs. Walter Anderson donated organ, 1954. Two sessions Sunday school started in 1955. In 1961 congregation pledged $61,000, for new building. The fiftieth anniversary celebrated in 1962. Rev. Bruce Foreman, pastor. Ground breaking exercises held in 1964.

In 1964, Rev. Charles E. Gruenwald, pastor, second year. Members, 377, church school enrollment, 283. Woman's Society of Christian Service, 70 members. They gave $757. Building valued at $49,200. Parsonage, $18,100.

public schools and institutions of higher learning as provided in the laws of most states.

When the Puget Sound Conference became separated from Oregon its members stepped boldly into the fight against intemperance. At the first session the Conference reaffirmed its faith in the traditional Methodist stand. In 1903 this body petitioned the American Congress to prohibit the sale of intoxicants in all places where the United States exercised control.

Three years later the group declared it a serious policy to elect to the Legislature saloonists, and political ringsters and expect them to enact satisfactory laws, such as the direct primary and local option. It called upon the Church to cease nullifying its own power by voting against itself.

By 1914 the Conference stood in sight of state-wise prohibition, and in 1918, the body heard a report that the National Board of Temperance, Prohibition, and Moral Reform had been victorious in its advocacy of bone-dry prohibition, anti-advertising legislation, strict legislation surrounding the army camps in the United States, and better restrictions against the social evil and drinking in France.

In 1921 the Conference thanked God, "that we have lived to see the day of victory, and the liquor traffic stands convicted by every tribunal and now is an outlaw in our land, nevertheless, eternal vigilance still is the price of liberty."

It was recognized that a long-ranged counterattack was under way by the liquor interests. Protests were registered against the subtle attack being made by glorifying drink in motion picture theatres, thus poisoning the minds of the young. The ministers pledged to oppose such procedure. The next year note also was taken of the unrelenting fight being made upon prohibition by the "press, magazines, and picture houses," in an attempt to nullify the Volstead Act and restore the saloon.

HALLER LAKE—1912

First Sunday school at Haller Lake met in vacant house at Bitter Lake Station, in 1912. Rev. W. H. Leach, Seattle Missionary Union, C. L. Evans, and George Stratmen steered the young school.

Church organized 1920, with 15 members. Missionary Union offered $1,000 for building if community would match it. People responded. In 1920 workmen finished Two Lakes Church, costing $3,000. Ladies promised pews. In 1924, under Rev. Raymond A. Partee, student pastor, membership doubled.

In 1926, name changed to St. Paul's Methodist Episcopal Church. In 1929, Rev. Theodore H. Palmquist, property sold, relocated at 128th and First Ave. N. E. Board of Home Missions granted $1,200. Building started March, 1930, dedicated, May.

In 1930, Rev. W. O. Pflaum built his own home. In 1934, charge on circuit with Ronald, Rev. William E. Callahan, pastor. In 1945, Rev. John C. Soltman, pastor, sold property for $17,000, acquired new location at 133rd and First Ave. N. E. Building completed, 1950, seated 250, social hall 200.

Rev. Ac Wischmeier became pastor in 1954. A youth center, under his direction was consecrated, December 8, 1957. Rev. John Updike, associate.

In 1964, Rev. Eugene W. Muench appointed for sixth year. Members, 1,503, church school enrollment, 1,321. Woman's Society members, 130, gave $1,019.

CONFERENCE DISSATISFIED WITH TREASURY DEPARTMENT
ENFORCEMENT

The Conference was dissatisfied with the results of enforcement under the United States Treasury Department. In 1926 hope was expressed that the time would soon come when enforcement would be placed where its objectives might more readily be achieved. The following year the Conference expressed gratification at the prospect of placing enforcement under Civil Service.

During the years the influence of groups opposed to liquor control convinced public opinion that the Eighteenth Amendment had failed. Millions had become eligible to vote who had no experience under the saloon system. Notwithstanding the fact that incidence of alcoholism had been lower under prohibition than at any other time, the weight of public opinion was on the side of repeal.

In 1933 the Conference noted that the proposal to repeal the Eighteenth Amendment, by action of the 1933 Legislature, had been submitted to voters of Washington. Inasmuch as no substitute had been provided, and the 1933 Legislature had repealed all laws regulating the traffic, and none could be enacted for two years, the Conference pledged to support the Prohibition Emergency Committee. It called upon every member of the church, to work, pray, and vote to retain the Eighteenth Amendment.

With heads bloody, but unbowed, the Pacific Northwest Conference, assembled at Vancouver in 1934, declared, "We reaffirm the attitude of the church that for the ultimate eradication of the evils of the liquor traffic, we rely upon the reenactment of prohibitory laws." It approved the plan outlined by the Anti-Saloon League, to separate the liquor traffic from all other business.

In 1935 the Conference appointed Rev. E. J. Huston, director of Temper-

---

SAMISH ISLAND—1912

First Sunday school on Samish Island was organized in 1912 in a one room schoolhouse by Mrs. J. T. Squires and Mrs. Charles Dever, who continued to lead until 1920. In 1913 Rev. J. Randolph Sasnett of Blanchard began holding preaching services in the community. Articles of incorporation were filed October 21, 1918. Trustees, J. T. Squires, Charles W. Dever, and Marian Barnes. Ladies Aid first organized 1912, 15 members.

First building erected in 1918 on property donated by the John Bernenston family. Rev. J. M. Wilder, pastor. Mrs. J. T. Squires and Mrs. Charles Dever solicited the funds. Some not able to give money provided labor. The Board of Church Extension provided $250 grant. Electric lights were installed in the building under Rev. Robert Thompson in the 1930's. Building was enlarged and improved in 1956 by Rev. M. M. Lehmann.

In 1962, congregation observed 50 years of service. Group, though small, felt that baptisms, weddings, funerals, social occasions under the Christian influence of many dedicated and devoted persons had proved what a great work a few members could accomplish.

In 1964 Rev. F. R. Owen was appointed for the fourth year. Members, 15; Sunday school enrollment, 24; Woman's Society membership, 22. Women gave $657.

ance Education. In 1937 the Anti-saloon League bowed out of Washington. That year, Huston reported that in February representatives of 14 Protestant denominations had met in Seattle to canvass the temperance situation.

Out of this Methodist-sponsored move came Washington Temperance Association, with major denominations cooperating. Chapin D. Foster, a Methodist, presided at the organization meeting, in September, 1937, when Rev. W. J. Herwig was elected Educational Director. This group, known after about 1960, as Alcohol Problems Association, became Washington's strongest bulwark against encroachments of the liquor traffic.

In 1946 the Committee on Public Reform deplored the fact that Methodists patronized restaurants and stores where liquor was sold. The following year the committee disapproved drinking by Methodists, both men and women. It also recommended nationalization of manufacture and sale of all alcoholic beverages.

CONFERENCE URGES TOTAL ABSTINENCE UPON ITS MEMBERS

In 1950, with renewed faith in the mission of the church to exterminate the liquor traffic, the Conference called upon church members to set an example of total abstinence. "If members are not ready to do this," the Committee affirmed, "they can hardly expect it to be done by others." Ministers were reminded of their responsibility to stand firm against social practices which threaten to undermine the lives of thousands of our people. Each local church was advised to raise a committee to keep the congregation informed on the issue.

The conference, in 1952, was deeply concerned about the situation involving strong drink. The Committee said, "The evil is not new, but new methods are being adopted by the traffic to work its way into our homes and, in far too many

CROWN HILL—1913

First Methodist Sunday school, Crown Hill, met in Divine's store, October 5, 1913, 56 present. In September, Rev. W. H. Leach, city missionary, Seattle Evangelistic Union, called meetings looking toward church organization. Committee on Church Location, C. H. Rood, and C. S. Sterling, appointed.

Frank W. and Alfred Shillestad offered lots east of cemetery. Committee decided to locate at 9th Ave., N. W. City Union donated $250. First service in new building, March 22, 1914. Rev. J. P. Marlatt, district superintendent, delivered sermon. Rev. W. H. Leach, organizing pastor.

Building which cost $1,500 burned, July 5, 1915. Congregation rebuilt larger church, same location. Twenty-eight men donated labor. Ladies Aid, organized, 1913, Mrs. Ann B. Cottrill, president, served dinners, solicited money. Building opened October 17, 1915, costing $1,200. Rev. George A. Landen, officiated.

Emanuel Norwegian-Danish Church, organized in Ballard, 1901, merged with Crown Hill, 1951. Under Rev. J. H. Berringer, plans laid for new educational unit. Completed under Rev. John Lukens, April 8, 1956.

In 1964, Rev. Floyd E. Green, pastor, second year. There were 395 members, 276 in church school. Seventy-five members of Woman's Society of Christian Service gave $4,853 to local work. Church property was valued at $31,000, parsonage at $27,900.

instances, the invasion is meeting with success. The beverage alcohol traffic thrives on battered morality, and beaten spirits and bruises and breaks the bodies of men. Retreat of any kind is unthinkable. The destiny of the public may be hanging in the balance. Moral fibre is wanting in high places and low. Principles become flabby when kept too long in a solution of alcohol. Conscience does not easily function in a society using liquor as its social custom."

That year the Conference urged opposition to liquor sponsorship of radio and television programs, boycott of motion pictures featuring drinking, and elimination of the sale of wine and beer in grocery stores.

In addition to legislative action the Conference proposed an intensive program of education. In 1956 the Committee on Temperance reported that a study conference had been held during the year, and that in the following months more than 100 churches had conducted classes among their members.

The Conference continued alert to all abuses of the liquor laws. In 1961 the body petitioned the manager of Century 21 World's Fair, at Seattle, not to permit the sale and consumption of alcoholic liquors on the grounds.

While the liquor situation in Washington and Northern Idaho looked bleak in the 1960's Methodists clung to the faith that eventually time will be ripe for the elimination of the traffic in beverage alcohol.

Northwest Methodists did not limit their opposition to the traffic in intoxicants to resolutions on the conference floor. Most pastors indicted the evil from their pulpits and cooperated with organizations committed to temperance.

Certain men were outstanding in their condemnation of the traffic in alcohol. Such a man was Rev. Lauren Kufus who went to Wenatchee in 1903. Saloons were open twenty-four hours a day, seven days a week. Gambling ran

---

MANSON—1913

Methodism born in Manson when, in 1913, Rev. C. C. Curry, of Chelan, organized first Sunday school in what later was public library. There were 17 present. L. H. Watson, first superintendent.

Church organized, October 18, 1915, with 28 members. Presiding elder, Rev. Robert Brumblay, and Rev. J. E. Strevey, of Chelan, officiated. The Ladies Aid, organized in 1915, changed name to Dorcas Society in 1922.

First trustees were, Sam Nicholson, S. L. Mechlin, Paul M. Ford, G. L. Barklay, C. C. Troxel.

In 1918, Rev. E. C. Corn, pastor, began plans for a building, on land donated by the "Land Company." With aid of $300 from Board of Church Extension, work began in June, 1918, and building, first occupied in 1919, was dedicated November 30, 1919, by Rev. J. W. Caughlin, district superintendent. Rev. J. D. Bird, pastor. First resident pastor, Rev. J. H. Hill, 1934.

Parsonage purchased in 1941, Rev. F. L. Lowther, pastor. New building, erected in 1949, cost $45,000. The incomplete building entered in 1950, dedicated in 1954 by Bishop A. Raymond Grant.

In 1964 Rev. Eugene W. Hibbard, appointed pastor for the eighth year. Members, 236, church school, 276. Members of Woman's Society of Christian Service, 56. They contributed $473. Church valued at $105,000, parsonage $11,000.

THESE MEN STOOD FIRM ON VITAL MORAL ISSUES

Rev. J. G.
Bringdale

Rev. Robert A.
Uphoff

ev. Newton E.
Moats

EVANGELISM AND MORAL REFORM

Northwest Methodism has stressed Evangelism and Moral reform. Typical of the many pastors who gave full time to evangelism is Rev. J. G. Bringdale, of the Norwegian-Danish conference. Certain other men either gave full time to liquor control or placed major emphasis on it in their ministry. Some of these are shown here.

Rev. W. J.
Herwig

Rev. E. J.
Huston

Rev. Charles
MacCaughey

riot. The pastor was a strong preacher and drew large crowds. He also was a deadly foe of liquor and gambling. When he turned his oratory against these evils the entire town listened. He remained in Wenatchee four years, making an indelible impression upon the conscience of the city.

Several conference members, at one time or another, engaged in temperance work. Notable among these was Rev. W. J. Herwig, who gave more than forty years to temperance promotion, beginning about 1907. He headed temperance organizations in Idaho, Iowa, Oregon, and Washington. Full-time leaders of temperance forces in Washington for shorter periods were: Rev. W. B. Eakin, Rev. C. W. Cook, Rev. John W. Frescoln, Rev. John Ovall, Rev. E. J. Huston, Rev. Robert LaMott, and Rev. Fred O. Hunt.

In the 1940's an attempt was made by Governor Mon C. Wallgren to induce the Legislature of Washington to liberalize the liquor laws. Rev. Newton E. Moats, pastor of First Methodist Church and head of the Temperance Committee of the State Council of Churches, teamed up with Rev. W. J. Herwig, then leading the Washington Temperance Association. They stumped the state in the interest of strict regulation of the traffic. For the time being the temperance forces won.

RIVERSIDE CHURCH—1913

Riverside Church first appeared in 1906 teamed with Alma. In 1908, Rev. W. R. Struble was supply pastor with Okanogan. The two had 32 members. In 1912 Rev. C. F. Graham was the supply pastor. In 1913 Rev. J. P. Armand was pastor. In 1914 it was with Okanogan with Rev. J. O. Hawk, pastor. There were 84 members and 154 in the church school. In 1916 Riverside was with Pine Creek, Rev. R. R. Martin pastor. In 1918 Riverside and Conconully were together, Rev. J. W. Downs supplying. In 1928 again with Conconully, Molson, and Loomis. Rev. John Moede, pastor. There were 56 members in Riverside. In 1935 again with Omak, Desautel, supplied by Rev. J. G. Wilkins. There were 49 members and 149 in the Sunday school. In 1960 it was teamed with Omak, Rev. Bruce B. Groseclose, pastor in his fourth year. There were 40 members, 25 in the Sunday school. There were 18 in the Woman's Society of Christian Service and they had given $44. In 1964 Rev. Paul F. Ashbrook, in first year as pastor. There were 47 members, 87 in the Sunday school. Thirteen women had given $129 to local work. The church building was valued at $18,500, and parsonage at $6,100.

SABBATH KEEPING ESSENTIAL TO CHRISTIAN VIRILITY

The Methodists believed in the sanctity of the Sabbath and that its rigid observance by Christian people was obligatory as a means of maintaining the spiritual virility of the Church.

Pursuant to this belief, the Committee on the Sanctity of the Sabbath, in 1871, urged that the utterances of ministers on the necessity to keep this day holy should be frequent and clear.

Two years later the committee recalled the origin of the Sabbath and its significance to Christians. It was said, "Its change from the seventh to the first

326

day of the week by the example of apostles and churches trained under their care, did not less serve to remind us of the great work of creation. But as the first was the day of Christ's resurrection and, therefore, called the Lord's Day, it incorporated with it, also, the memory of the greater work of redemption. The duty to keep constantly before the people the church's obligation to the Sabbath is too manifest to be questioned or neglected by any true minister of the gospel."

The Conference said, "We recognize that only in the maintenance of the sanctity of the Sabbath, rests the absolute safety of the nation. Also that its desecration promises absolute certainty of our national ruin."

As, with the passing of the years, more settlers came to the Northwest from many nations, desecration of the Sabbath became more deplorable. In 1881, the committee, headed by Rev. J. H. Acton and Rev. T. M. Reid, specified instances of violation of the holy day. They said, "All over the land the widespread disregard for this day exists. In the towns and cities merchants carry on their traffic. Saloons and restaurants reap the richest harvests of the week, while parks and beer gardens, revel with maudlin, drinking crowds. In the country men and women hold picnics, go on excursions, fish, hunt, visit, and lounge. This condition is not confined to the ranks of the vile and lawless. Many people of culture and intelligence, who hold pews in our churches, and support our ministry, seem to have no just conception of its requirements, and in some instances we fear, not a few church members frequently are guilty."

The responsibility of Christians to observe the Sabbath was emphasized at every session of the Conference, and the ministers asked to keep the subject before their people.

In 1903 the Conference said, "The Sabbath is the bulwark of our liberties

TRINITY, TACOMA—1913

Trinity, Tacoma founded 1913, but roots date to two earlier congregations. Fowler Church, organized in 1889, under inspiration of Rev. George C. Wilding, pastor First Church, who transferred several members instructing them to organize church in their community.

Rev. Benjamin F. Brooks, pastor, Fern Hill, became pastor of new congregation. First building located at East E. and 30th St. Ea. Trustees: Jeremiah H. Lister, J. W. Penguilly, Alfred Lister, E. Dement, H. W. Spaulding. Rev. F. A. LaViolette, pastor, enlarged church with aid from Board of Home missions and Church Extension.

McKinley Park Church, organized in 1906, by Rev. G. L. Cuddy, pastor at Fowler. Rev. James Clulow, city missionary, was first pastor. This church was merged with Fowler in 1913, to become Trinity.

New church located at East 35th and East F. Streets, dedicated, January 10, 1913. There were 150 members; church school, 424.

In 1918-23 additions made to church, Rev. Clifford D. Rarey, pastor. Guiding light and inspiration this church for half century was Alfred Lister. He was Superintendent church school, trustee, steward and in other places of leadership.

In 1964, Rev. Edward E. Smith, pastor, first year. Membership, 260, Sunday school 134, and 88 women in Woman's Society. They gave $1,143.

because it is the bulwark of our morality. Break down the defense of Christianity and liberty and law will perish with it."

HOME AND FAMILY STAND WITH THE CHURCH

Maintenance of the sanctity of the home and family, from the beginning, was a matter of deep concern to Northwest Methodists. Personal immorality that disregarded family responsibility was a glaring condition first faced by the missionaries. Therefore, the attitude of churchmen regarding this evil early was proclaimed.

Rev. Jason Lee and his associates deplored the readiness with which white men deserted their Indian wives. Rev. and Mrs. David Blaine[3] expressed revolt against such practices, and Rev. James Harvey Wilbur took note of a like condition in Walla Walla.

One of the great indictments against the use of alcohol was its effects upon family life, according to early churchmen. In 1873, for instance, the Pastoral Address declared that alcohol blights the happiness of homes. The 1876 Pastoral Address, written by Rev. John Flinn, exhorted the brethren to keep up the family altar. The effects of such a practice were considered important in training children in the Christian way of life.

Columbia River Methodists, in 1874, through the Pastoral Address, were exhorted, "As you love your children we intreat you earnestly to devote your time and means to the prosperity of the Sunday school. Let there be heroic efforts to save your children from ruin, and to save them for the Church and heaven."

In 1903 the Puget Sound Conference protested against the evils of divorce. "The divorce evil," it said, "has grown to gigantic proportions. In at least one of our largest counties, the ratio of divorce is more than one to four marriages."

Ministers were admonished to make a thorough investigation of the back-

NESPELEM—1914

Nespelem is headquarters of the Colville Indian Reservation Agency. Here, Joseph, greatest chieftain of the Nez Perce Tribe, spent his last years. He died in 1904 and his monument, gift of James J. Hill, stands in the Nez Perce Cemetery north of town.

Methodist work here began in 1914 when Rev. A. A. McGinnes reported 12 church members. No pastor was appointed that year, but in 1917, Rev. J. H. S. Holloman reported 17 members. Ten years later, Rev. R. T. Holland reported 13 members.

Work among the Indians here never has been notably successful under Methodist leadership. The above reports are typical. In 1938, Rev. Charles A. Burris reported 35 members, and in 1964, Rev. Laird V. Glascock reported 40. Church school enrollment was 59. Sixteen members were reported in the Woman's Society of Christian Service and they had contributed $647 to the local work. The church building was valued at $16,600 and parsonage, $6,300, with indebtedness of $570. The church paid the pastor $660 and $210 on World Service and Conference Benevolences. Grand total for all causes $2,054.

The church was served as part of a circuit with Grand Coulee the other point, in 1964. Farming, cattle raising are chief industries.

ground of divorced persons seeking to be remarried by them.

CONFERENCE ADVOCATES UNIFORM DIVORCE LAWS IN STATES

In 1909 the Conference advocated uniform divorce laws throughout the several states. The Columbia River Conference, in 1906, heard the committee report, "There is a sad lack of family religion. The family is not only the bond of the nation, but the strong arm of the church. The godless home is sure to breed a vicious and godless generation."

The reverent reading of God's Word by the head of the family and the leading by the father or mother in prayer was said to be essential to the moral and religious training of children.

Northwest Methodists continued this emphasis. In 1934 the Conference reaffirmed its belief in the sanctity of the home and deplored the modern tendency to break it up. Divisive forces brought by serious economic problems and recent changes in public moral ideals, it was thought, could be overcome only by a personal religious experience.

The Committee on Public Reform, in 1948, urged every Methodist home to set up a family altar, for Bible study and prayer. The conviction that family unity had lost none of its significance in moral society, is seen in recommendations made in 1949. To preserve family unity the Conference Board of Education was asked to increase its training courses on family counselling for ministers. A family relations clinic was proposed to deal with special cases of disrupted home life. Appreciation was expressed for family courts which had been set up by the state to which divorce applicants could be referred where children were involved.

When, in 1959, the Conference adopted a resolution approving planned parenthood, it gave evidence of its continued interest in home and family life. Also there was evidence that the Church

HIGHLAND PARK—1916

First Sunday school at Highland Park, Seattle, began in 1916, in various homes. In 1917, Rev. W. H. Leach, city missionary, began preaching in community. The church was organized in 1919, reporting 33 members in 1920. Rev. Dwight G. Bennett, student pastor appointed in 1922. In 1924, Rev. William C. Bowman, student at University of Washington, appointed.

Building, 14x24, erected previously on lots purchased by congregation. Building was enlarged and left incomplete with $10,000 debt. During depression of 1930's, church struggled against discouraging odds.

In 1947, Board of Home Missions and Church Extension offered to donate $6,053 if church would raise $4,000. Proposition accepted and, in 1948, church was free from debt. The Seattle Missionary Union assisted the project. Rev. T. W. Bundy was pastor from 1937 to 1957.

In 1952, a parsonage was purchased for $8,000. Under Rev. Rarden Virgen, 1957, the building was enlarged and consecrated, by Bishop Everett W. Palmer, in 1961. The church was located at S. W. 9th and Henderson, S. W.

In 1964, Rev. E. Vincent Smith, became pastor. There were 352 members, church school enrollment, 354. Woman's Society members, 87. They gave $777. Value of property $165,000. Parsonage $11,000.

was abreast of the times in its stand on this controversial issue.

PRIVATE AND PUBLIC MORALITY ARE ESSENTIAL

In the Pastoral Address, written by Rev. William Roberts, in 1877, it was said, "It has been the custom of Satan ever since the days of Job to deny the existence of moral desert, of actual virtue, but God has borne testimony and given evidence that moral virtue is a reality, a prime fact in the world, and the most precious product in the universe of God. By ordination of the Almighty and in accord, as we suppose, with the eternal fitness of things, the chief development of moral goodness is in the labors, trials, sufferings, and opportunities of earthly probation. Hence, the furnace, the rod, the chastening and conflict of battle has entered largely into the history of piety in all ages. Your case, brethren, is no exception to the general rule. Denying ungodliness and worldly lusts, let us strive to live soberly, righteously and godly in this present world."

Thus, the grounds for morals in private and public, and its eternal justification were stated by one of the greatest leaders of Northwest Methodism.

WISER LAKE—1916

The first appointment to Wiser Lake to appear in the conference minutes was that of Rev. C. M. Olsen in 1916. Rev. John M. Canse was district superintendent. In his conference report he said, a new building had been erected on lots previously purchased by the women of the church who also gave $300 for the building. In 1917 thirty members reported at Wiser Lake with 65 enrolled in the Sunday school.

District Superintendent Canse called the building a model church. The men had felled the timber, sawed the lumber valued at over $600, and contributed labor. The complete building was valued at $2,000. A memorial gift of $350 by Mrs. J. S. Smith and her daughter, Grace, of Bellingham helped pay for other material.

Rev. T. A. Graham was pastor in 1929. He reported 25 members and 63 in the Sunday school. The church building then was valued at $3500.

In 1939 Eureka and Wiser Lake were together with Rev. F. R. Gillett, pastor. There were 30 members, 67 in the Sunday school and ten in the Epworth League. In 1950 the appointment was attached to Lynden with Rev. Chester Blair as pastor. After 1953 Wiser Lake did not appear among the conference appointments.

Gambling, whether fostered by the community, or practiced in the seclusion of the back room in a saloon or gaming house, was ever considered by the Church a moral evil to be eliminated. In 1874 the Columbia River Conference lifted its voice against sinful amusements, games of chance, and especially against all gambling methods of raising money for religious purposes. "Whether our financial enterprises succeed or fail," it was said, "whether we live or die, let us adhere to the methods that are honorable and just. If we do this we shall not die."

In 1910 the crime prevention issue was introduced. Because crimes committed by the young, the social evil, cigarette smoking, incurable diseases, and the traffic in girls, were said to be on the increase, the Conference was asked heartily to endorse the work of prevention as outlined in the Constitution of the Woman's Christian Temperance Union.

The issues were state-wide. In 1907 the Columbia River Conference took its stand against an action of the Spokane City Council. The Council recently had adopted an ordinance prohibiting pool selling within the city. The promoters of the Spokane Inter-State Fair, on the plea of necessity for its financial success, had induced the City Fathers to amend the ordinance to permit pool selling for the two weeks of the fair. The ministers deplored this action and commended the State Grange and moral forces in Spokane in withdrawing their support.

Four years later eternal enmity was expressed against the evil of race track gambling.

FILTH IN RADIO, MOTION PICTURES, AND PUBLICATIONS OPPOSED

The Pacific Northwest Conference, in 1934, pledged its cooperation with all agencies seeking to eliminate the filthy, suggestive, and criminal, in publications, radio programs, and motion pictures wherever they appear. It also pledged cooperation with the League of Decency,[4] and urged pastors to win members to this principle. In 1957 members of local churches were urged to be alert in reporting violations of gambling laws and in obtaining strict enforcement at the local level.

METHODISTS DEFEAT GAMBLING MEASURE REFERENDUM NO. 34

Northwest Methodists, having ever stood for private and public morality, continued committed in 1964, when a bill permitting gambling, enacted by the 1963 Legislature, came before the voters of Washington as Referendum 34. When the bill was before the Legislature Methodists had led in lobbying against

FOUR LAKES—1917; MICA—1928

Four Lakes first appeared in 1917. Rev. J. D. Bird, pastor. In 1918 with Medical Lake there were 160 in Sunday school and 83 members. Three church buildings valued at $6,500. In 1920, Rev. F. L. Farnham supply. In 1928, Rev. Ralph I. Thomas, pastor. There were 61 members and 57 in Sunday school, one building valued at $2600. In 1939 with Hayford, Rev. J. Phillip Arman, Greenacres, was pastor. There were 22 members and 40 in Sunday school. One building valued at $1,000. In 1960 Rev. T. Orville Kelly reported 31 members, 100 in Sunday school. In 1963 church abandoned and building sold.

Mica first appeared in 1928, with Rev. S. E. Taft, pastor. In 1931 Rev. Robert Thompson also served Farmington. Total, 77 members. In 1932 with Four Lakes, Medical Lake. Rev. Dan Taylor, pastor. In 1939 with Rockford, Rev. W. W. Switzer reported 16 members, 25 in Sunday school, building valued at $1,000. In 1950, with Rockford, Rev. Cecil G. Rickard supply, reported 27 members, 44 in Sunday school. In 1960, with Rockford. Rev. Arthur E. Paltridge reported 27 members. In 1963 the church at Mica was abandoned by Pacific Northwest Annual Conference, building unused for years, was sold to a community church.

it. Rev. Paul J. Beeman, Public Relations Director, led the lobby.

In 1964 a committee of state heads of denominations, including the Council of Churches, issued a joint statement which concluded:

"It is time for all our citizens to realize that a vote for Referendum 34 is a vote for the legalization of commercialized gambling. A vote against Referendum 34 is a vote to keep our state as clean and free from corrupt forces as it has been for many years. We personally urge every citizen to vote against Referendum 34."

The statement was signed by The Right Reverend Ivol Ira Curtis, Bishop, Diocese of Olympia, Protestant Episcopal Church; The Rev. J. Henry Ernst, Seattle District Superintendent, The Methodist Church; The Reverend Clement F. Hahn, General Secretary, Washington-Northern Idaho Council of Churches; The Reverend A. G. Fjellman, President, Pacific Northwest Synod, Lutheran Church in America; Reverend Archie H. Hook, Minister and Superintendent, Washington-North Idaho Conference United Church of Christ; The Reverend George H. McCleave, Executive Secretary (retired) Presbytery of Seattle, United Presbyterian Church; Bishop Everett W. Palmer, Resident Bishop, The Seattle Area The Methodist Church; The Reverend Harold Penhalurick, Field Administrator, Synod of Washington, United Presbyterian Church; Rev. Earl H. VanDoren, Executive Secretary, Washington-North Idaho, The Christian Churches, Inc., (Disciples of Christ); Reverend E. Wayne Roberts, Acting Executive Secretary, American Baptist Churches of the Pacific Northwest.

A state-wide committee to oppose the Referendum was set up by churchmen. Methodist leaders were ready to introduce a resolution before the 1964 session of the Pacific Northwest Annual Conference, setting forth the attitude of the Church toward the measure. But laymen, supposedly in accord with the attitude of the Church, urged leaders to refrain from Conference action on the

---

FALL CITY—1918

Baptists built church at Fall City, 1898. Sunday school followed. Baptists sold building to Methodist Episcopal Church in 1918. Charge appeared in conference journal, 1918. Rev. G. L. Snyder, supplying. The following year, District Superintendent G. A. Landen, reported Snyder had disappeared during the year. Rev. S. V. Warren, Issaquah, had finished the year. Rev. Jarrett I. Beatty appointed in 1919.

Pastors during the following years were, Rev. B. W. Rinehart, Rev. W. E. Callahan, Rev. Richard Oates, Rev. L. C. Schultz, Rev. Nelson C. Pierce, Rev. John R. Butler.

In 1918 the parsonage was built with aid of $1,000 grant from Board of Church Extension. Name "Mary Ware Benedict Methodist Episcopal Church." Ladies Aid bought first parsonage in 1926, Rev. William E. Callahan, pastor. The church was moved across the street in 1929. New one, in 1948, cost $12,000. A new section was added in 1958, Rev. Ernest Barber, pastor, aided by $6,000 gift.

In 1961, sanctuary remodeled, redecorated, and divided chancel installed. Rev. George Pratt was pastor.

In 1964, Rev. George Pratt was appointed for seventh year. There were 177 members, 231 in church school. Woman's Society of Christian Service membership was 34. They gave $660. Church building valued at $36,000, and parsonage at $12,000.

ground that it would be more effective to appear before the public as a move sponsored by "good citizens."

In late August, Bishop Everett W. Palmer, episcopal head of the Seattle Area of The Methodist Church, received word that no one had been found to head the state-wide committee. Methodist layman, Wilfred R. Woods, editor and publisher of the Wenatchee Daily World, upon the insistence of Bishop Palmer, accepted the chairmanship of the Committee. But he found finances to undergird the committee's educational program difficult to raise.

Two weeks before election there was on hand only $500 of the $10,000 needed. The Bishop appealed to laymen of means and was successful. Therefore, a week prior to the polling date, state radios and televisions ran spot announcements during one day, and most of the newspapers carried advertisements paid for by the committee, in which the facts as seen by the churchmen were presented.

Armed with these facts and with a feeling that they had been misled by the claims of the proponents of the referendum, the electorate went to the polls and defeated the measure, by a majority of 117,000. Thus, in the eyes of churchmen, the state of Washington, for the time being, had been spared an influx of big-time gamblers and racketeers.

Bishop Everett W. Palmer issued a statement concerning the outcome in which he said: "Defeat of Referendum 34 is a compliment to the conscience and common sense of the electorate, a triumph for the churches, and a victory for the moral and spiritual well being of the state. It is heartening evidence that most people can be trusted to discern the truth despite clever attempts to confuse and mislead them. It sends the message loud and clear to the gambling interests and those politicians influenced by them, that the state of Washington is not to be had."

The Seattle Times called the defeat of the measure a Methodist victory.

SEAVIEW—1918

Seaview Methodist Protestant Church School organized 1918 by Rev. Leonard B. Smith, First Methodist Protestant Church. November 24, 1918, small chapel dedicated. In June, 1919, 20 members of First Methodist Protestant Church became charter members of Seaview Church.

Rev. O. B. Williams, first pastor. Five years later he reported 64 members. During his term, parsonage was acquired. Rev. R. N. Orrill, 1924-27 paid debt on parsonage. Celebration held in chapel, February 17, 1926. Church, costing $25,000 dedicated, February 6, 1927, by Rev. R. N. Orrill, assisted by other Methodist Protestant pastors. There were 310 members of church, 400 in school.

Rev. Theodore G. Betschler came in 1927. A neon-lighted cross was erected above church tower. His wife organized junior church, produced religious pageantry. In 1935, Moeller pipe organ dedicated to memory of Ben Baxley, long-time member.

Rev. Wilbur M. Snyder came in 1937, paid debt, celebrated in 1942. When the Methodist denominations were merged in 1939, group became "Seaview Methodist Church." Under the leadership of Rev. Roy Jenkins, 1956-61, chapel was renovated and an educational unit added to the plant.

In 1964, Rev. John C. Radmore was assigned for fourth year. Members, 388, church school enrollment, 360. Woman's Society members, 80, giving $1,190.

Indeed the Council of Churches, impressed by Methodist leadership in the anti-gambling move, selected Rev. Paul J. Beeman, public relations director for the Seattle Methodist Area as the council's first representative in the State Legislature in 1965.

THE METHODIST IDEAL IS A NEW MAN IN A NEW SOCIETY

Although Northwest Methodists have, at times, employed legal means to obtain some of their spiritual objectives, they ever have clung to the conviction that a new society depends upon new men, committed to the moral and spiritual principles of Christ. Their reason for appealing to law is similar to that given by Woodrow Wilson for resorting to war, namely, that force sometimes must be employed to hold evil men in check until they can be convinced of the virtue of acting in the interest of the common good.

The first objective of pioneer Methodists was personal piety based upon Christian experience. The Pastoral Address in 1878 urged Columbia River Methodists to keep in their hearts deep personal piety growing out of a complete consecration of heart and life to the work and worship of the Lord Jesus Christ.

The Pastoral Address further said, "Ours is a new country and offers many opportunities for the immigrant, but coupled with these are many temptations. The vast agricultural, mineral, and other resources, constantly present to the minds of Christian people the opportunities and advantages of the acquirement of wealth. We would say to you, remember the assurance of Scripture, 'They that would be rich fall into temptation and a snare, to many foolish and hurtful lusts, that has drawn them into destruction and perdition.'

"Be sure," the admonition continued, "that in all business transactions, you have the divine approval and, seeking first the kingdom of God and His righteousness, make worldly fortunes occupy

JULIAETTA, IDAHO—1920

Juliaetta, Idaho, organized in 1920, by Methodist Episcopal Church, South. Rev. Haskel Tudor, pastor, that year, reported 30 members of the church, building valued at $5,000. There were 20 organized women.

In 1938, last year before Methodist union, Juliaetta was served by Rev. J. E. Walbeck, who also served Arrow. There were 30 members but church building had dropped in value to $2,000, parsonage valued at $800.

In 1940, Juliaetta and Arrow still together were served by Rev. Melvin C. Pruitt, first year. There were 54 members and 107 in church school. In 1950, charge left to be supplied. Rev. E. Lonnie Williams, who had served the charge the preceding year, reported 31 members, 82 in church school, church valued at $4,000 and parsonage at $1,500.

In 1964, Juliaetta was with Kendrick, Rev. David A. Zaske, pastor, first year. He resided at Kendrick. There were 33 members, church school enrollment of 80. Twenty-eight members of the Woman's Society of Christian Service had raised $157 for the work of the church. Church building was reported to be worth $6,600 and parsonage $7,000.

The church had paid its pastor $960, and $187 to World Service and Conference Benevolences. Grand total of giving was $2407.

a secondary place." Deep and constant personal piety was admonished.

Personal piety, these leaders believed, exists, not for its own sake alone, but for the building of a strong society in a righteous nation.

Aggressive Evangelism Supported in 1905

Because of the persistence of this belief, in 1905, the Conference issued a statement favoring aggressive evangelism. "The spirit of Methodism is that of evangelism," it was said. "Whatever other denominations may do and whatever methods they may depend upon for the salvation of sinners and the extension of Christ's kingdom, Methodism dies when revival fires cease to burn upon her altars."

This faith was further emphasized in 1927 by the Puget Sound Conference in adopting the report of the Committee on Social Service. It was said, "The program of the kingdom contemplates not alone the saving of the individual but of society. These two ends are so intimately related that one cannot be realized without the other. We further believe that the reluctance to face the major sins of our time will continue and the church will grow more worldly and that there will be no real revival of religion until these matters are dealt with more definitely, intelligently and earnestly from our pulpits."

Similar views were expressed by the Columbia River Conference. In 1909 in a resolution it declared its hearty sympathy with every form of humanitarian activity, with all social and political reform. But the ministers were reminded that their primary mission was so to reveal God in Jesus Christ that those under their care should become partakers of the divine nature.

This emphasis was continued. In 1922, the body directed that the express effort of the coming year should be upon religious education and the spiritual truths of the Church that the people may be more firmly grounded in the doctrines of Methodism, and not so

CULDESAC, IDAHO—1925

Methodists made themselves felt in Culdesac, Idaho, in the early 1900's. Organization effected in 1925, when Rev. C. E. Miller, superintendent Moscow District, responding to urgent call, organized church. First pastor, Rev. Waldo W. Pierson. Early services held in old store building, later in Odd Fellow's Hall. Pierson followed by Rev. Henry R. Cross.

By 1930, membership was 59, Rev. S. E. Yaggy, pastor. Church planned building. Lots donated by Harry Clark, May 24, 1930. Building dedicated, 1931. Rev. Paul R. Campbell, 1932-34, also served Cottonwood, residing in that town. Rev. E. E. VanWert, served 1934-35, and built parsonage of lumber from wrecked church at Mohler.

Rev. Charles Thornton, 1946, supplied until his death in 1951. Church prospered, new members added, mid-week service became force in church.

Rev. A. K. Walborn, 1952-53, reorganized Methodist Youth Fellowship. Rev. F. B. Kenoyer, 1954, organized Daily Vacation Bible school. Parsonage given to church. Old one used for educational purposes. Rev. Jack Caldwell, 1959-60, brought records up to date. Rev. James Buckles, served two and one-half years and died. His wife was effective Bible teacher.

In 1964, Rev. Mack Farmer, pastor, membership, 91; church school 45. Nineteen members of Woman's Society gave $264. Value of church $10,500. Parsonage $7,500.

easily led astray by the nostrums offered by erratic religious leaders.

Five years later the Conference asserted that the chief job of the Church was to win men to Christ. "The supreme need of men," it said, "is a vital knowledge of God as He is revealed in Jesus Christ, and a consciousness of His abiding peace.'" This personal experience of God was said to be the only source of adequate ideals of living and the dynamic which alone can turn these ideals into reality.

The belief was expressed by the Conference in 1933 that substitutes for the Gospel are inadequate to satisfy the heart. "We believe," it was said, "that if the doctrines of Methodism were preached instead of eulogizing men of doubtful doctrines, we would again see sinners coming to our altars, repenting of their sins, and seeking peace with God."

Faith in the transforming power of Christ in the life of the individual and society was expressed in 1934. "We believe that the fundamental mission of the church is to awaken and foster the personal relationship between the individual and his God so clearly made real in the life and teachings of Jesus Christ. The reformed individual must antedate any successful social and economic reform."

On such faith Northwest Methodists always have stood.

Christ Is Central in the Christian Life

The foregoing would indicate that to the pioneer Methodists and their modern successors, Christ is considered to be central in the Church and all social achievement. It was to this end that Rev. James H. Wilbur spoke in 1871 when he authored a report on the State of the Church in which he said, "Do not forget, beloved brethren, that if we confess our sins, He is faithful and just to forgive us our sins and to cleanse us from all unrighteousness. Remember that the great want of the church right now is not more money nor more men,

---

FELLOWSHIP—1926

Fellowship Methodst Church born, 1926, when Rev. and Mrs. T. W. Bundy began meeting with group of Filipinos at First Methodist Church, Seattle, Sunday afternoons.

Church membership not among first objectives. Bible study and religious topics included in agenda. By 1930, married couples with children affiliated. Mrs. Bundy began Sunday school for children, assisted by Grandino Baaoa, local preacher.

The Bundys continued with the group until 1945. Grandino Baaoa, appointed to direct the Fellowship, now holding regular preaching services. An attempt to merge Filipino children with those of First Methodist Church, unsuccessful.

Filipino leaders, Bishop J. C. Baker, District Superintendent C. K. Mahoney, and Rev. Newton E. Moats, of First Church, decided upon separate organization. With aid of First Church, Methodist Union, and Board of Home Missions, a building acquired and opened for use, January, 1948, was dedicated by Bishop J. C. Baker and Rev. Edwar Lee, superintendent of Oriental Mission.

Rev. Peo Daba, first pastor. In 1950, name changed to "Fellowship Methodist Church." Daba was succeeded in 1952, by Rev. D. F. Gonzalo who, in 1964, was reappointed for the twelfth year. There were 44 members, 108 in Sunday school. Twenty members of Woman's Society, gave $50. Building valued at $15,000 and parsonage at $12,000.

but more of the power from on high." He spoke for the Conference.

Belief that the greatest victory for which to be thankful was the winning of men to Christ was seen in the report of the Committee on the State of the Church in 1894, which said, "We have great reason to praise God for the presence of the Holy Ghost in power with us in giving the conference 2,300 souls."

Fifty years later the Conference expressed confidence that the power of Jesus Christ to save men was unabated. It was said, "We believe that Christianity is the only hope of the world."

The Conference further gave utterance to the belief that the spirit of Christ must undergird all educational efforts and said it was believed that the moral training of youth was more important than mere technical training. Much of the crime of the day was attributed to training of the minds without moral and religious attitudes. The ministers pledged to give all possible support to the administrative officers of state normal schools and universities, in their efforts to strengthen the moral and religious life of their student bodies.

The Church and the Ministry Are of God

The belief that the Church and the ministry are of God was steadfastly held. Evidence of this faith is seen in the report on the State of the Church presented in 1872. It was said, "The Church of God is divinely instituted and for the perfection of the saints. For the edifying of the Church God has a divinely appointed and endowed ministry." The Church, it was said, includes all who profess faith in the Lord Jesus Christ and are spiritual.

The Pastoral Address to the Oregon Conference, in 1874, dealt with the minister and his work. It said, "The pastorate is an office appointed by the great head of the church. He said, 'I will set thee as a watchman unto the house of Israel.' Christ commissioned His min-

WAPATO JAPANESE—1927

Methodism among Japanese at Wapato, began in 1925 under leadership of Miss Mabel Brown, public school teacher. Miss Brown was aided by Misses Caroline Boyd, Rosemarie Chabert, Alice Sutton and Ilda Manring. In 1926 Mrs. Aya Okuda was appointed missionary to Wapato by Rev. Frank Herron Smith, superintendent Japanese Methodist Mission on Pacific Coast. Mrs. Okuda, assisted by Mrs. Will L. McGahan, Seattle, correlated Sunday school and held special preaching services. Church, organized in 1927, by March, 1928, had 76 members and 130 in Sunday school.

K. Wada, began building fund through use of "mite boxes," purchased building site in 1933. Cornerstone laid, fall 1934, Rev. Otoe So, Tacoma, officiating. Labor donated by members of congregation, ladies serving meals. Building dedicated March 17, 1937, by Rev. Frank Herron Smith, assisted by Rev. Y. Tsuda, Seattle, and Rev. Otoe So, Tacoma.

Building closed because of Japanese evacuation during war years. Few returned to take up work. Board of Home Missions, in 1954, through the recommendation of Rev. Frederick L. Pederson, associate general secretary, granted funds for renovation. Another grant in 1955 provided funds for materials. Members did work. Rev. Frank Woolridge appointed to supply congregation along with White Swan, in 1965.

isters to go into all the world and preach the gospel to every creature. Unto the office of the ministry we feel that we have been called by the Holy Ghost." The message further said of the duties of the pastor, "The pastor is a watchman stationed upon the walls of Zion to guard and keep it, an ambassador whose duty it is to make known to the perishing world the exact conditions upon which it may become reconciled to God—a shepherd, appointed to feed the church of God."

CHAPTER XVI

*Methodist patriotism has never been
questioned by responsible persons. How
Northwest Methodist leaders imple-
mented their loyalty to country is set
forth in—*

Men of Patriotic Fervor

NORTHWEST METHODISTS LOVE THEIR COUNTRY [1]

Love for country characterized Methodists from the beginning.
Naturally, Northwest pioneers of this faith brought with them strong
devotion to America, rendered more intense by the struggles and
hardships they endured in building Christian civilization here. They
experienced, first hand, bitter and sweet, disappointment and victory,
attending the business of establishing homes, schools, churches, commerce, and government in the erstwhile wilderness. They knew what
their country cost in blood, sweat, and tears.

Consequently they were jealous of every attitude, agency, habit, or
custom that threatened the civilization they sought to establish. That
was why they girded themselves for battle against gambling, the liquor
traffic, broken homes, neglect of the Sabbath, and immorality in
public and private. They were men of patriotic fervor, intolerant of
evil, but they loved God and country more than life.

NORTHWEST METHODISTS PLEDGE SUPPORT OF GOVERNMENT

Devotion of Northwest Methodists to the United States Government
and its institutions, began early to motivate their protests against evil.
All utterances by them, quoted in this chapter, were spoken into
current events affecting or threatening the welfare of their beloved
nation at the time spoken.

Methodism still was young in Washington and Oregon, when, in
1861, the Conference adopted a resolution setting forth its philosophy
regarding the relation of Christians to their country. The ministers
declared that since their dearest earthly hopes and interests were

involved in the preservation of the Government, therefore their safety and duty demanded that they support it against all enemies.

It was stated, "In the fearful struggle now going on between our government and those who are madly striving to subvert it there is no neutral ground to be occupied by ministers or people."

It was resolved, finally, that "As all our hope for success is in God, therefore, we will pray for the welfare of our countrymen, that our republic may emerge from the present ordeal, stronger and purer than ever before."

Following the Civil War, in 1866, the Conference resolved, "We are devoutly thankful that war is ended. The determined purpose of patriotism has been gloriously consummated in preventing our national boundaries from violation, and in retaining the undiminished number of states in one indissoluble union. We affirm the religious duty of all our citizens to uphold our national honor and liberties. We must remember that we are Christian men and bound by all principles of religious charity to extend the hand of kindness to the fallen."

In 1889 the Columbia River Conference reaffirmed loyalty to the country in endorsing the recommendations of the General Conference that a corps of chaplains be created for the United States Army, and expressed the hope that the bill establishing such a corps, then before Congress, might be enacted.

The sensitiveness of the Puget Sound Conference to its relation to the United States Government and its leaders was revealed in a resolution adopted on the occasion of the death of the president in 1901. The resolution said, "Whereas in the death of President William A. McKinley, the nation has been placed in mourning, and whereas the Governor of the State of Washington has issued a proclamation calling upon the people to meet in their churches on Thursday, the day of the President's funeral, and testify their sympathy for the living and

---

GRAND COULEE—1933

The church at Grand Coulee was begun, in 1933, as a cooperative project, among seven denominations, under state Council of Churches. Cooperating denominations include Presbyterian, Baptist, Congregational, Methodist, Disciples, United Presbyterian, and Evangelical and Reformed. Rev. Roy H. Murray, first pastor.

Land for first church site donated by Continental Land Company. Construction of building began, November, 1934. In October, 1935, incomplete but usable building dedicated. A year later two lots adjoining building donated for recreation by Howard Short. Borrowed piano for Christmas service, 1935.

Many unsuccessful job-seekers helped by women under name, "The Aiders" in 1936. Group became Ladies Aid in 1938 with 100 members. Eighteen denominations cooperated in 1938.

After war population dispersed and difficulties experienced. In 1958 the congregation became the Grand Coulee Methodist Church, Rev. Robert Pruitt, pastor. Rev. William E. Callahan, Jr., was superintendent of the Columbia River District. The church that year was attached to Nespelem to form a charge.

In 1964 membership was 97, with Sunday school enrollment, 91. There were 16 members in the Woman's Society of Christian Service who gave $643 to the local work. In 1964 Rev. Laird V. Glascock was reappointed for the third year.

sorrow for the dead, therefore, be it resolved that it is the sense of this body that in the death of the President the nation has lost a wise leader and Methodism a loyal member, we, therefore, recommend that on Thursday at ten o'clock, in this church, there will be held a memorial service."

Conference Pledges Support to Theodore Roosevelt

Then regarding the man, who already had succeeded to the presidency, the Conference said, "Whereas through a mysterious providence Honorable Theodore Roosevelt has become president of the United States, the office so lately occupied and so ably filled by President William A. McKinley, therefore resolved that, as representatives of the Methodist Episcopal Church in Western Washington, we pledge him our heartiest support in carrying out the principles embodied in the Constitution of the land. We will ever pray that our Heavenly Father may ever be his chief guide in administering the affairs of the nation."

A resolution adopted by the Columbia River Conference in 1917 bore evidence that devotion to the country was undiminished in Methodist hearts. The resolution invoked the blessing of God upon President Woodrow Wilson and his counselors, upon the soldiers at the front, and upon all who would sacrifice for the common good. The Conference also endorsed the plan to make food and other sources available to all through rationing and conservation.

Because of their devotion to America and its freedoms, the Conference, in 1933, declared its conviction regarding an issue which continued to grow more acute into the sixth decade of the century. The body deplored the methods of those who used such terms as "Bolshevism," "Communism" and "Un-Americanism," to prejudice the minds of the public against any change in the present

MALOTT—1935

A community Sunday school was organized in Malott in 1910 by Mrs. J. R. Everett, Mrs. Zona Burdett, and Mrs. L. C. Malott. Later, Mrs. C. H. McIntosh was superintendent.

The first regular Methodist services in the town were led by Rev. Daniel E. Taylor, pastor at Okanogan, in 1935. The church was organized, December 7, of that year by Rev. Paul H. Ashby, superintendent of the Spokane District.

Plans for building were laid in 1936 under leadership of Rev. W. S. T. Gray, and a basement excavated. The next year a flood refilled the basement, and swept away 105 sacks of cement. The congregation recovered and erected the building that year. Rev. Chester Finkbeiner, pastor.

Malott has been served with Okanogan or Riverside since its organization. An electric organ was installed in December, 1962, the gift of Mrs. A. A. Asmussen.

The following pastors served Malott between 1935 and 1964: Rev. Chester Finkbeiner, 1937; Rev. Erling Bergan, 1940; Rev. Mary Graves, 1941; Rev. John Finkbeiner, 1942; Rev. Everett M. Filbert, 1950; Rev. Mary Gruenwald, 1955; Rev. Aubrey Winsor, 1956; Rev. Paul Woodward, 1957; Rev. Floyd E. Wells, 1958; Rev. Robert Lyons, 1959; Rev. Alex Poobus, 1963.

Membership in 1964 was 38; church school enrollment was 53.

system. "We should keep secure the American principle of the right to protest, free speech and free press," it was said.

In 1936 the Conference issued another statement reaffirming the loyalty of the Church to the country. It was said, "We reaffirm those ideals which have made America a great nation. We dedicate ourselves to the building of a truly Christian citizenship. Not by revolution, but by natural processes, the incarnation of Christian principles in the society of today."

DEVOTION TO DEMOCRACY PROMPTS DRASTIC DECLARATIONS

The devotion of Northwest Methodists to democracy and its free institutions motivated many apparently drastic declarations. An early expression of love for freedom was issued by the Oregon Conference in 1866. That body declared, "We consider it a reason for profound thanksgiving to Almighty God, and we extend our heartiest congratulations to our whole people, that the changed condition of our 4,000,000 freed men of the South is recognized by the body of the people, and especially by the churches of the South."

The Social Service Committee, in 1938, expressed the stand of the Church on the cause of democracy. "The only basis upon which we believe our people can be guaranteed the greatest amount of liberty in the pursuit of happiness, is that of democracy founded upon the principles enunciated by Jesus," it was said. "We believe that every attempt to supplant this system has resulted in unhappiness and chaos, whether the attempt has carried the name, Communism, Nazism, or Fascism. We believe that respect for and observance of the law is fundamental in democracy."

The determination to preserve freedom and use it in the interest of national welfare was seen in a crisp statement adopted by the Conference in 1948. "We are determined that free preachers, oc-

OMAK—1939

Methodism entered Omak with organization of Sunday school, July 30, 1939. Meeting held in the Adventist church. Winston G. Emert was first superintendent. Three classes were taught by Raymond Gubser, Mrs. Karma Taylor, and Joan Emert.

The church was organized November 19, 1939 with 28 members. First trustees were, Frank S. Emert, Raymond Gubser, Richard M. Rockey, Roy Brown, and W. T. Archer. Rev. J. G. Wilkins, East Omak, organizing pastor. Rev. Ernest F. Harold, Spokane District, officiated.

Building site acquired January 22, 1941. Frame and roof of building erected that year. Rev. Darrell Iwerks was pastor. Building construction continued until completed in 1945, under Rev. Claude W. Groth. Loans of $10,000 from Board of Church Extension and $3,000 from local bank made completion possible. Pews, chairs, parsonage, other necessities, were acquired under the leadership of Rev. James A. Moore, who served eight years.

The congregation of East Omak merged in 1949. Under the leadership of Rev. Bruce Groseclose in 1956-59, improvements made. The building dedicated by Bishop A. Raymond Grant, April 26, 1959.

Rev. Paul F. Ashbrook was appointed for the first year in 1964. Membership, 266, church school enrollment, 125. Woman's Society membership, 45, and their gifts $1,457. Methodist Men, 23.

cupying free pulpits, preaching to free laymen, in a free land, shall be free to proclaim the free religion of Jesus Christ."

The Conference held that democracy should extend its liberties to all its people. This was suggested in a report on race relations in 1951, in which it was said, "We commend the progress being made along these lines in the South, and we commend certain labor unions who hire employees on the basis of ability rather than color. We commend the schools of Tacoma and other cities who have hired competent Negro teachers. We commend restaurant management which serves all well-behaved persons."

The Board of Social and Economic Relations, in 1953, said, "We feel that the greatest threat to America today is in the area of civil rights and religious liberties. Cited were McCarthyism, character assassinations, guilt by association, smear and fear techniques, the wide-spread misuse of Congressional Immunity, numerous investigations under way by Congressional Committees, the attack upon Bishop Oxnam, the proposed investigation of churches and ministers, and various other related problems."

METHODISTS HOLD NO DELUSIONS REGARDING TYRANNY OF COMMUNISM

Methodists held no delusions regarding the tyranny of Communism. In 1954 the Board of Social and Economic Relations said, "Since the close of the last war the world has witnessed the spread of Communism until today it controls a large proportion of the world's population. Communism is anti-God, and is in direct opposition to the principles of Christianity. Its growth and ruthless leadership is a threat to Christianity and to our Church. Upon us as Christians and citizens falls the responsibility of strengthening the Christian forces in this time of conflict."

Dealing with the problem of race, in 1956, the Commission on Civil Liberties

SANDPOINT, SEATTLE—1943

Rev. Harold O. Perry organized Sand Point Methodist Church, February 20, 1944, with 90 charter members. He had worked in community since 1943. First meeting held in pastor's home, and later, in community hall.

First building, financed through Seattle Missionary Union, Board of Home Missions and Church Extension, and local contributions, was consecrated by Bishop Bruce R. Baxter, January 6, 1946. Dr. and Mrs. Theodore Houk gave the organ which was used in first sanctuary and the one erected later. Cecil Bullock was organist, his wife, choir director.

First unit erected on lots donated by Dr. and Mrs. E. T. Porter, 4710 N. E. 70th St., cost $50,000.

In 1947-58, Rev. Robert Hicks, pastor, Fellowship Hall completed, in 1954, plans laid for new sanctuary adjoining first unit.

Rev. Merritt W. Faulkner became pastor in 1958. After a third building campaign, the new sanctuary was erected and consecrated in 1960. Chairman of building committee, Ernest W. Lehmann, was honored when the Fellowship Hall was officially designated, "Lehmann Hall."

In 1964, Rev. William A. Welch was appointed pastor for third year. There were 1,110 members, 760 in church school and 111 in Woman's Society of Christian Service. Building valued at $470,000. Parsonage, at $20,450.

approved the Supreme Court decision calling for the end of segregation in public education and transportation. On the same issue, in 1959, the Methodist Discipline was cited. The paragraph reads, "The Methodist Church must view the perplexing times and the problems which we face today in the light of the teachings of Jesus who taught us to love our neighbors and seek justice for them. We believe that God is father of all races and peoples, that all persons are of supreme value in the sight of God. We believe we should help save men from sin and every influence which would harm or destroy them."

The committee expressed its concern for the rise of anti-Communism groups using the same evil methods employed by Communism, and subscribing to the belief that the end justifies the means. "There can be no more dangerous fallacy," the report stated. "We stand firmly in opposition to such radical rightist groups as the John Birch Society and Christian Anti-Communists."

The Committee requested the United States Congress to amend the McCarran-Walker Law of 1953, to include a ten-year statute of limitations on deportations.

Northwest Methodists, firm believers in law and order, urged their members to uphold it. Witness a statement adopted by the Puget Sound Conference back in 1903. "We are appalled by the rising tide of anarchy which threatens the very foundations of our Government." The Conference said, "We believe that the recent exhibitions of mob violence in many parts of our country, are proofs of the general disregard for the sacredness of law and authority. We, therefore, urge upon our members, not only loyalty to all authority, but to exhibit greater activity in supporting men of integrity and honor in every place of public trust."

In 1928 the Columbia River Conference departed from its usual practice to call candidates by name. In a resolution presented by Rev. J. Randolph Sasnett,

---

CENTRAL UNITED PROTESTANT
RICHLAND—1944

Methodism first took root in Richland in 1908 when Rev. C. M. Carson became pastor. There were 42 members following year, 150 in church school and building valued at $2,500. In 1919, Richland, on Walla Walla District, Rev. J. W. Mayes, pastor. There were 159 members, 138 in church school.

In 1943, Rev. R. Kenneth Bell, pastor. There were 150 members, average church school attendance 57.

In 1944, Northwest Methodists found themselves providing leadership for a United Protestant Church at Richland, residential city for Hanford Atomic Energy project.

By 1945, population at Richland had leaped to 30,000. The situation called for action of the State Council of Churches, which decided upon a United Protestant Church under Methodist sponsorship. Plan called for Protestants of all denominations to belong to the church without forfeiting previous affiliations. Mission funds prorated among cooperating bodies represented in membership.

Church grew beyond expectations. Rev. Thomas Acheson became senior minister, Rev. R. Kenneth Bell, pastor since 1940, remained on staff as minister of education. Succeeding pastors, Rev. Roy L. Smith, Rev. Robert A. Uphoff, Rev. David Seaman, Rev. Melvin M. Finkbeiner. In 1964, Methodist membership was 1,560, almost 1,000 members representing other denominations.

344

THESE MEN EXEMPLIFIED METHODIST PATRIOTISM

Chaplain
Ralph W. D. Brown

Chaplain
E. Ray Attebery

Chaplain
Raymond Partee

Chaplain
Ernest P. Goulder

Chaplain
Dwight G. Bennett

Chaplain
Lloyd H. Doty

Chaplain
Forrest D. Tibbitts

Chaplain
Elmer E. Beckman

Chaplain
Herbert Eugene Miller

the body approved the candidacy of Honorable Herbert Hoover for president of the United States as against that of Mr. Alfred Smith, who stood on a platform pledged to destroy National Prohibition.

1953 CONFERENCE DISAPPROVES METHODS OF COMBATTING COMMUNISM

In 1953 the Conference disapproved methods of combatting Communism which ignored the law and rights of free people. The statement said, "We recognize that Communism is both an external and internal threat to our free society and needs to be guarded against. But the almost exclusive concentration of the American mind upon the threat of Communism is not healthy. It has produced a fanatical negativism, completely lacking in a constructive program of action. It has produced an emptiness which could easily be occupied by Fascist tyranny, in the name of security. We agree with the words of the General Assembly of the Presbyterian Church in the United States of America, stating, "Treason and dissent are being confused. The shrine of conscience and private judgment which God alone has the right to enter, are being invaded. Attacks utterly alien to our democratic traditions are being made upon citizens of integrity and social passion. Suspicion and accusation of disloyalty have increased alarmingly. Much of this deplorable situation is the result of methods used in investigating Communism. Many of these are in fact no different from Communistic methods. Truth is subtilely and silently dethroned by prominent public figures. In this form of warfare falsehood frequently is preferred to fact. The demagogue who lives by propaganda is coming into his own on a national scale. Truth is thus a captive in the land of the free. At the same time great words like love, peace, justice, and mercy, and the ideals undergirding them, are becoming suspect. We submit that if democracy resorts to lying in order to defeat Communism, it is itself defeated already."

HIGHLINE—1945

Highline Church had its beginnings, in 1945, when Miss Mary Shoemaker, a deaconess, began survey of church preferences. First Sunday school meeting held in home, February 2, 1946. Preaching began in 1945. Rev. Karl E. Ekaas, pastor. Rev. Carl K. Mahoney, superintendent, Seattle District.

Woman's Society of Christian Service began, January, 1945, with four women present. They were, Mrs. Eva McArthur, Miss Mary E. Shoemaker, Margaret L. Gay, and Mrs. Arthur Versoi.

Basement on First Ave. So. and So. 130th, was occupied in 1946. Superstructure completed in 1948, opened, October 15, with Bishop Gerald H. Kennedy, officiating. Parsonage acquired in 1951. Educational building completed in 1956 with aid of $40,000 loan. Board of National Missions also gave aid.

Pastors serving the church include, Rev. Wayne Wright, 1946; Rev. John H. Soltman, 1947; after dedication of the church, in 1948, Rev. Robert Elliott, served, 1949-51; Rev. C. Keith Mills, 1951-56; Rev. William F. Andrews, 1956-60.

In 1960, Rev. Alfred Carter became pastor. During the first four years of his ministry the membership increased from 464 to 656. Church school reached 522 and Woman's Society of Christian Service membership, totalled 114. They gave $717. Church building was worth $135,000, and parsonage value $24,000.

346

The committee was more optimistic a year later, although still concerned. The statement that year was, "The reversal of the influence of the demagogue has been a most heartening trend. Not that it has been entirely eliminated nor damage repaired at home and abroad, but a reaction has set in. This demonstrates the virility of our democracy. All signs now point to fairness in legislative inquiries. At the same time individual liberties suffered a number of deplorable defeats in the name of national security caused by a drop in the morale of our public servants. Individual firings carried out without allowing the dismissed a fair chance to face his accuser, is contrary to our concept of justice. Educational institutions also felt the demand for orthodxy and conformity. Academic freedom is civil liberties in the educational world. This has been subject to numerous restrictions.

NORTHWEST METHODISTS ESPOUSE THE CAUSE OF PEACE

Northwest Methodists believe that peace is the way of Christ and that war is not the final cure for the ills of the world. In keeping with this faith, the Social Service Committee in 1921 introduced a resolution calling for disarmament among the nations as a means of reducing the danger of war. In 1926 the Committee on the State of the Church in the Columbia River Conference, said, "Whereas we believe that the mind that was in Christ will never become the mind of our nation until our church and all its followers make peace one of their dominant desires. We, therefore, commend most heartily the plan submitted by the General Conference, that a committee on peace be established in every local church, and we urge our pastors, as agents of the Prince of Peace, to give their cooperation to those institutions which have as their goals the abolition of war."

The Social Service Committee of the Puget Sound Conference, two years later, declared, "There are no greater

SKYWAY—1946

Skyway Methodist Church, organized November 3, 1946, with 60 members. First planning meeting held at Market Basket Grocery store. First building committee members, Russell Hunt, Phil Bowman, Joe Clyde, Trygve Hoff, Jim Bassett, Tom Bratt, Jack Weber, Guy Starkey. Organizing pastor, Rev. Laura E. Butler; District superintendent, Rev. Carl K. Mahoney.

Woman's Society of Christian Service organized, October 31, 1946, Mrs. Paul McDowell, president. Four circles organized in 1948. First Men's president, Ed Carroll.

First building, a quonset hut, was placed on lots purchased by the Seattle Methodist Union. During pastorate of Rev. C. E. Miller, congregation decided need for church building. First crusade for building launched Easter, 1952. Offering for new building was $1,521. Rev. Nolan McClurg was pastor. First drive for pledges conducted under Rev. Harlan Jones in 1954. Under pastorate of Rev. Troy M. Strong, 1955-58, the building was consecrated in June, 1958. A new drive to raise funds to complete plant followed.

The church, under Rev. Robert Dibble, aided the Alaska University. In 1962, Rev. James Lane took steps to complete the plant. In 1964, he was assigned for the third year. Members, 281, church school enrollment, 122. Woman's Society members 32, gave $708.

obstructions to the destruction of the machines of war in our own day than the hesitation, reservations, and qualifications of Christian leaders and their followers." This report was submitted by Rev. J. E. Crowther, Rev. J. Herbert Geoghehan, and Rev. Robert Brumblay, who pledged themselves to the settlement of all disputes between nations by peaceful means.

One year later the Pacific Northwest Conference expressed the opinion that the League of Nations had justified itself in the prevention of war.

METHODISTS URGED TO PRAY FOR PEACE WITH JUSTICE

In 1941, with war raging in Europe and Pearl Harbor but six months away the Conference approved a declaration that, "We believe that God is the father of all mankind, and that His will, as revealed in Jesus Christ, is universal love, and that Christ's gospel involves a faith that evil can be overcome only with good. Let us be truly Christian in prayer. Penitence should be our deepest note, for we are all sinners before God. Let us pray, not for victory, but for peace with justice. Let us pray for greater faith in God, for more reliance upon the moral structure of the universe, which guarantees the insecurity of evil. The church sincerely desires that the United States stay out of war."

Many sincere Christians have felt that these statements for peace were too drastic. But those who advanced them justified their position by pointing to statements of Jesus in the Sermon on the Mount.

THE STATE MUST SERVE PERSONALITY

Northwest Methodists believe that personality is sacred and that all human institutions exist for its service. This was set forth in a report of the Social Service Committee in 1939. "We believe that the cardinal principle which Jesus laid

CENTRAL PARK, ABERDEEN—1948

First meeting to organize church at Central Park, Aberdeen, convened, January 12, 1948. First Sunday school, connected with American Sunday school Union. Baptists were active, but majority were Methodists, which determined denomination. In 1949, Rev. Joe Cleland, Hoquiam, began supplying. Remained until 1954. Meantime, 91 persons received as charter members, December 18, 1949. Sunday school attendance that day, 108. In December, 1950, there were 200 members, and $45,000 building under way. Woman's Society of Christian Service was active. Senior and Junior Methodist Youth Fellowship organized, May, 1951.

Second anniversary celebrated, December 16, 1951, Rev. Willard E. Stanton, district superintendent, preaching. Service in incomplete building. Twenty-one members brought total to 250. Board of Home Missions aided with $3,000.

In 1954, Rev. Bruce Groseclose, first full-time pastor. Followed, in 1956, by Rev. J. Dean King and, Rev. Erling Bergan in 1959. All worked at debt and membership. In 1961, church realized dream for new parsonage.

Woman's Society of Christian Service, organized, 1949, was tower of strength with church debt and local budget.

In 1964, Rev. Ronald R. Northrup, pastor, first year. Membership, 197, church school, 171. Woman's Society membership, 47, raised, $756. Building value, $46,650. Parsonage, $16,100. Raised for all purposes, $8,948.

348

down, the sacredness of human personality, issues finally in a form of human organization known as democracy, as opposed to dictatorships, such as Communism, Fascism, or Nazism. We call upon our people to seek to understand the philosophies of totalitarianism, so that with intelligence and faith, we may the better be able to meet the destructive tenets of their basic platforms. We affirm again our loyalty to our constitutional guarantees of freedom, and oppose all those official or self-constituted bodies, who, through their activities, seek to abridge these rights."

A Conference action in 1958, deploring the use of capital punishment, was based upon the concept of the sacredness of personality. The body recommended disciplines of a redemptive nature as a substitute for capital punishment.

CHRISTIANITY AND DEMOCRACY ARE MUTUALLY DEPENDENT

The mutual dependence of Christianity and democracy was implied in all the Church said and did in the interest of the Kingdom of God. As early as 1866 this faith was clearly set forth in a resolution presented by the Committee on the State of the Church. It said, "A living and active Christianity is the basis of our national prosperity and the security of our national life. We earnestly desire all our people to pray for its revival and diffusion all over our land."

This mutual dependence between Christianity and the Democratic state was outlined by Rev. William Roberts in his report on The State of the Church in 1877, in the second year of the second century of our national existence. He said, "Doubtless our first reliance under God must be in the conscience power of our people, and hence, everything that enlightens and educates the people and their conscience and increases the weight of individual responsibility, is to be coveted. Everything that benumbs and paralyzes the public

LEWISTON ORCHARDS—1948

Lewiston Orchards Church, organized, 1948. Twenty-one charter members. Rev. Ac C. Wischmeier, pastor, First Church, Lewiston, sponsor. In 1949, Rev. John Coan, pastor and in June, 1950, Rev. Merritt Faulkner. In 1951, Rev. Robert Horne appointed to Lewiston Orchards alone, and in December, same year, Rev. Truman Cotten, succeeded him and was in turn succeeded by Rev. Earl Lake, in 1957.

Church first met in Cantor's Hall, later in home of Mr. and Mrs. Leonard Ulrich. Ground broken for church, 1950 located east of Old Orchards Elementary school. Congregation occupied basement, September, 1953, and sanctuary, Easter, Sunday, 1956. Membership 200.

Charter members of the Lewiston Orchards Church were: Mr. and Mrs. Clarence A. Megenity, Mr. and Mrs. C. M. Ryle, Mr. and Mrs. Arnold M. Swinford, Mr. and Mrs. Clarence E. Van Trease, Mrs. Mary Jean Price, Mrs. Kate E. Burnell, Joanna Burnell, Mrs. Pearl Chapin, Mrs. Charlotte D. Ulrich, Douglas P. Clark, Mrs. Jacqueline B. Clark, Mrs. Mary Louise Williams, Howard Williams, Mr. and Mrs. Benjamin R. Goodhead, Mrs. Claude Jones, Mr. and Mrs. Walter S. Thornber.

In 1964, Rev. Eric L. Kallis, pastor, fourth year. Members, 288; church school enrollment, 249. Woman's Society, 43 members, gave $1,459. Value church, $104,800. Parsonage, $16,150.

conscience is destructive to public morality and the well being of society. He who obliterates moral distinctions is no friend either of the church or the state."

Roberts went on to say, "In view of these most obvious facts we most earnestly urge upon you carefully to study your duties as American citizens. These may never be overlooked or neglected without peril."

These words spoken in 1877 could, with profit, be pondered in 1965.

1945 PACIFIC NORTHWEST CONFERENCE APPROVES UNITED NATIONS PLAN

The idea of the United Nations was approved by the Pacific Northwest Conference in 1945 when the assembly that set it up was still at work in San Francisco.

A statement in 1953 serves to illustrate the attitude of the Conference toward that agency for peace. It was said, "Because efforts are continuously being made to discredit the United Nations we need just as continuously to emphasize the constructive aspects of its work."

The next year the United Nations was recognized as the agency through which the American Government could work to create good will among underdeveloped states. The report said, "As the people of underdeveloped countries tend to accept Communism as a short-cut to better living conditions we urge our Government, through the United Nations, to give greater support to self-help measures in these lands."

The following year another statement indicating approval of the United Nations appeared in connection with China. It was said, "We recognize that any country whose government has been established by aggression, should be given the right, under the United Nations plebiscite, to choose their government, and that when this has been

PIERCE, IDAHO—1949

Church at Pierce, Idaho, organized as United Protestant, under Methodist auspices, August 21, 1949. Rev. Joseph H. Beall, district superintendent. Eleven preparatory members received, twelve full members, three, Methodists, others Baptist, Lutheran, United Brethren, Episcopal. Twenty others later united.

Trustees: Daniel Kiley, Mrs. Art Brown, H. Kenneth Buick, Mrs. Lester Williamson, Mrs. Fred Owen. Rev. Fred Owen, pastor.

In 1950, Headquarters invited to joint ownership of parsonage. Steps taken to locate new church building site. Rev. Fred Owen, 1950, was succeeded by Rev. G. Edward Knight, Orofino. In 1953, Rev. James M. Lane, pastor, Peck, Pierce, Headquarters. In 1953 revived plans for new church. Work began, June 19, 1954. First service in basement, February 13, 1955. Sanctuary first used Easter, 1956. Grant of $2,000 from National Board of Missions. Church consecrated, May 12, 1957. Reverend Alden R. Graves, district superintendent, Rev. G. Edward Knight, Rev. James M. Lane, officiated.

Parsonage began, 1956, occupied Christmas, 1957. Conference granted $3,000. In 1961, Pierce entered Clearwater group ministry, twelve other churches, pastor, G. Edward Whitnett, chairman.

In 1964, Rev. M. Douglas Bobbitt, pastor, second year. Members, 46; church school, 94; Woman's Society, 16, gave $1,204. Building value, $43,000.

accomplished, they should be accorded a place in the United Nations if they desire. Granting of this choice is not only Christian, but in line with our own Declaration of Independence. Such a course would do much toward lessening tensions in Asia."

A resolution adopted in 1961, was interpreted as indicating the conditions upon which the Conference would be willing to see Red China admitted to the United Nations. It was said, "Whereas one uncooperative nation can endanger the continued existence of world populations, therefore, be it resolved that all nations be included in the United Nations when they are willing to abide by the charter of that body."

--◦◄{ CHAPTER XVII }►◦--

That Northwest Methodists from the beginning were convinced of essential unity of the Christian Church, and how they worked with other bodies to accomplish their common goals, are set forth in—

Men of Ecumenical Minds

NORTHWEST METHODISTS WELCOME CHRISTIAN FELLOWSHIP

The term "ecumenical," as used in this chapter, refers to the attitudes of Northwest Methodists toward other Christian denominations in all their relations with them. It is proposed here to report how these Methodists have felt and still feel toward other Christian bodies and what they think about cooperation with them, in various ways, including councils of churches, as well as organic church union. It is not within the province of this chapter to champion any one view.

From the earliest times Northwest Methodists welcomed fellowship with other Protestant bodies. Two years after Marcus Whitman established the mission at Waiilatpu, Jason Lee spent some days with him. The relationship between these two pioneer missionary leaders was warm and cordial. Some years later the Oregon Mission transferred its property at The Dalles to the American Board of Commissioners for Foreign Missions, under which Whitman served. After the tragedy at Waiilatpu, the property was returned to the Methodists.

During the pioneer years Protestant ministers and missionaries always were welcomed at the mission station on the Willamette. The Oregon Conference was born with a spirit of warmth and Christian fellowship toward other Protestants.

It is not surprising, therefore, to find the Oregon Conference, after the Church had entered the Puget Sound country, encouraging fraternal relationships across denominational lines. In 1858, for instance, the Oregon Conference appointed several of its members to bear fraternal greetings to other bodies. These were: Rev. William Roberts, to the Protestant Episcopal Church; Rev. F. S. Hoyt, to the New

School Presbyterian and Congregational Churches; Rev. Gustavus Hines, to the Cumberland Presbyterian Church; Rev. A. F. Waller, to the United Presbyterian Church; Rev. J. W. York, to the Baptist Church; Rev. Nehemiah Doane, to the United Brethren Church; and Rev. T. H. Pearne, to the Methodist Protestant Church.

That same year, Reverend Daniel Bagley, representing the Methodist Protestant Church in Oregon, presented greetings to the Annual Conference, and was invited to be seated within the bar of the Conference and to participate in its deliberations.

The general superintendent of Wesleyan Missions on Vancouver Island and British Columbia, Reverend Dr. Evans, in 1865, brought greetings to the Conference and likewise was invited to a seat within the bar of the Conference. Similar courtesies were extended in 1870 to Rev. W. H. Palmer of the United Brethren Church and to Rev. A. E. Russ of the Wesleyan Church of British Columbia.

This procedure was followed through the years by the Oregon, Columbia River, and Puget Sound conferences. In 1901 similar courtesy was extended to Rev. G. H. Gibbs, presiding elder of the Methodist Episcopal Church, South, and Rev. C. R. Howard, pastor of the southern church at Genesee, Idaho.

CONFERENCE SEEKS TO ELIMINATE FRICTION

The desire of the Columbia River Conference to avoid friction through cooperation or federation was expressed in conference action in 1911. A committee of three was appointed to meet with a like committee from the Columbia Conference of the Methodist Episcopal Church, South, to consider unnecessary cases of duplication, or possible federation and cooperation between churches within the identical territory occupied by the two Methodist Conferences.

The willingness of Methodists to cooperate did not mean that they could be "pushed around" by groups wishing

> **HEADQUARTERS, IDAHO—1950**
>
> Headquarters, Idaho first appeared as conference appointment in 1950, teamed with Pierce. Rev. Fred Owen, pastor and wife, Sophie, associate. These and other neighboring points had been allocated to the Methodist Church by Washington—Northern Idaho Council of Churches.
>
> In 1951, Rev. G. Edward Knight had served this charge from Orofino since October, 1949. He reported 19 members at Headquarters, 40 in church school. Twenty-seven members of Woman's Society of Christian Service had raised $250. There was neither church building nor parsonage. Headquarters had been invited by Pierce to share in ownership of a parsonage yet to be erected.
>
> In 1955, Peck, Pierce, Headquarters were teamed together, served by Rev. James M. Lane, fourth year. Headquarters had 31 members, and 73 in church school. According to report, women had raised $1,114.
>
> In 1960, circuit had entered Clearwater Group Ministry program. Rev. G. Edward Whitenett, pastor, first year. Church had 31 members, 110 enrolled in church school. Nineteen women had raised $460.
>
> In 1964, Rev. M. Douglas Bobbitt, pastor, second year. There were twelve members and 61 enrolled in church school. Average attendance, 13. Nine women raised $227. Paid pastor, $1,300. World Service and Conference Benevolences, $50. Raised for all purposes, $2,550.

to monopolize a field. It was in 1913 that the Conference resolved, "We advise comity in the encouragement of the spirit of fraternity among the various churches of the community and rejoice in the manifestation of increasing good fellowship among the various denominations. Nevertheless, we believe in many localities where our rights to exist as a church are disputed, we have a mission in the community to the end that the people may not be deprived of the privileges of an evangelical gospel."

A statement by the Conference in 1925 further indicated the willingness of Methodists to cooperate on the basis of need. It was said, "We believe our churches are looking forward to larger cooperation with other denominations. We believe that the rural church and rural church life in America is most hopeful. We rejoice in the recent statement of the Board of Bishops and the Department of Rural Work that in communities where the Methodist Episcopal Church has full responsibility, the Board of Home Missions and Church Extension should render aid and cooperate, adequately caring for the work. But where the responsibility is divided with other denominations, equal adjustment should be made in order that there not be competitive programs."

CONFERENCE LEARNS FROM FEDERATED CHURCHES

For decades the Conference participated in experiments with federated, community, and union churches. Results of such experiments were indicated in replies to a questionnaire addressed to all ministers of the Conference including copies for the use of laymen. Responses came from 160 pastors and 85 laymen. Among the former, 48 reported personal experiences with federated churches, while only six of the latter reported such contacts. Six pastors said Methodism grew stronger under the plan and 26 said communities were better served through federation whereby

---

AUDUBON PARK, SPOKANE—1951

Methodist Church at Audubon Park, Spokane, grew out of post war expansion of that city. A group of members of St. Paul and Central churches met in 1951 to discuss need for a church in that community. First sermon was delivered by Rev. Harold Bashor, district superintendent. Service held in French School Gymnasium, October 7, 1951. Fifty-eight attended worship and 138, Sunday school. Church organized, November 11, 1951, with 75 charter members. Twenty-five more united within six weeks.

Woman's Society of Christian Service was organized, 1952, Men's Brotherhood about the same time. December 6, 1953 ground broken for building on Driscoll Boulevard. Building, costing $93,000 was used for first service, June 13, 1954.

In following years, growth necessitated two worship services and three sessions of church school. Educational unit and chapel completed in 1962. Parsonage was occupied in fall of 1962.

Audubon Church meanwhile carried full share of district and conference activities, financial obligations.

Earliest pastors of church were Rev. David Almond, Rev. Roy Finch, Rev. Joseph H. Beall, Rev. Horace Mounts, Rev. William Franklin Summerour still pastor in 1964. Membership, 1964, 710, church school enrollment, 604. Woman's Society membership 91, paying $2,026.

Building, valued at $239,000 and parsonage at $23,400.

354

two or more denominations in a community came together and were served alternately by ministers of cooperating bodies. Forty-two said Methodism lost ground or disappeared, and 22 believed that communities were not better served through the arrangement.

A number of federated churches with Methodists involved were still functioning in 1964, while many no longer were alive. An example of this arrangement is seen at Kirkland, across Lake Washington from Seattle. In 1922 the Methodist Church there had 215 members, paying a salary of $2,700. The following year it became federated, an arrangement which continued until 1931, when Methodism disappeared from the community. That year Methodists reported 115 members and the pastor had received $1,650 on salary.

In 1959 Methodists in Kirkland invited the mother church to return to the field. Dr. Clark J. Wood, superintendent of the Seattle District, responded, reentering the community, without land, building or members. In 1960, 88 members were reported and in 1963 there were 222, and the pastor received $4,200 on salary.

Another example is that of Colville, on the Spokane District. This charge first appeared in the minutes as an appointment in 1860. In 1929 there were 226 members, and the church paid $2,300 salary. The first year of federation with a Congregational group, the church paid $1,500 to its pastor and reported 120 members. In 1950 the federation was dissolved. The 167 Methodist members that year paid the pastor $2,000. By 1964 there were 349 members and the pastor received $4,983 on salary.

The church at Ephrata on the Columbia River District, in 1931, entered into an informal combination with the Presbyterians to form a United Church. In 1942 the congregation voted to become a Community church under Methodist auspices.

The experience at Longview, on the Columbia River is of interest in that the

> **BROWNSVILLE—1951**
>
> The church at Brownsville first appeared among appointments in 1951. Rev. John Mathone, pastor, also served Silverdale. In 1952 this church was teamed with Tracyton, pastor, Rev. Thomas Slate. Combined membership of two churches was 85. The following year Brownsville reported 17 members, 39 in the church school. In 1955 membership had climbed to 18 and 65 were reported in church school.
>
> In 1960 the church was left to be supplied, but in 1961 Rev. R. B. Huddleston, pastor, reported 48 members with 86 in the church school. A building that year was reported to be valued at $20,000. The following year Huddleston reported 62 members with 103 in the church school.
>
> Brownsville was teamed with Tracyton in 1963 and 1964. Rev. Robert G. Calkins, pastor both years. In latter year he reported 67 members at Brownsville and 87 in church school. Eighteen members of the Woman's Society of Christian Service had raised $175 for local work. That year the building was valued at $25,000. No parsonage was reported, Tracyton being the residence of the pastor. The minister received $1,200 salary in 1964 and the church had paid $200 on World Service and Conference Benevolences, four dollars above asking and acceptance.

Methodists there cooperated to form a Community Church. The city, across the Cowlitz River from Kelso, is adjacent to the site of Monticello, which was an appointment in the Oregon Conference in the 1850's and 1860's. Some time after 1865 the town with its site was wiped out by a flood.

Thenceforward Methodists had no work there until Longview was founded in 1922. The church at Kelso, under the leadership of Pastor Earl E. Reisner, organized the first Sunday school there, holding regular preaching services. In 1922, church leaders of the town asked the Puget Sound Conference for a pastor. In 1923 Rev. E. H. Gebert was appointed. When he arrived at the town, however, he was informed that a majority had voted to establish an independent Community Church. Gebert stayed more than thirty years before his retirement, building a large congregation.

Other denominations entered Longview, including several which at first cooperated with the Community Church. In 1953, Methodists, with the approval of the Council of Churches, established a church in Columbia Valley Gardens, a new housing development, in Longview. In 1963 the congregation numbered 299.

BELLEVUE—1952

First Methodist services at Bellevue, held in Chapel of Flowers. Later, in school room. First superintendent of Sunday school, Jason Smith. First preaching service, July 20, 1952. Rev. J. W. Caughlan, preaching. Later services in library. Other meetings in homes. Church organized, October 5, 1952, 29 members. Rev. Owen J. Beadles, district superintendent.

The Woman's Society of Christian Service was organized, October, 1952. Mrs. Delbert Lewis, president. In 1954, Area Forward Movement donated $1,100 to purchase land, $15,000 more in 1954. Three acres on 108th Ave. N. E. where building later erected cost $12,000.

In 1954, Rev. H. Paul Smith, pastor, parsonage acquired and ground broken for church. Building was consecrated September 30, 1956. Rev. Kenneth Underwood came in 1960 and plans laid for completing educational unit. It cost $103,000. Ground was broken July 31, 1960.

This church did not let its own struggles lead it to forget others. Contributions in 1958 included six scholarships, $1,575 to Foreign Missions, and $247 to Alaska Methodist University, at Anchorage.

In 1964, Rev. Kenneth H. Underwood was appointed for fifth year. There were 1,059 members, with church school enrollment of 875. Woman's Society of Christian Service members, 157. They gave $1,340. Church building valued at $260,000.

FEDERATED CHURCHES NOT ALWAYS APPROVED

Federated churches have not always been approved by Conference leaders. In 1932 the Methodist Church at Kellogg, Idaho, entered into a plan of union with a Congregational group. Rev. Robert Brumblay, superintendent of the Spokane District of the Methodist Church, and the state executive of the Congregational Church, being informed of the proposal several months beforehand, advised against the union, but both congregations were determined to proceed with the plan. The matter was presented to the Annual Conference and the district superintendent appointed a committee to investigate in accordance with Rule 17 which provided for a committee on Federation to act.

The committee did not approve the merger, but advised that it would be better to let the matter stand for further investigation. In 1963, the united congregation numbered 230 against the 86 reported in 1932.

Rev. Alden R. Graves,[1] pastor at the time of the union, said, in 1964, that both congregations had been desperate. It was during depression years and, with so few members neither congregation could support a church. Graves suggested then and continued to hold that a better plan would have been to attach the Kellogg church to Wallace to form a circuit, but the authorities refused.

"The Kellogg congregation today is aggressive, forward looking and engaged in erecting a church building," Graves said.

When Dr. Paul H. Ashby, retired, expressed an opinion on federated churches he spoke out of a background of 55 years as a Methodist minister in the Northwest, seven years as district superintendent, and a like period as executive secretary of the Board of Conference Claimants. He followed Brumblay as superintendent of the Spokane District in 1935. In 1964 Ashby suggested that better than the usual federation would be a plan whereby the weaker denomination would withdraw from a community, turning over its property, good will, and membership to the stronger church. Compensation could come from a reciprocal arrangement in some other community. This he believed, would eliminate many problems resulting from alternate pastorates in federated churches. However, he pointed out that each decision must come after careful appraisal of conditions in the community.

Methodists Pilot a United Protestant Church

Through cooperation with the Washington and Northern Idaho Council of Churches, Northwest Methodists, in

MOSES LAKE—1952

Methodism started at Moses Lake, September 13, 1952, when seven teachers and 20 pupils began first Sunday school. The church was organized August 10, of that year, by Rev. William G. Berney, pastor. The 11 members increased to 48 by 1953. Methodist Youth Fellowship organized in August and Woman's Society of Christian Service in September, 1952.

First meetings were held in homes of church members, Berg and Hanson Funeral Home or the parsonage in Motel.

Two and one-half acres of land was acquired on Lakeview Terrace and ground breaking for the first church building took place November 14, 1954. Construction started in March, 1955. Contract called for $43,000. Building later completed by donated labor.

First financial campaign in 1952 to raise funds for conference-wide Forward Movement. First school of missions in 1953. Adult choir organized same year. Methodist Men organized in 1954 with 12 members. In 1956 church began self supporting budget.

In 1961, addition to the building started under leadership of Rev. Lloyd N. Alden.

Pastor in 1964, Rev. James B. Darcey. Church members, 293; church school, 197. Members of Woman's Society of Christian Service, 60. They gave $850. Methodist Men 23. Church building valued at $169,950.

THESE WERE NORTHWEST ECUMENICAL LEADERS

Rev. Jack M. Tuell

Rev. Gertrude L.
Apel

Rev. Robert J.
Huston

1944, found themselves providing leadership for a United Protestant Church at Richland, the residential city for workers at the Atomic Energy project at Hanford.

Methodists had maintained a church at Richland for years. But between 1943 and 1945 population in the town exploded from 243 to more than 30,000. The Federal Government built two churches, Catholic and Protestant, each a typical Army Chapel, seating about 650.

The situation called for action of the Council of Churches. This group decided upon a United Protestant Church under Methodist sponsorship. The plan called for Protestants of all denominations to belong to the church without forfeiting previous affiliations. Mission funds were prorated among cooperating bodies represented in the membership.

The church grew beyond expectation. Rev. Thomas Acheson became senior minister, and Rev. R. Kenneth Bell, pastor since 1939, remained on the staff as minister of education. Succeeding pastors were: Rev. Roy L. Smith, Rev. Robert Uphoff, Rev. David Seaman, and Rev. Melvin M. Finkbeiner. In 1964 the Methodist membership was 1,560 with almost a thousand members representing other denominations.

Rev. Earl L. Dean who succeeded Bell as minister of education appraised the plan as a good one for such a community. Rev. Robert A. Uphoff, senior minister for seven years beginning in 1950, said, "The plan offers an excellent solution for newly formed communities. It enables them to start a church with the blessing of all the cooperating denominations, without having a 'community' or non-denominational church or competitive churches.

"With the excellent cooperation of the major denominations, it would provide a pattern for a non-competitive ministry in the multitude of older, smaller communities that could and should support

---

LONGVIEW—1953

Sixty-five persons attended Sunday school first day, at Columbia Valley Gardens, Longview, 1953. May, 1954, there were 172 enrolled, thirty-five in Methodist Youth Fellowship. C. L. Byers, Longview Post Master, first superintendent. Rev. Harry L. Allen conducted first preaching service, September 13, 1953, and organized church with 47 members. Two lots purchased for $15,000. Church incorporated October 9, 1953. Ill health forced Allen to retire. Rev. G. Edward Knight succeeded, January 1, 1954.

First choir director, Mrs. Warren Coburn. Women organized, January 20, 1954. By May, 35 members. Government apartment building acquired as nucleus of first building, 1954. First services in building, August 15. Bishop A. Raymond Grant delivered sermon.

Methodist Men organized November 22, 1954. Electric organ installed, March 27, 1955, in memory of J. C. Haley, Tacoma businessman, by his family. Parsonage consecrated, September, 1957. Name "Longview Methodist Church" adopted, June, 1958. Rev. Lawrence A. Burdette, pastor, 1960. Thirty per cent of members tithed in November 1961.

Church began every member canvass each year. Rev. Kenneth B. McLagan, pastor, 1962-63.

In 1964, Rev. Edward C. Liebman, first year. Members, 312. Church school enrollment, 146. Woman's Society, 53, gave $914. Value of building, $61,500. Parsonage, $32,500.

one strong church. This 'pilot project' offers a new and hopeful way in which denominations can work together pending the coming of the day when, their function fulfilled, their importance recedes or disappears and the project may even bring the day measurably nearer."

METHODISTS WORK WITH COUNCILS OF CHURCHES [2]

The Washington and Northern Idaho Council of Churches had its roots back in the second decade of the century as a movement to promote Protestant Sunday schools. The first head of the Western Washington Sunday School Association was Rev. Walter Moore. He was succeeded by Rev. Herbert Loomis. When Miss Gertrude L. Apel became executive secretary, in 1930, the group took on aspects of a full-fledged council of churches.

From the earliest days of council history Northwest Methodists championed the movement, supporting it with leadership and finances. In 1931 the Pacific Northwest Annual Conference appointed as its representatives on the state board, Rev. M. J. Purdue, Rev. John G. Law, Rev. Robert Elmer Smith, and Rev. J. Ralph Magee. Thereafter the Conference steadily was represented on the board. Some Methodists served as presidents on state and local levels.

Among the 160 ministers responding to the questionnaire, 147 had cooperated with the council on local, and 123 on state level. One hundred and twenty-five said their congregations supported the National Council of Churches, and 102 had supported the World Council, mostly through World Service giving.

Sixty-nine ministers reported that they had held office in local or state councils, 22 had been presidents of various cooperating groups and 49 had served on committees. One hundred and forty felt that certain services can be rendered better through cooperation.

Ninety pastors said their youth had

MOUNTLAKE TERRACE—1953

Mountlake Terrace, a new community started about 1951, by 1956 had 8,000 inhabitants. The congregation first was called Christ Church, Edmonds in 1953. Rev. Henry R. Cross was first pastor. In 1954 there were 77 members and 225 in Sunday school. Eighteen members of Woman's Society of Christian Service gave $267. The church building was valued at $35,000, parsonage at $8,000. That year Rev. Roger K. Johnson became pastor.

In 1956 Johnson reported 156 members. Sunday school enrolled 467. The building was worth $48,000 and the parsonage $11,500. Thirty-one women in the Woman's Society of Christian Service had given $340. In 1959 there were 272 members, 555 in church school, and 43 in Woman's Society gave $328. The building was valued at $75,260. Had been improved and enlarged. Rev. Kenneth B. MacLagan became pastor that year.

In 1963, when Rev. O. James Garrett became pastor, he found 282 members and 285 enrolled in Sunday school. Twenty-nine members of Woman's Society had given $947.

In 1964 Rev. David A. Miles was pastor, first year. There were 314 members and 287 in church school. Thirty members of Woman's Society had given $861. Building was valued at $109,200. The parsonage at $9,200.

cooperated with the United Protestant Youth movement. Seventy-eight felt their youth were better Christians for the experience, and 69 felt their youth were better Methodists.

Women had cooperated with the Council of Churches-sponsored United Church Women in 125 instances, 106 felt the work done was profitable to the community and 96 felt the spiritual life and outlook of their women had been deepened. The replies of 85 laymen agreed closely with the views expressed by the ministers in their appraisal of local, state, national, and world councils of churches.

A greater percentage of laymen than ministers, however, criticized the National Council for its pronouncements on topics considered to be of political nature.

One minister, Rev. Donald Fife, pastor of Tibbetts Church, Seattle, expressed respect and unhesitating endorsement of the National and World Councils of Churches, yet he said he had misgivings concerning the tendency of some groups, such as United Protestant Youth, to draw leadership away from the local church. This statement, however, is not to be interpreted as disagreement with the statement of Rev. L. Marshall Campbell, youth director for the Conference Council, who favorably evaluated some of the work of the youth movement. He said, "A few years ago, in a state United Christian Youth Movement Conference, we were able as Methodist Youth Fellowshippers, to share our own tradition, history, and convictions, along with other Christians and all of us came away better informed about our own peculiarities and relationships."

Notwithstanding some criticisms which came from loyal and devoted leaders in local churches, 101 of the ministers who replied to the questions on ecumenicity, favored the National and World Councils of Churches. Some expressed no opinion and 140 felt that there are areas of service which can be rendered better through cooperation.

TRINITY, EAST WENATCHEE—1955

Rev. Ruth M. Lortz organized Trinity Church, East Wenatchee, in 1955, after extensive surveys. First Sunday school met in the town library. First preaching service held in town hall, October 2. Six persons uniting that day were, Lewis A. and Alice Clark, Robert E. and Barbara Lee, Mrs. Eva Pentamaki, and Miss Lucille Sprengle, a deaconess who assisted with early cultivation. Membership, 1956, 23. Rev. Danial E. Taylor was district superintendent.

Woman's Society of Christian Service organized in 1956. Five-acre building site purchased in 1955 aided by $2,000 grant from Conference Board of Missions. In 1956 a $4,000 grant from Home Mission Board, used to help building parsonage. A debt of $12,500 remained. Robert E. Lee was president of board of trustees when parsonage erected.

In 1963 church edifice was built with aid of $32,500 loan from Urgent Needs Appeal. Rev. Hubert E. Rhymes was pastor. After building went up a Wenatchee firm landscaped the grounds free and a gift of $900 provided sprinkling system.

In 1964 there were 109 members of church, 115 in Sunday school, 40 enrolled in Woman's Society of Christian Service. The women had contributed $592 to local work. Rev. Donald L. Russell, pastor in 1964.

The prevailing view of the Conference on the subject of pronouncements by the National and World Councils was stated in 1962 in a Pacific Northwest Conference resolution commending The Methodist Church on its historic support of interchurch cooperation and witness through local, state, national, and world councils of churches.

"We reaffirm our support of the Washington and Northern Idaho Council of Churches," the resolution read, "The National Council of Churches in the United States of America, and the World Council of Churches, and we affirm our support of the right and propriety of such councils and their properly constituted study groups to consider and speak responsibly, as autonomous bodies, on all matters of Christian faith and life, both personal and social as well as on matters of church order and work."

Unity of Spirit Stands Above Organic Union

Northwest Methodists long have favored moves to bring denominations together in organic union, but apparently the prevailing view is that organic union is of less importance than spiritual harmony. The openmindedness of the church in the Northwest toward union of Methodist groups was expressed in 1917 when the Columbia River Conference approved a resolution favoring union with the Methodist Episcopal Church, South, presented by the Columbia Conference of the latter denomination.

The sincerity of this approval was verified in 1939 when the three Methodist denominations came together to form The Methodist Church.

Interest of the Conference in further unification among other Methodist bodies was evidenced in replies of ministers and laymen to questions dealing with this subject. One hundred and fifteen favored such union conditionally while 29 expressed no condition. The prevailing view, however, was that such unification could and should come about

---

VIEW RIDGE, EVERETT—1955

This church was born in 1955, holding first services in the View Ridge public school. As a missionary project most of the financial support came from the Puget Sound District and the Pacific Northwest Annual Conference. The first pastor in 1955 was Rev. Henry Cross. In 1956 church was left to be supplied. In 1957 Rev. Paul B. L. Anderson was pastor. Rev. G. Paul Carr served in 1961-'62, and in 1963 Rev. Larry LaVelle became pastor. This is the only Protestant church serving the View Ridge area, a new suburban section of the city of Everett.

By 1964 the membership was 130. The church school enrolled 138 and 24 members of the Woman's Society of Christian Service gave $426 for the work of the church and the conference. Rev. Jack M. Tuell was district superintendent.

This church received a loan of $3,000, to complete and improve its building, from the Urgent Needs Appeal, in 1963. In appreciation the pastor wrote, "This loan has brought new life to the church, a real sense of accomplishment, and a growing awareness that many other Methodists had a hand in its completion. It has 'converted' sentiment to a definite can-do attitude, a real achievement."

only with complete meeting of minds on theology, church polity, organization, and administration. The view often was expressed that the divergencies of theological opinion between some Methodist groups would render such a merger unprofitable. There was agreement that there should be a spirit of fraternity and Christian harmony transcending theological and social views.

Among laymen replying, forty expressed unconditional approval or at least desire for unification among those Methodist groups agreeing upon such a plan, and 23 favored the idea conditionally.

Unification of Protestant Bodies not Favored

The question concerning unification between other Protestant bodies brought somewhat less enthusiastic response. While both laymen and ministers were agreed that the spirit of unity is urgent, organic unification was deemed neither desirable, necessary, nor possible in the immediate future. Twelve ministers and 40 laymen expressed approval without stating conditions, yet there was an evident feeling that denominational separation among Protestants, is not so much a sign of disunity as of democratic diversity, an expression of individual differences. There was firm reaction against any attempt to force all Christians into a common mold.

Two statements from ministers of the Conference are included here. Rev. J. Ray Neiser called attention to a matter which apparently was in the thinking of most ministers and laymen. He said, "A simple look at the history of the Christian movement shows that God has had his hand of blessings upon separate communions that have resurrected truths long ignored by the church at large, and in the revitalization of such truth the whole church has profited. Luther, taught salvation by faith, not by works; Wesley, surety of God's forgiveness, and the wholly consecrated life; and do we

---

WEST HIGHLANDS
KENNEWICK—1955

First Sunday school, West Highlands, Kennewick before 1947. Bruce Lampson, leader. Methodist church organized in 1955. Official Board, Bruce Lampson, chairman, E. T. Palmer, Ray Nelson, Dorsey Gilkerson, Nels Seaberg. Rev. David O. Beadles, first pastor, 1955.

Parsonage completed, October 1, 1956. Church October 14, congregation moved into basement of new parsonage, twenty present. Lampson's Sunday school moved to basement.

Fifty-nine charter members constituted first official congregation. First trustees, W. L. Pierce, Robert Zumhoff, J. H. Grigg, Jr., Leland Nitteberg, Bruce Lampson, Henry Henderson, John Clark, Robert Yoder, W. H. Willetts. Articles of Incorporation filed 1957. Rev. Robert F. Waller, pastor.

Woman's Society organized, April 14, 1957, Mrs. Robert McMullen, president. Senior Methodist Youth Fellowship organized, 1957. Mr. and Mrs. Robert McMullen, counsellors, assisted by Mr. and Mrs. John Pierson. Junior High group same year, Mr. and Mrs. John Nunn, counsellors, assisted by Mr. and Mrs. Dave Ashby. Incomplete new building consecrated, May 10, 1959, Bishop A. Raymond Grant. Organ installed, August 21, 1960.

In 1964, Rev. Charles Kent Echelbarger, pastor, second year. Membership 303. Church school enrollment, 398. Woman's Society members, 43, gave $445. Value of building, $82,000.

363

not have to admit that some of the 'sects' are now emphasizing almost the same things which Methodists did 100 years ago and by which it became a great church?"

A most thoughtful statement came from Dr. John B. Magee, Professor of Philosophy and Religion at the University of Puget Sound. He said, "I favor; more, I urge organic union between Methodist bodies now separated. Moreover, I believe that eventually most of the now separate Protestant bodies would present a better witness for their Lord if they were to demonstrate the brotherhood implicit in a single organism.

"I do not believe that simple merger is the answer to all questions. Any final union must carry into the larger church the values for which the separate groups previously existed. Only long and patient dialogue between the churches can arrive at such a union, and then, only if they are genuinely open to the leading of the Holy Spirit. The whole concept of a superorganization is foreign to the New Testament meaning of the Church as the body of Christ. But the present fragmentation is, if anything, even more of a contradiction.

"I believe that for most laymen the great Protestant denominations represent a single church, at least in the sense that they move freely from one to another—at least across many of the organizational boundaries. A good next step would be to establish such movement among the clergy so that a Methodist minister could spend five years as a Presbyterian minister and move back into Methodist Circles without penalty. I use this merely as an example as to what ought to happen for all the Protestant denominations. Perhaps a multiple ordination would facilitate this. I know that it would be for a time organizationally awkward, but organizations exist to serve higher ends. When they exist for themselves they blight the work of the Spirit.

"After a period in which ministers as well as laymen have moved about in various denominations, there should become evident eventually the most auspicious method of further unifying them into a single church."

364

Chapter XVIII

How success of the Urgent Needs Ap-
peal led by Bishop Everett W. Palmer,
Seattle Area, put new heart into Area
churches and promised greater achieve-
ments for the future is related in—

Men of Prophetic Insight

Urgent Needs Appeal Sets Pattern for the Future

This volume is intended to be history and not prophecy. Yet, developments in the Pacific Northwest Conference in the early 1960's certainly had prophetic implications.

This development was prophetic because its transforming effects on the morale of churches pointed to better things ahead. Because of it, district superintendents were given means to get on with church extension. Official members no longer shook their heads saying, "It cannot be done," but instead, they exclaimed, "This is the most amazing thing we have ever seen!"

Congregations no longer felt they had been led into impossible situations and left to carry depressingly heavy loads alone. Rather they said, "Since the conference cares so much, our part will be easier." At least that was the way of it in September, 1964.[1]

This miracle in Pacific Northwest history was symbolized by three letters, UNA, which being interpreted meant, "URGENT NEEDS APPEAL."

Conference-wide Needs Were Urgent

This is how it came about. When Bishop Everett W. Palmer was elected, in 1960, to head the new Seattle Area, he found the flow of Methodist progress retarded because of a bottleneck arising from urgent needs and paucity of funds.

In the Northwest population almost had doubled in the past twenty years, and still was growing faster than church membership. In fact, Methodist membership, percentage-wise, had lagged behind general population growth. Most growing edges were at Seattle, Bremerton, Bellingham, Everett, Tacoma, Olympia, Grays Harbor, Vancouver, Yakima and Wenatchee Valleys, The Columbia River Basin, and Spokane. Only thirty-one per cent of the 3,000,000 persons in Washington and Northern Idaho were affiliated with churches and a little above three per cent were Methodists.

Through comity agreements with the Council of Churches many communities had been allocated to Methodist care, but district superintendents had insufficient funds to organize, build churches, and provide pastors to occupy them. There was the further hazard that if Methodists did not meet their responsibilities to these new communities the people might go without the services of cooperating churches.

Moreover, older congregations in crowded cities were without off-street parking, forcing would-be worshipers, either to stay at home or go out of their communities for spiritual inspiration. There were small, established churches, "bursting at the seams" for lack of space to accommodate growing congregations and church schools.

Some churches were forced to move to make room for freeways, and others were housed in condemned buildings that must be abandoned for safety's sake. Other churches, poorly located, needed to move to the center of their constituency in order to serve persons for whom they were responsible.

Adding to the acuteness of these conditions was the fact that, for the most part, Methodist churches were without sufficient bank credit to borrow money to supplement the gifts of their members in building new houses for worship and Christian education.

The Bishop found the University of Puget Sound growing beyond its ability to provide facilities for its students.

Everett Deaconess Children's Home was at a point of transition. For years this institution had glorified the Chris-

LAKEWOOD, TACOMA—1955

The first Sunday school, Lakewood community southwest of Tacoma was organized in September 1955. It met in hall at Lakewood Center. First superintendent was Norris Kaldor. First preaching service, in 1955, by Rev. Jack Tuell. Also held in hall under Lakewood Theater, September 4, 1955. Church was organized same year, with 104 members.

Trustees, Lee Siler, P. T. Chaney, Al Schumacher, Al Lemcke. Organizing pastor, Rev. Jack M. Tuell. Rev. Clark J. Wood, district superintendent. Women, organized in 1955 with 28 members. Mrs. Harvey Boese was first president. First building erected in 1957, was social unit to be used until sanctuary could be built. In 1964, still being used as a sanctuary.

First building at 6900 Steilacoom Boulevard, S. W. Tacoma. Cost of first building $49,000. Rev. Jack M. Tuell, pastor. Chairman of trustees when erected, P. T. Chaney.

In 1964 Rev. Bruce G. Parker was pastor. There were 948 members and 657 in church school. Dr. Robert Whitaker was church school superintendent. Mrs. Connie Burke, president of the Woman's Society which had 122 members. Group paid $359 for local work. In 1960, second unit of church completed. An educational administrative building valued at $90,000. Sanctuary tentatively scheduled for construction in 1968.

tian faith and the Church through providing love and Christian training for homeless children. But in the early 1960's this program was altered. The home became a clinic for treatment of children suffering from emotional disturbances. They needed love, care, understanding, and treatment as much as ever. But money was lacking to construct essential buildings to replace outmoded and inadequate ones.

Thousands of Methodist students were crowding into state institutions of higher learning. A program for their spiritual and social care had been projected, but because of lack of funds, in some instances, the program was retarded for lack of parsonages for student ministers.

The Conference for fifty years had offered Christian training for youth through summer camps. Yet some of these were inadequate to meet growing needs. Others required relocation because urban populations had encroached upon their sites. This program also was in the midst of transition from the concept of district control to that of conference planned programs. New and larger tracts of land must be purchased at increasingly higher prices, if summer camping were to keep pace.

This situation was not new for it was typical of conditions under which Northwest Methodists had labored since 1834. There never had been a time when men and money had been equal to needs, or to the Methodist tendency to reach beyond its grasp.

NEED MATCHED BY DETERMINATION TO MEET IT

The situation in the new Seattle Area was matched by what Bishop Palmer and his co-workers determined to do about it.

Between September, 1960 and September, 1962, Bishop Palmer called the Conference into extraordinary session three times. The first, in 1960, was for the purpose of getting under way plans for an area headquarters building. The second session February, 1961, con-

WESLEY MEMORIAL, YAKIMA—1955

Wesley Memorial Church, Yakima, founded in 1955, through desire of local residents for church and hearty cooperation of First Church. Reverend Raymond H. Blanton, appointed in June, was housed in a parsonage in July.

With $30,000 and 28 members donated by First Church, these pioneer Methodists met at Nob Hill Garage in West Yakima, September 28, to organize a new church with 54 charter members.

The name Wesley Memorial Methodist Church was adopted by the Quarterly Conference October 17. Trustees were authorized to purchase site.

Other organization went forward with dispatch. Mrs. Lloyd Winkenwerder, elected president of Woman's Society of Christian Service. Methodist Men's Fellowship elected Jake Frank.

Trustees purchased lots on Glenside and Orchard Avenue, appointed Reinhold Eichler, building chairmen, and plans made for construction. Sanctuary was consecrated December 7, 1958, by Bishop A. Raymond Grant. Milton Stevenson was chairman of Board of Trustees. Rev. Harper Richardson, was pastor, and Russell Fulgham was church school superintendent.

In 1964, Rev. Robert C. Ward, was reappointed pastor for the third year. Membership was 259, church school enrollment, 160, Woman's Society of Christian Service membership, 40. They had given $635. Building was valued at $132,000 and parsonage at $24,500.

THESE CHURCHES INDICATE
METHODISM'S FORWARD LOOK

Robert Thorpe

Audubon Park Church
Spokane

Alderwood Manor

Lewiston Orchards,
Idaho

University Methodist Temple, Seattle

vened in Spokane and was designed to bring the Conference under the regular financial program through spiritual awakening of ministers and laymen. The third special session took the form of a conference-wide rally at the University of Puget Sound Fieldhouse, in September, 1962, to launch the campaign to raise $2,100,000 to meet urgent needs of the Conference.

The 3,000 Methodists who met in Tacoma went home to inspire 15,800 of their fellows to pledge $2,362,054 payable in forty months. By August 31, 1964, the midway point in the collection program, $1,152,932 had been paid, not quite half of the pledged goal. In the fall of that year every church in the Conference was asked to follow a carefully outlined plan to review its giving to UNA and take steps to see that final sums should equal the amount pledged in 1962.

HISTORY AND PROPHECY INSPIRE METHODISTS

A joyous and triumphant mingling of history and prophecy resulted from the fact that money paid on UNA was put to work immediately. Churches threatened with the spirit of defeat became aware of new life surging through the hearts of members.

By August 31, 1964, 53 churches, representing all districts, and eight conference institutions had received the miracle-working financial aid served with the love and concern of conference-wide Methodism. It was the love and concern, the knowledge that fellow Methodists cared, that gave the money personality and power.

The transforming power of love and the spirit of sharing were evident in every place where aid was received. Take a look, for instance, at Trinity Church, East Wenatchee, on the Columbia River District. The nine-year-old congregation first had met in a small chapel under the parsonage. Later they worshiped in the school library. But the growing congregation needed a new

UNITED, WALLA WALLA—1955

United Church, Walla Walla, born December 11, 1955. Charter service, January 30, 1956. Resulted from Grace Church, 1908, and Marvin Memorial, Southern Methodist Church, entering conference through Methodist Union, 1939.

First pastor of Grace, Rev. F. C. Baylor, in 1909, reported 20 members, 68 in Sunday school, 30 in Epworth League, one church building worth $2,000. In 1919, Rev. Hubert Vincent reported 60 members, 165 in two Sunday schools.

In 1929, Grace was with Valley Grove, Rev. W. H. Staines, pastor. There were 162 members. Ten years later, Rev. C. H. Cowdy received 85.

In 1940, Marvin Memorial, Rev. J. A. Hoffman, pastor, reported 183 members, 99 in church school.

In 1950, Grace was served by Rev. Aubrey W. Windsor, who reported 130 members. Marvin Memorial, supplied by Rev. Joseph L. Woodford, had 171 members, 137 in church school.

In 1955, at merger, Rev. Will W. Martin, pastor Grace, continued with united congregation. Through sale of Marvin property and loan from Board of National Missions, newly property acquired, Grace neighborhood. Rev. Truman Cotten, pastor.

In 1964, Rev. Donald E. Sattleberg, pastor, fourth year. Members, 220. Church school, 210. Woman's Society 108, gave $853. Value of church building $77,000. Parsonage, $21,000.

building immediately. Love provided a loan of $32,500 to enable this group to erect its first unit, a place of worship, study for the pastor, kitchen, and four classrooms.

Reaction in East Wenatchee was electric. Children flocked to the classrooms to fill them to overflowing. The pastor wrote, "Morale is at a new high. Long-suffering members are thrilled that we now have adequate room for worship and fellowship. The new building attracts newcomers and calls for the best in our 'old faithfuls.'"

The generosity of Methodists inspired generosity in the community. "It is thrilling to see how generous so many have been," the minister said. "Our five-acre plot is to be landscaped by a local contractor free. A gift of $900 will provide an automatic irrigation system. A member donated materials and labor for finishing walls and floors. Volunteers are completing the interior painting and installation of doors. Painting of the parsonage was completed by volunteers."

At Selah, on the same district, a $26,500 loan was used to refinance an old debt, complete the building and improve educational facilities. Response here was typical. The pastor reported that the loan had given the people of the church a new appreciation of the concern of the Conference in the local church program. "It has eased the morale problem caused by facing debt payments that could not be met, and a building standing in an unfinished state," the pastor said. "Our men have responded by donating many long hours of skilled labor."

Urgent Needs Program Works Miracles

On the Puget Sound District, Alderwood Manor received a $7,000 grant and loan of $22,775. This was to get this congregation born and into its cradle. In June, 1963, the Methodists had no church or congregation at Alderwood Manor. When Rev. Milton Andrews arrived on the scene following the Annual Conference session there was only a

WESLEY CHAPEL, SEATTLE—1956

The first preaching service for Wesley Chapel in Seattle was held in 1956, Rev. John W. Caughlan was the pastor. Service was held in building taken over from the Presbyterians and known as the Van Asselt Church. In January 1956, the church was organized with ten families in the charter membership. The Sunday school was organized in January 1956 with Mrs. Mary Edwards as the first Sunday school superintendent. The district superintendent at that time was Rev. Clark J. Wood. The women were organized almost immediately with ten charter members. Mrs. Gladys Smith who had transferred her membership from First Church, Seattle was the first president of the Woman's Society.

The building later was purchased from the Presbyterians. This congregation, located at the south end of Seattle's Beacon Hill, was served by Rev. L. Waine Bond, 1956-57; Rev. James E. Gossett, 1958-59; Rev. H. Robert Morton, 1960-61; Rev. Stanley R. Kuntz, 1962; Rev. G. Hurst Paul, 1963.

In 1964, Rev. Gene Ernst was pastor. There were 32 members and 15 enrolled in the church school. The church school superintendent was Floyd Green. President of the Woman's Society of Christian Service was Laura Hortney. The church building was valued at $7,800.

vacant lot to which to tie. First services were held in a farmhouse where 41 adults met in the living room and 19 children crowded the attic. At Christmas, in the unfinished basement of the new parsonage, 125 were in attendance and 165 were present at Easter.

Money granted and loaned from UNA was used to purchase a site and build a parsonage. It also provided a portable chapel and four Sunday school units.

Pastor Andrews wrote, "In March, when only five months old, we entered our stewardship drive. The goal for current operation budget and building payments was $11,120. We went over the top with $12,500 pledged. Our people had received freely and freely gave. The average family giving was $8 per week.

"Since Easter," Andrews said, "we have had to hold two services each Sunday, except for summer months. You just can't put a limit on a church that doesn't put a limit on God! Our slogan is, 'Working Today, Planning for Tomorrow, Building for Eternity.' After all, isn't that the heart of UNA?"

View Ridge, at Everett, on the Puget Sound District, used a loan of $3,000 for building and improvements. The pastor reported, "This loan has brought new life to this church, a real sense of accomplishment, and a growing awareness that many others had a hand in its completion. It has 'converted' sentiment to a definite 'can-do' attitude. This in itself is a real achievement, as well as completion of one of the handsomest of small churches."

Aldersgate, east of Lake Washington on the Seattle District, received a loan of $6,000 for a parsonage. A portable chapel and four class units were provided by UNA. This new Methodist Church at Eastgate served ten communities with a population in 1964 of 15,-000. The membership almost quadrupled the first year, to 130.

On Mercer Island, in Lake Washington, near Seattle, the church was

ST. PAUL, VANCOUVER—1956

Site picked for church in "Hazel Dell-Lake Shore" addition, Vancouver, by Quarterly Conference, First Church. Deeds, held in trust for new church. Congregation met for first time Hazel Dell Elementary school, September 8, 1957. Rev. C. Ellsworth Wilson, temporary pastor. Rev. M. M. Finkbeiner, district superintendent, speaker. Thirty-nine members joined that day. Mrs. W. G. Wanger elected superintendent Sunday school. Woman's Society, Methodist Youth Fellowship, followed. Charter Day fixed for December 1, 1957, 77 members received. Building committee presented plans for building that day. Ground broken, February 20, 1958. Articles of Incorporation filed. Sunday school teachers eagerly attended leadership training classes. District made money available for church and Forward Movement provided funds to build a parsonage. Congregation entered new building June 1958. Consecrated October 5, 1958. Bishop A. Raymond Grant, officiating. Rev. R. G. Calkins, pastor.

In 1960, two sessions of church school started. Daily Vacation Church school annual feature. Church supported the Urgent Needs Appeal in 1962 and pledged 30% more than quota.

In 1964, Rev. George Allen Odgers, pastor, fifth year. Membership, 117. Church school enrollment, 123. Woman's Society membership 27, gave $466. Building value, $39,000; parsonage, $18,750.

founded in 1962. Within twenty months there were 193 members. The church, seating 110, was filled at two services each Sunday morning. There were 16,000 people on the island and no other Methodist Church. The congregation was making use of four portable units, and used a grant of $10,000 and a $28,850 loan to purchase a site and building.

Pastor L. L. Dunnington, commented, "Our people are grateful for the help we have had from UNA. Now they want to go forward on their own."

On the Spokane District, Central Church, successor to the first Methodist Church established at Spokane Falls, received a $5,000 grant and a $15,000 loan from UNA to complete the interior of a new building. The exterior of the educational plant had been erected several years earlier, but the transient, downtown congregation could not pay for it. This is said to be the front door to Spokane Methodism.

Pastor James T. Albertson wrote, "The new sense of mission which our church has now achieved is not only restoring Central Church but is helping the restoration of Spokane District Methodism."

At Meade, on the same district, the church had met in a former tavern for years. New population trends indicated the need to move to a new location. With the aid of a $6,000 grant to purchase a 6-acre site, and the loan of a portable chapel and three classroom units, the congregation faced a new day. The pastor said, "Persons living near the new site who had not participated in the church at its old location now are calling on their neighbors to tell them of the coming of the church."

Lake Louise, on the Tacoma District, received a $10,000 grant and $8,000 loan to purchase a three-acre site near the high school and a shopping center. The district superintendent, Rev. Ac C. Wischmeier, said, "This is the next new church we plan to get started on the Tacoma District."

ST. ANDREWS, OLYMPIA—1958

First Sunday school, North Olympia, December 7, 1958, in home of Mr. and Mrs. J. W. Farmer, 308 Warren, with 40 children. Leaders, Mrs. Farmer, Mrs. J. K. Moore, and Mrs. Frank Bowen. Rev. Louis Kaub, Portland and Rev. Robert Albertson, University, Puget Sound, preached occasionally.

St. Andrews Church organized April 27, 1960, 26 members. First regular pastor, Rev. Cyril L. Payne. Rev. Ray Proudfoot, superintendent Tacoma District, organizing minister. Rev. Robert Gray Hess, 1960, succeeded, 1962, Rev. Robert Kinch. In 1961, new building planned. Urgent Needs Appeal fund loaned $25,000. With money raised locally building was completed by March, 1964, consecrated April 1964. By fall 1964 growing church school required two Sunday sessions church school. Two worship services also started.

Organization of congregation in north end of Thurston County had the blessing of pastor and congregation of First Church Olympia. Officials participated in planning from the start. Pastor Robert Uphoff, assigned his director of Christian Education and chairman of the Commission on Education to serve as consultants in plans from the beginning.

In 1964, Rev. Robert F. Kinch was pastor, third year. There were 146 members, 219 in church school, 34 in Woman's Society. Group paid $335. Building valued at $95,000.

Port Townsend, also on the Tacoma District, first appeared among the appointments of the Puget Sound District of the Oregon Conference in 1854. In 1964 it had more than 7,000 people. But the Methodist Church had never been strong. An allocation was scheduled for winter, 1964. The original church, erected in 1871, for 75 years had had various additions, making the building somewhat less than an architectural gem. The church was to be relocated.

The district superintendent reported, "Port Townsend is a growing city of largely unchurched people who can be reached." The pastor said, "Even the possibility of new facilities has caused our old men to dream dreams and our young men to lay plans."

Cosmopolis, on the Vancouver District, was the first community on Grays Harbor to receive a Methodist pastor in 1883. In 1920 the Methodists sold their old church on the railroad tracks, and purchased the abandoned Presbyterian building on the main street leading to Aberdeen. The building then was more than thirty years old.

PORTABLE UNITS AID MANY CHURCHES

This structure, in 1964, was so deteriorated that it was burned to make room for portable units provided by UNA. It was the first church to demonstrate that these units were portable. The first unit was hauled to the site from Hoquiam where it had been used while the church building there was under construction.

This community, originally built around a lumber mill, saw that means of support disappear in the 1930's. After the Second World War a pulp mill was erected on the site which provided a nucleus for the support of a growing population. A member of that church said, "Led by our young pastor, we see a bright future ahead."

Urgent Needs Appeal funds were used to make a loan of $15,000 available to St. Paul Church, Vancouver, to purchase

MARINE VIEW—1959

First Methodist Sunday school organized at Federal Way, February 22, 1959. Location assigned to Methodists in 1956, by the Council of Churches. First Sunday school superintendent was William R. Miller. First meeting to decide upon church, held in the home of Mr. and Mrs. C. L. Gove, November 30, 1958. Church organized, April 12, 1959, with 96 members. Rev. Gertrude L. Apel, organizing pastor. January 13, 1959, name "Marine View Methodist Church," selected. February 13, 1959, first service held in Federal Way school, Rev. Cyrus E. Albertson, First Church, Seattle, preaching. Attendance was 182. Woman's Society of Christian Service organized February 26, 1959 with eight members.

First Church, Seattle, donated lodge at near-by Epworth Heights, to church. Later, First Church donated $1,200; Tibbetts, $101; Renton, $200; Des Moines, $175; Rev. Clark J. Wood, district superintendent, $100; Kent, $100; The Methodist Union, 100 hymnals. A $35,000 loan and gift of $5,000 from Division of Church Extension; $6,000 from conference; and $6,000 from local church assured building on land previously purchased. Contract for $30,000, let in 1959. First unit consecrated, June, 1960.

In 1964, Rev. Gertrude L. Apel, pastor. Membership, 245, church school enrollment, 239. Woman's Society, 24, gave $450. Cottage from Epworth Heights used for week-day meetings.

a five-acre site, near both senior and junior high schools. The community had been allocated to the Methodists by the Council of Churches after the war. The suburban community was booming in 1964, and a population of 35,000 was foreseen.

The pastor of the church said, "The purchase of this new site is acting like magic on the people of St. Paul Church. After a trying and 'sickly' infancy, the church seems to be entering upon a healthy childhood, with prospects of becoming a robust church in the not-too-distant future."

On the Walla Walla District, birthplace of Eastern Washington Methodism, the new congregation at Burbank received a $15,000 loan to build a parsonage. Lapwai, Idaho, where Rev. Henry Spaulding, missionary associate of Dr. Marcus Whitman, established a work among the Nez Perces in 1836, is the oldest Christian Mission in Idaho. The very old building needed a new roof which members were unable to provide. The work was done, through a $1,000 UNA grant.

The new Riverview congregation at Pasco was made happy in the erection of an educational addition made possible by a $4,000 loan and a portable classroom unit. Afterwards the children attended Sunday school in an uncrowded room and parents were relieved to know their offspring were adequately served while their elders were at worship.

UNA AIDS METHODIST EDUCATIONAL INSTITUTIONS

Helping churches over crises was but one phase of the function of UNA. It also served to provide religious care for students. Since 1920 Northwest Methodists had attempted to follow their students to state institutions of higher learning. The problem had been adequately to finance this mission. The work, therefore, was classified among urgent needs and funds earmarked for that purpose. At Western Washington College of Education, Bellingham, the

---

ST. LUKE'S, BREMERTON—1959

First Sunday school organized in East Bremerton, September 7, 1958, in View Ridge School, with 155 present. Sponsored by Rev. Albert H. Wilson, pastor First Church, Bremerton. Allen Henderson elected superintendent.

First preaching service, February 1, 1959, 105 in attendance. St. Luke's Church organized, March 1, 1959; 73 members. Officers elected, Articles of Incorporation filed in May. There were 145 members.

Rev. Jerry Smith, ministerial student, served until conference, and followed by Rev. Vincent F. Hart, Jr., Woman's Society of Christian Service organized, August 26, 1959. Mrs. Allen Henderson, president.

In 1960, St. Luke's had 188 members of whom 119 had come from First Church. A loan from Board of Home Missions made a building possible in 1961. That year, Lawrence Bouchet, First Church, Seattle, gave two lots to his home church which deeded them to St. Luke's. First service in new building, September, 1962. Rev. Paul Malcom McCutcheon, pastor. Attendance 341.

In 1962, St. Luke's oversubscribed askings for Urgent Needs Appeal by 112%. Church consecrated, December 2, 1962, by Bishop Everett W. Palmer.

In 1964, Rev. Paul McCutcheon, pastor, third year. Members, 386. Church School enrollment, 338. Woman's Society of Christian Service, 66, giving $226. Building value $110,606.

OLD AREA CHURCHES IN NEW BUILDINGS

Mason Church
Tacoma

Grandview Church

Mt. Vernon Church

Tibbetts Church
Seattle

First Church
Vancouver, Washington

United Campus Christian Foundation needed money to complete its building. UNA provided $5,000 to remodel and redecorate the main floor, build a new stairway to the basement, and repair the apartment for the minister-director.

This aid inspired other groups to purchase new furniture. It also helped to lift morale of students and faculty and to elicit a more favorable attitude toward this campus ministry. The College came to regard the Foundation as a complement to the program and facilities on the campus.

The fund also contributed $2,500 toward the new Campus Christian Center at Eastern State College of Education at Cheney. After leaving the campus, a co-ed wrote, "The Lord gave me a wonderful family who could help, love, and understand me. This family is you."

The University of Puget Sound was scheduled to receive $400,000 from UNA funds to help erect a new science center. This would make it possible for the university to accept many more students seeking higher education under Christian auspices.

At midway point, the Deaconess Home at Everett had received only a small portion of the $50,000 grant allocated to it.

Three Conference summer youth camps had been aided by the midway point in UNA program. The new Arlington camp had received $9,000 for a down payment on a 230-acre site costing $30,000 in Snohomish County. Previously Northwest Washington Methodist Youth had met in a state-owned camp ground with little choice of dates. The new site promised to enable church groups to choose their own dates and carry on a year-round camping program.

A new home for the manager of the Lazy F. Ranch, near Ellensburg, was provided through a $9,711 grant from UNA. This released space for 10 additional campers. A new cement floor, foundation for the dormitory, fireplace, and chimney added to the attractiveness

LAKE WASHINGTON
KIRKLAND—1959

Lake Washington Church, Kirkland, was launched August 30, 1959, in Rose Hill School, Rev. Cyrus E. Albertson, preaching. Louis Keller appointed chairman of organizing committee.

Church school superintendent, Mrs. Gordon Skinner. Church organized, December 20, 1959, 27 members. Trustees were, Clyde Simmons, Louis Keller, Harold Dawley, Roy Barnett, Gordon Soma. By 1960, there were 65 members and 176 in church school. Rev. Wilbur M. Snyder, first pastor. In 1961, Louis Keller was appointed Conference Lay Leader.

First Methodist Youth Fellowship organized December, 1959, with eight members. For permanent location of church, a five-acre site was purchased at 7525-132d St. N. E. Ground broken, in July 1961 with Bishop Everett W. Palmer delivering the sermon. District Superintendent J. Henry Ernst spoke at the breaking of soil. The building was consecrated, unfinished, December 17, 1961. An organ was presented to the church by Mr. and Mrs. Ed. Van Winkle.

Congregation worshiped in first unit of unfinished building, February 11, 1962. In 1964, Urgent Needs Appeal granted $2,000, loaned $12,500 to complete building. That year, Rev. Jonathan W. King reappointed for fourth year. There were 270 members of church, 264 in church school. Woman's Society of Christian Service, 42. Church property valued at $97,000.

of the Twinlow Camp, in Idaho. "Twinlow Camp has been given a great boost and the many who see the work done are thrilled to have had a part in it," a leader wrote.

New Credit Program Insures Bright Future

A feature of the Urgent Needs Appeal promising much for the future was an endowment to provide credit for churches in the years ahead. One phase of this endowment was a fund of $100,000 for collateral guaranteeing repayment of loans provided by public banking institutions. This money, while drawing interest, served as a backlog against which credit was made available to the Conference. The other phase was a $1,100,000 permanent fund from which loans would be made directly to local churches to be repaid with interest. Through this endowment churches, hitherto without bank credit, became able to move ahead with building and improvement projects.

Still another prophetic feature of the program was the purchase at low prices of lots in new communities soon after such projects were begun. In some instances congregations were not established for some years, but when the churches were organized, not only did the Conference save money through early purchase, but sites were guaranteed for the congregation when the opportune time arrived.

UNA Undergirded by Stewardship and Public Relations

Additions to the conference staff, carrying bright promise for the future undergirding of the Urgent Needs Appeal, included directors of Public Relations and Stewardship. Filling the former office was Rev. Paul J. Beeman, responsible for keeping members of the church happily informed of the spiritual implications of the many conference projects.

Rev. James R. Bennett was given the important task of cultivating the giving potential of the people. His responsibility was to raise the spiritual level of the Church to the point that members would give not only of their means but themselves to the cause of Christ.

Thus was justified the prophetic UNA slogan, "Methodists Building for a Christian Future."

ADDITIONAL CHURCH HISTORIES

OTHELLO—1959

In 1959, Othello had been allotted, by Council of Churches, to another denomination. Mrs. Thomas R. Booker learned that many residents wanted a Methodist Church there. November 30, 1959 a meeting in the Washington Water Power Building authorized a survey which located 108 families desiring a Methodist Church.

Council of Churches gave consent. Rev. William Ritchie of Lind and Rev. Alfred Carter of Ritzville, served as counsellors. Organization was effected March 28, 1960, with 46 members.

First officers included: Roy Logan, charge lay leader; Clyde Pointer, church school superintendent; Thomas R. Booker, lay member of Annual Conference. Mrs. Thomas R. Booker, president of Woman's Society of Christian Service. Trustees were, Thomas R. Booker, O. L. Capps, Ralph Johnson, Claude Martin, George Sundgren, and Jonathan Wolff.

First regular pastor was Rev. Arthur Paltridge. Junior and Senior High groups were organized and Woman's Society of Christian Service set up, September 24, 1960, with 17 members.

In 1964 Rev. Donald L. Snyder was appointed pastor for third year. Church members, 108; church school, 86; Woman's Society, 21, with gifts of $228. Church building and equipment valued at $85,000. Parsonage and furnishings, $25,800. UNA grant of $5,000 and loan of $10,000 helped.

BROWN'S POINT, TACOMA—1959

The Brown's Point Methodist Church was organized June 6, 1959. The first pastor was Rev. James Shapland. Rev. Harold Simonson had begun preaching services in this community, in 1958. A Sunday school was organized, in 1959 with Mrs. Earl Mann, superintendent.

The first Official Board convened, June 11, 1959, at the home of Joe Baker, Lakota Beach. Earl D. Mann was elected Lay Leader. First anniversary dinner served December 5, 1959.

Dr. Clarence Utterback was chairman of the first building committee. Kick-off dinner for building fund drive, March 8, 1960. In 1960, congregation began holding services in the activities building. Ground breaking for new building, April 9, 1961. Building opened November of that year. Harold Peterson was chairman of Board of Trustees. Rev. R. Franklin Thompson, President University of Puget Sound, delivered the opening sermon. Rev. Ac C. Wischmeier, district superintendent. Building consecrated January 28, 1962, by Bishop Everett W. Palmer.

In 1964, Rev. Craig T. Harper, pastor third year. Members of church, 287. Church school enrollment, 150. Woman's Society of Christian Service members, 30. They gave $1,277. Building valued at $100,700. Parsonage, $16,500.

BURBANK-RIVERVIEW PASCO—1960

Burbank-Riverview churches, Pasco born in 1960. Grew out of Pasco's Greater Parish program launched in 1960, planned by Bishop Everett W. Palmer, general superintendent, Seattle Area, Rev. Ac C. Wischmeier, superintendent Walla Walla District, Rev. Randall Larson, pastor.

In December, 1960, at ceremonies at First Church, members of Riverview Parish were commissioned to serve section of the community. That year the assignments at conference had been to Pasco and Burbank-Riverview parish.

In 1961, Rev. Richard E. Nye, pastor both churches. At Riverview, he found 111 members, 183 in church school, no property. At Burbank, there were 38 members, 114 in church school, small church valued at $4,000.

The following year Riverview had 138 members, 150 in church school. A church building was valued at $16,000. At Burbank, there were 63 members, 105 in church school.

In 1963, Burbank, 78 members, 89 in church school. Church building worth $60,000. Riverview had 178 members, 171 in church school. Church building valued at $70,000, parsonage, $20,000.

In 1964, Rev. David Braun, pastor, 79 members at Burbank, 89 in church school. Pastor had received $2,000. Riverview paid pastor, $1,500, had 217 members, 180 in church school. Building valued at $80,000, parsonage $16,000.

ROYAL SLOPE—1960

Royal Slope came into being through Columbia Basin Irrigation project. Because of location water and population came late. Allocated to Methodists by State Council of Churches. Charge left to be supplied in 1960, but next year, Rev. P. R. Beiring reported church organized previous year with 25 members, which had increased to 28 by conference time. Church school enrollment, 92. Eight members of the Woman's Society of Christian Service had contributed $40 to local work.

Rev. Paul McConnell, appointed in 1961, a year later, reported 40 members with 94 in Sunday school. Ten members of Woman's Society had contributed $158. The church building was valued at $3,200. The congregation had paid the pastor $367, and to World Service and Conference Benevolences, $209.

In 1962, the charge was attached to Othello and Rev. Donald L. Snyder appointed pastor. The 1963 membership was 32 and Sunday school enrollment, 83. Church building was valued at $22,000, and parsonage at $3,000. Pastor had received $400 and World Service and Conference Benevolences, $238.

In 1964, Rev. Donald L. Snyder reappointed. Church membership, 33; church school enrollment, 83. Sixteen members of Woman's Society of Christian Service had paid $77. Total giving, $3,324, indicated spirit of sacrifice.

ALDERSGATE, BELLEVUE—1962

First organization meeting for church at Eastgate, in home of Mr. and Mrs. Paul Stickles, October 10, 1962. Rev. J. Henry Ernst presided. Jim Attebery elected chairman, Mrs. Paul Stickles, secretary, Robert Nickelson, treasurer. First service held in Eastgate real estate office, December 4, 1962. Twenty-nine members received. Two weeks later congregation moved to 148 S. E. Eastgate. Building at time was used by Lutheran congregation. Name Aldersgate chosen by Official Board January 7, 1963.

First Communion service held March 10, 1963. Church chartered by Annual Conference in June, 1963. Charles Allen, chairman of Official Board received charter for congregation. Rev. Reah Dougherty served as interim pastor until Rev. Albert J. Wilson was appointed in June.

September 22, 1963, congregation moved into portable building provided by Urgent Needs Appeal. Eleven acres of land, on Newport Way, purchased by Urgent Needs Appeal, cost $39,500. In September, 1963 membership 100.

In 1964, Rev. Albert J. Wilson, pastor, second year. There were 170 members of church, and 163 in church school. Woman's Society of Christian Service, members 110, gave $1,400. Building and land valued at $43,000. Congregation still housed in portables.

ALDERSGATE, TACOMA—1962

Aldersgate Church, Tacoma, was chartered September 16, 1962 with 80 members. Rev. Everett W. Palmer, Bishop of the Seattle Area, Rev. Ac C. Wischmeier, superintendent of Tacoma District, and Rev. James T. Burcham, pastor, led the service. Conference Board of Missions granted $10,000 for land and buildings, $4,000 for pastor's salary. Church began with five and one-half acres of land upon which were parsonage and small fruit packing shed, later converted into attractive sanctuary. Six portable Sunday school units were made available by Urgent Needs Appeal.

Ground work for church was done by Rev. John Damitio, University of Puget Sound student, under direction of Rev. Robert G. Albertson, director of Religious Activities at the University. The first Sunday school superintendent was Mrs. Dan Moffett and first president of Woman's Society of Christian Service, Mrs. Kenneth Higgins. First Board of Trustees included, Gene Wakefield, chairman, Floyd Chapman, Hubert Bisson, Ronald Damon, Barry Reid, Wayne Smith, Floyd Kriegel, Jack Sanguinetti and Robert Wakeman.

In 1964 membership was 130 and Sunday school enrollment, 145. Church building valued at $24,000 and parsonage at $26,500. In 1965 Rev. Jeffrey L. Smith was pastor. Mrs. Nels Bjarke was church school superintendent and her husband, chairman of trustees.

ALDERWOOD MANOR—1963

Alderwood Manor, in Southern Snohomish County, received its first Methodist pastor in June, 1963. When Rev. Milton P. Andrews, Junior, reached the charge he found neither lot nor congregation. His salary had been guaranteed by the Urgent Needs Appeal.

First service was held in a farmhouse with 41 adults in the living room, 19 children in attic. Urgent Needs Appeal provided $7,000 grant and loan of $22,750 to start the church. Money used to purchase building site and parsonage. By Christmas 1963 the congregation met in unfinished basement of the new parsonage, with 125 persons present. At Easter the crowd had grown to 165.

A portable chapel and four portable Sunday school units were made available by Urgent Needs Appeal. In March, 1965, the five-months old church began its stewardship drive. The goal for current operations and proposed building was set at $11,120. Campaign for funds resulted in pledges to the amount of $12,500, the average family giving being $8.00 per week.

Following Easter, 1964 two morning services became necessary.

MERCER ISLAND—1963

Mercer Island is in Lake Washington, Seattle's eastern boundary. In 1963, 16,000 persons resided there and there was no Methodist church. In 1962, Rev. L. L. Dunnington, retired Methodist minister from Iowa, began to cultivate this field and, January 6, 1963, organized a Methodist church with 106 members. He continued as first pastor.

Charles Gnehm became first chairman of Board of Trustees and Dave Brown first chairman of the Official Board. The church school was organized immediately with Mrs. Ellen Kelsey, superintendent. The Woman's Society of Christian Service was organized a year later with Mrs. Harriett Bold president.

A grant of $10,000 and a loan of $28,850 from Urgent Needs Appeal funds enabled the congregation to acquire an old church building and parsonage. The U.N.A. also made available four portable units for church school purposes. By 1964 the membership had climbed to 193 and a year later to 221. At that time church school enrollment was 186. Church value $60,000, parsonage $23,000.

ST. PETER'S CHURCH
BELLEVUE—1964

The first service for St. Peter's Church, Bellevue was held July 26, 1964, in temporary portable chapel provided by UNA of Pacific Northwest Conference, on the site previously selected as the permanent location for the congregation. The same day the Sunday school was organized with Mrs. T. E. Dunning, first superintendent. The church was organized in 1964 with 161 charter members. Trustees were M. L. Acre, T. O. Haga, S. M. Mark, Ralph Paasch, Llewelyn Pritchard. Rev. Frederick E. Still was first pastor and Rev. J. Henry Ernst, district superintendent.

The woman's organization was perfected that year with fifteen charter members. Mrs. Kenneth Breer was the first president. From July 1964 until March 1, 1965 the church had received more than 200 members. There were 130 in the church school. Rev. Frederick Still was the pastor. Mrs. Breer, president of the Woman's Society, reported 25 members of that organization. Pastor Still attributed the rapid growth of the church to the fact that he and the members of the congregation had visited from house to house confronting the people with their need for the church and the church's need for them. Twenty-five per cent of membership received the first year came on confession of faith.

Appendix I

EXPLANATORY NOTES

CHAPTER I—A MAN TO MATCH THE MOUNTAINS.

1—Jason Lee, Prophet of the New Oregon, Cornelius J. Brosnan, MacMillan, 1932. Missionary History of Pacific Northwest, Rev. Harvey K. Hines, March Printing Company, Portland, Oregon, 1899. Winning the Oregon Country, John T. Faris, Missionary Education Movement, 1911, Eaton and Mains. The Conquerors, Rev. Albert Atwood, Jennings and Graham, 1907. 2—Brosnan. 3—Brosnan. 4—Brosnan. 5—History of Washington, Clinton A. Snowden, Century History Company, N. Y., 1909. 6—Brosnan. 7—Atwood, 1907, quotes the Richmond family Bible as giving Mrs. Richmond's first name as America. This is sanctioned by Ezra Meeker, J. M. Canse, and by Brosnan. Favoring the name "Amelia" is a typed history of Methodism in Illinois, by James Leaton, in possession of the Historical Society of the Illinois Conference. Historian Charles J. Lotz quotes Leaton as saying Mrs. Richmond was the widow of Dr. Alexander Talley of the Mississippi Conference whom Richmond married in 1836, and that her name was Amelia. 8—Jason Lee, Prophet of the New Oregon, Brosnan.

CHAPTER II—MEN OF ACTION.

1—Manuscript minutes of Oregon Conference, 1853. Library of Willamette University. 2—Glimpses in Pioneer Life on Puget Sound, Rev. Albert Atwood, Denton Coryell Company, Seattle, 1903. 3—History of Washington, Snowden. 4—Atwood, 1903. 5—Autobiography Rev. D. G. LeSourd, manuscript in Library of University of Puget Sound. 6—Manuscript "Letters of David and Catharine Blaine," 1853-56. Library of University of Puget Sound, University of Washington, and Seattle Public Library. 7—History of First Methodist Protestant Church, Seattle, typed form, Dillis Ward. In Conference Archives at University of Puget Sound and Library of University of Washington. 8—Autobiography of Rev. D. G. LeSourd. 9—LeSourd. 10—Biographical sketch of Rev. John A. Tennant, on file at Lynden Church and Archives of Conference at University of Puget Sound. 11—LeSourd. 12—Brother Mack, autobiography of Rev. A. J. McNemee. Personal letters to Rev. Erle Howell. 13—Personal letter to Howell. 14—Autobiography, Rev. Andrew Anderson.

CHAPTER III—MEN OF GREAT HEARTS.

1—Snowden, History of Washington. 2—Snowden. 3—Snowden. 4—Judge E. V. Kuykendall, Address before Pacific Northwest Annual Conference, 1942, published in conference minutes of that year. 5—Kuykendall.

CHAPTER IV—GREAT HEARTS IN ACTION.

1—Letter by Charles MacCaughey—signed by his wife. 2—Scrap Book, "My Papa Was A Preacher Too," prepared by Mrs. L. C. Wright, Bellevue, Washington, contained an autobiography of Dr. Landen. 3—See Pearson's report to Puget Sound Annual Conference, 1909. 4—Bishop Leonard was killed in an airplane accident over Iceland in 1943 while on a tour of Europe in interest of the chaplaincy by order of President Franklin D. Roosevelt. 5—Puget Sound and Columbia River Conferences, in 1927, both took action favoring union of two bodies. 6—In 1934, Oregon and Puget Sound Conferences held joint session in Portland to observe centennial of coming to Oregon of Rev. Jason Lee. 7—See Manuscript on History of Methodist Protestants in Seattle, by Dillis Ward. 8—First Church in Seattle only church in conference with unbroken history since 1853, with possible exception of Church at Coupeville, successor to Whidbey Island Church. 9—Hillman and Lakeside, in 1921 were appointments on Seattle District, but by 1940 had been discontinued. Three churches in Ballard united in 1927 to become Trinity church. See individual history of Trinity, Seattle.

CHAPTER V—MEN OF FOREST AND PLAIN.

1—Brosnan, Hines, Snowden. 2—Letters of David and Catharine Blaine. 3—The Yakimas, Click Relander. Writings of Judge E. V. Kuykendall. 4—Snowden, History of Washington. 5—Winning of the Oregon Country, John T. Faris. 6—Snowden, Relander, Kuykendall. 7—Snowden. 8—Minutes of Oregon Conference, 1860. Reports to Bureau of Indian Affairs, 1860-61-62-63. Also Judge E. V. Kuykendall. 9—The Yakimas, p. 17-19, Click Relander. 10—Record left by Rev. C. M. Tate, with Nooksack Mission. 11—Brother Mack, A. J. McNemee. 12—The Yakimas, Relander. 13—Official Report of Yakima Indian Reservation, 1962, and Relander, in The Yakimas.

CHAPTER VI—MEN OF MANY TONGUES AND NATIONS.

1—Snowden, History of Washington. C. B. Bagley, History of Seattle and King County. 2—Bagley, History of Seattle. 3—Journal of Puget Sound Annual Conference, 1884. History of Pacific Swedish Mission, 1928. 4—History of German Methodism in Walla Walla—Robert Wentsch. Conference Archives. 5—Memorial Journal of Western Norwegian-Danish Methodism, Martin T. Larson, 1944. 6—Journal Puget Sound Annual Conferences, 1923-28. And Pacific Northwest Annual Conference, 1929-34.

CHAPTER VII—MEN OF WORLD OUTLOOK.

1—Conference journals. Volumes already named, by Snowden, Brosnan, Atwood, LeSourd, McNemee. Personal letters. Hines, Canse. 2—Councils of Churches Reports and others. 3—Blaine Letters, 1853-56. 4—Autobiography, D. G. LeSourd. 5—Brother Mack, A. J. McNemee. 6—Snowden, Hines. 7—Four Wagons West, Roberta Frye Watt. Binford and Mort, Portland, 1931.

CHAPTER VIII—MEN OF THE ITINERANCY.

1—Missionary History of Pacific Northwest, H. K. Hines, 1899. 2—Snowden—Volume III. Pages 18-19. 3—Life at Puget Sound, by Caroline C. Leighton, 1884. Lee Shepard, Boston. 4—D. G. LeSourd. 5—Published in Diamond Jubilee of Methodism in Pacific—1909. Edited by W. H. Leech. 6—Pioneer Campfire, 1914, by Rev. G. W. Kennedy. 7—Snowden. 8—Brother Mack. Rev. A. J. McNemee. 9—Letters of David and Catharine Blaine. 10—Journal of Puget Sound Annual Conference, 1892—Report of Presiding Elder, Rev. T. B. Ford.

CHAPTER IX—MEN OF LEARNING.

1—Conference Journals. 2—Blaine Letters. 3—Blaine Letters. 4—Albert Atwood, 1902.

CHAPTER X—MEN OF HIGHER EDUCATION.

1—Certain Members of Alumni of Olympia Collegiate Institute reported that the school was established in 1853. 2—In 1882, a school known as Olympia Collegiate Institute was accepted by the Conference, but there is no certain evidence in the minutes that it was the same school. Alumni tradition holds that it was. 3—Apparently this school had been operating or proposed by a local Vancouver group earlier. But the Conference journal records indicate this was the first year the Conference had operated it. 4—Rev. G. M. Erwin, who for a time was head of the Blue Mountain Institute, later, College, also for some time was superintendent of public schools for Oregon and still later, Alaska. 5—Royal D. Bisbee, probably a son of this man, was a missionary to India. 6—The incident was not dropped by Port Townsend. Apparently it was cause for resentment against the Annual Conference in the Methodist Church at that place. 7—This school was known as Goucher Academy. Reports that it was the predecessor of University of Puget Sound are in error. It was established as branch of the Tacoma School, but was short-lived. 8—This is the new Science Complex, to which the Pacific Northwest Annual Conference pledged $400,000 of Urgent Needs Appeal funds.

CHAPTER XI—MEN OF LOYALTY.

1—Records of the Initial Quarterly Conference of the Walla Walla Church, 1859. In conference Archives. 2—History of King County, Bagley. 3—9—Same. 10—Conference journal. Snowden, Information on file in Oregon Historical Society. 11—History of College of Puget Sound, Edward H. Todd. UPS Library. 12—Todd.

CHAPTER XII—WOMEN OF DEDICATION.

1—Letters of David and Catharine Blaine. 2—Report of Mrs. Robert McCaw, historian of Woman's Society of Christian Service, First Methodist Church, Seattle. 3—Historian for women of First Church, Ellensburg. 4—Reports of Historians for women of various churches. 5—Reports in Journals of Oregon, Columbia River, and Puget Sound Conferences. 6—Miss Black's report on file in Conference Archives. 7—See respective conference journals. 8—Annual Reports of Conference presidents of Woman's Society of Christian Service. In journals of respective years. 9—Report of Mrs. Ada Hanscom, historian for Rainier Beach Woman's Society, 1963. In Conference Archives.

CHAPTER XIII—MEN OF COMPASSION.

1—Most information in this chapter from Journals of respective conferences. 2—Information provided by office of Goodwill Industries, Seattle.

CHAPTER XIV—MEN OF BROTHERHOOD.

1—Doctrines and Discipline of the Methodist Church. 2—Pacific Swedish Mission Conference, adopted a resolution on peace and asked the English-speaking conferences to join them.

CHAPTER XV—MEN OF FAITH AND PURPOSE.

1—See Chapter I for criticism against Jason Lee. Also Brosnan, Appendix. 2—Address of Judge E. V. Kuykendall, Journal 1942. 3—See Blaine Letters. 4—The League of Decency was sponsored by the Roman Catholic Church in the early 1930's, in protest against indecency in radio, motion pictures, and publications. 5—Northwest Methodist emphasis on the Bible was presented in Chapter IX. It is included here to make the record of Methodist belief complete.

CHAPTER XVI—MEN OF PATRIOTIC FERVOR.

1—All quotations in this chapter are taken from the journals of the respective annual conferences of the years given.

CHAPTER XVII—MEN OF ECUMENICAL MINDS.

1—Rev. Alden R. Graves retired member of conference, Bayview Manor, Seattle. 2—Questionnaire dealing with phases of ecumenicity covered here was sent to all members of conference, with copies for laymen. This section summarizes replies. Shortage of space precludes use of most statements.

CHAPTER XVIII—MEN OF PROPHETIC INSIGHT.

1—Information for this chapter provided in a report of Rev. Paul Beeman to Bishop Everett W. Palmer, of the Seattle Area, at mid-way point in collections, August 31, 1964.

Appendix II

RECORD OF SESSIONS OF NORTHWEST METHODIST CONFERENCES

OREGON CONFERENCE SESSIONS, 1852-1883

No.	Year	Date	Place	Bishop	Secretary
1	1852	Sept. 2	Portland	Wm. Roberts	F. S. Hoyt
2	1853	Mar. 17	Salem	E. R. Ames	F. S. Hoyt
3	1854	Mar. 16	Belknap Settlement	Matthew Simpson	Wm. Roberts
4	1855	Aug. 1	Oregon City	O. C. Baker	Wm. Roberts
5	1856	Sept. 17	Portland	Levi Scott	Wm. Roberts
6	1857	Aug. 13	Corvallis	E. S. Janes	Wm. Roberts
7	1858	Aug. 11	Salem	Levi Scott	H. K. Hines
8	1859	Aug. 10	Albany	O. C. Baker	I. Dillon
9	1860	Aug. 22	Portland	E. R. Ames	Wm. Roberts
10	1861	Aug. 7	Eugene	C. S. Kingsley	Wm. Roberts
11	1862	Aug. 6	Vancouver, Wn.	Matthew Simpson	Wm. Roberts
12	1863	Aug. 12	Lebanon	E. S. Janes	Wm. Roberts
13	1864	Aug. 18	Salem	D. W. Clark	C. C. Stratton
14	1865	Aug. 10	Olympia, Wn.	Jas. H. Wilbur	C. C. Stratton
15	1866	Aug. 8	Albany	E. C. Benson	C. C. Stratton
16	1867	Aug. 7	Portland	E. Thompson	C. C. Stratton
17	1868	Aug. 13	Salem	Levi Scott	C. C. Stratton
18	1869	Aug. 5	Eugene	C. S. Kingsley	C. C. Stratton
19	1870	Aug. 25	Vancouver, Wn.	E. R. Ames	C. C. Stratton
20	1871	Aug. 9	First Ch. Portland	E. S. Janes	Wm. Roberts
21	1872	Aug. 29	Salem	R. S. Foster	H. K. Hines
22	1873	Sept. 3	Olympia, Wn.	J. T. Peck	H. K. Hines
23	1874	Aug. 12	First Ch. Portland	S. M. Merrill	L. M. Nickerson
24	1875	Aug. 11	Salem	J. T. Peck	John T. Wolfe
25	1876	Aug. 23	Albany	Wm. L. Harris	John T. Wolfe
26	1877	Aug. 29	Seattle, Wn.	Thomas Bowman	John T. Wolfe
27	1878	Aug. 28	Salem	E. G. Andrews	John T. Wolfe
28	1879	Aug. 20	First Ch. Portland	Gilbert Haven	John T. Wolfe
29	1880	Aug. 19	Eugene	I. W. Wiley	John T. Wolfe
30	1881	Aug. 29	East Portland	Wm. L. Harris	John T. Wolfe
31	1882	Aug. 23	Albany	J. F. Hurst	John T. Wolfe
32	1883	Aug. 22	Vancouver, Wn.	H. W. Warren	John T. Wolfe

COLUMBIA RIVER CONFERENCE SESSIONS

No.	Year	Date	Place	Bishop	Secretary
1	1874	July 30-Aug. 3	Walla Walla	Merrill, S. M.	H. K. Hines
2	1875	July 29-Aug. 2	The Dalles	Peck, J. T.	H. K. Hines
3	1876	Aug. 9-13	La Grande	Harris, William L.	H. K. Hines
4	1877	Aug. 16-19	Boise City	Bowman, Thomas	D. G. Strong
5	1878	Sept. 12-15	Dayton	Andrews, E. G.	W. G. Simpson
6	1879	Aug. 7-12	Walla Walla	Haven, Gilbert	W. G. Simpson
7	1880	Aug. 12-15	The Dalles	Wiley, I. W.	W. G. Simpson
8	1881	Aug. 4-11	Colfax	Wilbur, James H.	H. K. Hines
9	1882	Aug. 10-14	Baker City	Hurst, J. F.	G. M. Irwin
10	1883	Aug. 8-13	Walla Walla	Warren, H. W.	G. M. Irwin
11	1884	Sept. 4-8	The Dalles	Fowler, C. H.	G. E. Wilcox
12	1885	July 16-20	Spokane	Walden, J. M.	W. C. Gray
13	1886	July 14-20	Lewiston	Harris, Wm. L.	W. C. Gray
14	1887	Sept. 18-23	Walla Walla	Foster, R. S.	W. C. Gray
15	1888	Sept. 19-24	Moscow	Ninde, W. X.	W. C. Gray
16	1889	Sept. 18-23	Ellensburg	Bowman, Thomas	Henry Brown
17	1890	Aug. 27-31	Dayton	Vincent, J. H.	W. W. Van Dusen
18	1891	Sept. 16-23	Spokane	Fitzgerald, J. N.	W. W. Van Dusen
19	1892	Sept. 21-26	Walla Walla	Walden, J. M.	W. W. Van Dusen
20	1893	Sept. 14-18	Moscow	Goodsell, D. A.	Henry Brown
21	1894	Aug. 22-24	The Dalles	Joyce, I. W.	V. C. Evers
22	1895	Aug. 28-Sept. 2	Spokane	Bowman, Thomas	Henry Brown
23	1896	Sept. 2-6	North Yakima	Cranston, Earl	Henry Brown
24	1897	Aug. 25-30	Pendleton	Foss, Cyrus D.	E. H. Todd
25	1898	Aug. 31-Sept. 5	Pullman	McCabe, C. C.	E. H. Todd
26	1899	Sept. 6-11	Spokane	Vincent, J. H.	E. H. Todd
27	1900	Sept. 5-10	North Yakima	Andrews, E. G.	C. D. Nickleson

No.	Year	Date	Place	Bishop	Secretary
28	1901	Sept. 4-10	Walla Walla	Mallalieu, W. F.	C. D. Nickleson
29	1902	Sept. 3-8	Colfax	Cranston, Earl	C. D. Nickleson
30	1903	Sept. 2-7	Spokane	Hamilton, J. W.	John Evans
31	1904	Aug. 31-Sept. 5	The Dalles	Spellmeyer, Henry	John Evans
32	1905	Aug. 23-28	Moscow	McDowell, W. F.	John Evans
33	1906	Sept. 5-10	North Yakima	Warren, H. W.	John Evans
34	1907	Sept. 4-9	Spokane	Moore, David H.	Wm. DeWeese
35	1908	Sept. 9-14	Wenatchee	Hughes, E. H.	C. O. Kimball
36	1909	Sept. 1-7	Coeur d'Alene	Smith, Chas. W.	C. O. Kimball
37	1910	Aug. 31-Sept. 5	Spokane	Smith, Chas. W.	C. O. Kimball
38	1911	Aug. 30-Sept. 4	Spokane	Smith, Chas. W.	C. O. Kimball
39	1912	Aug. 28-Sept. 2	Ellensburg	Cooke, R. J.	C. O. Kimball
40	1913	Sept. 3-8	Walla Walla	Cooke, R. J.	John Evans
41	1914	Sept. 2-7	Pullman	Cooke, R. J.	Paul Little
42	1915	Sept. 1-6	Spokane	Cooke, R. J.	John Evans
43	1916	Sept. 6-10	Lewiston	Hughes, Matt. S.	John Evans
44	1917	Sept. 5-10	North Yakima	Hughes, Matt. S.	John Evans
45	1918	Sept. 4-8	Pendleton	Stuntz, **Homer C.**	John Evans
46	1919	Sept. 3-8	Spokane	Hughes, Matt. S.	John Evans
47	1920	Sept. 1-6	Moscow	Shepard, Wm. O.	John Evans
48	1921	Aug. 31-Sept. 5	Spokane	Shepard, Wm. O.	John Evans
49	1922	Aug. 30-Sept. 3	Ellensburg	Shepard, Wm. O.	John Evans
50	1923	Sept. 5-9	Spokane	Shepard, Wm. O.	John Evans
51	1924	Sept. 3-8	Wenatchee	Johnson, Eben S.	H. C. Vincent
52	1925	Sept. 9-14	Yakima	Shepard, Wm. O.	H. C. Vincent
53	1926	Sept. 8-12	Walla Walla	Leonard, A. W.	H. C. Vincent
54	1927	Sept. 7-12	Spokane	Shepard, Wm. O.	H. C. Vincent
55	1928	Sept. 4-9	Lewiston	Lowe, Titus	H. C. Vincent

PUGET SOUND CONFERENCE SESSIONS

1	1884	Aug. 21-25	Seattle	Fowler, Charles H.	Isaac Dillon
2	1885	Aug. 12-17	Tacoma	Walden, J. M.	John N. Dennison
3	1886	Aug. 12-16	Port Townsend	Harris, Wm. L.	John N. Dennison
4	1887	Sept. 7-12	Olympia	Foster, R. S.	Andrew J. Hanson
5	1888	Sept. 6-10	Seattle	Ninde, W. X.	Andrew J. Hanson
6	1889	Sept. 4-9	Vancouver	Bowman, Thomas	Andrew J. Hanson
7	1890	Aug. 28-Sept. 1	Whatcom	Newman, J. P.	George C. Wilding
8	1891	Aug. 26-31	Aberdeen	Fitzgerald, J. N.	George C. Wilding
9	1892	Aug. 17-22	Puyallup	Walden, J. M.	George C. Wilding
10	1893	Aug. 16-21	Seattle	Goodsell, D. A.	George C. Wilding
11	1894	Sept. 5-10	Tacoma	Joyce, I. W.	George C. Wilding
12	1895	Sept. 4-9	Seattle	Bowman, Thomas	George C. Wilding
13	1896	Sept. 9-14	Vancouver	Cranston, Earl	W. S. Harrington
14	1897	Sept. 2-6	Everett	Foss, Cyrus D.	W. S. Harrington
15	1898	Sept. 7-12	Tacoma	McCabe, C. C.	W. S. Harrington
16	1899	Sept. 13-18	Whatcom	Vincent, John H.	W. S. Harrington
17	1900	Sept. 12-16	Hoquiam	Andrews, E. G.	G. L. Cuddy
18	1901	Sept. 18-23	Olympia	Mallalieu, W. F.	G. L. Cuddy
19	1902	Sept. 17-22	Seattle	Cranston, Earl	G. L. Cuddy
20	1903	Sept. 23-28	Tacoma	Hamilton, J. W.	G. L. Cuddy
21	1904	Sept. 7-12	Montesano	Spellmeyer, Henry	G. L. Cuddy
22	1905	Sept. 13-18	Everett	McDowell, W. F.	G. L. Cuddy
23	1906	Sept. 19-24	Ballard	Warren, H. W.	G. L. Cuddy
24	1907	Sept. 11-16	Seattle	Moore, David H.	H. Williston
25	1908	Sept. 16-21	Tacoma	Hughes, Edwin H.	T. E. Elliot
26	1909	Sept. 8-13	Bellingham	Smith, Chas. W.	Robert C. Hartley
27	1910	Sept. 14-19	Centralia	Smith, Chas. W.	Robert C. Hartley
28	1911	Sept. 13-18	Tacoma	Smith, Chas. W.	Robert C. Hartley
29	1912	Sept. 11-16	Seattle	Cooke, R. J.	Robert C. Hartley
30	1913	Sept. 17-22	Olympia	Cooke, R. J.	Robert C. Hartley
31	1914	Sept. 9-14	Seattle	Cooke, R. J.	Robert C. Hartley
32	1915	Sept. 9-13	Seattle	Cooke, R. J.	Robert C. Hartley
33	1916	Sept. 13-18	Everett	Hughes, Matt. S.	Robert C. Hartley
34	1917	Sept. 12-17	Tacoma	Hughes, Matt. S.	Robert C. Hartley
35	1918	Sept. 10-15	Aberdeen	Stuntz, Homer C.	Robert C. Hartley
36	1919	Sept. 10-15	Seattle	Hughes, Matt. S.	Robert C. Hartley
37	1920	Sept. 8-12	Olympia	Shepard, Wm. O.	Robert C. Hartley
38	1921	Sept. 14-19	Tacoma	Shepard, Wm. O.	Robert C. Hartley
39	1922	Sept. 13-18	Vancouver	Burns, Chas. W.	Robert C. Hartley
40	1923	Aug. 28-Sept. 3	Puyallup	Shepard, Wm. O.	Robert C. Hartley
41	1924	Sept. 10-15	Bremerton	Johnson, Eben S.	Robert C. Hartley
42	1925	Sept. 16-21	Tacoma	Shepard, Wm. O.	Robert C. Hartley
43	1926	Sept. 15-20	Bellingham	Leonard, A. W.	Robert C. Hartley
44	1927	Sept. 14-19	Seattle	Shepard, Wm. O.	Robert C. Hartley
45	1928	Sept. 11-16	Tacoma	Lowe, Titus	Robert C. Hartley

PACIFIC NORTHWEST CONFERENCE OF THE METHODIST EPISCOPAL CHURCH

No.	Year	Date	Place	Bishop	Secretary
1	1929	Sept. 17-22	Spokane	Lowe, Titus	Robert C. Hartley
2	1930	June 17-23	Seattle	Smith, H. Lester	Robert C. Hartley
3	1931	June 16-22	Yakima	Blake, Edgar	Robert C. Hartley
4	1932	June 14-20	Tacoma	Lowe, Titus	Robert C. Hartley
5	1933	June 13-18	Seattle	Lowe, Titus	Robert C. Hartley
6	1934	June 19-24	Vancouver	Lowe, Titus	Robert C. Hartley
7	1935	June 18-23	Moscow, Idaho	Magee, J. Ralph	Robert C. Hartley
8	1936	June 16-21	Seattle	Lowe, Titus	Frederick L. Pedersen
9	1937	June 15-20	Centralia	Lowe, Titus	Frederick L. Pedersen
10	1938	June 14-19	Spokane	Lowe, Titus	Frederick L. Pedersen
11	1939	June 14-18	Bellingham	Brown, Wallace E.	Frederick L. Pedersen
				Brown, Wallace E.	Frederick L. Pedersen

PACIFIC NORTHWEST CONFERENCE OF THE METHODIST CHURCH

No.	Year	Date	Place	Bishop	Secretary
1	1939	June 14-18	Bellingham	Brown, Wallace E.	Fred'k L. Pedersen
2	1940	June 12-16	Tacoma	Martin, W. C.	Fred'k L. Pedersen
3	1941	June 11-15	Walla Walla	Baxter, Bruce R.	Fred'k L. Pedersen
4	1942	June 10-14	Yakima	Baxter, Bruce R.	Willard E. Stanton
5	1943	June 8-13	Chehalis	Baxter, Bruce R.	Willard E. Stanton
6	1944	June 13-16	Spokane	Baxter, Bruce R.	Willard E. Stanton
7	1945	June 14-18	Yakima	Baxter, Bruce R.	Willard E. Stanton
8	1946	June 12-16	Walla Walla	Baxter, Bruce R.	Willard E. Stanton
9	1947	June 10-15	Tacoma	Baxter, Bruce R.	Willard E. Stanton
10	1948	June 8-13	Tacoma	McConnell, Francis J.	Willard E. Stanton
11	1949	June 7-12	Tacoma	Kennedy, Gerald H.	Willard E. Stanton
12	1950	June 6-11	Tacoma	Kennedy, Gerald H.	Willard E. Stanton
13	1951	June 5-11	Tacoma	Kennedy, Gerald H.	Wayne D. Griffen
14	1952	June 10-15	Seattle	Kennedy, Gerald H.	Wayne D. Griffen
15	1953	June 9-14	Tacoma	Grant, A. Raymond	Wayne D. Griffen
16	1954	June 1- 6	Tacoma	Grant, A. Raymond	Wayne D. Griffen
17	1955	June 14-19	Walla Walla	Grant, A. Raymond	Wayne D. Griffen
18	1956	June 5- 8	Tacoma	Grant, A. Raymond	Wayne D. Griffen
19	1957	June 4- 7	Tacoma	Grant, A. Raymond	Wayne D. Griffen
20	1958	June 3- 6	Tacoma	Grant, A. Raymond	Wayne D. Griffen
21	1959	June 3- 7	Tacoma	Grant, A. Raymond	Wayne D. Griffen
22	1960	June 7-10	Tacoma	Grant, A. Raymond	Wayne D. Griffen
23	1961	June 13-18	Tacoma	Grant, A. Raymond	R. S. Dougherty
24	1962	June 12-17	Tacoma	Palmer, Everett W.	R. S. Dougherty
25	1963	June 11-16	Tacoma	Palmer, Everett W.	R. S. Dougherty
26	1964	June 9-14	Tacoma	Palmer, Everett W.	F. A. Rarden
				Palmer, Everett W.	F. A. Rarden

SESSIONS OF COLUMBIA, EAST COLUMBIA, AND NORTHWEST CONFERENCES OF THE METHODIST EPISCOPAL CHURCH, SOUTH

COLUMBIA CONFERENCE

No.	Place	Date	Bishop	Secretary
1	Corvallis, Ore.	1866	H. H. Kavanaugh	W. A. Finley
2	Rickreall Camp Ground, Ore.	1867	H. H. Kavanaugh	W. A. Finley
3	Roseburg, Ore.	1868	E. M. Marvin	W. A. Finley
4	Corvallis, Ore.	1869	E. M. Marvin	W. A. Finley
5	Dallas, Ore.	1870	W. M. Wightman	J. Emory
6	Santiam Camp Ground, Ore.	1871	J. C. Keener	W. A. Finley
7	Albany, Ore.	1872	H. N. McTyerie	J. Emory
8	Brownsville, Ore.	1873	D. S. Doggett	J. Emory
9	Dixie, Ore.	1874	G. F. Pierce	J. Emory
10	Albany, Ore.	1875	H. H. Kavanaugh	J. F. Curtis
11	Corvallis, Ore.	1876	E. M. Marvin	J. Emory
12	Walla Walla, Wash.	1877	E. M. Marvin	J. Emory
13	Roseburg, Ore.	1878	H. N. McTyerie	J. W. Compton
14	Albany, Ore.	1879	J. C. Keener	J. W. Compton
15	Weston, Ore.	1880	J. R. N. Bell	J. W. Compton
16	Corvallis, Ore.	1881	H. H. Kavanaugh	J. Emory
17	Walla Walla, Wash.	1882	R. K. Hargrove	J. W. Compton
18	Independence, Ore.	1883	R. K. Hargrove	J. W. Compton
19	Dayton, Wash.	1884	J. C. Granberry	J. Emory
20	Albany, Ore.	1885	R. K. Hargrove	J. W. Compton
21	Weston, Ore.	1886	J. C. Keener	J. W. Compton
22	Tangent, Ore.	1887	R. K. Hargrove	J. W. Compton

No.	Place	Date	Bishop	Secretary
23	Pendleton, Ore.	1888	C. B. Galloway	J. W. Compton
24	Dallas, Ore.	1889	R. K. Hargrove	J. W. Compton
25	Lebanon, Ore.	1890	E. R. Hendrix	G. S. Henleiter
26	Roseburg, Ore.	1891	W. W. Duncan	E. E. Phipps

EAST COLUMBIA CONFERENCE

No.	Place	Date	Bishop	Secretary
27	Palouse, Wash.	1892	W. W. Duncan	J. W. Compton
28	Pendleton, Ore.	1893	O. P. Fitzgerald	J. W. Compton
29	Spokane, Wash.	1894	O. P. Fitzgerald	J. W. Compton
30	Milton, Ore.	1895	A. W. Wilson	J. W. Compton
31	Dayton, Wash.	1896	R. K. Hargrove	J. W. Compton
32	Oakesdale, Wash.	1897	R. K. Hargrove	J. W. Compton
33	LaGrande, Ore.	1898	E. R. Hendrix	J. W. Compton
34	Heppner, Oregon	1899	W. W. Duncan	J. W. Compton
35	Dayton, Wash.	1900	W. W. Duncan	J. W. Compton
36	Weston, Ore.	1901	W. W. Duncan	J. W. Compton
37	Milton, Ore.	1902	W. W. Duncan	J. W. Compton
38	Walla Walla, Wash.	1903	H. C. Morrison	J. W. Compton
39	Spokane, Wash.	1904	H. C. Morrison	J. W. Compton
40	Milton, Ore.	1905	H. C. Morrison	J. W. Compton
41	Oakesdale, Wash.	1906	James Atkins	J. W. Compton
42	Walla Walla, Wash.	1907	James Atkins	J. W. Compton
43	Milton, Ore.	1908	James Atkins	J. W. Compton
44	Spokane, Wash.	1909	James Atkins	J. W. Compton
45	Walla Walla, Wash.	1910	R. G. Waterhouse	J. W. Compton
46	Heppner, Ore.	1911	R. G. Waterhouse	J. W. Compton
47	Troy, Idaho	1912	R. G. Waterhouse	J. W. Compton
48	Milton, Ore.	1913	R. G. Waterhouse	J. H. Dills
49	Weston, Ore.	1914	E. D. Mouzon	J. H. Dills
50	Oakesdale, Wash.	1915	W. R. Lambuth	J. H. Dills
51	Walla Walla, Wash.	1916	W. R. Lambuth	J. H. Dills
52	Spokane, Wash.	1917	W. R. Lambuth	J. H. Dills

NORTHWEST CONFERENCE

Organized by merging Columbia, East Columbia, and Montana Conferences

No.	Place	Date	Bishop	Secretary
53	Milton, Ore.	1918	H. M. DuBose	H. M. Law
54	Milton, Ore.	1919	H. M. DuBose	J. H. Dills
55	Spokane, Wash.	1920	H. M. DuBose	J. H. Dills
56	Portland, Ore.	1921	H. M. DuBose	J. H. Dills
57	Milton, Ore.	1922	H. M. DuBose	J. H. Dills
58	Milton, Ore.	1923	H. M. DuBose	J. H. Dills
59	Corvallis, Ore.	1924	H. M. DuBose	J. H. Dills
60	Spokane, Wash.	1925	H. M. DuBose	J. H. Dills
61	Corvallis, Ore.	1926	S. R. Hay	J. H. Dills
62	Milton, Ore.	1927	S. R. Hay	J. H. Dills
63	Milton, Ore.	1928	S. R. Hay	J. H. Dills
64	Coquille, Ore.	1929	S. R. Hay	J. H. Dills
65	Corvallis, Ore.	1930	A. J. Moore	J. H. Dills
66	Stevensville, Mont.	1931	A. J. Moore	J. H. Dills
67	Coquille, Ore.	1932	A. J. Moore	J. H. Dills
68	Troy, Idaho	1933	A. J. Moore	J. H. Dills
69	Milton, Ore.	1934	James Cannon, Jr.	J. H. Dills
70	Corvallis, Ore.	1935	James Cannon, Jr.	J. H. Dills
71	LaGrande, Ore.	1936	James Cannon, Jr.	J. H. Dills
72	Spokane, Wash.	1937	James Cannon, Jr.	J. H. Dills
73	Coquille, Ore.	1938	W. C. Martin	J. H. Dills
74	Milton, Ore.	1939	W. C. Martin	J. H. Dills

SESSIONS OF THE PACIFIC GERMAN CONFERENCE

NORTH PACIFIC GERMAN MISSION

No.	Place	Date	Bishop	Secretary
1	Eugene, Ore.	1888	W. X. Ninde	F. W. Buchholz
2	Tacoma, Wash.	1889	Thos. Bowman	F. W. Buchholz
3	Tacoma, Wash.	1890	John P. Newman	F. W. Buchholz
4	Seattle, Wash.	1891	J. N. Fitzgerald	G. J. Schultz
5	Portland, Ore.	1892	J. M. Walden	G. J. Schultz

386

NORTH PACIFIC GERMAN MISSION CONFERENCE

No.	Place	Date	Bishop	Secretary
1	Portland, Ore.	1892	J. M. Walden	G. J. Schultz
2	Spokane, Wash.	1893	D. A. Goodsell	M. A. Dehuff
3	Tacoma, Wash.	1894	J. W. Joyce	M. A. Dehuff
4	Salem, Ore.	1895	Thos. Bowman	M. A. Dehuff
5	Portland, Ore.	1896	Earl Cranston	M. A. Dehuff
6	Spokane, Wash.	1897	Cyrus D. Foss	M. A. Dehuff
7	Tacoma, Wash.	1898	C. C. McCabe	M. A. Dehuff
8	Portland, Ore.	1899	John H. Vincent	H. F. Lange
9	Salem, Ore.	1900	E. G. Andrews	H. F. Lange
10	Spokane, Wash.	1901	W. F. Mallalieu	H. F. Lange
11	Portland, Ore.	1902	Earl Cranston	H. F. Lange
12	Davenport, Wash.	1903	J. W. Hamilton	H. F. Lange
13	Seattle, Wash.	1904	H. Spellmeyer	H. F. Lange
14	Portland, Ore.	1905	W. F. McDowell	H. F. Lange

PACIFIC GERMAN CONFERENCE

No.	Place	Date	Bishop	Secretary
1	Portland, Ore.	1905	W. F. McDowell	H. F. Lange
2	Spokane, Wash.	1906	H. W. Warren	F. H. Luecke
3	Rosalia, Wash.	1907	D. H. Moore	H. F. Lange
4	Salem, Ore.	1908	E. H. Hughes	F. H. Luecke
5	Seattle, Wash.	1909	Chas. W. Smith	F. H. Luecke
6	Walla Walla, Wash.	1910	Chas. W. Smith	F. H. Luecke
7	Portland (Rodney Ave.)	1911	Chas. W. Smith	Fred Cramer
8	Spokane, Wash.	1912	R. J. Cooke	F. H. Luecke
9	Portland (First)	1913	R. J. Cooke	F. H. Luecke
10	Salem, Ore.	1914	R. J. Cooke	A. F. Hilmer
11	Walla Walla, Wash.	1915	R. J. Cooke	A. F. Cramer
12	Rosalia, Wash.	1916	Matt. S. Hughes	A. F. Cramer
13	Ritzville, Wash.	1917	Matt. S. Hughes	A. F. Cramer
14	Portland (Rodney Ave.)	1918	Homer C. Stuntz	A. F. Cramer
15	Spokane, Wash.	1919	Matt. S. Hughes	A. F. Cramer
16	Walla Walla, Wash.	1920	Wm. O. Shepard	A. F. Cramer
17	Portland (First)	1921	Wm. O. Shepard	A. F. Cramer
18	Rosalia, Wash.	1922	C. W. Burns	C. A. Wentsch
19	Metolius, Ore.	1923	Wm. O. Shepard	F. H. Luecke
20	Salem, Ore.	1924	Eben S. Johnson	A. F. Cramer
21	Spokane, Wash.	1925	Wm. O. Shepard	A. F. Cramer
22	Ridgefield, Wash.	1926	Chas. W. Burns	F. H. Luecke
23	Portland, Ore.	1927	Thomas Nicholson	F. H. Luecke
24	Walla Walla, Wash.	1928	Titus Lowe	F. H. Luecke

SESSIONS OF THE WESTERN NORWEGIAN-DANISH CONFERENCE

No.	Place	Date	Bishop	Secretary
1	Tacoma, Wash.	1890	J. P. Newman	J. L. Eriksen
2	Seattle, Wash.	1891	J. N. Fitzgerald	J. L. Eriksen
3	Portland, Ore.	1892	J. M. Walden	E. M. Stangeland
4	Moscow, Idaho	1893	D. A. Goodsell	E. M. Stangeland
5	Oakland, Calif.	1894	J. N. Fitzgerald	F. Hermans
6	Astoria, Ore.	1895	Thos. Bowman	F. Hermans
7	Tacoma, Wash.	1896	Earl Cranston	Joseph Olsen
8	Portland, Ore.	1897	C. C. McCabe	Joseph Olsen
9	Tacoma, Wash.	1898	C. C. McCabe	Joseph Olsen
10	Spokane, Wash.	1899	John H. Vincent	Joseph Olsen
11	Portland, Ore.	1900	E. G. Andrews	Joseph Olsen
12	Seattle, Wash.	1901	F. F. Mallalieu	Joseph Olsen
13	Astoria, Ore.	1902	Earl Cranston	Joseph Olsen
14	Tacoma, Wash.	1903	J. W. Hamilton	F. A. Scarvie
15	Ballard, Wash.	1904	W. F. McDowell	F. A. Scarvie
16	Portland, Ore.	1905	H. Spellmeyer	Joseph Olsen
17	Everett, Wash.	1906	H. W. Warren	Joseph Olsen
18	Seattle, Wash.	1907	David H. Moore	Joseph Olsen
19	Spokane, Wash.	1908	Edwin H. Hughes	Joseph Olsen
20	Ballard, Wash.	1909	Chas. W. Smith	F. A. Scarvie
21	Tacoma, Wash.	1910	Chas. W. Smith	F. A. Scarvie
22	Oakland, Calif.	1911	Edwin H. Hughes	F. A. Scarvie
23	Portland (Vancouver)	1912	R. J. Cooke	F. A. Scarvie
24	Astoria, Ore.	1913	R. J. Cooke	F. A. Scarvie
25	Seattle, Wash.	1914	R. J. Cooke	F. A. Scarvie
26	San Francisco, Calif.	1915	Edwin H. Hughes	F. A. Scarvie
27	Tacoma, Wash.	1916	Matt. S. Hughes	F. A. Scarvie
28	Everett, Wash.	1917	Matt. S. Hughes	F. A. Scarvie
29	Bellingham, Wash.	1918	W. O. Shepard	F. A. Scarvie
			(C. J. Larsen)	

No.	Place
30	Seattle (First)
31	Portland (First)
32	Seattle (Emmanuel)
33	Portland (Vanc.)
34	Los Angeles, Calif.
35	San Francisco, Calif.
36	Aberdeen, Wash.
37	Everett, Wash.
38	Oakland, Calif.
39	Tacoma, Wash.
40	Seattle (Emmanuel)
41	Bellingham, Wash.
42	San Francisco, Calif.
43	Portland (Vanc.)
44	Eureka, Calif.
45	Portland (First)
46	Los Angeles, Calif.
47	Seattle (First)
48	Oakland, Calif.
49	San Pedro, Calif.

Date	Bishop	Secretary
1919	Matt. S. Hughes	Abr. Vereide
1920	W. O. Shepard	Abr. Vereide
1921	W. O. Shepard	Abr. Vereide
1922	Chas. W. Burns	H. P. Nelsen
1923	Adna W. Leonard	H. P. Nelsen
1924	Eben S. Johnson	Abr. Vereide
1925	W. O. Shepard	Abr. Vereide
1926	Chas. W. Burns	J. G. Bringdale
1927	T. B. Nicholson	H. P. Nelsen
1928	Chas. W. Burns	H. P. Nelsen
1929	Titus Lowe	H. E. Andersen
1930	W. E. Brown	H. E. Andersen
1931	Frederick Leete	H. E. Andersen
1932	J. Ralph Magee	H. E. Andersen
1933	James C. Baker	F. Engebretsen
1934	James C. Baker	Martin T. Larson
1935	J. Ralph Magee	H. E. Andersen
1936	James C. Baker	H. E. Andersen
1937	James C. Baker	H. E. Andersen
1938	G. Bromley Oxnam	H. E. Andersen

THE PACIFIC SWEDISH MISSION CONFERENCE OF THE METHODIST EPISCOPAL CHURCH

Conference Sessions—1908 to 1928

No.	Year	Date	Place	Bishop	Secretary
1	1908	Sept. 2-6	Oakland, Calif.	Henry W. Warren	G. A. Werner
2	1909	Aug. 21-24	Seattle, Wash.	Charles W. Smith	G. A. Werner
3	1910	Sept. 15-18	San Francisco, Calif.	Edwin H. Hughes	G. A. Werner
4	1911	Sept. 7-10	Portland, Ore.	Charles W. Smith	G. A. Werner
5	1912	Sept. 5-8	Los Angeles, Calif.	Wm. O. Shepard	J. N. Burdell
6	1913	Oct. 2-5	Spokane, Wash.	R. J. Cooke	J. N. Burdell
7	1914	Sept. 10-13	Kingsburg, Calif.	F. J. McConnell	J. N. Burdell
8	1915	Sept. 9-15	San Francisco, Calif.	Edwin H. Hughes	J. N. Burdell
9	1916	Sept. 21-24	Tacoma, Wash.	Matt. S. Hughes	J. N. Burdell
10	1917	Sept. 20-23	Mt. Vernon, Wash.	Matt. S. Hughes	J. N. Burdell
11	1918	Sept. 6-9	Pasadena, Calif.	W. P. Thirkield	J. N. Burdell
12	1919	Sept. 18-21	Portland, Ore.	Matt. S. Hughes	J. N. Burdell
13	1920	Sept. 2-5	Los Angeles, Calif.	Adna W. Leonard	J. N. Burdell
14	1921	Sept. 7-11	Seattle, Wash.	Wm. O. Shepard	J. N. Burdell
15	1922	Sept. 28-Oct. 1	Berkeley, Calif.	Charles W. Burns	F. Ahnlund
16	1923	Sept. 27-30	Spokane, Wash.	Wm. O. Shepard	F. Ahnlund
17	1924	Oct. 9-12	Kingsburg, Calif.	Eben S. Johnson	F. Ahnlund
18	1925	Sept. 24-27	San Francisco, Calif.	Charles L. Mead	J. N. Burdell
19	1926	Sept. 2-5	Mt. Vernon, Wash.	Charles W. Burns	J. N. Burdell
20	1927	Sept. 1-4	Portland, Ore.	Thomas Nicholson	J. N. Burdell
21	1928	Sept. 19-23	Los Angeles, Calif.	Charles W. Burns	J. N. Burdell

Appendix III

GENERAL CONFERENCE DELEGATES 1856-1964

OREGON ANNUAL CONFERENCE 1856-1884

Year	Delegates	Reserves	Lay Delegates	Reserves
1856	William Roberts Thos. H. Pearne	James H. Wilbur Alvan F. Waller		
1860	Francis F. Hoyt Alvan F. Waller	J. H. Wilbur H. K. Hines		
1864	J. H. Wilbur Thos. H. Pearne	C. S. Kingsley John Flinn		
1868	Gustavus Hines H. C. Benson	A. F. Waller		
1872	John F. DeVore C. C. Stratton	Nehemiah Doane H. K. Hines		
1876	Nehemiah Doane	I. Dillon		
1880	P. M. Starr	I. Dillon		
1884	A. C. Fairchild	T. F. Royal		

PUGET SOUND ANNUAL CONFERENCE—1928

Year	Delegates	Reserves	Lay Delegates	Reserves
1888	D. G. LeSourd	I. Dillon		
1892	A. J. Hanson	T. J. Massey		
1896	T. B. Ford T. J. Massey	S. S. Sulliger Geo. C. Wilding		
1900	Wilmont Whitfield S. S. Sulliger	D. G. LeSourd W. S. Harrington		
1904	E. M. Randall Jos. E. Williams W. S. Harrington	B. F. Brooks A. B. Chapin S. S. Sulliger		
1908	G. A. Landen B. F. Brooks E. M. Randall S. S. Sulliger	D. L. Rader W. S. Harrington G. L. Cuddy		
1912	J. P. Marlatt W. H. W. Reese Thos. E. Elliott G. A. Landen	E. M. Randall S. S. Sulliger C. E. Todd		
1916	A. W. Leonard E. H. Todd G. W. Frame E. M. Randall	J. M. Canse Robert C. Hartley	C. E. Beach F. A. Hazeltine Will D. Pratt Henry R. King	Mrs. E. B. McFall N. D. Pollom C. H. Bennett
1920	J. E. Crowther J. C. Harrison R. J. Reid D. R. Martin	E. H. Todd J. M. Canse	N. D. Pollom F. A. Hazeltine C. E. Beach A. S. Elford	
1924	R. C. Hartley G. W. Frame T. W. Lane E. H. Todd	J. E. Milligan E. M. Hill R. J. Reid	Dix H. Rowland F. A. Hazeltine Clint W. Lee E. B. McFall	Harry Brown W. D. Pratt L. L. Bush
1928	J. Ralph Magee E. M. Hill Andrew Warner G. W. Frame	R. J. Reid J. T. McQueen	Charles A. Robbins John R. Wilkinson	C. L. Vaughn W. P. Hopping P. M Snider

COLUMBIA RIVER ANNUAL CONFERENCE 1876-1928

Year	Delegates	Reserves	Lay Delegates	Reserves
1876	J. H. Wilbur	H. K. Hines	*Joseph L. Carter	
1880	D. G. Strong	H. K. Hines	*Jonas W. Brown	
1884	W. S. Turner	J. H. Wilbur	*Norman Buck	**Mrs. H. K. Hines
1888	J. H. Wilbur	W. S. Turner	Wm. Mitchell	J. L. Reser
1892	G. M. Booth H. I. Rasmus	D. G. Strong Henry Brown	J. B. Sargent H. J. Cozine	Mrs. L. G. Sullivan Mrs. D. G. Strong
1896	G. M. Booth W. W. Van Dusen	T. A. Towner V. C. Evers	I. C. Libby H. C. Clark	J. W. Peter S. C. Cosgrove
1900	Math. H. Marvin Henry Brown	M. S. Anderson John Uren	Wm. Warner Dr. G. W. Libby	E. R. Headley H. G. Stratton
1904	George M. Booth M. H. Marvin	C. E. Gibson Henry Brown	Elton Fulmer R. J. Ginn	Mrs. Minnie Warner John Sarginson
1908	U. F. Hawk Robert Warner M. H. Marvin	O. W. Mintzer Henry Brown	John Sarginson L. V. Wells D. H. Cox	Mrs. Emma Curtis Almon Baker
1912	C. O. Kimball Robert Warner C. E. Gibson Walton Skipworth	Henry Brown A. A. Luce U. F. Hawk	R. L. Brainard D. H. Cox S. E. Notson Mrs. Luella Smith	H. S. Brode J. L. Hughes J. F. Corner Jas. C. Cunningham
1916	B. E. Koontz Robert Brumblay Robert Warner U. F. Hawk	H. O. Perry O. W. Mintzer	D. H. Cox L. R. Horton F. L. Daggett B. F. Kumler	Nina G. Blake F. L. Brainard Ethel Butts
1920	H. O. Perry J. W. McDougall W. H. H. Forsythe Andrew Warner	W. E. Armfield Robert Warner	A. W. Rugg R. L. Brainard Edward Jeklin Fred Kemp	J. L. Hughes D. H. Cox
1924	Robert Brumblay N. M. Jones Robert Warner W. E. Armfield	C. C. Curry H. O. Perry	D. H. Cox I. R. Boyd H. M. Fried G. W. York	R. L. Brainard John Isenhart Chas. Chamberlain
1928	Charles E. Miller A. A. Callender T. W. Jeffrey	H. O. Perry F. N. Morton	F. L. Pickett Grant E. Hunt C. M. Holtzinger	Chas. Chamberlain Ira R. Boyd Chas. E. Berg

* No official record. Names supplied from other sources.
** Said to be first woman delegate ever elected to Methodist Episcopal Church.

PACIFIC NORTHWEST ANNUAL CONFERENCE 1932-

1932	J. Ralph Magee John G. Law H. O. Perry T. W. Jeffrey Andrew Warner Thos. Acheson J. M. Adams	F. A. LaViolette A. A. Callender C. W. MacCaughey	Rufus Woods John B. Hazen Hary L. Brown P. M. Snider Hugh C. Gruwell F. L. Pickett F. A. Hazeltine	Logan H. Roberts W. Wayne Smith C. A. Robbins
1936	F. A. LaViolette Charles MacCaughey John B. Magee Paul H. Ashby J. Edgar Purdy	H. O. Perry R. L. Sprague R. S. Dum	Joseph B. Hall W. Wayne Smith Ferman L. Pickett Chapin D. Foster Charles A. Robbins	Mrs. Rufus Woods Ray W. Haskins P. M. Snider
1940	Charles MacCaughey Wilbur M. Snyder Carl K. Mahoney F. L. Pedersen		Chapin D. Foster Chas. A. Robbins Mrs. Paul Sweet Clinton R. Crook	
	JURISDICTION Joseph M. Adams Stanley G. Logan Cyrus E. Albertson	Owen J. Beadles J. Edgar Purdy Wm. C. Bowman	JURISDICTION Dwight S. Jeffers Mrs. Grace Cooper Joseph B. Hall	S. F. Stephenson Heber M. Fried Olaf A. Wiggin

Year	Delegates	Reserves	Lay Delegates	Reserves
	Roy L. Sprague	J. G. Bringdale	Fred Levering	Grover P. Davis
	Ernest F. Harold	Paul H. Ashby	P. M. Snider	Mrs. J. Hawkins
	Norman McCay			
1944	C. K. Mahoney		Chapin D. Foster	
	Fred L. Pedersen		Charles A. Robbins	
	Lynn A. Wood		Mrs. D. J. Lawson	
	Walter S. Gleiser		G. Robert Huston	
	JURISDICTION		JURISDICTION	
	Roy L. Sprague	P. Malcom Hammond	Elwood Ball	Ed J. Fuller
	Willard E. Stanton	Joseph M. Adams	P. M. Snider	J. B. Hall
	Stanley G. Logan	Richard D. Decker	Mrs. Paul Sweet	Mrs. D. C. Smith
	Jas. Brett Kenna	Daniel E. Taylor	Mrs. J. K. Kilgore	John W. Webster
	J. Henry Ernst		Dwight S. Jeffers	
1948	Carl K. Mahoney		Ethel Sprague	
	Wm. C. Bowman		Charles A. Robbins	
	Harold E. Bashor		Harry Rymond	
	George Poor		John W. Webster	
	JURISDICTION		JURISDICTION	
	J. Henry Ernst	Elwin H. Scheyer	Chapin D. Foster	Mrs. E. Paul Todd
	Willard E. Stanton	Richard D. Decker	Mrs. Harry E. Smith	Edward J. Fuller
	Newton E. Moats	Daniel E. Taylor	Jos. C. Beckman	G. Robert Huston
	James E. Milligan	W. E. Callahan	Dwight S. Jeffers	Mrs. J. D. Kilgore
	R. F. Thompson		Mrs. G. M. Cooper	
	Walter S. Gleiser		P. M. Snider	
1952	Owen J. Beadles		Thomas C. Hall	
	J. Henry Ernst		Mrs. H. C. Christopher	
	Willard Stanton		William E. Sander	
	Cyrus E. Albertson		Dr. S. Stephenson	
	JURISDICTION		JURISDICTION	
	George Poor	Joseph H. Beall	Chapin D. Foster	Louis A. Vimont
	Elwin Scheyer	Howard Buck	Mrs. D. C. Smith	Don H. Phipps
	Cecil Ristow	Ernest F. Harold	Roy Lutz	Edward J. Fuller
	Harold Bashor	Noel LeRoque	Ronald E. DuFresne	C. L. Barker
	Richard Decker		Joseph C. Beckman	
	John B. Magee		Dr. C. C. Berkey	
1956	J. Henry Ernst		Mrs. Thos. Swayze	
	Cyrus Albertson		Lyle Truax	
	R. F. Thompson		John Radkey	
	Dan Taylor		Eugene Simmons	
	Clark J. Wood			
	Owen J. Beadles			
	JURISDICTION		JURISDICTION	
	Cecil Ristow	John C. Soltman	Mrs. Larry Grimes	Gordon Clinton
	Alden Graves	Elwin Scheyer	Louis Vimont	Melvin Wingard
	Melvin Finkbeiner	Harold Bashor	Walter Seaman	Herman Klindworth
	George L. Poor	Willard Stanton	Mrs. Ralph Perkins	J. H. Warren
			A. W. Campbell	
			Walter Clore	
1960	Melvin Finkbeiner		Mrs. Thos. Swayze	
	Cecil Ristow		Lyle Truax	
	J. Henry Ernst		Gordon Clinton	
	John C. Soltman		Mrs. R. K. Smith	
	George Poor		Al Holte	
	JURISDICTION		JURISDICTION	
	W. E. Callahan, Jr.	John Magee	Harold Griffith	Roy P. Moller
	Clark J. Wood	Cyrus Albertson	Louis Vimont	Robt. G. Leonard
	Owen J. Beadles		Eric Hawkinson	Mrs. Tom Young
	R. F. Thompson		Willard A. Zellmer	Kenneth J. Jacobson
	Jack M. Tuell		Lawrence Lowther	Robt. F. Lewis
	R. S. Proudfoot		Mrs. W. D. Dingle	
1964	J. Henry Ernst		Robert Thorpe	
	Jack Tuell		Mrs. John Eby	
	John C. Soltman		Lyle Truax	
	Cecil Ristow		Roy Moller	
	William Ritchie		Willard Zellmer	
	JURISDICTION		JURISDICTION	
	George Poor	Ac Wischmeier	Al Holte	Merril Stover
	William Callahan	Frank Brown	Frank Robson	Mervin Wingard
	Robert A. Uphoff	Lynn Corson	Gordon Clinton	Frances Swayze
	Melvin Finkbeiner	Reah Dougherty	Mrs. R. K. Smith	Bertha Hartsell
	R. F. Thompson	Joe Walker	Mrs. Frank Little	Frank Coates
		Clark J. Wood	Donald Phipps	

Appendix IV

PRESIDING ELDERS AND DISTRICT SUPERINTENDENTS
With Districts and Years Served
1853-1964

Benjamin Close, Puget Sound Mission, 1853.
Thomas H. Pearne, Wallamet, 1853.
A. F. Waller, Columbia River, 1854.
William Roberts, Puget Sound Mission, 1854; 1863-65; Idaho Mission, 1867-70.
Gustavus Hines, Columbia River, 1855-58.
John F. DeVore, Puget Sound, 1855-58; 1870-73; Olympia, 1886.
James Harvey Wilbur, Columbia River, 1859; Walla Walla, 1860; Yakima Indian Mission
    District, 1867-75; The Dalles District, 1877-78; Pendleton, 1884.
Nehemiah Doane, Puget Sound, 1859-62.
Isaac Dillon, Wallamet, 1860-61; Walla Walla, 1866-67.
S. S. Kingsley, Wallamet, 1861-62.
John Flinn, Walla Walla, 1861-64.
C. G. Belknap, Puget Sound, 1863-65.
W. S. Lewis, Walla Walla, 1865.
Harvey K. Hines, Puget Sound, 1866-69; Walla Walla, 1870-73.
J. B. Calloway, Walla Walla, 1868-69.
Hugh Caldwell, The Dalles, 1873-76.
L. T. Woodward, Puget Sound, 1874-75.
S. G. Havermale, Walla Walla, 1874-76.
A. C. Fairchild, Puget Sound, 1875-78.
D. G. Strong, Walla Walla, 1877-80; Lewiston, 1886; Walla Walla, 1887-91.
L. J. Whitcomb, The Dalles, 1879-80.
Albert Atwood, Puget Sound, 1879-82.
W. S. Turner, Walla Walla, 1881-84.
G. C. Roe, The Dalles, 1881-83.
M. S. Anderson, Spokane, 1883-85.
D. G. LeSourd, Puget Sound, 1883; Seattle, 1884-86; Whatcom, 1890-92.
Frederick Bonn, German, 1883.
A. J. Hanson, Olympia, 1884-85; Vancouver, 1889-92.
Stephen Gascoigne, The Dalles, 1884-86.
Levi Tarr, Walla Walla, 1885.
N. E. Parsons, Walla Walla, 1886; Spokane, 1887-89.
H. D. Brown, Olympia, 1887-89.
T. J. Massey, Seattle, 1887; New Whatcom, 1893-95.
G. M. Booth, The Dalles, 1887-91; Columbia River, 1892-1900; The Dalles, 1902-05.
W. H. Drake, Seattle, 1888-90.
W. C. Gray, Columbia River, 1889.
Henry Rasmus, Spokane, 1890-91.
F. R. Spaulding, The Dalles, 1890.
Samuel Moore, Tacoma, 1890-94.
Olaff E. Olander, Swedish, 1890-92.
T. B. Ford, Seattle, 1891-95.
R. C. Moter, The Dalles, 1891-95.
W. W. Van Dusen, Spokane, 1892-97.
T. A. Towner, Walla Walla, 1892-97.
Spencer S. Sulliger, Vancouver, 1893-94; Chehalis, 1895; Olympia, 1896-98; Whatcom,
    1902-04; Bellingham, 1905-07: Vancouver, 1908-13; Tacoma, 1914-16.
Andrew J. Joslyn, Tacoma, 1895-1900.
Wilmont Whitfield, Seattle, 1895-1901.
John Johnson, Swedish, 1896-1901.
Robert Warner, The Dalles, 1896-1901.

C. E. Gibson, Moscow, 1898-99; Walla Walla, 1900-1905; Spokane, 1910-15.
Henry Brown, Spokane, 1898-1904.
Matthew H. Marvin, Walla Walla, 1898-1901.
J. E. Williams, Chehalis, 1899-1903.
W. S. Harrington, New Whatcom, 1899-1901; Seattle, 1902-1907.
O. W. Mintzer, Republic Mission, 1902-07; Upper Columbia, 1908-10.
B. F. Brooks, Tacoma, 1901-06.
John Ovall, Swedish, 1902-04.
George A. Landen, Centralia, 1904-07; Bellingham, 1908-13; Seattle, 1914-23.
U. F. Hawk, Spokane, 1905-09; 1916-20; Walla Walla, 1921-23.
Walton Skipwôrth, The Dalles, 1905-10.
Gabriel Sykes, Walla Walla, 1905-10.
Andrew Farrell, Swedish, 1905-06.
F. S. Pearson, Port Townsend, 1907; Olympia, 1908-09.
D. C. Franklin, Tacoma, 1907-08.
A. A. Luce, Coeur d'Alene, 1908-10.
J. P. Marlatt, Seattle, 1908-13.
Thomas E. Elliott, Tacoma, 1909-13; Vancouver, 1914-18.
Charles E. Todd, Olympia, 1910-15.
Bracken E. Koontz, Coeur d'Alene, 1911-15.
C. A. Hodshire, Columbia, 1911-12.
Harold O. Perry, The Dalles, 1911-16; Tacoma, 1929-31; Seattle-Tacoma, 1932-34.
Andrew Warner, Walla Walla, 1911-16; Tacoma, 1924-28.
Robert Brumblay, Wenatchee, 1913-18; Spokane, 1929-34.
J. M. Canse, Bellingham, 1914-20.
Jabez C. Harrison, Olympia, 1916-19.
D. Roland Martin, Tacoma, 1917-23.
Charles MacCaughey, Moscow, 1917-21; Puget Sound, 1936; Seattle-Tacoma, 1937-41.
H. F. Pemberton, The Dalles, 1917-21; Puget Sound, 1930-35.
N. M. Jones, Walla Walla, 1917-20; Spokane, 1921-23.
J. W. Caughlan, Wenatchee, 1919-21.
J. T. McQueen, Alaska, 1919-20; Vancouver, 1924-29.
Everett M. Hill, Vancouver, 1919-23.
George W. Frame, Bellingham, 1921-26.
C. C. Curry, Wenatchee, 1921-24.
W. H. H. Forsythe, Moscow, 1922-26.
Charles E. Miller, Moscow, 1924-26; Walla Walla, 1927-29.
Robert Elmer Smith, Spokane, 1924-27; Spokane and Northern, 1928.
Byron H. Wilson, Seattle, 1924-28.
A. A. Calender, Wenatchee, 1925-26; Western, 1927-28; Columbia River, 1929-30.
Robert J. Reid, Bellingham, 1927-28; Puget Sound, 1929.
Francis Ahnlund, Swedish, 1928-30.
J. Ralph Magee, Seattle, 1929-31.
Henry Young, Alaska, 1929.
Edward A. Wolfe, Vancouver, 1930-32.
Paul H. Ashby, Walla Walla, 1930-34; Spokane, 1935-37.
J. N. Burdell, Swedish, 1931.
Walter Torbet, Alaska, 1932-39.
Roy L. Sprague, Vancouver, 1933-36.
C. K. Mahoney, Seattle-Tacoma, 1935-36; 1942-47.
Joseph M. Adams, Walla Walla, 1935-40.
Stanley G. Logan, Puget Sound, 1937-42.
Ernest F. Harold, Vancouver, 1937; Spokane, 1938-40; Puget Sound, 1949-54.
Norman McCay, Vancouver, 1938-43.
Walter S. Gleiser, Spokane, 1941-45.
Frederick L. Pedersen, Walla Walla, 1941-46.
James E. Milligan, Puget Sound, 1943-48.
William C. Bowman, Vancouver, 1944-49.
Harold E. Bashor, Spokane, 1946-51; Puget Sound, 1955-60.
Joseph H. Beall, Walla Walla, 1947-52.
Owen J. Beadles, Seattle-Tacoma, 1948-53.

Willard E. Stanton, Vancouver, 1950-54.
Richard D. Decker, Spokane, 1952-57.
Daniel E. Taylor, Columbia River, 1953-56.
Alden R. Graves, Walla Walla, 1953-58.
Clark J. Wood, Seattle-Tacoma, 1954-59.
Melvin M. Finkbeiner, Vancouver, 1955-59.
William E. Callahan, Jr., Columbia River, 1957-62.
A. Maurice Chamberlin, Spokane, 1958-60.
Raymond S. Proudfoot, Tacoma, 1958-60.
Ac Chester Wischmeier, Walla Walla, 1959-60; Tacoma, 1960-64.
Robert A. Uphoff, Seattle, 1960.
W. Clyde Beecher, Vancouver, 1960—
Jack M. Tuell, Puget Sound, 1961—
J. Henry Ernst, Seattle, 1961—
Cecil F. Ristow, Spokane, 1961—
William H. Ritchey, Walla Walla, 1961—
Troy M. Strong, Columbia River, 1963—
Joe A. Harding, Seattle, 1965—
G. Richard Tuttle, Tacoma, 1965—

PRESIDING ELDERS AND DISTRICT SUPERINTENDENTS OF GERMAN CONFERENCES

George Hartung, Spokane, 1891-92; 1899-1900. Conf. Supt. 1900-03.
F. C. Bauer, Portland, 1894.
M. A. Dehuff, Spokane, 1894.
F. C. Jahn, Tacoma, 1894.
C. A. Priesing, Portland, 1898; 1905-06.
H. F. Lange, Spokane, 1898; 1904.
F. H. Lucke, Spokane, 1906-09.
Joseph Hepp, Portland, 1907-10.
A. J. Weigle, Spokane, 1910; Oregon 1921-22.
E. E. Hertzler, Pacific, 1912-16.
L. Gaiser, Pacific, 1917.
A. F. Hilmer, Pacific, 1918-23; Washington Dist. 1921-22.
A. F. Cramer, Pacific, 1924-28.

DISTRICT SUPERINTENDENTS OF PACIFIC SWEDISH MISSION CONFERENCE

Andrew Farrell, Washington District, 1908-09.
G. E. Kallstedt, Conference Supt. 1910-11.
J. O. Wahlberg, Conference Superintendent, 1912-16.
Anthony E. Lind, Washington District, 1917-20.
O. F. Linstrum, Pacific District, 1921-22. Conference Supt., 1923-24.
Francis Ahnlund, Northwest District, 1925-27; Swedish District Puget Sound Conference, 1928-30.

Appendix V

LIST OF MINISTERS WHO SERVED IN CONFERENCE
A. Conference Members
B. Supplies

CONFERENCE MEMBERS WHO SERVED IN WASHINGTON AND NORTHERN IDAHO

Aaasen, David L., 1957—
Abbott, George R., 1910-15 ; '19-'36
Abegglin, Walter, 1915
Acheson, Thomas, 1928-32 ; 1944-'51
Adam, Oscar M., 1948—
Adams, Charles C., 1954
Adams, J. H., 1870
Adams, James, 1956
Adams, Joseph M., 1913-46
Ahnlund, Francis, 1919-52
Ailward, F., 1884-87
Airheart, Walter L., 1908-16 ; '18-'21
Aiton, Alexander P., 1938-54
Aiton, Clinton A., 1950—
Albert, David J., 1893-95
Albertson, C. Gene, 1941-53
Albertson, Cyrus E., 1937-41 ; '49-'64
Albertson, James T., 1939—
Albertson, Robert G., 1952—
Albright, Ernest L., 1917-20
Albright, Henry, 1918-34
Alden, Leon Leslie, 1963—
Alden, Lloyd N., 1939—
Alderson, Christopher, 1858-60
Aleridge, M. C., 1892-93
Alford, Eugene C., 1891-98
Allen, F. T., 1902
Allen, Harry L., 1909-10 ; 1921-55
Allen, Robert H., 1922-51
Allen, T. F., 1903-13
Allen, W. A., 1921-23
Alling, Horatio, 1891-93
Allyn, J. H., 1866-89
Almon, David K., 1951—
Almond, George, 1939—
Altes, Edward F., Jr., 1961—
Andersen, H. Ernest*
Anderson, Andrew, 1884-16
Anderson, C. A., 1893-95
Anderson, Greabert*
Anderson, Hans E., 1915-51
Anderson, J. A., 1900-07
Anderson, J. S., 1913-16
Anderson, J. S.*
Anderson, John A., 1892-07
Anderson, John S., D.D., 1896-15
Anderson, Lewis N. B., 1883-'92, 1904-21
Anderson, Martin L., 1906-54
Anderson, Milton S., 1876-26
Anderson, O. R., 1906-18
Anderson, Paul B. L., 1957—
Anderson, Rudolph A., 1934—
Anderson, Virgil A., 1960-63
Anderson, W. S., 1882-83
Anderson, Willard B., 1908-19
Andrews, C. I., 1919-24
Andrews, Milton P., Jr., 1955—

Andrews, O. M., 1923-26
Andrews, William F., 1951—
Anthony, Oswald L., 1927-55
Arima, Sumikiyo, 1910
Armand, Jesse P., 1929—
Armfield, Wm. E., 1898-1925
Arms, M. Wesley, 1963—
Armstrong, Andrew J., 1915—
Armstrong, Clyde, 1963—
Armstrong, R. A., 1903-20
Arney, George, 1894-46
Aschenbrenner, A. J., 1928 ; 1949-'59
Ash, G. O., 1883-84
Ashbrook, Paul F., 1960—
Ashby, Paul H., 1909—
Ashby, Philip H., 1936-43
Askey, E. N., 1911-23
Asp, Waldo Bertram, 1962—
Atkins, Robert A., 1890-97
Atkinson, T. W., 1887-93
Attebery, E. Ray, 1920-44
Attenborough, Henry, 1911-48
Atwood, Albert, 1883-27
Austin, Samuel H., 1932-40
Avery, J. H., 1907-55
Avison, R. N., 1920-21
Ayers, Albert E., 1912-14

Babbidge, C. C., 1904-08
Babcock, Donald C., 1909-11
Bachman, Clyde P., 1958—
Baer, Arthur C., 1920-21
Bagley, Alvin W., 1897-02
Bagley, Daniel, 1862-05
Bailey, Floyd S., 1935
Baker, Edward, 1891, 1899, 1904-'58
Baker, S. A.,* M. P.
Baker, Wm. H., 1909-29
Baldwin, C. H., 1910-11
Baldwin, Donald W., 1942-50 ; 1951—
Baldwin, Fred L., 1910-30
Baldwin, Wilbur J., 1904-07
Ball, John R., 1903-13
Ball, W. B., 1909
Banks, L. A., 1884-87
Barber, Edward, Died 1914. M.E.S.
Barber, Ernest, 1924-'37 ; 1939—
Bargar, W. J., 1890-94
Barker, John P., 1894-1910
Barnhart, George W., 1894-98
Barrett, R., 1877-16
Bartholomew, W., 1882
Bartlett, P. E., 1903-46
Barton, N. G. B., 1897-02
Bashor, Harold E., 1921—
Bass, Harold J., 1939-55
Bassett, Wilfred C., 1914
Batcheller, W. W., 1905-13
Bates, Ernest J., 1907-29

Batschler, Thomas G., 1927-34
Bauman, A., 1909-15
Baxter, J. M., 1890-97
Beach, John C., 1905-08
Beach, King D., 1935-37
Beadles, David O., 1953-57
Beadles, Owen J., 1920-43 ; 1948—
Beal, Carl B., 1959—
Beall, Joseph H., 1919-53 ; 1956—
Beans, W. K., 1898
Beattie, David G., 1920-23
Beatty, Jarrett I., 1919-26
Beatty, Wm. T., 1922—
Beck, George W., 1912, Meth. Prot.
Beck, John A., 1910-18 ; 1926-28
Beckley, J. W., 1892 ; 1899-01 ; 1903
Beckman, Elmer E., 1933-'48 ; 1956—
Beecher, W. Clyde, 1955
Beeman, Paul J., 1961—
Beightol, H. L., 1898-40
Belknap, C. G., 1965-66
Bell, J. S., 1903-53
Bell, R. Kenneth, 1941-58
Bell, Walter B., 1905-14
Benadom, Wilfred O., 1887-52
Benedict, Daniel E., 1961—
Benedict, E. L., 1903-18
Benjamin, Rial, 1896-08
Bennet, A. G., 1922-29 ; 1936-51
Bennett, C. F., 1898-16
Bennett, Dwight G., 1921-46
Bennett, Geo. H., 1924-44
Bennett, James R., 1963—
Bennett, V. Ray, 1900-05
Benninger, S. S., 1911
Bent, Percy C., 1950—
Benton, Joel R., 1926-28
Berg, Darrell, 1951-60
Berg, George K., 1959-61
Bergan, Erling, 1924—
Berglund, Knute O., 1893-53
Bergman, E. E., 1910-18
Berney, William G., 1952—
Berringer, J. H., 1907-56
Berry, Geo. M., 1855-60
Berryman, Geo. E., 1926-33
Best, Horace W., 1921-24
Betts, Fred H., 1934-37
Betts, Will A., 1911-14
Biering, Paul, 1961—
Bigham, Elmer, 1964—
Biles, David W., 1961—
Bird, J. D., 1909-45
Bird, Matthew, 1888
Bisbee, R. E., 1884-92
Bisbee, Royal D., 1909-14
Bishop, W. E., 1945
Black, Harold W., 1947-48; 1954—

395

Black, Oliver W., 1924-40
Blackledge, L. Wayne, 1960-63
Blackwell, J. W., 1908
Blaine, David E., 1853-'66; 1884-00
Blair, Chester C., 1925—
Blaisdell, T. L., 1923-62
Blanpied, Charles, 1909-15
Blanton, Raymond H., 1948-60
Bleakley, W. S. J., 1957—
Bluett, James W., 1882-91
Bobbitt, Marion Douglas, 1963—
Bolick, Ralph, 1937-53
Bolin, C. M., 1909-14
Bond, L. Wayne, 1954-60
Bone, R. W., 1911-13
Bonn, Frederick, 1883-84
Booth, George Minor, 1882-05
Booth, R., 1870
Boothby, F. F., 1923-49
Bostrom, J., 1924-26
Botts, Charles E., 1900-01
Bowen, Arthur J., 1897
Bowen, Charles A., 1909-29
Bowen, Ira P., 1910-11
Bower, Edward, 1899-11
Bowers, Gerald, 1964
Bowman, William C., 1918-33; 1949-50
Bowser, Wellington, 1889-38
Boyd, Carl Richard, 1954—
Boylan, F. G., 1907-18
Brace, E. E., 1919-28
Brackenbury, A. C., 1899
Bradley, Geo. W., 1911-14
Bradley, W. F., 1906
Bradshaw, B. V., 1914
Bramble, L., Died 1912, M.E.S.
Branham, H. M. Died 1930, M.E.S.
Braun, David, 1961
Brentlinger, Bill L., 1958
Brewster, Bernard C., 1921-23
Bright, S. A., 1890-96
Bringdale, J. G., 1925-58
Brittain, Alfred Arthur, 1908-17
Britts, John H., 1887-04
Brizee, Robert, 1964
Broad, Thos., 1898
Brokaw, Sanford P., 1880-35
Bronson, E. V., 1909-21
Brooke, Bruce, 1964
Brooks, Benjamin F., 1884-34
Brown, Arthur W., 1898—
Brown, Benjamin F., 1905-21
Brown, C. J., 1891-94
Brown, Claude A., 1941-49
Brown, Frank E., 1954—
Brown, Fred R., 1909-10
Brown, H. D., 1887-92
Brown, Harrison D., 1896-05
Brown, Henry, 1885-31
Brown, M. R., 1891-20
Brown, Ralph W. D., 1925-45
Brugger, John G., 1922-29
Brumblay, Robert, 1907-43
Bruner, A. B., 1885-86
Bryan, Calvin H., 1917-22
Bryan, M. C., 1881-85
Buchanan, John E., 1959
Buchholz, F. W., 1886-88; 1891-93; 1899-1900; 1902-03; 1905
Buck, Howard P., 1936
Buck, Sylvester J., 1898-05
Buckner, N. S., 1892-94
Buehler, Adam, 1884-86; 1891-93; 1902-14
Bundy, T. Walter, 1916-18; 1924—
Burcham, James T., 1962—
Burdell, Joseph N., 1903-08; 1928-32
Burdette, Laurence A., 1955—

Burger, H. T., 1891
Burgoyne, W. Sherman, 1947-48
Burk, Loyd L., 1916-33
Burkhart, Roger Samuel, 1963
Burkholder, H. C., 1923
Burleson, John K., 1957
Burnett, James P., 1960-62
Burns, J. W., 1908-10
Burrill, Sanford L., 1875-79; 1895-09
Burris, C. A., 1916-49
Burrows, A. Edwin, 1899-03
Busching, Howard C., 1944-46
Bushong, James W., 1896-97
Butler, Frank, 1889-96
Butler, John R., 1927-61
Butler, Ralph H. R., 1942—
Butler, T. W., 1888-94
Buzzell, Frank L., 1889-98
Byars, W. Nesbett, 1914-20
Byrd, J. C., M.P., 1937-38

Cain, J. D., 1912-17
Caldwell, H., 1873
Caldwell, Jack L., 1957-62
Calkins, Robert G., 1954-61
Callahan, James, 1905-25
Callahan, Wm. E., Jr., 1927—
Callander, Asa A., 1909-37
Calloway, J. B., 1868-70
Cameron, D. W., 1883-03
Camp, F. W. P., 1911-26
Campbell, Arthur D., 1950—
Campbell, D. D., 1888-90
Campbell, Gilbert E., 1898
Campbell, L. Marshall, 1949—
Campbell, Paul R., 1925—
Canfield, F. M., 1920-38, M.E.S.
Canse, John M., 1907-54
Carithers, W. B., 1884-03
Carleton, L. W., died 1929, M.E.S.
Carli, Pete A., 1926-31
Carpenter, John L., 1901-12
Carr, Gabriel Paul, Jr., 1961-63
Carr, R. W., 1906
Carr, William Wallace, 1904-06
Carrick, J. G., 1914-33
Carroll, L. C., 1919-21
Carson, Charles M., 1905-29
Carter, Alfred W., 1943-45; 1948—
Carter, Duane E., 1906-61
Carter, J. H., 1902-47
Case, Edwin Max, 1962
Casey, M. A., 1905-10
Cast, F. J., 1907-08
Caughlan, John W., 1911—
Cecil, John K., 1912-30
Cederberg, Chas. A., 1912-14; 1928-38
Chamberlain, A. Morris, 1954-61
Chamberlain, Fred H., 1895-02
Chambers, L. Morgan, 1922-24
Chambers, W. E., 1912-14
Chan, Hon Fan, 1885-86
Chandler, Perry, 1891-23
Chaney, S. J., 1928-30
Chapin, Austin B., 1899-06
Chapin, E. B., 1902
Chapin, Russell, 1963—
Chapman, Joseph A., 1904-08
Chapman, W. T., 1871-75
Chappel, E. S., 1910-46
Chappell, Harry E., 1910-16
Chatterton, Harry, 1951-57
Chattin, W. C., 1867 and 1881
Cheleden, Algerdas, N., 1929-32
Chaney, S. J., 1929-35
Cherrington, F. B., 1890-94
Chester, Joseph, 1934-45; 1948-55
Chiles, Van Camp, 1965

Christensen, Andrew*
Clapp, Phillip S., 1928-34
Clark, A. W., 1924-27
Clark, D. L., 1923
Clark, F. M., 1903-08
Clark, Herbert C., 1898-21
Clark, R. S., died 1915, M.E.S.
Clark, Rolla C., 1913-22
Clark, Thomas, 1896-99, M.E.S.
Clark, W. C., died 1911, M.E.S.
Clarke, David L., 1910-29
Clarke, Wm. F., 1892-96
Clay, Russell, 1921-25
Claypool, Ernest V., 1891-98
Clayton, Henry, 1904-11, M.P.
Clayton, John, 1915-17
Clemens, B. G., 1920-43
Cloflin, E., 1884
Close, Benjamin, 1853-54
Clulow, James E., 1903-22
Coan, John B., 1943-64
Coates, Harry, 1939—
Cobb, J. B., 1940
Coberly, Charles S., 1902-05; M.E.S.
Cochran, L. G., 1899-00
Coffey, Geo., 1873
Cole, Charles G., 1943—
Coleman, Herbert T., 1897-00
Compton, J. W., died 1913, M.E.S.
Cone, Wendell J., 1939—
Conklin, Peter, 1905-07
Conner, Edward J., 1910-16; 1923-28, M.E.S.
Conrad, Carl J., 1956
Constien, W. W., 1912-13
Cook, Chas. C., 1892-97
Cook, Claude T., 1901-09
Cook, Frederick L., 1916-32
Cook, John F., 1905-41
Cool, Peter A., 1897
Cooper, Earl P., 1965
Cooper, George W., 1921-60
Cooper, Harvey O., 1913-18
Cooper, Kenneth L., 1948-50
Corn, E. C., 1913-26
Corner, Ivan H., Sr., 1953
Corson, Lynn H., 1961—
Cosper, William I., 1871-97
Cotten, Truman H., 1951—
Cotton, Earl B., 1952-56
Cottrell, Clark, 1912-53
Coulter, Joseph H., 1946-50
Countryman, Kenneth W., 1938—
Covington, Luther J., 1890-35
Covington, Melmoth A., 1891-31
Cowdrick, Harold G., 1945-56
Cowdy, Claude H., 1906-50
Cowell, Wm. I., 1906-12
Cox, Clay C., 1894-96
Cox, Wm. E., 1905-62
Craig, J. W., died 1933, M.E.S.
Craig, Stephen M., 1913-15
Cramer, A. F., 1912; 1917; 1919-27
Cramer, Donald G., 1960
Crawford, A. K., 1883-86
Crawford, James D., 1952—
Creel, H. B., 1898-00
Creesy, Charles L., 1905-07; 1915-65
Crenshaw, J. M., 1910-14
Cribb, Harold L., 1962—
Cromwell, Howard P., 1898-01
Cronkhite, Floyd E., 1955-60
Crooke, Chas. W., 1903-05
Crooks, Ira L., 1907-13
Cross, Benjamin P., 1913
Cross, H. P., 1913-15
Cross, Henry R., 1928—
Crowder, U. S., 1914-20

Crowther, James E., 1916-21; 1923-29
Crumley, J. Askew, 1957-57
Cuddy, George L., 1891-29
Culmer, C. C., 1887-92
Cummings, George A., 1950—
Cummins, Robert A., 1910-20
Cunningham, Albert B., 1919-23
Cunningham, Chas. E., 1890-99
Cupp, Harry T., 1956-58
Curry, Caleb C., 1907-30
Curry, G. L., before 1911. M. P.
Curry, Osborne A., 1894-95
Curtis, Chesley E., 1911-12
Curtis, G., died 1873, M.E.S.

Daba, Pio J., 1952-53
Dabritz, Robert E., 1950-56; 1958—
Dahlgren, Lewis, 1888-91
Dahlin, P. N., 1928-29
Dailey, Squire, 1900
Danford, Samuel A., 1928-37
Daniel, Will M., 1913-51
Daniel, William, 1896-01
Daniels, J. E., 1899-12
Dann, William G. R., 1911—
Darcy, James B., 1964
Darrow, Chas. W., 1891-14
Davenport, Charles R., 1954
Davidson, Eric A., 1891-94
Davies, Percy H., 1921-22
Davies, S. W., died 1899. M.E.S.
Davis, Ben H., 1953—
Davis, Clark D.,* M.P.
Davis, E. G., 1888-91
Davis, H. Copley, 1936-38
Davis,* L. A. died 1921, M.E.S.
Davis, Merritt C., 1903-12
Davis, Sprague, 1888-95
Davis, Walter M., 1909
Day, G. W., 1877-79
Day, George M., 1909-17
Day, Murlin W., 1946-48
Dean, Earl L., 1947—
Deardorff, J. G., 1866-69
DeBolt, W. W., 1944-56
Decker, Edwin G., 1913-17
Decker, Richard D., 1913—
Dehuff, M. A., 1902-03
Dell, Charles D., 1897-02
DeLong, Dow, 1917-42
Demoy, Abraham, 1898-02
Dennison, J. N., 1871-92
Dennison, James M., 1892-31
Denny, C. T., 1911
DePartee, J. N., 1910
Derby, Alfred E., 1914-26
Derrick, Columbus, 1884-86
DeVore, John F., 1853-89
DeVries, Harvey M., 1955—
DeWeese, William, 1887-33
Dews, Walter M., 1905-44
De Yoe, J. Willard, 1924-25
Dibble, J. Robert, 1958
Dill, John H., 1909-26
Dill, R. A., 1883-84
Dillon, Isaac, 1877-02
Dills, John Henderson, 1903-06; 1912-17; 1924-34. M.E.S.
Dimick, Geo. D., 1895-59
Dixon, Harold E., 1939-51
Doak, James E., 1950—
Doane, Nehemiah, 1860-84
Doane, Orville L., 1895-04
Dobbs, J. W., 1884-88
Dobson, John M., 1898-02
Dodd, Elmer L., 1908-09
Dodds, Marcus, 1921
Dodsworth, Marmaduke, 1916-21; 1942-47; 1953-65
Dorwin, Jay C., 1907-37

Doty, Lloyd A., 1938—
Dougherty, Reah S., 1949—
Douglas, James S., 1859-65
Downs, T. H., 1903-07
Drake, Francis E., 1889-17
Drake, F. G., 1901-07
Drake, Walter H., 1887-05
Driver, Henry W., 1911-14; 1923-50
Driver, Samuel M., 1879-92
Dudley, E., 1879
Duff, C. A., 1914
Dum, Ray S., 1931-37
same as Ray S. Dunn
Dunkelberger, Kenneth H., 1934-45
Dunlap, R. E., 1923-26
Dunlap, R. V. B., 1905-54
Dupertius, Sam, 1905-18
Durbahn, J., 1904-05; 1907-08
Dyer, Theodore L., 1891-13

Eads, Abram, 1874-06
Eakin, W. B., 1887-57
Earl, Robert R., 1898-09
Earle, Harry G., 1916-24
Easton, Charles, 1909-13
Eaton, Manson M., 1916-33
Ebright, Donald F., 1958—
Eccles, Robert S., 1942-51
Echelbarger, Charles Kent, 1960—
Ecker, Francis A., 1905-37
Eddings, Lawrence, 1965
Edwards, J. R., 1893-04
Ekaas, Karl N., 1929—
Eklund, Abel, 1916-18
Elayer, E. W., 1903-05
Elder, Joshua, 1854
Elder, Martin P., 1907-13
Eldridge, Wm. S., 1904
Ellefsen, P. M.*
Ellington, J. J., 1935—
Ellington, William D., 1955—
Elliott, F., 1865
Elliott, Robert E., 1947-56
Elliott, Thos. E., 1893-01; 1903-20
Ellsworth, D. M., 1891-17
Elrey, Charles H., 1898-10
Elvigen, H.*
Elworthy, Henry B., 1902-46
Emery, T. W., 1917-37
Emmel, Henry B., 1911-20
Engebretsen, Frederick, 1928-29
Engle, David West, 1959-61
Ensley, Milton, Jr., 1959-60
Enslow, Fred A., 1906-07
Erickson, E. W., 1903-48
Ericson, Rudolph, 1919-22
Eriksen, Carl*
Erikson, Karl, 1886-89
Ernst, Ed. G., 1937-42
Ernst, J. Henry, 1928—
Eskildsen, Ludvig, 1952—
Esslinger, William, 1883-84
Estabrook, C. M., 1938—
Euster, William, 1890-96; 1902-09
Eva, James, 1886-89
Evans, John, 1894-52
Evans, N., 1893-22
Evans, W. C., 1900-40
Everett, G. W., 1908
Everett, James H., 1899-01
Evers, Volney C., 1889-19
Ewing, Seldon H., 1906-24

Fahs, Rolando Z., 1888-23
Fairchild, A. C., 1862-63; 1867-68; 1870-73; 1875-79
Falk, Erik Gusley, 1898-05
Fallis, George V., 1917-24

Fancher, W. M., died 1897, M.E.S.
Farmer, Mack, 1950-57; 1963—
Farrell, A., 1883-30
Faulkner, Merritt W., 1944—
Faulkner, O. E., 1913-25; 1946-58
Feak, Jacob, 1887-25
Feese, G. H., 1890-97
Ferguson, G. G., 1883-03
Ferris, Charles, 1889
Fertig, Noah Ellis, 1905-06
Fertig, Thomas H., 1892-33
Field, J. J.*
Field, O. T., 1900-40
Fife, Donald M., 1943—
Filbert, Everette M., 1926—
Finch, Roy R., 1951-56
Finkbeiner, Chester, 1934—
Finkbeiner, James, 1964—
Finkbeiner, John, Jr., 1938-45
Finkbeiner, Melvin M., 1948—
Finkbeiner, Raymond R., 1927; 1942-50
Finlayson, Bruce, 1947
Finley, F. E., 1911-12
Finney, John M., Jr., 1938
Fisher, Charles W., 1943-61
Fisher, Donald Clive, 1962—
Fleenor, Henry C., 1890-91
Flenner, J. D., 1877-85
Flenner, L. Warner, 1924-26
Flesher, John W. 1897-12
Fletcher, Albert E., 1924
Flinn, John, 1862-06
Flood, James R., 1924-26
Flowers, F. W.* died 1907, M.E.S.
Flynn, John N., 1962—
Foley, W. B., 1928-31
Forbes, William Garrett, 1906-09; 1916-17; 1927-29, M.E.S.
Forch, Adam S., Sr., 1951
Ford, Charles, 1890-95
Ford, Eugene, 1950-59
Ford, T. B., 1890-96; 1909-12
Ford, W. T., 1894-98
Foreman, Bruce E., 1959—
Foreman, John P., 1965
Forsberg, Clarence J., 1953-57
Forsberg, Donald G., 1958—
Forster, Fletcher, 1952—
Forsyth, W. H. H., 1905-51
Forsythe, W. M., 1921-30
Fox, E. S., 1909-16
Fox, Fred E., 1955—
Fox, James, 1964
Frame, George W., 1895-46
Franklin, DeWitt C., 1906-29
Franklin, W. J., 1857
Frederick, Arthur L., 1943—
Freeman, Carl O., 1895-98
Freeman, John B., 1952—
Freeman, Mark, 1928-59
Frescoln, John W., 1901-14
Frisbie, F. F., 1913-22
Fry, W. H., 1899-10
Fujimura, Shiroku, 1930
Fulkerson, E. Robert, 1908-41
Fuller, Enos H., 1891-01
Fulmer, Chas. Ellis, 1891-48
Fulmer, W. Paul, 1937—
Fysh, Richard, 1885-87

Gable, Geo., 1899-05
Gailey, Ralph A., 1899-22; 1924-58
Gaiser, Ludwig, 1898-01; 1904-17; 1919-20
Galbraith, B. N., 1902-61
Gallaher, Byron C., 1917-60
Gallaher, Morgan R., 1913-54
Gambill, Thos. J., 1903-11; 1917-29

Gamble, W. J., 1912
Ganaway, W. H., 1898-00
Gardner, Harry E., 1914-28; 1932—
Gardner, Paul, 1909
Garland, Charles R., 1927-29
Garner, Kenneth A., 1959
Garrett, O. James, 1956—
Garrison, Charles H., 1964
Garver, J. E., 1912-24
Garver, L. J., 1886-87
Gascoigne, Stephen, 1881-95
Gates, E. H., 1913
Gates, Ernest F., 1954-56
Gaylor, Henry W., Jr., 1954-56
Gebert, Edward H., 1914-33
Geisler, Charles W., 1905-48
Gellerman, A. B. L., 1901-08
Gelvin, Harry E., 1913-15
Geoghegan, John H., 1911-30
George, David E., 1879-24
George, George P., 1943-63
George, W. P., 1891-95
Getty, William J., 1907-09
Getzendaner, J. Wm., 1922-23
Gibbs, George Harold, 1889-92; 1894-01; 1917-18; 1921-27. M.E.S.
Gibson, C. E., 1887-33
Gibson, John F., 1919-25
Giesey, Earl M., 1912-22
Gift, L., 1868
Gilbert, Cyrus L., 1905-11
Gilbert, Levi, 1890-92
Gill, J. M.,* M.P. 1910-15
Gill, Oliver J., 1951
Gillespie, W. G., 1912-14
Gillett, Frank R., 1908-18; '21-'51
Gilmer, Karl R., 1908-25
Givler, H. V., 1899-02
Gjerding, E. B., 1905
Glasgow, R. L.,* died 1922 M.E.S.
Glass, Robert C., 1899-15
Glasscock, Laird V., 1937—
Gleiser, Walter S., 1914-22, 1937
Glenk, J. Wesley, 1899-56
Goddard, W. H., 1859
Golding, William E., 1887-88
Gonzalo, Dionicio F., 1953—
Goodell, Ira M., 1891-97
Gooding, James G., 1906-07
Goodnough, Frank E., 1929—
Goodpasture, T., 1877
Gornall, Robert E., 1906-30
Gornall, Wm., 1918-43
Gossett, James E., 1958-64
Goto, Masaji, 1949
Goto, Taro, 1935
Gould, H. F., 1903-04, M.P.
Gould, John Allen, 1901-02
Goulder, Chas. N., 1903-22
Goulder, Ernest P., 1933-52; 1957—
Gowan, H. N., 1898-01
Graham, Olin M., 1924-35; 1945-53
Graham, Thomas A., 1906-34
Granberg, Olaf ,1900-15
Grandey, Joseph L., 1912-22
Grant, Frank R., 1963
Graves, Alden R., 1926—
Gray, Albert L., 1896-97
Gray, Andrew E., 1928-32
Gray, Emanuel A., 1926-28
Gray, W. C., 1883-94
Gray, William S. T., 1936—
Gray, Wm. W., 1892-94
Graybeal, Howard L., 1932-36, M.E.S.
Green, Elwin P., 1895-97
Green, Floyd E., 1958—
Green, Henry T., 1920-24

Green, Paul F., 1918-21; 1923-59
Green, W. T., 1905-10
Green, Wm. J., 1911-20
Greening, H. E., 1909-51
Greenlee, Samuel H., 1904-05
Greenslade, James, 1881-02
Greer, G. H., 1867-74
Gregg, Albert S., 1893-01
Gregory, John R., 1902-05
Gregory, Thomas D., 1894-01
Griffen, Wayne D., 1940—
Griffith, Llewellen, O., 1934-36
Grigsby, L. M., 1926-30
Grimes, Edwin Oglesby, 1917-34
Grissom, A. F., 1911-19
Gritton, E. L., 1920. M.E.S.
Grosclose, Kelvin, 1964
Groseclose, Bruce B., 1944—
Groth, Claud W., 1925-48
Groves, Everett L., 1944-48; 1955—
Gruenewald, Charles E., 1950-55; 1960
Gruenwald, F. A., 1914-17
Gruwell, E. T., 1930-52
Guiler, F. A., 1906-46
Guiler, Samuel S., 1898-18

Hadley, Roy O., 1896-14
Haga, K. L., 1918-25
Hager, John, 1887
Haguja, Paul, 1949
Haines, Henry L., 1939-51
Haley, Frank H., 1938—
Hall, Clyde J., 1937
Hall, John O.* died 1935
Hall, Joseph A., 1914-16; 1917-24, 1937. M.E.S.
Hall, William A., 1879-16
Halladay, E. C., 1907-09
Halsey, Peter Waldron* died 1937
Hamilton, Quincey K., 1952-57
Hamlin, Paul E., 1952—
Hammond, A. C., 1909-15
Hammond, Blaine G., 1951—
Hammond, Percy M., 1936-49
Hancock, 1875
Hancock, Frank, 1903-16
Hanks, John, 1900-07; 1912
Hanlein, W. S., 1898-25
Hanna, Earl W. D., 1920-47
Hansen, C. Lyng, 1891-93
Hansen, Hans, 1891-01
Hansen, Martin* Died 1907
Hansen, N. L., 1897-00
Hanson, A. J., 1884-97
Hanson, C. Lyng* Died, 1913
Hanson, Hilmer W., 1926—
Haratani, Iwakichi, 1917
Harbison, Geo. B., 1917-26
Hardie, Thomas, 1924-26
Harding, Joe A., 1962—
Hardison, A.* Died 1883. M.E.S.
Hardy, Thomas, 1925
Harmon, C. G., 1895-07
Harold, Ernest F., 1922-55
Harper, B. Frank, 1890-91
Harper, Craig T., 1963—
Harper, Edward Johnson, 1932-33. M.E.S.
Harrington, J. E., 1905
Harrington, Wm. S., 1895-16
Harris, Ernest O., 1896-62
Harris, P. C. L., 1891-93
Harrison, C. S., 1884
Harrison, Jabez C., 1910-26; 1945—
Harschman, Hardwick W., 1941-53
Hart, B. H., 1928-42
Hart, Earl D., 1928-35

Hart, Edward A., 1922-35
Hart, James H., 1910-22
Hart, Thomas, 1909-11
Hart, Vincent S., Jr., 1957—
Hartley, Robert C., 1900-36
Hartman, Philip D., 1928-31; 1934-39, M.E.S.
Hartsell, Henry J., 1908-14
Hartshorn, A. W., 1914-17
Hartung, Geo., 1888-93; 1900-17
Harvey, H. Grant, 1950—
Harvey, John F., 1916-18
Harvey, Julius C., 1903-32
Harvey, Pharis J., 1962—
Hassel, David C.*
Hatten, Chas. T., 1910—
Haueisen, H., 1908-13; 1919-20
Hauge, C. N., 1887-28
Haugland, P. O.*
Haven, Grant C., 1890-03
Havens, Clyde H.* M.P.
Haver, H. S.* Died 1933
Havermale, S. G., 1873-79
Hawk, J. O., 1909-51
Hawk, Nathaniel S., 1909-18
Hawk, Raymond F., 1917-20
Hawk, U. F., 1895-47
Hawley, A. L., 1898-23
Hayden, Frank L.* M.P.
Hayes, F. M., 1909-14
Hayes, T. P.* Died 1910
Haygood, John A., 1956
Hayward, Eugene R., 1891-96
Hayward, Richard A., 1950-60
Hebblethwaite, Harold, 1944-46
Heggen, O.*
Heidelbaugh, Martin V., 1900
Heineck, Geo. E., 1913-26
Heinsman, Z. K., 1884-88
Heist, A. A., 1921-26
Helgesen, H.*
Helm, James W., 1885-29
Helmick, Daniel M., 1907-34
Henderson, J. L., 1884
Henderson, Wm. H., 1896-13
Henry, A. H., 1904-08
Henry, W. W., 1891-96
Hepp, Joseph, 1891-93; 1898-01; 1903; 1907-10; 1914-16
Herd, Archie M., 1921-29
Herrick, John S., 1912-28; 1961—
Herrington, J. E., 1905-15
Herrmann, J. M., 1906; 1908-14
Hersh, Edgar C., 1964
Hertzog, Fred, 1939-53
Hertzog, William H., 1951—
Herwig, W. J., 1899-21
Hess, Allen O., 1910-14
Hess, John L., 1906-11
Hess, Robert G., 1956—
Hibbard, Eugene W., 1957—
Hickerson, J. M. P., 1891-98
Hicks, Benjamin L., 1896-07
Hicks, H. W., 1890-92
Hicks, J. H., 1916
Hicks, Luverne C., 1926-38
Hicks, Robert W., 1945—
Hierholzer, John, 1965—
Hika, Yasutaki, 1939
Hilbish, J. M., 1913-14
Hill, Everett M., 1906-28; 1929-51
Hill, J. W., 1885
Hill, James A., 1920-51
Hill, John D., 1915
Hill, Wm. E., 1885
Hilmer, August F., 1908-36
Hilton, G. O.* Died 1871. M.E.S.
Hines, Gustavus, 1861-72
Hines, Harvey K., 1867-01
Hingley, J. B., 1924
Hints, William B., 1928-31

LaVelle, Larry, 1963—
LaViolette, Francis Alex, 1893-35
Law, John G., 1910-32
Law, Wm. G., 1930-33
Lawrence, Jabill C., 1898-03
Lawrence, Roderick Q., 1957-59
Lawson, Norman R., 1955—
Lawson, Thomas, 1909-30
Leach, J. B., 1856-57
Leach, John D., 1926-30
Leach, John E., 1882-91
Leard, John Hitchcock, 1879-80
Leavenworth, H. C., 1907-46
LeCornu, John, 1879-15
Lee, Alton E., 1923-25
Lee, Frederick C., 1902-08
Lee, Robert C., 1895-97
Leech, William Henry, 1892-36
Leeds, Robert B., 1963
Leonard, Adna W., 1910-43
Leppert, David, 1907
Leps, Evald, 1955-60
LeRoque, Noel C., 1949-55
LeSourd, David G., 1881-25
LeSourd, Gilbert Q., 1911-35
Levedahl, J. H., 1902-06
Lewellen, J. D., 1908-57
Lewis, Francis R., 1946—
Lewis, W. S., 1865
Lewtas, John, 1900-15
Libby, J. C., 1883-84
Liebman, Edward Charles, 1964
Lindstrum, Gustaf, 1915-18
Lindstrum, Oscar L., 1879-26
Linnemann, Lawrence J., 1948—
Lippert, David, 1908-10
Lippincott, B. C., 1859-62
Little, Paul, 1907-16
Lockhart, E. B., 1906-08 ; 1915-16
Lockhart, James C., 1898-01
Lockwood, George, 1946-49
Logan, Stanley G., 1913-58
Long, John Fletcher, 1907-52
Longbrake, E. H., 1913-18 ; 1929-32
Loomis, A. J., 1882
Looney, Floyd L., Sr., 1950-56
Lortz, Miss Ruth M., 1926—
    First woman member of conf.
Lovejoy, Irving R., 1895-02
Lovett, Miller C., 1952-62
Lowther, Frank L., 1920—
Loy, F. W., 1886-94
Loy, Harry H., 1916-17
Luark, M., 1871
Luce, A. A., 1905-14
Luce, Albert W., 1910-36
Luce, Willis A., 1907-41
Ludwick, Wm. M., 1888-24
Ludwig, Thomas F., 1955—
Luecke, F. H., 1892-03 ; 1904-13 ; 1920 ; 1932-33
Lukens, Robert J., 1948-52
Lund, Clarence H., 1935—
Lundegaard, E. J., 1900-03
Luscombe, Herbert G., 1946—
Luse, Carl A., 1889-97
Lynch, A. H.* M.P.
Lyon, Robert J., 1953—

McAbee, Earl W., 1919-52
McAllister, J. J., 1901-26
McAllister, N. S., 1857-58
McArthur, Walter A., 1960—
McBride, G. M., 1910-11
McCallum, F. E., 1883
McCallum, John W., 1961—
McCarthy, Charles F., 1896-00
McCausland, C. L., 1920. M.E.S.
McCay, Norman, 1922-53

McClurg, Edward, 1943-47 ; 1960—
McClurg, Nolan J., 1947—
McConnell, Carl Francis, 1926-31 ; 1933-34 ; M.E.S.
McConnell, Paul W., 1960—
McCormac, J., 1879-81
McCulloch, Roy S., 1923-62
McCutcheon, Paul M., 1962—
McDermoth, Chas., 1885-03
McDonald, J. M., 1892-95
McDougall, John W., 1916-24
McEvers, Edward, 1892-01
McEwen, Marshall L., 1913-16
McFarland, D. C.* Died 1916. M.E.S.
McFarland, Ira J., 1927—
McFarland, Robert D., 1945-48
McFeron, Thomas C., 1935-37
McGaffee, R. Clinton, 1942—
McGee, Carl H., 1955—
McGill, Oscar H., 1902-32
McGill, T. J., 1875
McGraw, Eugene, 1943-47
McGuire, D. Stanley, 1927-31
McInturff, D. N., 1895-96
McKain, Hunter, 1942-45 ; 46
McKain, William F., 1909
McKay, J. F.* Died 1912. M.E.S.
McKee, J. A., 1947—
McKee, Stanley, 1922
McKeene, J., 1896
McKenzie, Alex. J., 1919-22
McLaughlin, C. W., 1914-19
McMillan, W. B., 1884-08
McMullen, T. E., 1890-96
McNamee, Hastings, 1898-01
McNees, John A., 1923—
McNemee, A. J., 1876-36
McOmber, Ed., 1907-13
McPheeters, Harry A., 1926-28
McPheeters, William, 1872
McQueen, James T., 1900-49
McShane, G. A., 1915-18
McShane, J. E., 1914-19
McVicker, Donavan E., 1959—
McWatters, Wm., 1894-16

Maag, G. A., 1908-13 ; 1921-28 ; 1932-39
Maas, Wm. F., 1901 ; 1915-20
MacArthur, Walter A., 1960—
MacCaughey, Chas. W., 1903-22 ; 1926-48
Machida, Tamotsu, 1941
Mackey, Harold, 1964
MacLagan, Kenneth B., 1959—
MacLean, A. R., 1923-24
Madsen, Carl B., 1927-28
Magee, Bishop J. Ralph, 1921—
Magee, John B., Jr., 1937—
Magee, John B., Sr., 1932-39
Magee, John Homer, 1924-39
Magill, Thos., 1874
Magin, Louis A., 1923-29
Mahaffie, W. H., 1889-94 ; 1922
Mahana, J. B., 1881-84
Mahoney, C. K., 1932-48 ; 1950-61
Makino, Akira, 1953
Mallory, W. W., 1891-93
Malloy, W. L.* Died 1916. M.E.S.
Manier, R. H., 1888-01
Manley, Tracy W., 1955—
Mann, Henry B., 1903-40
Mann, John H., Jr., 1965
Mann, S. H., 1868
March, Ralph C., 1904-07
Marcy, Milton A., 1941-51
Marks, William, 1886-92
Marlatt, Joseph P., 1894-99 ; 1904-37
Marsh, Albert H., 1889-29

Marsh, Waldo B., 1905-14
Martin, A. W., 1925-49
Martin, Claudius B., 1911-12 ; 1918-26
Martin, D. Roland, 1914-24
Martin, Haven, 1938-45
Martin, James H., 1895-36
Martin, Louis V., 1948-52 ; 1953—
Martin, Ray R., 1917-63
Martin, Thomas Ray, 1959—
Martin, William M., 1914-62
Martinsen, Christian*
Marvin, Matthew H., 1888-28
Mason, A. B., 1915
Mason, Ray W., 1909-54
Massey, A., 1888
Massey, Richard H., 1888-11
Massey, Thomas J., 1886-97
Mathews, George, 1886
Mattershead, 1895-96
Matthews, James, 1886-04
Matthews, Robert E., 1946-48
Matthews, Samuel, 1855-59, 1874
Mattney, J. J., 1916-32
Maulden, Robert W., 1922—
Maxfield, W. H.* Died 1884. M.E.S.
Maxwell, J. W., 1888-93
Mayes, Henry, 1886
Mayes, J. W., 1905-10 ; 1914-26
Mead, George F., 1887-03
Meier, Kermit I., 1965
Melby, P. N.*
Menord, H. T., 1933
Merrill, H. R., 1906-10
Metcalf, H. L., 1935
Michael, F. G.* Died 1902. M.E.S.
Michel, H. F., 1891-93 ; 1900-24
Michener, Herbert W., 1900-64
Miffin, M. H. L., 1901
Miles, David Lee, 1964
Miles, H. H., 1920-22
Miller, Arthur H., 1901-09
Miller, C. E., 1914-59
Miller, C. H., 1902
Miller, Charles D., 1911-21
Miller, Clement H., 1886-00 ; 1924-28
Miller, Ernest L., 1928-29
Miller, Herbert E., 1941—
Miller, Ivan L., 1945-47
Miller, J. W., 1896-43
Miller, J. Wesley, 1871
Miller, John W., 1858
Miller, John Willard, 1911-35
Miller, M. C.* Died 1884. M.E.S.
Miller, William O., 1897
Milligan, James E., 1905-28 ; 1940—
Mills, C. Keith, 1951-56
Mills, Ira A., 1895-98
Miner, M. M., 1889-95
Mink, George, 1958—
Mintzer, Olin W., 1892-34
Misner, Peter L., 1956-64
Mitchell, Douglas C., 1961—
Mitchell, J. H., 1907
Mitchell, Leonard H., 1909-10
Mitchell, Melville A., 1894-95
Mitchell, Wm. C., 1896-04
Miyake, Joe, 1929
Moats, Newton E., 1939-49 ; 1962—
Mobbs, Horatio M., 1890-06
Moede, John D., 1922-58
Moehring, J. G., 1888-90 ; 1891-10
Moles, John Wesley, 1904-33
Moller, Donald R., 1958—
Money, P. C., 1908-36
Monroe, Andrew, 1904-24
Monroe, William Harry, 1937-56

SUPPLIES

(Date represents year
of beginning)

Cissna, E. E., 1919
Clausen, J. H.*
Cleland, J. W., 1947
Clements, Mrs. Wilma H., 1943
Clulow, Mrs. Nellie, 1920
Coats, Dorton, 1944
Cobb, Walter A., 1941
Cocks, T. C., 1922
Cole, Geo. B., 1909
Cole, W. Z., 1915
Compton, G. A., 1906
Cook, A. H., 1911
Cook, A. L., 1932
Cook, L. D., 1912
Cook, Mrs. Nellie, 1945
Cook, W. D., 1910
Coons, S. F., 1898
Coop, Charles, 1902
Cooper, Fred W., 1904
Corner, David, 1964
Cotton, Mrs. Earl B., 1952
Cowley, T. J., 1920
Cox, A. M., 1892
Cox, George, 1949
Coy, Gladys, 1947
Cozier, B. F. W., 1898
Craig, J. K., 1908
Craig, Thomas C., 1894
Craven, C. W., 1909
Cravens, Adele, 1947
Cravens, Isaac, 1905
Crawford, Miss Gladys, 1945
Crocker, J. H., 1919
Cronkhite, Frederick H., 1953
Crooks, James, 1909
Crown, F. A. C., 1920
Crumley, Arthur, 1895
Cunningham, Meade L., 1897
Curl, H. T., 1890
Currier, A. E., 1924
Curry, R. W., 1908
Curtis, F. G., 1899
Cydrus, Floyd, 1943
Cydrus, Mrs. Floyd, 1949

Dailey, W. F., 1902
Damon, Vern L., 1954
Daniel, Earl, 1913
Davids, O. R., 1908
Davies, L. C., 1908
Davis, A. E., 1903
Davis, Lafayette, 1908
Davis, Margaret, 1945
Davis, O. R., 1907
Daws, Bessie F., 1941
Dawson, J. P., 1876
Dawson, R. H., 1889
Day, Calvin V., 1946
Dealy, Mrs. Gertrude, 1944
DeArmand, Milton, 1938-54
Delano, Dann, 1887
Denning, Ernest W., 1937
Dennis, Orville, 1937
Derry, E. R., 1913
Dettmers, H. A., 1947
De Voe, Dennis, 1951
Dickey, Charles J., 1936
Dillinger, L., 1901
Dittmar, Charles A., 1959
Dixon, Joe, 1947
Dockstader, C. E., 1949
Dockstader, Charles A., 1945
Dodson, Karen, 1965
Dodsworth, Ruth Ann, 1946
Doran, John, 1901
Douglas, L. C., 1914
Douglas, Thomas F., 1915
Downs, F. G., 1917
Downs, W. J., 1917
Dray, Calvin H., 1858
Dunlap, R., 1881
Dunlap, R. R., 1888

Dunnington, L. L., 1963
Duvall, R. Fenton, 1950

Earl, D., 1927
Earl, S. D., 1877
Easson, William, 1950
Eastland, J. M., 1902
Eaton, E. H., 1906
Eckels, Wilson, 1941
Elexander, Boaz, 1923
Elkins, John H., 1955
Elkins, Walter P., 1952
Eller, Jay, 1944
Ellison, Herbert G., 1948
Elmer, Harold J., 1953
Emerson, A. E., 1894
English, Albert, 1921
Ernst, David Leroy, 1963
Ernst, Gene Allan, 1963
Erwin, J. C., 1914
Esterborg, Joseph, 1897
Estes, Burl, 1945
Evans, B. B., 1892
Evans, Evan R., 1909
Evans, Robert C., 1945

Farnham, F. L., 1920
Faubion, N. G., 1909
Ferguson, R. J., 1906
Field, Fred M., 1948
Field, Mrs. O. T., 1941
Finlay, Miss Alice, 1947
Finlayson, Donald, 1933
Finney, Ivan J., 1956
Fischer, E. Harlan, 1957
Fisher, F. O., 1908
Fleisher, E. H., 1888
Fliesher, Harry, 1926
Fluharty, Orril A., 1946
Fly, E. M., 1904
Forbes, W. M., 1919
Ford, Arthur, 1943
Ford, J. F., 1913
Forkner, R. A., 1918
Frederick, Allen M., 1913
Frederiksen, E.*
Freeland, B. R., 1887
Fulford, F. C., 1937

Gaiser, L., 1932
Galbraith, G. M., 1900
Gamble, W. T., 1919
Garner, W. S., 1921
Garver, James E., 1912
Gavin, Wm., 1941
Gearhart, Clyde M., 1943
Geizentanner, J., 1895
George, Henry, 1896
Getty, Robert, Jr., 1938
Gilbert, W. J., 1900
Gillespie, C. S., 1948
Gillespie, W. G., 1912
Glasspool, G. E., 1926
Gleason, Charles, 1939
Glenn, David, 1933
Glenn, Don H., 1964
Gobbell, I. H., 1904
Goddard, Stanley, 1951
Gooderham, W. H., 1904
Goodnow, W. W., 1929
Goodwin, E. H., 1894
Gordon, S. G., 1915
Gough, J. B., 1910
Gouldin, Raymond, 1951
Graff, William G., 1964
Graham, G. L., 1915
Graham, George F., 1904
Graham, T. P., 1924
Gravenor, G. H., 1947
Graves, Calvin J., 1945
Graves, Mrs. Mary, 1941
Graves, Paul, 1964

Gray, A. L., 1896
Green, Charles A., 1965
Green, Floyd C., 1952
Green, Mrs. Mary T., 1920
Greene, W. Thomas, 1905
Greenstreet, F. M., 1911
Gregory, J. C., 1918
Gregory, W. W., 1894
Grindle, S. T., 1913
Groth, Francis L., 1951
Gruenwald, Mary, 1954
Gustafson, J. J., 1904

Hadley, Harvey, 1886
Haggerman, C. E., 1884
Haggert, B. W., 1924
Haggerty, Wm., 1924
Haines, Mrs. Elmer, 1950
Haines, Hazeldean, 1944
Hall, Bertram, 1922
Hall, Tom C., 1952
Hallam, J. H., 1916
Hanchett, John, 1949
Hankins, N. S., 1916
Hankinson, Victor E., 1948
Hanna, J. L., 1920
Hannan, Thomas, 1955
Hansen, Hans, 1899
Harding, H. J., 1911
Hardwick, J. T., 1904
Harpst, Henry, 1901
Harris, C. C., 1917
Harris, Charles, 1951
Harris, Frank E., 1940
Harrison, G. H., 1911
Hartranft, H. C., 1910
Hartzell, Bertha Pease, 1951
Hastings, A. D., 1896
Hatch, William, 1897
Hatfield, Robt., 1894
Hawk, Mrs. U. F., 1924
Hawkins, "Daddy", 1886
Hawley, F. D., 1916
Haworth, L. M., 1897
Hawthorne, W. B., 1932
Hay, Hugh, 1928
Hayes, Ezra, 1906
Hayworth, L. M., 1891
Hazelton, T. J., 1901
Hearne, Floyd R., 1923
Hecox, Don, 1957
Hegg, Theodore, 1946
Heitman, Isaac, 1894
Helaas, D. M., 1945
Helgeson, G. S., 1915
Helm, I. D., 1908
Henderson, E. R., 1900
Henry, D. P., 1917
Henry, Gerald, 1938
Henry, Gordon, 1885
Hereford, C. M., 1927
Herrick, Bernard, 1954
Hester, J. C. P., 1894
Hickman, Miss Charlotte, 1944
Higasheda, Seichi, 1907
Higgins, Geo. H., 1925
Higgins, Malcom, 1950
Hill, Benjamin A., 1883
Hill, C. V. E., 1906
Hiller, J. M., 1907
Hoare, W. H., 1915
Hodge, Marshall, 1949
Holiday, C. L., 1918
Hollar, H. W., 1902
Holsopple, Donald G., 1962
Honen, Grant C., 1897
Hoover, Amos T., 1955
Hopper, Milton W., 1953
Horton, Richmond H., 1951
Houchens, Walter O., 1906
Houlston, T., 1910
Howard, H., 1919

Wallace, James N., 1908
Walling, Harry E., 1949
Walsh, E. W. G., 1911
Walter, C. W., 1911
Walter, J. J., 1901
Walters, H. C., 1912
Walters, Oren, 1964
Waltman, Victor E., 1895
Walton, G. P., 1952
Walton, W. T., 1895
Wanamaker, H. S., 1922
Ward, Russell, 1952
Warren, A., 1887
Warren, Thos., 1895
Watson, S. H., 1915
Weaver, Ethel, 1943
Weaver, M. W., 1910
Weber, W. C., 1914
Weeks, Orville, 1933
Weidner, C. E., 1930
Weller, J. F., 1919
Wellington, L. G., 1907
Wellington, William, 1911
Wells, Sterling, 1954
Werth, Wilmer, 1940
Westbrook, Delos, 1942
Westfall, G., 1882

Wetherell, R. S., 1934
Whipkey, A. J., 1900
White, Geo. W., 1894
White, James F., 1947
White, John P., 1941
White, Raymond F., 1965
Whitlock, W. E., 1938
Whitmore, M., 1879
Wilder, Hoyt G., 1917
Wilhelm, Mrs. L. W., 1922
Wilkins, I. G., 1941
Wilkins, James, 1939
Wilkinson, C. C., 1909
Willey, F. G., 1919
Williams, A. C., 1904
Williams, Edgar Lonnie, 1948
Williams, Ethel, 1921
Williams, H. F., 1886
Williams, R. G., 1939
Williams, W. T., 1880
Williamson, A. C., 1906
Willis, V. T., 1903
Wilson, Allan B., 1938
Wilson, W. L., 1908
Winsor, Aubrey W., 1947
Winsor, James, 1894

Withnell, W. A., 1918
Wolf, E. L., 1930
Wolfe, Aaron, 1927
Wolfe, E. L., 1924
Wood, D. Hugh, 1953
Wood, George, 1912
Wood, Hazel, 1949
Wood, Henry, 1902
Wood, O. B. D., 1911
Wood, Ralph, 1949
Wooldridge, Frank, 1965
Worsham, John, 1900
Wright, J. Taylor, 1907

Yaggy, S. E., 1930
Yandle, H. T., 1909
Yates, Lawrence, 1952
Yeomans, A. J., 1927
Yockey, S. H., 1905
Yost, J. J., 1920
Yost, John, 1957

Zedecker, A. P., 1914
Zeller, James, 1948
Zenor, W. T., 1888
Zimmerman, DeWane, 1951
Zottnick, James, 1954

M.P.—Methodist Protestant.
M.E.S.—Methodist Episcopal Church South.
* Ministers whose years of service were not available.

Appendix VI

LIST OF MISSIONARIES

A. of General Board of Missionaries
B. of Woman's Division
C. Deaconesses
D. Chaplains in Armed Forces

MISSIONARIES FROM THE SEATTLE AREA WITH THE DIVISION OF WORLD MISSIONS

Allen, Rev. and Mrs. Harry L.—Chile
Bell, Rev. and Mrs. William W.—India
Bisbee, Rev. and Mrs. Royal D.—Japan
Blakney, Rev. and Mrs. Richard B.—Sarawak
Bundy, Rev. and Mrs. T. Walter—The Philippines
Dodsworth, Rev. and Mrs. Marmaduke—Malaysia
Farrand, Miss Fannie—Chile
Freeman, Rev. and Mrs. Mark—Sumatra
Fulkerson, Rev. and Mrs. E. R.—Japan
Harvey, Rev. and Mrs. Pharis S.—Japan
Herrick, Rev. and Mrs. John S.—Bolivia
Herrmann, Rev. and Mrs. Carl C.—India
Irle, Mr. and Mrs. Charles A.—South America
Jackson, Rev. and Mrs. Frank A.—Africa
Jackson, Rev. and Mrs. Keith W.—Japan

Jenkins, Rev. and Mrs. Linden B.—Malaysia
Kaemmer, Rev. and Mrs. John E.—S. E. Africa
Kinch, Rev. and Mrs. Francis M.—Chile
Knowlton, Mrs. Roger H.—Argentina
Martin, Rev. and Mrs. Arthur W.—China
Murphy, Rev. and Mrs. U. G.—Japan
Persons, Rev. and Mrs. Maurice E.—Congo
Peterson, Mrs. Robert F.—North India
Pflaum, Rev. and Mrs. William O.—Chile
Powell, Mrs. Lyall—India
Root, Mr. and Mrs. Stephen E.—S. E. India
Schaad, Mr. and Mrs. Lloyd O.—Angola
Spaulding, Rev. and Mrs. F. R.—Brazil
Strunk, Rev. and Mrs. Leon F.—Brazil

WITH THE WOMAN'S DIVISION

Addington, Patsy—Malaysia
Ballard, Dr. and Mrs. Jack—Pakistan
Bartling, Clara—S. E. Africa
Bedell, Mary—China
Brandt, Adeline—Korea
Brown, Lora Lee—Brazil
Corner, S. Marie—India
Curry, Mary Jane—Africa
Dingle, Leila—Philippines
Endow, Masaka—Japan

Gibson, Clara—Mexico
Hobson, Ruby—India
McCall, Meriel—India
Martin, Margaret—Korea
Moffatt, Margaret—India
Rexroth, Emma—India
Richardson, Ann—Japan
Sandberg, Winifred C.—Nepal
Warne, Eleanor—Japan
Woods, Murden—Pakistan

DEACONESSES OF THE SEATTLE AREA

A—Associate
P—Probation

Adron, Doris
Alexander, Stella
Anderson, Luna E.
Atwood, Helen
Aubin, Mabel—P
Austin, Amy
Bakhouse, Eileen
Barr, Rebecca
Bartling, Clara—P
Beggs, Ruth
Belknap, Rachel
Berger, Mary Alice—P
Berry, Alda—A
Bird, Edith B.
Black, Bertha A.
Black, Elizabeth
Blanchard, Luella M.
Bollinger, Esther
Boney, Elizabeth T.
Brown, Clara A.

Brown, Mary E.
Brown, Minnie
Burbank, Ada
Burch, Eva
Butts, Ethel H.
Cady, Anna M.
Carpenter, Anna H.
Carter, Maude
Chaffee, Jane
Chick, Sophia Eunice
Colton, Mildred
Comstock, Mary J.
Cook, Margaret
Conner, Iva
Cooper, Kate M.
Courtnage, Donna Etta
Curnick, Mary A.
Davies, Margaret
Daws, Bessie F.
DeLong, Edyth—A

Denno, Alice R.
deVries, Evelyn
Dingle, Leila
Dickinson, Lorraine—P
Donaldson, Zoe
Douglas, Beulah
Dove, Winifred
Egbert, Gertrude
Ellis, Lillian B.
Elmer, Hulda
Elson, Jennie
Enley, Bertha E.
Falconer, Margaret
Fifield, Elizabeth
Fleming, Isabel
Fogle, Ruth A.
Forbing, Ruby
Foy, Ethel Lou—A
Furth, Helen
Gasser, Jennie M.

Gegna, Laura A.
Gibson, Celia
Gibson, Clara
Giles, Carrie
Guilkey, Ethel
Glandon, Ethel V.
Gleason, Dorothy
Gleiser, Nellie
Glenk, Esther M.—P
Glenk, Charlotte—P
Godfrey, Louise
Gooch, Bessie M.
Good, Mary E. S.—A
Graham, Ruth
Gruenwald, Mary
Gwynn, Jennie
Hall, Miss E. H.
Hammerly, Margarite
Hanson, Opal
Harding, Dorothy
Harris, Ella Mae
Hepburn, Mary
Hewson, Margarite E.
Hickock, Alice J.—P
Hoffman, Charlotte
Hoffman, Ida
Holcomb, Bertha B.
Horton, Isabella
Howell, Agnes
Howland, Charlotte
Hulbert, Ruby
Ingersol, Ifa M.
Iverson, Asselle
Johnson, Effie D.
Johnston, Jeanette
Jones, Elizabeth
Kastenbader, Pearl
Kiehlbauch, Annette
Kimbrell, Dorothy
Kinch, Alberta
King, Mary
Kinison, M. Blanch

Kiser, Gail Marie
Kissell, Hattie
Klein, Edna
Kling, Ida M.
Kortemeyer, Clara O.—P
Kraut, Helen Marie
Kuter, Susan E.
LaDuke, Dollie E.
Langdon, Lillian
Larson, Viola
Lewis, Emma E.
Lewis, Mrs. Nellie B.
McFarlane, Rebecca
McFerrin, Verna
Maltby, Addie E.
Menzies, Bell M.
Merrick, Nina M.
Milbert, Katherine
Moore, Clara E.—P
Morse, Olga
Murrell, Ruth
Nayhart, Mabel
Newberry, Edna
Nymeyer, Jennie M.
Nymeyer, Edith
Palmer, Orva
Pease, Bessie
Pease, Bertha
Peterson, Christine
Peterson, Lottie
Pollom, Ethel
Reich, Bertha
Reoua, Laura A.
Rogers, Bertha M.
Rogers, Naomi
Rosendahl, Belle—A
Ross, Ione
Rounds, Marion—P
Russell, Dorothy
Sawtell, Bertie
Schacht, Helen M.
Schwinn, May

Seager, Jennie M.
Sexton, Edna
Shoemaker, Mary
Shrader, Willie
Sigerson, Mrs. Jeanette M.
Smick, Alice—A
Smith, Alice
Smith, Jennie E.
Smith, Sadie
Smith, Winifred
Sorenson, Anna
Spoce, Nora—A
Sprengle, Lucile
Steffer, Pearl Ann
Stevenson, Mary
Stieger, Dora
Stringer, Gertrude A.
Strunk, Cora M.
Swanson, Alma
Swartzlander, Wilma
Sweet, Mary B.
Swift, Ella Lois
Tate, Frances—P
Teachman, Corabell
Thurman, Ruth
Trapp, Ida
Trumbull, Jennie
Venema, Mary
Vince, Faith—P
Waller, Genevieve
Ward, Georgia—P
Wattam, Fannie
Whipple, Daisy
White, Edith—P
Wilder, Agnes
Williams, Mildred
Wolf, Marie
Wolfer, Ora
Yates, Elizabeth
Yocum, Elva
Yokel, Rachel P.
York, Frankie P.

CHAPLAINS WITH THE ARMED FORCES OF THE UNITED STATES

Albertson, Gene
Attebery, E. Raymond
Beckman, Elmer E.
Bennett, Dwight G.
Berry, George W.
Bolick, Ralph W.
Bronson, E. V.
Brown, Ralph W. D.
Doty, Lloyd A.
Earle, Harry G.
Franklin, W. J.
Fulmer, W. Paul

Garner, Kenneth A.
Goulder, Ernest P.
Isackson, Fred R.
Jernberg, Marvin G.
Johnson, C. F.
Johnson, John P.
Jordan, Marvin E.
Lewis, Francis R.
Lund, Clarence H.
Miller, H. Eugene
Partee, Raymond A.
Poindexter, T. Earl

Raynor, J. O.
Seiber, Richard A.
Skarbo, Martin
Smith, S. Raynor, Jr.
Storey, David A.
Sulliger, Spencer S.
Sutherland, Calvin J.
Tanquary, Oliver L.
Tibbitts, Forrest D.
Walker, Joe E.
Wood, Clark J.
Wright, Wayne

Appendix VII

OTHER NORTHWEST METHODIST BODIES

The Methodist Episcopal Church and its successor, the Methodist Church, has not been the only Methodist body serving in the Northwest. Five other groups, bearing the name and carrying the Wesleyan banner, have sought to spread the gospel in Washington and Northern Idaho for three quarters of a century.

Each group follows closely the Methodist tradition of organization, administration, and doctrines. Although differing in emphasis and in certain aspects of the faith, their common heritage makes for a sense of oneness between them that transcends divergent views.

Strongest of these bodies is the Free Methodist Church. This denomination, organized in 1860 in New York, grew out of a conviction that the church had become too worldly. Shortly after its birth its ministers entered the State of Washington and won a following. In 1964 there were seventy congregations in the Northwest, with 5,800 members.

Superintendent of the Pacific Northwest Conference, Washington, British Columbia and Alaska, is Dr. Stanley Watkins with headquarters in Seattle. He said the denominational emphasis of his church is expressed in its constitution as follows:

"The Free Methodists are a body of Christians who profess to be in earnest to get to heaven by conforming to all the will of God as made known in His Word. They do not believe that either God or the Bible have changed to accommodate the fashionable tendencies of the age. The conditions of salvation as they teach are the same that they were in the days of the apostles."

The Wesleyan Methodist Church had a congregation in Seattle. This body was founded in 1843 in protest against slavery and the Episcopacy. After the Civil War, the church, because of differences in spiritual reform, maintained a separate existence. It stands for entire sanctification and opposes the liquor traffic and the use of tobacco. Its doctrines mainly correspond closely with traditional Methodist belief. Candidates for membership are required to disavow the use, sale, or manufacture of tobacco or alcoholic beverages.

Three other Methodist bodies were represented in Washington. The strongest, the African Methodist Episcopal Church, dates its national beginning to 1787 when a group of Negro members withdrew from the Methodist Episcopal Church because of the practice of discrimination in the parent body. The denomination, with more than a million members, was second largest Methodist body in the United States. The first church was located at Philadelphia. The denomination was formally organized in 1816. Following the Civil War membership spread rapidly in the South. By 1964 it had congregations in most of the states of the Union.

The first society of the denomination in the Northwest, The First African Methodist Episcopal Church, Seattle, was organized in 1890. In 1964, it was by far the largest organization of that body in the Northwest. Its membership was 1,500.

Other African Methodist Episcopal congregations in Washington were: Walker Chapel, Seattle; Allen, Tacoma; Bethel, Spokane; Bethel, Yakima; Ebenezer, Bremerton; Bailey, Everett; and Moses Lake Mission. Total membership in Washington in 1963 was 2,183. Although Idaho had no congregation in the bounds of the Seattle Area of the Methodist Church, there were churches at Pocatello and Boise. The presiding officer was Bishop Howard Thomas Primm. The presiding elder of the Puget Sound Conference, in 1965, was Rev. L. F. Greene of Seattle. The Rev. John H. Adams was pastor of First Church in Seattle.

The Christian Methodist Episcopal Church had four congregations in Washington. This was the former Colored Methodist Episcopal Church, organized in New Orleans in 1866. By mutual agreement between the Negro members of the Methodist Episcopal Church, South, and their white brethren this group was granted its request to become a separate body of Methodists.

In 1965 Rev. Henry Y. Sideboard was pastor of Bethel Christian Methodist Church, Seattle. Other churches were at Tacoma, Spokane, and Pasco.

411

The African Methodist Episcopal Zion Church, in 1965, had in Seattle one congregation, Ebenezer Church, with fifty members. The pastor was Rev. Joseph Jones. The congregation was organized in 1928. The body dates nationally to 1796, when a group of Negro members, protesting discrimination in the John's Street Methodist Church in New York City, organized a new body. The first church, built in 1800, was called Zion Church. This suggested the term Zion which was included in the denominational name in 1848. In 1949 the body had 520,175 members in the United States.

Appendix VIII

CHARGES AND DISTRICTS

CHARGES BY 1965 DISTRICTS
WITH PASTORS LISTED CHRONOLOGICALLY

COLUMBIA RIVER DISTRICT
BUENA
1908, J. M. Huggins
1910, W. E. Ragan (S)
1913, C. C. Curry
1915, J. O. Johnson
1916, F. N. Morton
1917, Chas. E. Miller
1919, Fred Stilwell
1920, Andrew J. Armstrong
1923, Hubert Vincent
1924, M. H. Staines
1927, O. A. Scott
1930, W. M. Martin
1932, Daniel S. Kerr
1935, Paul R. Campbell
1940, W. H. Monroe
1941, Vern A. Spicker
1943, Robert H. Allen
1946, TBS
1947, T. M. Krause (S)
1948, R. S. McCulloch
1950, Floyd L. Looney
1953, Columbia R. D.
1954, R. S. McCulloch (S)
1954, Robert W. Maulden (R)
1957, Marion Koth (S)
1962, Waldo B. Asp
1965, Wm. Wilford Beckstead (S)

LIBERTY
1900, Rev. Sanford Burwell,
    E. H. Rubicam
1901, T. G. Stull
1903, B. J. Hoadley
1905, G. R. Short (S)
1906, H. O. Perry
1906, W. E. Ragan
1907, W. L. Wilson
1908, TBS
1909, John Huggins,
    John Mountain
1910, Wilmer E. Ragan
1913, Henry Attenborough
1914, William Nash
1917, E. T. Reid
1919, E. L. Wolff
1921, E. S. Williamson
1922, J. E. Garner
1923, Hubert C. Vincent
1925, C. M. Carson
1927, Fred L. Post
1930, John D. Moede
1932, T. Earl Poindexter
1934, Harry Gardner
1938, P. Malcolm Hammond
1940, I. M. Brubacher (S)
1942, P. M. Hammond
1943, Robert L. LaMott
1946, Wm. W. Martin
1948, TBS
1950, not listed
1952, TBS
1953, C.R.D., Ben H. Davis
1954, G. H. Rickard (S)
1957, Marion Koth (S)
1962, Waldo B. Asp
1965, Wm. Wilford Beckstead (S)

CASHMERE
1904, Fred W. Cooper (S)
1905, L. N. B. Anderson
1906, H. T. Robinson
1908, M. J. Perdue
1911, O. W. Mintzer
1914, J. C. Harvey
1917, C. C. Curry
1921, J. S. Bell
1925, J. D. Lewellen
1927, E. F. Stidd
1929, Ernest Barber
1932, Harry F. Gardner
1934, F. N. Morton
1936, Waldo W. Pierson
1939, Andrew Warner
1940, Chester Finkbeiner
1945, Ivan L. Miller
1947, Clyde J. Hall
1950, R. Kenneth Bell
1953, C.R.D.
1954, Floyd L. Looney, Sr.
1955, Clinton A. Aiton
1961, John McCallum
1965, James A. Moore

CHELAN
1891, L. M. Hayworth (S)
1892, M. R. Brown
1895, B. E. Koontz
1898, R. D. Osterhout
1899, J. T. Hoyle and
    D. W. Thurston (S)
1900, A. Y. Skee (S)
1903, J. C. Harvey
1906, William Hoskins
1909, Melvin Rumohr
1910, W. A. Luce
1912, C. C. Curry
1913, C. W. Monson
1914, J. C. Snowden
1915, J. E. Streevy
1917, E. C. Corn
1918, J. O. Hawk
1919, J. D. Bird
1920, J. R. Jeffrey
1921, Henry Attenborough
1925, H. J. Wood
1928, J. L. Rentfro
1931, F. N. Morton
1934, Oliver Black
1936, Francis Kinch
1937, R. Z. Newton
1939, James A. Moore
1941, L. V. Glasscock
1945, Hubert C. Vincent
1952, J. J. Ellington
1953, C.R.D.
1959, Roger K. Johnson
1964, Dan E. Benedict

EAST WENATCHEE
1955, Ruth M. Lortz (S)
1956, Ruth M. Lortz member
1957, Clyde P. Bachman
1961, Hubert Rhymes (S)
1964, Donald L. Russell

ELLENSBURG
1884, S. W. Richards
1884, Ira Wakefield
1885, Henry Brown
1886, Henry Mayes
1887, C. C. Culmer
1888, John W. Maxwell
1890, R. H. Manier
1891, M. R. Brown
1892, M. S. Anderson
1893, Nathan Evans
1895, Robert Warner
1896, M. H. Marvin
1898, J. S. Smith
1900, John Hanks
1902, Wm. Park
1904, F. C. Lee
1906, Wm. DeWeese
1909, W. P. Jinnett (S)
1911, J. W. Caughlan
1913, Nathan Evans
1914, R. D. Snyder
1916, W. B. Young
1922, J. W. Caughlan
1925, O. M. Andrews
1926, E. F. Stidd
1927, J. R. Sasnett
1929, Olin M. Graham
1935, Ernest E. Tuck
1936, F. L. Pedersen
1941, W. M. Martin
1946, R. L. LaMott
1947, Hardwick W. Harschman
1952, Miller C. Lovett
1953, C.R.D.
1955, Assoc. Ronald A. Hummel
1959, Assoc. John E. Buchanan
1962, Geo. L. Poor
1962, Assoc. Donald Cramer

EPHRATA
1904, H. O. Perry
1905, S. H. Yockey (S)
1907, A. A. Moore
1909, W. E. Thompson
1910, P. C. Money
1911, J. P. Armand
1912, (E. F. Oman) and
    C. A. Huff
1913, J. W. Wright
1914, W. W. Strite
1915, G. L. Graham (S)
1916, A. A. Moore (S)
1919, H. W. Best (S)
1921, J. F. Weller (S)
1922, Dow DeLong
1924, Thos. W. Emery
1926, TBS
1927, O. L. Anthony
1929, H. S. Randall
1931, Wm. Gornall
1932, E. S. Williamson
1933, Donald Finlayson (S)
1936, TBS
1937, J. M. Robinson (S)
1938, Robt. B. Shaw
1940, Hubert C. Vincent

413

1945, Laird V. Glasscock
1953, Calvin Sutherlin
1957, Fred E. Fox
1964, Robert H. Ortmeyer

GRANDVIEW
1909, W. L. Wilson (S)
1910, F. M. Hayes
1911, John E. Williams
1911, H. J. Wood
1915, Willis A. Luce
1917, Louis Thomas
1918, F. L. Cook
1920, O. A. Scott
1922, J. D. Lewellen
1925, V. A. Spicker
1927, Daniel Kerr
1932, Wm. Martin
1936, Earl McAbee
1940, Earl E. Reisner
1949, Howard P. Buck
1952, Herbert G. Luscombe
1953, C.R.D.
1959, Ritchie D. Ocheltree
1961, Charles Davenport

LEAVENWORTH
1904, F. W. Cooper (S)
1905, L. N. B. Anderson
1906, M. Rumohr
1909, J. O. Hawk
1910, J. P. Armand
1911, J. O. Hawk and
      M. A. Jeffords
1913, Chas. Snowden
1914, C. A. Duff
1915, F. L. Moore
1918, A. H. Morton
1919, Wm. Hoskins
1922, A. E. Derby
      Ralph I. Thomas
1928, C. M. Carson
1929, TBS
1930, C. A. Burris
1931, O. W. Mintzer (S)
1934, C. G. Scannell (S)
1935, TBS
1936, Erling Bergan
1940, TBS
1941, John M. Finney
1944, LaVern E. Tooley
1949, Stanley D. Trefren (S)
1950, Floyd E. Wells
1953, Charles M. Estabrook
1957, Edwin F. Rode
1960, Oscar A. Olsen
1964, Ritchie D. Ocheltree

MABTON
1907, Wilmer E. Ragan (S)
1908, W. L. Wilson (S)
1910, M. C. Newell
1912, W. A. Pratt
1913, W. A. Luce
1915, J. W. Mayes
1918, Henry Attenborough
1919, Harlan Stone
1922, Hubert Vincent
1923, R. S. McCulloch
1925, M. L. Anderson
1927, C. M. Carson
1928, K. O. Pearson
1930, John Moede
1932, T. Earl Poindexter
1934, W. G. R. Dann
1936, C. H. Cowdy
1939, Geo. W. Almond
1940, Earl E. Reisner
1948, S. E. Hornibrook
1949, Ruth M. Lortz
1953, C. R. Dist.
1955, Mrs. Gertrude Dealy (S)

1956, Wm. M. Martin (R)
1959, J. D. Stout (S)
1961, Bill L. Brentlinger
1963, Billy H. Parrish
1964, Oren Walters (S)
1965, James E. Doak

MANSON
1915, J. E. Strevey
1917, E. C. Corn
1918, J. O. Hawk
1919, J. D. Bird
1920, J. R. Jeffrey
1921, Henry Attenborough
1924, M. A. Soper (S)
1925, H. J. Wood
1928, J. L. Rentfro
1931, Fred N. Morton
1932, J. A. Hill
1936, B. C. Gallaher
1939, Frank L. Lowther
1944, Geo. W. Schreiner (S)
1948, Fred O. Hunt
1951, Revelle E. Roach
1953, C.R.D.
1955, Laurence Burdette
1957, Eugene W. Hibbard

MONITOR
1911, J. E. Clulow
1913, C. A. Huff
1914, W. W. Strite
1915, M. A. Jeffords
1916, L. N. B. Anderson
1918, E. E. Cissna (S)
1920, G. E. James
1922, John Moede
1923, C. B. Martin
1925, James Opie
1926, Wm. W. Switzer
1929, U. C. Smothers
1933, R. A. Gailey
1936, Percy E. Pike
1939, Andrew Warner
1940, E. E. VanWert (S)
1941, Wendell Cone
1944, Dewane E. Lamka (S)
1945, Darrell L. Iwerks
1947, Raymond F. Pilcher (S)
1953, C.R.D.
1953, H. L. Rollert (S)
1958, Clyde P. Bachman
1961, Hubert Rhymes (S)
1964, Donald L. Russell
1965, Graham O. Hutchins

MOSES LAKE
1952, William G. Berney
1953, C.R.D.
1957, Gregory Zimmer
1959, Lloyd N. Alden
1964, James B. Darcy

BRIDGEPORT
1902, W. E. Beach (S)
1903, No record
1904, J. C. Beach (S)
1906, P. R. McMahon (S)
1907, J. F. Cook
1908, J. B. Smith (S)
1909, J. J. Pacey
1910, A. S. Redfern
1911, R. T. Holland
1912, J. H. Dill
1913, E. C. Corn
1915, S. G. Logan
1917, C. H. Schreiber
1918, Harry A. Wann
1919, Alfred E. Derby
1922, C. L. Lowther (S)
1923, John Moede
1926, C. A. Burris

1929, Chester Blair
1933, Percy E. Pike
1936, TBS
1937, Frank L. Lowther
1939, Loren Jones (S)
1943, I. V. Parker (S)
1944, Jewell F. Pyles (S)
1949, Ruth Belknap (S)
1950, John B. Coan
1953, Columbia River Dist.
1958, James D. Crawford
1961, E. Vincent Smith
1962, Raymond L. Poindexter
1965, John Hierholzer

OKANOGAN, First
1909, L. L. Hursey (S)
1910, George F. Graham
1910, A. S. Redfern
1910, Perry Wilson
1911, C. T. Denny and
      John J. Pacey
1912, J. W. Wright
1913, Ernest F. Oman
1914, J. O. Hawk
1916, A. F. Kroneman
1918, E. J. Snell
1919, Owen J. Beadles
1922, George E. James
1923, J. A. Hill
1928, C. A. Pickering
1929, B. C. Gallaher
1934, Daniel Taylor
1936, William S. T. Gray
1937, Chester Finkbeiner
1940, Erling Burgan
1941, John Finkbeiner
1942, R. R. Finkbeiner
1950, E. M. Filbert
1953, C.R.D.
1955, Paul T. Woodward
1958, Floyd E. Wells
1959, Robert J. Lyon
1963, Alex Poobus
1965, Robert F. Kinch

MALOTT
1934, Daniel E. Taylor
1937, Chester Finkbeiner
1940, Erling Bergan
1941, John Finkbeiner
1942, Raymond Finkbeiner
1950, Everett M. Filbert
1953, C.R.D.
1954, not listed
1956, TBS
1957, Paul T. Woodward
1958, Floyd E. Wells
1959, Robert J. Lyon
1965, Robert F. Kinch

RIVERSIDE
1906, J. C. Beach
1907, W. R. Struble (S)
1908, L. L. Hursey (S)
1909, G. F. Graham (S)
1910, J. M. Rush (S)
1912, G. F. Graham (S)
1913, J. P. Armand
1914, J. O. Hawk
1916, R. R. Martin and
      H. A. Wann
1918, W. J. Downs (S)
1919, TBS
1920, J. S. Taylor (S)
1921, Albert English (S)
1922, TBS
1923, Harry Fleischer (S)
1926, John Moede
1930, C. W. Groth
1932, J. P. Armand
1934, H. R. Cross

1937, E. E. Van Wert
1938, L. G. Wellington (S)
1939, I. G. Wilkins (S)
1941, Hazeldee Mowry (S)
1943, C. W. Groth
1944, Floyd Cydrus (S)
1948, Frank Sutton (S)
Geo. Lees (S)
1949, Benjamin Peters **(S)**
1950, Mrs. Elmer Haines (S)
1953, C.R.D., James Moore
1954, Mary Gruenwald
1955, TBS
1957, Bruce B. Groseclose
1960, S. Christian Thele
1963, Dewey Alan Knowles
1964, Paul F. Ashbrook
1965, Robert F. Kinch

OMAK
1925, G. E. Heineck
1926, Geo. E. Berryman
1928, R. T. Holland
1931, No record
1932, J. P. Armand
1934, H. R. Cross
1937, E. E. Van Wert (S)
1938, L. G. Wellington (S)
1939, I. G. Wilkins (S)
1940, Hazeldee Mowry (S)
1944, Miss Ruth Belknap (S)
1948, James A. Moore
1952, Combined with Central
1953, C.R.D.
1956, Bruce B. Groseclose
1960, S. Christian Thele
1963, Dewey Alan Knowles
1964, Paul F. Ashbrook

NESPELEM
1912, Rev. W. A. Talbert (S)
1913, Rev. A. A. McGinnis (S)
1914, Rev. Israel Putnam (S)
1915, W. E. Thompson
1916, Rev. J. H. S. Hallam (S)
1917, Geo. O. Harbison
1919, no pastor
1920, Rev. Raymond Acheson
1921, C. T. Hatten
1924, Roy Jenkins
1926, R. T. Holland
1928, J. W. Poolton
1933, C. H. Schreiber
1937, C. A. Burris
1949, Verne Brooks (S)
1950, Loval R. Phillips
1952, G. T. Walton (S)
1953, C.R.D. Mrs. Hortense
Bennett (S)
1954, Mrs. Hortense Anable (S)
1955, Amos T. Hoover (S)
1957, TBS
1957, R. W. Pruitt (S)
1959, James M. Lane
1962, Laird V. Glasscock
1965, Paul F. Ashbrook

CONCONULLY
1900, A. W. Trine
1904, I. V. Parker
1905, A. W. Trine
1907, J. F. Redfern
1908, A. S. Redfern
1910, J. J. Pacey
1911, G. F. Graham (S)
1912, C. M. Bolin
1913, H. C. Kohr
1914, C. W. Geisler
1917, J. F. Ford (S)
1918, J. W. Downs (S)
1919, not listed
1923, Harry Fleischer (S)

1925, not listed
1926, John D. Moede
1930, C. W. Groth
1932, J. P. Armand
1934, H. R. Cross
1937, E. E. Van Wert
1938, L. G. Wellington (S)
1939, Chester Finkbeiner
1940, Walter Pearson (S)
1941, Darrell Iwerks
1942, C. W. Groth
1945, Floyd Cydrus (S)
1948, Geo. Lees
1949, Benjamin Peters (S)
1950, Mrs. Elmer Haines
1953, C.R.D. James Moore
1954, Mary Gruenwald
1956, TBS
1957, not listed
1965, Paul F. Ashbrook

OROVILLE
1898, J. H. Martin
1902, O. W. Mintzer
1903, A. W. Trine
1905, C. L. Creesy
1905, J. L. Hess
1906, J. A. Smith
1907, Robert Thompson
1908, Mrs. Robert Thompson
1909, James Callahan
1910, A. Bauman
1912, R. T. Holland
1913, A. H. Morton
1915, W. W. Strite
1916, F. L. Cook
1917, U. C. Smothers
1918, R. R. Martin
1920, James Opie
1922, A. F. Kroneman
1926, D. Stanley McGuire
1927, J. H. Dill
1929, C. A. Pickering
1932, T. Emery
1935, W. Richards
1937, E. E. Van Wert
1938, T. H. Stanley (S)
1940, W. W. Peters
1942, Verne L. Chapman
1944, H. L. Rollert **(S)**
1953, C.R.D.
1953, John M. Jones (S)
1956, TBS
1957, Joseph L. Woodford
1961, Clyde P. Bachman
1965, J. Dean Stout

OTHELLO
1958, Arthur E. Paltridge
1962, C.R.D.
1962, Donald L. Snyder

ROYAL SLOPE,
ROYAL CITY, etc.
1956, TBS
ROYAL SLOPE
1957, TBS
1958, Raymond L. Poindexter
1960, TBS
1961, Paul McConnell
1962, Donald L. Snyder

PATEROS
1905, J. C. Beach
1907, J. F. Cok
1908, C. J. Steiner (S)
1909, D. L. Clarke
1910, M. Rumohr
1911, P. C. Money
1914, G. E. James
1917, E. J. Snell (S)
1918, Chas. H. Schreiber

1921, U. G. Beadles (S)
1922, F. H. Brown (S)
1923, Ralph I. Thomas
1926, G. E. James
1928, J. A. Hill
1934, J. P. Armand
1936, TBS
1937, F. C. Fulford (S)
1938, O. L. Kendall
1939, Percy E. Pike
1941, Claude W. Groth
1942, Stewart E. Sparrow (S)
1946, TBS
1947, Verne L. Chapman (S)
1948, TBS. Walter G. Sloan
1952, Raymond H. Blanton
1953, C.R.D.
1955, Harlan D. Jones
1957, David L. Aasen
1959, H. Grant Harvey
1960, TBS
1961, Hortense Anable (S)
1962, Paul W. McConnell

PROSSER
1895, Henry Moys
1897, S. L. Burrill
1900, A. C. Brackenbury
1901, E. H. Rubicam
1902, J. E. Williams
1905, W. C. Smith
1908, H. N. Rounds
1910, F. E. Smith
1913, G. A. Tylor (S)
1915, Geo. R. Moorhead
1919, T. A. Graham
1922, J. W. Mayes
1923, M. R. Gallaher
1927, R. L. LaMott
1929, O. L. Anthony
1932, B. A. Hylton
1934, W. G. R. Dann
1936, C. H. Cowdy
1939, Geo. W. Almond
1940, John A. Hoffman
1942, John W. Kuller
1947, M. Chester Morgan
1953, C.R.D.
1953, Laird V. Glasscock
1958, Herbert E. Miller
1962, Tracy W. Manley

SELAH
1909, C. Springer (S)
1910, J. K. Craig (S)
1912, H. C. Clark
1914, M. L. Anderson
1916, M. R. Gallaher
1918, Joseph W. Mayes
1921, C. A. Hodshire
1923, Chas. L. Creesy
1926, D. S. Kerr
1927, M. H. Staines
1928, Geo. E. James
1930, J. Homer Magee
1933, U. C. Smothers
1935, J. A. Hoffman
1939, J. L. Rentfro
1940, Robt. H. Allen
1944, Vern A. Spicker
1951, Blaine G. Hammond
1953, C.R.D.
1957, Ralph H. Richardson
1960, Edwin B. Towle
1964, Edgar C. Hersh

SUNNYSIDE
1908, H. O. Perry
1911, J. D. Lewellen
1912, M. H. Marvin
1914, C. C. Curry
1917, Andrew Warner

1920, Robert Brumblay
1922, Alexander R. Maclean
1923, George H. Bennett
1924, Louis Thomas
1926, Charles Creesy
1929, J. Fletcher Long
1931, H. J. Wood
1934, Harry Gardner
1938, P. Malcolm Hammond
1943, Robert L. LaMott
1946, Wm. M. Martin
1953, C.R.D.
1953, G. Richard Tuttle
1960, William F. Andrews

TOPPENISH
1898, Zenas Bolton (S)
1900, S. L. Burrill
1901, W. H. McKnight
1902, J. J. Calloway
1905, A. C. Williamson (S)
1906, Joseph W. Mayes
1908, J. M. Huggins
1910, F. R. Spaulding
1911, A. A. Callender
1913, C. C. Curry
1914, J. O. Johnson
1916, F. N. Morton
1917, Chas. E. Miller
1924, U. F. Hawk
1925, John H. Secor
1927, O. A. Scott
1930, Wm. M. Martin
1932, Daniel S. Kerr
1935, Paul R. Campbell
1940, Wm. H. Monroe
1941, Vern A. Spicker
1943, Robert H. Allen
1946, TBS
1946, C. Herbert Picht
1949, Earl E. Reisner
1953, C.R.D.
1957, Norman R. Lawson
1961, Truman Cotten
1963, Harold W. Black

WATERVILLE
1887, James W. Bluett
1888, H. F. Williams
1889, Frank L. Buzzell
1889, W. J. White
1890, L. M. Haworth
1892, M. R. Brown
1895, B. E. Koontz
1898, F. B. Utter
1900, B. L. Hicks
1901, R. D. Osterhout
1902, F. T. Allen
1904, H. O. Perry
1907, J. E. Daniels
1908, F. B. Utter
1908, P. C. Money
1910, J. O. Hawk
1911, N. S. Hawk
1913, Gabriel Sykes
1918, G. E. Heineck
1919, Gabriel Sykes
1920, E. C. Newham
1922, John Evans
1924, W. G. R. Dann
1926, TBS
Federated. Meth. pastors:
1928, W. W. Pierson—'31
1937, Dwight Bennett—'42
1945, Lew Brown (S)
1946, TBS
1947, Joe Dixon
1948, TBS
1948, W. O. Benthin (S)
1951, J. Dean King
1953, C.R.D.
1956, TBS

1961, Federated
1962, W. J. Brooks (BAPT.)

WENATCHEE
1895, M. R. Brown
1896, B. L. Hicks
1897, H. T. Coleman
1898, C. F. B. Runyon (S)
1899, J. T. Hoyle
1900, F. B. Utter
1903, L. R. Kufus
1907, H. L. Beightol
1910, M. L. Sanders
1912, N. M. Jones
1915, W. H. H. Forsyth
1917, R. Warner
1919, R. Warner and
      H. Attenborough
1921, R. E. Smith
1924, N. M. Jones
1925, H. O. Perry
1929, Norman McCay
1932, Stanley G. Logan
1937, Wm. B. Young
1940, Jos. H. Beall
1945, Assoc., Darrel L. Iwerks
1947, Willard E. Stanton
1950, James T. Albertson
1953, C.R.D.
1960, G. Richard Tuttle
1965, J. Henry Ernst

WHITE SWAN
1861, first reported
1873, James H. Wilbur
      Geo. Waters, Asst.
1873, Thos. Pearne, Asst.
1884, D. L. Spaulding (S)
1886, G. C. Roe
1887, S. Gascoigne
1890, M. R. Browers (S)
1891, J. W. Helm
1896, G. M. Booth, Asst.
1915, S. M. Nickle
1916, A. M. Lambert (S)
1919, A. H. Morton
1920, M. L. Anderson
1921, M. A. Soper (S)
1922, no pastor
1923, R. T. Holland
1926, John A. McNees
1932, R. V. B. Dunlap
1938, Chas. T. Hatten
1942, Eugene McGraw
1944, Chas. Austun (S)
1947, R. S. McCulloch
1948, C. S. Gillespie (S)
1950, J. S. Huntley (S)
1952, A. G. Rugger
1952, Harry E. Gardner
1953, C.R.D.
1956, Fred R. Owen
1961, E. F. Altes, Jr.
1963, Thomas F. Ludwig
1965, Frank Wooldridge (S)

WAPATO, Japanese
1927, Mrs. Aya Okuda
1929, Zentaro Hirota
1933, Miss Grace Kiyo Takahashi
1935, Lester Suzuki
1936, Isao Tanaka
1938, Andrew Kuroda
1941, Casper Y. Horikoshi
      until 1942
1945, Miss Azalia Peet until 1946
1947, Miss Alice Finlay
      until 1948
1950-'52, Masaji Goto
1953, Akira Makino
1955, Alpha Takagi
1955, Shigeo Shimada
1958, Weichi Oyanagi

1961, Robert Yamashita
1963, Clyde Armstrong
1964, Oren Walters
1965, Frank Wooldridge (S)

WINTHROP
1903, W. E. Beach
1904, A. W. Trine
1904, J. C. Beach
1906, W. E. Beach
1906, W. L. Singer (S)
1911, M. P. Stoute (S)
1912, Perry Wilson
1912, Fred Greenstreet
1912, James S. Taylor
1913, Chas. M. Bolin
1914, Isaac B. Ricketts (S)
1916, M. R. Brown
1919, Alfred Derby
1919, O. W. Mintzer
1920, I. V. Parker
1920, Miss Gertrude Apel (S)
1923, Floyd R. Hearne (S)
1924, Ralph I. Thomas
1926, A. A. Moore
1928, Misses Gail Kiser and
      Bessie Pease
1930, Clark Cottrell
1932, John A. McNees
1945, Hunter McKain
1946, Wendell Cone
1947, J. N. Snow (S)
1948, Wendell J. Cone
1952, J. D. Crawford
1953, C.R.D.
1955, John H. Elkins
1956, J. D. Stout
1958, Robert E. Dabritz

TWISP
1904, A. W. Trine
1905, W. E. Beach (S)
1906, No record
1907, M. D. Berg (S)
1909, D. L. Clarke
1910, No record
1911, M. P. Stout (S) &
      F. M. Greenstreet (S)
1912, J. S. Taylor (S)
1913, C. M. Bolin
1914, I. B. Ricketts (S)
1916, M. R. Brown
1919, TBS
1923, Floyd R. Hearne (S)
1924, Ralph I. Thomas
1925, L. W. Flenner
1926, A. A. Moore (S)
1928, Gail Kiser (S) and
      Bessie Pease (S)
1930, Clark Cottrell
1932, John McNees
1945, Wendell J. Cone
1952, J. D. Crawford
1953, C.R.D.
1955, John H. Elkins (S)
1956, J. D. Stout
1958, Robert E. Dabritz

YAKIMA, First
1873, Geo. W. Kennedy
      No record of pastors 'til
1879, G. W. Shaffer
1880, Richard Barrett
1883, D. G. Strong
1885, Richard Fysh
1886, Wm. E. Golding
1888, John Uren
1891, Robert Warner
1895, N. Evans
1897, U. F. Hawk
1899, John H. Wood
1903, W. H. Selleck
1904, A. H. Henry
1907, C. E. Gibson

416

1910, W. H. Selleck
1913, W. F. Ineson
1919, R. E. Smith and
    J. F. Stillwell
1921, E. E. Brace
1922, W. B. Young
1927, John G. Law
1932, C. K. Mahoney
1935, Chas. MacCaughey
1936, J. Edgar Purdy
1939, Lynn A. Wood
    Assoc. H. W. Hebbleth-
    waite
1946, Assoc. K. H. Underwood
1949, Rector W. Johnson
    Assoc. Don L. Swerdfeger
1953, C.R.D.
1954, Owen J. Beadles
1955, Assoc. J. M. Finney
1957, Assoc. L. A. Burdette
1962, Joe A. Harding
1964, Assoc. J. W. Workman, Jr.
1965, Ac C. Wischmeir

WESLEY MEMORIAL
1955, Raymond H. Blanton
1958, Austin H. Richardson
1962, Robert C. Ward

PUGET SOUND DISTRICT
ALDERWOOD MANOR
1963, Milton P. Andrews, Jr.

ARLINGTON
1894, G. L. Cuddy
1895, George W. Frame
1898, Isaac Dillon
1899, John Britts
1901, G. D. Dimick
1903, William J. Rule
1904, C. A. Owen
1906, S. G. Jones
1908, J. W. Kern
1911, F. W. P. Camp
1913, A. A. Brittain
1915, F. A. Guiler
1917, G. C. Squires (S)
1920, TBS
1921, W. J. Rule
1924, Robert H. Allen
1925, E. E. Reisner
1929, V. A. Spicker
1930, F. R. Gillett
1937, J. C. Hofstetter
1940, Frank C. Abbott (S)
1942, C. E. Rayburn
1945, H. W. Driver
1948, Bertram Robins
1950, Arnt O. Quall
1953, J. Philip Porter
1955, John Mathone (S)
1959, C. W. Johnson (S)
1962, Rollin E. Stierwalt
1965, Clyde P. Bachman

DARRINGTON
1903, TBS
1906, A. B. Towne (S)
1913, J. S. Sneethen (S)
1914, Al P. Zedecker (S)
1915, B. V. Bradshaw (S)
1917, C. E. Sanders
1918, Roy M. Owen (S)
1919, R. L. Wolfe (S)
1921, F. A. C. Crown (S)
1923, TBS
1924, A. E. Currier (S)
1925, Paul Campbell (S)
1928, Philip S. Clapp
1929, V. A. Spicker (S)
1930, F. R. Gillett
1937, J. C. Hofstetter

1941, Frank C. Abbott (S)
1942, TBS
1943, L. Clyde Bennett (S)
1944, Pierce Roberts (S)
1947, R. A. Gailey
1948, William Park
1950, Arnt O. Quall
1951, Mrs. Nellie Cook (S)
1952, O. I. Borseth (S)
1955, Gregory A. Zimmer
1957, Thomas F. Ludwig
1960, C. W. Johnson
1962, Rollin E. Stierwalt
1965, Clyde P. Bachman

COUPEVILLE
1853, Wm. B. Morse
1856, Jas. S. Smith
1857, TBS
1858, H. C. Rhodes
1859, Wm. D. Nichols (S)
1860, J. H. B. Royal
1861, TBS
1863, Christopher Alderson
1865, S. H. Todd
1867, F. Elliott
1868, H. Patterson
1870, G. H. Greer
1873, J. W. Kuykendall
1874, Martin Judy
1875, B. J. Sharp
1876, Thomas Magill
1878, Wallace Hurlburt
1879, N. A. Starr
1880, T. B. Goodpasture
1881, TBS
1882, G. A. Landen
1884, W. H. Zellers
1885, W. B. McMillan
1888, E. J. Moore
1889, C. C. Culmer
1890, Wm. H. Wilson
1892, W. F. Clarke
1895, W. H. Leech
1896, J. W. White
1898, W. B. McMillan
1899, G. A. Sheafe
1901, J. H. Kevan
1903, C. B. Seely
1907, C. N. Goulder
1908, R. C. Hartley
1912, W. B. Bell (S)
1914, W. W. Switzer
1917, TBS
1918, W. L. Airheart
1920, B. W. Rhinehart
1923, T. C. Cocks (S)
1924, W. J. Rule
1926, TBS
1927, O. W. Mintzer (S)
1929, J. R. Butler
1932, R. A. Partee
1935, B. H. Hart
1938, J. F. Long
1944, Delos Westbrook (S)
1945, E. Ray Kaemmer
1946, H. E. Greening
1948, Henry Cross
1953, Ritchie D. Ocheltree
1956, Wayne T. Wright
1963, Truman H. Cotten

EDMONDS
1909, C. W. Stevens (S)
1909, L. C. Carroll
1910, Charles Easton
1911, J. W. Wright
1913, R. Z. Fahs
1913, E. V. Bronson
1915, S. G. Jones
1917, T. H. Jorgenson
1918, S. G. Jones

1919, C. E. Preston (S)
1927, J. H. Berringer
1932, O. L. Anthony
1934, J. R. Butler
1936, Chas. E. Sanders
1941, Oliver L. Tanquary
1944, Henry Haines
1951, Raymond S. Proudfoot
1958, Robert W. Hicks
1962, David L. Aasen
1963, Assoc. M. Chester Morgan

EVERETT, First
1892, A. H. Marsh
1892, B. B. Evans (S)
1892, Horace Williston
1895, E. V. Claypool
1896, F. E. Drake
1898, Irving Lovejoy
1902, E. B. Chapin
1905, M. A. Casey
1908, W. H. H. Forsythe
1910, W. H. W. Rees
1913, J. P. Marlatt
1917, E. M. Randall
1921, Robert J. Reed
1927, F. A. LaViolette
1929, Harlan R. Stone
1935, W. B. Young
1937, Joseph Chester
1941, Joseph M. Adams
1945, J. C. Harrison
1950, E. A. Wolfe
1954, A. Maurice Chamberlin
1958, Harold C. Williams
1964, Paul E. Peterson

EVERETT, GRACE
1907, Summit Ave., TBS
1909, Grace, W. G. R. Dann (S)
1911, W. W. Switzer
1913, J. L. Grandey
1915, A. W. Hartshorn
1917, E. V. Bronson
1918, T. H. Jorgenson
1920, J. F. Long
1921, C. E. Sanders
1924, J. M. Weaver
1925, Richard Decker
1928, C. H. Cowdy
1930, E. W. D. Hanna
1931, G. W. Frame (S)
1936, John H. Secor
1941, Henry R. Cross
1943, J. Ray Neiser (S)
1947, K. W. Larrison
1950, Jack M. Tuell
1952, Fletcher Forster
1953, C. Ellsworth Wilson
1954, Samul A. Carlson (S)
1959, Everett M. Richey (S)
1964, David Corner
1965, Raymond E. Poindexter

EVERETT, VIEW RIDGE
1955, Henry R. Cross
1956, TBS
1957, Paul B. L. Anderson
1961, G. Paul Carr
1963, Larry LaVelle

LAKEWOOD
1951, Arnt O. Quall
1952, absent
1953, J. Philip Porter
1955, John Mathone
1956, out
1957, E. Clifford Newham
1963, Robert B. Leeds

LANGLEY
1901, TBS

1902, W. F. Dailey (S)
1903, G. W. Stroop (S)
1904, TBS
1909, A. J. McNemee
1910, J. B. Gough (S)
1911, TBS
1912, J. A. Chapin (S)
1913, TBS
1915, A. J. McNemee
1916, A. Robertson (S)
1918, TBS
1919, R. D. Cady (S)
1920, TBS
1921, A. H. Carlson (S)
1922, TBS
1927, B. E. Jacobs (S)
1928, TBS
1930, Payson Peterson (S)
1931, TBS
1933, R. A. Partee
1935, TBS
1939, Haven R. Martin
1940, TBS
1941, John Mathone (S)
1943, TBS
1947, Bruce Finleyson
1949, Harold Slocum (S)
1952, L. B. Jenkins
1954, Hilmer Hanson
1958, TBS
1959, J. Dean Stout
1961, Bruce Wakeman
1964, K. B. MacLagan

MARYSVILLE
1890, John Flinn
1891, A. H. Marsh
1892, J. W. Patterson
1894, C. E. Cunningham
1895, George W. Frame
1898, G. D. Dimick
1901, G. A. Landen (S)
1902, L. J. Covington
1903, G. D. Dimick
1904, H. G. Ward
1907, R. D. Snyder
1909, S. S. Guiler
1910, W. W. Switzer
1911, P. H. Ashby
1914, K. R. Gilmer
1918, V. C. Evers (S)
1919, J. H. Avery
1920, J. M. Hixson
1923, T. H. Jorgenson
1927, F. M. Bushong (S)
1930, L. C. Shultz
1937, Harry E. Greening
1941, W. O. Pflaum
1944, T. L. Blaisdell
1946, H. G. Luscombe
1952, E. Clifford Newham
1956, Howard P. Buck
1959, Lloyd A. Doty

MONROE
1896, J. W. Patterson
1898, T. L. Dyer
1900, A. H. Marsh
1901, R. M. Schoonmaker
1904, W. J. Rule
1907, S. V. Warren
1909, H. Jones
1911, W. I. Cowell
1912, E. W. Erickson
1913, H. C. Leavenworth
1915, P. H. Raymond
1917, H. O. Cooper
1918, F. M. Bushong (S)
1923, E. D. White
1926, J. M. Hixson
1927, E. J. Bates
1929, G. F. Hopkins

1931, R. H. Allen
1932, T. L. Blaisdell
1934, H. L. Allen
1938, David A. Storey
1942, S. Raynor Smith, Jr.
1944, B. A. Hylton
1946, John P. Johnson
1950, Carl K. Mahoney
1951, Neil C. Neilson, Jr. (S)
1952, Fred O. Hunt
1953, Roy L. Kuhns
1955, Forrest D. Tibbitts
1962, Oren D. Watson
1963, Harold O. Perry

MOUNTLAKE TERRACE
1952, Robert Ward
       Christ Ch., Edmonds
1953, Henry R. Cross
1955, Mountlake Terrace
1955, Roger K. Johnson
1958, To Seattle Dist.
1959, Kenneth B. MacLagan
1960, John E. Haygood
1963, O. James Garrett
1964, David L. Miles
1965, Donald R. Kaelin

OAK HARBOR
1892, Crescent Harbor
1892, J. L. Parmeter
1893, C. E. Cunningham
1894, R. M. Schoonmaker
1897, TBS
1898, W. S. Hanlein (S)
1901, McClellan Reed
1902, H. W. Michener
1906, E. B. Reese
1909, J. M. Hixson
1910, C. H. Baldwin
1911, H. P. Waldron
1913, B. Waddington
1916, B. N. Galbraith
       combined with Oak Harbor
1921, B. N. Galbraith
1936, W. G. R. Dann
1938, Carroll H. Sprague
1939, Philip H. Ashby
1940, C. E. Rayburn
1942, N. M. Jones
1944, Henry Attenborough
1947, K. W. Countryman
1952, Darrel L. Iwerks
1960, Calvin Moore

SNOHOMISH
1884, C. Derrick
1885, G. R. Osborn
1886, J. W. Dobbs
1887, B. F. Brooks
1889, Charles F. Teeter (S)
1890, TBS
1891, G. H. Feese
1892, F. E. Drake
1893, D. G. LeSourd
1895, A. J. Hanson
1897, R. Z. Fahs
1900, Edward McEvers
1901, G. A. Sheafe
1904, C. B. Sears
1908, F. M. Clark
1909, H. K. Vann
1910, Richard Oates
1913, D. S. Kerr
1916, F. L. Moore
1918, W. T. Randolph
1919, D. A. Storey
1923, F. R. Gillett
1925, L. C. Shultz
1929, A. W. Brown
1935, H. E. Nelson
1938, W. Paul Fulmer

1940, R. B. Shaw
1943, N. M. Jones
1946, L. B. Jenkins
1948, Geo. Cox (S)
1951, Milton C. De Armand
1954, Paul G. Perkins
1960, Wilfred L. Johnson
1963, S. Christian Thele

STANWOOD
1887, Andrew J. McNemee
1889, W. H. Johnson
1889, M. C. Van Tyne (S)
1890, John W. White
1892, J. W. Patterson
1894, C. E. Cunningham
1896, G. D. Dimick
1897, C. A. Williams
1900, R. M. Schoonmaker
1901, John Britts
1903, E. B. Reese
1906, C. A. Owens
1907, W. S. Hanlein
1910, TBS
1911, J. H. Dill
1912, W. J. Rule
1913, W. M. D. Riggs (S)
1914, J. S. Sneethen (S)
1915, E. V. Bronson
1917, F. A. Guiler
1919, J. W. Reynolds
1923, L. C. Davies (S)
1924, John A. Logan (S)
1925, W. H. Pascoe (S)
1928, Paul R. Campbell
1929, S. V. Warren
1931, J. D. Bird
1934, A. W. Smith
1937, Jas. A. Reeder
1939, Bertram Robins (S)
1948, H. W. Driver
1951, J. Ray Neiser
1954, Wendell J. Cone
1961, Roy Jenkins
1963, Robert J. Lyon

SULTAN
1891, TBS
1893, A. J. McNemee
1894, TBS
1895, O. Doane
1896, J. W. Patterson
1898, T. L. Dyer
1900, A. H. Marsh
1901, TBS
1902, J. A. Nutter
1903, B. N. Galbraith
1904, S. H. Greenlee
1905, H. C. Wilson
1906, J. M. Wilder
1908, H. K. Kline
1910, TBS
1911, A. N. Raven (S)
1912, E. M. Fly (S)
1913, D. A. Storey
1914, E. E. Simmons
1915, H. L. Richardson
1916, TBS
1917, A. P. Basher (S)
1918, TBS
1919, Fred L. Post (S)
1920, W. J. Rule
1921, J. W. Kern
1923, J. H. Bennett (S)
1925, TBS
1928, L. J. Butcher (S)
1929, TBS
1930, J. D. Bird
1931, A. W. Luce
1936, TBS
1938, Gerald Henry (S)
1940, J. Ray Neiser

418

1943, S. M. Berney
1944, B. A. Hylton
1945, Paul Woodward
1946, TBS
1947, Robert R. Potts (S)
1950, Robert K. Shartz (S)
1952, Everett M. Richey
1956, TBS
1957, John K. Burleson
1960, Thomas F. Ludwig
1964, Jesse Modahl (S)
1965, Clarence H. Lund

INDEX
1954, Everett M. Richey
1956, TBS
1957, John K. Burleson
1960, Thomas F. Ludwig
1964, Jesse Modahl (S)
1965, Clarence H. Lund

ALLEN
1924, C. B. Seely (S)
1927, J. F. Redfern (S)
1928, J. D. Bird (S)
1930, O. W. Black
1931, TBS
1934, Allen Chamberlain (S)
1935, TBS
1943, Mrs. Gertrude C. Dealy (S)
1945, John Mathone
1944, John W. Kuller
1950, Malcolm Higgins (S)
1951, Samuel A. Carlson
1954, Arno M. Hutchinson, Jr.
1957, Alfred S. Palmer
1960, Clarence H. Lund
1965, Herbert G. Luscombe

BLANCHARD
1910, TBS
1911, H. C. Carter
1912, Randolph Sasnett (S)
1915, J. L. Grandey
1917, J. M. Wilder
1921, Clark Cottrell
1923, A. M. Frederick (S)
1925, P. E. Pike
1928, J. D. Bird (S)
1930, A. W. Smith
1931, E. W. D. Hanna
1933, Robert Thompson (S)
1937, TBS
1938, W. M. Richards
1940, TBS
1941, Ralph Stevens (S)
1942, S. N. Berney (S)
1943, TBS
1944, Thomas Slate
1947, Absent
1948, John W. Kuller
1949, TBS
1950, Donald P. Sandel (S)
1951, Stanley Goddard
1952, Russell Ward (S)
1954, TBS
1955, Wilfred Johnson
1956, E. C. Kreitlow (S)
1960, Clarence H. Lund
1965, Herbert G. Luscombe

ANACORTES
1890, TBS
1891, Chas. McDermoth
1893, F. M. Pickles
1895, F. S. Wright
1896, TBS, Seattle D.
1897, C. J. Kallgren
1899, M. A. Covington
1900, Rial Benjamin
1901, W. S. Hanlein
1907, Daniel S. Kerr

1910, W. M. Dews
1912, G. A. Sheafe
1913, E. W. Erickson
1916, V. C. Evers
1918, J. F. Long
1920, G. F. Pollock
1925, A. W. Smith
1927, O. W. Black
1930, R. A. Partee
1932, Jas. A. Moore
1934, O. L. Anthony
1935, Allan Chamberlain (S)
1937, Everett M. Hill
1938, Decatur N. Lacy
1944, W. H. Monroe
1948, Lawrence J. Linnemann
1952, Paul G. Perkins
1954, Charles R. Davenport
1961, Carl Richard Boyd

AVON
1884, W. B. McMillan
1886, F. M. Pickles (S)
1890, Liberty E. Wornom
1892, C. E. Cunningham
1893, G. F. Mead
1894, J. R. Edwards
1896, F. S. Wright
1897, A. H. Marsh
1900, J. H. Kevan
1901, S. S. Guiler
1905, R. D. Cady (S)
1906, B. W. Rinehart
1908, J. W. Glenk
1909, C. C. Pratt
1910, TBS
1911, H. C. Carter
1912, A. F. Stearns
1914, A. O. Quall (S)
1922, L. C. Davies (S)
1923, C. B. Seely
1928, A. W. Smith
1931, R. T. Holland
1937, F. F. Boothby
1940, Merrill Hurd (S)
1945, L. C. Bennett & wife (S)
        Hortense Bennett (S)
1949, L. E. Larson (S)
1951, Hortense Bennett (S)
1953, Louis H. Kaub
1959, R. W. Pruitt
1963, R. Clinton McGaffee

BAYVIEW
1891, Ira N. Goodell
1893, F. M. Pickles
1895, not listed
1896, F. S. Wright
1897, W. M. Daniel
1899, TBS
1900, T. J. Redfern
1902, C. A. Owens
1904, R. M. Schoonmaker
1906, H. K. Kline
1908, TBS
1909, E. O. Harris
1911, Charles Easton
1912, L. C. Schultz
1914, G. F. Pollock
1917, F. M. Bushong (S)
1918, TBS, C. E. Sanders
1921, W. M. D. Riggs (S)
1922, L. H. Miller
1924, TBS
1925, B. V. Bradshaw
1927, J. F. Redfern
1928, J. D. Bird
1930, TBS
1931, E. D. W. Hanna
1933, Robert Thompson
1937, F. F. Boothby
1940, not listed

1945, L. C. Bennett (S)
        wife Hortense (S)
1949, TBS & L. E. Larson (S)
1950, Donald P. Sandel
1951, Martin Ramsey
1952, Hortense Bennett (S)
1953, Ernest F. Gates
1954, Louis H. Kaub
1956, M. M. Lehmann
        no active church
1958, TBS
1959, M. M. Lehmann
1960, R. W. Pruitt
1963, R. Clinton McGaffee

BURLINGTON
1903, J. W. Kern
1905, T. F. Allen
1906, E. J. Smith
1908, J. H. Carter
1912, W. M. Dews
1916, W. E. Cox
1920, L. C. Shultz
1925, F. R. Gillett
1926, Richard Oates
1929, O. W. Black
1934, H. J. Wood
1936, B. N. Galbraith
1941, H. E. Greening
1943, J. P. Johnson
1945, H. R. Cross
1948, E. Maxwell Strange
1949, K. N. Ekaas
1954, J. Ray Neiser
1962, James E. Doak
1965, William E. Strance

LA CONNER
1884, B. F. Brooks
1886, E. J. Moore
1888, J. W. White
1890, John M. Baxter
1891, P. C. L. Harris
1892, Sprague Davis
1894, O. A. Curry
1895, W. F. Clarke
1896, R. H. Massey
1897, F. H. Chamberlain
1899, Edward McEvers
1900, C. A. Williams
1903, George Arney
1905, C. N. Goulder
1907, J. W. Glenk
1909, C. C. Pratt
1911, E. O. Harris
1912, J. W. Kern (S)
1914, H. E. Chappell
1916, J. M. Hixson
1918, C. E. Sanders
1921, W. M. D. Riggs (S)
1922, L. H. Miller (S)
1924, TBS
1925, R. V. Bradshaw (S)
1927, C. V. Seely (S)
1928, A. W. Smith
1930, R. A. Partee
1931, R. T. Holland
1939, H. W. Hanson
1947, C. Smith Yndestad
1949, Wm. E. Whitlock (S)
1951, Martin Ramsey (S)
1952, R. V. B. Dunlap
1953, Ernest F. Gates (S)
1958, TBS
1959, K. W. Larrison
1961, Fred R. Owen

SAMISH ISLAND
1943, Gertrude C. Dealy (S)
1946, L. C. Bennett
1949, TBS
1949, Donald P. Sandel (S)
1951, Stanley Goddard (S)

1952, Russell Ward
1954, TBS
1955, M. M. Lehmann (S)
1958, not listed
1959, M. M. Lehmann
1960, R. W. Pruitt
1961, Fred R. Owen

MOUNT VERNON, FIRST
1888, W. M. Ludwick
1889, Charles McDermoth
1891, TBS
1892, B. F. VanDeVenter
1893, F. W. Loy
1894, B. F. Brooks
1897, R. H. Massey
1899, A. E. Burrows
1900, J. W. Kern
1902, R. L. Wolfe
1904, A. W. Brown
1908, S. G. Jones
1909, H. G. Ward
1911, H. E. Greening
1914, F. L. Baldwin
1918, Paul H. Ashby
1920, C. E. Todd
1925, P. H. Raymond
1929, G. W. Frame
1931, O. J. Beadles
1933, H. C. Kohr
1935, C. L. Creesy
1938, Harry E. Gardner
1942, Raymond S. Rees
1944, Elwin H. Scheyer
1945, William Twiddy
1947, Roy Jenkins
1948, Victor Phillips
1953, Carroll H. Sprague
1964, Fred E. Fox

MOUNT VERNON, GRACE
Pleasant Ridge
1888, L. Dahlgren
1889, O. E. Olander
1892, C. A. Anderson
1894, John A. Anderson
1896, B. Howe
1898, J. Johnson
1900, C. J. Nelson
1903, Ch. Johnson (S)
1904, J. H. Levedahl
1906, John Johnson
1912, O. N. Johnson

SKAGIT CITY
1898, J. Johnson
1904, K. O. Berglund
    now GRACE
1908, K. O. Berglund
1909, E. G. Landin
1912, S. Moody
1918, J. A. Willman
1922, J. N. Burdell
1932, G. A. Nelson
1937, C. J. Nelson
1944, Thos. Slate
1948, Wallace R. Johnson (S)
1948, Alfred Palmer (S)
1953, D. Hugh Wood (S)
1954, Russell Ward (S)
1962, Marvin E. Maddux (S)
1965, Raymond F. White (S)

SEDRO WOOLEY (Central
Methodist)
1884, W. B. McMillan
1887, B. N. L. Davis
1886, "Daddy" Hawkins
1887, F. M. Pickles
1890, Riley T. Baldwin (S)
1891, G. L. Cuddy
1896, C. A. Williams

1897, G. D. Dimick
1898, F. M. Pickles
1899, R. H. Massey
1901, TBS
1902, John H. Carter
1905, S. G. Jones
1906, H. W. Michener
1908, R. L. Wolfe
1910, D. S. Kerr
1913, B. W. Rinehart
1916, M. B. Phillips
1918, B. F. Brooks
1919, C. I. Andrews
1920, E. D. White
1922, A. M. Steele
1924, E. J. Bates
1927, R. V. B. Dunlap
1932, C. E. Miller,
    O. L. Anthony
1935, O. L. Anthony
1937, Elmer E. Beckman
1939, C. L. Walker
1943, Milo E. Morris
1944, Wayne D. Griffen
1948, TBS
1949, Miss M. Koth (S)
1952, R. Clinton McGaffee
1957, Harlan D. Jones
1961, Joseph O. Patterson

BELLINGHAM, ALDERSGATE
1889, G. C. Boswell
1890, Frank W. Loy
1892, W. B. McMillan
1893, Charles McDermoth
1896, F. H. Chamberlain
1897, F. S. Wright
1899, J. W. Kendall
1901, C. B. Sears
1903, E. W. Ericson
1906, J. A. Sutton
1908, E. J. Smith
1911, W. E. Cox
1913, H. L. Townsend
1917, P. H. Ashby
1918, L. C. Schultz
1920, T. H. Jorgenson
1923, J. M. Hixson
1926, R. V. B. Dunlap
1927, A. O. Quall
1937, I. J. McFarland
1944, Herbert E. Luscombe
1946, Paul Woodward
1949, Hortense Bennett (S)
1951, Ernest F. Gates
1953, Alfred S. Palmer (S)
1957, Don Kaelin (S)
1961, Ritchie D. Ocheltree
1962, Fairhaven, First Church
1964, Aldersgate, John R.
    Qualley

BELLINGHAM, EUREKA
1905, J. W. Flesher
1905, Alfred Brittain
1906, J. W. Martin,
    F. A. Guiler
1909, J. W. Glenk
1911, G. C. Squire
1915, C. M. Sullivan (S)
1916, Roy M. Owen (S)
1918, C. B. Sears
1919, W. D. Turkington (S)
    G. B. Mehl (S) &
    H. Howard (S)
1920, Robt. G. Pike (S)
1921, Harold E. Bashor
1926, W. J. Rule
1930, John H. Avery
1936, W. J. Rule
1937, Frank R. Gillett
1943, R. A. Stevens (S)

1945, Wm. Phillips (S)
1946, J. C. Snowden
1947, Harlan R. Stone
1950, Paul G. Perkins
1952, John W. Kuller
1956, TBS, Joe Patterson
1961, T. H. Roddey (S)
1962, not listed

BELLINGHAM,
    GARDEN STREET, FIRST
1884, "WHATCOM"
    J. W. Dobbs
1886, L. J. Garver
1887, G. R. Osborn
1888, D. G. LeSourd
1890, Thomas J. Massey
1892, C. C. Cook
1896, T. J. Massey
1897, C. McDermoth
1898, F. E. Drake
1899, S. S. Sulliger
1902, J. W. Frescoln
1904, J. W. Flesher
1907, Wm. B. McMillan
1908, J. A. Sutton
1909, W. T. Randolph
1912, N. M. Temple
1915, E. M. Hill
1916, Geo. C. King
1919, T. E. Elliott
1920, J. E. Harrison
1926, Chas. MacCaughey
1929, Andrew Warner
1931, Thos. W. Jeffrey
1936, Chas. J. Dickey (S)
1936, Ed. A. Wolfe
1939, Jas. E. Milligan
1943, Roy L. Smith
1947, Alexander P. Aiton
1949, Daniel E. Taylor
1953, Clarence J. Forsberg
1955, Assoc. W. E. Strance
1956, Assoc. Calvin Moore
1957, Donald Swerdfeger
1960, Assoc. Robert Irwin
1963, Joe Walker
1963, Assoc., Donovan E.
    McVicker

BLAINE
1871, M. J. Luark
1874, J. N. Dennison
1875, T. J. McGill
1876, A. J. McNemee
1877, T. B. Goodpasture
1878, C. Derrick
1879, T. B. Goodpasture
1880, J. A. Tennant
1883, Levin Johnson (S)
1884, B. F. VanDeVenter
1885, A. Warren (S)
1886, William Zellers
1887, A. Warren (S)
1888, James Eva, ½ yr.
1888, A. Warren (S)
1888, W. R. Warren
1889, W. M. Ludwick
1890, George Kindred
1891, W. H. Mahaffie, 5 mos.
1891, J. McKeen
1891, B. B. Evans
1891, A. Warren
1892, W. F. Loy
1893, J. W. White
1896, H. D. Wadsworth
1898, J. W. Kendall
1899, A. J. Whitfield
1901, J. W. Frescoln
1902, O. H. McGill
1903, C. B. Sears
1904, G. A. Sheafe

1907, C. B. Seely
1912, R. C. Hartley
1915, J. F. Long
1918, G. F. Pollock
1920, G. C. Squire
1923, F. M. Bushong (S)
1927, T. H. Jorgenson
1928, C. B. Seely
1934, G. E. James
1936, Bertram Robins (S)
1939, F. L. Groth (S)
1940, K. L. Countryman
1941, B. N. Galbraith
1945, Donald Bishop (S)
1946, TBS
1947, J. Warne Sanders
1951, Linden B. Jenkins
1952, Harold Slocum
1954, Clarence H. Lund
1960, TBS
1961, Mack Farmer (S)
1963, William G. Graff (S)

CUSTER
1905, TBS
1906, J. H. Berringer (S)
1909, G. C. Poolton
1910, B. W. Rinehart
1913, N. E. Wood
1915, A. A. Brittain
1917, G. F. Pollock
1918, A. F. Grissom
1919, G. B. Mehl (S)
1920, W. M. D. Riggs (S)
1921, J. W. Moles (S)
1927, T. H. Jorgensen (S)
1928, C. B. Seely
1934, G. E. James
1936, Bertram Robins
1938, Allan B. Wilson
1939, Kenneth W. Countryman
1942, R. S. McCulloch
1944, Donald Bishop (S)
1946, R. V. B. Dunlap
1947, Dennis DeVoe (S)
1949, Hazel Wood, TBS (S)
1950, T. H. Roddy (S)
1955, Donald J. Roraback
1956, Everett M. Richey
1959, John Mathone
1963, Jesse L. Tooley (S)

NO. BELLINGHAM
1915, J. M. Hixson
1916, W. P. Rutledge (S)
1917, TBS
1918, J. W. Moles (S)
1921, L. H. Miller (S)
1922, C. B. Sears (S)
1925, H. L. Allen
1926, Harry A. McPheeters
1927, R. B. Parcel
1930, Dow DeLong
1931, A. W. Smith
1934, E. H. Scheyer
1937, W. Paul Fulmer
1938, Lloyd A. Doty (S)
1940, W. H. H. Forsyth
1943, Henry R. Cross
1945, R. S. McCulloch (S)
1946, L. C. Shultz (S)
1947, Harlan R. Stone
1950, Paul G. Perkins
1952, John W. Kuller
1956, TBS
1957, Joseph Patterson
1959, John Mathone (S)
1963, Jesse L. Tooley (S)

FERNDALE (United)
1884, B. F. VanDeVenter
1885, not listed

1889, Geo. Kindred (S)
1890, John Britts
1891, W. R. Warren
1892, L. E. Wornom
1893, J. L. Parmeter
1895, A. H. Marsh
1897, A. J. Whitfield
1898, J. W. Patterson
1900, C. J. Kallgren
1905, S. S. Guiler
1909, J. W. Moles
1912, J. C. Harrison
1915, M. B. Phillips
1916, R. L. Sprague
1918, E. J. Bates
1921, G. B. Mehl (S)
1923, Harry L. Allen
1926, Harry A. McPheeters
1927, R. B. Parcel
1930, Dow DeLong
1931, A. W. Smith
1934, E. H. Scheyer
1937, W. Paul Fulmer
1938, Lloyd A. Doty (S)
1940, W. H. H. Forsyth
1943, Henry R. Cross
1945, R. J. L. McKelvey (S)
1946, C. Gene Albertson
1953, Ernest F. Gates (S)
1954, Henry Martynse (S)
1956, Robert L. Irwin
1960, No appt. United
1961, Ivan R. Smith (S)
1963, John A. Haygood

LYNDEN
1884, G. R. Osborn
1885, John Flinn
1887, John Tennant
1890, Charles F. Teeter
1892, M. A. Covington
1893, W. J. Barger
1894, Wm. McWatters
1895, F. H. Chamberlin
1896, Wm. Daniels (S)
1897, John Thomas
1898, John Britts
1899, W. C. Mitchell
1900, C. E. Botts
1901, R. L. Wolfe
1902, J. W. Kern
1903, B. W. Rinehart
1906, A. J. Whitfield
1908, J. M. Wilder
1911, Herbert Jones
1914, P. H. Ashby
1917, W. O. Benadom
1921, E. O. Grimes
1923, D. A. Storey
1925, T. L. Blaisdell
1928, T. A. Graham
1931, Robert C. Hartley
1935, J. F. Long
1936, M. J. Perdue
1940, Paul R. Campbell
1949, Chester C. Blair
1953, Floyd E. Wells
1958, James N. Updike
1963, Marvin E. Jordan

NOOKSACK
1884, G. R. Osborn
1885, John Flinn
1889, John W. Patterson
1891, not listed
1903, TBS
1905, C. W. Stevens (S)
1907, H. L. Richardson
1910, J. C. Harrison (S)
1912, E. O. Harris
1914, L. C. Shultz
1918, J. M. Hixson

1920, J. H. Avery
1923, G. C. Squire
1927, F. L. Lowther
1931, F. F. Boothby
1937, Arnt O. Quall
1942, Clarence H. Lund
1945, Kenneth W. Countryman
1947, Byron C. Gallaher
1949, Paul T. Woodward
1952, Marion Koth (S)
1955, Ben H. Davis
1959, Samuel Carlson (S)
1963, Murray V. Hyde

NOOKSACK INDIAN MISSION
1874, Rev. C. M. Tate (S)
    of Canada
1876, A. J. McNemee
1884, TBS
1888, John Flinn
1889, John W. Patterson
1891, J. A. Tennant
1892, A. H. Marsh
1895, J. L. Parmeter
1898, O. L. Doane
1899, C. A. Owens
1902, T. J. Hazelton (S)
1903, F. J. Brown
1908, H. L. Richardson (S)
1910, O. R. Anderson
1913, W. J. Gilbert
1917, B. V. Bradshaw (S)
1928, TBS
1929, S. G. Thero (S)
1938, R. S. McCulloch
1942, W. T. Beatty
1944, not listed
1952, Hilmer W. Hanson
1954, Marmaduke Dodsworth
1959, Hortense Anable (S)
1960, TBS
1961, M. Dodsworth
1962, Samuel A. Carlson
1963, Marmaduke Dodsworth

SUMAS
1891, J. W. Patterson
1891, C. C. Culmer
1892, TBS
1895, J. L. Parmeter
1896, TBS
1897, D. W. Thurston
1898, S. J. Buck
1899, TBS
1900, T. J. Hazelton (S)
1902, H. G. Ward
1904, J. H. Kevan
1905, E. V. Smith
1907, J. W. Kern
1908, B. W. Rinehart
1910, E. J. Huston
1912, J. L. Grandey
1913, W. W. Switzer
1914, A. W. Hartshorn
1915, J. R. Sasnett
1916, G. C. Poolton
1917, H. H. Newman
1919, K. R. Gilmer
1920, TBS
1924, H. L. Richardson (S)
1926, D. S. McGuire (S)
1928, F. L. Lowther
1930, not listed
1931, F. F. Boothby
1937, not listed
1938, R. S. McCulloch
1942, W. T. Beatty
1945, H. L. Richardson (S)
1947, Hilmer R. Hanson
1954, Marmaduke Dodsworth
1959, Hortense Anable (S)
1960, TBS

1961, David Roddy (S)
1962, TBS
1963, Stanley R. Kuntz (S)

SEATTLE DISTRICT
BELLEVUE, ALDERSGATE
1962, Rhea S. Dougherty
1963, Albert J. Wilson

BELLEVUE, FIRST
1952, John W. Caughlan (R)
1954, TBS
1955, H. Paul Smith
1958, Seattle D.
1960, Kenneth H. Underwood

BELLEVUE, ST. PETER'S
1963, Frederick E. Still
1965, Paul J. Beman

BOTHELL
1886, A. Atwood
1889, L. E. Wornom
1890, Geo. R. Osborn
1891, H. Alling
1892, Arthur Crumley
1895, William Metcalf
1896, J. McKeene
1897, A. J. McNemee
1898, Rowland Hughes
1899, Jno. W. Kern
1900, T. L. Dyer
1901, Chas. E. Lambert
1901, A. J. Whipkey
1902, Lorenzo Jean (S)
1903, S. J. Buck
1904, Wm. S. Eldridge (S)
1904, F. H. Calder (S)
1906, Richard Oates
1907, J. H. Carter
1908, H. W. Michener
1911, H. C. Leavenworth
1913, A. W. Brown
1916, B. W. Rinehart
1919, O. F. Krieger
1922, A. H. Thompson
1924, Chas. A. Bowen
1926, Joseph H. Beall
1930, V. A. Spicker
1931, U. F. Hawk
1933, C. L. Walker
1937, Elwin H. Scheyer
1943, Robert B. Shaw
1948, Harry E. Rarey
1951, J. Warne Sanders
1960, S. Raynor Smith, Jr.
1962, J. Allan Justad

DES MOINES
1889, Rev. M. Sampson (S)
1892, S. S. Guiler (S)
1894, E. D. White, also
    Robt. Hatfield ()
1895, W. T. Walton (S)
1897, A. S. Gregg. TBS
1899, William Daniel
1900, S. J. Buck
1903, R. W. Paul
1907, TBS
1908, J. C. P. Hester (S)
1909, E. H. Rubicam
1910, F. A. Guiler
1913, W. J. Rule
1915, A. F. Grissom
1917, J. W. Kern
1919, G. R. Abbott
1921, S. V. Warren
1922, J. I. Beatty
1924, W. H. Leech
1928, D. A. Storey (S)
1931, W. M. Dews

1932, J. H. Berringer
1937, C. E. Miller, Assoc.
1945, T. Earl Poindexter
1951, W. H. Hertzog
1957, Ernest P. Goulder
1958, Seattle District
1961, Assoc. Robert Kinch
1962, Rudolph A. Anderson
1965, Craig T. Harper

FALL CITY
1886, A. J. McNemee (S)
1887, Ed. H. Stayt (S)
1888, A. Atwood
1889, W. H. Johnstone
1890, TBS
1892, not listed
1918, G. L. Snyder (S)
1919, Jarrett I. Beatty
1922, A. Earl Lee (S)
1923, B. W. Rinehart
1927, Wm. E. Callahan, Jr.
1929, L. C. Shultz
1930, Richard Oates (S)
1932, Nelson Pierce
1933, Waldo W. Pierson
1936, J. R. Butler
1938, Harry L. Allen
1944, Revelle E. Roach
1946, David Kline
1949, W. E. Menold (S)
1950, John Kuller
1952, Robert Walker
1953, TBS
1954, Ernest Barber
1958, Geo. C. Pratt

FEDERAL WAY,
MARINE VIEW
1959, Gertrude L. Apel (S)

KENT
1854, called White River,
    D. E. Blaine
1855, no record
1860, D. L. Spaulding
1861, B. C. Lippincott
1862, TBS
1863, N. Doane
1865, C. G. Belknap
1866, R. C. Smith
1867, H. B. Lane
1868, G. H. Greer
1870, S. H. Mann
1872, A. C. Fairchild
1873, W. I. Cosper
1874, Albert Atwood
1877, B. J. Sharp (S)
1879, D. L. Spaulding
1881, TBS
1882, not listed
1883, A. K. Crawford
1884, John Flinn
1885, B. F. VanDeVenter
1889, Became Kent, R. Z. Fahs
1891, W. H. Drake
1893, C. E. Fulmer
1896, E. E. Morris
1901, A. J. Whitfield
1903, F. E. Drake
1905, C. A. Williams
1908, Geo. A. Sheafe
1911, V. C. Evers
1913, Richard Oates
1915, W. O. Benadom
1917, H. L. Townsend
1918, S. S. Sulliger
1924, H. E. Gardner
1928, George R. Abbott
1933, N. M. Jones
1935, H. C. Kohr
1936, Wm. E. Callahan, Jr.

1942, Wilbur M. Snyder
1944, Earl W. McAbee
1952, Robert H. Ortmeyer
1959, Paul E. Hamlin
1964, Carroll H. Sprague

KIRKLAND, Lake Washington
1960, Donald E. Sattelberg
1961, Jonathan W. King
1965, Ritchie D. Ocheltree II

MERCER ISLAND
1963, L. L. Dunnington (S)

REDMOND
1895, B. F. Luse (S)
1896, no record in mins.
1908, TBS
1909, F. A. Guiler
1910, H. C. Carter (S)
1912, T. Houlston (S)
1915, Angus McLean (S)
1916, R. G. Pike
1918, TBS
1922, R. J. Allen (S)
1923, TBS
1925, J. W. Walker (S)
1926, Ralph W. D. Brown
1927, Wm. E. Callahan
1928, Nelson C. Pierce
1933, Waldo W. Pierson
1936, John W. Butler
1938, Harry L. Allen
1944, Revelle E. Roach
1949, E. Maxwell Strange
1950, C. E. Rayburn
1953, Robert J. Lyon
1959, Peter L. Misner
1964, Frank A. Jackson

RENTON
1899, TBS
1903, F. H. Calder (S)
1904, Roland Hughes
1906, R. Z. Fahs
1909, R. L. Sprague
1911, O. F. Krieger
1914, M. B. Phillips
1915, R. L. Wolfe
1917, D. P. Henry (S)
1920, A. F. Stearns
1921, A. M. Steele
1922, E. D. White
1923, J. W. Reynolds
1925, G. R. Abbott
1928, Paul F. Green
1932, Ernest Barber
1934, W. H. H. Forsythe
1938, C. L. Creesy
1940, Roy Jenkins
1947, William Twiddy
1948, W. Harry Monroe
1956, Lawrence J. Linnemann
1960, Assoc. Charles Gruenwald
1963, Charles Gruenwald left
1961, Earl L. Dean

KENNYDALE
1907, T. L. Dyer
1910, W. E. Williams
1911, C. W. Walter (S)
1912, H. C. Walters (S)
1913, D. Earl (S)
1915, W. H. Hoare (S)
1916, R. C. Hartley
1917, TBS
1918, W. H. Hoare (S)
1919, F. G. Willey (S)
1920, Ray Atteberry
1921, A. M. Herd
1923, W. S. Garner (S)
1924, B. W. Haggert (S)

1925, J. M. Weaver
1926, A. W. Luce
1928, Hugh Hay (S)
1929, C. E. Challeden (S)
1930, K. O. Pearson
1934, TBS
1935, not listed
1936, W. H. H. Forsythe
1938, Charles L. Creesy
1940, TBS
1941, Charles Gleason (S)
1943, Irving Sylvia (S)
1945, John W. Caughlan (R)
1949, Albert Richardson (S)
1950, Ernest Barber (R)
1952, Paul D. Brown (S)
1954, Edwin F. Rode
1956, Henry R. Cross
1958, John B. Freeman
1960, Gregory A. Zimmer
1964, John K. Burleson

SEABOLD
1957, Donald G. Cramer (S)
1958, John A. Haygood
1960, Justin I. Morrill

SEATTLE, INNER CITY
MINISTRY
CAPITOL HILL
1864, Daniel Bagley
1886, S. A. Baker
      H. M. Sexton
      M. Skidmore
      Clark D. Davis
      W. M. Kellogg
      Frank Whitman
      T. Plummer Revelle
      A. Norman Ward
      J. M. Gill
      R. T. Tyson
      Leonard B. Smith
1924, George Beck
      A. E. Fletcher
      W. P. Roberts
      R. N. Orrill
      Frank L. Hayden
      Clyde H. Havens
      A. H. Lynch
      J. C. Byrd
1939, Alexander G. Bennett
1942, W. Raymond Wilder
1950, J. J. Ellington
1952, Erwin G. Ranton
1956, Ritchie D. Ocheltree, Sr.
1959, Fred O. Hunt
1963, Donald L. Swerdfeger

FELLOWSHIP, FILIPINO
CHURCH
1926, T. Walter Bundy
1945, Grandino Baaoa (S)
1947, Pio J. Daba
1953, D. F. Gonzalo

GRACE
1889, called "Jackson St."
      W. H. Mahaffie
1890, H. D. Brown
1891, changed to Grace
      W. B. McMillan
1892, T. W. Butler
1894, W. T. Ford
1896, J. W. Bushong
1897, W. H. Selleck
1901, Edward McEvers
1902, R. C. Glass
1904, George Gable
1905, W. H. R. Forsythe
1906, W. T. Randolph
1909, E. H. Todd
1910, J. H. Secor

1913, W. O. Benadom
1915, Richard Oates
1916, W. H. Baker
1920, F. A. C. Crown (S)
1921, E. W. Erickson
1925, E. R. Attebery
1940, Arthur S. Morton
1946, John M. Finney
1949, J. E. Milligan
1952, Wayne D. Griffen
1957, Linden B. Jenkins
1958, Robert B. Shaw
1962, Robert F. Vahey

SOUTH PARK, formerly
SHAW MEMORIAL
1893, N. S. Buckner
1894, S. Davis
1895, W. T. Walton (S)
1896, A. S. Gregg
1897, A. W. Bagley (S)
1898, A. J. Whitfield
1899, Rowland Hughes
1902, T. L. Dyer
1904, Rial Benjamin
1905, V. C. Evers
1908, O. H. McGill
1911, Horace Williston
1913, R. G. Pike (S)
1915, J. M. Dennison
1918, T. W. Bundy
1919, Rudolph Ericson
1920, J. H. Geoghegan
1921, Joseph Olsen (S)
1922, F. E. Cain
1923, E. E. Reisner
1925, J. Homer Magee
1926, J. M. Weaver
1928, G. A. Sheafe
1929, D. A. Storey
1930, B. W. Rinehart
1931, R. W. D. Brown
1933, Mrs. L. E. Pontius (S)
1936, Elsie Mitchell (S)
1937, Wayne Sprague
1938, Frank C. Abbott (S)
1939, Merrill Hurd (S)
1940, Ralph Butler
1950, Bessie Pease (S) and
      Annette Kiehlbauch (S)
1953, South Park
1955, D. L. Rothweiler (R)
1958, James E. Gossett
1960, H. Robert Morton
1962, John Wesley Martin (S)
1964, Robert F. Vahey

NORTH BROADWAY,
SEATTLE, formerly HAVEN
1890, Geo. H. Feese
1891, E. D. White
1893, Supplied
1895, W. H. Drake
1897, TBS
1898, J. M. Dennison
1903, A. J. Whitfield
1904, Charles N. Goulder
1905, F. E. Drake
1907, W. O. Benadom
1908, W. W. Batcheller
1909, E. E. Morris (S)
1911, W. H. Baker
1914, B. F. Brooks
1916, E. W. Erickson
1921, F. E. Cain (S)
1922, E. M. Randall
1924, A. H. Thompson
1925, A. H. Lathrop
1926, Ray R. Martin
1929, E. T. Gruwell
1936, Frank Abbott (S)
1938, E. M. Hill (S)

1939, J. A. Reeder (S)
1941, Walter Torbet (S)
1944, John Henry Soltman
1947, Darrell Iwerks
1952, George Nafus (S)
1953, Carl K. Mahoney
1954, J. C. Snowden
1956, L. Wayne Bond
1958, G. Hurst Paul (S)
1963, Gene Allan Ernst (S)
1965, Wesley N. Yamaka

WESLEY PARISH or
WESLEY CHAPEL
1955, John W. Caughlan
1956, L. Wayne Bond
1958, James E. Gossett
1960, H. Robert Morton
1962, Stanley R. Kuntz (S)
1963, G. Hurst Paul (S)
1964, Gene Allan Ernst (S)
1965, Wesley N. Yamaka

BLAINE MEMORIAL, Japanese
1904, Genhichi Tsuruta
1905, Seimei Yoshioka
1914, Munetsugu Obayashi
1918, Tokuji Komuro
1921, Yuzuru Yamaka
1931, Yasaburo Tsuda
1941, Tamotsu Machida
      Relocated
1954, Juhei C. Kono

English or Nisei Division,
BLAINE MEMORIAL
1931, T. W. Bundy
1938, Everett Thompson
1946, Lester Suzuki
1949, Paul Haguja
1954, Frederick Yasaki
1958, Wesley Yamaka
1964, Harry Murakami

BRYN MAWR
1909, org., no pastor
1910, R. L. Sprague
1911, O. F. Krieger
1913, Earl Daniel (S)
1914, R. L. Wolfe
1915, R. C. Hartley
1917, D. P. Henry (S)
1919, R. G. Pike (S)
1920, A. F. Stearns (S)
1921, A. M. Steele
1922, Archie M. Herd
1923, W. S. Garner (S)
1924, Wm. Haggerty (S)
1925, J. M. Weaver
1926, J. Homer Magee
1927, G. A. Sheafe
1929, A. H. Lathrop
1930, K. O. Pearson
1931, B. W. Rinehart
1935, Fred Thompson
1939, Wayne Sprague
1942, Robert Marshall Putt (S)
1943, J. R. Butler
1947, L. V. Martin
1950, TBS
1951, Truman Cotten (S)
1951, Clinton A. Aiton
1955, Frank A. Jackson
1964, K. W. Larrison

CROWN HILL, SEATTLE
1913, W. H. Leech
1916, W. H. Thomas (S)
1919, Earl McAbee (S)
1921, John Tingling (S)
1922, F. E. Cain (S)
1923, W. H. Pascoe

1925, C. O. Burnett (S)
1926, F. R. Gillett
1928, W. T. Randolph
1932, R. L. LaMott
1936, Wayne Sprague
1938, Clarence Lund
1942, Chas. E. Sanders
1943, J. H. Berringer (S)
1947, C. E. Miller
1948, Robert Lukens
1952, Nolan J. McClurg
1957, S. Christian Thele
1960, Harold W. Black
1963, Floyd E. Green

SEATTLE, FIRST
1853, David E. Blaine
1856, W. B. Morse
1857, W. J. Franklin
1858, C. Alderson
1860, no appt.
1861, B. C. Lippincott
1862, Daniel Bagley
1863, N. Doane
1865, C. G. Belknap
1866, R. C. Smith
1867, H. B. Lane
1868, G. H. Greer
1870, S. H. Mann
1872, A. C. Fairchild
1873, W. I. Cosper
1874, A. Atwood
1877, Isaac Dillon
1879, J. F. DeVore
1881, W. C. Chattin (S)
1881, W. S. Harrington
1883, J. N. Dennison
1886, A. J. Hanson
1888, D. D. Campbell
1890, Levi Gilbert
1892, W. P. George
1893, William A. Shanklin
1896, Edwin M. Randall
1902, Assoc. George Gable
1904, Fletcher Wharton
1906, W. H. W. Rees
1910, A. W. Leonard
1912, W. H. Leech, City Misn.
1916, J. E. Crowther
1918, J. R. Sasnett, Assoc.
1920, V. A. Spicker, Assoc.
1921, J. Ralph Magee
1924, J. Homer Magee, Assoc.
1928, F. L. Pedersen, Assoc.
1929, Earl Hoon
1932, John B. Magee
1936, Cyrus Wright, Assoc.
1939, Newton E. Moats
1944, William Twiddy, Assoc.
1945, Erle Howell, Assoc.
1947, Harold N. Nye, Assoc.
1949, Cyrus E. Albertson
1951, Donald Baldwin, Assoc.
1953, Troy M. Strong, Assoc.
1961, Robert A. Uphoff
1961, Assoc. Francis M. Kinch
1962, Assoc. Carl H. McGee
1964, Assoc. E. Max Case
1965, Assoc. R. A. Anderson

GREEN LAKE
1900, A. E. Burrows
1902, Rial Benjamin
1904, R. C. Glass
1907, E. L. Benedict
1912, F. A. LaViolette
1916, D. R. Martin
1917, R. J. Reid
1921, A. H. Lathrop
1922, G. V. Fallis
1924, E. M. Hill
1928, N. M. Jones

1932, E. T. Randall
1935, J. J. Ellington
1937, Edw. J. Huston
1938, Alden R. Graves
1944, W. W. Pierson
1945, Donald M. Fife
1949, Alexander P. Aiton
1951, Carl K. Mahoney
1953, Earl L. Dean
1961, Wayne D. Griffen

HALLER LAKE
1924, Raymond Partee
1927, P. M. Resor (S)
1928, T. H. Palmquist (S)
1930, Wm. O. Pflaum
1934, Wm. E. Callahan
1936, Decatur N. Lacey
1937, Wayne Sprague
1938, L. R. Lake (S)
1940, Gerald Henry (S)
1941, John H. Secor (S)
1945, John C. Soltman
1954, Ac C. Wischmeier
1956, Assoc. James N. Updike
1958, Assoc. Donald E. Sattelberg
1959, Eugene M. Muench
1960, Assoc. James P. Burnett
1962, Assoc. W. W. Pierson (R)
1963, Assoc. David L. Ernst (S)
1965, Assoc. John P. Foreman

HIGHLAND PARK, SEATTLE
1919, John Tingling (S)
1921, Dwight G. Bennett (S)
1923, T. S. Leland (S)
1924, Wm. C. Bowman
1927, W. T. Randolph
1928, E. L. Boothby (S)
1929, Russell Bisnet (S)
1930, G. C. Poolton
1931, R. W. D. Brown
1934, Clark J. Wood
1935, Frank Abbott (S)
1936, Paul B. VanZee (S)
1937, T. Walter Bundy
1957, Rarden W. Vergin
1962, Donald C. Fisher
1964, E. Vincent Smith

HIGHLINE, SEATTLE
1945, K. N. Ekaas
1945, Wayne Wright
1946, Named HIGHLINE
1947, John Henry Soltman
1948, K. N. Ekaas
1949, Robert E. Elliott
1951, C. Keith Mills
1956, William F. Andrews
1960, Alfred W. Carter

MAGNOLIA formerly BETHEL, SEATTLE
1906, Roy L. Sprague
1908, F. E. Drake (S)
1911, J. M. Dennison
1915, J. A. Badcon (S)
1922, W. H. Pasco (S)
1923, G. G. Howse (S)
1924, W. S. Garner (S)
1925, W. T. Randolph
1926, A. H. Lathrop (S)
1928, E. W. Erickson (S)
1929, Ray R. Martin
1930, A. H. Lathrop (S)
1932, R. L. LaMott
1933, E. J. Huston
1934, Lila Marston (S)
1936, Elsie Mitchel (S)
1937, John B. Magee, Jr.
1938, E. J. Walker (S)
1940, Milo Morris (S)

1942, Geo. A. Sheaf (S)
1943, R. S. Ridgway (S)
1945, Clyde L. Walker (S)
1946, E. M. Strange (S)
1947, Wm. O. Pflaum
1951, H. W. Driver
1955, Harry L. Slick
1957, Geo. Almond (R)
1959, MAGNOLIA
1962, Paul J. Beeman
1963, Everett L. Groves
1964, Richard E. Nye

QUEEN ANNE (formerly BATTERY STREET)
1882, Isaac Dillon
1884, Louis Albert Banks
1886, J. H. Skidmore
1887, F. W. Loy
1889, Alfred Inwood
1893, G. A. Landen
1894, E. R. Hayward
1895, H. D. Brown
1902, F. E. Drake
1903, O. H. McGill
1905, became Queen Anne
1907, T. E. Elliott
1909, D. C. Franklin
1912, W. M. Jeffers
1915, G. C. King
1916, F. A. LaViolette
1917, C. D. Rarey (S)
1919, R. N. Orrill
1923, James E. Milligan
1928, A. G. Bennett
1929, C. A. Wright
1936, Wm. M. Bowman
1944, Wilbur M. Snyder
1953, Charles W. Fisher
1959, M. Chester Morgan
1959, F. E. Wells, Assoc. (S)
1961, Wade Springboarn (S)
        Assoc., one yr.
1963, Robert F. Waller

RAINIER BEACH
1903, F. H. Calder (S)
1903, John R. Ball
1905, W. A. Scott
1906, Herbert Jones
1907, E. Victor Smith
1909, TBS
1910, Horace Williston
1911, J. M. Wilder
1914, R. L. Wolfe
1915, R. C. Hartley
1917, G. C. Poolton
1918, R. G. Pike (S)
1919, Jas. Clulow (S)
1920, Mrs. Nellie Clulow (S)
1922, T. L. Blaisdell (S)
1925, E. W. Erickson
1928, Richard Decker
1929, F. E. Goodnough
1932, R. L. Jenkins
1933, M. L. Sanders
1935, Fred Thompson
1936, TBS, D. N. Lacy
1937, J. H. Berringer
1943, J. R. Butler
1947, George Gable
1949, John W. Caughlan
1952, Donald J. Roraback (S)
1955, Milton P. Andrews, Jr.
1961, Geo. A. Cummings

RAVENNA
1903, T. P. Revelle
1903, H. J. Hartsell
1904, Henry Carlyon (S)
        G. L. Curry
1911, S. S. Benninger

424

1912, Robert Asa Smith (S)
Geo. W. Beck
1924, W. L. Hoffman
1931, W. H. Hodges
1942, Wayne L. Sprague (S)
1946, D. L. Rothweiler
1954, John P. Johnson
1959, Louis V. Martin

RIVERTON
1907, Cyrus L. Gilbert
1908, R. L. Sprague
1910, G. M. Irwin (S)
1911, John Tingling (S)
1912, TBS
1913, J. H. McIntosh (S)
1915, John Tingling (S)
1916, J. M. Dennison
1917, TBS
1919, A. P. Basher (S)
1920, J. L. Hanna (S)
1921, W. S. Garner (S)
1922, Mrs. A. D. Newell (S)
1925, E. L. Wolfe (S)
1927, B. W. Rinehart
1930, D. A. Storey
1931, W. M. Dews
1932, F. A. Ecker
1934, Frank Abbott (S)
1935, R. C. Hartley
1936, Philip H. Ashby
1938, Frank E. Abbott (S)
1940, Merlyn Northfelt
1943, Don M. Fife
1945, Jas. Randle
1946, Chas. L. Pegram (S) and
H. Donell Miller (S)
1947, E. M. Strange (S)
1948, Victor E. Hankinson (S)
1950, Robert L. La Mott
1952, TBS
1953, Joseph C. Chester
1955, Mary McKee Chester (S)
1959, David L. Aasen
1962, Harold L. Cribb
1962, Assoc. C. W. Thompson (S)

RONALD
1909, Carl J. Kallgren
1910, J. T. Wright (S)
1911, W. W. Shenk
1913, J. A. Badcon (S)
1914, J. W. Kern
1915, J. T. Wright (S)
1916, W. P. Owens (S)
1917, C. B. Seely
1918, TBS
1919, J. S. VanWinkle
1920, J. J. Yost (S)
1921, K. L. Haga
1923, R. H. Allen
1924, F. L. Baldwin
1926, A. W. Brown
1929, W. E. Callahan
1934, T. L. Blaisdell
1936, F. N. Morton
1938, Waldo Pierson
1944, R. H. Ortmeyer
1947, H. C. Kohr
1948, Frank Haley
1951, Darrell E. Berg
1955, Assoc. Arthur S. Morton
1960, Edward McClurg
1962, Merritt W. Faulkner

SAND POINT, SEATTLE
1943, Harold O. Perry
1947, Robert Hicks
1958, Merritt W. Faulkner
1962, William A. Welch

SEAVIEW, SEATTLE
1919, Leonard B. Smith

1919, A. B. Williams
1925, R. N. Orrill
1927, Thos. G. Batschler
1934, Richard N. Orrill
1935, Wilbur M. Snyder
1942, Harlan R. Stone
1944, H. C. Kohr
1947, Robert Ortmeyer
1952, Wayne T. Wright
1956, Roy Jenkins
1961, John C. Radmore

SKYWAY
1945, Laura Butler (S)
1945, Hillcrest, E. Laura Butler
1950, Skyway, Nolan J. McClurg
1952, Harlan D. Jones
1955, James H. Thompson
1956, Troy M. Strong
1958, J. Robert Dibble
1962, James M. Lane

TIBBETTS, SEATTLE
1909, P. H. Ashby
1911, W. B. Bell
1912, J. F. Long
1915, E. D. White
1920, R. A. Gailey
1922, A. W. Brown
1926, C. C. Curry
1930, J. H. Beall
1935, R. A. Partee
1937, C. L. Walker
1939, E. E. Beckman
1944, D. N. Lacy
1950, LeRoy H. Walker
1951, Francis M. Kinch
1958, Troy M. Strong
1963, Anthony R. Perrino
1964, Donald M. Fife

TRINITY, SEATTLE
1925, J. W. Caughlan
1931, E. J. Huston
1934, Ernest Barber
1936, A. G. Bennett
1939, Harlan R. Stone
1942, Harry E. Gardner
1946, George L. Poor
1950, Assoc. Bertha P. Hartsell
Assoc. Roger K. Johnson
1956, Lloyd F. Holloway
1958, Rudolph A. Anderson
1958, Assoc. Robert Gray Hess
1960, Alin E. Parrett
1961, Assoc. Dewey Knowles
1964, Assoc. Gregory A. Zimmer

UNIVERSITY TEMPLE,
SEATTLE
1891, John R. Edwards
1899, called Brooklyn ch.
Horace Williston
1900, A. E. Burrows
1901, Rial Benjamin
1902, Called University ch.
W. H. Leech
1907, J. M. Canse
1910, E. M. Hill
1914, C. A. Bowen
1918, A. H. Lathrop
1919, TBS
1920, Arch Tremayne
1920, Assoc. T. J. Gambill
1921, Assoc. S. G. Logan
1923, J. E. Crowther
1926, Assoc. Paul F. Breen
1927, Assoc. U. F. Hawk
became University Temple
1928, Assoc. J. M. Weaver
1929, R. H. Schuett
1930, Assoc. L. C. Hicks

1932, Geoffrey W. Stafford
1938, James Brett Kenna
1943, Assoc. John B. Magee, Jr.
1945, Cecil F. Ristow
1951, Assoc. James E. Milligan
(R)
1960, Assoc. in Ed., Fred Rarden
1961, Lynn H. Corson
1962, Harry L. Williams, Assoc.
1963, Education, John Flynn
1964, Assoc. Edwin B. Towle

WOODLAND PARK
1903, TBS
called W. Green Lake ch.
1905, W. W. Batcheller
Became Woodland Park ch.
1906, W. W. Batcheller
1908, M. P. Elder
1910, A. W. Brown
1913, V. C. Evers
1916, Richard Oates
1919, Raymond S. Reese
1924, F. L. Pedersen
1928, H. F. Pemberton
1930, C. E. Miller
1932, M. J. Perdue
1936, H. C. Kohr
1944, J. M. Finney
1946, Harold C. Williams
1951, Don L. Swerdfeger
1957, Reah S. Dougherty
1962, Owen J. Beadles

SNOQUALMIE
1885, A. J. McNemee
1892, R. M. Schoonmaker
1893, H. H. Walkington
1895, Arthur Crumley (S)
1897, G. F. Mead
1898, A. J. McNemee
1903, TBS
1904, H. D. Waldron (S)
1905, G. Anderson (S)
1906, R. W. Merrill (S)
1907, Martin P. Elder
1908, I. D. Helm (S)
1909, J. T. Wright (S)
1910, George R. Abbott
1912, J. F. Keating
1913, S. A. Rhyndress (S)
1914, A. P. Basher (S)
1915, E. G. Ranton (S)
1917, F. W. P. Camp
1918, TBS
1919, V. A. Spicker
1920, Bert Waddington
1922, J. H. Beall
1926, T. A. Graham
1928, W. M. Dews
1931, M. R. Gallaher
1936, John Long
1938, Benj. H. Hart
1941, Geo. Almond
1943, Ernest Barber
1946, E. Clifford Newham
1952, Lawrence J. Linnemann
1956, Myron H. Sharrard
1962, Howard P. Buck

VASHON
1885, TBS
1886, G. R. Osborn
1887, B. R. Freeland (S)
1888, R. H. Massey
1889, C. R. Pomeroy
1891, TBS
1892, C. R. Pomeroy
1893, W. H. Leech
1895, W. H. Wilson
1896, S. P. Brokaw
1897, C. E. Fulmer

1898, G. G. Ferguson
1900, J. T. Smith
1901, A. H. Marsh
1902, J. R. Edwards
1904, J. W. Moles
1907, Harris G. Ward
1909, S. V. Warren
1910, H. K. Kline
1912, J. E. Milligan
1916, R. A. Gailey
1919, E. H. Gebert
1920, J. H. Berringer
1923, TBS
1926, T. W. Bundy
1927, C. E. Preston (S)
1929, E. M. Randall (S)
1935, Elsie Mitchell (S)
1936, E. M. Hill (S)
1937, Frank McAllister (S)
1938, Ethel Williams (S)
1940, E. M. Hill (S)
1942, Arnt O. Quall
1945, John H. Secor (S)
1947, Ira J. McFarland
1949, Paul D. Brown (S)
1952, Paul T. Woodward
1955, Bessie Pease (S),
  Annette Kiehlbauch (S)
1956, G. Hurst Paul (S)
1958, Henry Cross
1961, Fred Cronkite (S)
1962, Fred A. Rarden
1965, Harlan D. Jones

WOODINVILLE
1898, Rowland Hughes
1899, John W. Kern
1900, T. L. Dyer
1901, Chas. E. Lambert
1902, Lorenzo Jean (S)
1903, S. J. Buck
1904, Wm. S. Eldridge
1904, F. H. Calder (S)
1906, Richard Oates
1907, J. H. Carter
1908, H. W. Michener
1911, H. C. Leavenworth
1913, A. W. Brown
1916, B. W. Rinehart
1919, O. F. Krieger
1922, A. H. Thompson
1924, C. A. Bowen
1926, Jos. H. Beall
1930, V. A. Spicker
1932, William Park
1941, Wilson Eckles (S)
1944, Simeon M. Berney (S)
1946, K. W. Larrison (S)
1947, Harold O. Perry
1948, John Mathone (S)
1949, J. Smith Yndestad
1952, Robert K. Shartz
1953, Adam S. Forsch, Sr. to
  Seattle Dist.
1959, Mary McKee Chester (S)
1960, Donald G. Forsberg
1963, Newton E. Moats (R)

SPOKANE DISTRICT
BONNERS FERRY, IDAHO
1902, J. M. Eastland (S)
1904, L. N. B. Anderson
1905, R. C. Moter
1906, E. R. Henderson (S)
1908, Ralph Chaffee (S)
1909, E. R. Henderson (S)
1910, J. L. Moore
1911, J. J. Pacey
1913, A. W. Roberts
1915, H. T. Robinson
1916, J. A. Hoffman
1917, U. S. Crowder

1918, No record
1919, J. F. Gibson
1920, A. H. Morton
1923, R. W. Mason
1927, Dow DeLong
1930, J. R. Norton
1932, W. T. Beatty
1936, Wm. Gornall
1938, M. R. Gallaher
1942, Percy E. Pike
1945, Ralph M. Walsh (S)
1948, TBS
1949, Neils A. Christensen (S)
1955, W. B. Nelson (S)
1956, Bernard E. Mott (S)
1959, Wm. Franklin Summerour
1963, M. Wesley Arms

CHENEY
1880, G. W. Strong
1880, Theodore Hoagland
1881, G. W. Strong
1882, J. W. Bluett
1884, George E. Wilcox
1886, Theodore Hoagland
1887, James Greenslade
1888, M. H. Marvin
1889, J. W. Bluett
1890, F. L. Young
1891, R. H. Manier
1896, O. A. Noble
1899, W. H. Fry
1900, D. W. Raines
1901, John P. Barker
1904, A. W. Roberts
1906, M. L. Sanders
1907, W. E. Thompson
1909, R. D. Snyder
1911, H. C. Kohr
1918, M. M. Eaton
1919, C. B. Martin
1920, C. L. Creesy
1923, H. J. Wood
1925, J. L. Rentfro
1928, Ralph I. Thomas
1931, John Secor
1936, Supply Cong.
1937, Orville Dennis (S)
1942, Harold J. Bass
1947, Fred Field (S)
1953, TBS
1954, David K. Almon
1957, TBS
1959, Charles A. Dittmar (S)
1961, K. W. Larrison
1964, Howard S. Pitts

CHEWELAH
1906, E. H. Eaton (S)
1907, H. F. Pemberton
1908, E. R. Anderson (S)
1909, J. L. Rollins
1909, A. F. Kroneman
1913, D. E. Faulkner
1916, Orland A. Scott
1918, E. T. Reid
1919, G. B. Harbison
1920, W. A. Pratt
1921, H. W. Best
1922, J. F. Weller (S)
1923, Gertrude Apel (S)
1929, Wm. Park
1931, Thos. W. Emery
1933, C. A. Pickering
1934, D. G. Bennett
1937, H. Copley Davis
1938, R. W. Mason
1943, Jas. A. Moore
1948, TBS
1949, Ronald K. Johnson
1956, Roy L. Kuhns
1957, Harry T. Cupp

1957, Fred Riehle (S)
1960, Raymond L. Poindexter
1962, Charles W. Johnson (S)
1965, Paul W. Kidwell (S)

VALLEY
1910, A. F. Kroneman
1913, O. E. Faulkner
1915, T. F. Douglas (S)
1917, T. W. Emery
1918, Wm. Wellington (S)
1920, J. D. Bird
1921, TBS
1922, J. F. Weller (S)
1923, Gertrude Apel (S)
1929, Wm. Park
1931, Thos. W. Emery
1933, C. A. Pickering
1937, Marion Rounds (S)
1938, TBS
1939, Ruth Lortz (S)
1941, No record
1942, Walter A. Pierson
1943, Jas. A. Moore
1948, TBS
1949, Ronald K. Johnson
1956, Roy L. Kuhns
1957, Harry T. Cupp
1958, Fred Riehle (S)
1960, Raymond L. Poindexter
1962, Chas. W. Johnson (S)
1965, Paul W. Kidwell (S)

CLARK FORK, IDAHO
1913, William Daniel
1915, Robt. Thompson (S)
  not in minutes until
1919, TBS
1921, J. R. Bouger (S)
1923, J. H. Dill
1924, A. H. Morton
1927, Mrs. Nellie Nally (S)
1930, TBS
1931, F. J. Long (S)
1932, A. H. Morton
1933, R. W. Maulden
1935, TBS
1936, I. V. Parker
1937, TBS
1938, Robt. W. Maulden
1939, A. H. Morton
1941, Mrs. Mary Graves (S)
1949, Loval Phillips (S)
1950, TBS
1952, E. F. G. Meyer (S)
1956, Louis Ray (S)
1958, N. U. Stout (S)
1961, Arlen J. Rhoads (S)
1963, Merritt R. Metcalf (S)
1965, Donald W. Baldwin

HOPE, IDAHO
1908, G. A. Wells
1909, No record
1910, R. C. Moter
1913, W. M. Daniel (S)
1919, TBS
1915, Robt. Thompson (S)
1917, J. A. Hoffman
1918, R. C. Moter
1919, TBS
1920, A. F. Patterson (S)
1921, J. R. Bouger (S)
1923, J. H. Dill
1924, A. H. Morton
1927, Mrs. Nellie Nally (S)
1930, TBS
1931, F. J. Long (S)
1933, R. W. Maulden
1935, TBS
1936, I. V. Parker (S)
1937, TBS

1938, Robt. H. Allen
1939, A. H. Morton
1941, Mrs. Mary Graves (S)
1949, Loval Phillips (S)
1950, TBS
1952, E. F. G. Meyer (S)
1956, Louis Ray (S)
1958, N. U. Stout (S)
1961, Arlen Rhoads (S)
1963, Merritt R. Metcalf (S)
1965, Donald W. Baldwin

COEUR D'ALENE, IDAHO
1890, T. A. Towner
1892, M. C. Aleridge
1893, W. W. Henry
1894, J. H. Feak
1894, G. G. Muller
1896, T. G. Hodgson
1904, John P. Barker
1907, William H. Fry
1910, U. F. Hawk
1912, W. H. H. Forsyth
1915, N. M. Jones
1917, B. E. Koontz
1919, J. D. Llewellen
1922, Ira L. Ketchum
1925, Orland A. Scott
1927, Ernest F. Harold
1930, Edwin T. Randall
1933, Ralph I. Thomas
1937, Willard E. Stanton
1942, Chester C. Blair
1949, Forrest D. Tibbitts
1955, Victor Phillips
1958, Laird V. Glasscock
1962, Myron H. Sharrard

ATHOL, IDAHO
1906, S. W. Shirly (S)
1907, F. R. Spaulding
1908, G. A. Wells
1909, C. S. Price
1910, I. P. Bowen and A. O. Hess
1912, J. A. Smith
1914, A. E. Derby (S)
1915, W. M. Daniel (S)
1917, E. R. Derry (S)
1918, Ambrose King (S)
1919, TBS
1920, A. W. Luce
1922, J. H. Crocker (S)
1923, No record
1925, Floyd Burke (S)
1927, Carl B. Madsen
1928, Roy Jenkins
1929, John Hoffman
1932, Wm. Gornall
1936, R. B. Shaw
1937, TBS
1938, Harry L. Slick
1939, Mark Freeman
1941, Louis McConnell (S)
1943, Kenneth Lawson (S)
1944, Erling Bergan
1946, TBS
1946, Theodore Hegg (S)
1947, M. R. Gallaher
1948, Geo. J. Lees (S)
1952, Raymond Gouldin (S)
1953, TBS
1954, Clarence R. Pierce
1955, Fred H. Cronkhite (S)
1960, not listed
1963, Myron H. Sharrard

COLVILLE (Federated)
1886, TBS
1888, R. R. Dunlap (S)
1889, TBS
1891, Sidney Smith
1893, TBS

1894, J. C. Kirkman
1895, J. C. Hester (S)
not in records until
1904, TBS
1905, J. E. Harrington
1906, TBS
1907, H. A. Sheldon
1908, A. H. Morton
1909, Geo. A. Wells
1912, M. L. Sanders
1915, E. C. Corn
1916, J. S. Bell
1919, R. H. Allen
1920, G. E. Whitten
1922, F. L. Cook
1925, Henry Attenborough
1928, M. M. Eaton
1930, Federated
1930, Everett Hunt (S)
1938, Chester C. Blair
1943, Arthur Ford (S)
1947, Donald W. Baldwin
1950, H. Eugene Miller
1954, Kenneth W. Countryman
1963, Robert L. Irwin

DAVENPORT
1882, W. S. Anderson
1883, F. L. Young
1884, N. E. Parsons
1885, J. H. Shepherd
1888, F. L. Young
1890, W. O. Benadom
1892, G. G. Muller
1894, W. B. Eakin
1897, T. H. Fertig
1898, H. B. Creel
1899, R. C. Moter
1900, B. T. Pick
1901, Stacey A. Smith (S)
1901, J. J. McAllister
1903, H. N. Rounds
1904, H. A. Sheldon
1907, E. McOmber
1910, R. A. Gailey
1912, Wm. Hoskins
1913, Geo. W. Bradley
1914, Chas. E. Miller
1915, Fred E. White
1920, G. A. Wells
1921, J. A. Hill
1923, C. A. Hodshire
1926, A. F. Kroneman
1936, R. S. McCulloch
1938, T. Earl Poindexter
1941, Erling Bergan
1944, J. Dean King
1951, TBS
1952, James E. Doak
1956, Eugene Ford
1959, Donald R. Yates
1961, Joseph L. Woodford

DEER PARK
1902, TBS
1903, E. R. Henderson (S)
1906, M. S. Anderson
1908, TBS
1909, Herbert P. Ide
1910, J. A. Smith
1911, W. A. Pratt & A. Owen (S)
1912, L. N. B. Anderson
1915, TBS
1916, F. W. Cooper (S)
1917, H. C. Clark
1919, E. S. Williamson
1920, E. E. Cissna (S)
1921, Dow DeLong
1922, U. O. Beadles (S)
1923, C. E. Auger (S)
1924, L. W. Flenner

1925, TBS
1926, Wm. Hoskins
1928, Geo. A. Wells
1929, W. J. Osborne (S)
1931, M. L. Anderson
1934, F. L. Lowther
1937, L. G. Wellington (S)
1939, Ruth M. Lortz (S)
1944, Louis McConnell (S)
     & Roy Saferite (S)
1945, Loren E. Jones
1946, Claud H. Cowdy
1950, TBS
1951, Eugene Ford
1953, TBS
1954, Don Kaelin (S)
1957, James M. Lane
1959, James E. Doak
1962, Carl B. Beal

WILD ROSE
1923, TBS
1924, Wm. Wellington (S)
1926, TBS
1928, W. J. Osborne (S)
1931, M. L. Anderson
1934, F. L. Lowther
1935, Ruth Lortz (S)
1936, F. L. Lowther
1937, L. G. Wellington (S)
1939, Ruth M. Lortz (S)
1944, Louis McConnell (S)
1945, Loren E. Jones
1946, Claude H. Cowdy
1950, TBS
1951, Eugene Ford
1953, TBS
1954, Don Kaelin
1957, James M. Lane
1958, TBS
1959, James E. Doak
1962, Carl B. Beal

EDWALL
1909, TBS
1910, H. T. Robinson
1912, J. Charles Snowden
1913, G. W. Bradley
1914, E. J. Snell
1917, W. M. Daniel
1919, TBS
1920, Jas. Callahan
1921, TBS
1922, W. A. Pratt
1923, John E. Garver
1924, John E. Williams
1927, J. C. Harvey
1933, Clark Cottrell
1937, Everett M. Filbert
1943, Loren E. Jones
1945, Miss Gladys Crawford (S)
1948, Ralph M. Walsh
1950, Clyde J. Hall
1956, Bessie Pease (S) and
     Annette Kiehlbauch (S)
1960, Dean C. Kallender
1963, John Mathone (S)

GREENACRES
1908, R. B. Martin (S)
1909, J. E. Daniels (S)
1911, T. H. Fertig and
     W. E. Thompson
1913, M. R. Brown
1913, Robt. Thompson (S)
1915, A. J. Neufeld (S)
1916, J. P. Armand and
     E. R. Derry (S)
1919, TBS
1922, Edw. Baker
1927, Robt. W. Maulden
1931, F. L. Lowther

427

1934, B. C. Gallaher
1936, R. A. Gailey
1937, Ernest W. Denning (S)
1938, John Finkbeiner, Jr.
1940, C. M. Estabrook
1941, Mark Freeman
1944, Milton DeArmand (S)
1945, Ray Mason
1949, Erling Bergan
1950, TBS
1951, William Burke (S)
1953, Arthur D. Campbell
1958, Louis E. Ray (S)
1959, Richard H. N. Yost
1962, J. Robert Dibble
1965, Paul G. Perkins

RATHDRUM, IDAHO
1900, T. G. Hodgson
1901, No record
1902, C. T. Cook
1904, J. H. Martin
1906, J. S. Bell
1909, A. Warner
1910, T. H. Fertig and
     C. W. Monson
1911, A. W. Luce
1913, N. S. Hawk
1915, H. S. Randall
1917, J. G. Carrick
1919, G. E. James
1920, J. C. Harvey
1923, D. L. Clark
1924, W. B. Eakin
1925, Loyd Burke
1926, Carl B. Madsen (S)
1928, Roy Jenkins
1929, John Hoffman
1932, Wm. Gornall
1936, R. B. Shaw (S)
1937, TBS
1938, Harry L. Slick
1939, Mark Freeman
1941, Louis McConnell (S)
1943, Erling Bergan
1948, TBS
1948, George Lees (S)
1952, Raymond Gouldin (S)
1953, TBS
1954, Clarence R. Pierce
1955, Fred G. Cronkhite (S)
1960, not listed
1962, J. Robert Dibble
1965, Paul G. Perkins

HARTLINE
1891, G. G. Muller
1892, Edward Smith
1893, L. W. Haworth (S)
1894, J. C. Taylor
1896, Walter Williams (S)
1897, D. L. Spaulding
1899, R. A. Gailey
1901, A. H. Miller
1903, J. L. Carpenter
1904, J. E. Daniels
1907, C. C. Curry
1910, Hazen Oakes and
     E. F. Williams
1911, G. W. Bradley
1913, J. O. Hawk
1914, P. C. Money
1916, G. E. Heineck
1918, Ed Baker
1920, TBS
1921, E. L. Wolff
1923, W. A. Pratt
1924, Joined with Almira
1925, C. B. Martin
1926, Roy Jenkins
1928, Carl B. Madsen
1929, Geo. A. Wells

1930, E. S. Williamson
1933, Roy H. Murray
1935, TBS
1936, W. W. Switzer
1939, C. M. Estabrook
1940, Clifford Knight
1942, Mrs. J. Dean King (S)
1945, Chas. L. Thornton (S)
1946, E. H. Tetwiler (S)
1948, Miss Gladys V. Crawford
     (S)
1949, TBS
1950, G. H. Rickard (S)
1952, Cecil Rickard (S)
1953, C.R.D.
1954, TBS
1955, Amos T. Hoover (S)
1956, Mrs. Hortense Anable (S)
1959, Wm. M. Martin (R)
1963, Mrs. Wm. M. Martin (S)
1965, Mack E. Farmer

GRAND COULEE
1933, R. H. Murray
1957, R. W. Pruitt
1959, James M. Lane
1962, Laird V. Glasscock
1965, Mack E. Farmer

KELLOGG, IDAHO, (United)
1910, G. A. Tyler
1911, W. J. Gamble (S)
1913, A. F. Kroneman
1916, E. C. Corn
1917, J. E. Strevey
1919, G. O. Parish
1920, C. B. Martin
1922, James Opie
1923, M. M. Eaton
1926, J. C. Harvey
1927, E. S. Williamson
1930, A. R. Graves
1938, O. P. Shenefelt (S)
1944, Stanley D. Trefren
1948, TBS
1949, John Hanchett (S)
1952, Roy Jenkins
1953, TBS
1954, Bernard Herrick (S)
1956, no appt.
1959, Everett L. Groves
1963, TBS
1964, Robert H. McPherson UCC
     (S)

LIND
1901, F. E. Drake
1902, L. R. Kufus
1903, E. W. Elayer
1904, J. S. Bell
1907, H. N. Rounds
1908, W. C. Smith
1909, W. A. Luce
1910, F. L. Moore
1912, C. W. Johnson (S)
1913, J. W. Mayes
1915, A. S. Black (S)
1916, Hubert C. Vincent
1917, B. C. Gallaher
1918, J. W. Poolton
1920, C. W. Geisler
1923, C. M. Carson
1925, J. J. Prichard (S)
1926, Burchard A. Hylton
1928, H. S. Randall
1929, John Seethoff
1933, J. D. Moede
1934, R. S. Wetherell (S)
1935, TBS
1937, S. E. Yaggy
1938, J. H. Bennett (S)
1941, W. E. Whitlock (S)

1943, Mrs. Wm. H. Clements (S)
1944, W. W. DeBolt
1945, TBS
1946, Robert W. Hicks
1947, Wm. H. Ritchey
1953, Spokane D.
1961, Martin T. Larson
1964, Roger K. Johnson

MEAD
1908, L. W. Putnam
1909, W. C. Smith
1910, R. A. Armstrong
1911, Wm. Wellington (S)
1914, C. M. Carson
1916, A. J. Neufeld (S)
1918, R. A. Forkner (S)
1920, E. A. Bradley (S)
1921, Wm. Wellington (S)
1924, C. W. Geisler
1925, Geo. H. Higgins (S)
1926, Frank James (S)
1927, J. D. Lewellen
1929, Mark Freeman
1936, No record
1938, Milton DeArmand (S)
1940, E. E. Van Wert (S)
1942, Arthur R. Treman (S)
1943, Jewell F. Pyles (S)
1944, Harry L. Slick
1947, Enoch E. Willman
1950, TBS
1951, John D. Moede
1954, TBS
1955, Roy L. Kuhns
1956, Austin G. Rugger
1958, F. B. Kenoyer (S)
1963, Ronald C. Kurtz

GREENBLUFF
1925, George H. Higgins (S)
1926, S. E. Taft (S)
1927, Wm. Wellington (S)
1934, TBS
1935, Wm. Wellington (S)
1940, Milton DeArmand (S)
1941, E. E. Van Wert (S)
1942, Arthur R. Treman (S)
1943, Jewell F. Pyles (S)
1944, Harry L. Slick
1946, Forrest D. Tibbitts
1949, TBS
1950, Roy C. Saferite
1951, DeWane Zimmerman (S)
1952, Charles M. Estabrook
1953, Marvin G. Jernberg
1954, TBS
1955, Mrs. Charleen Schmidt (S)
1959, F. B. Kenoyer (S)
1960, not listed
1963, Ronald C. Kurtz

MEDICAL LAKE (Federated)
1898, S. F. Coons (S)
1900, P. A. King (S)
1901, no record
1904, M. S. Anderson
1905, C. B. Rees (S)
1907, S. H. Yockey (S)
1908, Chas. Elrey
1909, H. C. Hartranft (S)
1910, D. L. Clark (UG)
1913, T. H. Fertig
1914, W. M. Martin
1916, Henry Attenborough
     and T. W. Emery
1917, J. D. Bird
1919, TBS
1920, F. L. Farnham (S)
1921, TBS
1922, H. S. Wanamaker (S)
1927, W. B. Eakin

1928, TBS
1929, A. G. Child (S)
1931, Roy Keeling (S)
1932, Dan Taylor
1933, not listed
1935, L. G. Wellington (S)
1936, T. C. McFeron
1937, J. P. Armand
1938, TBS
1939, not listed
1940, Frank Harris (S)
1943, Donald W. Baldwin
1944, Dorton Coats (S)
1945, Burl Estes (S)
1948, Marshall Hodge (S)
1950, Mrs. T. J. Bennett (S)
1952, Enoch E. Willman
1953, TBS
1954, Albert W. Richardson
1957, Aubrey W. Winsor (S)
1959, James Y. Horton
1961, Congregational pastor
1962, Charles Billups (UCC) (S)

NEWPORT (Federated)
1903, J. S. Bell
1904, L. N. B. Anderson
1905, A. H. Morton
1908, H. T. Robinson
1909, N. S. Hawk
1911, J. E. Weigle
1911, and A. E. Ayers
1913, F. R. Spaulding
1916, M. H. Needham (S)
1917, J. F. Reid (S)
1918, A. J. Neufeld
1921, TBS
1922, W. B. Eakin
1923, Geo. E. James
1926, Dow DeLong
1927, John R. Butler
1929, Percy E. Pike
1933, Chester C. Blair
1938, Laird V. Glasscock
1941, Lloyd Doty
1942, J. E. Walbeck
1944, Wendell Cone
1946, Gale A. Putnam (S)
1947, William T. Beatty (R)
1950, Gene Ford (S)
1951, Ray W. Mason
1954, TBS
1955, Floyd L. Looney
1956, J. A. McNees
1958, Ruth Lortz
1961, Paul Biering (S)
1963, Charles A. Pobanz (S)
  UCC

RITZVILLE
1889, G. E. Wilcox
1890, C. E. Ford
1891, TBS
1892, W. W. Henry
1893, J. H. Feak
1894, T. G. Hodgson
1896, F. B. Utter
1897, B. L. Hicks
1898, TBS
1899, J. H. Everett
1900, T. H. Fertig
1903, C. G. Harmon
1904, B. E. Koontz
1908, F. H. Winter
1909, W. Hoskins
1912, R. A. Gailey
1914, C. W. Williams
1917, M. J. Perdue
1919, R. D. Snyder
1921, W. C. Reuter
1922, H. S. Randall
1926, W. G. R. Dann

1930, Henry Attenborough
1935, Richard Decker
1943, Clifford C. Knight
1951, Alfred Carter
1960, Alfred J. Waln
1963, James N. Updike

ROCKFORD
1884, Theodore Hoagland
1886, James Greenslade
1887, T. A. Towner
1889, M. H. Marvin
1890, C. E. Gibson
1893, W. A. Shanklin
1894, F. B. Utter
  and A. V. E. Waltman (S)
1896, John P. Barker
1898, B. E. Koontz
1900, A. W. Roberts
1902, R. D. Osterhout
1903, TBS
1904, C. T. Cook
1905, A. Y. Skee (S)
1906, E. A. McKinney (S)
1907, W. H. Rogers
1908, J. F. Redfern
1909, E. V. Bronson
1910, J. L. Hess and
  J. W. Poolton
1912, W. C. Evans
1915, J. A. Hoffman (S)
1917, C. M. Carson
1919, J. F. Weller (S)
1921, M. L. Anderson
1923, H. C. Vincent
1924, Robt. W. Maulden
1925, TBS
1926, John H. Dill (S)
1927, Chas. H. Schreiber
1930, J. P. Armand
1931, G. A. Wells
1933, C. E. Auger (S)
1935, Wm. O. Pflaum
1938, C. M. Estabrook
1939, W. W. Switzer
1941, I. G. Wilkins (S)
1943, Frank E. Harris (S)
1944, Ruth M. Lortz (S)
1949, TBS
1950, Cecil G. Rickard (S)
1952, Hubert C. Vincent
1955, James D. Crawford
1958, TBS
1959, Arthur E. Paltridge
1960, Fred Riehle (S)
1963, Glen A. Rudolph

ROCKLYN
1884, Adam Buehler
1886, F. W. Buchholz
1887, Ass't. Adam Buehler
1888, Ass't., Carl Jans
1888, J. G. Moehring
1890, Carl Jans
1892, F. H. Luecke
1893, Adam Buehler
1897, Joseph Hepp
1901, G. A. Jahns
1904, L. Gaiser
1907, G. J. Sohm
1908, Charles H. Weise
1908, L. Gaiser
1909, G. S. Roeder
1914, W. F. Maas
1917, G. A. Maag
1918, A. F. Cramer
1924, E. J. Traglio
1926, T. N. Hostetler
1927, R. R. Finkbeiner
1928, H. B. Mann
1939, Darrel Iwerks
1941, Milton DeArmand (S)

1945, Mrs. (J. D.) Millie L.
  King (S)
1951, TBS
1952, Lawrence Yates (S)
  (Presby.)
1953, TBS
1954, Lawrence Yates (S)
  (Presby.)
1958, Robert Roberts (S)
1958, Lawrence E. Yates (S)
  (Presby.)

ROSALIA
1888, Geo. Hartung
1899, W. J. Herwig
1901, P. J. Sehnert
1903, G. J. Sohm
1904, G. A. Jahns
1908, H. F. Michel
1909, L. Gaiser
1913, J. C. Mueller
1916, C. A. Wentsch
1927, A. F. Hilmer
1931, J. C. Hofstetter
1937, D. E. Carter
1947, Charles G. Cole
1950, Charles W. Fisher
1953, Chester C. Blair
1963, G. Edward Knight

THORNTON
1891, C. E. Gibson
  W. A. Tickner
  W. C. Evans
1905, T. H. Fertig
  E. McEvers
  F. R. Spaulding
  W. F. Bradley
1906, J. M. Huggins
1908, M. L. Anderson
1909, Hazen Oakes
1910, Herbert P. Ide
1911, J. W. Miller
1912, J. H. Martin
1913, H. T. Robinson
1915, John Dill
1916, J. J. Mattney
1917, J. W. Poolton
1918, Mrs. Agnes D. Newell (S)
1919, J. J. Mattney
1923, R. C. Acheson
1924, Erling Bergan
1925, Ed Baker
1926, W. A. Pratt
1927, Will M. Daniel
1930, C. H. Schreiber
1931, William Iley (S)
1932, Claud W. Groth
1933, R. W. Mason
1934, C. W. Geisler
1935, L. C. Bennett (S)
  Lilla M. Marston (S)
1936, J. E. Williams
1938, S. E. Yaggy (S)
1940, Perry McArthur (S)
  W. A. Pratt
1941, Lilla Marston (S)
1944, Luther G. Baker, Jr. (S)
1945, H. G. Cowdrick
1947, H. A. Dettmers (S)
1948, Herbert G. Ellison (S)
1949, Clark M. Smith
1952, Charles W. Fisher
1953, Chester C. Blair
1964, G. Edward Knight

ST. JOHN
1905, Charles MacCaughey
1906, T. G. Williams
1907, F. H. Walker
1908, J. L. Hess
1908, C. A. Smith

429

1911, H. S. Randall
1913, E. H. Gates
1913, M. R. Gallaher
1916, J. Callahan
1917, R. F. Hawk
1918, T. H. Fertig
1920, J. F. Gibson
1922, Wm. Gornall
1924, Chas. H. Schreiber
1927, F. F. Boothby
1929, B. A. Hylton
1930, B. E. Koontz
1933, R. W. Mason
1935, Erling Bergan
1936, Roy Murray
1937, TBS
1938, J. Earl Secord
1942, Andrew Warner
1943, John D. Moede
1945, Edward Smyth (S)
1946, William H. Phillips (S)
1947, Sylvan W. Sherrell (S)
1950, John Morange (S)
1953, not listed
1954, Albert E. Van Andel (S)
1956, James E. Doak
1959, Aubrey W. Winsor (S)
1961, Daniel E. Benedict
1964, David W. Biles

SANDPOINT, IDAHO
1900, J. H. Martin
1901, J. C. Reid
1902, R. A. Armstrong
1903, W. Hoskins
1906, J. C. Harvey
1909, R. Warner
1911, W. Skipworth
1912, G. A. Wells
1916, Chas. MacCaughey
1917, M. L. Sanders
1918, W. Nesbitt Byars
1920, T. H. Fertig
1922, C. B. Martin
1923, H. W. Driver
1925, TBS
1926, Joel R. Benton
1928, J. Fred Stilwell
1931, R. W. Maulden
1936, W. T. Beatty
1938, Robt. H. Allen
1939, Henry Attenborough
1941, Percy E. Pike
1942, Lloyd A. Doty
1944, John Finkbeiner
1945, Floyd E. Wells
1950, Frank L. Lowther
1957, Carl H. McGee
1962, Richard H. N. Yost
1965, Fred A. Rarden

SPOKANE,
AUDUBON PARK
1945, Calvin J. Graves (S)
1946, TBS
1947, Milton DeArmand
1948, no appt.
1951, TBS
1952, David K. Almon
1954, Roy Finch
1956, Joseph H. Beall
1959, Horace H. Mounts
1963, Wm. Franklin Summerour

CENTENARY (formerly
Union Park)
1892, Perry Chandler
1893, W. S. Turner
1895, G. C. Haven
1899, C. E. Todd
1900, S. F. Coons (S)
1900, J. L. Carpenter (S)

1901, H. M. Mobbs
1902, M. R. Brown
1907, E. B. Lockhart
1908, H. A. Sheldon
1910, J. G. Law
1915, C. D. Rarey
1915, J. P. Armand
1916, G. A. Wells
1918, Fred E. White
1920, G. O. Parish
      Became CENTENARY
1921, G. O. Parish
1923, R. D. Snyder
1924, Thomas Hardie
1925, D. S. Kerr
1926, M. M. Eaton
1928, Alden R. Graves
1930, O. F. Krieger
1931, E. H. Winfield
1933, J. Homer Magee
1936, R. W. Maulden
1941, E. C. Newham
1946, Ernest Barber
1949, John M. Finney, Jr.
1955, Harold W. Black
1957, Armon F. Lathrop
1959, Geo. K. Berg
1961, Wendell J. Cone
1965, Jonathan M. King

SPOKANE, CENTRAL from
1st Ch. & Vincent
1876, TBS
1877, S. G. Havermale
1879, J. H. Leard
1880, M. S. Anderson
1882, TBS
1884, R. E. Bisbee
1885, S. W. Richards
1886, W. C. Gray
1887, A. G. Wilson
1891, W. A. Shanklin
1892, Henry Rasmus
1895, D. N. McInturff
1896, H. D. Stauffer
1897, P. A. Cool
1901, A. R. Lambert
1903, Henry Rasmus
1910, W. A. Betts
1912, F. B. Short
      "Central"
1918, J. M. Walters
1922, L. Morgan Chambers
1918, J. M. Walters
1924, Thomas Jeffrey
1926, T. W. Jeffrey and
      Assoc. E. H. Winfield
1928, T. W. Jeffrey
1931, R. S. Dunn
1937, Carl K. Mahoney
1942, Chas. MacCaughey
1947, Thos. Acheson
1949, Noel C. LeRoque
1955, Clyde Beecher
1958, Assoc. William F.
      Summerour, 1 yr.
1960, James T. Albertson
1963, Assoc. John A. McNees
      (R) 1 yr.

CORBIN PARK
1886, J. W. Compton
1889, R. B. Swift
1900, A. L. Thoroughman
1903, John H. Dills
1907, W. L. Killian
1907, R. K. Triplett
      J. H. Bennett
      W. A. Orr
1912, H. S. Shangle
      C. L. McCausland
      S. C. Rogers

1917, C. R. Howard
1920, C. R. Sims
1921, W. L. Reid
1922, C. A. Rexroad
1927, P. D. Hartman
1930, E. J. Harper
1931, C. F. McConnell
1933, Carl Francis McConnell
1935, Howard L. Graybeal
1937, W. Raymond Wilder
1942, John Finkbeiner, Jr.
1944, Chas. W. Fisher
1946, Forrest D. Tibbitts
1949, TBS
1950, R. Fenton Duvall (S)
1956, Everett E. Peterson (S)
1958, Arthur E. Paltridge (S)
1959, Frank L. Lowther (R)
1959, Assoc. Robert R. Roberts,
      1 yr.
1960, Richard Wrangle
1962, TBS
1963, Homer Saxton (S)
1965, James T. Burcham

DISHMAN, Washington
1910, A. McClintock (S)
1911, J. C. Snowden
1911, Thos. Lawson
1912, M. R. Brown
      merged with Opportunity
1914, W. S. Whitsett
1916, W. M. Martin
1917, J. Callahan
1918, J. F. Reid (S)
1919, Chas. T. Hatten
1921, J. O. Hawk
1923, W. B. Eakin
1924, Edw. Baker
1925, D. L. Clark
1926, Alden R. Graves
1928, John Hoffman
1929, J. H. Secor
1930, Mrs. N. B. Nally (S)
1933, F. L. Lowther
1934, Ruth M. Lortz (S)
1936, H. C. Davis (S)
1936, Mark Freeman
1939, H. L. Slick
      became Spokane Valley

FOWLER MEMORIAL
1908, T. H. Fertig
1910, H. F. Pemberton
1912, T. C. Mountain
1913, J. W. Miller
1914, S. M. Nickle
1915, H. J. Wood
1916, W. P. Jinnett
1917, S. G. Logan
1922, Vern A. Spicker
1925, Wm. Martin
1927, Thomas Lawson
1930, R. W. Mason
1933, U. F. Hawk
1937, T. Earl Poindexter
1939, Jas. T. Albertson
1943, George Almond
1946, Chas. L. Creesy
1953, Roy Jenkins
1956, James A. Moore
1965, H. Robert Morton

HAYS PARK
1907, Paul Little
1909, J. S. Bell
1911, Walter L. Airheart
1914, J. W. Miller
1916, Joseph Adams
1921, H. S. Randall
1922, B. E. Koontz
1925, F. L. Cook

430

1927, Charles R. Garland
1929, W. B. Foley
1931, R. S. McCulloch
1936, Hubert C. Vincent
1940, Frank Haley
1942, Warren W. Peters
1944, Quentin Leisher (S)
1946, Donald W. Baldwin
1947, W. Sherman Burgoyne
1948, Melvin M. Finkbeiner
1955, Everett L. Groves
1959, Herbert G. Luscombe
1961, Harlan D. Jones
1965, James T. Burcham

HIGHLAND PARK,
JAPANESE
1902, Genhichi Tsuruta
1905, Seimei Yoshioka
1907, Sadakichi Murakata
Kenshu Yoshioka
Maaki Kata
1915, Seijiro Uemura
1919, Shu Takada
1921, no minister
1923, Mrs. Aya Okuda
1928, Rev. Mr. Nishibuchi
1929, Joe Miyake
1931, Miss Yuki Kuwahara
1933, Miss Mary Oyama
1934, Shigeo Tanabe
1935, Taro Goto
1938, Seiichi Niwa
1940, J. B. Cobb
1945, Taro Goto
1949, Masaji Goto
1950, Shigeo Shimada

HILLYARD
1891, Lee A. Johnson
1893, N. E. Parsons
1894, M. R. Brown
1895, G. C. Haven
1897, J. C. Kirkman
1898, W. B. Eakin
1899, George Gable (S)
1901, B. E. Koontz
1905, Charles Elrey
1906, H. L. Beightol
1907, H. B. Elworthy
1910, C. A. Hodshire
1911, R. D. Snyder
1912, C. W. Williams
1913, M. J. Perdue
1915, Edward Baker
1918, J. E. Strevey
1920, H. J. Wood
1923, J. C. Harvey
1926, Frank James (S)
1927, J. D. Lewellen
1929, Mark Freeman
1937, Edw. G. Ernst
1941, Henry Attenborough
1944, Harry L. Slick
1947, Enoch E. Willman
1952, TBS
1953, Robert L. LaMott
1955, John A. McNees
1960, H. L. Rollert
1964, James Thuirer (S)

LIBERTY PARK, Spokane
1905, J. W. Robinson (S)
1906, A. Monroe
1910, A. S. Mulligan
1911, T. D. Moore
1915, I. L. Ketchum
1916, L. N. B. Anderson
1917, M. M. Eaton
1918, H. C. Kohr
1921, John Robertson
1925, H. W. Driver

1929, E. Clifford Newham
1933, Fred L. Pedersen
1937, J. Henry Ernst
1941, Harry Coates
1944, Merritt W. Faulkner
1950, Alfred Carter
1951, Ritchie D. Ocheltree, Sr.
1953, Robert R. Rings
1959, Clifford J. Pine
1962, Rarden W. Vergin

MORAN
1900, S. F. Coons (S)
1900, & C. T. Cook (S)
1901, No record
1903, V. T. Willis (S) &
A. A. McGinnis (S)
1904, J. C. Kirkman
1906, J. C. Lawrence
1909, T. Hart
1910, E. Baker
1911, J. M. Huggins
1912, A. W. Roberts
1913, John Evans
1915, J. H. Dill
1917, G. E. James
1919, C. M. Carson
1920, G. B. Harbison
1922, H. W. Best
1923, F. L. Moore
1926, Harry Fliesher (S)
1927, J. Fred Stilwell
1928, Wm. Gornall
1929, T. W. Emery
1931, W. J. Osborne (S)
1932, E. C. Newham
1933, C. E. Auger (S)
1935, T. C. McFeron (S)
1936, S. E. Yaggy (S)
1937, A. L. McConnell (S)
1938, Ernest P. Goulder
1939, Edwin D. Rounds
1940, Stewart E. Sparrow (S)
1942, Gene Lander (S)
1943, Chas. W. Fisher
1944, Kenneth Lawson (S)
1945, John D. Moede
1948, Mrs. Floyd Cydrus (S)
1952, Floyd E. Cydrus
1953, TBS
1955, James I. McLimans (S)
1956, TBS
1959, Floyd E. Cydrus
1960, F. H. Cronkite (S)
1961, Wendell J. Cone
1964, Kenneth Lawson &
Rarden Vergin

MANITO
1909, J. C. Lawrence
1910, C. W. Monson &
H. B. Elworthy
1912, J. W. Miller
1913, A. McClintock (S)
1915, R. W. Mason (S)
1917, A. E. Derby
1918, Thos. Lawson
1919, M. L. Sanders
1920, Ira L. Ketchum
1922, Ernest Harold
1927, E. E. Brace
1928, S. A. Danford
1929, Ralph I. Thomas
1933, Ernest P. Goulder
1939, Edwin D. Rounds
1941, James Moore
1943, Charles G. Cole
1947, Ralph W. Bolick
1951, Eugene W. Muench
1959, Robert Ortmeyer
1960, Assoc. A. K. Walborn (S)
1 yr.

1964, Paul Hamlin

METZGER MEMORIAL
1909, Andrew Monroe
1909, J. L. Hess
1910, W. E. Armfield
1913, Thos. Lawson
1918, J. Philip Armand
1919, B. E. Koontz
1922, C. B. Rees (S)
1923, Wm. Hoskins
1924, C. E. Powell
1925, R. W. Maulden
1927, M. L. Anderson
1930, TBS
1931, E. C. Newham
1932, R. S. McCulloch
1936, H. C. Vincent
1940, Wendell Cone
1941, James T. Albertson
1943, Geo. Almond
1945, Roy C. Saferite
1951, DeWane Zimmerman (S)
1952, Charles M. Estabrook
1953, Marvin G. Jernberg
1954, Cecil G. Rickard (S)
1956, Orin D. Watson
1959, C. Ellsworth Wilson
1960, T. Orville Kelley (S)
1961, A. K. Walborn (S)
1963, Wayne R. Schaub

OPPORTUNITY
1907, F. R. Spaulding
1908, Supply
1909, R. B. Martin
1910, A. J. Baldwin (S)
1912, W. E. Thompson
1913, M. R. Brown
1914, W. S. Whitsett
1916, W. M. Martin
1917, J. Callahan
1918, J. R. Reid (S)
1919, C. T. Hatten
1921, Marcus Dodds
1922, W. D. Price
1923, J. G. Carrick
1926, Alden R. Graves
1928, John Hoffman
1929, J. H. Secor
1932, R. H. Murray
1933, David Glenn (S)
1934, B. C. Gallaher
1936, H. C. Davis (S)
1936, Mark Freeman
1939, H. L. Slick
merged with Dishman to become
Spokane Valley

ST. PAUL'S
1888, R. E. Bisbee
1889, TBS
1890, W. C. Gray
1891, W. T. Euster
1892, Henry Brown
1893, F. A. LaViolette
1894, W. T. Euster
1896, C. E. Todd
1900, W. H. Fry
1905, C. E. Gibson
1906, E. M. Hill
1910, W. H. Forsyth
1913, U. F. Hawk
1916, J. W. McDougall
1920, R. N. Avison
1921, F. L. Wemett
1923, L. A. Magin
1928, S. J. Cheney
1931, R. L. Smith
1935, H. O. Perry
1940, E. F. Harold
1949, E. J. Aschenbrenner

431

1959, Anthony R. Perrino
1960, Assoc. John A. McNees, 1 yr.
1963, Lloyd F. Holloway

SPOKANE VALLEY
1939, H. L. Slick
1943, Mark Freeman
1947, Everett M. Filbert
1950, Stanley D. Trefren
1952, Kenneth W. Countryman
1954, H. Eugene Miller
1957, David K. Almon
1962, Donald G. Northdurft

TEKOA
1900, J. C. Kirkman
1901, J. LeCornu
1902, F. G. Drake
1903, W. H. Henderson
1906, C. Elrey
1907, C. C. Babbidge
1908, J. A. Smith
1909, R. A. Armstrong
1910, R. O. Hadley
1912, A. O. Hess & K. R. Gilmer (S)
1913, E. L. Wolff
1915, W. C. Evans
1917, C. H. Bryan
1919, S. E. Taft
1921, M. H. Marvin
1922, Wm. Hoskins
1923, E. T. Randall
1925, R. S. McCulloch
1926, Edward Baker
1929, Geo. W. Cooper
1930, Geo. A. Wells
1931, Chas. H. Schreiber
1932, G. A. Wells
1934, E. E. Beckman
1937, Clark Cottrell
1940, Paul G. Perkins
1942, Morgan R. Gallaher
1946, Marvin Jordan
1951, Roy R. Finch
1953, Spokane D.
1954, Ralph M. Walsh
1956, Paul E. Hamlin
1959, Gregory A. Zimmer
1960, H. Grant Harvey
1963, Raymond B. Huddleston (S)

FARMINGTON
1888, G. E. Wilcox
1889, TBS W. R. Phelps (S)
1890, Grant C. Haven
1892, William DeWeese
1893, Ed McEvers
1894, Thos. C. Craig (S)
1895, Thos. H. Fertig
1896, A. W. Trine (S)
1897, R. M. Moore
1899, M. S. Anderson
1900, J. C. Kirkman
1902, F. G. Drake
1903, W. H. Henderson
1906, Chas. Elrey
1907, L. G. Wellington
1908, J. F. Redfern
1910, F. N. Morton
1913, J. W. Poolton
1915, H. C. Clark
1917, J. H. Dill
1918, P. C. Money
1919, D. L. Clarke
1921, F. L. Moore
1923, M. L. Anderson
1925, K. O. Pearson
1926, F. F. Boothby
1927, W. A. Pratt

1929, TBS. Robert Thompson (S)
1932, C. W. Groth
1933, G. A. Wells
1934, S. H. Austin
1936, TBS. J. H. Bennett
1938, E. J. Smith
1945, I. V. Parker (S) & Mrs. Jean Treman (S)
1946, Orril A. Fluharty (S)
1949, Clark M. Smith (S)
1952, Roy R. Finch
1954, Ralph M. Walsh
1956, Paul E. Hamlin
1959, Gregory A. Zimmer
1960, H. Grant Harvey
1963, Raymond B. Huddleston (S)

WALLACE, IDAHO
1894, W. H. Selleck
1897, M. R. Brown, J. W. Craig (S) & Grant C. Honen (S)
1900, P. A. Cool
1902, H. M. Mobbs
1904, L. Carpenter
1906, F. H. Winter
1906, Chas. MacCaughey
1908, C. A. Williams
1911, C. C. Curry
1913, W. A. Luce
1914, M. Helmick
1919, R. F. Hawk
1920, M. L. Sanders
1922, Thos. Lawson
1927, Wm. Martin
1930, Wm. C. Bowman
1933, Earl W. McAbee
1937, A. F. Kroneman
1939, Francis M. Kinch
1942, E. M. Filbert
1947, TBS
1947, Alfred Carter
1950, Ralph M. Walsh
1951, Adam S. Forch, Sr.
1953, C. E. Rayburn
1955, W. W. DeBolt
1956, A. K. Walborn (S)
1958, TBS
1959, L. Wayne Bond
1960, TBS
1961, Kenneth Lawson (S)
1964, Franklin A. Nash, Jr.

BURKE, IDAHO
1942, Everette M. Filbert
1947, TBS
1947, Alfred Carter
1950, Ralph M. Walsh
1951, Adam S. Forch, Sr.
1953, C. E. Rayburn
1955, W. W. DeBolt
1956, A. K. Walborn (S)
1958, TBS
1959, L. Wayne Bond
1960, TBS
1961, Kenneth Lawson (S)
1964, Franklin A. Nash, Jr.

TACOMA DISTRICT
ALGONA
1910, Samuel Dupertius
1911, J. W. Blackwell
1913, E. M. Giesey
1914, J. W. Walker
1915, M. H. Marvin
1916, G. L. Cuddy
1917, Lloyd Burk
1919, C. C. James
1921, David G. Beattie
1922, W. H. Thomas
1923, H. Williston

1925, Clark Cottrell
1929, A. A. Moore
1930, James A. Moore
1932, J. C. Harvey
1933, E. R. Phelps
1935, F. L. Amos
1936, R. Huddleston (S)
1937, A. L. McConnell (S)
1939, R. G. Williams (S)
1941, W. E. Callahan
1942, D. L. Rothweiler
1943, E. M. Hill
1944, O. E. Faulkner (S)
1946, D. Richardson (S)
1948, P. Brown (S)
1949, H. Sellers (S)
1949, A. Warner (R)
1951, Dennis DeVoe
1952, TBS
1953, Eric Kullberg (S)
1954, TBS
1955, Sterling Wells (S)
1956, Richard Seiber (S)
1957, TBS
1958, Don Moller
1959, Jeff Smith
1960, TBS
1961, Jeff Smith (S)
1962, William D. Ellington Combined with Pacific

AUBURN
1888, R. Z. Fahs
1890, H. T. Curl (S)
1891, S. P. Wilson
1892, W. H. Jennings
1893, R. M. Schoonmaker
1894, G. D. Dimick
1898, S. S. Guiler
1899, S. J. Buck
1900, A. J. Whipkey (S)
1901, L. Jean (S)
1902, J. T. Smith
1903, R. Z. Fahs
1906, J. M. Weaver
1909, A. W. Brown
1910, F. L. Moore
1911, J. W. Miller
1912, Clarence B. Seely
1914, E. E. Bergmann
1915, F. A. Ecker
1918, C. I. Andrews
1919, Joel Vigus
1922, Harlan Stone
1926, Wm. Park
1929, Richard D. Decker
1935, Arthur S. Morton
1935, Chas. Huddleston (S)
1938, Wayne T. Wright
1942, Francis Kinch
1945, Robert W. Maulden
1950, Myron H. Sharrard
1956, John M. Finney, Jr.
1961, Norman R. Lawson
1964, Assistant, Don H. Glen (S) Paul Graves (S)

BLYN
1916, Charles McLaughlin
1917, A. M. Frederick
1920, W. L. Airheart
1921, E. J. Bates
1924, T. W. Bundy
1925, J. M. Ammundson (S)
1928, D. S. McGuire
1930, Ben H. Hart
1935, Virgil A. Kraft
1937, Decatur N. Lacy
1938, W. G. R. Dann
1947, not listed
1954, Fletcher Forster
1957, J. Dean Stout

1959, Robert C. Ward
1962, To Tacoma Dist.,
 V. S. Hart, Jr.
1962, combined with Sequim

BREMERTON, FIRST
1899, TBS
1900, McC. Reed
1901, George Arney
1903, C. A. Williams
1905, J. H. Carter
1907, Richard Oates
1910, R. L. Wolfe
1912, T. F. Allen
1913, E. G. Decker
1916, B. F. Brooks
1918, F. A. LaViolette
1920, Assoc. E. V. Bronson
1921, Assoc. J. F. Long
1922, Alex G. Bennett
1928, P. H. Ashby
1930, Roy L. Sprague
1933, Andrew Warner
 (Temporary)
1934, Joseph Chester
1937, Martindale Woods
1943, Richard Decker
1952, Harold E. Bashor
1955, Fred E. Fox
1956, Assoc. Geo. R. Wolverton
1957, Albert J. Wilson
1958, to Tacoma Dist.
1963, Kenneth W. Peterson

BREMERTON, ST. LUKE'S
1959, Vincent S. Hart, Jr.
1962, Paul W. McCutcheon

CHIMACUM
1892, TBS
1893, not listed
1894, TBS
1903, A. Davis (S)
1906, TBS
1907, H. C. Leavenworth
1909, J. H. Avery
1910, J. L. Kendall
1912, TBS
1913, A. J. McNemee (S)
1915, A. M. Frederick (S)
1917, Thaddeus Lowe (S)
1918, F. F. Frisbie
1920, Clark Cottrell
1921, J. H. Hicks (S)
1925, TBS
1926, Ira J. McFarland (S)
1928, P. E. Pike
1929, R. A. Gailey
1933, J. F. Long
1935, E. E. Reisner &
 W. O. Pflaum
1938, M. W. Northfelt
1940, Raymond L. Otto (S)
1941, John P. White (S)
1942, Ralph Stevens (S)
1943, Various supplies
1946, F. F. Boothby &
1947, W. G. R. Dann (S's)
1952, Wendell J. Cone
1956, Harold Slocum
1957, Geo. L. Poor
1962, To Tacoma Dist.
1962, Ritchie D. Ocheltree, II
1965, John H. Mann, Jr.

EATONVILLE
1896, TBS
1903, O. L. Doane
1905, S. S. Howell (S)
1906, A. M. Brown (S)
1907, T. J. Lewis (S)
1908, R. G. B. Parcel (S)

1909, TBS
1910, J. J. Calloway (S)
1912, G. L. Cuddy
1913, J. H. Avery
1914, E. B. Reese
1916, C. H. Wood
1917, F. H. Walker
1918, TBS
1919, A. W. Smith (S)
1921, Harry E. Gardner
1924, C. L. Walker
1928, Mark Freeman
1929, Roy Jenkins
1933, H. E. Greening
1937, W. T. Beatty
1942, D. A. Storey
1944, Ira J. McFarland
1947, J. W. Reynolds
1957, Arno M. Hutchinson, Jr.
1958, on Tacoma Dist.
1958, Dorwin Secord
1961, Arthur S. Morton
1963, Alfred S. Palmer (S)

GIG HARBOR
1892, organized
1893, C. W. Darrow (S)
1894, C. T. Jones (S)
1896, not listed
1897, S. P. Brokaw
1900, A. B. L. Gellerman
1902, C. F. Bennett
1903, not listed
1904, A. J. McNemee
1905, Samuel Dupertius (S)
1906, TBS
1907, A. A. Brittain (S)
1908, J. M. Rush (S)
1909, TBS
1910, E. J. Matthews (S)
1911, W. J. Green
1913, G. M. Day
1914, T. C. Newby
1916, C. D. Miller
1917, Paul Jones
1918, J. W. Blackwell (S)
1919, Wm. Richards (S)
1920, David G. Beattie (S)
1921, Russell Clay
1922, TBS
1922, Herbert West (S)
1924, Forrest Tibbitts
1925, F. C. Petersen (S)
1926, A. M. Frederick
1927, TBS
1928, J. C. Dorwin
1930, E. L. Wolf (S)
1931, TBS
1932, S. V. Warren (S)
1936, Geo. F. Pollock
1938, TBS
1940, G. W. Frame (S)
1944, Arthur W. Smith (S)
1946, TBS
1947, Robert J. Kennedy (S)
1948, John B. Magee, Jr.
1956, Assist. Don F. Cramer (S)
1961, Kenneth W. Peterson
1963, Bruce Foreman

HADLOCK
1893, T. E. Elliott
1894, M. A. Mitchell
1895, H. H. Ashbaugh (S)
1896, C. G. Morris (S)
1898, John Thomas
1899, TBS
1903, A. E. Davis (S)
1906, TBS
1907, H. C. Leavenworth
1909, J. H. Avery
1910, J. L. Kendall

1911, not listed
1945, Freeman F. Boothby (S)
1947, W. G. R. Dann
1952, Wendell J. Cone
1954, Harold Slocum
1956, TBS
1957, Geo. L. Poor
1962, To Tacoma Dist.
1962, Ritchie D. Ocheltree, Jr.
1965, John H. Mann, Jr.

MILTON
1902, James E. Milligan (S)
1903, H. H. Newman
1904, J. A. Nutter
1904, T. J. Gambill
1905, W. O. Pflaum
1906, J. L. Kendall
1907, Samuel Dupertius
1910, C. Warren Jones
1912, H. E. Moore
1913, Chas. D. Miller
1914, R. C. Clark
1915, Cassius H. Wood (S)
1915, John W. Blackwell
1916, Frank R. Gillett
1916, Harry G. Earl
1917, C. C. Moore
1918, Herbert West
1919, Loren Sheffler
1920, Thomas A. Swayze (S)
1921, B. F. Brooks
1922, L. T. Cruver (S)
1923, Forrest Tibbitts
1924, Ernest Goulder
1928, A. A. Moore
1929, Louella M. Wilhelm (S)
1940, Everett M. Hill
1941, Bessie Pease (S)
1942, D. L. Rothweiler
1943, Don Hugh Glenn (S)
1950, Pierce Roberts (S)
1956, Harry E. Gardner (R)
1961, Jack E. Wright, Jr.

OLYMPIA, FIRST
1853, Benjamin Close
1854, William Roberts
1855, John F. DeVore
1856, I. Dillon
1858, John W. Miller
1859, TBS
1860, Nehemiah Doane
1861, Christopher Alderson
 & G. W. Roork
1862, A. C. Fairchild
1863, C. G. Belknap
1864, D. E. Blaine (nominal
 appt.)
1865, C. C. Stratton
1866, TBS
1867, G. H. Greer
1868, S. H. Mann
1870, A. C. Fairchild
1872, Wm. McPheeters
1873, L. T. Woodward
1874, J. T. Wolfe
1877, Albert Atwood
1878, William Roberts
1879, J. McCormac
1881, D. G. LeSourd
1883, D. W. Cameron
1885, A. B. Bruner
1886, R. H. Massey
1888, G. A. Landen
1890, Thos. B. Ford
1891, F. E. Drake
1892, S. A. Bright
1894, A. J. Joslyn
1895, George H. Feese
1897, O. W. Mintzer
1899, R. C. Glass

1902, J. W. Satterthwaite
1905, F. A. LaViolette
1907, J. W. Flesher
1908, C. E. Todd
1910, C. A. Bowen
1914, N. M. Temple
1917, J. H. Secor
1919, A. H. Lathrop
1921, J. M. Canse
1925, O. F. Krieger
1928, Elijah H. Longbrake
1931, S. J. Chaney
1935, Robert Brumblay
1939, Paul H. Ashby
1945, H. E. Bashor
1946, A. P. Aiton
1947, Wm. E. Callahan, Jr.
1957, Robert A. Uphoff
1960, Walter A. McArthur

OLYMPIA, ST. ANDREWS
1960, Robert G. Hess
1962, Robert F. Kinch
1965, Donald E. Sattelberg

ORTING
1889, C. F. Teetor
1889, John H. Britts
1890, W. J. Bargar
1892, C. F. Teetor
1894, W. M. Welch
1895, W. H. Jordan
1896, W. M. Welch
1899, Robt. R. Earl
1900, H. W. Michener
1901, H. W. Holler (S)
1902, Joel Vigus
1905, W. M. Ludwick
1907, F. A. Ecker
1912, Roy Sprague
1914, J. H. Carter
1915, R. V. B. Dunlap
1916, Jas. E. Milligan
1918, E. O. Grimes
1921, W. O. Benadom
1926, C. H. Cowdy
1928, Ira J. McFarland
1933, J. T. McQueen
1938, Frank Haley
1940, L. C. Shultz
1946, Arnt O. Quall
1950, Mack Farmer (S)
1952, TBS
1953, Joseph L. Woodford
1957, Roderick I. Lawrence
1959, John C. Radmore
1961, Elmer E. Beckman
1963, Donald R. Moller

PACIFIC
1906, Rev. J. M. Weaver
1908, Harry L. Allen
1909, Samuel Dupertius
1911, J. W. Blackwell (S)
1913, E. M. Giesey
1914, J. W. Walker (S)
1915, M. H. Marvin (S)
1916, G. L. Cuddy (S)
1917, Lloyd Burk
1919, C. C. James (S)
1921, David G. Beattie
1922, W. H. Thomas
1923, H. Williston
1925, Clark Cottrell
1928, A. A. Moore (S)
1930, James Moore
1932, Earl P. Phelps (S)
1934, E. L. Boothby (S)
1935, Frederick L. Amos (S)
1936, Raymond Huddleston (S)
1937, Rev. O. E. Faulkner (S)
1938, A. L. McConnell (S)

1939, R. G. Williams (S)
1940, not listed
1941, W. E. Callahan, Jr.
1942, D. L. Rothweiler
1943, E. M. Hill
1944, Dewane Lamka (S)
1945, Francis Kinch, (Mrs.) (S)
1946, O. E. Faulkner
1947, Douglas Richardson (S)
1948, Paul D. Brown (S)
1949, Harold Sellers (S)
1950, Andrew Warner (S)
1951, Dennis DeVoe (S)
1952, Eric Kulberg (S)
1954, Sterling Wells (S)
1956, Richard Seiber
1958, Don Moller
1959, Jeff Smith
1962, William D. Ellington

PARKLAND
1902, Horace Williston
1903, J. M. Wilder
1906, E. W. Erickson (S)
1909, H. C. Leavenworth
1910, Henry T. Yandle (S)
1911, John H. Avery
1912, C. Warren Jones
1913, Samuel Dupertius
1914, Clark Cottrell
1915, Chas. D. Miller
1916, Lloyd Burk
1917, Marmaduke Dodsworth
1919, F. S. Pearson
1922, A. M. Frederick (S)
1923, Joel Vigus
1926, Forrest D. Tibbitts
1929, W. J. Scott
1932, Clark J. Wood
1934, James A. Moore
1936, Walter S. Jamieson (S)
1940, Bessie Pease (S) &
      Annette Kiehlbauch (S)
1943, R. M. Putt (S)
1944, George W. Cooper
1951, Alexander P. Aiton
1953, William F. Andrews
1956, Donald G. Northdurft
1956, Assoc. J. C. Snowden (R)
      1 yr.
1959, Donald G. Northdurft
1962, Arthur D. Campbell

PORT ANGELES
1889, A. J. McNemee
1890, Wm. R. Warren
1891, J. M. Baxter
1895, Joseph Mattershead
1896, C. E. Cunningham
1898, George W. Frame
1902, C. E. Fulmer
1904, Horace Williston
1905, George F. Graham (S)
1906, TBS
1907, G. H. Simons (S)
1908, J. M. Hixson (S)
1909, H. J. Hartsell (S)
1910, M. B. Phillips
1914, Herbert Jones
1915, T. T. Sharpe
1917, E. O. Grimes
1918, U. S. Crowder
1920, J. R. Norton
1922, Erle Howell
1935, J. H. Beall
1940, M. J. Perdue
1943, James T. Albertson
1950, W. Raymond Wilder
1952, Oscar M. Adam
1958, Lloyd F. Holloway
1962, To Tacoma Dist.
1963, Robert R. Rings

PORT ORCHARD (formerly
   Sidney)
1890, John Jensen
1892, F. S. Pearson
1895, H. H. Walkington
1896, O. L. Doane
1898, R. M. Schoonmaker
1900, S. P. Brokaw
1902, R. Hughes
1903, Sidney became Port
      Orchard
1903, Rowland Hughes
1904, H. Carlyon (S)
1905, H. P. Waldron
1907, F. R. Gillett
1910, G. C. Poolton
1912, C. J. Kallgren
1913, C. A. Lindholm
1916, E. O. Harris
1918, K. L. Haga
1921, Earl W. D. Hanna
1922, Wm. C. Bowman (S)
1924, A. M. Herd
1926, W. M. Richards (S)
1930, A. S. Morton (S)
1932, J. R. Butler
1934, H. W. Driver
1938, Truman L. Blaisdell
1940, Haven R. Martin
1942, Carroll Sprague
1947, Geo. Almond
1957, Wayne D. Griffen
1958, To Tacoma Dist.
1961, Harvey M. deVries

PORT TOWNSEND, TRINITY
1854, W. B. Morse
1871, A. Laubach
1872, George H. Greer
1873, John Rea (S)
1876, B. J. Sharpe (S)
1877, John Parsons
1878, N. A. Starr
1879, W. I. Cosper
1882, S. H. Todd
1883, N. Doane
1884, Isaac Dillon
1886, J. N. Dennison
1891, S. S. Sulliger
1893, E. R. King
1893, W. O. Benadom
1898, Wm. H. Leech
1902, J. A. Sutton
1905, Horace Williston
1908, C. N. Goulder
1909, Jay C. Dorwin
1913, F. W. P. Camp
1914, J. M. Wilder
1917, L. D. Cook (S)
1917, J. E. McShane
1919, R. L. Sprague
1920, Clark Cottrell
1921, L. C. Davies (S)
1922, A. O. Quall
1927, J. M. Hixson
1929, R. A. Gailey
1933, J. F. Long
1935, Earl E. Reisner
1938, W. O. Pflaum
1941, C. E. Sanders
1942, R. C. McGaffee
1946, Harlan R. Stone
1946, TBS
1947, Henry Attenborough
1948, Linden B. Jenkins
1951, Bertram Robins (S)
1960, John K. Burleson
1964, William H. Holmes, Jr.

PUYALLUP
1884, G. A. Landen
1886, B. F. Brooks

1887, J. W. Dobbs
1888, Sprague Davis
1889, not listed
1889, T. J. Massey
1890, Edward J. Moore
1893, A. J. Hanson
1895, E. V. Claypool
1898, W. O. Benadom
1903, M. A. Covington
1904, W. B. McMillan
1907, G. W. Frame
1911, J. W. Satterthwaite
1913, J. H. Secor
1917, N. M. Temple
1919, Edwin E. Brace
1921, T. W. Lane
1924, C. D. Rarey
1926, H. R. Stone
1929, E. J. Huston
1931, A. A. Callender
1935, P. H. Raymond
1941, Joseph Chester
1944, Harry Coates
1950, Oliver J. Gill
1955, Harvey M. deVries
1957, Assoc. Bruce Hollingsworth
1961, Randall W. Larson

SEQUIM
1897, L. M. Haworth (S)
1898, TBS
1899, W. M. Welch
1900, TBS
1902, A. H. Marsh
1904, TBS
1905, A. J. McNemee
1907, C. F. Bennett
1908, A. Davis (S)
1910, C. N. Goulder (S)
1911, A. B. Simpson (S)
1913, R. C. Johnson
1915, F. F. Frisbie
1916, C. W. McLaughlin (S)
1917, W. H. W. Rees, Jr.
1918, R. C. Hartley
1920, W. L. Airheart
1921, E. J. Bates
1924, T. W. Bundy
1925, J. M. Ammundson (S)
1928, D. S. McGuire (S)
1930, B. H. Hart
1935, V. A. Kraft
1937, Decatur N. Lacy
1938, Wm. G. R. Dann
1945, Margaret Davis (S)
1946, R. Clinton McGaffee
1952, TBS
1952, Fletcher Forster
1957, J. Dean Stout
1959, Robert C. Ward
1962, To Tacoma Dist.
1962, Vincent S. Hart, Jr.

SHELTON
1885, Gordan Henry (S)
1886, W. H. Johnson (S)
1887, Became Shelton
1887, G. F. Mead (S)
1889, TBS
1890, Henry C. Fleenor
1891, TBS
1892, J. M. P. Hickerson
1894, F. M. Wheeler
1897, L. J. Covington
1899, W. B. McMillan
1900, M. S. Anderson (S)
1901, W. B. McMillan
1904, S. G. Jones
1905, George Arney
1907, J. C. Dorwin
1909, C. L. Gilbert

1911, R. H. Reid
1912, R. C. Johnson
1913, Seymour Williams
1916, Bertie Waddington
1920, W. H. Thomas (S)
1922, Nelson C. Pierce
1926, J. H. Avery
1927, F. A. Ecker
1932, Forrest D. Tibbitts
1936, V. A. Spicker
1939, Robert Brumblay
1941, Robert W. Maulden
1945, Hardwick W. Harschman
1947, Wayne Wright
1952, Robert B. Shaw
1955, Charles T. Hatten
1959, Robert R. Rings
1963, Horace H. Mounts

SILVERDALE
1906, R. W. Carr
1907, H. P. Waldron
1908, H. R. Merrill (S)
1909, R. A. Curry (S)
1910, G. Anderson (S)
1913, F. F. Frisbie (S)
1915, J. H. Hicks (S)
1918, J. W. Walker (S)
1920, H. E. Kelly
1922, M. G. Tennyson (S)
1924, J. R. Flood
1925, W. S. Garner (S)
1926, W. C. Sage (S)
1930, Mary McKee
1935, T. W. Emery
1937, Henry R. Cross
1941, Hardwick W. Harschman
1943, D. L. Rothweiler
1946, Burchard A. Hylton
1948, Dennis Stiles, Jr. (S)
1950, John Mathone
1955, J. Philip Porter
1958, To Tacoma Dist.
1960, Paul G. Perkins
1965, William D. Ellington

SOUTH COLBY
1888, G. R. Osborn
1890, not listed
1892, A. J. McNemee
1893, TBS
1894, George Arney
1895, TBS
1902, Henry Wood (S)
1903, TBS
1904, G. Anderson (S)
1905, J. W. White (S)
1906, W. R. A. Scott (S)
1907, A. J. McNemee
1909, TBS
1910, J. Boyce (S)
1911, TBS
1912, E. H. Rubicam
1914, E. O. Harris
1916, F. F. Frisbie
1918, N. V. Moore (S)
1919, S. V. Warren
1921, Frederick Amos (S)
1923, R. W. Maulden
1924, TBS
1925, J. A. Badcon (S)
1926, J. D. Bird (S)
1927, G. A. Sheafe (S)
1928, A. W. Luce (S)
1929, TBS
1930, A. S. Morton (UG)
1932, J. R. Butler
1934, H. W. Driver
1938, Truman L. Blaisdell
1940, Haven R. Martin
1942, Carroll Sprague
1943, John Mathone

1945, Fred W. Hertzog
1947, Mark Freeman
1950, Bertram Robins
1951, William E. Whitlock
1952, John B. Freeman
1954, Karl N. Ekaas
1958, Tacoma Dist.
1958, TBS
1959, Ralph H. R. Butler

SPANAWAY
1908, TBS
1909, A. A. Metcalf (S)
1910, H. T. Yandle
1911, J. W. Walker (S)
1912, F. C. Thompson
1913, Rolla Clark
1915, J. H. Berringer
1916, TBS
1917, Hoyt G. Wilder (S)
1918, M. Dodsworth
1919, TBS
1920, Nelson C. Pierce (S)
1922, A. M. Frederick (S)
1923, Joel Vigus
1924, not listed
1928, F. D. Tibbitts
1929, W. J. Scott
1932, Frances Camp (S)
1933, Orville Weeks (S)
1936, W. S. Jamieson
1940, Bessie Pease (S) &
      Annette Kielbauch (S)
1943, Everett Lowther (S)
1945, Louis Martin
1946, Laura Butler (S)
1946, Roy McMillan (S)
1947, James F. White
1948, Arthur Campbell
1950, Byron Brady (S)
1951, Alexander P. Aiton
1953, William F. Andrews
1956, Donald G. Northdurft
1956, Assoc. J. C. Snowden (R)
1956, Geo. Nafus (S)
1962, John R. Qualley
1964, Alan F. Nubling

SUMNER
1888, Sprague Davis
1890, A. E. Davis (D)
1891, E. R. Hayward
1892, W. W. Gray
1894, G. A. Landen
1896, A. L. Gray (S)
1897, J. M. P. Hickerson
1898, George Arney
1901, A. L. Gray (S)
1903, Horace Williston
1904, A. B. L. Gellerman
1906, T. A. Graham
1907, W. B. Bell
1909, J. W. Miller
1911, F. L. Moore
1912, F. S. Pearson
1914, R. L. Sprague
1916, W. M. Dews
1918, M. B. Phillips
1920, G. F. Hopkins
1924, Richard Oates
1926, O. M. Graham
1929, Harry L. Allen
1931, D. E. Carter
1937, L. C. Shultz
1940, W. Paul Fulmer
1941, Marmaduke Dodsworth
1946, Harry E. Gardner
1950, E. Rae Kaemmer
1955, Tracy W. Manley
1962, Edward McClurg

ALDERSGATE, TACOMA
1962, James T. Burcham

435

1963, Became Aldersgate
1965, Jeffrey L. Smith

ASBURY
1891, Horace Williston
1892, W. H. Johnstone
1893, R. Z. Fahs
1896, G. L. Cuddy
1903, D. G. LeSourd
1906, J. T. McQueen
1911, J. W. Flesher
1912, J. H. Carter
1915, R. V. B. Dunlap
1919, Richard Oates
1924, G. F. Hopkins
1925, G. F. Pollock
1928, T. L. Blaisdell
1932, W. M. Dews
1935, R. A. Anderson
1940, N. M. Jones
1942, F. H. Haley
1944, H. L. Allen
1949, Donald S. Lamka
1952, Robert G. Albertson
1957, Blaine G. Hammond
1958, Assoc. L. Wayne Bond,
1 yr.
1962, H. Eugene Miller

BETHANY
1907, J. C. Reed (S)
1909, W. B. Anderson
1910, J. W. Blackwell
1911, James E. Milligan
1912, F. A. Ecker
1915, W. H. Selleck
1917, D. S. Kerr
1920, E. H. Gebert
1922, E. J. Huston
1929, J. D. Lewellen
1930, J. T. McQueen
1933, Ernest E. Tuck
1935, Erle Howell
1939, Ernest Barber
1943, J. J. Ellington
1950, Jabez C. Harrison
1951, Harry Coates
1957, Elmer E. Beckman
1961, William G. Berney
1964, Lloyd N. Alden

BROWN'S POINT
1959, James E. Shapland
1960, Virgil A. Anderson
1963, Craig T. Harper

CALVARY
1901, J. R. Edwards
1904, F. L. Tuttle (S)
1905, T. J. Gambill
1907, O. L. Kendall
1909, W. O. Pflaum
1911, R. L. Sprague
1912, H. K. Kline
1914, T. H. Jorgensen
1915, Herbert Jones
1916, S. V. Warren
Changed to 64th St. Ch.
1918, J. Pascoe (S)
1920, D. S. Kerr
1923, T. A. Graham
1926, G. C. Poolton
1928, G. F. Pollock
1933, Ira J. McFarland
1935, Everette M. Filbert
1935, Became CALVARY
1937, Raymond Huddleston (S)
1938, James T. McQueen
1940, Fred Hertzog (S)
1941, R. L. Otto (S)
1946, William D. Williams
1949, Percy E. Pike

1959, Edward E. Smyth (S)
1964, Elmer J. Church (S)

EPWORTH
1890, Jno. W. Maxwell
1891, TBS
1892, G. H. Feese
1895, D. G. LeSourd
1903, Edward H. Todd
1905, A. B. Chapin
1906, W. W. Shenk
1908, W. O. Benadom
1911, W. T. Randolph
1914, W. H. W. Rees
1917, E. N. Askey
Assoc. H. G. Earle
1920, Andrew Warner
1924, R. S. Rees
1928, Thos. Acheson
1932, Paul Green
1934, E. F. Harold
1937, W. S. Gleiser
1940, H. O. Perry
1943, Martindale Woods
1945, Francis Kinch
1951, Harold C. Williams
1958, S. Raynor Smith, Jr.
1960, LaVern E. Tooley

FERN HILL
1890, Thos. E. McMullen
1891, F. M. Wheeler
1893, L. J. Covington
1895, F. S. Pearson
1899, S. G. Jones
1900, Horace Williston
1903, J. M. Wilder
1906, E. W. Erickson
1909, H. C. Leavenworth
1911, J. A. Sutton
1913, T. A. Graham
1914, R. V. B. Dunlap
1915, J. H. Berringer
1920, Harry L. Allen
1922, Clyde L. Walker
1924, O. M. Graham (UG)
1926, N. C. Pierce (UG)
1928, E. O. Grimes
1929, Robert L. LaMott
1932, A. S. Morton
1935, D. S. Kerr
1938, Wayne Sprague
1939, B. C. Gallaher
1942, John R. Butler
1943, Andrew Warner
1945, Francis F. Ohse
1947, Andrew Warner
1948, Wayne D. Griffen
1952, Donald W. Baldwin
1959, Adam S. Forch, Sr.
1963, Wilfred L. Johnson

FIRCREST
1914, E. H. Gebert (S)
1915, C. D. Miller
1916, L. L. Burk
1917, Hoyt G. Wilder (S)
1918, C. M. Phoenix (S)
1919, TBS
1926, S. S. Sulliger (S)
1927, W. E. Stanton
1928, Mrs. L. W. Wilhelm (S)
1929, TBS
1931, not listed
1932, TBS
1938, not listed
1942, Don Lamka
1943, Don H. Glenn (S)
1944, A. W. Smith
1945, TBS
1946, O. L. McDonald (S)
1947, Robert W. Huston (S)

1949, Dennis DeVoe (S)
1951, Geo. W. Cooper
1953, Don F. Utterback
1959, Bruce E. Foreman
1963, Charles E. Gruenwald

TACOMA, FIRST
1873, W. T. Chapman
1874, C. H. Hoxie
1876, Martin Judy
1878, John Parsons
1879, Enoch Dudley
1880, D. L. Spaulding
1880, J. W. Miller
1881, J. F. DeVore
1884, J. F. Ward
1885, TBS
1886, T. J. Massey
1887, D. G. LeSourd
1888, TBS
1889, G. C. Wilding
1891, F. B. Cherington
1894, J. P. Marlatt
1899, H. V. Givler
1902, D. L. Rader
1904, J. P. Marlatt
1908, M. A. Casey
1910, T. W. Lane
1912, E. M. Randall, Assoc.
1915, D. H. Trimble
1915, J. C. Zeller, Assoc.
1918, R. H. Schuett
1922, Herbert B. Rhodes
1926, L. M. Grigsby
1929, J. Franklin Haas
1934, King D. Beach
1937, Cyrus E. Albertson
1941, Milton A. Marcy
1951, Clark J. Wood
1954, Frank E. Brown
1957, Assoc. John C. Radmore
1960, Assoc. Glade McClish (S)
1961, Lawrence J. Linneman
1964, Assoc. Milford M. Oliver
(S)

GRACE
1903, H. H. Newman
1904, Arthur H. Miller (S)
1905, Joel Vigus
1909, W. B. Ball
1911, S. G. Jones
1913, W. B. Anderson
1914, G. M. Day
1916, W. J. Green
1917, A. F. Stearns
1920, A. P. Rolan (S)
1921, R. R. Martin (S)
1922, Stanley McKee
1923, C. P. Johnson
1924, TBS
1925, O. J. Beadles (UG)
1926, Harry A. Wann
1927, Joel Vigus
1932, Geo. F. Hopkins
1934, Geo. F. Pollock
1936, H. J. Wood
1938, O. E. Faulkner (S)
1943, Charles Gleason (S)
1945, F. C. Fulford (S)
1946, TBS
1947, H. Gene Upton (S)
1948, TBS
1947, H. Gene Upton (S)
1948, TBS
1949, Bruce Parker
1950, Don H. Glenn (S)
1954, TBS
1955, E. Smyth
1959, J. C. Snowden (R)
1960, TBS
1961, Wayne Blackledge

436

1962, Fred W. Hertzog

LAKEWOOD
1955, Jack M. Tuell
1961, Bruce G. Parker

LESOURD
1911, C. N. Goulder
1913, Clark Cottrell
1914, C. D. Miller
1915, A. J. Armstrong (S)
1916, H. E. Gardner
1917, W. F. Pool (S)
1918, TBS
1920, T. A. Swayze (S)
1921, B. F. Brooks (S)
1926, TBS
1927, W. E. Stanton (S)
1928, W. E. Stanton
1929, H. E. Bashor
1931, T. L. Blaisdell
1932, T. A. Graham (S)
1933, Geo. F. Hopkins (R)
1938, D. S. Kerr (R)
1939, Miss Marion Rounds (S)
1941, G. F. Hopkins (R)
1942, Barent Johnson (S)
1944, F. C. Fulford (R)
1950, Willis L. Carruth (S)
1956, Edwin F. Rode
1958, Donald G. Forsberg
1960, L. W. Blackledge
1962, H. Robert Morton
1965, Donald R. Moller

MASON
1891, Horace Williston
1891, Charles E. Fulmer
1893, Edward J. Moore
1894, A. Horace Keeler
1895, Charles S. Revelle
1900, George G. Ferguson
1902, George A. Landen
1904, Melmoth A. Covington
1905, Joseph W. Satterthwaite
1909, James A. Sutton
1910, Fred L. Baldwin
1912, E. L. Benedict
1913, Robert J. Reid
1917, Joseph P. Marlatt
1921, TBS, Norman McCay
1922, Assoc. E. H. Gebert
1924, J. G. Law
        Assoc. F. W. Tolles (UG)
1925, Assoc. Harry E. Rarey
        (UG)
1927, Robert Brumblay
1929, Charles MacCaughey
1935, Roy Leslie Smith
1943, Stanley G. Logan
1945, J. Henry Ernst
1955, Assoc. Ludwig Eskildsen
1955, Assoc. Charles T. Hatten
        (R)
1960, Assoc. Paul Campbell
1961, John C. Soltman
1964, Assoc. F. L. Pedersen (S)

ST. PAUL'S
1890, Benj. F. Brooks
1894, H. Williston
1899, F. S. Wright
1900, C. S. Revelle
1902, G. W. Frame
1907, C. E. Todd
1908, W. B. Marsh
1913, E. J. Smith
1914, W. H. Baker
1916, W. T. Randolph
1918, J. E. Milligan
1923, P. H. Ashby
1925, John F. Long

1928, M. J. Perdue
1932, Frank E. Goodnough
1939, Ernest P. Goulder
1942, William E. Callahan, Jr.
1947, Harold J. Bass
1955, Robert B. Shaw
1957, Nolan J. McClurg

SUMMIT
1903, William M. Welch
1907, O. R. Davis (S)
1910, John H. Avery
1912, H. E. Moore
1913, T. C. Newby
1914, A. F. Stearns
1917, J. W. Reynolds
1918, H. E. Gardner
1919, Roy M. Owen
1920, L. A. Sheffler (S)
1922, Lloyd L. Burk
1923, J. H. Avery
1926, Mrs. A. D. Newell (S)
1927, Joel M. Wilder (S)
1929, P. R. Campbell
1931, G. F. Hopkins
1933, Ira J. McFarland
1935, Orville Weeks (S)
1936, H. J. Wood
1942, Robt. Ridgeway (S)
1943, H. W. Driver
1945, A. O. Quall
1946, Bessie Pease (S) &
        Annette Kiehlbauch (S)
1948, J. R. Butler
1952, TBS
1953, John Christensen (S)
1955, John E. Besant
1958, Floyd E. Cronkite (UG)
1960, TBS
1961, Douglas C. Mitchell

TRINITY, TACOMA
    Combination of Fowler and
    McKinley Park
1913, F. L. Moore
1916, J. C. Dorwin
1918, C. D. Rarey
1924, G. A. Landen
1926, O. J. Beadles
1931, W. H. H. Forsyth
1934, V. A. Spicker
1936, Forrest Tibbitts
1941, J. W. Caughlan
1945, Eugene W. Muench
1949, R. L. LaMott
1950, John P. Johnson
1954, C. Ellsworth Wilson
1957, Allen C. Lambert
1960, Orin D. Watson
1962, E. Vincent Smith
1964, Edward E. Smyth (S)

WHITNEY MEMORIAL
JAPANESE
1907, Seichi Higasheda (S)
1909, Fusao Sakaizawa
1910, Sumikiyo Arima
1912, Shinichiro Kurihara
1914, Saburo Nomi
1915, Maaki Kato
1917, Iwakichi Haratani
1923, Seiji Izaka
1930, Shiroku Fujimura
1933, Otoe So
1937, Goro Uzaki
1939, Yasutaki Hika
1940, Seiichi Niwa
1942, Evacuated
1953, Alpha Hajime Takagi
1962, Robert M. Yamashita

TRACYTON
1905, R. W. Carr

1906, H. P. Waldron
1907, H. R. Merrill
1908, R. W. Curry (S)
1909, G. Anderson (S)
1913, F. F. Frisbie (S)
1915, TBS
1916, J. H. Hicks (S)
1918, J. W. Walker (S)
1920, H. E. Kelly
1922, TBS
1924, J. R. Flood
1925, W. S. Garner (S)
1926, W. C. Sage (S)
1930, Mary McKee (S)
1935, Thos. W. Emery
1937, Henry R. Cross
1941, Hardwick W. Harschman
1943, D. L. Rothweiler
1946, Burchard A. Hylton
1948, Thos. Slate
1958, To Tacoma Dist.
1958, Robert L. LaMott
1960, TBS
1961, R. B. Huddleston (S)
1963, Robert G. Calkins (S)

BROWNSVILLE (formerly
    Browning)
1951, John Mathone (S)
1952, Thomas Slate
1952, BROWNSVILLE
1958, To Tacoma Dist.
1958, Robert L. LaMott
1960, TBS
1961, R. B. Huddleston (S)
1963, Robert G. Calkins

TUMWATER
1884, A. K. Crawford
1885, Robert Phillips
1886, Ebenezer Hopkins (S)
1888, J. I. Smith
1889, G. F. Mead
1891, W. H. Johnstone
1892, R. H. Massey
1896, E. Hopkins
1902, TBS
1903, E. Hopkins
1904, R. L. Ludlum (S)
1905, TBS
1906, G. F. Graham (S)
1909, TBS
1910, A. Davis (S)
1911, W. J. Gilbert (S)
1913, TBS
1914, W. H. W. Rees, Jr.
1915, W. C. Webber (S)
1916, J. W. Walker (S)
1919, J. H. Hicks (S)
1921, Mrs. L. M. Wilhelm (S)
1927, Chester Blair (S)
1929, J. M. Hixson
1934, J. D. Bird
1937, C. B. Seely (R)
1938, John R. Butler
1939, TBS
1941, not listed
1942, TBS
1944, Mrs. Nellie Cook (S)
1950, Tom B. Cherrington (S)
1952, TBS
1954, Robert H. Keller, Jr. (S)
1955, Don H. Glenn (S)
1957, J. C. Snowden (R)
1958, To Tacoma Dist.
1961, H. Gordan Castell (S)
1964, Doyle E. Shields

YELM, Community ch. prior to
    1910
1910, H. P. Waldron
1911, E. Hopkins (S)

437

1912, J. W. Blackwell (S)
1914, J. J. Jones
1915, W. H. W. Rees, Jr.
1917, C. W. McLaughlin
1919, C. B. Seely
1920, W. P. Rutledge
1921, A. W. Smith (S)
1925, E. W. D. Hanna
1929, Harold E. Nelson
1934, J. H. Ernst
1937, Edwin D. Rounds
1939, Howard P. Buck
1942, Hunter McKain
1943, Geo. H. Huber
1945, George F. Lockwood
1948, William Richards
1952, TBS
1953, Tracy W. Manley
1955, Everette M. Filbert
1957, Evald Leps
1960, J. Philip Porter
1965, Rollin E. Stierwalt

VANCOUVER DISTRICT
ABERDEEN, Central Park
1950, J. W. Cleland (S)
1954, Bruce Groseclose
1956, J. Dean King
1959, Erling Bergan
1964, Ronald R. Northrup

ABERDEEN, FIRST
1883, S. D. Lougheed
1884, J. H. Stuntz
1884, John Patterson
1885, Charles McDermoth
1888, A. Kershaw
1889, T. W. Butler
1892, A. J. Joslyn
1894, S. Alonzo Bright
1896, Melmoth A. Covington
1897, Oscar A. Smith
1899, Charles McDermoth
1903, Thomas E. Elliott
1904, William E. Thompson
1906, Wilmot Whitfield
1907, F. A. LaViolette
1909, B. F. Brooks
1911, J. T. McQueen
1915, W. T. Randolph
1916, E. M. Hill
1919, C. W. Huett
1920, A. H. Thompson
1921, Aaron Allen Heist
    Assoc. A. E. Hart
1923, Henry T. Greene
1924, G. V. Fallis
1924, J. R. Sasnett,
    Asst. Bessie F. Daws
1927, W. H. H. Forsyth
1931, J. W. Coughlan
1936, Laverne Hicks
1938, N. M. Jones
1940, R. A. Anderson
1945, Martindale Woods
1948, Roy Jenkins
1952, W. Raymond Wilder
1955, LaVerne E. Tooley
1956, Elmer E. Beckman
1957, Harold W. Black
1958, Assoc. J. W. Cleland (S)
    ended 1959
1960, TBS
1961, Floyd E. Green
1963, Howard W. Yoder

CAMAS, FIRST
1886, TBS
1887, W. H. Drake
1888, T. W. Butler
1889, F. M. Pickles
1891, James Matthews

1893, Ebenezer Hopkins
1894, D. M. Ellsworth
1895, Isaac Heitman
1896, William McWatters
1897, TBS
1900, W. J. Rule
1901, E. C. Parker
1904, J. C. Reed (S)
1905, B. L. Hicks
1906, C. H. Cowdy (S)
1907, TBS
1908, E. J. Huston
1909, Seymour Williams
1911, H. L. Townsend
1913, Horace Williston
1915, D. A. Storey
1918, F. A. Ecker
1921, D. E. Carter
1922, George W. Cooper
1925, C. E. Todd
1930, M. L. Sanders
1933, Robert Elmer Smith
1937, Howard Seymour
1940, Geo. L. Poor
1946, Elmer Beckman
1948, Robert B. Shaw
1952, Waldo W. Pierson
1962, Paul E. Peterson
1964, R. Marshall Campbell

CAMAS, FERN PRAIRIE
1873, J. H. Allyn
1874, Samuel Matthews
1875, N. A. Starr
1876, T. M. Reese
1878, John Flinn
1881, Columbus Derrick
1882, J. M. Sweney
1883, G. G. Ferguson
1886, W. H. Drake
1887, F. M. Pickles
1888, T. W. Butler
1889, F. M. Pickles
1891, James Matthews
1893, Ebenezer Hopkins
1894, D. M. Ellsworth
1895, L. E. Wornom
1898, E. O. Harris
1902, F. E. Smith
1905, M. L. Hardingham
1906, W. E. Rossman
1912, S. V. Warren
1916, J. H. Avery
1919, TBS
1920, B. G. Clemens
1925, John Place
1929, L. C. Davies (S)
1930, C. H. Cowdy
1931, B. G. Clemens
1934, J. M. Canse (S)
1935, L. O. Griffith
1936, T. L. Blaisdell
1938, Kenneth H. Dunkelberger
1939, Robert Getty, Jr. (S)
1940, Howard A. Seymour
1941, Geo. L. Poor
1942, Howard P. Buck
1944, Geo. L. Poor
1945, Percy E. Pike
1949, Roy L. Kuhns
1951, Charles Harris
1952, Earl B. Cotton
    Assoc., Mrs. E. B. Cotton
1954, Francis L. Groth
1957, W. S. J. Bleakley
1959, Floyd E. Green
1961, TBS
1962, Mrs. Dorothy Northcutt
    (S)

CASTLE ROCK
1883, T. M. Reese

1884, John Laity
1885, M. Burlingame
1886, E. L. Hughes
1887, Dan DeLano (S)
1888, W. T. Zenor
1889, C. P. Stayton
1890, Melmoth A. Covington (S)
1892, W. M. Ludwick
1893, E. L. Hughes
1895, James Matthews
1896, W. H. Jordan
1898, W. M. Ludwick
1899, R. C. Hartley
1901, W. M. Ludwick
1903, F. M. Clark
1906, T. F. Allen
1907, W. J. Getty
1909, J. E. Murphy
1910, A. A. Brittain
1912, B. N. Galbraith
1914, D. A. Storey
1915, Frank Sutton
1916, W. J. Rule
1917, W. E. Rossman (S)
1920, F. R. Gillett
1923, E. O. Grimes
1925, S. V. Warren
1926, T. J. Hazelton (S)
1928, R. H. Allen
1929, H. J. Harding (S)
1935, R. B. Parcel
1937, Howard Buck
1939, H. E. Nelson
1940, L. C. Bennett (S)
1941, W. M. Richards (S)
1948, Geo. F. Lockwood
1949, M. K. Skarbo

CENTRALIA
1880, W. P. Williams (S)
1882, J. E. Leach
1883, G. R. Osborn
1885, A. K. Crawford
1886, J. W. Kepler
1887, C. P. Stayton
1888, C. C. Culmer
1889, Sprague Davis
1890, A. J. Joslyn
1892, T. E. McMullen
1893, F. E. Drake
1895, O. A. Smith
1896, I. R. Lovejoy
1897, Charles McDermoth
1899, E. H. Fuller
1900, J. W. Miller
1905, F. S. Pearson
1907, A. J. Joslyn
1908, Robert J. Reid
1913, A. A. Luce
1914, D. Roland Martin
1916, George W. Frame
1920, E. N. Askey
1923, O. M. Andrews
1925, J. M. Canse
1926, C. A. Bowen
1929, Philip H. Raymond
1935, Neil M. Jones
1938, Paul H. Ashby
1939, Erle Howell
1945, R. A. Anderson
1949, Chas. T. Hatten
1955, S. Raynor Smith, Jr.
1958, Bruce G. Parker
1961, Clinton A. Aiton

CHEHALIS
1884, TBS
1885, D. W. Cameron
1887, C. P. Stayton
1888, C. C. Culmer
1889, E. J. Moore
1890, Robert A. Atkins

1892, J. W. Maxwell
1893, E. D. White
1894, J. E. Williams
1896, T. E. Elliott
1898, G. A. Sheafe
1899, F. E. Drake
1900, M. V. Heidelbaugh
1902, F. S. Pearson
1905, C. S. Revelle
1906, R. L. Wolfe
1907, T. F. Allen
1909, F. A. LaViolette
1912, Fred L. Baldwin
1914, E. J. Smith
1917, J. A. Sutton
1919, A. J. McKenzie
1924, E. M. Randall
1927, T. J. Gambill
1929, S. G. Logan
1932, Norman McCay
1933, O. J. Beadles
1937, J. J. Ellington
1939, Harry Coates
1941, J. H. Ernst
1945, O. M. Graham
1949, D. M. Fife
1953, Walter S. Gleiser
1964, Harold C. Williams

COSMOPOLIS
1883, S. D. Lougheed (S)
1884, J. H. Stuntz
1885, Charles McDermoth
1888, A. Kershaw (S)
1889, W. I. Cosper
1890, TBS
1893, W. H. Jordan
1894, J. M. P. Hickerson
1896, W. M. Ludwick
1898, N. M. Temple
1900, S. G. Jones
1902, R. D. Snyder (S)
1903, J. F. Redfern
1904, W. H. Gooderham (S)
1905, C. C. Babbidge
1906, E. L. Bower
1907, W. J. Gilbert (S)
1909, H. T. Yandle (S)
1911, E. E. Simmons
1912, L. D. Cook (S)
1913, K. R. Gilmer
1914, A. Robertson (S)
1915, J. J. Jones
1916, J. W. Miller
1917, T. P. Jimison (S)
Didn't serve
N. V. Moore supplied
1918, Erle Howell
1922, Harry L. Allen
1923, Paul F. Green
1925, F. A. Ecker
1927, J. W. Reynolds
1929, Lila M. Marston (S)
1934, Wilbur Walker (S)
1935, T. A. Olson (S)
1936, F. S. Bailey
1937, J. P. Armand
1938, C. R. Mitchell (S)
1939, N. M. Jones
1940, F. L. Cook (S)
1941, TBS
1945, A. J. Armstrong
1947, J. W. Cleland (S)
1949, Murray V. Hyde
1953, Charles Gruenwald
1955, Carl J. Conrad
1956, Donald R. Yates
1959, Donovan E. McVicker
1961, James D. Crawford
1962, Hortense Anable (S)
1964, TBS
1965, Milford M. Oliver (S)

ELMA
1884, A. Anderson (S)
1887, W. I. Cosper
1888, C. P. Stayton
1889, C. A. Snelling (S)
1890, Chas. E. Cunningham
1891, T. E. McMullen
1892, Andrew Anderson
1894, W. H. Jordan
1895, L. J. Covington
1897, C. C. Pratt
1899, F. S. Pearson
1902, J. M. Weaver
1903, John Lewtas
1906, F. M. Clark
1908, J. W. Frescoln
1911, G. A. Sheafe
1912, J. W. Miller
1913, T. T. Sharpe
1915, T. H. Jorgenson
1917, G. V. Fallis (S)
1919, B. Waddington
1920, R. V. D. Dunlap
1921, F. A. Ecker
1925, E. O. Grimes
1928, M. L. Sanders
1930, J. D. Lewellen
1935, A. W. Brown
1937, G. E. Knight
1939, L. N. Alden
1944, Bruce Groseclose
1947, Robert LaMott
1949, Ira McFarland
1951, Roy L. Kuhns
1954, S. Christian Thele
1957, Geo. A. Cummings
1961, Herbert G. Luscombe
1965, Edgar Lee Starr, Jr.

MCCLEARY
1912, R. H. Reed
1913, E. R. Tracy
1914, L. D. Cook (S)
1917, C. F. Johnson
1919, L. D. Cook (S)
1920, Earl Hanna (S)
1921, Geo. W. Cooper
1922, Earl Hanna (S)
1923, Clark Cottrell
1924, R. A. Gailey
1926, R. H. Allen
1928, T. J. Hazelton
1929, J. W. Reynolds
1937, G. E. Knight
1939, L. N. Alden
1944, B. B. Groseclose
1946, J. S. Randle
1947, John R. Butler
1948, R. L. LaMott
1949, Geo. Gable (S)
1951, Roy L. Kuhns
1954, S. Christian Thele
1956, Mack Farmer
1957, Alex Poobus (S)
1963, H. Grant Harvey
1965, Edgar Lee Starr, Jr.

SATSOP
1896, L. J. Covington
1897, C. C. Pratt
1899, F. S. Pierson
1902, J. M. Weaver
1903, John Lewtas
1904, M. B. Phillips
1906, E. L. Hughes
1907, N. V. Moore (S)
1909, E. B. Reese
1910, J. H. Dill
1911, W. G. R. Dann
1913, H. P. Waldron
1914, J. W. Reynolds

1915, Richard D. Decker
1916, C. A. Lindholm (S)
1917, Erle Howell
1918, C. W. McLaughlin (S)
1919, J. H. Beall
1921, C. H. Cowdy
1922, S. V. Warren
1925, TBS
1926, Miss Ethel Williams (S)
1927, TBS
1928, John Evans (S)
1930, J. D. Lewellen
1935, H. J. Harding (S)
1942, Murray Hyde
1943, Wm. A. Andersen (S)
1944, Lloyd N. Alden
1944, Charles Creesy
1946, Bruce B. Groseclose
1947, Robert L. LaMott
1948, J. D. Lewellen
1956, John W. Kuller
1959, Alex Poobus
1963, H. Grant Harvey
1965, Edgar Lee Starr, Jr.

GOLDENDALE
1873, H. Caldwell
1875, J. W. Kuykendall
1876, J. C. Kirkman
1877, G. C. Allender
1878, W. T. Koontz
1880, G. C. Roe
1881, G. E. Wilcox
1882, S. W. Richards
1884, M. C. Bryan
1885, John Uren
1886, J. W. Bluett
1888, L. J. Whitcomb
1889, G. G. Ferguson
1890, E. McEvers
1892, J. M. McDonald
1895, U. F. Hawk
1897, Nathan Evans
1901, C. D. Nickelsen
1902, H. B. Elworthy
1904, Henry Brown
1906, Perry Chandler
1907, W. P. Jinnett
1909, Wm. DeWeese
1912, W. F. Ineson
1913, E. H. Longbrake
1914, W. L. Airheart
1916, H. T. Greene
1918, Louis Thomas
1922, John E. Garver
1923, M. L. Sanders
1925, D. A. Storey
1928, R. C. Young
1933, R. H. Allen
1937, Clyde J. Hall
1947, Bruce B. Groseclose
1951, T. Earl Poindexter
1953, Edwin B. Towle
1958, Arthur D. Campbell
1962, Robert G. Hess

HOQUIAM, FIRST
1890, A. L. Waiker (S)
1891, E. V. Claypool
1892, C. S. Revelle
1895, A. H. Keeler
1896, J. M. P. Hickerson
1897, F. M. Wheeler
1898, T. E. Elliott
1901, J. W. Satterthwaite
1902, W. O. Benadom
1904, E. L. Benedict
1907, O. H. McGill
1908, C. A. Williams
1911, E. N. Askey
1913, J. A. Sutton
1917, W. W. Switzer

1920, P. H. Ashby
1923, J. H. Geoghegan
1928, John F. Long
1929, C. W. Stark
1931, E. M. Hill
1936, J. H. Magee
1939, V. A. Spicker
1941, W. S. T. Gray
1945, H. P. Buck
1948, Lloyd Alden
1951, Bruce G. Parker
1958, Paul R. Campbell
1961, Chas. Kent Echelbarger
1963, Fred O. Hunt

KALAMA
1889, T. M. Reese (S)
1890, Chas. P. Stayton
1891, A. J. McNemee
1892, John Flinn
1893, C. A. Luse
1894, A. F. Wilson
1895, C. C. Pratt
1897, C. B. Seeley
1899, O. L. Doane
1902, J. W. Glenk
1903, Thomas A. Stamp
1904, N. M. Temple
1906, R. D. Snyder
1907, W. E. Cox
1911, J. W. Frescoln
1912, R. V. B. Dunlap
1914, G. C. Poolton
1916, A. W. Brown
1919, B. F. Brooks
1920, L. D. Cook (S)
1922, J. F. Long
1923, Loyd Burk
1924, TBS
1925, T. J. Cowley (S)
1926, TBS
1927, A. M. Herd
1928, T. H. Jorgenson
1932, C. E. Sanders
1936, J. H. Avery
1940, F. F. Boothby
1942, Clark Cottrell
1944, W. B. Lamb
1946, O. L. McDonald
1948, C. Groth
1949, L. G. Melone (S)
1950, Percy C. Bent
1957, Murray V. Hyde
1963, Donald D. Larson

KELSO
1887, E. L. Hughes
1888, F. M. Pickles
1889, C. P. Stayton
1891, J. I. Smith
1893, G. G. Ferguson
1895, S. P. Brokaw
1896, George A. Sheafe
1898, C. E. Fulmer
1902, S. G. Jones
1904, R. L. Wolfe
1906, F. L. Moore
1908, N. M. Temple
1911, E. J. Smith
1913, E. L. Benedict
1915, J. T. McQueen
1916, H. E. Greening
1918, O. F. Krieger
1919, B. W. Rinehart
1920, E. E. Reisner
1922, W. W. Switzer
1925, M. L. Sanders
1926, C. D. Rarey
1931, L. C. Hicks
1935, C. E. Miller
1937, Harold Bashor
1945, Wm. S. T. Gray

1947, C. H. Sprague
1954, Edward A. Wolfe
1958, Ludwig Eskildsen

LONGVIEW
1953, Harry L. Allen
1954, G. Edward Knight
1960, Lawrence A. Burdette
1962, Kenneth B. MacLagan
1964, Edward C. Liebman
1965, Wendell J. Cone

LYLE
1927, W. H. Mills (S)
1928, TBS
1929, not listed
1930, probably with
    White Salmon
1932, Earl McAbee
1933, Roy L. Jenkins
1935, C. W. Stark
1938, Jos. W. Reynolds
1943, B. C. Gallaher
1945, Geo. P. George
1951, Francis Groth (S)
1952, TBS
1953, Francis L. Groth
1954, Leonard J. Ruff (S)
1955, Miss Bertie Sawtell (S)
1956, TBS
1957, Miss Bertie Sawtell
1958, John E. Besant (S)
1961, James A. Mott (S)
1964, Everett M. Richey (S)

J. D. TRAILER CITY
1959, Hubert Vincent (R)
1961, James A. Mott
1964, Everett M. Richey
    no congregation. Served by
    pastor at Lyle.

MONTESANO
1859, J. S. Douglas
1860, W. J. Franklin
1862, TBS
1863, H. C. Rhoades
1864, TBS
1868, H. B. Lane
1870, C. H. Hoxie
1871, W. T. Chapman
1872, Ira F. Ward
1873, T. M. Reese
1874, W. I. Cosper
1877, J. H. Allyn
1878, Thomas Magill
1879, M. Whitmore
1880, Thomas Magill
1882, S. D. Lougheed
1883, W. H. Zellers
1884, W. I. Cosper
1887, D. W. Cameron
1889, A. H. Marsh
1889, F. E. Drake
1891, H. D. Brown
1892, E. V. Claypool
1892, A. M. Cox
1893, N. P. Tedrick
1893, W. H. Jennings
1895, Irving R. Lovejoy
1896, Oscar A. Smith
1897, Edward H. Todd
1899, John W. Miller
1900, E. Hale Fuller
1901, W. E. Thompson
1903, J. W. Flesher
1904, W. O. Benadom
1907, George A. Sheafe
1908, A. J. Joslyn
1909, T. F. Allen
1912, R. L. Wolfe
1914, O. F. Krieger

1917, R. C. Hartley
1918, W. M. Dews
1920, F. L. Baldwin
1924, G. C. Poolton
1926, C. M. Van Marter
1930, J. M. Canse
1933, W. E. Stanton
1937, J. M. Canse
1938, E. E. Reisner
1940, C. L. Creesy
1946, Geo. H. Huber
1949, Paul R. Campbell
1959, Linden B. Jenkins
1961, Harold E. Bashor

MORTON
1892, Benjamin F. Woods
1893, C. P. Stayton
1893, Wm. J. Rule
1894, Isaac Heitman (S)
1896, TBS
1897, TBS
1899, E. L. Bower
1906, William Porter
1907, O. R. Anderson
1909, C. W. Craven (S)
1910, D. A. Storey (S)
1912, Charles D. Miller
1913, Martin A. Isdahl (S)
1913, J. W. Walker
1914, F. C. Thompson
1918, John Orkney (S)
1918, Horace H. Williston
1920, Lloyd Burk
1922, T. C. Cocks (S)
1923, A. M. Lambert (S)
1925, Joseph W. Reynolds
1927, J. H. Avery
1929, C. E. Preston (S)
1931, W. B. Hawthorn (S)
1931, Elwin H. Scheyer
1934, O. H. Whitesides
1940, Wm. M. Richards (S)
1941, Donald W. Baldwin
1943, Charles E. Sanders
1944, J. H. Avery
1945, Byron C. Gallagher
1947, J. Charles Snowden
1951, Chas. A. Dockstedder (S)
1952, Walter P. Elkins (S)
1955, Harry W. Chatterton
1957, Everette M. Filbert
1963, Samuel A. Carlson (S)

OCEAN PARK
1918, T. J. Cowley (S)
1922, J. C. Lawrence (S)
1923, H. Albright
1929, M. R. Gallaher
1931, Henry Albright
1934, Boudinst Seeley
    (Presby) (S)
1934, Fred H. Betts
1936, L. C. Bennett (S)
1938, Robert E. Thomas
1939, Harold E. Dixon
1951, Erling Bergan
1959, Bernard E. Mott (S)
1960, Jack Caldwell
1961, Donald Krogh (S)
1963, J. Fred Stilwell (R)

OCEAN PARK INSTITUTE
1939, Harold E. Dixon
1953, Erling Bergan
1959, Bernard E. Mott (S)
1961, Donald Krogh (S)
1963, J. Fred Stilwell (R)

CHINOOK
1895, TBS
1896, not listed

1897, James Matthews
1899, Wm. J. Rule
1900, W. J. Gilbert (S)
1901, B. N. Galbraith (S)
1903, William McWatters
1905, M. B. Phillips
1906, John F. Long (S)
1908, TBS
1909, L. S. Chapman (S)
1910, E. E. Bergman
1911, T. T. Sharpe
1913, J. H. Geoghegan
1915, J. W. Reynolds
1917, C. H. Cowdy
1922, J. C. Lawrence
1923, H. Albright
1929, M. R. Gallaher
1931, Henry Albright
1934, Boudinst Seeley (S)
1934, Fred H. Betts
1936, L. C. Bennett
1938, TBS
1939, Harold E. Dixon
1947, R. W. Campbell (S)
1950, TBS
1951, Erling Bergan
1959, Bernard E. Mott (S)
1960, Jack Caldwell
1961, Donald Krogh (S)
1963, J. Fred Stilwell (R)

RANDLE. First known as
VANCE
1890, J. N. Taylor (S)
1891, TBS
1892, B. F. Woods
1894, TBS
1900, E. L. Bower (S)
1901, TBS
1904, E. L. Bower (S)
1906, TBS
1907, O. R. Anderson
1909, TBS
Became RANDLE
1910, D. A. Storey (S)
1912, Roy B. Parcel
1914, W. J. Green
1916, F. E. Reddick
1918, E. L. Albright
1919, J. W. Blackwell (S)
1923, C. C. James
1927, TBS
1928, Clark Cottrell
1930, J. W. Reynolds
1931, T. A. Graham
1932, G. E. James
1934, G. A. Wells
1937, O. L. Anthony
1942, J. H. Avery
1947, K. L. Cooper
1949, Jesse L. Tooley (S)
1956, Pierce Roberts (S)
1959, Albert W. Richardson (S)
1961, Henry R. Cross (R)
1964, James A. Mott

RAYMOND
1904, W. E. Cox
1907, R. L. Wolfe
1908, A. W. Brown
1909, J. M. Weaver
1914, H. E. Greening
1916, Geo. F. Hopkins
1920, Chas. A. Bowen
1922, Wm. Park
1926, W. O. Benadom
1928, D. E. Carter
1931, David A. Storey
1934, Harold E. Nelson
1935, T. Arthur Olsen
1939, Daniel E. Taylor

1944, Lloyd N. Alden
1946, E. Rae Kaemmer
1950, Harry E. Gardner
1952, Austin G. Rugger
1956, Erwin G. Ranton
1957, Raymond Parish
1960, Kenneth B. MacLagan
1962, TBS
1963, John A. Larsson

EAST RAYMOND
1914, George Abbott
1913, TBS
1914, George Abbott
1915, W. J. Rule
1922, TBS
1925, Claud Groth (S)
1929, not listed
1932, D. A. Storey
1934, Chester Finkbeiner
1937, O. A. Cheek (S)
1938, Chester Boddy (S)
1939, Clark M. Smith
1941, Walter A. Cobb (S)
1942, Wm. A. Anderson (S)
1943, Harry E. Greening (S)
1946, TBS
1947, E. Rae Kaemmer
1950, Harry E. Gardner
1952, Austin G. Rugger
1956, Erwin G. Ranton
1957, see Raymond Parish
1960, Kenneth B. MacLagan
1962, TBS
1963, John A. Larsson

LEBAM
1909, W. M. Dews
1910, B. N. Galbraith
1912, George Abbott
1915, W. J. Rule
1916, J. F. Harvey
1917, T. C. Newby
1918, J. H. James (S)
1919, A. F. Kline (S)
1922, W. T. Beatty
1924, Clark Cottrell
1925, Claud Groth (S)
1926, W. B. Lamb (S)
1929, Geo. W. Cooper
1929, H. E. Greening
1934, Chester Finkbeiner
1937, Bennie Howe
1939, Clark M. Smith (S)
1940, Walter Lobb
1942, Wm. A. Anderson (S)
1943, Harry Greening (S)
1946, TBS
1947, James S. Randle
1950, R. W. Campbell (S)
1954, Arnt O. Quall
1959, John Morange (S)
1960, Clark M. Smith (S)
1962, Merritt R. Metcalf (S)
1963, not listed

MENLO
1915, F. C. Thompson
1918, J. H. James (S)
1922, W. T. Beatty
1924, Clark Cottrell
1925, Claud Groth (S)
1926, W. B. Lamb (S)
1929, H. E. Greening
1930, not listed
1931, C. W. Stark
1934, Chester Finkbeiner
1937, O. A. Cheek (S)
1938, Chester Boddy (S)
1939, Clark M. Smith (S)
1941, Walter B. Lobb (S)
1942, not listed

1944, Harry E. Greening (S)
1946, TBS
1947, James S. Randle
1950, R. W. Campbell (S)
1951, Harry E. Gardner
1952, Austin G. Rugger
1954, Arnt O. Quall
1958, See Raymond Parish
1960, Kenneth B. MacLagan
1962, TBS
1963, John A. Larsson

WILLAPA
1888, TBS
1889, R. H. Dawson (S)
1890, Sprague Davis
1891, E. L. Hughes
1893, James Matthews
1895, Rial Benjamin
1897, J. M. Dennison
1898, E. C. Parker
1899, Wm. McWatters
1901, W. J. Gilbert (S)
1902, B. M. Anslow (S)
1903, TBS
1907, W. T. Greene
1908, S. P. Brokaw
1909, W. M. Dews
1910, J. S. Simmons (S)
1918, E. B. Reese
1919, A. F. Kline (S)
1922, TBS
1925, Claud Groth (S)
1929, H. E. Greening
1930, J. C. Lawrence
1932, D. A. Storey
1934, Chester Finkbeiner
1937, TBS
1938, Chester Boddy (S)
1939, Clark M. Smith
1941, Walter V. Lobb (S)
1942, Wm. A. Anderson (S)
1943, Harry E. Greening (S)
1946, TBS
1947, E. Rae Kaemmer
1950, Harry E. Gardner
1952, Austin G. Rugger
1956, Erwin G. Ranton
see Raymond Parish
1960, Kenneth B. MacLagen
1962, TBS
1963, John A. Larsson

RIDGEFIELD
1908, Ezra Hayes (S)
1909, TBS
1910, Evan R. Evans (S)
1911, J. H. Harding (S)
1912, Wm. Vimont (S)
1913, E. J. Bates
1915, Harvey O. Cooper
1917, V. A. Spicker
1919, TBS
1920, J. B. Stark (S)
1921, Lorenzo Johnson
1923, D. E. Carter
1925, W. T. Beatty
1928, C. E. Sanders
1932, T. H. Jorgensen
1936, TBS
1937, Wayne T. Wright
1938, L. C. Bennett (S)
1941, John R. Butler
1942, Samuel A. Linge
1944, Theo. H. Jorgensen
1946, Jesse L. Tooley
1949, Burchard A. Hylton
1951, Geo. Gable (S)
1953, Milton W. Hopper (S)
1955, Walter P. Elkins (S)
1961, Donavan E. McVicker
1964, Edward F. Altes, Jr.

ROCHESTER
1891, TBS
1894, J. N. McDonald (S)
1895, not listed
1896, A. Anderson
1915, F. W. P. Camp
1917, TBS
1918, H. E. Kelly
1920, C. B. Seely
1923, T. J. Hazelton (S)
1925, W. B. Lamb (S)
1926, TBS
1927, Lloyd L. Burk
1929, C. L. Vaughn (S)
Became part of Oakville,
Porter, Rochester charge
1931, J. E. Williams
1934, D. A. Storey
1938, H. W. Driver
1943, J. D. Lewellen
1946, W. B. Lamb
1948, Loren E. Jones
1950, Austin G. Rugger
1952, Marvin G. Jernberg
1953, Everett L. Groves
1955, Thomas P. Hannan (S)
1957, Albert W. Richardson
         (S)
1959, E. Rae Kaemmer
1960, Albert Van Andel (S)

LITTLE ROCK
1871, J. F. Ward
1873, C. H. Hoxie
1874, T. M. Reese
1875, Thomas Magill
1876, William Butt
1877, W. I. Cosper
1879, C. Derrick
1881, John Flinn
1884, A. K. Crawford
1885, Robert Phillips
1886, Ebenezer Hopkins
1888, J. I. Smith
1890, G. F. Mead
1891, W. H. Johnstone
1892, H. F. Tyler
1893, R. H. Massey
1896, A. Anderson
1902, E. H. Thompson (S)
1903, Charles H. Myers
1904, R. J. Irwin
1905, Chester Bennett
1907, Wm. Ludwick
1909, J. H. Dill
1910, W. D. Cook (S)
1911, R. W. Nelson (S)
1913, A. M. Frederick (S)
1915, J. W. Walker (S)
1916, R. W. Curry (S)
1917, Clarence Harris (S)
1918, J. H. Hicks (S)
1921, Mrs. L. M. Wilhelm (S)
1925, O. B. Wood (S)
1926, L. C. Davies
1927, Harry A. Wann,
         Chester Blaire
1928, Robert Smiley (S)
1929, J. M. Hixson
1931, Loyd Mabom (S)
1932, Corabelle Teachman (S)
1933, Bessie Pease &
         Annette Kielbauch (S'S)
1936, Dewane Lamka (S)
1937, Arthur Smith
1938, Hazeldee Mowry
1940, Wilmer Werth
1942, Clarence B. Seely
1946, W. B. Lamb (S)
1948, TBS
1948, Clark Cottrell
1950, Tom Cherrington (S)

1951, Ivan J. Kinney (S)
1957, Albert W. Richardson (S)
1959, Eric Kaemmer
1960, Albert Van Andel (S)

OAKVILLE
1889, A. Anderson
1892, Ebenezer Hopkins
1893, A. S. Gregg
1894, F. C. Butler
1896, E. O. Harris
1898, TBS
1899, G. J. Taylor
1901, V. R. Bennett
1902, E. L. Hughes
1906, Seldon H. Ewing
1907, E. L. Bower
1908, K. R. Gilmer
1909, W. J. Gilbert (S)
1911, C. B. Martin
1912, E. E. Simmons (S)
1914, F. W. P. Camp
1917, TBS
1918, H. E. Kelly
1920, C. B. Seely
1923, T. J. Hazelton (S)
1925, W. B. Lamb (S)
1926, TBS
1927, Lloyd Burk
1929, T. J. Hazelton (S)
1931, J. E. Williams
1934, D. A. Storey
1938, H. W. Driver
1943, TBS
1944, J. D. Lewellen
1948, Loren E. Jones
1950, Austin G. Rugger
1952, Marvin G. Jernberg
1953, James S. Randle
1961, Ruth M. Lortz
1965, Albert E. VanAndel (S)

SKAMOKAWA
1886, Harvey Hadley (S)
1888, John Nebone (S)
1889, E. L. Hughes
1891, C. A. Luse
1893, John Flinn
1894, John Tonkins
1895, TBS
1896, J. I. Smith
1898, A. W. Brown
1900, J. H. Everett
1901, W. McWatters
1902, A. M. Brown (S)
1905, R. O. Matthews (S)
1906, R. J. Ferguson (S)
1907, TBS
1908, Wm. Hatch (S)
1909, A. B. Hotchkiss
1910, G. M. McBride
1911, R. S. Reese
1912, TBS
1913, William Vimont (S)
1914, Olaf Grandberg (S)
1916, E. J. Boddy (S)
1917, TBS
1918, R. C. Blackler (S)
1919, H. J. Harding (S)
1920, Lorenzo H. Johnson
1921, H. J. Harding (S)
1922, TBS
1927, E. L. Wolff
1928, TBS
1929, W. B. Lamb (S)
1944, Jesse L. Tooley (S)
1946, Murray V. Hyde
1949, TBS
1950, Mrs. Ruth S. Smutz (S)
1951, TBS
1952, Thos. C. Hall (S)
1955, Thomas F. Ludwig

1957, TBS
1958, William M. Richards (S)
1960, John Freeman
1965, Alex Poobus

GRAY'S RIVER
1888, T. H. Stimson (S)
1889, not listed
1889, T. H. Stimson (S)
1892, T. J. Hughes (S)
1893, B. F. Woods
1894, A. J. McNemee
1897, Wm. McWatters
1899, J. Wesley Glenk
1902, TBS
1903, Isaac Heitman (S)
1904, A. M. Brown (S)
1906, Wm. Hatch (S)
1908, W. T. Greene
1909, Evan R. Evans (S)
1910, John J. Jones
1911, H. E. Chappell
1914, A. F. Grissom
1915, E. J. Bates
1918, H. Albright
1919, TBS
1920, John Place
1921, J. H. Beall
1922, TBS
1923, T. J. Cowley
1924, TBS
1927, E. L. Wolff (S)
1928, W. B. Lamb (S)
1934, Dow DeLong
1944, Jesse L. Tooley
1946, Murray V. Hyde
1949, TBS
1950, Mrs. Ruth S. Smutz (S)
1951, TBS
1952, Andrew M. Olson
1958, Harry Walling (S)
1960, John Freeman
1965, Alex Poobus

SOUTH BEND
1871, J. N. Dennison
1873, Ira F. Ward
1874, W. T. Chapman
1875, C. Shepard
1876, J. P. Dawson (S)
1876, N. A. Starr
1878, James Matthews
1880, T. M. Reese
1882, J. M. Sweeney
1882, C. Derrick
1884, J. E. Leach
1886, James Matthews
1890, Sprague Davis
1892, Luther J. Covington
1893, Robert A. Atkins
1894, T. E. Elliott
1896, Robert C. Lee
1897, J. N. Dennison
1898, Charles A. Owens
1898, J. T. Smith
1899, C. B. Seeley
1903, Chas. Revelle
1905, R. D. Snyder
1906, N. M. Temple
1908, Frank L. Moore
1909, H. L. Townsend
1910, R. V. B. Dunlap
1912, J. W. Frescoln
1913, J. C. Dorwin
1916, H. W. Michener
1919, F. L. Baldwin
1920, Percy H. Davies
1922, Walter M. Dews
1925, Roy B. Parcel
1927, George W. Cooper
1929, Robert H. Allen
1931, C. W. Stark

442

1935, Dow DeLong
1937, W. H. Monroe
1940, J. D. Lewellen
1942, Daniel E. Taylor
1943, Lloyd N. Alden
1946, Paul G. Perkins
1950, TBS
1951, Fred Owen,
    Assoc., Mrs. Fred Owen (S)
1956, Robert G. Calkins
1959, Orin D. Watson
1960, Bernard E. Mott (S)
1964, John W. Martin (S)
1965, Loval R. Phillips (S)

BAY CENTER
1871, John N. Dennison
1873, Ira F. Ward
1874, W. T. Chapman
1875, C. Shepard
1876, J. P. Dawson (S)
1876, N. A. Starr
1878, James Matthews
1880, T. M. Reese
1882, J. M. Sweeney
1882, C. Derrick
1884, J. E. Leach
1886, James Matthews
1891, D. M. Ellsworth
1892, S. P. Brokaw
1894, C. A. Luse
1896, Rial Benjamin
1898, W. H. Jordan
1900, Arthur W. Brown
1904, Robert C. Hartley
1907, B. N. Galbraith
1910, Scott E. Winebrenner
1911, C. H. Cowdy
1917, A. B. Hotchkiss
1918, E. B. Reese
1919, not listed
1922, J. C. Lawrence (S)
1929, not listed
1934, C. W. Stark
1935, Dow DeLong
1937, W. H. Monroe
1940, J. D. Lewellen
1942, TBS
1944, R. W. Campbell (S)
1947, L. A. Tolles (S)
1948, Paul G. Perkins
1951, Fred Owen
    Assoc., Mrs. F. R. Owen
    (S)
1956, Robert G. Calkins
1959, Orin D. Watson
1960, Bernard E. Mott (S)
1964, John W. Martin (S)
1965, Loval R. Phillips (S)

STEVENSON
1909, TBS
1911, E. W. G. Walsh (S)
1912, H. J. Harding (S)
1919, TBS
1920, Seldon Ewing
1923, J. C. Lawrence (S)
1927, Assist., Miss Anna
    Lawrence (S)
1929, Lloyd Burk
1933, F. H. Leucke
1934, E. Williams
1936, Federated
    Ethel Williams (S)
1938, C. W. Stark
1940, S. A. Linge
1942, R. V. B. Dunlap
1943, J. W. Reynolds
1947, J. H. Avery
1950, James S. Randle
1952, J. C. Snowden
1954, Robert F. Waller

1957, R. Clinton McGaffee
1963, Melvin V. Olson
1965, Russell Chapin (UG)

VANCOUVER, EAST
1907, Ezra Hayes
1907, Alfred Bates (S)
1908, E. R. Tracy
1909, J. H. Berringer
1915, Horace Williston
1918, J. B. Stark (S)
1919, Arthur W. Brown
1922, Earl E. Reisner
1923, Earl W. D. Hanna
1925, B. G. Clemens
1926, G. H. Quigley (S)
1927, Ethel Williams (S)
1928, W. W. Mills (S)
1931, J. W. Reynolds
1932, T. H. Jorgensen
1933, C. H. Cowdy
1937, Roy B. Parcel
1939, Lloyd C. Parsons
1941, Ac Wischmeier
1946, Lloyd N. Alden
1949, Harry L. Allen
1953, M. Chester Morgan
1958, Joe W. Walker
1963, William E. Callahan, Jr.
1964, Assoc., Waldo W. Pierson

VANCOUVER,
EAST MILL PLAIN
1886, G. G. Ferguson
1887, W. H. Drake
1888, T. W. Butler
1889, F. M. Pickles
1891, James Matthews
1892, C. A. Snelling (S)
1892, D. M. Ellsworth
1895, L. E. Wornom
1898, E. O. Harris
1902, F. E. Smith
1905, W. E. Rossman
1912, S. V. Warren
1916, J. H. Avery
1919, W. H. Selleck
1920, B. G. Clemens
1925, John Place
1929, L. C. Davies
1930, C. H. Cowdy
1936, T. H. Jorgenson
1942, H. P. Buck
1945, C. A. Brown
1948, TBS
1948, Harry E. Walling (S)
1958, Floyd E. Green
1961, Walter P. Elkins (S)
1962, Marion Koth (S)
1965, James L. Reynolds

VANCOUVER, FIRST CH.
1853, C. S. Kingsley
1854, J. Garrish
1855, Samuel Matthews
1857, C. O. Hosford
1859, John Fletcher DeVore
1862, James O. Raynor
1862, R. C. Smith
1863, Harvey K. Hines
1866, G. C. Roe
1867, D. L. Spaulding
1867, W. P. Nichols
1868, Conington G. Belknap
1870, T. A. Wood
1871, William Ingold Cosper
1873, John Wesley Miller
1874, J. F. DeVore
1876, R. S. Stubbs
1877, G. W. Day
1878, Martin Judy
1880, L. Albert Banks

1883, F. M. Robertson
1885, Robert Phillips
1886, J. H. Skidmore
1888, A. J. Joslyn
1890, E. M. Wheeler
1891, George C. Wilding
1896, Joseph E. Williams
1899, Edward H. Todd
1903, William E. Thompson
1904, Thomas E. Elliott
1907, B. F. Brooks
1909, William Park
1910, John M. Canse
1914, W. T. Randolph
1915, E. L. Benedict
1918, A. H. Thompson
1920, G. W. Frame
1921, J. P. Marlatt
1923, F. A. LaViolette
1927, G. W. Frame
1929, Raymond S. Reese
1935, Martindale Woods
1937, Fred C. Taylor
1944, Daniel E. Taylor
1949, Olin M. Graham
1954, John C. Soltman
1954, Assoc., Donald R. Yates
1957, Assoc. Fred L. Waller
1961, Frank E. Brown
1962, 2d Assoc., Donald G.
    Holsopple (S) 1 yr.
1965, Fred L. Waller, ninth
    year. Assoc.

ORCHARDS CHURCH,
VANCOUVER
1882, John Flinn
1892, D. M. Ellsworth
1893, C. C. Pratt
1895, Wm. McWatters
1896, W. J. Rule
1898, A. Demoy
1900, J. T. McQueen
1902, C. F. Bennett
1904, C. C. Babbidge
1905, W. J. Gilbert (S)
1907, Claude Cowdy
1908, Ernest J. Bates
1911, E. B. Reese
1914, Roy B. Parcel
1918, D. A. Storey
1919, H. Albright (S)
1923, TBS
1924, Mrs. Sadie Porter (S)
    (Mrs. J. H.)
1940, Lloyd C. Parsons
1941, K. H. Dunkelberger
1945, Claude A. Brown
1949, C. E. Dockstader (S)
1951, Mrs. Ruth Smutz (S)
1952, Earl B. Cotton &
    Mrs. Earl B. Cotton (S)
1956, Jesse L. Tooley (S)
1963, Loval R. Phillips (S)
1965, Charles A. Green (S)

ST. PAUL (Formerly
HAZEL DELL)
1957, C. Ellsworth Wilson
1958, Became St. Paul
1959, Robert G. Calkins
1961, Geo. Allen Odgers

SALMON CREEK
1853, James Gerrick (S)
1856, Samuel Matthews
1857, C. O. Hosford
1859, J. F. DeVore
1862, James O. Raynor
1862, R. C. Smith
1863, Harvey K. Hines
1866, G. C. Roe

443

1867, D. L. Spaulding
1867, W. D. Nichols
1868, W. Pitner (S)
1869, H. F. Williams (S)
1870, T. A. Woods (S)
1871, W. I. Cosper
1872, Samuel Matthews
1873, J. H. Allyn
1875, N. A. Starr
1876, T. M. Reese
1878, John Flinn
1881, Columbus Derrick
1882, J. M. Sweeney
1883, G. G. Ferguson
1886, C. P. Stayton
1887, John Britts (S)
1889, Wm. C. Hockett
1890, Samuel P. Brokaw
1892, G. G. Ferguson
1893, James I. Smith
1896, G. J. Taylor (S)
1897, E. L. Hughes
1901, C. F. Bennett
1902, TBS
1903, C. C. Babbidge (S)
1905, W. J. Gilbert (S)
1907, C. H. Cowdy (S)
1908, E. J. Bates (S)
1909, not listed
1911, P. H. Raymond
1914, J. H. Avery
1916, H. H. Rama (S)
1917, F. S. Pearson (S)
1918, J. B. Stark (S)
1920, G. W. Hoy
1921, J. M. Wilder
1927, B. G. Clemens
1931, J. W. Reynolds
1934, T. J. Hazelton (S)
1935, J. E. Williams
1937, O. A. Cheek (S)
1938, K. H. Dunkelberger
1941, A. C. Wischmeier
1942, T. H. Jorgenson
1944, S. A. Linge (S)
1948, Claude Brown
1949, C. E. Dockstader (S)
1953, T. Earl Poindexter
1961, Donald W. Baldwin
1964, Martin T. Larson

WASHOUGAL
1896, W. J. Rule
1899, Charles Parker
1901, TBS
1902, not listed
1903, J. C. Reed
1905, B. L. Hicks
1906, Claude Cowdy
1907, E. J. Huston
1909, Became Washougal
1910, Ernest Bates
1912, W. E. Rossman
1916, Vern Spicker
1917, David Moore (S)
1918, Roy B. Parcel
1924, C. E. Sanders
1928, E. D. Hart
1931, T. J. Hazelton (S)
1933, L. O. Griffith
1936, T. L. Blaisdell
1938, Robert Getty (S)
1939, K. H. Dunkelberger
1944, Howard P. Buck
1945, Percy E. Pike
1949, Roy L. Kuhns
1951, Ira J. McFarland
1953, Joe W. Walker
1955, E. Rae Kaemmer
1959, Bill Brentlinger
1961, J. Dean Stout
1965, Kermit I. Meier

WHITE SALMON
1908, J. K. Craig (S)
1909, H. C. Clark
1912, TBS
1913, M. P. Stout
1914, E. T. Reid
1916, F. R. Jackson
1917, C. A. Smith
1918, M. H. Staines (S)
1920, R. T. Holland
1923, A. W. Clark
1924, TBS
1925, R. C. Young
1928, W. T. Beatty
1930, Earl McAbee
1933, Roy Jenkins
1935, C. W. Stark
1938, J. W. Reynolds
1943, B. C. Gallaher
1945, Geo. P. George (S)
1957, Oscar A. Olsen
1960, Alfred S. Palmer
1963, Alfred J. Waln

WINLOCK
1884, C. E. Haggerman (S)
1884, David Matter (S)
1885, J. I. Smith (S)
1886, D. W. Cameron
1887, W. C. Hockett (S)
1889, A. H. Marsh (S)
1890, Wm. M. Ludwick
1892, R. A. Atkins
1893, W. H. Wilson
1894, S. P. Brokaw
1895, G. G. Ferguson
1896, C. A. Luse (S)
1897, G. G. Ferguson
1898, W. M. Ludwick
1901, E. L. Hughes
1902, M. V. Heidelbaugh
1903, T. F. Downs
1905, J. F. Redfern
1906, M. B. Phillips
1908, John F. Long
1909, W. I. Cowell
1911, S. E. Winebrenner
1912, R. S. Reese
1919, R. V. B. Dunlap
1920, W. M. Dews
1922, C. H. Cowdy
1926, H. L. Allen
1929, R. B. Parcel
1936, Ira J. McFarland
1938, Dow DeLong
1941, H. Eugene Miller
1942, Clyde Gearhart (S)
1946, L. E. Jones
1948, Milton Winkler (S)
1950, John H. Avery
1951, J. C. Snowden
1952, TBS
1953, William M. Richards
1956, O. James Garrett (S)
1962, L. Wayne Blackledge
1963, Edgar Lee Starr, Jr.
1965, Richard H. N. Yost

PE ELL
1893, L. E. Wornom
1895, E. L. Hughes
1897, G. J. Taylor (S)
1899, Abraham Demoy
1900, J. D. Wasson
1901, John Lewtas (S)
1903, E. L. Benedict
1904, J. F. Redfern
1905, F. E. Smith
1906, W. I. Cowell
1907, R. E. Hartley
1908, C. F. Bennett
1910, S. V. Warren

1912, A. A. Brittain
1913, Frank Sutton
1915, J. H. Geoghegan
1916, F. L. Pedersen
1917, E. L. Albright
1918, F. S. Pearson
1919, R. G. Pike (S)
1920, TBS
1922, Andrew Monroe (S)
1924, P. T. Graham (S)
1925, not listed
1927, TBS
1928, Earl W. McAbee
1929, not listed
1931, TBS
1932, Bessie Pease (S) &
       Annette Kiehlbauch (S)
1933, TBS
1938, not listed
1939, Clark M. Smith
1940, TBS
1947, James S. Randle
1950, R. W. Campbell (S)
1955, Evald Leps (S)
1957, Donald A. Bishop (S)
1959, Pierce Roberts (S)
1961, TBS
1962, Merritt R. Metcalf (S)
1963, TBS
1964, Edgar Lee Starr, Jr.
1965, Richard H. N. Yost

WALLA WALLA DISTRICT
ASOTIN
1882, J. W. Rigby
1884, H. W. Waltz
1886, Z. K. Heinsman
1888, Richard Barrett
1889, F. B. Utter
1890, Jonathan Swaine
1891, TBS
1892, D. E. George
1893, C. E. Gibson
1895, J. P. Barker
1897, John LeCornu
1899, J. C. Kirkman
1900, W. M. Spoor
1901, J. S. Anderson
1907, John Evans
1909, Paul Little
1913, J. S. Bell
1916, O. W. Mintzer
1918, Wm. Gornall
1919, J. G. Carrick
1923, F. F. Boothby
1926, S. E. Hornibrook
1935, TBS
1936, J. D. Lewellen
1940, Ralph W. Bolick
1943, Geo. P. Keeling (S)
1947, William H. Phillips (S)
1948, Clark M. Smith (S)
1949, John E. Besant (S)
1955, Hubert C. Vincent
1956, TBS
1957, Donald Krogh (S)
1958, TBS
1961, G. Ogston (S)
1962, TBS
1963, Errol Stevens
1965, David L. Miles (UG)

ANATONE
1902, C. M. Carson
1903, Henry Martin
1905, E. J. Snell
1907, J. L. Hess
1907, S. E. Boselly (S)
1908, Lafayette Davis (S)
1909, J. H. Artz (S)
1912, A. C. Hoover
1913, G. F. Pinkham (S)

1914, J. H. Artz
1916, H. A. Wann
1916, J. J. Mattney
1920, Will M. Daniel
1921, H. J. Betten (S)
1922, F. M. Cass (S)
1923, C. A. Pickering
1925, C. W. Geisler
1927, E. M. Filbert
1928, P. J. Armond
1930, D. Stanley McGuire
1930, J. G. Carrick
1931, S. E. Yaggy
1936, Merrill Hurd
1939, Wm. E. Whitlock
1940, Ralph Bolick
1941, J. E. Walbeck
1942, Clark M. Smith
1943, Guy A. Lewis (S)
1946, TBS
1947, Mason S. Osborne
1948, John D. Moede
1950, TBS
1951, Harry Chatterton (S)
1955, Vern L. Damon (S)
1957, Donald Krogh (S)
1958, Thos. C. Slate
1964, John W. Simmons (S)
1965, David L. Miles (UG)

BENTON CITY, Originally KIONA
1900, J. J. Calloway (S)
1902, E. H. Rubicam
1906, F. L. Tuttle (S) &
    J. J. Calloway (S)
1907, A. Kershaw (S)
1908, C. M. Carson
1910, M. C. Newell (S)
1911, TBS
1912, W. A. Pratt
1913, J. M. Crenshaw &
    J. D. Bird
1914, N. E. Wood
1916, Jos. Olsen (S)
1919, E. L. Wolff
1920, J. S. Rhodes (S)
1922, S. J. Beer (S)
1923, Became BENTON CITY
1926, Bessie Thompson (S)
1928, K. O. Pearson
1930, Erling Bergan
1931, E. M. Filbert
1935, TBS
1936, C. W. Geisler (S)
1940, E. A. Schwenk (S)
1941, J. A. Hoffman
1942, Howard A. Dettmers (S)
1943, John W. Kuller
1945, George Nafus
1949, Edwin B. Towle
1953, Louis V. Martin
1959, Donald Baldwin
1961, John Earl Lake

BURBANK
1960, Randall W. Larson
1960, Assoc., Paul F. Ashbrook
1961, Richard E. Nye
1964, Bruce Brooke

CLARKSTON
1900, W. B. Eakin
1903, J. W. Spangler
1904, J. E. Williams
1905, T. H. Fertig
1908, Edw. Baker
1910, H. L. Beightol
1911, S. M. Nickle
1913, W. P. Jinnett
1916, C. A. Hodshire
1920, J. E. Garver

1922, Louis Thomas
1924, Ray R. Martin
1926, Fred L. Cook
1928, Hubert C. Vincent
1933, B. E. Koontz
1937, John Moede
1943, Ray W. Mason
1944, Don Lamka
1945, Erwin G. Ranton
1952, Reah S. Dougherty
1957, Guy L. Roberts
1960, G. Edward Knight
1963, Kenneth W. Countryman

Clearwater Group Ministry
COTTONWOOD
1896, Thos. D. Gregory
1897, A. W. Roberts
1898, W. M. R. Pitt (S)
1899, TBS. J. B. Bucholz (S)
1901, J. E. Daniels
1902, C. E. Gibson
1903, Joseph Toms (S)
1904, R. D. Osterhout
1905, Robert Sykes
1907, A. S. Rickel
1907, George A. Pease (S)
1910, W. M. D. Riggs
1911, A. Kershaw
1911, E. C. Newham
1912, E. J. Snell
1915, E. Arthur Gruenwald
1917, L. E. Taber
1919, Marion W. Sligor
1921, F. M. Cass (S)
1923, Dean C. Poindexter
1924, Robert Thompson
1926, C. A. Pickering
1927, J. J. Mattney
1930, Phillip S. Clapp
1931, Paul Campbell
1935, J. D. Moede
1938, C. W. Groth
1940, C. A. Brown
1945, Roy L. Kuhns
1949, Reah S. Dougherty
1952, Ludvig Eskildsen
1955, J. Earl Lake
1957, Carl Richard Boyd
1961, Billy Parrish
1963, Mack A. Farmer
1965, Charles W. Johnson (S)

NEZ PERCE
1896, J. E. Williams
1898, Jacob Sargent (S)
1899, J. E. Daniels
1901, James Greenslade
1902, C. E. Gibson
1903, G. W. Taylor (S)
1904, Lyda M. Herrick (S)
1904, R. D. Osterhout
1905, Campbell Tavener
1907, W. G. Light
1908, C. W. Everett
1909, W. H. Zeller
1910, TBS
1911, George A. P. Jewell
1912, F. R. Spaulding
1913, T. D. Moore
1913, U. C. Smothers
1914, F. H. Fertig
1918, C. B. Martin
1919, Mark Pike
1923, John A. Hoffman
1925, TBS
1926, E. M. Filbert
1927, Trevor Orton
1928, Miss Corabell Teachman
    (S)
1930, Phillip S. Clapp
1932, Paul Campbell

1935, John Moede
1937, C. W. Groth
1940, C. A. Brown
1945, Roy L. Kuhns
1949, Reah S. Dougherty
1952, Ludvig Eskildsen
1955, J. Earl Lake
1957, Carl Richard Boyd
1961, Billy Parrish
1963, Mack A. Farmer
1965, Charles W. Johnson (S)

KENDRICK
1891, F. B. Utter
1892, TBS
1894, Trevor Orton (S)
1895, R. Norris (S)
1896, C. D. Bell (S)
1898, E. A. Thomas
1899, W. H. Zellers
1900, J. E. Williams (S)
1901, F. J. James
1902, W. C. Mitchell (S)
1904, G. A. Pease (S)
1906, J. L. Hess
1907, W. G. Light (S)
1908, J. S. Taylor (S)
1910, A. Kershaw (S) &
1910, J. H. Hart
1911, W. M. D. Riggs (S)
1912, J. K. Craig (S)
1915, J. J. Mattney
1916, H. B. Emmel
1918, J. C. Gregory (S)
1919, M. L. Anderson
1920, H. W. Mort
1922, C. A. Pickering
1923, J. W. Poolton
1924, C. D. Bell
1926, Lester E. Taber
1929, Claud W. Groth
1930, Corabelle Teachman (S)
1931, E. J. Smith
1933, Elmer E. Beckman
1934, T. E. Poindexter
1937, T. J. Pryor (S)
1938, W. S. T. Gray
1941, Roy Murray
1945, William E. Bishop
1946, Jos. H. Coulter
1950, TBS
1951, Fred C. Schmidt (S)
1957, John Yost
1958, Ernest F. Gates (S)
1961, David Braun
1964, David A. Zaske

JULIAETTA, IDAHO
1920, Haskel Tudor
    M. E. Ch. South
1921, no info.
1927, W. G. Forbes
1930, no info.
1936, J. E. Walbeck
1939, Louis V. Martin (S)
1940, Melville C. Pruitt
1941, Roy Murray
1945, Charlotte Hickman (S)
1946, Joseph H. Coulter
1948, Edgar Lonnie Williams (S)
1950, TBS
1952, Frederick C. Schmitt (S)
1957, John Yost (S)
1958, Ernest F. Gates (S)
1961, David Braun
1964, David A. Zaske

LELAND
1890, H. S. Hornbuckle
1891, H. T. Burger
1892, H. S. Hornbuckle
1893, Edwin Palmer

1897, William O. Miller
1902, C. H. Miller
1903, C. S. Coberly
1905, W. G. Forbes
1907, J. W. Compton
1909, J. T. Hoyle
1910, J. N. DePartee
1912, C. U. Cross
1913, H. P. Nelson
1914, J. A. Hall
1918, J. V. Roberts
1919, E. L. Whiddon
1920, J. A. Hall
1923, I. P. Kelly
1924, C. J. Taber
1925, G. H. Gibbs
1927, J. E. Walbeck
1932, Howard L. Graybeal
1935, H. L. Metcalf
1937, J. A. Hall
1938, J. E. Walbeck
1941, W. E. Bishop &
    Roy Murray
1943, Clark Smith
1945, Enoch Willman
1946, J. H. Coulter
1950, Lonnie Williams
1951, George F. Calvert
1952, TBS
1961, Carl Beal
1962, Daniel P. Smith
1965, David A. Zaske

OROFINO, IDAHO
1900, R. D. Osterhout
1901, P. A. King (S) &
    T. C. Craig (S)
1905, J. S. Taylor (S)
1906, W. H. Zeller
1907, A. W. Aubrey (S)
    & I. L. Crooks
1909, Thomas Lawson
1910, W. A. Pratt
1911, J. H. Hart
1913, F. N. Morton
1916, U. C. Smothers &
    R. D. Osterhout
1917, J. S. Anderson
1918, F. L. Moore
1919, J. A. Hoffman
1922, J. F. Gibson
1923, Wm. M. Martin
1925, E. S. Williamson
1927, Vern A. Spicker
1929, H. W. Driver
1934, Geo. W. Cooper
1944, Kenneth H. Underwood
1946, Fred R., and Mrs. Owen
    (S) Assoc.
1949, G. Edward Knight
1954, L. Marshall Campbell
1959, William E. Strance
1961, James H. Thompson

CAVENDISH, IDAHO
1939, J. E. Walbeck
1941, Clark M. Smith (S)
1942, TBS
1943, Enoch E. Willman
1944, Roy H. Murray
1945, TBS
1946, Fred R. Owen &
    Mrs. F. R. Owen (S)
1949, G. Edward Knight
1954, L. Marshall Campbell
1959, William E. Strance
1960, Carl Beal
1962, Daniel P. Smith

PECK, IDAHO
1907, J. B. Bucholz (S)
1910, A. M. Lambert (S)

1912, H. E. Galvin
1913, H. O. Worthen
1914, H. B. Emmel
1916, H. W. Best (S)
1918, TBS
1920, S. B. Chase (S)
1922, Bertram Hall (S)
1923, J. G. Brugger (S)
1924, C. D. Bell (S)
1925, TBS
1926, K. O. Pearson
1928, V. A. Spicker
1929, H. W. Driver
1934, Geo. W. Cooper
1941, Mrs. Lilla M. Marston (S)
1942, TBS
1946, Fred R. Owen and
    Mrs. Owen (S)
1949, G. Edward Knight
1953, James M. Lane
1957, Don Hecox (S)
1958, See Pierce Parish. TBS
1960, Carl B. Beal
1962, Daniel P. Smith
1965, Oren W. Walters (S)

LAPWAI, IDAHO
1898, Geo. Waters
    Methodists withdrew,
    favor of Presbyterians.
1910, Meth. Ch., So.
1911, E. J. Conners
1915, No records available
1920, Star J. Maxwell (S)
1936, Stephen J. Reuben (S),
    Assoc.
1939, Star J. Maxwell (S)
    Stephen Reuben, Assoc. (S)
1939, Mrs. R. W. Albright (S)
    Director Ed.
1940, Stephen J. Reuben (S)
1944, Charlotte Hickman (S)
    Bible teacher
1945, Charlotte Hickman (S)
    Stephen Reuben Assoc. (S)
1946, TBS. Adele Cravens (S)
1947, Conrad Owen (S)
1948, TBS
1950, Frederick C. Schmidt (S)
1954, F. B. Kenoyer (S)
1959, Jack L. Caldwell
1960, James A. Buckles (S)
1963, James H. Thompson
1965, Oren W. Walters (S)

CULDESAC, IDAHO
1924, John A. Hoffman
1925, Waldo W. Pierson
1928, Henry R. Cross
1929, TBS
1930, S. E. Yaggy (S)
1931, Paul Campbell
1933, TBS
1935, C. W. Groth
1937, Lloyd H. Smith (S)
1938, Ben Howe
1939, Fred Hertzog (S)
1940, TBS
1944, Prof. W. W. Myers (S)
1946, Chas. L. Thornton (S)
1952, A. K. Walborn (S)
1954, Firman B. Kenoyer (S)
1959, Jack L. Caldwell
1960, James A. Buckles (S)
1963, Mack A. Farmer
1965, Oren W. Walters (S)

PIERCE, IDAHO
1949, Fred R. Owen
1951, TBS
1953, James M. Lane
1957, E. Harlan Fischer (S)
1958, See Pierce Parish

1958, Carl B. Beal (S)
1960, C. Edward Whitenett
1963, Mack E. Farmer
1964, M. Douglas Bobbitt

HEADQUARTERS, IDAHO
1950, Fred R. Owen
1951, TBS
1953, James M. Lane
1957, E. Harlan Fischer (S)
1958, See Pierce Parish
1958, Carl Beal (S)
1960, C. Edward Whitenett
1963, Marion Douglas Bobbitt

COLFAX
1873, TBS
1876, M. S. Anderson (S)
    Part time TBS
1878, M. S. Anderson
1879, W. S. Turner
1880, No record
1881, D. G. Strong
1883, G. E. Wilcox
1884, J. W. Bluett
1886, W. S. Turner
1887, M. M. Waltz
1888, R. H. Manier
1889, R. C. Moter
1891, John Uren
1892, Wm. Euster
1894, E. H. Todd
1898, M. A. Covington
1899, J. W. Flesher
1901, U. F. Hawk
1902, C. D. Nickelsen
1903, U. F. Hawk
1904, Wilmot Whitfield
1905, F. C. Lee
1906, Henry B. Elworthy
1907, John P. Barker
1910, N. M. Jones
1912, R. D. Snyder
1913, Wm. Hoskins &
    P. J. Armond
1914, O. W. Mintzer
1915, John G. Law
1919, A. A. Callander
1922, O. A. Scott
1925, J. S. Bell
1928, H. J. Wood
1931, J. L. Rentfro
1933, E. C. Newham
1940, Earl McAbee
1944, L. J. Linnemann
1949, Kenneth H. Underwood
1954, Victor Phillips
1955, Martin Larson
1961, Milton P. Andrews
1963, Chester C. Blair

CONNELL
1901, J. W. Beckley &
    P. J. Sehnert
1902, P. J. Sehnert
1905, George Hartung
1907, C. H. Woltersdorf
1909, George Hartung
1909, H. Haueisen
1911, Hugo Woehl
1912, H. Haueisen
1914, G. S. Roeder
1916, E. Julius Traglio
1924, George J. Kleinbach
1926, G. A. Maag
1933, J. D. Moede
1935, E. J. Smith
1938, R. L. LaMott
1939, Myron H. Sharrard
1943, F. L. Lowther
1946, Waldo W. Piersen
1952, Howard P. Buck

1956, LaVern E. Tooley
1960, Darrell L. Iwerks

DAYTON
1873, H. B. Lane
1874, G. W. Kennedy
1875, A. J. Joslyn
1878, S. G. Havermale
1879, J. D. Flenner
1881, J. B. Mahana
1883, L. J. Whitcomb
1885, J. C. Richmond (S)
1886, Richard Fysh
1887, L. N. B. Anderson
1888, E. H. Fleisher
1889, W. T. Ford
1892, Edward McEvers
1893, Perry Chandler
1895, F. A. LaViolette
1896, Walton Skipworth
1898, Alfred Thompson
1901, A. L. Hawley
1902, John Uren
1903, J. J. McCallister
1904, W. E. Armfield
1905, H. B. Elworthy
1906, C. G. Harmon
1907, J. S. Anderson
1908, C. A. Housel
1910, A. W. Roberts
1912, J. M. Huggins
1913, H. L. Beightol
1914, A. A. Callander
1919, J. C. Harvey
1920, F. L. Cook
1922, E. S. Williamson
1925, Thomas Hardy
1926, Thomas W. Emery
1928, B. A. Hylton
1929, B. E. Koontz
1930, B. A. Hylton
1931, Harold E. Bashor
1935, Roy Jenkins
1940, E. Clifford Newham
1941, W. H. Monroe
1943, E. L. Groves
1948, Mason S. Osborne
1950, Robert W. Maulden
1954, Linden B. Jenkins
1957, Marvin E. Jordan
1963, Adam S. Forch, Sr.

FINLEY
1911, H. N. Rounds
1912, H. N. Rounds &
E. M. Landis (S)
1913, J. M. Crenshaw &
J. D. Bird
1914, N. E. Wood
1915, C. B. Bichener (S)
1916, C. A. Burris
1919, connected with Hover
1923, C. W. Geisler
1924, E. L. Wolff
1925, Robert Thompson (S)
1929, Erling Bergan
1931, J. A. Alford (S)
1933, TBS
1935, S. E. Hornibrook (S)
1938, J. E. Williams
1939, E. A. Schwenk (S)
1941, J. H. Bennett (S)
1943, Clark M. Smith (S)
1946, Guy A. Lewis (S)
1947, Pierce Roberts (S)
1950, TBS
1952, TBS
1954, Vern L. Damon (S)
1955, David O. Beadles
1957, Robert F. Waller
1958, Clark M. Smith
1960, Geo. Allen Odgers

1961, Thomas Ray Martin
1965, Leon L. Alden

GARFIELD
1881, W. J. White
1888, F. L. Young
1889, G. E. Wilcox
1889, W. R. Phelps (S)
1890, G. C. Haven
1891, Wm. DeWeese
1893, Edward McEvers
1894, T. C. Craig (S)
1895, T. H. Fertig
1896, A. W. Trine (S)
1898, John P. Barker
1899, John LeCornu
1901, J. S. Smith
1902, A. L. Hawley
1904, P. Conklin
1905, Edwin B. Lockhart
1907, Howard C. Kohr
1910, A. W. Luce
1911, Charles W. Monson
1913, C. W. Williams
1914, R. A. Gailey
1916, M. L. Sanders
1917, W. C. Evans
1918, P. C. Money
1919, D. L. Clarke
1919, Henry Attenborough
1921, Wm. Gornall
1922, Marion W. Sligar
1924, Lloyd L. Burk
1925, Fred L. Post (S)
1927, John E. Williams
1928, B. C. Gallaher
1929, C. C. James (S)
1932, John A. Hoffman
1935, U. C. Smothers
1936, Ernest W. Denning (S)
1937, James Wilkins (S)
1939, H. J. Bass
1941, J. E. Secord
1944, Harold G. Cowdrick
1946, TBS
1947, H. Gravenor (S)
1950, W. Wayne Smith (S)
1955, Frank Sturtevant (S)
1956, James Adams
1957, Thomas R. Martin
1958, J. D. Stout
1959, Hubert Rhymes (S)
1961, Linden B. Jenkins
1963, Jerry F. Smith

GRANGEVILLE, IDAHO
1877, J. D. Flenner
1879, W. A. Hall
1881, T. A. Towner
1882, G. E. Wilcox
1883, W. A. Hall
1885, J. C. Teeter
1886, W. A. Hall
1886, TBS
1887, D. E. George
1888, A. Maxey (S)
1892, F. L. Buzzell
1894, A. L. S. Bateman
1896, William C. Mitchell
1897, T. D. Lewis (S)
1897, W. H. Zellers (S)
1897, W. A. Hall
1898, C. F. McCarthy
1899, W. B. Eakin
1900, J. S. Anderson
1901, O. W. Mintzer
1902, J. S. Smith
1904, T. H. Fertig
1905, John E. Williams
1906, D. C. Sanderson (S)
1907, Edward Baker
1908, A. W. Roberts

1909, John Evans
1910, Ira L. Crooks
1911, G. E. James
1912, W. W. Constien
1913, W. P. Jinnett
1914, R. E. Gornall
1916, H. J. Wood
1919, H. S. Randle
1922, R. R. Martin
1924, Ernest Barber
1930, Presby. Sidney A. Walker (S)
1936, Nelson C. Pierce
1940, Presby. W. O. Benthin (S)
1946, Harold W. Black
1948, TBS
1949, LaVern E. Tooley
1955, Guy L. Roberts
1957, William G. Berney
1961, William E. Strance
1965, Lawrence Eddings

WHITEBIRD
1908, G. W. Everett
1909, Israel Putnam (S)
1909, John Moore
1910, Will Daniel
1912, A. O. Hess
1913, J. F. Ford (S)
1914, J. A. Smith
1915, J. C. Erwin (S)
1916, L. C. Douglas
1917, J. S. Andersen
1918, L. E. Taber
1919, W. J. Gamble
1922, TBS
1923, R. D. Osterhout
1923, John G. Brugger
1926, Everett M. Filbert
1928, TBS
1929, Ernest E. Barber
1932, TBS
1934, S. A. Walker (S) Presby.
1938, Nelson Pierce
1941, Claude A. Brown
1945, Roy L. Kuhns
1948, TBS
1949, LaVern Tooley
1955, Guy L. Roberts
1957, Wm. G. Berney
1961, William E. Strance
1965, Lawrence Eddings

KAHLOTUS
1921, K. O. Pearson
1922, TBS
1925, Bessie Thompson (S) (Mrs. Robert J.)
1926, TBS
1928, A. J. Armstrong
1929, Robert Thompson
1930, John Seethoff
1934, R. S. Wetherell (S)
1935, R. C. Jacobs (S)
1942, M. H. Sharrard
1944, F. L. Lowther
1946, Waldo W. Pierson
1949, Floyd C. Green (S)
1951, Norman Steinig (S)
1954, A. K. Walborn (S)
1956, Loval R. Phillips (S)
1959, James A. Mott (S)
1961, Darwin E. Secord (S)
1963, Frederick B. Riehle (S)
1965, Mrs. William M. Martin (S)

KENNEWICK, FIRST
1902, E. H. Rubicam
1903, John E. Williams
1904, A. N. Sanford
1905, F. L. Tuttle (S)

447

1906, J. H. Wood
1908, L. N. B. Anderson
1909, B. F. Brown
1912, C. D. Rarey
1915, C. E. Miller
1917, J. C. Harvey
1919, H. J. Wood
1920, J. E. Strevey
1922, A. A. Callander
1925, F. N. Morton
1931, J. Fletcher Long
1933, H. C. Vincent
1936, Henry Attenborough
1939, R. L. LaMott
1943, John B. Coan
1949, Ac C. Wischmeier
1954, Kenneth H. Underwood
1960, H. Paul Smith
1960, Assoc. Geo. Allen Odgers, 1 yr.
1961, Thomas R. Martin
1962, Robert W. Hicks
1965, Assoc. Melvin V. Olson

KENNEWICK, W. HIGHLANDS
1955, David O. Beadles
1957, Robert F. Waller
1958, West Highlands
1963, Charles Kent Echelbarger

LACROSSE
1906, W. F. Bradley
1907, E. J. Snell
1911, L. W. Putnam
1912, Thomas Lawson
1913, George H. Pease
1915, Charles L. Creesy
1917, H. S. Randall
1919, James Opie
1921, Ed Baker
1922, Chas. H. Schreiber
1924, William Gornall
1925, John A. Hoffman
1928, Henry Attenborough
1930, W. G. R. Dann
1934, Burchard A. Hylton
1937, Roy H. Murray
1941, Dow DeLong
1942, Fred R. Owen
1946, Frank L. Lowther
1950, Mason S. Osborne
1952, Paul E. Hamlin
1956, Ronald K. Johnson
1960, Howard P. Buck
1962, J. Ray Neiser

LEWISTON, FIRST, IDAHO
1876, G. W. Shaffer
1879, J. W. Rigby
1882, TBS
1883, Levi Tarr
1885, W. S. Turner
1886, George Mathews
1887, TBS
1888, G. O. Ash
1889, L. J. Whitcomb
1891, TBS
1892, G. C. Haven
1893, Henry Brown
1898, Walton Skipworth
1901, S. A. Smith
1902, J. R. Gregory
1904, W. W. Carr
1905, W. T. Euster
1907, R. J. Reid
1908, Chas. MacCaughey
1909, J. C. Harvey
1910, C. W. Williams
1912, W. C. Reuter
1914, E. H. Longbrake
1916, R. D. Snyder
1918, H. T. Green

1920, H. T. and Mrs. H. T. Green (S) (Mary T.)
1922, Mark Pike
1925, Edw. A. Wolfe
1930, C. C. Curry
1931, E. F. Harold
1935, L. C. Hicks
1936, J. W. Caughlan
1941, J. J. Ellington
1943, P. M. Hammond
1946, Ac Chester Wischmeier
1949, John B. Coan
1950, Merritt W. Faulkner
1958, Edwin B. Towle
1960, Bruce B. Groseclose

LEWISTON ORCHARDS
1949, John B. Coan
1950, Merritt W. Faulkner
1951, Robert M. Horne
1952, Truman Cotten
1957, J. Earl Lake
1961, Eric L. Kallis
1965, Thomas Ray Martin

MOSCOW, IDAHO
1876, M. S. Anderson
1878, David E. George
1880, E. C. Rigby
1881, M. C. Bryan
1883, Theodore S. Hoagland
1884, John C. Kirkman
1885, James Greenslade
1886, W. B. Carithers
1889, W. A. Tickner
1890, N. S. Parsons
1892, John Uren
1897, George M. Booth
1902, W. T. Euster
1905, William H. Fry
1907, A. A. Luce
1908, B. E. Koontz
1911, Robert Warner
1917, Harold O. Perry
1925, N. M. Jones
1928, William Hints
1931, J. Edgar Purdy
1936, H. F. Pemberton
1937, Owen J. Beadles
1942, W. E. Stanton
1946, Ernest P. Goulder
1952, David Seaman
1957, Ellsworth M. Tilton
1960, Rudolph A. Anderson
1962, S. Raynor Smith, Jr.

PALOUSE
1877, M. S. Anderson
1879, D. E. George
1880, W. J. White
1881, M. C. Bryan
1882, Theodore Hoagland
1883, G. O. Ash
1884, W. B. Carithers
1886, F. L. Young
1888, L. N. B. Anderson
1889, TBS
1891, G. C. Haven
1892, TBS
1893, J. C. Warren
1894, Wm. Rasmus (S)
1895, C. E. Todd
1896, G. G. Muller
1898, W. C. Beightol
1899, W. C. Reuter
1900, J. S. Smith
1901, J. E. Williams
1902, Chas. Elrey
1904, D. W. Raines
1905, M. C. Davis
1907, C. W. Williams
1908, W. B. Young

1911, E. Baker
1913, A. A. Callander
1914, J. F. Cook
1915, N. S. Hawk
1917, C. L. Creesy
1920, W. M. Martin
1923, S. J. Osborne (S)
1924, Wm. Daniel
1925, Hubert C. Vincent
1928, Thomas W. Emery
1929, F. F. Boothby
1931, B. A. Hylton
1932, John Moede
1933, J. L. Rentfro
1939, Ralph W. Bolick
1940, Dow DeLong
1941, H. J. Bass
1942, J. Earl Secord
1943, Arthur R. Treman (S)
1944, Mrs. Wilma E. Clements (S)
1946, Calvin V. Day (S)
1947, Don Aeschliman
1949, Ralph Wood (S)
1951, Federated. TBS
1952, L. Marshall Campbell
1954, Vernon Kirstein (S)
1955, TBS
1958, not listed
1960, TBS
1961, Ernest Gates (S)
1962, Donald D. Larson
1963, not listed
1964, E. James Cain (S) Baptist

PASCO, FIRST
1891, S. M. Dayton
1892, E. L. Miller (S)
1893, Henry Moys
1894, no appt.
1895, J. Geizentanner (S)
1897, S. C. Smith (S)
1898, J. J. Calloway (S)
1900, no preacher
1901, E. H. Rubicam
1902, C. W. Williams
1903, A. N. Sanford
1904, F. L. Tuttle (S)
1905, J. F. Cook
1906, A. A. Metcalf (S)
1908, W. H. Henderson
1909, Andrew Kershaw (S)
1910, A. O. Hammond
1911, J. D. Bird
1913, Frank R. Spaulding
1914, B. F. Koch
1916, J. D. Cain
1916, C. H. Bryan
1917, Robt. H. Allen
1920, M. M. Eaton
1923, James Opie
1926, B. E. Koontz
1927, U. F. Hawk
1929, E. M. Hill
1931, Chas. L. Creesy
1935, H. Bashor
1937, Ray A. Partee
1942, Chas. T. Hatten
1946, Assoc. Ruth A. Dodsworth
1949, Rudolph A. Anderson
1958, Randall W. Larson
1960, Assoc. Paul F. Ashworth, 1 yr.
1961, John M. Finney, Jr.

PASCO, RIVERVIEW
1960, Randall W. Larson
1960, Assoc. Paul F. Ashbrook
1961, Richard E. Nye
1964, David Braun

448

POMEROY
1883, W. T. Koontz
1884, F. E. McCallum
1885, L. J. Whitcomb
1887, A. C. Spencer
1888, John LeCornu
1889, J. C. Kirkman
1892, M. M. Miner
1893, T. H. Fertig
1895, F. L. Buzzell
1897, N. E. Parsons
1898, James C. Lockhart
1900, R. J. Reid
1903, D. C. Sanderson (S)
1906, A. W. Roberts
1908, A. S. Mulligan
1910, Andrew Monroe
1914, W. C. Reuter
1915, O. W. Mintzer
1916, J. O. Johnson
1917, F. N. Morton
1925, John Robertson
1926, L. C. Hicks
1930, O. A. Scott
1931, H. L. Allen
1934, W. E. Callahan, Jr.
1936, W. M. Martin
1941, Forrest Tibbitts
1944, Myron H. Sharrard
1950, Thos. Acheson
1951, Clifford C. Knight
1952, Lloyd N. Alden
1959, John P. Johnson
1964, Everett L. Groves

PULLMAN
1887, W. J. White
1888, W. R. Phelps
1889, C. E. Gibson
1890, L. N. B. Anderson
1891, M. S. Anderson
1892, H. M. Mobbs
1892, M. H. Marvin
1895, W. H. Bast (S)
1896, Edward J. Smith
1898, B. F. Cozier (S)
1899, E. H. Rubicam
1899, O. W. Mintzer
1901, J. W. Flesher
1903, Gabriel Sykes
1905, G. Grant Stewart
1906, M. H. Marvin
1909, Robert Brumblay
1913, J. W. Caughlan
1919, John G. Law
1923, Norman McCay
1929, Joseph Adams
1935, H. R. Stone
1939, J. J. Ellington
1941, Ernest P. Goulder
1943, Alden R. Graves
1953, Don M. Fife
1964, William G. Berney

RICHLAND, CENTRAL
1906, F. L. Tuttle (S) &
    J. J. Calloway (S)
1907, A. Kershaw (S)
1908, C. M. Carson
1910, H. N. Rounds
1911, A. C. Hammond &
    L. L. Hursey (S)
1912, C. H. Schreiber
1913, W. E. Kloster (S)
1914, J. C. Erwin (S)
1915, C. A. Smith
1917, H. R. Stone
1919, Orland A. Scott
1920, B. C. Gallaher

1924, W. J. Scott
1926, J. W. Poolton
1928, W. J. Scott
1929, TBS
1930, E. M. Filbert
1935, W. C. Rhea (S)
1938, Will M. Daniel
1941, Kenneth Bell (S)
1944, Thos. Acheson &
    Kenneth Bell, Assoc.
1947, Roy L. Smith &
    Kenenth Bell
1950, Robert A. Uphoff
1954, Assoc. Guy L. Roberts
1955, Assoc. Oliver J. Gill
1955, Assoc. Carl H. McGee
1957, David Seaman
1957, Assoc. Oliver J. Gill
1960, Melvin M. Finkbeiner
1962, Assoc. Ronald A. Hummel
1964, Assoc. O. James Garrett

WAITSBURG
1860, Geo. M. Berry
1861, John Flinn
1866, J. G. Deardorff
1866, J. L. Reeser
1867, Chas. H. Hoxie
1868, L. Gift
1869, J. L. Reeser
1869, W. H. Goddard
1870, C. H. Hoxie
1870, J. H. Adams
1872, F. Elliott
1873, W. T. Koontz
1875, Theo Hoagland
1878, E. C. Warren
1879, M. S. Anderson
1880, T. A. Towner
1881, Jno LeCornu
1882, N. E. Parsons
1883, J. C. Kirkman
1884, N. E. Parsons
1886, G. G. Ferguson
1887, Henry Moys
1888, D. E. George
1888, W. T. Robinson
1890, Wellington Bowzer
1891, Jno Whisler
1892, J. C. Warren
1893, Lee A. Johnson
1896, Wm. DeWeese
1897, J. S. Anderson
1900, C. G. Harmon
1903, T. H. Fertig
1904, M. H. Marvin
1906, Jno Williams
1907, Robt. Brumblay
1909, Chas. MacCaughey
1911, H. L. Beightol
1913, Paul Little
1916, H. F. Pemberton
1917, W. P. Jinnett
1918, J. E. Garver
1920, C. A. Hodshire
1921, T. A. Graham
1922, D. S. Kerr
1925, Wm. Gornall
1928, Jno Williams
1931, Erling Bergan
1935, H. Attenborough
1936, R. L. LaMott
1938, P. G. Perkins
1940, C. W. Groth
1941, W. W. Switzer
1945, L. Paul Jaquith (S)
1947, Aubrey W. Winsor (S)
1949, Revelle E. Roach

1952, Warren A. Sherk
1953, Murray V. Hyde
1957, Jack L. Caldwell
1959, Loval R. Phillips (S)
1963, Bill L. Brentlinger
1965, Earl P. Cooper

WALLA WALLA, PIONEER
Formerly First
1859, Geo. M. Berry
1861, John Flinn
1863, W. J. Franklin
1864, TBS
1866, J. G. Deardorf
1867, John S. Reeser (S)
1868, J. B. Calloway
1869, J. T. Wolfe,
    C. H. Hoxie
1870, H. C. Jenkins
1872, J. W. Miller
1873, S. G. Havermale
1874, C. W. Grannis
1875, W. Whitfield,
    S. L. Burrill
1876, D. G. Strong
1878, W. G. Simpson
1880, G. M. Irwin
1883, W. C. Gray
1884, J. D. Flenner
1885, D. G. Strong
1886, Henry Brown
1889, W. W. VanDusen
1892, V. C. Evers
1896, W. C. Reuter
1899, L. A. Johnson
1902, M. H. Marvin
1903, TBS
1904, Henry Brown
1905, Wilmot Whitfield
1906, W. E. Thompson
1908, M. L. Sanders
1910, C. O. Kimball
1913, J. F. Robinson
1916, A. H. Lathrop
1917, Pioneer
1917, C. A. Bowen
1918, T. W. Lane
1921, J. W. Caughlan
1922, Robert Brumblay
1927, W. B. Young
1929, Robt. E. Smith
    Conferences united
1933, Ed A. Wolfe
1936, Norman McCay
1938, Alexander P. Aiton
1946, Walter S. Gleiser
1953, Albert J. Wilson
1957, Forrest W. Werts
1962, David K. Almon

WALLA WALLA, UNITED
Formerly Marvin Memorial
1920, Bert A. Powell
1926, C. F. McConnell
1931, M. S. Shangle
1933, H. T. Menord
1934, P. D. Hartman
1937, J. S. Shangle
1939, J. A. Hoffman
1940, Clark Cottrell
1942, J. C. Snowden
1946, Edward Smith
1947, Joseph L. Woodford (S)
1953, Wm. M. Martin
1956, United with Grace
1956, Harry T. Cupp
1957, Truman H. Cotten
1961, Donald E. Sattelberg

DISCONTINUED CHARGES ALPHABETICALLY, PASTORS CHRONOLOGICALLY

ABERDEEN SOUTH SIDE
1927-'28, Miss Bessie Daws (S)

ABERDEEN, TRINITY
1909, TBS
1910, H. Liffiton
1911, TBS
1912, H. C. Carter (S)
1914, C. W. McLaughlin (S)
1916, TBS
1920, Mrs. Agnes D. Newell (S)
1923, TBS

ACME
1906, A. A. Brittain (S)
1907, H. L. Richardson
1908, TBS
1909, Charles Beachy
1910, O. A. Quall (S)
1912, James Sneed (S)
1913, J. J. Jones
1914, R. W. Curry (S)
1916, W. D. Riggs (S)
1918, TBS
1919, H. L. Richardson
1923, B. V. Bradshaw (S)
1924, TBS
1926, G. C. Squire
1927, F. L. Lowther (S)
1928, W. J. Rule
Abandoned

ADDY
1906, E. H. Eaton (S)
1907, J. C. Beach
1908, H. F. Pemberton
1909, Paul Gardner
1910, H. C. Hartranft (S)
1911, L. G. Wellington (S)
1913, F. J. Osborne
1917, W. J. Downs (S)
1918, W. A. Withnell (S)
1919, G. B. Harbison
1920, W. A. Pratt
1921, Jas. Callahan
1922, H. J. Betten (S)
1923, A. F. Patterson (S)
1930, J. C. Brugger (S)
1931, T. W. Emery
1933, C. A. Pickering
1934, D. G. Bennett
1937, H. Copley Davis
1938, Chester C. Blair
1940, J. Philip Armand
1941, Walter Pierson
1943, Jas. A. Moore
1945, A. A. Moore (S)
1948, TBS
1949, no appt.
1950, Ronald K. Johnson
1956, Roy L. Kuhns
1957, TBS

ALASKA MISSION, JUNEAU
1903, F. A. LaViolette
1918, H. E. Greening
1921, W. A. Allen
1924, Richard Decker
1925, G. W. Cooper
1926, R. A. Gailey
1928, Henry Young (S)
Abandoned

ALASKA MISSION,
KETCHIKAN
1903, TBS
1924, C. N. Van Marter
1926, M. L. Sanders
1928, Clyde Walker
Abandoned

ALASKA MISSION, NOME
1919, Richard Decker (S)
1923-'24, Not listed
1925, A. M. Herd
1926, TBS
1927-'28, R. Z. Newton
Abandoned

ALASKA MISSION,
SEWARD CITY
1903, TBS
1904, Not listed
1911, L. H. Pedersen
1914, Not listed
1919, R. B. V. Dunlap
1925, T. P. Graham (S)
1928, R. A. Gailey
Abandoned

ALBION (GUY)
1893, F. B. Utter
1894, E. A. Thomas
1895, not listed
1901, T. C. Craig (S)
1902, TBS
1903, J. T. Hardwick (S)
1904, J. C. Lawrence
1906, P. E. Bartlett
1909, R. A. Gailey
1910, John P. Barker
1911, T. C. Mountain
1912, Wm. DeWeese
1913, Wm. Hoskins
1914, J. P. Armand
1915, F. D. Hawley
1916, M. L. Anderson
1917, M. C. Newell
1918, Robt. Thompson
1920, C. M. Carson
1922, K. O. Pearson
1925, Erling Bergan
1927, John G. Brugger
1930, TBS
1931, B. A. Hylton
1932, John D. Moede
1933, J. L. Rentfro
1934, Mert Lampson
1936, Carroll H. Sprague
1938, T. J. Pryor (S)
1939, Robt. H. Allen
1940, TBS
1942, Edward M. Saldin (S)
1944, TBS
1945, Earl R. Shoup (S)
1953, TBS
1954, Martin G. Stuck (S)
1955, Abandoned

ALMIRA
1904, J. E. Daniels
1905, No record
1906, L. N. B. Anderson
1907, J. E. Herrington
1908, R. W. Curry (S)
1909, J. J. Callahan
1911, L. W. Nixon
1912, J. O. Hawk
1913, C. W. Geisler
1914, J. D. Llewellen
1918, Wm. Hoskins
1919, E. T. Reid
1920, T. W. Emery
1922, A. P. Rolan (S)
1923, John E. Williams
1924, W. A. Pratt
Joined Hartline
1925, C. B. Martin
1926, Roy Jenkins

1928, Carl B. Madsen
1929, Geo. A. Wells
1930, E. S. Williamson
1933, Roy H. Murray
1935, TBS
1936, W. W. Switzer
1939, C. M. Estabrook
1940, Clifford Knight
1942, Mrs. J. Dean King (S)
1945, Chas. L. Thornton (S)
1946, E. H. Tetwiler (S)
1948, Miss Gladys V. Crawford
(S)

AMBOY
1898, W. E. Stearns (S)
1899, A. M. Brown (S)
1900, TBS
1902, Chas. Coop (S)
1903, TBS
1905, C. W. Geisler
1906, Samuel Dupertius (S)
United Brethren took over

APPLETON
1924, W. B. Lamb (S)
1925, TBS
1927, W. W. Mills (S)
1928, TBS
Abandoned

ARROW, IDAHO
1936, J. E. Walbeck
1939, Louis V. Martin (S)
1940, Melville C. Pruitt
1941, Roy H. Murray
1945, TBS
1946, Joseph Coulter
1949, not listed

ARTONDALE
1912, W. J. Green
1913, G. M. Day
1914, T. C. Newby
1915, G. S. Helgeson (S)
1916, Paul Jones
1917, John H. Insel (S)
1918, TBS
1919, T. A. Swayze
1920, David G. Beattie (S)
1921, Russell Clay
1922, TBS
1923, Herbert West (S)
1924, F. D. Tibbitts
Abandoned

BAINBRIDGE ISLAND
1913, C. J. Kallgren

BALLARD
1895, W. H. Johnstone
1896, J. W. Miller
1897, B. F. Brooks
1901, A. J. Joslyn
1906, W. H. Forsyth
Discontinued

BARNESTON
1907, H. R. Merrill
1908, W. B. Anderson
1909, TBS
1910, F. R. Gillett
1911, Not listed
1912, M. P. Elder
1913, E. M. Fly (S)
1914, W. C. Weber
1915, J. S. Sneethen (S)

1917-'18, TBS
Abandoned

BATTLE GROUND
1918, W. P. Rutledge
Sold to Community Church

BELFAST CIRCUIT
1909, E. O. Harris
1910, Not listed
1915, TBS
1916, S. S. Guiler (S)
1918, C. L. Holiday (S)
1920, Abandoned

BELLEVIEW
1892, TBS
1893, Abandoned

BELLINGHAM CIRCUIT
1904, C. W. Stevens (S)
1905, A. A. Brittain (S)
1906, E. P. Hughes (S)
1907, C. A. Owens
1909, L. H. Mitchell
1910, TBS
1911, G. H. Harrison (S)
1912, H. L. Richardson
1913, G. F. Pollock (S)
1914, E. R. Tracy
Abandoned

BENGE
1936, TBS
1937, Ralph Bolick
1939, James Wilkins (S)
1940, W. E. Whitlock
1941, TBS
1942, John Hoffman
1945, TBS
1949, Clifford C. Knight
1949, Spokane D.
1950, no appt.

BERLIN, Whatcom District
1902, J. Taylor Wright (S)
1903, Abandoned

BETHEL, Kitsap County
1892, F. S. Pearson
1895, H .H. Walkington
1896, O. L. Doane
1897, not listed
1909, G. Anderson (S)
1910, TBS
1912, E. H. Rubicam
1913, G. Anderson (S)
1914, C. A. Lindholm
1916, TBS
1917, W. P. Owens (S)
1918, K. L. Haga
1919, Abandoned

BLACK RIVER CIRCUIT
1891, Ebenezer Hopkins

BOISTFORT
1892, W. C. Hockett (S)
1901, A. M. Brown (S)
1902, W. C. Hockett (S)
1903, TBS
1906, C. W. Geisler
1915, D. A. McComb (S)
1932, Bessie Pease (S) &
       Annette Kiehlbauch (S)
1933, TBS
1934, not listed
1938, Dow DeLong
1940, TBS
1941, not listed
1943, TBS

BOSTON HARBOR
1915, C. F. Bennett, Nominal
       Appt.

BOULEVARD HEIGHTS
1946, TBS
1947, no appt.

BRINNON
1906-'08, TBS
Abandoned

BUCKLEY
1890, Ezra H. Stafford
1891, F. M. Pickles
1892, E. R. Hayward
1894, W. Ludwick
1895, Rowland Hughes
1898, G. F. Meade
1899, J. W. White
1901, J. T. Smith
1902, S. P. Brokaw
1903, James T. McQueen
1906, H. F. Pemberton
1907, J. L. Kendall
1908, A. A. Brittain
1910, F. R. Gillett
1912, D. A. Storey
1913, G. C. Poolton
1914, B. N. Galbraith
1916, Seymour Williams
1918, TBS
1919, E. L. Albright
1920, H. Williston
1923, J. W. Blackwell (S)
1925, T. J. Gambill,
       Asst. W. E. Stanton
1927, Harold Nelson
Abandoned

BUCODA
1884, J. L. Henderson
       C. S. Harrison
       D. W. Cameron
1885, A. K. Crawford
1887, A. Anderson
1889, J. I. Smith
1891, J. W. Maxwell
1892, W. H. Wilson
1893, F. M. Wheeler
1894, Ebenezer Hopkins
1895, I. R. Lovejoy
1897, Ebenezer Hopkins
1902, D. L. Matson (S)
1903, W. M. Ludwick
1905, R. T. Irwin
1906, W. E. Williams
1907, C. C. Hull (S)
1908, T. A. Graham
1909, E. R. Tracy
1911, A. F. Grissom
1912, G. M. Day
1913, Geo. Morris (S)
1917, W. J. Gilbert (S)
1919, W. O. Owen (S)
1920, A. M. Frederick (S)
1922, C. C. James
1923, E. A. Blakeslee (S)
1925, J. C. Dorwin
1926, W. S. Garner (S)
1927, A. M. Frederick (S)
1930, O. W. Mintzer
1931, TBS
1933, not listed
1934, C. B. Seely
1935, Jean Jones (S)
1936, J. W. Reynolds
1937, E. D. Rounds
1939, J. R. Butler
1941, William Werth (S)
1942, Erle Howell
Sold in 1943

BURTON
1901, J. T. McQueen
1903, E. L. Bower
1904, Harry K. Kline (S)
1905, H. F. Pemberton
1906, R. J. Irwin
1908, W. E. Williams
1909, G. M. Day
1911, H. E. Moore
1912, J. H. Avery
1913, W. J. Green
1914, H. P. Waldron
1915, C. H. Wood
1916, E. H. Gebert
1918, J. W. Reynolds
Abandoned

CAMANO
1908, TBS
1909, A. J. McNemee
1910, J. B. Gough (S)
1911, TBS
1912, J. A. Chapin (S)
1913, TBS
Abandoned

CARBONADO
1891, TBS
Abandoned

CARLTON
1904, F. B. Utter
1914, I. B. Ricketts (S)
1923, Ralph I. Thomas
1930, Clark Cottrell
1932, John McNees
1945, Wendell J. Cone
1952, J. D. Crawford
1953, Col. Riv. Dist.
1954, not listed

CARROLTON
1890, Thos. M. Reese (S)
1891, A. J. McNemee
1892, Not listed
1909, TBS
1910, Alfred Bates (S)
1911, J. K. Boyd (S)
1912, W. E. Williams
1913, TBS
Abandoned

CARSON
1924, J. C. Lawrence (S)
1929, Lloyd Burk
1932, TBS
1934, J. E. Williams
1935, TBS
1936, not listed
1937, TBS
1938, C. W. Stark (S)
1940, Samuel A. Linge (S)
1942, R. V. B. Dunlap
1943, Joseph W. Reynolds

CASTLE ROCK CIRCUIT
1906, F. A. Enslow
Abandoned

CATLIN
1892, C. P. Stayton
1894, G. G. Ferguson
1895, S. P. Brokaw
1896, George A. Sheafe
1898, C. E. Fulmer
1902, S. G. Jones
Merged with Kelso in 1904

CEDAR FALLS
1914, W. C. Weber (S)
1915, J. S. Sneethen (S)
Abandoned

CENTRALIA CIRCUIT
1887, A. Anderson
1889, not listed
1909, C. H. Cowdy
1911, C. D. Miller

CHEHALIS CIRCUIT
1897, N. M. Temple (S)
1898, TBS
1899, F. G. Curtis (S)
1900, G. M. Galbraith (S)
1922, D. E. Carter

CLEAR LAKE
1903, TBS
1906, A. A. Brittain (S)
Closed

COLUMBIA
1898, W. J. Rule
1899, E. C. Parker
1901, TBS
Abandoned

COLUMBIA RIVER MISSION
1885, H. Hadley (S)
1886, TBS
1887, TBS
Abandoned

COWEMAN
1889, T. M. Reese (S)
1890, No report
Abandoned

COWLITZ
1884, TBS
1885, M. Burlingame (S)
1886, E. L. Hughes
1887, Not in appts.

DEMING
1911, A. O. Quall (S)
1912, James Sneethen
1913, J. J. Jones
Abandoned

DISAUTEL
1945, Charley A. Burris
1949, Verne Brooks (S)
1950, Loval R. Phillips
1952, G. P. Walton (S)
1953, C. R. D. No appt.
1954, Mary Gruenwald (S)
1956, not listed

DOCKTON
1912, J. H. Avery
1913, W. J. Green
1914, H. P. Waldron
1915, C. H. Wood
1917, E. H. Gebert
1918, J. W. Reynolds
1919, Wm. Bowman (S)
1920, Nelson C. Pierce (S)
1922, J. W. Sutton
Abandoned

DOWNS
1904, A. A. Moore
1906, R. A. Armstrong
1909, M. P. Stout (S)
1911, TBS
1913, not listed

DRYAD
1908, C. F. Bennett
1909, C. C. Wilkinson (S)
Abandoned

DUNGENESS
1884, S. D. Lougheed (S)

1887, TBS
1888, A. J. McNemee
1889, N. A. Baker (S)
1890, Wm. Slack (S)
1891, George Kindred
1893, W. M. Ludwick
1894, TBS
1895, R. C. Lee
1896, Edwin L. Brown (S)
1897, R. M. Schoonmaker
1898, H. D. Wadsworth
1899, W. M. Welch
1901, TBS
1902, A. H. Marsh
1903, TBS
1904, George F. Graham
1905, Walter Bell
1907, TBS
1908, J. W. Burns
1909, H. R. Merrill
1910, A. J. McNemee (S)
1913, R. C. Johnson
1915, Paul Jones
1916, TBS
1917-19, A. M. Frederick (S)
Abandoned

DUVALL
1892, TBS
1893, A. J. McNemee
1894, TBS
1909, TBS
1910, W. Whitfield (S)
1911, N. E. Wood
1913, C. A. Owens
1916, W. M. Hoare
1918, TBS
1919, F. E. Cain (S)
1921, Geo. R. Abbott
1925, Earl W. McAbee
1927, W. D. McDowell (S)
1929, E. W. D. Hanna
1931, A. N. Cheleden
1932, R. Z. Newton
1936, TBS
1937, Jas. M. Pendleton
1939, Henry L. Haines (S)
1942, Delos Westbrook (S)
1944, Wilson R. Eckels (S)
1945, Delos Westbrook (S)
1946, Dennis Stiles, Jr. (S)
1946, F. E. Pitcher (S)
1950, Ernest F. Gates (S)
1951, Oscar Rensberg (S)
1952, F. E. Pitcher (S)
1956, Adam S. Forch, Sr.
    4th year with Woodinville
1957, not listed

**EADONIA-SALKUM, LATER
TOLEDO CIRCUIT**
1889, C. A. Luce
1891, E. H. Fuller
1892, John Tonkins
1894, C. G. Morris
1896, A. J. Whitfield
1898, Chester F. Bennett
1901, A. M. Brown (S)
1903, F. W. Tisdale
1906, L. G. Knight
1906, E. L. Hughes
1910, C. H. Cowdy
1911, J. J. Jones
1912, A. F. Grissom
1914, A. F. Kline (S)
1915, John F. Mobley (S)
    membership transferred to
    Winlock

EAST CLALLAM
1893, TBS
1896, C. E. Cunningham (S)

1898, George W. Frame
1902, C. E. Fulmer
1904, not listed
1908, J. H. Avery (S)
1909, J. W. Burns
1910, TBS
1911, TBS
Abandoned

EAST SOUND
1887, James Eva
1888, TBS
1889, John Flinn
1890, Wm. H. Johnstone
1891, T. L. Dyer
1893, D. J. Albert
1894, J. W. Patterson
1896, Ira A. Mills
1898, Robert R. Earl
1899, H. G. Ward
1900, W. M. Daniels
1901, R. H. Massey
1904, TBS
1905, S. V. Warren
1907, J. W. Moles
1909, G. F. Pollock (S)
1910, W. B. Anderson
1912, J. J. Jones
1913, F. H. Walker
1917, TBS
1922, TBS, Abandoned

EDGEWOOD
1902, TBS
1905, W. O. Pflaum (S)
1906, J. L. Kendall
1907, S. Dupertius

EDISON
1888, TBS
1889, Wm. R. Warren
1890, TBS
1891, not listed
1910, TBS
1911, H. C. Carter
1912, Randolph Sasnett (S)
1915, J. L. Grandey
1917, J. M. Wilder
1921, Clark Cottrell
1923, A. M. Frederick (S)
1925, P. E. Pike (S)
1928, J. D. Bird (S)
1930, A. W. Smith
1931, E. W. D. Hanna
1933, Robert Thompson (S)
1935, not listed
1945, L. C. Bennett, and
    wife, Hortense (S)
1946, not listed

ENDICOTT
1888, C. E. Gibson
1889, W. R. Phelps (S)
1890, TBS
1891, James Greenslade
1893, not listed
1894, D. L. Spaulding (S)
1897, M. S. Anderson (S)
1898, TBS
1899, J. H. Martin
1901, J. C. Kirkman
1903, Roy D. Hadley
1905, E. A. McKinney (S)
1906, F. H. Walker
1907, Hazen Oakes
1909, W. H. Rogers
1912, C. W. Geisler
1913, J. H. Hart
1914, Wilfred C. Bassett
1915, M. C. Newell
1917, Wm. M. Martin
1921, Will M. Daniel

1925, S. E. Hornibrook
1926, TBS
1927, Fred Jenkins (S)
1928, TBS
1929, B. A. Hylton
1930, not listed
1931, TBS
1932, W. C. Weber (S)
1933, M. H. Sharrard
1936, TBS
1937, Ralph Bolick (S)
1939, James Wilkins (S)
1940, W. E. Whitlock (S)
1941, TBS
1942, John Hoffman
1943, Fred R. Owen
1945, Sophie Owen (S)
    (Mrs. Fred R.)
1946, Frank L. Lowther
1950, Abandoned

ENUMCLAW
1894, TBS
1895, George A. Sheafe
Abandoned

EVERETT, HOPKINS
    MEMORIAL
1911, A. H. Cook (S)
1913, W. H. W. Rees, Jr.
1914, P. H. Raymond
1915, Roy Owens (S)
1916, E. B. Reese
1917, T. H. Jorgenson
1918, TBS
1919, W. J. Rule (S)
1920, H. M. Campbell (S)
Abandoned

EVERETT, PINEHURST
1911, A. H. Cook (S)
Abandoned

EVERETT, SALEM
1944, D. M. Helaas (S)
1946, N. M. Jones
1947, TBS
1948, E. C. Kreitlow
1951, Robert C. Ward
1953, Abandoned

EVERETT, WESLEYAN
1911, A. H. Cook (S)
Abandoned

FELIDA
    LAKE SHORE
1906, Ezra Hayes (S)
1908, Alfred Bates (S)
1909, P. H. Raymond
1910, J. H. Geoghegan
    Became FELIDA
1913, TBS
1914, F. E. Reddick (S)
1916, T. C. Newby
1917, J. F. Harvey
1918, F. E. Reddick
1921, J. M. Wilder
1926, B. G. Clemens
1929, W. W. Mills (S)
1931, Jos. W. Reynolds
1934, K. H. Dunkelberger
1935, T. J. Hazelton (S)
1937, TBS
1938, H. G. Campbell (S)
1939, K. H. Dunkelberger
1940, L. C. Bennett (S)
1941, John R. Butler
1942, Samuel A. Linge (S)
1944, Sylvan W. Sherrell (S)
1944, Theo. H. Jorgenson
1946, Austin G. Rugger

1947, Duane E. Carter
1957, C. Ellsworth Wilson
1958, TBS
1959, W. S. J. Bleakley (S)
1961, not listed

FERRY
1892, G. Westfall (S)
1893, Not listed
1894, W. J. Rule (S)
Abandoned

FINNISH MISSION,
ABERDEEN
1924-1928, E. A. Hart
1935, Abandoned

FIRWOOD
1912, Clark Cottrell
1913, C. D. Miller
1914, E. H. Gebert (S)
1915, H. E. Gardner
1917, W. F. Pool
1918, TBS

FISHER'S AND
FOURTH PLAIN
1892, D. M. Ellsworth
1895, L. E. Wornom
1898, E. O. Harris
1902, F. E. Smith
1905, M. L. Hardingham
1906, W. E. Rossman
1909, Dee Orchards

FOOTHILLS
1940, Milton DeArmand with
    Green Bluffs & Mead (S)
1941, E. E. Van Wert (S)
1942, Arthur R. Treman (S)
1943, Jewell F. Pyles (S)
1944, Eugene A. McDowell (S)
1946, H. Clifton R. Reeve (S)
1948, TBS
1950, TBS
1951, Raymond Gouldin (S)
1952, TBS
1957, Austin G. Rugger
1959, not listed

FOREST CENTER
1948, TBS
1949, Ronald Johnson
1950, no appt.

FOREST GROVE
1914, W. J. Gilbert (S)
1917, B. V. Bradshaw (S)
1918, TBS
1919, Abandoned

FOSTER
1908, R. L. Sprague
1909, Abandoned

FOUR LAKES
1919, TBS
1920, F. L. Farnham
1921, TBS
1922, H. S. Wanamaker (S)
1927, W. B. Eakin
1928, Ralph I. Thomas
1929, A. G. Child (S)
1931, Roy Keeling (S)
1932, Dan Taylor
1934, TBS
1935, L. G. Wellington (S)
1937, J. P. Armand
1940, Frank Harris (S)
1942, Paul D. Brown (S)
1943, C. M. Estabrook
1946, John Jantzen (S)

1948, no appt.
1949, Ronald Treibel (S)
1950, TBS
1951, Homer Perry (S)
1952, Robert Leep (S)
1953, Raymond Gouldin (S)
1954, TBS
1959, T. Orville Kelley (S)
1960, TBS
1961, K. W. Larrison
1963, not listed

FRANCES
1900, Abraham Demoy

FRIDAY HARBOR
1891, C. E. Cunningham
1892, G. F. Mead
1893, I. N. Goodell
1894, T. L. Dyer
1898, J. W. White
1899, C. J. Kallgren
1900, S. S. Guiler
1901, Henry Harpst (S)
1903, J. H. Kevan
1904, C. C. Pratt
1907, Herbert Jones
1909, S. G. Jones
1911, T. A. Graham
1912, F. H. Walker
1913, A. Robertson
1914, E. H. Rubicam
1916, D. S. Kerr
1917, TBS
1918, Abandoned

GARDNER'S
1897, A. M. Brown (S)
1904, TBS. Abandoned

GATE CITY
1891, TBS, Abandoned

GENEVA
1891, J. W. Patterson
1892, Abandoned

GERMAN, ABERDEEN
1891, TBS
1892, not listed

GERMAN, ADDY, WASH.
1899, W. J. Bucholz
1906, not listed
1908, G. S. Roder
1909, not listed

GERMAN, BICKELTON
1898, Ludwig Gaiser
1899, not listed

GERMAN, CENTRALIA
1891, Adam Buehler
1894, J. C. Jahn
1895, not listed
1899, G. W. Roder
1906, not listed

GERMAN, CHEHALIS
1891, Adam Buehler
1892, not listed

GERMAN, CHENEY
1893, Adam Buehler
1898, not listed
1899, W. J. Herwig
1900, not listed
1901, P. J. Sehnert
1902, not listed
1909, G. A. Maag
1910, not listed

453

GERMAN, CONNELL CIRCUIT
1908, H. Hauisen
1910, not listed

GERMAN, DAVENPORT
1898, Joseph Hepp
1901, George A. Jahn
1904, Ludwig Gaiser
1908, G. A. Maag
1911, H. Hauisen (S)
1912, A. F. Cramer
1918, TBS
1919, A. F. Hilmer
1924, E. J. Traglio
1926, L. N. Hostettler
1927, R. R. Finkbeiner
1928, H. B. Mann

GERMAN, DOUGLAS
1899, Ludwig Gaiser
1900, not listed

GERMAN, EDWALL
1901, Wm. F. Maas (S)
1902, W. J. Herwig
1904, G. S. Roder
1906, C. A. Wentsch
1909, J. M. Hermann
1915, G. A. Maag
1917, A. J. Weigle
1919, H. Hauisen (S)
1921, TBS
1923, not listed

GERMAN, ELK
1924, H. B. Mann
   not listed further

GERMAN, EVERETT
1901, Joseph Schweirtlich
1903, TBS
1904, H. B. Mann
1906, George S. Roder
1908, C. H. Weigle
1909, H. F. Michel
1910, not listed

GERMAN, FAIRDALE
1902, Geo. S. Roder
1903, not listed

GERMAN, FAIRHAVEN
1891, Hans Hansen
1893, no record
1894, TBS
1898, Hans Hansen
1899, Joseph Schweirtlich
1900, H. F. Michel
1901, Joseph Schweirtlich
1902, not listed
1907, Bellingham
1907, J. M. Hermann
1909, H. F. Michel
1910, not listed

GERMAN, GENESEE
1908, P. J. Sehnert
1909, not listed

GERMAN, HARRINGTON
1891, Carl Jans
1892, F. H. Luecke
1893, Adam Buehler
1898, not listed
1907, G. J. Sohm
1908, L. Gaiser
1909, G. S. Roder
1912, not listed

GERMAN, HATTON
1900, J. W. Beckley
1901, not listed

GERMAN, HILLYARD
1907, TBS
1908, not listed

GERMAN, KENNEWICK
1907, George Hartung
1909, not listed

GERMAN, KENT
1901, Hans Hansen
1902, not listed

GERMAN, KETTLE FALLS
1907, G. A. Jahn
1908, not listed

GERMAN, KRUPP
1907, C. A. Wentsch
1909, J. M. Hermann
1912, not listed

GERMAN, LACAMAS
1891, J. W. Beckley
1892, not listed

GERMAN, MILAN
1899, W. J. Bucholz
1902, not listed

GERMAN, MORAN
1904, P. J. Sehnert
1905, not listed

GERMAN, MOSCOW, IDAHO
1905, J. A. Jahn
1906, Carl Jahn
1907, S. J. Taft
1908, P. J. Sehnert
1913, John A. Beck
1919, L. Gaiser
1920, John Seethoff
1921, TBS
1924, not listed

GERMAN, ODESSA
1898, H. E. Michel (S)
1899, not listed
1902, W. J. Herwig
1904, not listed
1907, G. J. Sohm
1908, not listed
1909, G. S. Roder
1912, not listed

GERMAN, PARADISE
1910, H. Hauisen (S)
1911, Hugo Wohl (S)
1913, H. Hauisen (S)
1914, G. S. Roder
1915, E. J. Traglio
1924, George J. Kleinbach
1926, G. A. Maag
1928, not listed

GERMAN, PORT TOWNSEND
1891, TBS
1892, not listed

GERMAN, RATHDRUM,
IDAHO
1904, P. J. Sehnert
1907, TBS
1909, L. Gaiser
1910, John A. Beck (S)
1913, TBS
1914, William E. Kurtz
1916, H. G. Schmid
1918, TBS, 1919, not listed

GERMAN, RICHLAND
1909, George Hartung

1910, TBS
1911, discontinued

GERMAN, RIDGEFIELD
1891, J. W. Beckley
1893, not listed
1894, Hans Hansen
1898, J. G. Moehring
1901, Ludwig Gaiser
1902, George S. Roder
1903, G. A. Maag
1905, E. J. Traglio
1909, H. B. Mann
1911, H. G. Schmid
1913, P. J. Sehnert
1917, Hugo Wohl
1923, A. J. Weigle
1926, G. S. Roder
1929, Oregon Conference
1932, Pacific Northwest Conf.
became BETHEL
1932, F. H. Luecke
1933, T. H. Jorgenson
1936, TBS
1937, Wayne Wright
1938, H. B. Mann
1941, Ac C. Wischmeier
1942, T. H. Jorgenson
1947, G. D. Lauby (S)
1950, TBS
1952, E. A. Lieske (S)
1954, James Zotnick
1956, TBS
1957, Abandoned

GERMAN, RITZVILLE
1891, H. F. Michel
1894, not listed
1898, Ludwig Gaiser
1901, Carl Jahn
1905, J. C. Mueller
1913, Ludwig Gaiser
1917, A. F. Cramer
1918, G. A. Maag
1921, H. B. Mann
1924, H. L. Wohl
1926, George J. Kleinbach
1929, Oregon Conf.
1932, Pacific Northwest Conf.

GERMAN, ROSALIA
1900, P. J. Sehnert
1902, TBS
1903, G. J. Sohm (S)
1904, G. A. Jahns
1908, H. F. Michel
1909, L. Gaiser
1913, J. E. Muller
1916, C. A. Wentsch
1927, A. F. Hilmer
1929, Oregon Conf.
1932, Pacific Northwest Conf.

GERMAN, SEATTLE
1891, C. A. Priesing
1893, Joseph Hepp
1894, no record
1895, J. G. Moehring
1898, Hans Hansen
1899, Joseph Schweirtlich
1901, Joseph Hepp
1903, F. H. Luecke
1906, J. N. Hermann
1907, A. J. Weigle
1910, F. H. Luecke
1913, H. G. Schmid
1916, Joseph Hepp
1917, F. M. Maas
1919, A. J. Weigle
1920, TBS
1923, H. L. Wohl
1924, Discontinued

GERMAN, SNOHOMISH
1892, C. H. Priesing
1893, Joseph Hepp
1899, not listed
1908, J. N. Hermann
1909, H. F. Michel
1910, TBS
1911, not listed

GERMAN, SPOKANE
1891, A. L. Koeneke
1898, H. F. Lange
    W. J. Herwig
1899, J. W. Beckley
1900, George Hartung
1904, J. Durbahn
1908, G. J. Sohm
1909, C. A. Wentsch
1916, H. F. Lange
1926, A. J. Weigle
1928, E. J. Aschenbrenner
1929, Oregon Conf.
1932, Pacific Northwest Conf.
1932, A. F. Hilmer
1933, Discontinued

GERMAN, SPOKANE CIRCUIT
1891, F. W. Bucholz
1899, not listed
1903, H. B. Mann
1904, Discontinued

GERMAN, TACOMA
1891, Joseph Hepp
1893, no record
1894, J. C. Jahn
1895, no record
1898, Carl Jahn
1899, J. W. Roder
1901, H. F. Michel
1908, C. H. Weise
1909, F. H. Luecke
1909, Charles Holtkamp
1910, A. J. Weigle
1914, Joseph Hepp
1917, F. M. Maas
1918, not listed

GERMAN, WALLA WALLA
1883, Wm. Esslinger
1887, John Hager
1888, Albert Koenike
1888, Joseph Hepp
1891, John G. Moehring
1895, H. F. Michel
1897, F. W. Buchholz
1898, John Wesley Roeder
1899, Hans Hansen (S)
1900, Carl A. Wentsch
1904, H. F. Lange
1905, Carl Jahn
1906, H. F. Lange
1916, John C. Mueller
1924, George S. Roeder
1926, John A. Beck
1929, George J. Kleinbach
1947, Abandoned

GERMAN, WARDEN, WASH.
1908, George Hartung
1909, not listed

GERMAN, WHATCOM
1891, Hans Hansen
1893, not listed
1900, H. F. Michel
1901, not listed

GERMAN, YAKIMA
1906, TBS
1907, not listed

GIFFORD, IDAHO
1902, A. A. Newman (S)
1903, M. C. Davis
1904, Joseph Toms (S)
1905, TBS
1907, C. W. Geisler
1908, Andrew Kershaw (S)
1909, W. F. McKain
1910, J. S. Taylor (S)
1911, Henry Attenborough
1912, TBS
1913, M. C. Newell (S)
1915, TBS
1917, no record
1921, Ethel Williams (S)
1922, Bertram Hall (S)
1923, W. J. Gamble (S)
1925, Waldo W. Pierson
1926, John G. Brugger
1927, Harry Fliesher (S)
1928, TBS
1935, C. W. Groth
1937, Lloyd H. Smith (S)
1938, Ben Howe
1939, Fred Hertzog
1940, TBS
1944, W. W. Meyers (S)
1946, Chas. L. Thornton (S)
1949, no appointment
Discontinued

GOLD BAR
1910, J. W. Wright (S)
1911, O. B. D. Wood (S)
1913, H. L. Richardson
1915, E. E. Simmons
1916, TBS
1917, A. P. Basher (S)
1918, TBS
1919, Fred L. Post (S)
1920, W. J. Rule
1921, J. W. Kern
1923, J. H. Bennett (S)
1924, not listed
1930, J. D. Bird
1931, A. W. Luce
1937, not listed
1938, TBS
1939, Gerald Henry (S)
1940, TBS
1941, J. Ray Neiser (S)
1943, S. M. Berney (S)
1944, not listed

GOSHEN
1899, C. A. Owen (S)
Abandoned

GREENBANK
1955, Ritchie D. Ocheltree
1956, Wayne Wright
1958, Abandoned

HAMILTON
1892, TBS
1904, Henry Harpst (S)
1905, H. K. Kline (S)
1906, O. I. Bennett (S)
1907, J. H. Mitchell (S)
1910, Leroy C. Shultz
1912, C. A. Lindholm (S)
1913, TBS
1914, B. V. Bradshaw (S)
1915, Thomas Trevor (S)
1916, TBS
1917, W. E. Loyle (S)
1918, TBS
1919, W. M. Forbes (S)
1920, A. C. Baer
1921, Geo. W. Hoy
1922, W. M. D. Riggs (S)
1923, T. F. Bissell (S)

1924, Oliver W. Black (S)
1927, A. W. Smith
1928, C. B. Sears (S)
1931, E. W. D. Hanna
1933, C. E. Miller
1934, TBS
1937, O. W. Black
1939, Chas. Gleason (S)
1940, L. R. Lake (S)
1943, TBS
1945, L. R. Lake (S)
1946, L. R. Lake
1947, Wayne D. Griffen
1948, Miss Marion Koth (S)
1952, R. Clinton McGaffee
1957, not listed

HATTON
1900, J. W. Beckley
1901, Henry Martin (S)
1902, J. E. Daniels
1903, B. L. Hicks
1905, L. W. Putnam
1907, W. H. Henderson
1908, John F. Cook
1910, A. H. Morton
1912, H. T. Robinson
1913, Geo. James
1914, Albert W. Luce
1915, Chas. H. Schreiber
1917, C. W. Geisler
1918, J. Fred Stilwell
1919, A. C. Childs (S)
1920, K. O. Pearson
1921, C. W. Geisler
1922, Burchard A. Hylton
1923, C. M. Carson
1925, J. J. Prichard (S)
1926, B. A. Hylton
1927, Andrew J. Armstrong
1929, Robert Thompson
1930, John Seethoff
1933, J. D. Moede
1935, E. J. Smith
1938, Robert L. LaMott
1939, M. H. Sharrard
1944, Frank L. Lowther
1946, Waldo W. Pierson
1948, TBS
1950, no appointment
merged with Connell

HAYFORD
1930, A. G. Child (S)
1931, Roy Keeling (S)
1932, Dan Taylor
1934, TBS
1935, L. G. Wellington (S)
1937, J. P. Armand
1940, Frank Harris (S)
1942, Paul D. Brown (S)
1943, C. M. Estabrook
1946, John Jantzen (S)
1948, no appt.
1949, Ronald Treibel (S)
1950, TBS
1951, Homer Perry (S)
1952, Robert Leep (S)
1953, Raymond Gouldin (S)
1954, TBS
1959, not listed

HEISSON
1913, H. O. Cooper

HIGHLAND
1945, TBS
1947, Owen L. McDonald (S)
1948, no appt.

HOOD'S CANAL MISSION
1885, TBS

1886, Not listed
1890, listed in separate Swedish Dist. TBS
1891, TBS
1893, Abandoned

HORSESHOE BEND
1945, TBS
1947, no appt.

HOUGHTON
1886, Albert Atwood
1889, L. E. Wornom
1890, Arthur H. Marsh (S)
1891, Abandoned

HOVER
1920, C. A. Burris
1922, TBS
1923, C. W. Geisler
1924, E. L. Wolfe
1924, Robert Thompson (S)
1929, Erling Bergan
1931, J. A. Alford (S)
1933, TBS
1935, S. E. Hornibrook (S)
1938, J. E. Williams (S)
1939, TBS
1940, E. A. Schwenk (S)
1941, J. H. Bennett (S)
1943, Clark M. Smith (S)
1946, Guy A. Lewis
1947, Pierce Roberts
1949, Abandoned

HUSUM
1934, Roy Jenkins
1935, C. W. Stark
1936, not listed
1938, Jos. W. Reynolds
1942, B. C. Gallaher
1945, George P. George (S)
1947, no appt.

ILWACO
1893, H. Hadley (S)
1894, R. A. Atkins
1897, D. M. Ellsworth
1898, Enos H. Fuller
1899, Sprague Davis
1901, F. E. Smith
1902, E. O. Harris
1903, E. Charles Parker
1905, Geo. F. Pollock
1906, H. C. Townsend
1907, Wm. J. Rule
1908, TBS
1910, J. F. Keating (S)
1912, A. F. Kline (S)
1914, J. H. James (S)
1915, V. A. Spicker
1916, T. J. Cowley (S)
1919, E. B. Reese
1920, T. J. Cowley (S)
1921, F. L. Pedersen
1924, TBS
1925, Federated, TBS
1927, Henry Albright
1928, A. M. Herd

ISSAQUAH
1895, H. D. Wadsworth
1896, TBS
1897, W. R. King (S)
1899, L. J. Covington
1902, J. T. Redfern
1903, A. J. McNemee
1904, S. J. Buck
1905, W. B. Marsh
1908, Horace Williston
1909, C. A. Owens

1913, S. G. Jones
1915, R. G. Pike (S)
1916, Charles F. Johnson (S)
1917, A. F. Grissom
1918, S. V. Warren
1919, TBS
1923, Archie M. Herd
1924, TBS
1925, J. H. Beall
1926, T. A. Graham
Abandoned

JOHN'S RIVER
1887, A. Marshion (S)
1888, I. C. Pratt (S)
1889, Frank C. Butler (S)
1890, not listed
Abandoned

JUNIATA
1916, R. G. Pike (S)
Abandoned

KAPOWSIN
1906, A. M. Brown (S)
1907, T. J. Lewis
1910, J. J. Calloway (S)
1912, G. L. Cuddy

KELSO CIRCUIT
1910, J. K. Boyd (S)

KENT CIRCUIT
1895, TBS
1905, TBS
1915, William Leber (S)

KIRKLAND
1891, TBS
1894, H. D. Wadsworth
1895, TBS
1897, A. J. McNemee
1898, D. M. Ellsworth
1899, Rial Benjamin
1900, R. Z. Fahs
1903, J. M. Weaver
1906, F. R. Gillett
1907, F. L. Drake
1908, H. J. Hartsell
1909, F. A. Guiler
1910, H. C. Carter (S)
1911, T. Houlston (S)
1912, R. W. Bone
1913, Frank Hancock
1914, W. E. Chambers (S)
1915, A. Robertson (S)
1916, R. G. Pike (S)
1918, R. A. Gailey
1920, F. W. P. Camp
1921, N. M. Temple
1922, Chas. A. Bowen
1924, J. W. DeYoe
1925, TBS
1926, C. E. Newberry (S)
1929-32, Dwight G. Bennett
Abandoned

KLABER
1924, John Place
1925, Mrs. A. D. Newell (S)
1926, T. J. Cowley
1929, not listed

KNAPPTON
1922, J. Thomas Cowley (S)
1924, TBS
Abandoned

LA CENTER
1900, Levin Johnson (S)
1901, A. Demoy
1902, W. J. Gilbert (S)

1906, O. R. Anderson
1907, TBS
1911, J. H. Harding (S)
1912, Grant Smurr (S)
1913, E. L. Hughes
1916, A. F. Kline (S)
1919, TBS
1920, W. O. Shields (S)
1921, Miss Ruth Bollinger (S)
1922, TBS
1925, J. M. Wilder
1927, W. T. Beatty
1928, C. E. Sanders
Abandoned

LACKAMAS
1909, E. J. Bates
Abandoned

LAKESHORE
1906, Ezra Hayes (S)
1908, Alfred Bates (S)
1909, P. Raymond

LAKE VIEW
1888, TBS
1889, not in Appt. list.

LAKEWOOD
1910, TBS
1911, W. J. Rule (S)
1913, W. M. D. Riggs (S)
1914, J. S. Sneethen (S)
1915, E. V. Bronson
1916, E. B. Reese (S)
1918, TBS
1919, G. C. Squire
1920, W. J. Rule
1924, Robert A. Allen
1925-28, E. E. Reisner
Abandoned

LAMONA
1905, A. A. Moore
1906, R. A. Armstrong
1909, M. P. Stout (S)
1911, TBS
1913, not listed
1916, Harry A. Wann
1917, W. A. Pratt
1918, not listed
1919, J. H. Crocker (S)
1921, Frank Peterson (S)
1922, R. W. Curry (S)
1924, not listed
1926, Ruth Lortz (S)
1928, not listed
1929, J. C. Harvey (S)
1931, not listed
1934, C. A. Pickering
1935, not listed
1938, T. Earl Poindexter
1940, Darrell Iwerks
1941, not listed
1942, Abandoned

LELAND
1892, TBS
1894, H. W. Michener (S)
1895, not in Appt. list
1906-08, TBS
Abandoned

LESTER
1899, H. W. Michener
Abandoned

LEWIS RIVER
1884, G. G. Ferguson
1886, not in Appt. list
Abandoned

456

LIFE BOAT MISSION
1909, James Crooks (S)
1911, Discontinued

LISABEULA
1912, J. H. Avery
1913, W. J. Green
Abandoned

LITTELL
1905, TBS
1909, C. C. Wilkinson (S)
1910, E. L. Hughes (S)
1911, W. E. Williams
1912, TBS
1913, S. T. Grindle (S)
Abandoned

LONGVIEW—COMMUNITY
1923, E. H. Gebert
1928, E. H. Gebert
Abandoned

LOPEZ ISLAND
1886, Isaac Dillon
1888, TBS
1889, A. J. McNemee
1890, Andrew J. McNemee
1891, W. W. Mallory
1892, G. F. Mead
1893, T. L. Dyer
1895, F. S. Wright
1896, I. Dillon
1897, H. H. Walkington
1898, Robert R. Earl
1899, H. G. Ward
1902, E. B. Reese
1903, Thomas J. Gambill
1904, B. N. Galbraith
1905, O. J. Bennett (S)
1906, C. C. Pratt
1907, E. O. Harris
1909, TBS
1910, A. F. Stearns (S)
1912, W. G. Gillespie (S)
1914, Chas. Sanders
1917, TBS
1919, E. E. Simmons
1920, L. C. Davies (S)
1921, TBS
1922, A. D. Shaw (S)
1923, H. D. Suhm (S)
1924, Percy E. Pike (S)
1925, TBS
1927, D. Earl (S)
Abandoned

LYMAN
1889, TBS
1890, not listed
1900, TBS
1909, Leroy C. Shultz
1912, C. A. Lindholm (S)
1913, TBS
1914, B. V. Bradshaw (S)
1915, A. P. Basher (S)
1917, W. E. Loyle (S)
1918, TBS
1919, W. M. Forbes (S)
1920, A. C. Baer
1921, Geo. W. Hoy
1923, T. F. Bissell (S)
1924, Oliver W. Black (S)
1926, not listed
1927, A. W. Smith (S)
1928, C. B. Sears (S)
1931, E. W. D. Hanna
1933, C. E. Miller
1934, TBS
1937, O. W. Black
1939, Chas. Gleason (S)
1940, L. R. Lake (S)

1943, TBS
1946, Discontinued

McKENNA
1919, C. B. Seely
1920, W. P. Rutledge
1921, A. W. Smith (S)
1925-28, E. W. D. Hanna
Abandoned

McKINLEY PARK
1908, E. H. Rubicam
1909, J. E. Milligan
1911, W. O. Pflaum
1912, Ernest J. Bates
combined with Fowler to make
Trinity.

MALONE
1917, G. V. Fallis (S)
1919, B. Waddington
1920, R. D. Cady (S)
1921, F. A. Ecker
1925, TBS
1928, John Evans (S)

MANSFIELD
1909, J. B. Smith
1911, C. Snowden
1912, John H. Dill
1913, G. F. Graham (S)
1914, C. W. Johnson (S)
1915, A. W. Luce
1917, R. R. Martin
1918, Thomas Emery
1920, U. C. Smothers
1921, J. D. Bird
1923, John Moede
1926, C. A. Burris
1928, B. H. Hart
1930, R. Z. Newton
1932, Robert Thompson
1933, Percy E. Pike
1935, C. D. Scannell
1936, Ruth M. Lortz (S)
1939, A. L. McConnell
1941, T. H. Stanley (S)
1942, Gail M. Kiser (S)
1945, William O. Cary (S)
1946, Eugene C. Lasater (S)
1950, R. V. B. Dunlap
1952, G. H. Rickard (S)
1963, C. R. Dist.
1954, TBS
1954, L. R. Phillips (S)
1956, N. U. Stout (S)
1958, TBS
1959, Patrick Myrick (S)
1960, E. Vincent Smith
1962, not listed.
To another denomination

MAPLE FALLS
1905, TBS
1906, E. V. Smith
1907, J. W. Kern
1908, TBS
1910, O. A. Quall
Abandoned

MARYSVILLE, Later CATLIN
1891, C. P. Stayton
1892, Abandoned

MATLOCK
1897, TBS
Abandoned

MAYFIELD
1902, W. T. Green (S)
1907, R. J. Ferguson (S)
1909, H. E. Chapman (S)

1910, E. L. Hughes (S)
1912, A. F. Grissom
1913, Wm. Porter
1914, TBS
1916, E. L. Hughes
1917, W. J. Rule

MAYTOWN
1914, A. M. Fredrick (S)
1915, J. W. Walker (S)
1916, R. W. Curry (S)
1917, TBS
Abandoned

MAZAMA
1944, John A. McNees
1945, Wendell J. Cone
1947, J. N. Snow
1948, no appointment

MEEKER
1893, TBS
Abandoned

METHOW
1915, S. H. Watson &
       S. G. Gordon (S's)
1916, G. E. James (S)
1917, E. J. Snell
1918, Chas. H. Schreiber
1921, U. G. Beadles (S)
1922, F. H. Brown (S)
1923, Ralph I. Thomas
1926, G. E. James
1929, J. A. Hill
1934, J. P. Armand
1936, TBS
1937, F. C. Fulford (S)
1938, O. L. Kendall
1939, Percy E. Pike
1941, Claude W. Groth
1942, Stewart E. Sparrow (S)
1946, TBS
1947, Verne L. Chapman (S)
1948, TBS
1948, Walter G. Sloan
1952, Raymond H. Blanton
1953, C. R. Dist.
1953, John M. Jones (S)
1954, not listed

MICA
1928, S. E. Taft
1929, Charles H. Schreiber
1930, J. P. Armand
1931, Robert Thompson
1932, Dan Taylor
1934, C. E. Auger (S)
1935, Thos. C. McFeron (S)
1936, S. E. Yaggy (S)
1937, A. L. McConnell (S)
1938, C. M. Estabrook
1939, W. W. Switzer
1941, I. G. Wilkins (S)
1943, Frank E. Harris (S)
1944, Ruth M. Lortz (S)
1949, TBS
1950, Cecil G. Rickard (S)
1952, TBS
1953, Frederick H. Cronkhite (S)
1955, James I. McLimans (S)
1956, TBS
1959, Arthur E. Paltridge
1960, TBS
1961, Fred Riehle (S)

MIDLAND
1906, J. L. Kendall
1907, O. R. Davis (S)
1909, A. A. Metcalf (S)
1912, H. E. Moore
1915, Clark Cottrell

457

1916, M. Dodsworth (S)
1917, H. E. Gardner
1918, TBS
1919, Roy M. Owen
1922, J. C. Dorwin
1923, J. H. Avery
Abandoned

MOHLER
1902, Henry Brown
1903, No record
1904, T. J. Hazelton (S)
1905, Fountain Walker
1906, A. A. Moore
1907, R. A. Armstrong
1909, M. P. Stout (S)
1910, J. Charles Snowden
1911, George Bradley
1912, J. D. Cain
1913, George E. James
1914, M. R. Brown
1916, Harry A. Wann
1917, W. A. Pratt
1918, James Callahan
1920, J. H. Crocker (S)
1921, Frank Peterson (S)
1922, R. W. Curry (S)
1924, not listed
1926, Ruth M. Lortz (S)
1928, TBS
1929, J. C. Harvey (S)
1932, Clark Cottrell
1935, H. B. Mann
1938, TBS
1939, T. Earl Poindexter
1940, Darrell Iwerks
1941, Milton DeArmand
1944, TBS
1945, Mrs. Millie L.
   (Mrs. J. D.) King (S)
1949, Abandoned

MONTESANO CIRCUIT
1888, W. I. Cosper
1889, not listed

MOSSY ROCK
1890, J. N. Taylor (S)
1891, TBS
Abandoned

NAPAVINE
1894, William J. Rule
1896, Alfred J. Whitfield
1897, Meade L. Cunningham (S)
1900, Edward L. Bower
1905, W. Thomas Greene (S)
1907, R. J. Ferguson
1909, H. E. Chappell (S)
1911, W. E. Williams
1913, S. T. Grindle
1914, A. F. Kline
1916, E. L. Hughes
1920, F. L. Lowther
1921, J. Place
1925, Mrs. Agnes D. Newell (S)
1926, T. J. Cowley (S)
1929, H. L. Allen
1930, Roy B. Parcel
1935, Ira McFarland
1937, Dow DeLong
1940, not listed
1942, Abandoned. Trans. to
   Winlock

NASELLE
1922, J. Thos. Cowley (S)
1924, TBS
1925, R. B. Parcel
Abandoned

NEVADA MISSION
1890, B. F. VanDeVenter

1891 not on Appt. list
Abandoned

NEWAUKUM
1902, TBS
1905, W. T. Green (S)
Abandoned

NEWCASTLE
1893, Alfred Inwood
Abandoned

NORTH RICHLAND
CONSTRUCTION CAMP
1948, Kenneth H. Underwood
1949, Eugene W. Muench
1951, no appointment

NORTH RIVER
1887, O. S. Sanders (S)
1888, TBS
1889, Not listed
Abandoned

NORWEGIAN-DANISH,
ABERDEEN
1892, church erected
   H. S. Waaler
   O. Heggen
   J. J. Field
   T. Larsen
   Frank Larsen
   O. T. Field
   H. Ernest Andersen
   Hagbert Elvigen
   Andrew Christensen
   Christian Martinsen
   Andrew Rogne
   A. Stromme
   E. Fredriksen
   Greabert Andersen
   C. H. Lund
   Joseph Bowdoin
   J. Avery
1925, Bishop W. O. Shepard
   presided at conference.

NORWEGIAN-DANISH,
BELLINGHAM, GLADSTONE
1889, J. S. Andersen
1892, C. L. Westberg
1894, J. M. Waage
1896, C. M. Hauge
1898, D. Heggen
1901, J. Jacobsen (Fairhaven)
1903, O. T. Field
1905, John Nilsen
1908, P. M. Melby
1909, John J. Field
1911, John H. Clausen
1914, F. Engebretsen
1918, John Johnson
1920, John Nelsen
1921, A. Rogne
1923, P. O. Haugland
1925, O. T. Field
1932, M. K. Skarbo
1936, Clarence H. Lund
1938, H. W. Hanson
1939, O. T. Field to 11/28/40
1940, Mrs. O. T. Field (S)
1953, Andrew Odegaard
1954, Closed

NORWEGIAN-DANISH,
BELLINGHAM,
NEW WHATCOM
1890, Rev. O. Heggen
1899, built church, dedicated.
1923, United with Fairhaven

NORWEGIAN-DANISH,
BLAINE, IDAHO
1887, Church dedicated
   Carl Eriksen
   C. L. Westberg
   J. S. Andersen
   Joseph Olson
   P. N. Melby
   J. J. Field
   O. T. Field
   J. Clausen
   Melvin L. Olson
   N. L. Hansen
   A. Sleipness
   A. Smedstad
   H. Helgesen
   Erling Bergan
   J. S. Andersen

NORWEGIAN-DANISH, COVE
1905, C. Aug. Petersen
   from First Seattle
1905, Carl Eriksen
   J. G. Bringdale
   John Nelsen
   O. O. Twede
   F. A. Scarvie
   H. P. Nelsen
   C. Aug. Petersen
   A. H. Stromme
   Martin T. Larson
   H. E. Andersen
   Oscar B. Jensen
1943, H. O. Jacobson (S)
1950, TBS
1951, Paul D. Brown (S)
1952, Paul T. Woodward
1955, Ira J. McFarland (R)
1959, TBS
1961, Fred Cronkite (S)
1962, Discontinued

NORWEGIAN-DANISH,
EMANUEL, SEATTLE
1900, C. N. Hauge
1901, C. Aug. Petersen
1902, E. L. Nanthrup
1905, E. Gjerding
1906, E. L. Nanthrup
1909, P. M. Melby
1913, C. J. Larsen
1914, Joseph Olsen
1915, F. A. Scarvie
1916, L. C. Knudsen
1917, F. L. Trelstad
1922, C. A. Petersen
1923, F. A. Scarvie
1924, David C. Hassel
1929, R. Petersen
1931, H. O. Jacobsen
1938, K. N. Ekaas
1941, J. P. Johnsen
1943, J. S. Yndestad
1947, Earl L. Dean
1948, H. C. Kohr (S)
1950, combined with Crown Hill

NORWEGIAN-DANISH,
EVERETT
1892, P. M. Ellefsen
1944, Pastors since 1892:
   P. M. Ellefsen
   O. Heggen
   O. O. Twede
   Carl Larsen
   Carl Eriksen
   F. A. Scarvie
   J. J. Field
   E. L. Nanthrup
   Gottfred Nelson
   Andrew Christensen
   O. T. Field

458

H. E. Andersen
H. P. Nelsen
H. Elvigen
Martin T. Larson
A. H. Stromme
Alfred Amundsen
1944, P. A. Norleman

**NORWEGIAN-DANISH,
BELLINGHAM, FAIRHAVEN**
1890, J. S. Andersen
1923, sold and united with
New Whatcom
C. L. Westberg
J. M. Waage
C. M. Hauge
O. Heggen
John Jacobsen
O. T. Field
John Nelson
P. M. Melby
J. J. Field
J. H. Clausen
F. Engebretsen
1918, John Johnson
John Nilsen
A. Rogne
P. O. Haugland
O. T. Field
M. K. Skarbo
Clarence H. Lund
H. W. Hanson
O. T. Field
Mrs. O. T. Field (S)

**NORWEGIAN-DANISH,
FIRST SEATTLE**
1889, C. J. Larsen
1890, Lewis Walby
1891, M. Hansen
1893, E. J. Lundegaard
1896, Greabert Anderson
1898, C. N. Hauge
1901, C. Aug. Petersen
1903, Frank A. Scarvie
1905, J. J. Petersen
1907, Joseph Olsen
1908, C. Lyng Hansen
1913, C. Aug. Petersen
1916, Abraham Vereide
1923, J. O. Hall
1926, H. S. Haver
1929, H. E. Andersen
1932, H. P. Nelsen
1936, Martin K. Skarbo
1944, Chas. A. Dockstader (S)
1951, Discontinued

**FRAGARIA,
NORWEGIAN-DANISH**
1921, F. A. Scarvie
H. P. Nelson
C. Aug. Peterson
M. T. Larson
Andrew Odegaard
1929, H. E. Anderson (S)
1949, Mark Freeman
1950, Bertram Robbins
1951, Thos. C. Slate
1952, out
1953, Karl N. Ekaas
1955, out. Abandoned

**NORWEGIAN-DANISH,
LA CENTER**
1891, C. N. Hauge founder &
builder

**NORWEGIAN-DANISH,
MOSCOW, IDAHO**
1886, Carl Eriksen

**NORWEGIAN-DANISH,
OLALLA**
1895, TBS
1913, J. P. Bancroft (S)
Abandoned

**NORWEGIAN-DANISH,
PORT TOWNSEND**
1889, J. S. Anderson

**NORWEGIAN-DANISH,
ROCKFORD**
1889, J. C. Paulsen
1890, church built

**NORWEGIAN-DANISH,
SOUTH BEND**
1890, Rev. Carl Erikson
Rev. & Mrs. Frank Larsen

**NORWEGIAN-DANISH,
SPOKANE**
1889, E. M. Stangeland
C. N. Hauge
C. Lyng Hansen
L. Walby
N. L. Hansen
E. J. Lundegaard
H. P. Nelsen
C. Aug. Peterson
Abraham Vereide
Andrew Christensen
Gottfred Nelson
O. T. Field
A. Odegaard
Hilmer W. Hansen
Frederick Engebretsen
Hagbert Elvigen
1944, A. Odegaard

**NORWEGIAN-DANISH,
STEVENS STREET,
SPOKANE**
1889, C. J. Larsen
1889, E. M. Stangeland
1890, C. N. Hauge
1891, Chris Lyng Hansen
1893, L. Walby
1897, N. L. Hansen
1900, E. J. Lundegaard
1903, H. P. Nelsen
1907, C. Aug. Peterson
1910, Abraham Vereide
1912, Andrew Christensen
1914, Gottfred Nelson
1917, H. P. Nelsen
1919, no minister
1920, O. T. Field
1925, Andrew Odegaard
1927, H. W. Hansen
1928, F. Engebretsen
1929, no minister
1932, Andrew Odegaard
1951, TBS
1952, Abandoned

**NORWEGIAN-DANISH,
TACOMA**
1882, J. C. Larsen
1884, C. J. Larsen
C. N. Hauge
E. J. Lundegaard
Greabert Anderson
E. B. Gjerding
H. P. Nelsen
Joseph Olsen
N. L. Hansen
P. O. Haugland
G. A. Storaker
R. B. Langness
R. P. Peterson

J. G. Bringdale
M. L. Olson
K. N. Ekaas
1944, J. T. McQueen (R)
In P.N.W. conf.

**NORWEGIAN-DANISH.
WOOLMER, TROY, AND
BEAR CREEK, IDAHO**
Served by preachers from Blaine.
Carl Eriksen built churches.
Properties disposed of about
1902.

OAK POINT
1911, Alfred Bates (S)
1913, TBS
1914, Olaf Grandberg
1915, TBS
Abandoned

OCOSTA
1890, TBS
1892, Not listed
Abandoned

OMAK, CENTRAL
1941, Darrel Iwerks
1942, Claude W. Groth
1945, Floyd Cydrus (S)
1948, James A. Moore
1952, United with First

ONECHO
1932, Earl R. Shoup (S)
1945-48 with Albion
1953, TBS
1954, Martin G. Stuck (S)
1955, not listed
Discontinued

ORILLA
1899, TBS
1901, J. W. Ball (S)
Abandoned

**OSBORN CIRCUIT,
LATER RANDLE**
1889, Jasper Taylor (S)
1892, B. F. Woods
1893, W. J. Rule
1894, C. P. Stayton
1895, TBS

OSO CIRCUIT
1909, J. W. Kern
1910, A. B. Towne (S)
1913, J. S. Sneethen (S)
1914, A. P. Zedaker (S)
1915, B. V. Bradshaw (S)
1917, C. E. Sanders
1920, R. L. Wolfe
1921, F. A. C. Crown (S)
1923, TBS
1924, A. E. Currier (S)
1925, not in Appts. list
1928, J. F. Smith (S)
Abandoned

OSTRANDER
1904, R. L. Wolfe
1906, F. L. Moore
1908, N. M. Temple
1911, E. J. Smith
1913, E. L. Benedict
1915, J. T. McQueen
1916, D. E. Carter
1919, F. W. P. Camp
1920, G. B. Mehl (S)
1921, F. L. Lowther
1925, T. J. Hazelton (S)
1928, Earl W. McAbee
Abandoned

OYSTERVILLE
1884, H. Hadley
1885, TBS
1886, James Matthews
1888, not listed
1890, James Matthews
1891, D. M. Ellsworth
1892, S. P. Brokaw
1894, C. A. Luse
1929, not listed
1931, Henry Albright
1934, Fred H. Betts
1936, L. C. Bennett (S)
1938, TBS
1939, Harold E. Dixon
1951, no appt.
   not listed since

PARADISE VALLEY, IDAHO
1903, Trevor Orton
1945, Chas. L. Thornton (S)
1946, Ralph M. Walsh
1948, TBS
1949, no appt.
1950, Neils A. Christensen (S)
1952, none

PARK
1911, J. W. Walker (S)
Abandoned

PAUL STEVENSON
MEMORIAL
1910, Arthur A. Metcalf
1911, F. H. Walker
Abandoned

PENINSULAR CIRCUIT
1895, J. H. Avery
1896, James Matthews
1904, TBS
1912, M. B. Phillips
1913, TBS
1916, H. A. Liffiton (S)
1918, TBS

PESHASTIN
1945, George Schubert (S)
1947, no appointment

PIONEER
1886, C. P. Stayton
1887, John Britts (S)
1889, Wm. C. Hockett
1890, Sam'l P. Brokaw
1892, G. G. Ferguson
1893, James P. Smith
1894, J. I. Smith
1896, G. J. Taylor (S)
1897, E. L. Hughes
1901, A. Demoy
1902, W. J. Gilbert (S)
1905, TBS
1906, Ezra Hayes (S)
1909, TBS
1910, Evan R. Evans (S)
1918, A. F. Kline (S)

PLEASANT VALLEY
1900, T. M. Reese (S)
1901, TBS
1906, J. B. Stark (S)
1907, TBS. Abandoned

PORT ANGELES
LINCOLN HEIGHTS
1895, J. H. Avery
1905, J. A. Voris (S)
1906, TBS
1908, J. H. Avery
1909, H. R. Merrill

1910, M. B. Phillips
1911, TBS

PORTER
1908, TBS
1909, K. R. Gilmer (S)
1910, R. W. Curry (S)
1911, TBS
1913, H. P. Waldron
1914, J. W. Reynolds
1916, C. A. Lindholm (S)
1917, Erle Howell
1918, C. W. McLaughlin (S)
1919, J. H. Beall
1920, R. D. Cady (S)
1922, S. V. Warren
1925, TBS
1934, D. A. Storey
1936, not listed
1938, H. W. Driver
1942, TBS
1945, J. D. Lewellen (S)
1948, no appt.

PORT ORCHARD HEIGHTS
1945, Fred W. Hertzog
1947, Mark Freeman
1948, Abandoned

PROEBSTEL
1910, E. B. Reese
1911, TBS
1912, George Wood (S)
1913, E. G. Smurr (S)
1914, J. F. Mobley (S)
1915, TBS
1916, R. B. Parcel
1921, W. E. Rossman (S)
1923, C. O. Larson (S)
1924, TBS
1925-27, Mrs. J. H. Porter (S)

QUARTERMASTER
1892, TBS
Abandoned

QUILCENE
1891, TBS
Abandoned

QUILLAYUTE MISSION
1885, TBS
1887, Not listed
1892, TBS
1897, TBS

QUINAULT
1896, TBS
Abandoned

RAINIER
1892, TBS
1893, F. C. Butler
1894, TBS
1895, Not listed
1896, TBS
1898, Clarence G. Morris
1901, E. Hopkins
1903, TBS
1905, Robert T. Irwin (S)
1906, W. E. Williams
1907, TBS
1908, J. W. Blackwell (S)
1910, H. P. Waldron
1911, A. F. Grissom (S)
1912, G. M. Day
1913, J. W. Miller
1914, Geo. Morris (S)
1917, W. J. Gilbert (S)
1919, J. F. Smith (S)
1922, Herbert West
1923, Not listed

1924, E. A. Blakesley (S)
1925-27, E. W. D. Hanna
Abandoned

ROCHE HARBOR
1892, P. C. L. Harris
1893, I. N. Goodell
1894, T. L. Dyer
1898, J. W. White
1899, C. J. Kallgren
1900, S. S. Guiler
1901, Henry Harpst (S)
1903, J. H. Kevan
1904, C. C. Pratt
1905, Not listed
1907, Herbert Jones
1909, S. G. Jones
1911, T. A. Graham
1912, F. H. Walker
1913, A. Robertson (S)
1914, TBS
Abandoned

ROY
1898, Thomas R. McDonald (S)
Abandoned

SALISHAN
1945, Harold C. Williams
1946, K. N. Ekaas
1947, no appt.
Preaching discontinued after war

SALKUM
1886, J. E. Smith
1888, Chas. Atkins (S)
1889, TBS
1890, Carl A. Luse
1891, Not listed
1892, G. Westfall (S)
1893, John Tonkins
1894, W. J. Rule (S)
Abandoned

ST. MARIES, IDAHO
FEDERATED
1900, E. R. Henderson (S)
1902, J. H. Martin
1904, R. A. Gailey
1905, J. L. Carpenter
1907, A. Warner
1909, H. F. Pemberton
1910, Andrew Warner
1911, J. C. Harvey
1914, A. Monroe
1917, N. S. Hawk
1918, W. C. Reuter
1921, R. D. Snyder
1923, Thos. Hardie
1924, Chas. E. Gibson
1925, E. C. Newham
1929, Wm. Gornall
1931, No record
1932, S. Herbert Austin
1934, J. R. Norton (S)
1936, S. D. Trefren
1938, W. E. Whitlock (S)
1939, E. E. Van Wert (S)
1940, T. H. Stanley (S)
1941, TBS
1942, Paul G. Perkins
1946, TBS
1947, W. O. Benthin (S)
1948, TBS
1948, Raymond H. Blanton
1950, William Easson (S)
1952, no appt.

SAN JUAN ISLAND
1884, J. A. Tennant
1887, Not listed
1918, TBS

1920, L. C. Davies (S)
1921, TBS
Abandoned

SARA
1931, C. E. Sanders
1932, J. W. Reynolds
1933, not listed
1934, Kenneth H. Dunkelberger
1935, T. J. Hazelton (S)
1937, TBS
1938, H. G. Campbell (S)
1939, K. H. Dunkelberger
1940, L. C. Bennett
1941, John R. Butler
1942, Samuel A. Linge (S)
1944, Theo. H. Jorgensen
1944, Samuel A. Linge (S)
1946, Jesse L. Tooley
1949, Burchard A. Hylton
1951, Richmond H. Horton (S)
1952, Paul H. Wood (S)
1953, Harold J. Elmer (S)
1954, Earl B. Cotton &
    Mrs. Earl B. Cotton (S)
1955, not listed
1959, Walter P. Elkins
1962, not listed

SEATTLE, ASBURY
1889, E. S. Stockwell
1890, TBS
1891, Horatio Alling
1892, N. S. Buckner
1893, W. H. Drake
1894, T. E. McMullen
1895, Not listed
1897, W. H. Wilson
1898, Rial Benjamin
1899, Horace Williston
1900, A. E. Burrows
1903, not listed
1906, William Park
1909, J. W. Satterthwaite
1911, G. W. Frame
1916, C. E. Todd
1920, W. W. Switzer
1922, O. F. Krieger
1925, J. M. Adams
1930, Charles Creesy
1931, V. A. Spicker
1934, R. W. D. Brown
1936, P. M. Hammond
1938, W. H. H. Forsythe
1940, J. C. Hofstetter
1943, W. H. Hodges
1945, Abandoned

BALLARD PARK, SEATTLE
1907, H. L. Townsend

SEATTLE, BAY VIEW
1906, Henry Ward
1908, H. L. Townsend
With Ballard Park

BEACON HILL, SEATTLE
1893, W. P. George
1895, Abandoned

CALVARY, SEATTLE
1909, W. H. Leech
1911, E. D. White
1915, J. C. Harrison
1916, J. R. Sasnett
1918, Wm. Park
1922, W. T. Randolph

SEATTLE,
CHINESE MISSION
1892, TBS
1895, not listed. Abandoned

SEATTLE, CITY MISSION
1891, E. S. Stockwell
1892, not listed
1903, TBS
1904, J. M. Dennison
1905, C. J. Kallgren
1909, C. J. Kallgren and
    W. W. Batcheller
1912, W. H. Leech
1924, TBS
1925, R. W. D. Brown
Abandoned

SEATTLE, COLUMBIA
1892, T. W. Butler
1893, Not listed
1898, W. J. Rule
1899, E. C. Parker (S)
Abandoned

SEATTLE, FOOTE MEMORIAL
1911, J. T. Wright (S)
1914, TBS
1915, T. W. Bundy
1918, Nathan Evans

SEATTLE,
FREMONT MISSION
1889, E. S. Stockwell
1890, Not listed
1895, T. E. McMullen
1896, W. H. Wilson
1903, Nathan Evans
1904, William Park

GILMAN PARK, SEATTLE
1890, Eugene S. Stockwell
1891, R. Z. Fahs
1892, E. R. King
1893, W. H. Johnstone
    J. R. Edwards
1894, TBS
1907, W. H. H. Forsyth
1908, J. W. Flesher
1911, B. F. Brooks
1914, E. M. Randall
1917, E. J. Smith
1919, G. V. Fallis
1921, Rudolph Ericson, Assoc.
1922, F. A. LaViolette
1923, J. H. Berringer

SEATTLE, HILLMAN
1903, Lorenzo Jean (S)
1904, J. H. McIntosh (S)
1906, H. C. Wilson
1908, George C. Poolton
1909, R. Z. Fahs
1912, W. B. Anderson
1913, F. A. Guiler
1915, J. W. Kern (S)
1917, James Clulow (S)
1921, J. H. Geoghegan
1923, Boaz Elexander (S)
1924, L. M. Briggs (S)
1925, Rene Howe (S)
1926, J. S. Andrews (S)
1927, A. J. Yeomans (S)
1928, A. J. Yeomans (S)
Abandoned

LAKESIDE, SEATTLE
1907, H. C. Wilson
1908, George C. Poolton
1910, W. H. Baker
1911, H. J. Hartzell
1914, Frank Hancock
1916, H. H. Newman
1917, C. D. Miller
1919, J. H. Geoghegan
1920, F. G. Willey
1921, James Clulow

1922, J. H. Geoghegan
1926, E. A. Gray (U.G.)

SEATTLE, LATONA
1893, W. H. Drake
1894, T. E. McMullen
1895, W. H. Drake
Abandoned

SEATTLE, MADISON &
JACKSON ST.
1889, W. H. Mahaffie
1891, C. R. Pomeroy
1892, Horatio Alling
1893, M. A. Covington
1896, W. T. Ford
1897, A. S. Gregg
1909, C. A. Bowen
1910, William Park
1911, E. E. Bergman
1913, W. E. Cox
1916, Guy A. McShane
1919, G. C. Poolton
1924, W. M. Dews
1928, F. R. Gillett
Abandoned

MADRONA HEIGHTS,
SEATTLE
1903, O. A. Smith (S)
1904, TBS
1907, J. W. Spangler (S)
1908, C. L. Gilbert
1909, J. M. Dennison
1910, Joined Grace, Seattle

OLD TRINITY, SEATTLE
1890, Sedwick A. Bright
1892, S. P. Wilson
1893, N. P. Tedrick
1896, W. S. Harrington
1899, A. B. Chapin
1902, F. C. Lee
1904, Nathan Evans
1906, D. C. Franklin
1907, W. H. Leech
1908, V. C. Evers
1911, W. O. Benadom
1913, J. W. Frescoln
1915, G. A. McShane
Discontinued. Half to
    Queen Anne Ch.

SEATTLE, OPEN DOOR
1926, E. A. Gray
1929, E. M. Randall (S)
1930, TBS
1931, W. O. Pflaum
1935, T. W. Bundy
1936, D. N. Lacy
1937, J. H. Berringer
1940, J. W. Reeder (S)
1941, Merlyn Northfelt
1943, Robt. S. Ridgway
1944, K. N. Ekaas
1946, Clyde L. Walker
1947, K. N. Ekaas
1948, Bessie Pease (S),
    Annette Kiehlbauch (S)
1950, TBS
1951, TBS

S. E. SEATTLE
1903, Lorenzo Jean (S)
1906, H. C. Wilson

SEATTLE, ST. JOHN'S
1910, H. J. Hartsell

SEATTLE, ST. PAUL (Colored)
1908, J. N. Wallace (S)
1909, TBS
Abandoned

461

SIXTY-SECOND STREET,
SEATTLE
1906, Roy L. Sprague
1908, TBS
1909, G. W. Carr (S)
1911, Wilmot Whitfield
1912, John Tingling (S)
1914, M. L. McEwen
1916, J. T. Wright (S)
1917, C. B. Seely
1919, Nathan Evans (S)
1922, R. W. Maulden
1923, J. A. Badcon (S)
combined with Trinity

VALENTINE, SEATTLE
1901, J. W. Ball (S)
1902, F. H. Calder (S)
Discontinued

WESLEY, SEATTLE
1893, N. S. Buckner
1894, S. Davis
1895, called So. Seattle
    A. S. Gregg
1897, A. W. Bagley
1898, A. J. Whitfield
1899, Rowland Hughes
1901, M. H. L. Miffin
1902, F. S. Thomas
1903, Henry Ward
1905, R. W. Paul
1906, V. C. Evers
1913, M. L. McEwen
1914, John Tingling (S)
1919, W. F. Pool
1922, F. E. Cain (S)
1923, E. E. Reisner
1925, Granius Austin (S)
1926, J. M. Weaver
1928, George Martin (S)
1929, B. F. Lawrence (S)
1932, G. A. Sheafe (S)
1935, H. R. Bowman (S)
1936, Frank McAllister (S)
1938, Kenneth W. Countryman
1939, Merrill Hurd (S)
1940, E. Laura Butler (S)
1943, Ralph Butler
1944, T. E. Poindexter
1945, Paul Brown (S)
1946, Francis Lewis (S)
1947, Bernice Moore (S)
1948, Kenneth Peterson (S)
1949, Rudolph Malek (S)
1950, Richard A. Hayward (S)
1951, TBS
1952, Floyd C. Green (S)
1954, TBS
1954, John W. Caughlan
1956, C. W. Thompson (S)
1962, Merged with Riverton

SHELTON CIRCUIT
1890, TBS
1892, not listed
1898, TBS
1909, A. Anderson
1914, Seymour Williams
1916, TBS
1918, Abandoned

SILVER LAKE
1886, T. M. Reese (S)
1887, not listed
Abandoned

HOQUIAM, SIMPSON AVE.
METH. CH.
1907, Alfred Bates (S)
1907, Ernest J. Bates
1908, M. B. Phillips

1910, H. L. Richardson
1911, J. C. Reed (S) not listed
1911, E. R. Tracy
1913, H. A. Liffiton (S)
1915, C. W. McLaughlin
1916, N. S. Hankins (S)
1918, C. C. Harris (S)
1919, E. O. Harris
1919, J. F. Smith (S)
1920, M. R. Brown
1920, E. W. Anacher (S)
1922, Henry J. Harding (S)
1929, Robert C. Hartley
1931, Corabelle M. Teachman (S)
1932, E. M. Hill
1934, T. A. Olsen
1935, Floyd S. Bailey
    (not listed)
1936, J. P. Armand
1937, John D. Bird (S)
1938, J. Homer Magee
1939, V. A. Spicker
1941, Wm. S. T. Gray
United with First Methodist
Church of Hoquiam, May 1942.

SKAGIT
1884, W. B. McMillan
1885, W. H. Zellers
1886, TBS
1887, F. M. Pickles
1888, L. Dahlgren
1889, not listed

SKAGIT CITY—
SWEDISH DISTRICT
1900, John Johnson
1904-07, K. O. Berglund
Abandoned

SKAMOKAWA,
SWEDISH DIST.
1891-95, TBS. Abandoned

SNOHOMISH CIRCUIT
1887, A. J. McNemee
1888, Not listed
1889, TBS
1890, Not listed
Abandoned

SOUTH PRAIRIE MISSION
1885, F. Ailward (S)
1886, Jas. Eva (S)
1887, TBS
1888, E. L. Hughes
1889, John Vrooman (S)
1890, TBS
1893, Rowland Hughes
1895, W. M. Ludwick
1896, Wm. Welch (S)
1897, Rowland Hughes
1898, G. F. Meade
1900, J. W. White
1901, E. L. Bower
1903, F. H. Merrick (S)
1904, TBS
1905, F. A. Ecker
1907, W. E. Williams
1908, W. A. Scott (S)
1909, A. A. Brittain
1910, Roy B. Parcel
1912, W. O. Pflaum
1913, F. C. Thompson
1914, W. B. Anderson
1915, B. N. Galbraith
1916, Seymour Williams
1917, TBS
1919, E. L. Albright (S)
1920, H. Williston
1923, J. W. Blackwell (S)
1925, not listed

1927, Harold Nelson
1928, W. O. Benadom (S)
Abandoned

SPIKETON
1912, D. A. Storey

SPOKANE, EPWORTH
1909, J. O. Johnson
1914, H. L. Beightol
1919, E. C. Corn
1921, J. M. Adams
1922, E. C. Newham
1925, C. E. Gibson
1926, J. Fred Stilwell
1927, D. L. Clarke
1929, Frank L. Moore
1936, P. D. Brown (S)
1938, Wm. Gornall
1939, Wendell Cone
1941, Wm. Gavin (S)
1942, Alva Snyder (S)
1943, Alfred Carter
1945, L. G. Baker, Jr. (S)
1949, Ray W. Mason
1951, TBS
1952, No appt.

FOURTH AVENUE, SPOKANE
1937, U. F. Hawk
1942, Quentin Leisher (S)
1944, Frank E. Harris (S)
1946, Charles M. Estabrook
1950, no appt.
1951, TBS
1952, no appt.

SPOKANE, VINCENT
CHURCH
1895, M. H. Marvin
1896, W. B. Hollingshead
1898, W. K. Beans
1900, G. H. Jones
1901, J. J. Walter (S)
1902, H. D. Kimball
1906, C. O. Kimball
1910, H. C. Kohr
1911, E. Naftzger
1912, J. K. Cecil
1918, joined Central Church

SQUAK MISSION
1885, A. J. McNemee (S)
Abandoned

STARBUCK
1893, TBS
1894, James Greenslade
1895, W. T. Koontz
1896, John LeCornu
1897, J. C. Lawrence
1899, James Greenslade
1900, TBS
1901, not listed
1902, J. C. Lawrence
1904, Charles MacCaughey
1905, C. G. Harmon
1906, F. G. Drake
1907, J. L. Hess
1908, not listed
1908, S. E. Boselly (S)
1909, A. A. Callander
1911, F. R. Spaulding
1912, W. M. D. Riggs
1913, John LeCornu
1913, J. M. Hilbish
1914, A. Frank Roberts (S)
1914, L. C. Douglas (S)
1919, A. M. Lambert
1922, J. Wm. Getzendaner
1923, J. J. Mattney
1926, G. E. Glasspool (S)
1927, C. W. Geisler

1931, Harold Bashor
1935, Roy Jenkins
1940, E. Clifford Newham
1941, W. H. Monroe
1943, Everett L. Groves
1948, Mason S. Osborne
1950, Robert W. Maulden
1952, not listed

STARTUP
1910, J. W. Wright (S)
1911, O. B. D. Wood (S)
1913, H. L. Richardson
1915, E. E. Simmons

STEILACOOM
1853, John F. DeVore
1855, TBS
1856, G. M. Berry
1858, J. W. Franklin
1859, J. H. B. Royal
1860, Christopher Alderson
1861, Does not appear
1867, H. Patterson
1868, TBS
1870, H. Patterson
1873, S. H. Mann
1874, C. H. Hoxie
1876, no appt.
1897, T. M. McDonald (S)
Abandoned. 1908 monument
   erected.

STELLA
1911, Alfred Bates (S)

SUNNYDALE
1897, TBS
1901, S. J. Buck
1903, Ralph W. Paul
1905, C. L. Gilbert
1908, R. L. Sprague
1909, W. T. Greene
1910, F. A. Guiler
1920, J. L. Hanna (S)
1922, Mrs. A. D. Newell

**BEAR CREEK, SWEDISH
DIST., IDAHO**
1891, TBS
1893, not in appt. list
1897, K. O. Berglund
1900, Emanuel Johnson (S)
Abandoned

CEDARHOME, (SWEDISH)
1887, A. Farrell
1888, O. E. Olander
1890, L. Dahlgren
1892, C. J. Johnson
1895, Emanuel Johnson
not listed John Johnson
not listed John A. Anderson
not listed E. Johnson
not listed A. Farrell
1906, J. N. Burdell
1908, K. O. Berglund
1910, S. Moody
1912, K. O. Berglund
1918, S. Moody
1922, Eric Nelson
1925, K. O. Berglund
1929, Abandoned

SWEDISH DES MOINES
1890, TBS
1891, Not listed
Abandoned

SWEDISH EDMONDS
1903, C. V. Abrahamson (S)
1906, E. Johnson
Abandoned

SWEDISH EVERETT
1893, TBS
1894, John Johnson
1895, TBS
1897, Not listed
1900, TBS
1902, C. V. Abrahamson (S)
1904, E. Johnson
1906, TBS
1907, Andrew Farrell

**FIRST SWEDISH, CALVARY,
SEATTLE**
1883, Andrew Farrell
1886, O. E. Olander
1889, N. G. Nelson
1891, John Johnson
1895, O. E. Olander
1896, C. J. Kallgren
1897, N. G. Barton
1897, C. O. Freeman
1898, E. G. Falk
1902, J. H. Levedahl
1904, John Johnson
1906, S. Moody (S)
1910, O. W. Westling
1912, J. N. Burdell
1915, John Bostrom
1916, C. G. Westerdahl
1919, Francis Ahnlund
1949, Richard Nagle
1951, TBS
Combined with Capitol Hill

**SWEDISH FREMONT,
SEATTLE**
1890, TBS
1892, not listed
1902, E. G. Falk
1903, Joseph N. Burdell
1904, John Ovall
1906, TBS
1907, E. G. Landin
Abandoned

GUY, SWEDISH DISTRICT
1899, TBS
Abandoned

SWEDISH, NORA—ALBION
1902, TBS
1903, Gustaf E. Carlson
1905, Ossian Johnson
1906, TBS
Abandoned

OLYMPIA, SWEDISH
1903, TBS
1904, Charles Johnson (S)
1905, A. J. Gustafson
1906, J. H. Burdell
Abandoned

PLEASANT RIDGE, SWEDISH
1890, Olaff E. Olander
1892, C. A. Anderson
1896, Bernt Howe
1899, TBS
1900, C. J. Nelson
1903, Charles Johnson
1904, J. H. Levedahl
1906, John Johnson
1908, Abandoned

PORT TOWNSEND, SWEDISH
1890-'92, TBS
Abandoned

**SWEDISH DISTRICT,
SEATTLE**
1890, Nicholas G. Nelson
1891, TBS
1892, John Johnson

1895, TBS
1896, Carl J. Kallgren
1897, C. O. Freeman
1898, E. Gustav Falk
1902, J. H. Levedahl
1904, John Johnson
1906, S. Moody (S)

**SOUTH BEND, SWEDISH
DIST.**
1890, TBS
1892, E. A. Olson (S)
1893, TBS
1895, C. J. Johnson
1896-1903, TBS
1904, C. V. Abrahamson (S)

SPOKANE, SWEDISH DIST.
1890, TBS
1894, K. O. Berglund
1896, TBS
1897, Joseph Esterborg (S)
1898, TBS
1900, Olaf Granberg
1901, TBS
1903, Ossian Johnson
1905, G. E. Carlson
1906, J. A. Willman

TACOMA, SWEDISH DIST.
1890, TBS
1891, E. A. Davidson
1892, TBS
1893, Knut O. Berglund
1894, Bernt Howe
1896, John A. Anderson
1897, J. A. Anderson
1898, TBS
1899, C. J. Nelson
1900, TBS
1902, John Ovall
1904, A. J. Gustafson (S)
1906, J. H. Burdell
Abandoned

SWEDISH VENERSBORG
1910, John Ovall
1914, Eric Nelson (S)
1922, John Ovall
1925, E. Nelson (S)
1926, J. Bostrom
1927, E. Nelson (S)
1928, Eric Nelson (S)
1935, C. C. James (S)
1936, TBS
1937, Eric Nelson (S)
1938, C. C. James (S)
1939, TBS
1940, Nels Nelson (S)
1941, not listed
1942, TBS
1945, A. Burns (S)
1946, TBS

**SWEDISH DIST., WHATCOM
& FAIRHAVEN**
1890, TBS
1892, Not listed
1892, TBS
1896, Bernt Howe
Abandoned

TACOMA, ARLINGTON
1909, Joel Vigus
1914, Clarence B. Seely
1918, J. C. Dorwin
1920, W. B. Hawthorne (S)
1924, J. H. Hicks
1930, U. O. Beadles (S)
1932, W. B. Hawthorne (S)

TACOMA, ARLINGTON
1942, Richard Adamson (S)
United with Asbury

TACOMA, CENTRAL
1889, W. B. McMillan
1891, Horace Williston
1892, E. E. Morris
1896, F. A. LaViolette
1899, H. McNamee
1900, F. E. Drake
1902, G. G. Ferguson
1903, James Clulow
1906, J. W. Miller
1909, E. W. Erickson
1912, T. A. Graham
1913, E. E. Bergman
1914, Joel Vigus
1919, H. W. Michener
1923, J. P. Marlatt
1925, A. W. Martin (S)
1926, H. E. Bashor
Abandoned

TACOMA CIRCUIT
1884, J. F. DeVore
1885, not listed

EAST TACOMA
1889, B. F. Brooks
1890, not listed
Abandoned

TACOMA ENGLISH MISSION
1885, TBS
1886, Not listed
1890, David D. Campbell
1904, TBS
1905, B. F. Brooks (P.E.)
1906, James Clulow
1907, P. E., D. C. Franklin
1909, J. L. Kendall
1909, Joel Vigus
1914, C. B. Seely
1917, Wm. Park
1918, J. C. Dorwin
1922, TBS
1923, Harold Nelson
1924, R. M. Owen (S)

TACOMA, EPWORTH MISSION
1908, T. C. Newby (S)
Abandoned

TACOMA, FIRWOOD
1911, G. M. Day
Abandoned

FOWLER, TACOMA
1890, TBS
1891, G. F. Mead
1892, W. R. Warren
1895, W. M. Welch
1896, J. R. Edwards
1898, F. M. Wheeler
1900, F. A. LaViolette
1903, G. L. Cuddy
1910, F. S. Pearson
1912, F. L. Moore
Combined with McKinley Park
& named Trinity

TACOMA, OLD TOWN
1890, Richard H. Massey
1892, W. J. Bargar
1893, Not listed
Abandoned

TACOMA, PARK AVENUE
1892, E. H. Fuller
1893, TBS
1897, A. Munroe (S)
1899, J. T. Smith
1900, W. A. Alger (S)
1901, W. M. Welch
1903, TBS

1904, F. L. Tuttle
1905, Henry Ward
1906, G. H. Newland (S)
1907, W. O. Pflaum
1908, TBS
1912, W. H. W. Rees, Jr.
1913, R. Decker (S)
1915, E. H. Gebert
1916, G. S. Helgeson (S)
1917, M. Dodsworth
1918, TBS
Discontinued

TACOMA, SECOND
1893, E. H. Fuller
1895, F. M. Pickles
1898, John Edwards
1900, John R. Edwards
1901, C. W. Darrow
1902, A. B. L. Gellerman
1904, J. M. Rush
1905, J. E. Reed (S)
1908, J. L. Kendall
1909, TBS
Abandoned

SOUTH TACOMA
1886, T. J. Massey
1887, G. A. Landen
1888, W. B. McMillan
1889, not listed

TACOMA, UNIVERSITY PLACE
1911, C. W. Darrow
1913, J. E. Weigle
1914, John Lewtas
1915, A. J. Armstrong (S)
1916, TBS
1917, TBS
Abandoned

TACOMA, VINCENT
1916, H. G. Earle
1917, C. C. Moore
1918, TBS
1919, A. F. Stearns
1920, A. P. Rolan (S)
1921, R. R. Martin (S)

TACOMA, WESLEY
1893, E. H. Fuller
1894, A. S. Gregg
1895, C. S. Revelle
1899, C. W. Darrow
1901, W. M. Welch
1902, J. W. Ball
1903, C. F. Bennett
1905, J. E. Milligan
1909, C. W. Blanpied
1910, TBS
1911, G. M. Day
1912, C. N. Goulder
1925, TBS
1928, F. L. Baldwin (S)

WEST TACOMA CIRCUIT
1885, J. F. DeVore
1886, G. A. Landen
1887, Combined with
South Tacoma Cir.
1887, G. A. Landen
1888, R. H. Massey
1890, not listed. Into 1st Ch.

TENINO (Federated)
1909, E. R. Tracy
1911, R. W. Bone (S)
1912, B. Waddington
1913, J. W. Miller
1916, Richard Decker
1919, J. F. Smith (S)
1920, J. W. Sutton (S)

1921, S. Raynor Smith (S)
1922, Herbert West
1923, TBS
1929, not listed
1931, TBS
1934, J. W. Reynolds
1938, John R. Butler
1940, TBS
1941, Paul E. Ratsch (S)
1942, TBS
1946, H. E. Turley (S)
1947, C. M. Gearhart (S)
1948, no appt.

THOMAS
1908, G. M. Irwin (S)
1911, John Tingling (S)
1912, TBS
1913, J. H. McIntosh (S)
1916, TBS
Abandoned

TIETON VIEW
1944, Robert C. Evans (S)
1946, TBS
1947, no appt.

TOLEDO
1886, J. I. Smith
1888, Not listed
1890, Carl A. Luse
1891, Not listed
1894, C. G. Morris (Circuit)
1896, A. J. Whitfield (S)
1897, G. G. Ferguson
1898, C. F. Bennett (S)
1901, A. M. Brown (S)
1903, TBS
1904, F. W. Tisdale
1905, TBS
1906, B. L. Hicks
1907, E. L. Hughes
1910, C. H. Cowdy
1911, J. J. Jones
1912, A. F. Grissom (S)
1914, A. F. Kline (S)
1915, J. F. Mobley (S)
Abandoned

TOLEDO CIRCUIT
1912, E. L. Hughes (S)
Abandoned

TWINLOW, IDAHO
1939, Mark Freeman
1941, not listed
1943, Erling Bergan
1948, no appt.

VALLEY
1944, Robert C. Evans (S)
1946, TBS

VALLEY CHAPEL
1916, R. F. Hawk
1917, W. Byars
1918, J. F. Weller (S)
1919, TBS
1923, H. C. Vincent
1930, Thos. W. Emery
1931, W. J. Osborne (S)
1932, not listed
1942, Gene Lander (S)
1943, Charles W. Fisher
1944, Ruth Lortz (S)
1945, John D. Moede
1948, TBS
1949, no appt.

VAN ASSELT
1895, A. S. Gregg
Abandoned

VANCOUVER, Bethany
1915, Horace Williston
1918, J. B. Stark (S)

VANCOUVER CIRCUIT
1891, C. S. Snelling (S)
1892, not listed
1893, C. C. Pratt (S)
1896, William J. Rule
1898, Abraham Demoy
1899, TBS
1900, J. T. McQueen
1901, C. F. Bennett
1902, TBS
1903, C. C. Babbidge (S)
1905, W. J. Gilbert (S)
1907, C. H. Cowdy (S)
1908, E. Bates (S)

VANCOUVER, IRVINGTON
1907, Alfred Bates (S)
1908, E. R. Tracy
1909, J. H. Berringer
1914, J. H. Berringer

VANCOUVER, WESLEY
1909, TBS
1911, R. M. Schoonmaker,
1913, J. H. Berringer
Abandoned

VAUGHN
1889, TBS
1892, F. C. Butler
1893-'96, TBS
Abandoned

WALLA WALLA CIRCUIT
1877, G. W. Shaffer
1879, J. LeCornu
1880, Records missing
1883, A. J. Joslyn
1884, W. T. Koontz
1885, S. M. Driver
1888, G. G. Ferguson
1889, G. W. Rigby
1891, not listed
1895, Wm. DeWeese
1896, James Greenslade
1898, TBS
1899, J. C. Walker
1900, W. P. Jinnett (S)
1901, C. Maxson (S)
1902, W. H. Zeller
1904, A. H. Miller
1905, James E. Murphey
1908, Lester Long (S)
1909, Geo. B. Cole (S)
1912, Harvey O. Cooper
1913, Seldon H. Ewing
1915, J. K. Craig (S)
1917, J. E. Garver

WALLA WALLA, GRACE
1909, F. G. Boylan
1910, S. E. Baselly (S)
1912, Geo. E. James
1913, John LeCornu
1915, TBS
1917, not listed
1920, H. C. Vincent
1922, A. J. Armstrong
1923, B. C. Gallaher
1928, M. H. Staines
1933, E. J. Smith
1935, Wm. Daniel
1938, Louis V. Martin (S)
1939, C. H. Cowdy
1946, Clark M. Smith
1948, James Zeller (S)
1949, Aubrey W. Winsor (S)
1956, Became United Meth.
1956, Harry T. Cupp

WALLACE CIRCUIT
1900, G. F. West
1901, TBS
1902, J. A. Nutter
1903, B. N. Galbraith
1904, S. H. Greenlee
1905, H. C. Wilson
1906, J. M. Wilder
1908, H. K. Kline
Abandoned

WALVILLE
1913, Frank Sutton
1915, J. H. Geoghegan
1918, F. C. Thompson
1922, M. W. Forsythe
1924, W. T. Beatty
1925, F. L. Lowther
1927, E. W. McAbee
Discontinued

WAUKON
1923, James McDowell (S)
1924, J. E. Williams
1927, J. C. Harvey
1929, not listed
1939, Everett M. Filbert
1942, not listed
1944, Loren E. Jones
1945, Miss Gladys Crawford (S)
1948, Ralph M. Walsh
1949, no appt.

WAYSIDE
1900, H. George (S)
1901, TBS
1909, G. F. Pinkham
1910, M. R. Brown
1910, C. E. Curtis
1911, Wm. Wellington (S)
1911, R. A. Armstrong
1913, C. M. Carson
1914, Wm. Wellington (S)
1918, A. W. Luce
1919, TBS
1920, Ray Acheson (S)
1921, E. L. Quien (S)
1922, A. B. Calder
1923, TBS
1924, Wm. Wellington (S)
1926, TBS
1928, W. J. Osborne (S)
1931, M. L. Anderson
1934, not listed
1936, F. L. Lowther
1937, John Finney
1938, Milton DeArmond (S)
1939, not listed
1947, Claud H. Cowdy
1948, no appt.

WEST KITTITAS
1887, J. H. Feek
1888, Matthew Bird
1893, John Evans
1894, B. E. Koontz
1895, Edward Smith
1896, Edward Baker
1898, W. H. Henderson
1901, F. L. Johns
1904, J. E. Murphey
1905, S. E. Hornibrook
1906, C. F. Cook
1907, C. M. Carson
1911, S. E. Hornibrook
1912, C. L. Lowther (S)
1914, H. C. Clark
1915, I. E. Turner
1917, Wm. W. Nash
1926, John F. Roper
1927, E. F. Stidd

WILKESON
1912, W. O. Pflaum
1913, F. C. Thompson
1919, Loyd Burk
1920, TBS
1921, T. J. Gambill
1927, C. C. James
Abandoned

WINONA
1919, J. J. Mattney
1920, TBS
1921, not listed
1924, C. H. Schreiber
1925, S. E. Hornibrook
1927, Fred Jenkins
1928, TBS
1929, B. A. Hylton
1930, TBS
1932, W. C. Weber (S)
1933, M. H. Sharrard
1936, Ralph Bolick (S)
1939, James Wilkins (S)
1940, W. E. Witlock (S)
1941, TBS
1942, John A. Hoffman
1943, not listed
1944, Fred R. Owen
1945, Mrs. F. R. Owen (S)
1946, Frank L. Lowther
1950, Mason S. Osborne
1952, Paul E. Hamlin
1956, Ronald K. Johnson
1960, not listed
Abandoned

WISER LAKE formerly
LAUREL
1903, Chas. W. Stevens (S)
1905, Alfred A. Brittain
1906, Victor Charroin (S)
1906, E. P. Hughes (S)
1907, C. A. Owens
1909, L. H. Mitchell
1910, A. O. Quall
1910, Geo. H. Pease (S)
1911, Geo. H. Harrison (S)
1912, Harry L. Richardson
1913, Geo. F. Pollock
1914, E. R. Tracy
1915, C. M. Sullivan (S)
1915, C. M. Olsen (S)
1918, H. L. Richardson
1919, C. B. Sears
1921, Franklin Van Gorder (S)
1922, C. B. Sears
1927, W. J. Rule
1928, L. J. Covington
1929, T. A. Graham
1931, R. C. Hartley
1935, John F. Long
1936, M. J. Perdue
1937, Frank R. Gillett
1943, Harry L. Richardson (S)
1946, Geo. W. Rosenhall (S)
1947, Harlan R. Stone
1950, Chester C. Blair
1951, not listed
1952, Chester C. Blair
1953, Floyd E. Wells
1958, James N. Updike
1961, out

WOODLAND
1889, John Jensen
1890, M. C. Van Tyne (S)
1891, John Flinn
1892, G. G. Ferguson
1893, James P. Smith
1894, J. I. Smith
1896, J. G. Taylor (S)

1903, TBS
1904, TBS
Abandoned
WYNOOCHIE
1889, W. I. Cosper
1890, TBS
1891, Not listed
1899, W. E. Stearns (S)
Discontinued
YACOLT
1904, TBS

1905, C. W. Geisler
1906, Samuel Dupertius
1907, TBS
1908, Wm. Porter (S)
1913, H. O. Cooper
1915, J. H. James (S)
1916, Seldon Ewing
1917, W. P. Rutledge
1920, E. B. Reese
1924, TBS
1925, TBS

1927, TBS
Discontinued

YAKIMA, BROADWAY
1946, TBS
1947, Gladys Coy (S)

YORK
1903, Lorenzo Jean (S)
1904, J. H. McIntosh (S)
Abandoned

466

Appendix IX

ALPHABETICAL LIST OF INDIVIDUAL CHURCH HISTORIES

467